THE LOOK SOLUTION

Print

LOOK delivers all the key terms and all the content for the **Interpersonal Communications** course through a visually engaging and easy-to-review print experience.

Digital

MindTap enables you to stay organized and study efficiently by providing a single location for all your course materials and study aids. Built-in apps leverage social media and the latest learning technology to help you succeed.

1 Open the Access Card included with this text.

2 Follow the steps on the card.

3 Study.

Student Resources

- Interactive eBook
- Flashcards
- Chapter Review Cards
- Matching Activities
- Multiple Choice Quizzes
- Video Quizzes
- Critical Thinking Questions
- Chapter Review Questions
- Online Glossary
- Polling Questions

Students: **nelson.com/student**

Instructor Resources

- MindTap Progress App provides insight into student's performance and level of engagement
- Engagement Tracker
- Instructor Companion Site
- PowerPoint® Slides
- Updated Test Bank
- LMS Integration
- Instructor Prep Cards
- Assignable Activities

Instructors: **nelson.com/instructor**

NELSON

This edition of LOOK is dedicated to Lennon Mae Catherine Payson,
the newest little communicator in our family.

— Aunt Judy

**LOOK: Looking Out, Looking In,
Third Canadian Edition**

by Ronald B. Adler, Judith A. Rolls,
and Russell F. Proctor II

VP, Product and Partnership Solutions:
Anne Williams

Publisher, Digital and Print Content:
Leanna MacLean

Executive Marketing Manager:
Amanda Henry

Content Development Manager:
Lisa Berland

Photo and Permissions Researcher:
Julie Pratt

Senior Production Project Manager:
Natalia Denesiuk Harris

Production Service:
MPS Limited

Copy Editor:
Jessie Coffey

Proofreader:
MPS Limited

Indexer:
MPS Limited

Design Director:
Ken Phipps

Higher Education Design PM:
Pamela Johnston

Interior Design:
Cathy Mayer

Interior Images:
Tablet and smartphone vector
mockup over white, vector
illustration: Nexusby/Shutterstock

Cover Design:
Trinh Truong

Cover Image:
TommL/iStockphoto

Compositor:
MPS Limited

Library and Archives Canada Cataloguing in Publication Data

Adler, Ronald B. (Ronald Brian), 1946–, author
    LOOK : looking out, looking in / Ronald B. Adler, Judith A. Rolls, Russell F. Proctor II. — Third Canadian edition.

Includes bibliographical references and index.
ISBN 978-0-17-670012-6 (paperback)

    1. Interpersonal communication—Textbooks. I. Rolls, Judith A. (Judith Ann), author II. Proctor, Russell F., author III. Title.

BF637.C45A335 2017   158.2
C2016-906703-3

ISBN-13: 978-0-17-670012-6
ISBN-10: 0-17-670012-9

Brief Contents

© AlaskaStockRM/All Canada Photos

Eric Pelaez/Stone/Getty Images

© Arctic Photo/All Canada Photos

Contents

The Canadian Press/Andrew Vaughan

JGI/Tom Grill/Blend Images/Getty Images

MANDY GODBEHEAR/Shutterstock.com

Jaimie Duplass/Shutterstock.com

Rebecca Drobis/Blend Images/Getty Images

SpeedKingz/Shutterstock.com

Ikonoklast Fotografie/Shutterstock.com

Frank Gaertner/Shutterstock.com

A FIRST LOOK
AT INTERPERSONAL COMMUNICATION

LEARNING OUTCOMES

LO1 Assess the needs (physical, identity, social, and practical) that communicators are attempting to satisfy in a given situation or relationship.

LO2 Apply the transactional communication model to a specific situation.

LO3 Describe how communication principles and misconceptions are evident in a specific relationship.

LO4 Describe the degree to which communication is qualitatively impersonal or interpersonal, as well as the consequences of this level of interaction.

LO5 Identify the types of relational messages you exchange during communication with others.

LO6 Diagnose the effectiveness of various communication channels in a specific situation.

LO7 Determine your level of communication competence in a specific instance or relationship.

LO1
Why We Communicate

As human beings, we are clearly wired for interaction and most of us wouldn't opt to live in isolation. In fact, isolation is so painful it is used as a punishment in penal systems. Bob Kull studied the effects of isolation by secluding himself on an island off the coast of Chile while he was gathering data for his Ph.D. dissertation at the University of British Columbia. He concluded that while there were moments of bliss, it was hard to escape the spiritual and emotional darkness to which he was subjected.[1]

It appears that what human beings really want is communication and relationships. This need for connection and interaction seems even more pronounced today. People are in constant touch with friends, family, and colleagues through the various miracles of technology and feel cut off from the world without their electronic devices. In fact, in an international study covering 10 countries throughout the world, 1000 university students attempted to go 24 hours without using cell phones, going on Facebook, e-mailing, texting, and so forth. The results showed that the majority of students felt lonely, bored, or they didn't know what to do with themselves. They felt that their phones offered connection and comfort. Some students were so addicted that they suffered severe withdrawal symptoms. Across countries, students likened these symptoms to those experienced by drug addicts.[2]

Regardless of how we interact with others, it is clear that communication is a very rewarding activity. And, if you think about it, we actually communicate to fulfil our physical needs, identity needs, social needs, and to attain practical goals.

What do you THINK?

I think I am an effective communicator.

1   2   3   4   5   6   7

strongly agree   strongly disagree

Mick Stevens The New Yorker Collection/The Cartoon Bank

Physical Needs

It's hard to believe that communication affects our physical health and medical researchers have provided considerable evidence of this. For example, it is common practice in birthing centres across Canada to place newborns immediately in skin-to-skin contact with their mothers. Referred to as the *golden hour*, this contact (and the resulting breastfeeding) helps new moms bond with their infants and improves infant survival rates.[3] Further, breastfeeding during the *golden hour* lowers rates of "ear infections, asthma, diabetes, childhood leukemia and Sudden Infant Death Syndrome (SIDS)."[4] In situations where new mothers are incapacitated for some reason, skin-to-skin with fathers works as well.[5]

Positive interpersonal relationships in adulthood also lead to better health. We know that socially isolated people are four times more susceptible to the common cold[6] and three times more likely to die prematurely while marriage, friendships, and religious and community ties increase longevity.[7] Compared to their married counterparts, divorced men and women have higher cancer rates.[8] Even, the death of a close relative increases the likelihood of your own death.[9]

It appears that a life that includes positive relationships leads to better health. Socializing for 10 minutes a day, for example, improves memory and boosts intellectual function,[10] and stress hormones decline the more often people hear expressions of affection.[11] This might account for why the Canadian Health Network's definition of wellness is broad-based and recognizes the importance of social support and close personal relationships.[12] This stance is acknowledged elsewhere, as well. A hospital in Ireland opened a pub on its premises to help short- and long-term residents meet their social needs. Because much of Irish life centres on the pub, the facility affords an opportunity for seniors to interact with the other daily patrons. The pub provides a more inviting atmosphere than sitting in a residents' lounge, with nothing to see or do.[13]

Identity Needs

In addition to helping us survive, communication is the only way we learn who we are; our sense of identity comes from our interactions with others. Learning if we're intelligent, creative, skilled, or inept does not come from looking in the mirror but from seeing how others react to us.

Deprived of communication, we would have no sense of ourselves. Perhaps you have read about the famous "Wild Boy of Aveyron" case. The boy was discovered in January 1800 in France, digging for vegetables in a village garden. Having spent his childhood with no human contact, he couldn't speak, he uttered only weird cries, and he had absolutely no identity as a human being. As author Roger Shattuck put it, "The boy had no human sense of being in the world. He had no sense of himself as a person related to other persons."[14] Only with the influence of a loving "mother" did the boy begin

Macduff Everton/Getty Images

to behave—and, we can imagine, think of himself—as a human. Like the boy of Aveyron, we enter the world with little or no sense of identity and we learn who we are through others.

Social Needs

Besides helping to define who we are, communication also satisfies a whole range of social needs that include pleasure, affection, companionship, escape, relaxation, and control.[15]

Research suggests a strong link between effective interpersonal communication and happiness. In a study of over 200 college students, the happiest 10 percent described themselves as having a rich social life.[16] In another study, women reported that "socializing" was more satisfying than virtually any other activity.[17] Married couples who are effective communicators are reported to be happier than less skilful couples.[18]

The film *Cast Away* captures the pain of being isolated from communication with others.

In spite of knowing that communication is vital to social satisfaction, many people aren't very successful at managing their interpersonal relationships. One study revealed that 25 percent of the 4000-plus adults surveyed knew more about their dogs than about their neighbours' backgrounds.[19] Research also suggests that the number of close friendships we have is in decline. A 1985 study reported that North Americans had an average of 2.94 close friends, but 20 years later, that number had dropped to 2.08.[20] It's also worth noting that educated individuals had larger and more diverse networks than those with less education. Because positive relationships with others are so vital, some theorists argue that they may be our single most important source of satisfaction and emotional wellbeing, and that this holds across cultures.[21]

Invitation to Insight

Setting Your Communication Goals

Take the survey below to rate your present interpersonal communication skills. Afterwards, develop three to five communication goals you would like to achieve during this course.

1 = Strongly Disagree; 2 = Disagree; 3 = Undecided; 4 = Agree;
5 = Strongly Agree

1. I am a good communicator.

   1   2   3   4   5

2. I have a positive attitude about myself and my abilities.

   1   2   3   4   5

3. I can empathize with others.

   1   2   3   4   5

4. I express my emotions well.

   1   2   3   4   5

5. I express myself well.

   1   2   3   4   5

6. I am aware of the nonverbal messages I am sending and receiving.

   1   2   3   4   5

7. I am a good listener.

   1   2   3   4   5

8. I self-disclose to my friends and family.

   1   2   3   4   5

9. I can communicate assertively when necessary.

   1   2   3   4   5

10. I handle conflict well.

   1   2   3   4   5

You're tattooed on my skin
Don't know where you end
and I begin
You're tattooed on my soul
Are you the part that makes
me whole

—Damhnait Doyle and
Christopher Ward,
"Tattooed"*

*Reprinted with permission from Damhnait Doyle, care of Jones & Co., and with the permission of Christopher Ward.

Practical Goals

Finally, communication is used most often to satisfy our **instrumental goals**: getting things done. Some instrumental goals are quite basic. For example, communication is the tool that lets you tell the hairstylist to take just a little off the sides or makes it possible to negotiate household duties. Other instrumental goals are more important. Career success is a prime example. One study showed that the ability to speak and listen effectively was among the top factors that helped university graduates find jobs.[22] On-the-job communication is just as important. The Conference Board of Canada, in its *Employability Skills 2000+* pamphlet, identified a set of characteristics required "to enter, stay in, and progress in the world of work." Of these, basic communication skills such as speaking, listening, reading and writing, problem solving, demonstrating positive attitudes and behaviours toward others, adaptability, and teamwork all fall within the rubric of good interpersonal communication.[23]

Psychologist Abraham Maslow suggested that the physical, identity, social, and practical needs we have been discussing fall into five hierarchical categories, each of which must be satisfied before moving on to the next.[24] See **Figure 1.1**. The most basic of these needs are *physical*: air, water, food, rest, and the ability to reproduce. The second level is *safety*: protection from threats to our well-being. Beyond physical and safety needs are the *social* needs we have mentioned already. The third level has to do with *self-esteem*: the desire to believe that we are worthwhile, valuable people. The final category described by Maslow is *self-actualization*: the desire to develop our potential to the maximum, to become the best person we can be. As you go through your day, take a moment to assess which communication need others may be trying to satisfy when they communicate with you. You might find this exercise quite revealing.

Instrumental goals
Goals aimed at getting things done.

Linear communication model
A characterization of communication as a one-way event in which a message flows from sender to receiver.

Sender
The creator of a message.

Encode
The process of putting thoughts into symbols, most commonly words.

Message
Information sent from a sender to a receiver.

Channel
The medium through which a message passes from sender to receiver.

Receiver
One who notices and attends to a message.

Decode
The process in which a receiver attaches meaning to a message. Synonymous with interpretation.

Noise
External, physiological, or psychological distractions that interfere with the accurate transmission and reception of a message.

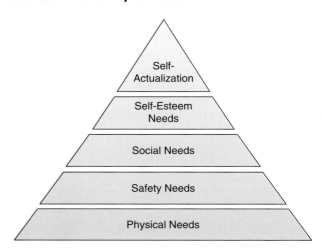
LO2
The Process of Communication

We've been discussing *communication* as though the meaning of this word were perfectly clear. Before going further, we need to explain just what happens when people exchange messages. This will introduce a working vocabulary that will be used throughout the text.

A Linear View

In the early days of studying communication as a social science, researchers thought of communication as something that a sender "does" to a receiver, and this resulted in a **linear communication model**.

According to the linear model shown in **Figure 1.2**,

a **sender** (the person creating the message)
encodes (puts thoughts into symbols, usually words) a
message (the information being transmitted), sending it through a
channel (the medium through which the message passes) to a
receiver (the person attending to the message) who
decodes (makes sense of the message), while contending with
noise (distractions that disrupt transmission).

Notice how the vocabulary in **Figure 1.2** sounds like the language of electronic media. There is a linear, machinelike quality to it. In reality, we know that interpersonal communication is much more complicated than

FIGURE 1.2
Linear Communication Model

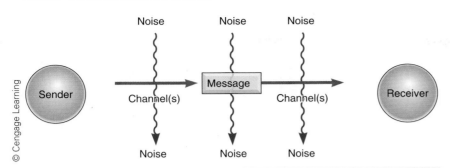

© Cengage Learning

the basics of sending and receiving messages. That is why more advanced models have been developed. Of particular interest is the transactional model of communication.

A Transactional View

The **transactional communication model** (**Figure 1.3**) expands the linear model to better capture communication as a uniquely human process. Some concepts and terms from the linear model are retained in the transactional model, while others are enhanced, added, or eliminated.

The transactional model uses the word *communicator* instead of *sender* and *receiver*, thus reflecting the simultaneous nature of communication. Consider, for example, what might occur when you and a housemate negotiate chores. As soon as you begin to hear (receive) the words sent by your partner, "I want to talk about cleaning the kitchen . . ." you grimace and clench your jaw (sending a nonverbal message of your own while receiving the verbal one). This reaction leads your housemate to interrupt herself defensively, sending a new message: "Now wait a minute . . ." You can see from the example how both individuals simultaneously send and receive messages.

FIGURE 1.3
Transactional Communication Model

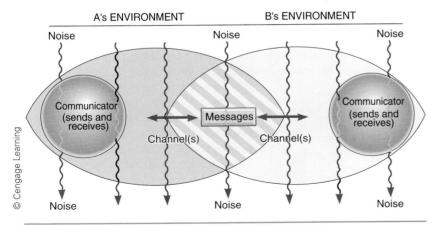

© Cengage Learning

A transactional model also shows that communicators often occupy different **environments**—fields of experience that affect how they understand others' behaviour. In communication terminology, *environment* refers not only to a physical location but also to the personal experiences and cultural background that participants bring to a conversation.

Consider some factors that might contribute to different environments:

- Person A might belong to one ethnic group and person B to another.
- A might be rich and B poor.
- A might have lived a long, eventful life and B might be young and inexperienced.
- A might be passionate about a subject and B indifferent to it.

Environments are not always obvious. Notice how the model in **Figure 1.3** shows that the environments of A and B overlap. This area represents the background that the communicators have in common. As the shared environment becomes smaller, communication becomes more difficult. For example:

- Bosses who have trouble understanding the perspective of their employees are less effective managers, and workers who do not appreciate the challenges of being a boss are more likely to be uncooperative.
- Parents who have trouble recalling their youth are likely to clash with their children, who have no idea that parenting is such a huge responsibility.
- Members of a dominant culture who have never been part of a minority may not appreciate the concerns of people from non-dominant cultures, whose own perspectives make it hard to understand the cultural blindness of the majority.

Communication channels play a significant role in the transactional model, and their importance can be seen in the following example: Should you say "I love you" in person? On Facebook?

> **Transactional communication model**
> A characterization of communication as the simultaneous sending and receiving of messages in an ongoing, irreversible process.
>
> **Environment**
> The field of experiences that lead a person to make sense of another's behaviour.

By renting space on a billboard? Via e-mail? In a voice mail? In a text message? Channel selection matters even more when sending breakup messages. A recent study of 1000 cellphone users found that 45 percent had used their phones to end a relationship—usually by text![25]

The transactional model also retains the concept of noise but broadens its focus. In the linear model, the focus is on noise in the channel—what is known as **external noise**—such as loud music or too much cigarette smoke in a crowded room. But in the transactional model, noise also resides *within* communicators.

Interpersonal communication
A continuous transactional process involving participants who occupy different but overlapping environments and create relationships through the exchange of messages, many of which are affected by external, physiological, and psychological noise.

This includes **physiological noise**—biological factors that interfere with accurate reception, such as illness, fatigue, hearing loss, and so on—and **psychological noise**: forces within that interfere with the ability to understand a message accurately. For instance, a student might become so upset that he failed a test that he is unable (or unwilling) to understand where he went wrong. Psychological noise can cause many communication problems. See **Table 1.1** for more examples of noise.

For all the insights they offer, models can't capture some important features of interpersonal communication. A model is a "snapshot," but communication more closely resembles a "motion picture." In real life it's difficult to isolate a single discrete "act" of communication from the events that precede and follow it.[26] Consider the *Zits* cartoon. If you read only the final frame, Jeremy appears to be the victim of his mother's nagging. If you then read the first three frames, you might conclude that if Jeremy were more responsive to his mother, she might not need to be so persistent. And if you watched the two of them interact over the days and weeks preceding the incident in this cartoon, you would have a larger (but still incomplete) picture of the relational history that contributed to this event. In other words, the communication pattern that Jeremy and his mother have created together contributes to the quality of their relationship.

The relationships between the characters on the television show *How I Met Your Mother* illustrate the transactional nature of interpersonal "communication."

TABLE 1.1
Some Examples of Noise

External Noise
Sounds, running motors, talking, music, smoke, temperature, perfumes, smells, visual distractions, clothing, lighting, language, nonverbal communication, culturally diverse mannerisms

Physiological Noise
Pain, hunger, fatigue, visual problems, pounding heart, body temperature, thirst, itch, twitching, hearing loss, numbness, dizziness

Psychological Noise
Embarrassment, anger, disappointment, confusion, nervousness, inadequacies, fear, joy, pressure, boredom, pessimism, optimism, apathy, shame

This leads to another important point: Transactional communication isn't something that we do *to* others; rather, it is an activity that we do *with* them. In this sense, person-to-person communication is rather like dancing with a partner in that it depends on another person's involvement. And like good dancing, successful communication doesn't just depend on the partner who's leading. Both partners must coordinate their movements. Likewise, the way you communicate almost certainly varies from one partner to another.

Now the definition of *communication* can be summarized. **Interpersonal communication** is a continuous transactional process involving participants who occupy different but overlapping environments and create relationships through the exchange of messages, many of which are affected by external, physiological, and psychological noise.

© King Features Syndicate. Reprinted with permission – Torstar Syndication Services

Communication Principles and Misconceptions

Before we look at the qualities of interpersonal communication, it's important to define what communication is, what it isn't, what it does, and what it can't accomplish.

Communication Principles

Based on what you've learned so far, it's possible to draw several important conclusions about interpersonal communication.

Communication Can Be Intentional or Unintentional

Some communication is clearly intentional: You plan your words carefully before asking for a big favour or offering criticism. Some scholars argue that only intentional messages like these qualify as communication, but others hold that even unintentional behaviour is communicative. Suppose, for instance, that a friend overhears you muttering complaints to yourself. Even though you didn't intend for her to hear your remarks, they certainly carried a message.

In addition, we unintentionally send many nonverbal messages. You might not be aware of your sour expression or sigh of boredom, but others see and hear them nonetheless. The debate continues about whether unintentional behaviour should be considered communication, and it's unlikely that the issue will ever be settled in the near future.[27] In *LOOK*, we will examine the communicative value of both intentional and unintentional behaviour.

Communication Is Irreversible

At times, we've all said something we immediately regretted and wished that the words could have been erased. But, alas, that's impossible. While an apology can mollify hurt feelings or further explanation can clear up a misunderstanding, the impression you've created cannot be erased. It is no more possible to "unreceive" a message than to "unsqueeze" a tube of toothpaste. Words said and deeds done are irretrievable.

It's Impossible Not to Communicate

Many theorists agree that it is impossible not to communicate because whatever you do—whether you speak or remain silent, confront or avoid—you provide others with information about your thoughts and feelings. In this sense, we are like transmitters that can't be shut off. We constantly send messages.

This explains why the best way to enhance understanding is to discuss your intentions and your interpretations of the other person's behaviour until you have negotiated a shared meaning.

Communication Is Unrepeatable

Because communication is an ongoing process, it is impossible to repeat an event. A certain smile that worked well when you met a stranger last week might not work with one you encounter tomorrow: It might feel stale or be inappropriate for a different person or occasion. Even with the same person, you can't recreate an event. Why? Because neither of you is the same person. You've both lived longer and the behaviour isn't original. Your feelings about each other may have changed. You need not constantly invent new ways to act around familiar people, but realize that the "same" words and behaviours are different each time they are spoken or performed.

Communication Has a Content and a Relational Dimension

Practically all exchanges operate on two levels: the content level and the relational level. The **content dimension** involves the information being explicitly discussed. The content of "Turn left at the next corner" or "You can buy that for less online" is obvious. The **relational dimension** expresses how the parties feel toward one another.[28] Imagine, for example, two ways of saying, "It's your turn to do the dishes": one that is demanding and another that is matter-of-fact. The different tones of voice can send very different relational messages.

Sometimes the content dimension of a message is all that

> **Content message**
> A message that communicates information about the subject being discussed.
>
> **Relational message**
> A message that expresses the social relationship between two or more individuals.

Andresr/Shutterstock.com

matters. For example, you probably aren't concerned about the service rep's feelings about you as long as you get your car fixed. At other times, the relational dimension message is important. This explains why arguments can develop over apparently trivial subjects like whose turn it is to wash the dishes or how to spend the weekend.

Communication Misconceptions

Along with understanding the communication principles, avoiding the following misconceptions can save a good deal of interpersonal trouble.[29]

More Communication Is Always Better

Although not communicating enough can cause problems, there are also situations when *too much* communication is a mistake. Sometimes excessive communication is unproductive, like when two people "talk a problem to death" without making progress. As one book puts it, "More and more negative communication merely leads to more and more negative results."[30] Even too much noncritical communication can backfire. Pestering a prospective employer or texting too many "call me" messages to a friend can generate a negative reaction.

QUALITY TIME   Gail Machlis

Drawing by Gail Machlis, *Quality Time*, 21 July 1994. Quality Time © 1994 Gail Machlis. Reprinted with permission of the artist. All rights reserved.

Meanings Are in Words

It's a big mistake to assume that saying something is the same thing as communicating it. The words that make perfect sense to you can be interpreted in entirely different ways by others. For example, one of the authors told an acquaintance that she enjoyed painting at her summer cottage. The acquaintance asked if she did landscape, still life, abstract. But she had to disappoint the person by saying that it was just routine upkeep around the house—some years the deck needed a face lift, other years the doors and window frames needed a touch-up.

Successful Communication Always Involves Shared Understanding

There are times when successful communication comes from not completely understanding one another. For example, we are often deliberately vague about something. Perhaps you find a friend's new tattoo grotesque, but when asked how you like it, you say, "Wow, that's really unusual." In such cases, clarification is sacrificed for the sake of kindness and relational maintenance.

Some research shows that satisfying relationships depend in part on flawed understanding. Couples who *think* their partners understand them are more satisfied with each other than those who *actually* understand what the other person says and means.[31]

A Single Person or Event Causes Another's Reaction

Another common misconception is thinking that any single thing we say or do causes a particular outcome when, in fact, many factors affect how others will react to your communication. If you lose your temper and say something to a friend that you immediately regret, your friend's reaction depends on a host of events besides your

unjustified remark. These include her frame of mind at the moment (uptight or mellow), elements of her personality (judgmental or forgiving), your relational history (supportive or hostile), and so forth. Because communication is a transactional, ongoing, collaborative process, it's usually a mistake to think that any event occurs in a vacuum. For instance, you're talking with your friend and she breaks her pen. She glares at you and says, "Now look what you've made me do." Clearly, there's more going on with her than your immediate conversation.

Communication Can Solve All Problems

Sometimes even the best-planned, best-timed communication won't solve a problem. Imagine asking an instructor to explain why you received a poor grade on a project that you believe deserved top marks. The instructor outlines the reasons for your low grade and sticks to that position after listening to you carefully. Has communication solved the problem? Hardly.

LO4
The Nature of Interpersonal Communication

Now that you have an understanding of the communication process, it's time to look at what makes some types uniquely interpersonal.

Two Views of Interpersonal Communication

Communication scholars define interpersonal communication in two ways: quantitatively and qualitatively.[32] A **quantitative** definition focuses on the number of people involved and includes *any* interaction between two people, usually face to face. Two people interacting is referred to as a **dyad**, and this type of interaction is called *dyadic* communication. So, in a quantitative sense, the terms *dyadic communication* and *interpersonal communication* are interchangeable. Using a quantitative definition, a sales clerk talking to a customer or a police officer issuing a ticket are interpersonal acts because they involve two people and are probably **impersonal** in nature. For instance, a clerk might tell you to have a nice day without even looking at you.

Some scholars argue, however, that it's not quantity that distinguishes interpersonal communication, it is *quality*.[33] Using a qualitative definition, interpersonal communication occurs when people treat one another as unique individuals, regardless of the context or the number of people involved. Several features distinguish qualitative interpersonal communication from less personal communication. These features include uniqueness, irreplaceability, interdependence, disclosure, and intrinsic rewards.[34]

Quantitative definition of interpersonal communication
Impersonal communication, usually face to face, between two individuals.

Dyad
Two people interacting.

Impersonal communication
Behaviour that treats others as objects rather than as individuals.

Qualitative definition of interpersonal communication
Communication in which the parties consider one another as unique individuals rather than as objects. Such communication is characterized by minimal use of stereotyped labels; by unique, idiosyncratic rules; and by a high degree of information exchange.

Characteristics of Qualitative Interpersonal Relationships

The first feature is *uniqueness*. **Qualitative** interpersonal relationships are characterized by the development of unique rules and roles, and, therefore, every relationship that you have is different. In one, you might exchange good-natured insults, whereas in another you are more formal. Likewise, you might handle conflicts as they arise with one friend and withhold resentments until they build up and explode with another. One communication scholar coined the term *relational culture* to describe people in close relationships who create their own unique ways of interacting.[35]

A second feature of qualitatively interpersonal relationships is *irreplaceability*. Because interpersonal relationships are unique, they can't be replaced. This explains why we usually feel so sad when a relative dies

Even the "closest" relationships can become impersonal over time.

Photodisc/Thinkstock

or a love affair cools down. No matter how many other relationships we have, that particular one can't ever be replaced.

Interdependence is a third feature of qualitatively interpersonal relationships. This simply means that the other's experiences affect you as well. While this can bring pleasure, at other times it may be a burden. But interdependence goes beyond the level of joined fates—our very identity depends on the nature of our interaction with others. As Kenneth Gergen explains, "One cannot be 'attractive' without others who are attracted, a 'leader' without others willing to follow, or a 'loving person' without others to affirm with appreciation."[36]

A fourth feature is **disclosure** of personal information. While we don't typically reveal much about ourselves in impersonal relationships, we tend to disclose private thoughts and feelings when we're in a qualitative interpersonal relationship.

The final feature of interpersonal communication is **intrinsic rewards**. That simply means that spending time with friends, lovers, and others is enjoyable and personally rewarding.

Because relationships that are unique, irreplaceable, interdependent, disclosing, and intrinsically rewarding are rare, qualitatively interpersonal communication is relatively scarce. Considering the number of people with whom you communicate daily (classmates, neighbours, etc.) or the amount of time engaged in online bantering, personal relationships are by far in the minority.

Communicators who strive to acquire a large number of "friends" on social networking websites like Facebook and Twitter are engaging in superficial, impersonal relationships. As one critic put it, "The idea . . . is to attain as many of these not-really-friends as possible . . . Like cheap wine, 'friends' provide a high that can only be sustained by acquiring more and more of them. Quantity trumps quality."[37]

Personal and Impersonal Communication: A Matter of Balance

Most relationships aren't either interpersonal or impersonal; they fall somewhere on a continuum between these two extremes. You might appreciate the unique sense of humour of a grocery clerk or connect on a personal level with the person cutting your hair. Or a demanding, by-the-book boss might be warm and easy going with her family.

Just as there's a personal element in many impersonal settings, we also communicate in impersonal ways with the people we care most about. When we're distracted, tired, busy, or just not interested, we don't want to be personal. In fact, interpersonal communication is rather like rich food—it's fine in moderation, but too much can make you uncomfortable.

The personal–impersonal balance in relationships also changes over time. New lovers talk excessively about their feelings, but as time passes, their communication becomes more routine. While interpersonal communication can make life worth living, it isn't possible or desirable all the time. The challenge is to balance the two types.

Invitation to Insight

How Personal Are Your Relationships?

Use the characteristics of qualitatively interpersonal communication to think about your own relationships.

1. Make a list of several people who are close to you—family members, people you live with, friends, co-workers, and so on.
2. Use the scales below to rate each relationship. To distinguish the relationships from one another, use a different color of ink for each one.
3. Consider comparing your results with those of classmates or friends.

After completing the exercise, ask yourself the important question: How satisfied are you with the answers you have found?

Uniqueness

1	2	3	4	5
Standardized, habitual				Unique

Replaceability

1	2	3	4	5
Replaceable				Irreplaceable

Dependence

1	2	3	4	5
Independent				Interdependent

Disclosure

1	2	3	4	5
Low disclosure				High disclosure

Intrinsic rewards

1	2	3	4	5
Unrewarding				Rewarding

LO5
Communicating about Relationships

Clearly, relationships and the messages we exchange can be complex. As you further explore interpersonal communication, it is important to understand the kinds of messages we send to one another.

Content and Relational Messages

Earlier in the chapter, we noted that every message has a content and a relational dimension. The **content** refers to the subject being discussed while relational messages make statements about how the parties feel toward one another.[38] While the content dimension consists of the words in the message, the relational dimension isn't discussed, and often we're not conscious of it. Sometimes we're unaware of relational messages because they match our beliefs about the amount of respect, control, and affection that is appropriate. For example, you probably wouldn't be offended if your boss told you to do a certain job, because you agree that supervisors have the right to direct employees. But if the message was delivered in a condescending or sarcastic tone, you would probably be offended. Your complaint wouldn't be with the order but with how it was delivered. That's the relational message and these can be divided into four different categories: affinity, immediacy, respect, and control.

Types of Relational Messages

There are four categories or relational messages: affinity, immediacy, respect, and control.

Affinity

Affinity refers to the degree to which people like or appreciate one another.[39] Not surprisingly, affection is the most important ingredient to express liking in romantic relationships.[40] But not all affinity messages are positive: A glare or an angry word shows the level of liking just as clearly as a smile or profession of love.

Immediacy

Immediacy refers to the degree of interest and attention that we feel toward and communicate to others. Not surprisingly, immediacy is an important element of relationships.[41] We express a great deal of immediacy through nonverbal behaviours such as eye contact, facial expression, tone of voice, or the distance we put between ourselves and others.[42] Immediacy is expressed through language when we say things like, "We have a problem," instead of "You have a problem."

Respect

While respect might seem identical to affinity, the two attitudes differ.[43] Although affinity involves liking, **respect**

"Fine. Sit there and check your messages. Perhaps it will give you something to contribute to the conversation."

involves esteem. It's possible to like others without respecting them. You might have a good deal of affection for some friends, yet not respect the way they act in certain situations. Or, conversely, it's possible to respect someone you don't like. You might hold an acquaintance in high esteem for being hardworking and honest but not enjoy that person's company.

Respect is an extremely important ingredient in relationships, and it's a better predictor of relational satisfaction than liking or loving.[44] Sometimes, being respected is more important than being liked. Being taken seriously is a vital ingredient of self-esteem.

Control

A final dimension of relational communication involves **control**—the degree to which the parties in a relationship have the power to influence one another. Some types of control involve conversation—who talks, interrupts, or changes the topic most often.[45] Another dimension involves decisions: who determines what will happen in the relationship.

Relational problems arise when the people concerned have different ideas about the distribution of control. If you and a friend each push for your own idea, problems are likely to arise. Of course, it can be just as difficult when neither person wants to make

Content message
A message that communicates information about the subject being discussed.

Affinity
The degree to which people like or appreciate one another.

Immediacy
The degree of interest and attention that we feel toward and communicate to others.

Respect
The social need to be held in esteem by others.

Control
The degree to which the parties in a relationship have the power to influence one another.

CHAPTER 1 A First Look at Interpersonal Communication

"Richard, we need to talk. I'll e-mail you."

Aaron Bacall The New Yorker Collection/The Cartoon Bank

a decision: "What do you want to do tonight?" "I don't know . . . why don't you decide." "No, you decide."

People in healthy relationships handle the distribution of control in a flexible way. They shift between one-up, one-down, and straight-across roles. For instance, Kyle may handle decisions about car repairs and menu planning while Ashley manages the finances and child care. When a decision is important to one partner, the other willingly gives in, knowing that the favour will be returned. When issues are important to both partners, they try to share power equally. But when an impasse occurs, each will make concessions in a way that keeps the overall balance of power equal.

Metacommunication

Social scientists use the term **metacommunication** to describe the verbal and nonverbal messages that people exchange about their relationship.[46] In other words, metacommunication is communication about communication—"I wish we could stop arguing so much." Metacommunication is essential in successful relationships, and sooner or later you'll have to talk about what is going on between you.

Metacommunication is useful for solving conflicts because it enables you to shift discussion from the content level to relational questions, where most interpersonal problems lie. Further, metacommunication can

Metacommunication
Messages that people exchange, verbally or nonverbally, about their relationship—communication about communication.

Social Media
Collectively describes all the channels that makes remote personal communication possible.

reinforce the satisfying aspects of a relationship: "I really appreciate it when you compliment my work in front of the boss." Such comments let others know that their behaviour is appreciated and boost the odds that the behaviour will be continued.

LO6
Social Media and Interpersonal Communication

Clearly, face-to-face conversation isn't the only way people create and maintain personal relationships. Today, communicators rely heavily on **social media** to connect with others. These include instant messaging, e-mailing, blogging, and tweeting, or using Skype, Facebook, MySpace, and so forth. A great example of this is Canadian astronaut Chris Hadfield. You may recall that he went into space in December 2012 for several months and during that time he used social media to entertain and inform Canada, and the world, about life in zero gravity. Further, he played his guitar, sang songs, and tweeted breathtaking photos of earth taken from his "out of this world" vantage point. Many people felt as if they had gotten to know him. Examples like this may account for why researchers are finding that the difference between face-to-face and virtual relationships is eroding.[47]

Benefits of Social Media

A growing body of research reveals that mediated communication isn't the threat to relationships that some critics once feared.[48] For example:

- According to one study, some media tools offer "low-friction" opportunities to create, enhance, and rediscover social ties." These benefits outweigh the costs.[49]
- Staying in touch with current friends and family members while still connecting with old friends they have lost are major reasons for using social media.[50]

Source: NASA, Canadian Space Agency, 2013.

Social Networking, Survival, and Healing

Dean Drobot/Shutterstock.com

If you dig enough, you'll find little bits and pieces of my life scattered across the Net. For many people, this sort of transparency is unnerving. For me, it's always been a source of comfort in the storm that has been my life. Throughout 20 years of drinking and drugs, I've always had cyberfriends who, for reasons I can't explain, have stayed up late and saved me more times than I can count.

When I made the decision—or more accurately, when the decision smashed down upon me—to get sober, I was terrified, embarrassed, and angry. I certainly didn't think I needed anyone to help me.

Sometime near the end of the third month, the last bits of my sanity were gone. I couldn't function any longer. That's when I turned to the Web. I began to post what I've been told was an ever-increasing series of erratic blurbs—some directly to FriendFeed and others on Twitter, Facebook, and MySpace.

Those messages started a dialogue that took on a life of its own. I began to get e-mails, phone calls, text messages, tweets, and other digital notes from people around the world. Some offered kind words. Some offered support. Many people shared their own stories of addiction. In my darkest times, these notes would come. And always, without question, they pulled me back from the brink.

Many of these messages were from people I have known for years. Another handful came from childhood friends and people I'd grown up with. Some I had known well; many I had not. Others came from complete strangers. I have no idea how they found me.

The moment when I knew I'd be okay came one night during a cross-country drive. The phone rang as I blew through Tennessee, but I didn't recognize the number so I let it go to voice mail. When I pulled into a gas station, I listened to the message. The woman on the phone didn't leave her name, and to this day I have no idea who she was. She told me about her father and his drinking. She told me that she was proud of me for getting sober and that she wanted me to keep trying. Already tenuous with my emotions, I sat on the side of the road crying. I listened to that message dozens of times, over and over.

The encouragement kept coming: strangers leaving messages about their lives, encouraging me to keep going. Throughout the next few months, my life became a 24-hour shower of love. There wasn't one free moment that wasn't taken up by someone making sure that my dumb ass wasn't back at the bar, that I wasn't looking for ways to die, and that I was doing the right thing. I still couldn't bring myself to leave the house. I rarely left my couch. I couldn't communicate with most people. But I was never alone.

AA keeps me sane. But social media got me there. Without that far-reaching network of people—friends and strangers alike—I wouldn't be here today.

Brad K.

Reprinted with permission from Brad King.

- Text-only formats can minimize perceptual differences resulting from gender, social class, ethnicity, and age.[51]
- More than 80 percent of social media users are involved in some kind of voluntary group or organization which is substantially more than non-users.[52]
- Facebook users are more trusting, have more close friends, and get more support from friends than non-users.[53]

It's important to note that social media isn't a replacement for face-to-face interaction. College students who frequently use instant messaging found face-to-face communication better "in terms of satisfying individuals' communication, information, and social needs."[54] However, mediated communication can promote and reinforce relationships in that if you regularly communicate with friends and family online, you're likely to call and see them more often.[55]

Ariel Skelley/Blend Images/Getty Images

JGI/Tom Grill/Blend Images/Getty Images

Using social media can increase both the quantity and the quality of interpersonal communication for several reasons. First, it is easier to maintain relationships.[56] Busy schedules can make it tough for people separated by long distances and multiple time zones to connect. However, the *asynchronous* nature of e-mail allows us to share information in a way that otherwise would be impossible. Communicators don't have to connect in real time. Instant messaging is another way to keep in touch: Discovering that a friend or relative is online is "like walking down the street and sometimes running into a friend," says Laura Balsam, a New York computer consultant.[57] Even when face-to-face communication is convenient, some people find it easier to share personal information via mediated channels. Sociolinguist Deborah Tannen describes how e-mail can transform the quality of relationships when individuals begin connecting online.[58] Experiences like these explain why Steve Jobs, the co-founder of Apple, suggested that personal computers be renamed

"*inter*personal computers."[59] Although social media can enhance relationships, Barry Wellman from the University of Toronto notes that most people typically incorporated all the avenues of communication.[60]

Challenges of Social Media

Despite its benefits, social media presents several challenges, as is explained below.

Leaner Messages

Face-to-face communication is rich because it abounds with nonverbal cues that help clarify the meanings of one another's words and offer hints about each person's feelings.[61] By comparison, most mediated communication is a much leaner channel for conveying information. For instance, imagine you haven't heard from a friend in several weeks and you decide to ask, "Is anything wrong?" Your friend replies, "No, I'm fine." If you received this message as a face-to-face response, it would contain a rich array of cues to interpret the message: facial expressions, vocal tone, and so on. Compare that response to a text message that contains only words. At least a phone message would give you a few vocal cues.

Because most mediated messages are leaner than the face-to-face variety, they can be harder to interpret. As receivers, it's important to clarify our interpretations before jumping to conclusions. As senders, we need to be aware of the many different ways our words can be interpreted by others.

The absence of nonverbal cues also allows cyber-communicators to carefully manage their identities. Further, Joseph Walther identifies a phenomenon that he calls "hyperpersonal" communication—accelerating the discussion of personal topics and relational development beyond what normally happens in face-to-face interaction.[62] This may explain why some communicators who meet online "rush" into marriage. Others have difficulty shifting to a face-to-face relationship.[63] Finally, recall the study of the 1000 students around the world who went 24 hours without connecting with others via technology. Although this proved extremely difficult, some participants said they found that their communication was actually deeper and more satisfying in the face-to-face context.[64]

Disinhibition

The tendency to transmit messages without considering their consequences can be especially great in online communication, where we don't see, hear, or sometimes even know the target of our remarks. This is referred to as **disinhibition** and it can take two forms.

The first is volunteering personal information you may not want some receivers to see. A quick scan of home pages on Facebook, MySpace, or Friendster reveals images and texts that could prove embarrassing in some contexts: "Here I am just before my DUI arrest." This may not be the kind of thing you want prospective employers or certain family members to see.

In addition to offering personal information about their life, individuals on mediated communication are more direct—often in a critical way—than they would be in face-to-face interaction.[65] Worse still can be the ramifications of sexting when the relationship goes awry.

Permanence

Nothing really goes away on the Internet. A regrettable text message, e-mail, or web posting can be archived virtually forever. Even worse, it can be retrieved and forwarded in ways that can only be imagined in your worst dreams. The best advice is to take the same approach with social media messages that you take in person: Think twice before saying or posting something you may later regret.

Competence in Social Media

In addition to the interpersonal competence discussed so far, social media competence calls for a unique set of skills.

Think Before You Post

Because the Internet never forgets, personal information posted today can, and perhaps will, haunt you in the future. Obviously, this can be especially damaging to your career. According to some surveys, 70 percent of recruiters rejected candidates based on online information such as photographs, comments by and about the candidate, and membership in groups.[66] Similarly, during the 2015 federal election campaign, we saw candidates from the Liberal, Conservative, and NDP parties drop out of the race after posts containing inappropriate material were discovered.[67] But the stories don't stop there. A 16-year-old British girl lost her job for complaining on Facebook, "I'm so totally bored!!" A 66-year-old Canadian psychotherpist was permanently banned from visiting the United States after a border guard's Internet search found that he had written an article in a philosophy journal describing his experiences with LSD 30 years earlier.[68] While the case can be made that such treatment is unfair, the point is that a little discretion now might save a lot of trouble later on.

Be Considerate

The unique nature of social media calls for a special set of civil appropriate behaviours which many refer to as "netiquette." Here are a few.

Disinhibition
The tendency to transmit messages without considering their consequences.

Somos/Veer/Getty Images

The Joy of Tech™   by Nitrozac & Snaggy

Signs of the social networking times.

What Makes an Effective Communicator?

It's easy to recognize good communicators and even easier to spot poor ones. But what are the characteristics of effective communication? Answering this question has been a leading challenge for communication scholars, and they have identified some important and useful information about communication competence.[70]

Communication Competence Defined

Communication competence involves achieving one's goals in a manner that, ideally, maintains or enhances the relationship in which it occurs.[71] This definition may seem vague and wordy, but it is guided by several important characteristics described below.

There Is No "Ideal" Way to Communicate

Just as there are many kinds of beautiful music or art, so are there many kinds of competent communication. Some very successful communicators are serious whereas others use humour, some are gregarious whereas others are quiet, and some are straightforward whereas others hint diplomatically. One way to learn new, effective ways of communicating is by observing models, but don't try to copy others, as it won't reflect your own style or values.

Respect the Needs of Your Face-to-Face Conversational Partner

If you have been texting since you could master a keyboard, you may not realize that face-to-face conversational partners get insulted when you start texting. As one observer put it, "While a quick log-on may seem, to the user, a harmless break, others in the room receive it as a silent dismissal. It announces, 'I'm not interested.'"[69]

Keep Your Tone Civil

If you've ever posted a snide comment on a blog, shot back a nasty reply to a text or instant message, or forwarded an embarrassing e-mail, you know that it is easier to behave badly when the recipient isn't right in front of you. One way to improve behaviour in asynchronous situations is to ask yourself a simple question before you post, send, or broadcast something: Would you deliver the same message in person? If the answer is no, you may want to hold off before hitting the "enter" key.

Don't Intrude on Bystanders

We have all has been exposed to moviegoers whose screens distract others, to people who speak so loudly on their phones that you can't hear your conversational partner, or to pedestrians who are more focused on their handheld devices than watching where they're going. These should also serve as our cues for us to treat others more respectfully when we're using technological devices.

Communication competence

The ability to accomplish one's personal goals in a manner that maintains or enhances the relationship in which it occurs.

When it comes to communication competence, TV character Dr. Sheldon Cooper (played by Jim Parsons) clearly lacked interpersonal communication skills. He did, however, demonstrate professional competencies.

Competence Is Situational

Communication that is competent in one setting might be a colossal blunder in another. The insulting jokes you trade with friends might be offensive to family members or co-workers.

Because competent communication behaviour varies so much from one situation and person to another, it's more accurate to talk about *degrees* or *areas* of competence.[72] For example, you might deal quite skilfully with peers but feel clumsy interacting with people who are older, wealthier, or more educated than you are. Your competence level with one person may even vary from situation to situation. So, rather than think that you are a terrible communicator in general, it's more accurate to say that you handle some situations better than others.

Competence Can Be Learned

To some degree, biology is destiny when it comes to communication style.[73] Studies of identical and fraternal twins suggest that traits including sociability, anger, and relaxation seem to be a partial function of our genetic makeup. However, biology isn't the only factor that shapes how we communicate. Because communication involves a set of skills that anyone can learn, skill training has been found to help people in a variety of professions.[74] Further, college students typically become more competent communicators over the course of their studies.[75] In other words, just like there are things you can do to improve your golf swing, so too can you improve your communication competence level through education and training. Even reading this book will help you become more competent.[76]

Characteristics of Competent Communicators

Even though competent communication varies from one situation to another, scholars have identified several common denominators that characterize effective communication.

A Wide Range of Behaviours

Effective communicators possess a wide range of behaviours.[77] To understand the importance of having a large communication repertoire, imagine that someone you know repeatedly tells jokes—perhaps racist, sexist, or ageist ones—that you find offensive. You could respond in a number of ways. You could

- say nothing, figuring that the risks of bringing the subject up would be greater than the benefits.
- ask a third party to say something to the jokester about the offensiveness of the stories.
- hint at your discomfort, hoping your friend will get the point.
- joke about your friend's insensitivity, counting on humour to soften the blow of your criticism.
- express your discomfort in a straightforward way, asking your friend to stop telling the offensive jokes, at least around you.
- demand that your friend stop.

With this choice of responses, you could pick the one that has the best chance of success. But if you were able to use only one or two of these responses, say always

I'M UNEMPLOYED AND I DRIVE AN ELECTRIC CAR.

THESE ARE MY ABS. I TALK TOO MUCH ABOUT MYSELF AND I'M NOT ROMANTIC.

scottadams@aol.com
www.dilbert.com
© 2001 United Feature Syndicate, Inc.

I REALIZE IT'S A LONG SHOT BUT DOES ANY OF THAT TURN YOU ON?

keeping quiet or always hinting, your chances of success would be greatly reduced. Poor communicators are easy to spot because of their limited range of responses. Some are chronic jokers, others are always belligerent, and still others are quiet in almost every situation. Like a chef who can prepare only a few dishes, these people are forced to rely on a small range of responses again and again, whether or not they are successful.

Having a repertoire of options available to manage unwanted offers of help is something many people with disabilities have learned.[78] Some options include performing a task quickly, before anyone has the chance to intervene; pretending not to hear the offer; accepting in order not to seem rude or ungrateful; using humour to deflect the person; declining the offer with thanks; and assertively refusing help from those who won't take no for an answer.

Ability to Choose the Most Appropriate Behaviour

Simply possessing a large range of communication skills is no guarantee of success; you have to know when to use which skill. To help make this decision, consider the following three factors: context, goal, and knowledge of the person.

The communication ***context***—time and place—will almost always influence how you act. For example, the sombre, low-key communication style one finds at a funeral would be out of place at a graduation party.

Your ***goal*** will also shape the approach you take. Inviting a new neighbour over for a cup of tea or coffee would be the right approach if you want to encourage a friendship. If you want to maintain your privacy, it would be wiser to be polite but cool.

Your ***knowledge of the other person*** should shape your approach. If, for instance, a person was very sensitive or insecure, your response might be supportive and cautious. With an old, trusted friend, you could be blunt. The social niche of the other party can also influence your communication. You would probably act differently around the president of your institution than you would toward a classmate, even in identical circumstances.

Skill at Performing Behaviours

There is a big difference between knowing *about* a skill and being able to put it into practice. It is necessary to perform the required skill effectively.[79] Like any other skills—playing a musical instrument or learning a sport, for example—you will pass through four stages on your road to communication competence.[80] See the skill builder below.

SKILL BUILDER

Stages in Learning Communication Skills
Learning any new skill requires moving through several levels of competence.

1. Beginning Awareness
The first step is becoming aware of a new and better way of behaving. Just as a tennis player learns a new serve that can improve power and accuracy, so should reading bring you new information about *communication competence*.

2. Awkwardness
Just as you were awkward when you first tried to ride a bicycle or drive a car, so may your initial attempts at communicating in new ways also be awkward. As the saying goes, "You have to be willing to look bad if you want to get good."

3. Skilfulness
If you keep working at your new skill, you'll reach a point where you can do it but it won't be natural to you. You'll still need to think about what you're doing. As an interpersonal communicator, you can expect this stage of skilfulness to be marked by a great deal of thinking and planning. But you'll find that you're getting increasingly good results.

4. Integration
Integration occurs when you're able to perform well without thinking about it. The behaviour becomes automatic, a part of your repertoire.

FIGURE 1.4
Stages in Learning Communication Skills

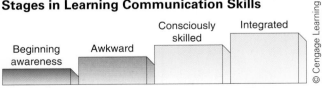

© Cengage Learning

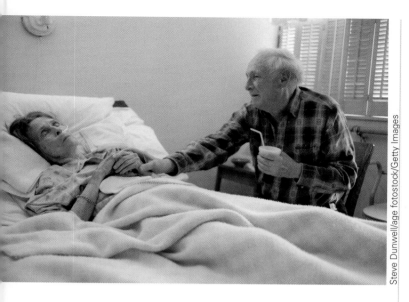
Steve Dunwell/age fotostock/Getty Images

complexity can increase competence, imagine that a long-time friend seems angry with you. One possible explanation is that your friend is offended by something you've done. Another possibility is that something upsetting has happened to your friend. Or perhaps nothing is wrong; you're just being overly sensitive. Considering the issue from several angles might prevent you from overreacting or misunderstanding the situation and thus increase the odds of resolving the problem constructively.

Cognitive complexity
The ability to construct a variety of frameworks for viewing an issue.

Empathy
The ability to project oneself into another person's point of view, so as to experience the other's thoughts and feelings.

Self-monitoring
The process of attending to your own behaviour and using these observations to shape the way you behave.

Cognitive Complexity

Social scientists use the term **cognitive complexity** to describe the ability to construct a variety of frameworks for viewing an issue.[81] To understand how cognitive

Empathy

Empathy involves feeling and experiencing another person's situation almost as they do. This ability is so important that some researchers have labelled empathy the most important aspect of communication competence.[82] Getting a feel for how others view the world is a useful and important way to become a more effective communicator.

Self-Monitoring

Although increased cognitive complexity and empathy help you understand others better, **self-monitoring** is one way to understand *yourself*. Self-monitoring describes the process of paying close attention to your own behaviour and using your observations to shape the way you behave. Self-monitors can separate a part of their consciousness and observe their behaviours from a detached viewpoint, making observations such as:

"I'm making a fool of myself."
"I'd better speak up now."
"This approach is working well. I'll keep it up."

Although too much self-monitoring can be problematic, communicators who are aware of their behaviour and the impression it makes are more skilful communicators.[83] They are more accurate in judging others' emotional states, better at remembering information about others, less shy, and more

---

Invitation to Insight

Self-Monitoring Inventory

These statements concern personal reactions to a number of situations. No two statements are exactly alike, so consider each statement carefully before answering. If a statement is true or mostly true as applied to you, circle the T. If a statement is false or not usually true as applied to you, circle the F.

1. I find it hard to imitate the behaviour of other people. T F
2. I guess I put on a show to impress or entertain people. T F
3. I would probably make a good actor. T F
4. I sometimes appear to others to be experiencing deeper emotions than I actually am. T F
5. In a group of people, I am rarely the center of attention. T F
6. In different situations and with different people, I often act like very different persons. T F
7. I can argue only for ideas I already believe. T F
8. To get along and be liked, I tend to be what people expect me to be rather than anything else. T F
9. I may deceive people by being friendly when I really dislike them. T F
10. I'm not always the person I appear to be. T F

Scoring: Give yourself 1 point for each of questions 1, 5, and 7 that you answered F. Give yourself 1 point for each of the remaining questions that you answered T. Add up your points. If you are a good judge of yourself and scored 7 or above, you are probably a high self-monitoring individual; 3 or below, you are probably a low self-monitoring individual.

Mark Snyder, "The Many Me's of the Self-Monitor," *Psychology Today* (March 1982): 34. *Psychology Today* © Copyright 1982. www.Psychologytoday.com

---

instead of doing all the talking, using language that makes sense to the other person, and being open to change after hearing the other person's ideas. Effective communicators also care about *the message*. They are sincere, know what they are talking about, and demonstrate verbally and non-verbally that they care about what they say.

Competence isn't a trait that people possess or lack, but rather it's a state that we achieve more or less frequently. The goal is to boost the percentage of times when you communicate in ways outlined in this section.

Competence in Intercultural Communication

As our world becomes more multicultural, the likelihood of interacting with people from different backgrounds is greater than ever. As a result, it's important to understand that competent behaviour in one culture might be considered completely inept, or even offensive, in another.[85] Customs like belching after a meal or appearing nude in public that might be appropriate in some parts of the world would be considered outrageous in others. However, most differences are more subtle. For example, self-disclosing and speaking clearly, which is valued among North Americans, may be considered aggressive and insensitive by many people in Asian countries, who see subtlety and indirectness as appropriate.[86]

Even within a single society, co-cultures may have different notions of appropriate behaviour. For instance, students from the Mi'kmaq nation have said in class that avoiding eye contact when speaking with their elders demonstrates respect. However, when this same behaviour is directed toward non-Aboriginal authority figures

assertive. By contrast, low self-monitors don't even recognize their incompetence. They are blissfully ignorant of their shortcomings and more likely to overestimate their skills.[84] For example, experimental subjects who scored in the lowest quartile on joke-telling skills were more likely than their funnier counterparts to grossly overestimate their sense of humour.

In terms of self-monitoring, how do you see yourself: High? Low? Medium? Take the Self-Monitoring Inventory in the Invitation to Insight box to see if the results match up with your self-assessment.

Commitment

One feature that distinguishes effective communication—at least in qualitatively interpersonal relationships—is commitment. This commitment shows up in at least two ways. The first is *commitment to the other person*, which is revealed in a variety of ways: spending time with a person instead of rushing, listening carefully

such as university professors, deans, or judges, it may be perceived as insolence rather than the courtesy it is meant to convey. Competent communicators are able to adapt their style to suit the individual and cultural preferences of others.[87]

In addition to the characteristics of competent communication, communicating with people from different cultural backgrounds calls for several additional ingredients.[88] First, it helps to know the rules of a specific culture. For example, the kind of self-deprecating humour that North Americans find amusing is likely to fall flat in the Middle East.[89] But beyond the basics, there's also attitudes and skills called "culture-general" that help communicators build relationships with people from other backgrounds.[90] For example, imagine you've just been hired to work in a Japanese-owned company in Canada that has manufacturing operations in Mexico and customers around the world. You'll be surrounded by co-workers, supervisors, and clients from cultures and co-cultures different from yours. To communicate effectively in different cultural settings, it would be helpful to possess the following attributes.

Motivation

The desire to communicate successfully with strangers is an important start. People high in willingness to communicate with people from other cultures report a greater number of "intercultural" friends than those who are less willing to reach out.[91] Motivation is particularly important in intercultural interactions because they can be quite challenging at times.

Tolerance for Ambiguity

A tolerance for ambiguity will make it possible to accept equivocal and sometimes incomprehensible messages that characterize intercultural communication. In Asian cultures, for instance, reticence is valued. However, you might interpret an unwillingness to talk as a lack of friendliness. In cross-cultural situations like this, ambiguity is a fact of life, and a challenge.

Open-Mindedness

It's one thing to tolerate ambiguity, but it's another to become open-minded about cultural differences. When communication styles don't match those of our own culture, we have a tendency to think of them as "wrong." For example, you might find that women are not regarded with the same level of equality that we experience here in Canada or that a practice of kickbacks and bribery doesn't jibe with our notions of what is ethical. In these situations, principled communicators don't usually compromise deeply held beliefs about what is right. At the same time, competence requires you to recognize that people who behave differently are following different rules.

LiudmylaSupynska/iStock/Thinkstock

Knowledge and Skill

The rules and customs of one group might be quite different from another's. When travelling in Latin America, for example, you'll find that meetings don't begin or end at their scheduled time and that it takes participants quite a while to "get down to business." Rather than seeing this as irresponsible and unproductive, you'll want to recognize that the meaning of time is different in that culture. Likewise, the gestures others make, the distance they stand from you, and the eye contact they maintain have ambiguous meanings that you'll need to learn and adopt.

To gain intercultural competence, you'll want to engage in *mindfulness*—awareness of your own behaviour and that of others.[92] Communicators who lack this quality blunder through intercultural encounters *mindlessly*, oblivious of how their own behaviour may confuse or offend others and of how behaviour they consider weird may be simply different. In a mindful state, you can use three strategies to move toward a more competent style of intercultural communication.[93] **Passive observation** involves noticing the behaviours used by members of a different culture and then using these insights to communicate in ways that are most effective. **Active strategies** include reading, watching films, and asking experts or members of the other culture how to behave, as well as taking intercultural communication courses.[94] The third strategy, **self-disclosure**, involves volunteering personal information to people from the other culture with whom you want to communicate. One type of self-disclosure is to confess your cultural ignorance: "This is very new to me. What's the right thing to do in this situation?" This approach can be risky, given that some cultures may not value candour and self-disclosure as much as others. Nevertheless, most people are pleased when strangers attempt to learn the practices of their culture, and they are usually more than willing to offer information and assistance.

iStockphoto/Thinkstock

Communication in the Workplace

Interpersonal communication is also important in our professional lives. Organizational communication theory tells us that communication activities create patterns that affect organizational life and that organizational cultures are created through communication processes.[95] Employers know that communication affects employee satisfaction and general productivity. One study of 2500 Canadian workers reported that the strongest correlate of a healthy work environment was communication.[96] A study of the IT sector revealed that interpersonal communication is the most important factor in terms of promotion to management positions.[97]

On-the-job communication skills can even make the difference between life and death. One police department cited "bad communication" among the most common reasons for shooting errors by its officers.[98] Communication skills are just as essential for doctors, nurses, and other medical practitioners.[99] Researchers discovered that "poor communication" was the root of over 60 percent of reported medical errors—including death, serious physical injury, and psychological trauma.[100] Other research revealed a significant difference between the communication skills of physicians who had no malpractice claims against them and doctors with claims.[101]

In addition, today's workplace is managing several generations of workers: baby boomers (born 1946 to 1966), Generation X (born 1967 to 1979), Generation Y (born 1980 to 1995), and Millennials. According to Paula Allan of Toronto's FGIWorld, a firm that helps organizations address their mental, physical, and social health issues, each group has its "own set of values, view of authority, work and communication style, and expectation of leadership and work environment."[107] It's easy to understand how clashes could arise based on generational placement, and this presents a challenge in today's work world.

Hero Images/Getty Images

READY TO STUDY?

IN THE BOOK, YOU CAN:

❏ Rip out the Chapter in Review card at the back of the book to have the key terms and Learning Objectives handy, and complete the quizzes provided (answers are at the bottom of the back page).

ONLINE YOU CAN:

❏ Stay organized and efficient with MindTap—a single destination with all the course material and study aids you need to succeed. Built-in apps leverage social media and the latest learning technology. For example:

   ❏ Listen to the text using ReadSpeaker.

   ❏ Use pre-populated Flashcards as a jump start for review—or you can create your own.

   ❏ You can highlight text and make notes in your MindTap Reader. Your notes will flow into Evernote, the electronic notebook app that you can access anywhere when it's time to study for the exam.

   ❏ Prepare for tests with a variety of quizzes and activities.

Go to **nelson.com/student** to access these digital resources

Endnotes

1. Interview with Vicki Gabereau, CTV Canadian Television, March 19, 2003; and B. Kull (2004). "My Year Alone in the Wilderness." *Canadian Geographic*, 124, 2–12. The interview and article, plus more about Bob Kull's experience, are available at www.bobkull.org. Accessed August 1, 2007. Also see R. Kull (2008). *Solitude: Seeking Wisdom in Extremes.* Novato, CA: New World Library.

2. S. Moeller (2011). "The World Unplugged," http://theworldunplugged.wordpress.com. Accessed November 12, 2012.

3. D. J. Annibale & R. L. Bissinger (2010). "The Golden Hour." *Advances in Neonatal Care, 10.* doi: 10.1097/ANC.0b013e3181e9e244, http://journals.lww.com/advancesinneonatalcare/Fulltext/2010/10000/The_Golden_Hour.1.aspx. Accessed September 24, 2015.

4. Sandford Health (2012, January). "The Golden Hour: Giving Your Newborn the Best Start." *Sanford Health.* https://www.sanfordhealth.org/Stories/View/44a97e6f-d477-4c44-accb-915f52acfcc5. Retrieved September 24, 2015.

5. K. Erlandsson, A. Dsilna, I. Fagerberg, & K. Christensson (2007). "Skin-to-Skin Care with the Father after Cesarean Birth and Its Effect on Newborn Crying and Prefeeding Behaviour." *Birth, 34,* 105–114.

6. S. Cohen, W. J. Doyle, D. P. Skoner, B. S. Rabin, & J. M. Gwaltney (1997). "Social Ties and Susceptibility to the Common Cold." *Journal of the American Medical Association, 277,* 1940–1944.

7. C. H. Kroenke, L. D. Kubzansky, E. S. Schernhammer, M. D. Holmes, & I. Kawachi (2006). "Social Networks, Social Support, and Survival After Breast Cancer Diagnosis." *Journal of Clinical Oncology,* 24, 1105–1111; H. Litwin & S. Shiovitz-Ezra (2006). "Network Type and Mortality Risk in Later Life." *Gerontologist,* 46, 735–743; C. F. Mendes de Leon (2005). "Why Do Friendships Matter For Survival?" *Journal of Epidemiology and Community Health, 59,* 538–539.

8. J. Lynch (1977). *The Broken Heart: The Medical Consequences of Loneliness* (pp. 239–242). New York: Basic Books.

9. W. D. Rees & S. G. Lutkins (1967). "Mortality of Bereavement." *British Medical Journal,* 4, 13.

10. O. Ybarra, O. E. Burnstein, P. Winkielman, M .C. Keller, M. Manis, E. Chan, & J. Rodriguez (2008). "Mental Exercising Through Simple Socializing: Social Interaction Promotes General Cognitive Functioning." *Personality and Social Psychology Bulletin, 34,* 248–259.

11. K. Floyd & S. Riforgiate (2006). "Human Affection Exchange: XII. Affectionate Communication Is Related to Diurnal Variation in Salivary Free Cortisol." *Western Journal of Communication, 75,* 351–368.

12. Public Health Agency of Canada (October 1, 2002). "Our Relationships Influence our Physical Health." Canadian Health Network, www.canadian-health-network.ca/servlet/ContentServer?cid=1039795127660&pagename=CHNRCS% 2FCHNResource%2FCHNResourcePageTemplate&c=CHNResource&lang=En. Retrieved July 12, 2006.

13. K. Ritchie (November 15, 2005). "A Nursing Home with a Twist." Australian Broadcasting Corporation, www.abc.net.au/am/content/2005/s1506885.htm. Accessed July 12, 2006.

14. R. Shattuck (1980). *The Forbidden Experiment: The Story of the Wild Boy of Aveyron* (p. 37). New York: Farrar, Straus & Giroux.

15. R. B. Rubin, E. M. Perse, & C. A. Barbato (1988). "Conceptualization and Measurement of Interpersonal Communication Motives." *Human Communication Research, 14*, 602–628.

16. E. Diener & M. E. P. Seligman (2002). "Very Happy People." *Psychological Science, 13*, 81–84.

17. D. Kahneman, A. B. Krueger, D. A. Schkade, N. Schwartz, & A. A. Stone (n.d.). "A Daily Measure." *Science, 306*, 1645.

18. U.S. Rehman & A. Holtzworth-Munroe (2007). "A Cross-Cultural Examination of the Relation of Marital Communication Behaviour to Marital Satisfaction." *Journal of Family Psychology, 21*, 759–763.

19. J. Rochmis (n.d.). "Study: Humans Do Many Things." *Wired magazine* online, www.wired.com/culture/lifestyle/news/2000/02/34387. Accessed July 13, 2010.

20. M. McPherson, L. Smith-Lovin, & M. E. Brashears (2006). "Social Isolation in America: Changes in Core Discussion Networks over Two Decades." *American Sociological Review, 71*, 353–375. See also M. McPherson, L. Smith-Lovin, & M. E. Brashears (2008). "The Ties That Bind Are Fraying." *Contexts, 7*, 32–36.

21. H. T. Reis & S. L. Gable (2003). "Toward a Positive Psychology of Relationships." In C. L. Keyes & J. Haidt (Eds.). *Flourishing: The Positive Person and the Good Life* (pp. 129–159). Washington, DC: American Psychological Association.

22. D. B. Curtis, J. L. Winsor, & R. D. Stephens (1989). "National Preferences in Business and Communication Education." *Communication Education, 38*, 6–14. See also M. S. Peterson, "Personnel Interviewers' Perceptions of the Importance and Adequacy of Applicants' Communication Skills," *Communication Education 46* (1997): 287–291.

23. Conference Board of Canada (2000). Employability Skills 2000+. www.conferenceboard.ca/education/learning-tools/employability-skills.htm. Accessed July 12, 2006.

24. A. H. Maslow (1968). *Toward a Psychology of Being.* New York: Van Nostrand Reinhold.

25. P. Mychalcewycz (February 12, 2009). "Breaking Up Via Text Message Becoming Commonplace, Poll Finds." www.switched.com. Accessed May 30, 2010.

26. See, for example, R. K. Shelly (1997). "Sequences and Cycles in Social Interaction." *Small Group Research, 28*, 333–356

27. See R. Buck & C. A. VanLear (2002). "Verbal and Nonverbal Communication: Distinguishing Symbolic, Spontaneous, and Pseudo-Spontaneous Nonverbal Behaviour." *Journal of Communication 52*, 522–541; T. Clevenger Jr. (1991). "Can One Not Communicate? A Conflict of Models." *Communication Studies 42*, 340–353. For a detailed rationale of the position argued in this section, see G. H. Stamp & M. L. Knapp (1990). "The Construct of Intent in Interpersonal Communication." *Quarterly Journal of Speech 76*, 282–299.

28. J. P. Dillard, D. H. Solomon, & M. T. Palmer (1999). "Structuring the Concept of Relational Communication." *Communication Monographs, 66*, 49–65; P. Watzlawick, J. Beavin, & D. Jackson (1967). *Pragmatics of Human Communication.* New York: Norton.

29. For a similar list of characteristics, see J. C. McCroskey & V. P. Richmond (1996). *Fundamentals of Human Communication: An Interpersonal Perspective.* Prospect Heights, IL: Waveland.

30. A. Sillars (1998). "(Mis)Understanding." In B. H. Spitzberg and W. R. Cupach (Eds.). *The Dark Side of Close Relationships.* Mahwah, NJ: Erlbaum.

31. J. C. McCroskey & L. Wheeless (1976). *Introduction to Human Communication* (p. 5). Boston: Allyn and Bacon. See also D. H. Cloven & M. E. Roloff (1991). "Sense-Making Activities and Interpersonal Conflict: Communicative Cures for the Mulling Blues." *Western Journal of Speech Communication, 55*, 134–158. See also D. Stiebel (1997). *When Talking Makes Things Worse! Resolving Problems When Communication Fails.* Kansas City, MO: Andrews and McMeel.

32. M. V. Redmond (1995). "Interpersonal Communication: Definitions and Conceptual Approaches." In M. V. Redmond (Ed.). *Interpersonal Communication: Readings in Theory and Research* (pp. 4–11). Fort Worth, TX: Harcourt Brace.

33. See, for example, G. R. Miller & M. Steinberg (1975). *Between People: A New Analysis of Interpersonal Communication.* Chicago: SRA; J. Stewart & C. Logan (1998). *Together: Communicating Interpersonally*, 5th ed. New York: McGraw-Hill.

34. For further discussion of the characteristics of impersonal and interpersonal communications, see Arthur P. Bochner (1984). "The Functions of Human Communication in Interpersonal Bonding." In C. C. Arnold & J. W. Bowers (Eds.). *Handbook of Rhetorical and Communication Theory* (p. 550). Boston: Allyn and Bacon; S. Trenholm & A. Jensen (1992). *Interpersonal Communication*, 2nd ed. (pp. 27–33). Belmont, CA: Wadsworth; J. Stewart & G. D'Angelo (1998). *Together: Communicating Interpersonally*, 5th ed. (p. 5). New York: McGraw-Hill.

35. J. Wood (1997). *Relational Communication*, 2nd ed. Belmont, CA: Wadsworth.

36. K. J. Gergen (1991). *The Saturated Self: Dilemmas of Identity in Contemporary Life* (p. 158). New York: Basic Books.

37. M. Daum (March 7, 2009). "The Age of Friendaholism." *Los Angeles Times*, B 13.

38. See P. Watzlawick, J. H. Beavin, & D. D. Jackson (1967). *Pragmatics of Human Communication.* New York: Norton; W. J. Lederer & D. D. Jackson (1968). *The Mirages of Marriage.* New York: Norton.

39. See, for example, R. A. Bell & J. A. Daly (1995). "The Affinity-Seeking Function of Communication." In M. V. Redmond (Ed.). *Interpersonal Communication: Readings in Theory and Research.* Fort Worth, TX: Harcourt Brace.

40. M. Dainton (1998). "Everyday Interaction in Marital Relationships: Variations in Relative Importance and Event Duration." *Communication Reports, 11*, 101–143.

41. S. A. Myers & T. A. Avtgis (1997). "The Association of Socio-Communicative Style and Relational Types on Perceptions of Nonverbal Immediacy." *Communication Research Reports, 14*, 339–349.

42. For a thorough examination of this topic, see Chapter 11, "Nonverbal Immediacy," in V. P. Richmond & J. C.

McCroskey (2004). *Nonverbal Behaviour in Interpersonal Relationships,* 5th ed. Boston: Allyn and Bacon.

43. T. S. Lim & J. W. Bowers (1991). "Facework: Solidarity, Approbation, and Tact." *Human Communication Research, 17,* 415–450.

44. J. R. Frei & P. R. Shaver (2002). "Respect in Close Relationships: Prototype, Definition, Self-Report Assessment, and Initial Correlates." *Personal Relationships, 9,* 121–139.

45. M. T. Palmer (1989). "Controlling Conversations: Turns, Topics, and Interpersonal Control." *Communication Monographs, 56,* 1–18.

46. Watzlawick et al., op. cit.

47. L. Rainie & J. Anderson (2008). *The Future of the Internet III: How Experts See It.* Washington, DC: Pew Internet & American Life Project.

48. See pewinternet.org. The site updates regularly with current studies.

49. J. Anderson (2010, July 2). *The Future of Social Relations.* Washington, DC: Pew Internet and American Life Project.

50. A. Smith (2011, November 15). *Why Americans Use Social Media.* Washington, DC: Pew Internet and American Life Project.

51. K. Hampton (2009, November 4). *Social Isolation and New Technology.* Washington, DC: Pew Internet and American Life Project.

52. L. Rainie (2011, January 18). *The Social Side of the Internet.* Washington, DC: Pew Internet and American Life Project.

53. K. Hampton (2011, June 16). *Social Networking Sites and Our Lives.* Washington, DC: Pew Internet and American Life Project.

54. A. J. Flanagin (2005). "IM Online: Instant Messaging Use Among College Students." *Communication Research Reports, 22,* 175–187.

55. J. Boase, J. B. Horrigan, B. Wellman, & L. Rainie (January 2006). *The Strength of Internet Ties.* Washington, DC: Pew Internet & American Life Project.

56. M. Dainton & B. Aylor (2002). "Patterns of Communication Channel Use in the Maintenance of Long-Distance Relationships." *Communication Research Reports, 19,* 118–129.

57. M. Marriott (1998). "The Blossoming of Internet Chat." *New York Times* online.

58. D. Tannen (May 16, 1994). "Gender Gap in Cyberspace." *Newsweek,* 52–53.

59. D. Kirkpatrick (March 23, 1992). "Here Comes the Payoff from PCs." *Fortune,* 93–102.

60. B. Wellman (2004). "Three Ages of Internet Studies: Ten, Five and Zero Years Ago." *New Media and Society, 6,* 123–129.

61. K. S. Surinder & R. B. Cooper (2003). "Exploring the Core Concepts of Media Richness Theory: The Impact of Cue Multiplicity and Feedback Immediacy on Decision Quality. *Journal of Management Information Systems, 20,* 263–299.

62. J. Walther & A. Ramirez (2010). "New Technologies and New Directions in Online Relating." In S. W. Smith & S. R. Wilson (Eds.). *New Directions in Interpersonal Communication Research* (pp. 264–284). Los Angeles: Sage.

63. A. Ramirez & S. Zhang (2007). "When Online Meets Offline: The Effect of Modality Switching on Relational Communication." *Communication Monographs, 74,* 287–310.

64. S. Moeller (2011). "The World Unplugged," http://theworldunplugged.wordpress.com. Accessed November 12, 2012.

65. S. A. Watts (2007). "Evaluative Feedback: Perspectives on Media Effects." *Journal of Computer-Mediated Communication, 12,* http://jcmc.indiana.edu/vol12/issue2/watts.html. Accessed June 1, 2009.

66. S. Sheppard (2010). "Cyber screening." *HR Management,* 15.http://www.hrmreport.com/article/Cyber-screening/#.

67. CBC Radio Interview (2015, October 3). "Michael Schlossberg in a discussion of his 2015 book—*Tweets and Consequences: Social Media Disasters in Politics and How You Can Avert a Career Ending Mistake.* South Carolina: Strategic Media Books."

68. J. Rosen (2010, July 25). "The Web Means the End of Forgetting." *New York Times Magazine,* 30–35.

69. M. Bauerlein (2009, September 4). "Why Gen-Y Johnny can't read nonverbal cues." *Wall Street Journal.* http://online.wsj.com/article/SB10001424052970203863204574 34849320178.html.

70. For a thorough review of this topic, see B. H. Spitzberg & W. R. Cupach (1989). *Handbook of Interpersonal Competence Research.* New York: Springer-Verlag.

71. For a thorough discussion of the nature of communication competence, see B. H. Spitzberg & W. R. Cupach (2002). "Interpersonal Skills." In M. L. Knapp & J. A. Daly (Eds.). *Handbook of Interpersonal* Communication, 3rd ed. Thousand Oaks, CA: Sage. S. R. Wilson & C. M. Sabee (2003). "Explicating Communicative Competence as a Theoretical Term." In J. O. Greene & B. R. Burleson (Eds.). *Handbook of Communication and Social Interaction Skills.* Mahwah, NJ: Erlbaum.

72. B. H. Spitzberg (1991). "An Examination of Trait Measures of Interpersonal Competence." *Communication Reports, 4,* 22–29.

73. J. J. Teven, V. P. Richmond, J. C. McCroskey & L. L. McCroskey (2010). "Updating relationships between communication traits and communication competence." *Communication Research Reports, 27,* 263–270.

74. Brown, R. F., Bylund, C. L., Gueguen, J. A., Diamond, C., Eddington, J., & Kissane, D. (2010). Developing patient centred communication skills training for oncologists: Describing the content and efficacy of training. *Communication Education, 59,* 235–248; Hyvarinen, L., Tanskanen, P., Katajavuori, N., & Isotalus, P. (2010). A method for teaching communication in pharmacy in authentic work situations. *Communication Education, 59,* 124–145.

75. R. B. Rubin, E. M. Perse, & C. A. Barbato (1988). "Conceptualization and Measurement of Interpersonal Communication Motives." *Human Communication Research, 14*, 602–628.

76. S. P. Morreale & J. C. Pearson (2008). "Why Communication Education is Important: The Centrality of the Discipline in the 21st century." *Communication Education, 57(2)*, 224–240.

77. D. Hemple (2005). "Invitational Capacity." In F. van Emeren & P. Houtlosser. *The Practice of Argumentation* (pp. 337–348). Amsterdam, the Netherlands: John Benjamins.

78. D. O. Braithwaite & N. Eckstein (2003). "Reconceptualizing Supportive Interactions: How Persons with Disabilities Communicatively Manage Assistance."*Journal of Applied Communication Research, 31*, 1–26.

79. B. R. Burleson (2007). "Constructivism: A General Theory of Communication Skill." In B. B. Whaley & W. Samter (Eds). *Explaining Communication: Contemporary Theories and Exemplars* (pp. 105–128). Mahwah, NJ: Erlbaum.

80. D. B. Wackman, S. Miller, & E. W. Nunnally (1976). *Student Workbook: Increasing Awareness and Communication Skills* (p. 6). Minneapolis, MN: Interpersonal Communication Programs.

81. B.R. Burleson & S.E. Caplan. (1998). "Cognitive Complexity." In J. C. McCroskey, J. A. Daly, M. M. Martin, & M. J. Beatty (Eds.). *Communication and Personality: Trait Perspectives* (pp. 233–286). Creskill, NJ: Hampton Press.

82. J. M. Wiemann & P. M. Backlund (1980). "Current Theory and Research in Communication Competence." *Review of Educational Research, 50*, 185–199; S. G. Lakey & D. J. Canary (2002). "Actor Goal Achievement and Sensitivity to Partner as Critical Factors in Understanding Interpersonal Communication Competence and Conflict Strategies." *Communication Monographs, 69*, 217–235. See also M. V. Redmond (December 1985). "The Relationship between Perceived Communication Competence and Perceived Empathy." *Communication Monographs, 52*, 377–382; M. V. Redmond (1989). "The Functions of Empathy (Decentering) in Human Relations." *Human Relations, 42*, 593–605.

83. Research summarized in D. E. Hamachek (1987). *Encounters with the Self*, 2nd ed. (p. 8). Fort Worth, TX: Holt, Rinehart and Winston. See also J. A. Daly, A. L. Vangelisti, & S. M. Daughton (1995). "The Nature and Correlates of Conversational Sensitivity." In M. V. Redmond (Ed.). *Interpersonal Communication: Readings in Theory and Research*. Fort Worth, TX: Harcourt Brace.

84. D. A. Dunning & J. Kruger (December 1999). "Unskilled and Unaware of It: How Difficulties in Recognizing One's Own Incompetence Lead to Inflated Self-Assessments." *Journal of Personality and Social Psychology, 77*, 1121–1134.

85. See Y. Y. Kim (1991). "Intercultural Communication Competence: A Systems-Theoretic View." In S. Ting-Toomey & F. Korzenny (Eds.). *Cross-Cultural Interpersonal Communication*. Newbury Park, CA: Sage; G. M. Chen & W. J. Sarosta (1996). "Intercultural Communication Competence: A Synthesis." In B. R. Burleson & A. W. Kunkel (Eds.). *Communication Yearbook 19*. Thousand Oaks, CA: Sage.

86. J. K. Burgoon & N. E. Dunbar (2000). "An Interactionist Perspective on Dominance-Submission: Interpersonal Dominance as a Dynamic, Situationally Contingent Social Skill." *Communication Monographs, 67*, 96–121.

87. L. Chen (1997). "Verbal Adaptive Strategies in U.S. American Dyadic Interactions with U.S. American or East-Asian Partners." *Communication Monographs, 64*, 302–323.

88. See, for example, C. Hajek & H. Giles (2003). "New Directions in Intercultural Communication Competence: The Process Model." In B. R. Burleson & J. O. Greene (Eds.). *Handbook of Communication and Social Interaction Skills*. Mahwah, NJ: Erlbaum; S. Ting-Toomey & L.C. Chung (2005). *Understanding Intercultural Communication*. Los Angeles: Roxbury.

89. M. Kalliny, K. Cruthirds, & M. Minor (2006). "Differences between American, Egyptian and Lebanese Humour Styles: Implications for International Management." *International Journal of Cross-Cultural Management, 6*, 121–134.

90. L. A. Samovar, P. E. Porter, E. R. McDaniel, & C. S. Roy (2013). *Communication Between Cultures*, 8th ed. Belmont, CA: Wadsworth.

91. J. W. Kassing (1997). "Development of the Intercultural Willingness to Communicate Scale." *Communication Research Reports, 14*, 399–407.

92. J. K. Burgoon, C. R. Berger, & V. R. Waldron (2000). "Mindfulness and Interpersonal Communication." *Journal of Social Issues, 56*, 105–128.

93. C. R. Berger (1979). "Beyond Initial Interactions: Uncertainty, Understanding, and the Development of Interpersonal Relationships." In H. Giles & R. St. Clair (Eds.). *Language and Social Psychology* (pp. 122–144). Oxford: Blackwell.

94. L. J. Carrell (1997). "Diversity in the Communication Curriculum: Impact on Student Empathy." *Communication Education, 46*, 234–244.

95. S. W. Littlejohn & K. Foss (2005). *Theories of Human Communication*, 8th ed., pp. 266–268. Belmont, CA: Thomson Wadsworth.

96. G. S. Lowe, G. Schellenberg, & H. S. Shannon (2003). "Correlates of Employees' Perceptions of a Healthy Work Environment." *American Journal of Health Promotion, 17*, 390–399.

97. H. Solomon (1999). "Soft Skills Key to IT Success, Execs Say." *Computing Canada, 25*, 1.

98. "Harper's Index" (December, 1994). *Harper's*, 13.

99. L. B. Mauksch, D. C. Dugdale, S. Dodson, & R. Epstein (2007). "Relationship, Communication, and Efficiency in the Medical Encounter." *Archives of Internal Medicine, 168*, 1387–1395; F. Holmes (2007). "If You Listen, the Patient Will Tell You the Diagnosis." *International Journal of Listening, 21*, 156–161.

100. *Sentinel Event Statistics* (2008). Oakbrook Terrace, IL: Joint Commission on Accreditation of Healthcare.

101. W. Levinson, D. Roter, & J. P. Mullooly (1997). "Physician-Patient Communication: The Relationship with Malpractice Claims Among Primary Care Physicians and Surgeons." *Journal of American Medical Association, 277,* 553–559. See also H. P. Rodriguez, A. C. Rodday, R. E. Marshall, K. L. Nelson, W. H. Rogers, & D. G. Safran (2008). "Relation of Patients' Experiences with Individual Physicians to Malpractice Risk." *International Journal for Quality in Health Care, 20,* 5–12.

102. See, for example, N.M. Hindi, D.S., Miller, & S.E. Catt (2004). "Communication and Miscommunication in Corporate America: Evidence from Fortune 200 Firms." *Journal of Organizational Culture, 8,* 13–26.

103. See, for example, A. L. Darling & D. P. Dannels (2003). "Practicing Engineers Talk about the Importance of Talk: A Report on the Role of Oral Communication in the Workplace," *Communication Education, 52,* 1–16.

104. D. A. Nellermoe, T. R. Weirich, & A. Reinsteinv (1999). "Using Practitioners' Viewpoints to Improve Accounting Students' Communications Skills." *Business Communication Quarterly, 62,* 41–60.

105. August 22, 1999. *Santa Barbara News-Press,* J1

106. J. Richman (September 2, 2002). "The News Journal of the Life Scientist." *The Scientist, 16,* 42.

107. P. Allen (September, 2004). "Welcoming Y." *Benefits Canada,* 51–53.

COMMUNICATION AND IDENTITY: CREATING AND PRESENTING THE SELF

LEARNING OUTCOMES

LO1 Describe the relationship among self-concept, self-esteem, and communication.

LO2 Understand how to change your self-concept.

LO3 Explain how self-fulfilling prophecies shape the self-concept and influence communication.

LO4 Compare and contrast the perceived self and the presenting self as they relate to identity management.

LO5 Describe the role that identity management plays in both face-to-face and online relationships.

LO1
Communication and the Self

How would you describe yourself? Take a moment to make a list of all the characteristics that define you. Refer to the list below to get you started. You'll use your list as you read this chapter, so try to complete it now.

Your moods or feelings (e.g., happy, angry, excited, nervous, insecure, confident)

Your appearance (e.g., attractive, female, trans, short, tall, dark)

Your social traits (e.g., friendly, quiet, funny, outrageous)

Talents you have or do not have (e.g., musical, creative, nonathletic)

Your intellectual capacity (e.g., smart, visual learner, philosophical, average, mathematically inclined)

Your strong beliefs (e.g., religious, environmentalist, political, feminist)

Your social roles (e.g., parent, co-worker, girlfriend, student, crafter)

Your physical condition (e.g., healthy, underweight, strong, have a disability)

Now look at what you've written. How did you define yourself? As a student? A man or woman or a trans person? By your appearance? Your beliefs? Your social roles? There are many ways of identifying yourself but the words you've chosen probably represent your most important characteristics. In other words, this would be a description of the "real you."

What do you THINK?

My perception of myself matches how others see me.

1	2	3	4	5	6	7
strongly agree						strongly disagree

So, how does this self-analysis relate to interpersonal communication? The short answer is that who you are both reflects and affects your communication with others. The long answer involves everything from biology to socialization to culture to gender. But, first, let's look at two terms that are basic to the relationship between the self and the communication: self-concept and self-esteem.

Self-Concept and Self-Esteem

There's a good likelihood that the list you created included emotional descriptions such as happy or sad, confident or nervous. Such characteristics show that how you *feel* about yourself is a big part of who you think you are. How we think and feel about ourselves are important components of the self and we'll examine these now.

Self-Concept

Who you think you are can be described as your **self-concept**: the relatively stable set of perceptions you hold about yourself.

If a mirror could reflect not only your physical features but other aspects of yourself—emotional states, talents, likes, dislikes, values, roles, and so on—the reflection you'd see would be your self-concept.

You probably recognize that the self-concept list you recorded earlier is only a partial one. To complete a full description, you'd have to add items until your list ran into hundreds of words.

This self-concept you've described thus far is extremely important. To see just how important it is, try the "Take Away" exercise on the left.

For most people, this exercise dramatically illustrates just how fundamental the concept of self is. Even when the item being abandoned is an unpleasant one, it's often hard to surrender. When students are asked to let go of their most central feelings or thoughts, they exclaim that, "I wouldn't be *me* without that." Of course, this proves our point: The concept of self is perhaps our most fundamental possession, for without a self-concept it would be impossible to relate to the world.

Self-concept
The relatively stable set of perceptions individuals hold about themselves.

Self-esteem
The part of the self-concept that involves evaluations of self-worth.

Yuriy Rudyy/Shutterstock.com

Invitation to Insight

Take Away

1. Find a comfortable spot where you can think without being interrupted. This exercise can be done in a group with the leader giving instructions, or you can do it alone by reading the directions yourself when necessary.

2. Close your eyes and get a mental picture of yourself. Besides visualizing your appearance, include in your image less observable features—your disposition, your hopes, your concerns—including all the items you described in the first exercise.

3. Keep this picture in mind, but now imagine what would happen if the last item on your list disappeared from your makeup. How would you be different? Does giving up that item leave you feeling better or worse? How hard was it to let go of that item?

4. Now, without taking back the item you just abandoned, give up the next-least-important item on your list and see what difference this makes to you. After pausing to experience your thoughts and feelings, give up each succeeding item on your list one by one.

5. After you've abandoned the number one feature of who you are, take a few minutes to add back the parts of yourself you abandoned, then read on.

Self-Esteem

While self-concept describes who you think you are, **self-esteem** involves evaluations of self-worth. A hypothetical communicator's self-concept might include being quiet, argumentative, or self-controlled. The individual's self-esteem would be determined by the value that person places on these qualities. Consider the following:

Quiet "I'm a coward for not speaking up" *versus* "I enjoy listening more than talking."

Argumentative "I'm pushy, and that's obnoxious" *versus* "I stand up for my beliefs."

Self-controlled "I'm too cautious" *versus* "I think carefully before I say or do things."

others; they think that the only way to look good is to put others down.

Having high self-esteem has obvious benefits, but it doesn't guarantee interpersonal success.[1] While people with exaggerated self-esteem may *think* they make better impressions on others or have better friendships and romantic lives, neither impartial observers nor objective tests verify these beliefs. Instead, people with an inflated sense of self-worth may irritate others by coming across as condescending know-it-alls, especially when their self-worth is challenged.[2]

However, self-esteem can be a starting point for positive behaviours and interactions. **Figure 2.1** shows the cycles that may begin from both positive and negative self-evaluations. These patterns often become self-fulfilling prophecies which are discussed later in the chapter. In all, it's good to have a balanced self-concept where you recognize your strengths and weaknesses. You'll have good self-esteem if you have more strengths than weaknesses and view them in a positive light.

Table 2.1 summarizes some important differences between communicators with high and low self-esteem. Such differences make sense when you realize that people who dislike themselves are likely to believe that others won't like them either. They imagine that others view them critically, then accept these imagined or real criticisms as proof that they are unlikable people. Sometimes this low self-esteem is manifested in hostility toward

Biological Roots of the Self-Concept

How did you become the kind of communicator you are? Were you born that way or were you a product of your environment? As you'll now see, both play a major role in determining the way you are.

TABLE 2.1
Differences between Communicators with High and Low Self-Esteem

People with High Self-Esteem

1. Likely to think well of others.
2. Expect to be accepted by others.
3. Evaluate their own performance more favourably than people with low self-esteem.
4. Perform well when being watched: are not afraid of others' reactions.
5. Work harder for people who demand high standards of performance.
6. Inclined to feel comfortable with others they view as superior in some way.
7. Able to defend themselves against negative comments of others.

People with Low Self-Esteem

1. Likely to disapprove of others.
2. Expect to be rejected by others.
3. Evaluate their own performance less favourably than people with high self-esteem.
4. Perform poorly when being watched: are sensitive to possible negative reactions.
5. Work harder for undemanding, less critical people.
6. Feel threatened by people they view as superior in some way.
7. Have difficulty defending themselves against others' negative comments: are more easily influenced.

From HAMACHEK. *ENCOUNTERS WITH THE SELF, 3E.* © 1987 South-Western, a part of Cengage Learning, Inc. Reproduced by permission. www.cengage.com/permissions

FIGURE 2.1
The Relationship between Self-Esteem and Communication Behaviour

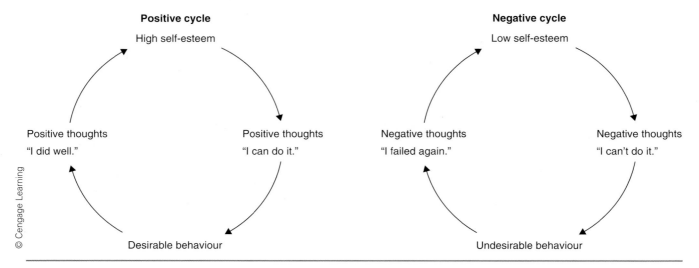

Positive cycle
High self-esteem
Positive thoughts "I did well."
Positive thoughts "I can do it."
Desirable behaviour

Negative cycle
Low self-esteem
Negative thoughts "I failed again."
Negative thoughts "I can't do it."
Undesirable behaviour

© Cengage Learning

Biology and the Self

Take another look at the "Who am I?" list you developed, and you will almost certainly find some terms that describe your **personality** — characteristic ways that you think and behave across a variety of situations. Your personality tends to be stable throughout your life, and often it grows more pronounced over time.[3] Research suggests that personality is actually part of our genetic makeup.[4] For example, people who were judged shy as children still show a distinctive reaction in their brains as adults when they encounter new situations.[5] In fact, we now know that biology accounts for personality traits such as extroversion,[6] shyness,[7] assertiveness,[8] verbal aggression,[9] and overall willingness to communicate.[10] It's not that we're born with a self-concept, but our personality traits may influence how we come to see ourselves.

Personality
Characteristic ways that you think and behave across a variety of situations.

Social scientists have grouped personality traits into five primary categories, and these categories are recognized in cultures as diverse as German and Chinese.[11] Take a look at **Table 2.2**[12] and identify the terms that best describe your personality. While labels like "neurotic" and "antagonistic" can be hard to acknowledge, the descriptors underneath them may be more typical of you. You will notice that several dimensions of these personality types relate to communication.

Also, keep in mind that these traits are not an either–or matter but rather a matter of degree. You are not shy *or* sociable, argumentative *or* agreeable, self-controlled *or* spontaneous. It's more likely that your personality fits somewhere along a continuum for each trait. You may be somewhat shy, a little argumentative, or moderately self-controlled.

Further, while you may have a disposition toward traits like shyness or aggressiveness, you can still control how you actually communicate. More and more research

TABLE 2.2
The "Big Five" Personality Traits

Extroverted	Open	Conscientious	Agreeable	Neurotic
Sociable	Imaginative	Careful	Courteous	Worried
Fun-loving	Independent	Reliable	Selfless	Vulnerable
Talkative	Curious	Persevering	Trusting	Self-pitying
Spontaneous	Broad interests	Ambitious	Cooperative	Impatient
Introverted	**Not Open**	**Undirected**	**Antagonistic**	**Stable**
Reserved	Unimaginative	Careless	Rude	Calm
Sober	Conforming	Undependable	Selfish	Hardy
Quiet	Incurious	Lax	Suspicious	Self-satisfied
Self-controlled	Narrow interests	Aimless	Uncooperative	Patient

Leo Cullum The New Yorker Collection/The Cartoon Bank

suggests that personality is flexible, dynamic, and shaped by experiences.[13] For example, shy people learn to reach out to others, and aggressive individuals learn to communicate in more sociable ways. As one author put it, "Experiences can silence genes or activate them. Even shyness is like Silly Putty once life gets hold of it."[14]

Socialization and the Self-Concept

Other people play a major role in shaping our self-concept. If, for example, you grew up on a deserted island, you would have no way of knowing if you were smart, attractive, short, tall, mean, skinny, fat, and so forth. Even if you could view your reflection in a mirror, you still wouldn't know how to evaluate your appearance without appraisals from others or people with whom to compare yourself. In fact, people play a major role in shaping how we regard ourselves. This process of shaping occurs in two ways: reflected appraisal and social comparison. To gain insight into this notion, try the Invitation to Insight exercise.

Reflected Appraisal

Sociologist Charles Cooley used the metaphor of a mirror to identify the process of **reflected appraisal** in that each of us develops a self-concept that reflects the way we believe others see us.[15] In other words, we are likely to feel less valuable, lovable, and capable to the degree that others have communicated ego-busting signals, and we will probably feel good about ourselves to the degree that others affirm our value.[16] The self-concept that you described in the list at the beginning of this chapter is a product of the messages you have received throughout your life.

Reflected appraisal begins early in life and children learn to judge themselves by the messages they receive. Some of these are positive: "You're so cute!" "I love you." "What a smart girl." Other messages are negative: "What's the matter with you? Can't you do anything right?" "You're a bad boy." "Leave me alone. You're driving me crazy!" Because children are trusting souls, they have no other way of viewing themselves and they accept these evaluations at face value. Referring to the cartoon on the next page, you can just imagine the type of self-concept that little chick will have.

These same principles continue later in life, especially when messages come from **significant others**—people whose opinions we especially value. A look at the ego boosters and ego busters you described in the previous exercise will show that the evaluations of a few especially important people can be powerful. Family members are the most obvious type of significant other, and their ego busters can be particularly hurtful as a result.[17] Imagine

Reflected appraisal
The theory that a person's self-concept matches the way the person believes others regard him or her.

Significant other
A person whose opinion is important enough to affect one's self-concept strongly.

Invitation to Insight

"Ego Boosters" and "Ego Busters"
This exercise should help you identify how others have shaped your self-concept and how you shape the self-concept of others.

1. Recall someone in your life who was an "ego booster"—someone who helped enhance your self-esteem by acting in ways that made you feel accepted, competent, worthwhile, important, appreciated, or loved. This person needn't have played a crucial role in your life as long as the role was positive. A family member with whom you've spent most of your life can be an "ego booster," but so can the stranger on the street who spontaneously offers an unexpected compliment.

2. Now recall an "ego buster"—someone who acted in large or small ways to reduce your self-esteem.

3. This time, recall instances when you were an ego booster to someone else—when you intentionally or unintentionally boosted another's self-esteem. Think of times when your actions left another person feeling valued, loved, needed, and so on.

4. Finally, recall instances when you were an ego buster. What did you do to diminish another's self-esteem? Were you aware of the effect of your behaviour at the time? Your answers might show that some events we intend as boosters have the effects of busters.

The Canadian Press/Andrew Vaughan

how difficult it must be for a young boy to come out to his family if he grew up hearing slurs and derogatory comments about people who are gay. Others can have an equal impact: a special friend, a professor, or perhaps an acquaintance whose opinion you value. The importance of significant others becomes clearer when you ask yourself how you feel about yourself as a student, as a person attractive to others, as a competent worker. You'll find that your self-evaluations were probably influenced by the way others regarded you.

The impact of significant others is especially strong during adolescence. Whether or not teenagers are included

Social comparison
Evaluation of oneself in terms of or by comparison to others.

Reference groups
Groups against which we compare ourselves, thereby influencing our self-concept and self-esteem.

in or excluded from peer groups is a crucial factor in their self-concept development.[18] Fortunately, parents who understand this notion can help them develop a strong self-concept.[19] After the age of 30, however, most people are not as influenced by significant others and their self-concepts don't change radically, at least not without a conscious effort.[20]

Social Comparison

While the messages of others shape our self-concept, so too does **social comparison**: evaluating ourselves in terms of how we compare with others.

Feelings of *superiority* or *inferiority* depend on whom we are comparing ourselves with,[21] particularly in today's media-saturated world. For instance, research shows that young women who regularly compare themselves with ultra-thin models develop negative appraisals of their own bodies.[22] In one study, young women's perceptions of their bodies changed for the worse after watching just 30 minutes of televised images of the "ideal" female form.[23] Men who compare themselves to media-idealized male physiques also evaluate their bodies negatively.[24] Even popular TV makeover shows—with their underlying message of "you must improve your appearance"—can lead viewers to feel worse about themselves.[25] It's not likely that many of us will be as beautiful as an air-brushed, Photoshopped picture of a popular movie star, as agile as a professional athlete, or as wealthy as a billionaire. Nonetheless, many people judge themselves against such unreasonable standards and suffer accordingly.[26] These distorted self-images can lead to serious behavioural disorders such as depression, anorexia nervosa, and bulimia.[27]

Social comparison also allows us to decide if we are *similar to* or *different from* others. A child who is interested in acting but lives in a setting where drama is regarded as weird will accept this label unless there is support from others. Likewise, adults who want to improve the quality of their relationships but are surrounded by friends and family who don't recognize or acknowledge the importance of these matters may think of themselves as oddballs. Thus, it's easy to recognize that the **reference groups** against which we compare ourselves play another important role in shaping our self-concepts. However, not every part of one's self-concept is shaped by others. If, for instance, you visited a Thai restaurant and then cooked a similar meal at home that had the same authentic taste and texture, you might consider yourself an adept chef.

While some features of the self are immediately apparent, the *significance* we attach to them depends greatly on the opinions of others. For example, we once heard a woman in her 80s describing her youth. "When I was a girl, we didn't worry about weight. Some people were skinny and others were plump, and we pretty much accepted the bodies God gave us." In those days it was unlikely that weight would have found its way onto the

"Now look what you've done!"

Lee Lorenz The New Yorker Collection/The Cartoon Bank

Whitney Thore, star of the TLC reality show *My Big Fat Fabulous Life*, doesn't let her size stop her from loving herself and living her life to the fullest.

The Self-Concept Is Subjective

The first characteristic of the self-concept is that it is subjective. It's our own personal view of ourselves and because of that, it may well be distorted. For example, researchers found that there is no relationship between the way college students rate their ability as interpersonal communicators, public speakers, or listeners and their true effectiveness.[28] In all cases, they rated their communication skills higher than their actual performance warranted. In another study, men ranked themselves on their ability to get along with others,[29] and defying mathematical laws, all subjects put themselves in the top half of the population; 60 percent rated themselves in the top 10 percent of the population; and an amazing 25 percent in the top 1 percent. The men also had lofty appraisals of their leadership and athletic abilities. Other research shows that perceptions of superiority tend to increase over time![30] The same holds for Internet daters. They too often have a "foggy mirror"—and see themselves more positively than others do.[31]

Not all distortion of the self-concept is positive. Many people view themselves more harshly than the objective facts warrant. We all experience temporary cases of the "uglies," convinced that we look much worse than we actually do. But people are more critical of themselves when they experience negative moods than when they feel more positive.[32] Although we all suffer occasional bouts of self-doubt, some people suffer from long-term or even permanent states of excessive self-doubt and criticism.[33] Such a chronic condition can influence how they approach and respond to others.

There are several reasons for distorted evaluations. One is ***obsolete information***. We cling to past failures even though they don't predict failure in the future. Likewise, your past successes don't guarantee future success. Perhaps your jokes were once well received but are now considered offensive, racist, or sexist.

self-concept list you constructed because it wasn't considered significant. This is not the case today: The popular media continually promote the latest diet fads and television ads are filled with scenes of slender, "happy" people. No wonder everyone wants to "lose a few pounds." While this campaign may stem from the need to be fit and healthy, thinness is considered desirable only because others tell us it is. In societies where obesity is the ideal, extremely heavy people regarded themselves as beautiful. In the same way, the fact that one is single or married, solitary or sociable, aggressive or passive takes on meaning depending on the interpretation that society attaches to those traits.

By now you might be thinking, "I'm shy or lack confidence because of the way others have treated me. I can't help being what I am." To an extent, you are a product of your environment, but having a poor self-concept in the past is no reason for continuing to do so in the future. You *can* change your attitudes and behaviours, as you'll soon read.

Characteristics of the Self-Concept

Now that we know more about where the self-concept comes from, let's look at some of its characteristics.

Distorted feedback can also create a self-image that is worse or better than the facts warrant. Overly critical parents can foster a negative self-image. Or the remarks of cruel friends, uncaring teachers, excessively demanding employers, or even memorable strangers can have a lasting effect. Other distorted messages are unrealistically positive. For instance, a child's inflated ego may be based on the praise of doting parents and a boss's inflated ego might come from the praise of obsequious subordinates.

Another cause of a negative self-concept is based on **perfection**. For example, children's stories and advertisements imply that the way to be a hero, the way to be liked and admired, is to show no flaws. Parents perpetuate this myth when they refuse to admit when they are wrong or when they are being unfair. Children quickly learn that a "well-adjusted, successful" person has no faults. Naively believing that other people are perfect contributes greatly to a negative self-concept.

Because perfection doesn't exist, expecting to achieve it is a sure ticket to an unnecessarily poor self-concept. For example, one study out of McMaster University and the University of Montreal found that women who exercised in front of mirrors expressed greater anxiety about their physical appearance than women who didn't. The authors concluded that standing in front of a mirror enhances self-awareness, but when the self is not quite up to the ideal, negative self-evaluations occur.[34]

A final reason why people sell themselves short is connected to **social expectations**. Canadians are, for the most part, modest people who consider talking about their strengths to be bragging, confusing this with the people who boast about achievements they haven't accomplished.[35] This convention leads us to focus on shortcomings rather than accomplishments. It's acceptable to proclaim that you failed to achieve a goal, but to express your pride at a job well done is considered boastful. Eventually, we begin to believe our disparaging remarks and see ourselves as much worse than we actually are. To avoid falling into the trap of becoming overly critical, try to recognize your strengths. Give the "Invitation to Insight" exercise a try.

Bojan Milinkov/Shutterstock.com

Cognitive conservatism
The tendency to seek and attend to information that conforms to an existing self-concept.

Invitation to Insight

Recognizing Your Strengths

1. In groups of three to five people, share five personal strengths or accomplishments. These needn't be momentous feats—it's perfectly acceptable to talk about some part of yourself that leaves you feeling pleased or proud. You might say that instead of procrastinating, you completed an assignment before the due date, that you spoke up in class even though you were afraid of disapproval, or that you bake a fantastic chocolate cake.

2. To help you get started, consider the following:
   a. How have you grown in the past year? How are you more skilled or wise, or a better person than you previously were?
   b. What features do you possess that make your friends and family appreciate you?

3. Did you have a hard time thinking of things to share? Would it have been easier to list the things that are *wrong* with you? If so, was this because you are a wretched person or because you tend to stress your defects and ignore your strengths? Consider how such a habit can affect your self-concept. Then ask yourself why it would be better to express your strengths more often.

The Self-Concept Resists Change

Although we all change, there is a tendency to cling to an existing self-concept by seeking out and attending to information that conforms to our existing self-concept. This is referred to as **cognitive conservatism**. For example, both college students and married couples with high self-esteem seek out partners who view them favourably and those with negative self-esteem seek out people who view them unfavourably.[36] It appears that we are less concerned with learning the "truth" about ourselves than with reinforcing a familiar self-concept.

We're often reluctant to revise a previously favourable self-concept because we honestly believe that the old truth still holds, in spite of the facts to the contrary. A student who did well in earlier years but now has failed to study might be unwilling to

© www.CartoonStock.com

Tim Tadder/Corbis/Getty Images

admit that the label "good scholar" no longer applies. Or a worker might resent a supervisor's mentioning increased absences and low productivity. Such individuals are not lying to themselves; they just don't get it.

The tendency to cling to an outmoded self-perception even holds when the new image is more favourable. One former student with physical features that mirrored the North American culturally accepted notion of beauty characterized herself as "ordinary" and "unattractive"—even when classmates tried to tell her otherwise. When questioned, she described how she had to wear thick glasses and braces from childhood into her late teens and how she had been teased constantly. Even though the braces were gone and she wore contacts, she still saw herself as ugly and brushed aside our compliments. She insisted that we were just being nice but she knew how she *really* looked. This student exemplifies how we deny ourselves a much happier life when we resist change by clinging to obsolete pictures of ourselves.

Another problem arising from an obsolete self-concept is self-delusion and lack of growth. If you hold an unrealistically favourable picture of yourself, you won't see the real need for change and the opportunity to learn new skills, change a relationship, or improve your physical condition. You'll stay with the familiar and comfortable delusion that everything is all right. As time goes by, this delusion will be harder to maintain, which will lead to a third type of problem: defensiveness. In fact, the problem of defensiveness is so great that it is examined in detail in a later chapter.

LO2
Changing Your Self-Concept

If you're not happy with parts of your self-concept, take comfort in the fact that we have the power to change a great deal of our communication-related traits.[37] When you're young, it seems as if you're still growing your self-concept. But what happens as you age? Does your self-concept stay the same? The answer is no, it does not. It changes just like

our lives do. In fact, some people refer to the self-concept as coming in waves. You're feeling great about yourself and your accomplishments but life delivers you a blow or some trying challenges and it may take a dip for a while. For example, when women undergo treatment for breast cancer, they view their physical selves more negatively.[38] This can result in a decline in the their self-esteem level. Regardless of your age or the situation you're in, although there's no quick method for becoming the person you'd like to be, we can offer several suggestions that will help you move closer to your goals.

How To Change Your Self-Concept
Have a Realistic Perception of Yourself

Unrealistic perceptions sometimes come from giving yourself more credit than you deserve or from being overly self-critical. An unrealistically poor self-concept can also arise from the inaccurate feedback of others. Perhaps you receive an excessive number of prickly messages and not enough fuzzy, warm messages. Workers with overly critical supervisors, children with cruel "friends," and students with unsupportive teachers are all prone to low self-concepts owing to excessively negative feedback. If you fall into this category, it's important to seek out more supportive people who will acknowledge your assets as well as your liabilities. Doing so is often a quick and sure boost.

Have Realistic Expectations

It's important to determine if some of your dissatisfaction might come from expecting too much of yourself. Expecting to communicate perfectly, handle every conflict productively, be totally relaxed and skillful in conversations, or be 100 percent helpful when others have problems is unrealistic. Nobody can do that. Expecting perfection is to doom yourself to unhappiness.

Rather than feel miserable, realize that you are probably a better, wiser, or more skilled person than you used to be. Thinking like this can be very satisfying.

Have the Will to Change

We often say that we want to change, but we're not really willing to work at it. Sometimes we maintain an unrealistic self-concept by claiming that we "can't" be the person we'd like to be when in fact we're simply not willing to do what's required. Check out the Skill Builder titled "Reevaluating Your Can'ts" to see how many of your can'ts are actually won'ts. You can change if you make an effort.

Have the Skill to Change

Trying isn't always enough. In some instances you're not sure how to change. To remedy this, you can seek advice—from books, from the Internet, and from instructors, counsellors, other experts, and, of course, friends. A second method is to observe models—people who handle themselves in the ways you would like to master. Watch what people you admire do and say, not to copy them but rather to adapt their behaviours to fit your personal style. You might also try to take Gardner's advice in the movie *The Pursuit of Happyness*.

Influences on Identity

How we view ourselves and others is also influenced by diversity, culture, and gender.

Diversity

The challenges and opportunities that come from diversity are becoming more apparent in our increasingly diverse society. Unlike Americans, who attempt to shed their ethnicity, Canadians celebrate differences. Immigrants coming to Canada retain their language, customs, and religion and thus add to the

richness of our land. For example, in 2011, there were 6,775,800 foreign born individuals in Canada.[39] This represents approximately 20.6 percent of the population, or one in six of us. Predictions by Statistics Canada suggest that by 2031, 25 to 28 percent of the population will be visible minorities.[40]

In *The Pursuit of Happyness*, Christopher Gardner (Will Smith) uses persuasive communication skills and determination to overcome poverty and build a better life for himself and his son. In Gardner's words, "If you want somethin', go get it. Period."

SKILL BUILDER

Reevaluating Your "Can'ts"

1. Choose a partner and take turns making and listing statements that begin with "I can't . . ." Try to focus your statements on your relationships with family, friends, co-workers, students, and even strangers—anyone with whom you have a hard time communicating. Below are some sample statements:

   "I can't be myself with strangers I'd like to get to know at parties."
   "I can't stay off Facebook for more than a few hours."
   "I can't bring myself to ask my supervisor for the raise that I think I deserve."
   "I can't ask questions in class."

2. Notice your feelings (self-pity, regret, concern) as you make and reveal each statement to your partner.

3. Now repeat aloud each statement you've just made, except this time change each "can't" to a "won't." After each sentence, tell your partner whatever thoughts you have about what you've just said.

4. After you've finished, decide whether "can't" or "won't" is more appropriate for each item and explain your choice to your partner.

5. Are there any instances when your decision that you "can't" do something was the only force keeping you from doing it? If so, then you may be buying into a self-fulfilling prophecy. This notion will be discussed later in the chapter.

Old Wisdom Finds Home in New Nunavut Schools

Eva Aariak had a problem. The young Inuk woman from Arctic Bay—in what is now Nunavut—had received a good education away from home, attending a hands-on vocational school in Churchill, Manitoba, and courses at Algonquin and Kemptville colleges in Ontario. She had learned bookkeeping and typing, and had even helped launch a weather rocket during an internship with the National Research Council.

But she was back home with her newborn and she realized she needed an amautik—the distinctive Inuit parka with a built-in baby pouch. Yet in all her schooling, no one had ever taught her to make one.

"All the time I was away from home left me not learning my own culture and my own language," Aariak says.

She tried to learn from elders but they used technical terms in Inuktitut to describe the different stitches essential in making the parka. Aariak could not understand—she hadn't studied Inuktitut past elementary school. She had to ask her mother to make her amautik.

When Aariak was both premier and education minister for Nunavut, she built an education system that combines the skills young people need to work in the 21st century with a solid grounding in their language, culture, and the traditional skills that even today are necessary for life in Canada's far north.

The Nunavut education system still faces major challenges. Aariak says they desperately need 300 more Inuktitut language teachers, and many people still have a strong distrust of formal education—a legacy of residential schools. Low attendance and drop-out rates are still a problem.

"We have still a long way to go yet, but we have accomplished so much," says Aariak. It's a fitting symbol for how Nunavut is finding a place for old knowledge in new schools. And, it's finding the resources to do so. Kieran Oudshoorn of CBC News posted on February 17, 2016 that Nunavut schools were adding 10 new teachers in the 2016–17 academic year.

Craig and Mark Keilburger

Adapted from "Nunavut Education–Old Wisdom in New School," by Craig and Marc Kielburger. From http://www.weday.com/global-voices/nunavut-education-old-wisdom-in-new-school.

Canada's "self-concept" is changing. As Oxman-Martinez and Hanley write, "These changes demand a revision of our national image, our sense of what is Canadian, to fully reflect this racial and ethnic diversity."[41]

Language is another feature of diversity that affects self-concept and this is particularly evident in Canada. In an attempt to maintain the distinct Québécois culture, Bill 101 made French the official language in Quebec. Francophones clearly recognize that to lose your language is to lose your sense of self. If your primary language is not the majority one, or when it lacks prestige, the sense of being a member of what social scientists call the "outgroup" is strong. At this point, the speaker of a non-dominant tongue can react in one of two ways: either to feel pressured to assimilate by speaking the "better" language or to refuse to accommodate to the majority language and maintain loyalty to the ethnic tongue.[42]

In either case, the self-concept is affected. On one hand, the feeling is likely to be, "I'm not as good as speakers of the native language," and on the other, the belief is, "There's something unique and worth preserving in my language." This experience is exemplified by Canada's First Nations people, who during the 1950s and 1960s were forced to speak English in residential schools. This resulted in the loss of their language and related cultural norms. It is only in recent years that Canada's Aboriginal peoples are reclaiming their identity and language. This is very important. One study revealed that strong cultural identity was more important to the academic success of young First Nations students living in northern Quebec than their self-esteem level.[43] Providing culturally based curricula can ensure the success of Indigenous youth and inform other students at the same time.

When it comes to self-concept and Indigenous people, it is also important to note the government's implementation in December 2015 of a national inquiry into murdered and missing Indigenous women. For five years, all requests for this inquiry had been denied even though Indigenous women make up "4 percent of Canada's female population but 16 percent of all the women murdered in the country."[44] Perhaps this new policy will help First Nations people feel more respected in their own country.

Another example of self-concept and diversity comes from a student from Bangladesh. He told us that becoming a Canadian immigrant is a super boost to the self-concept. Individuals who are accepted into Canada are very proud of this achievement and are showered with respect from their relatives at home.

You don't need to travel overseas to appreciate the influence of ethnicity on the self. Within societies, co-cultural identity plays an important role in how people see themselves and others, and how they communicate. If society keeps reminding us that ethnicity is important, then we begin to think of ourselves in those terms.

Culture

Our self-concept is also shaped by the culture in which we have been reared.[45] Most Western cultures are highly individualistic, whereas Asian ones tend to be collectivistic. When asked to identify themselves, Canadians, Americans, Australians, and Europeans would probably respond by giving their first name, surname, street, town, and country. Many Asians do it the other way around.[46] If you ask Hindus for their identity, they will provide their caste as well as their name and village. The Sanskrit formula for identifying oneself begins with lineage and goes on to state family and house, and ends with one's personal name.[47] If you asked members from collectivistic cultures to make a "Who am I?" list, there would be far more group references than those from individualistic cultures.[48]

These naming conventions aren't just cultural curiosities; they reflect a way of viewing oneself. In collective cultures, people gain identity through group associations. Feelings of pride and self-worth are not shaped solely by what an individual does, but also by behaviours of other members of the community. This linkage explains the traditional Asian denial of self-importance—a strong

Jon Feingersh/Blend Images/Getty Images

contrast to the self-promotion that is common in individualistic Western cultures.[49] In Chinese written language, for example, the pronoun I looks very similar to the word for "selfish."[50] **Table 2.3** summarizes some differences between individualistic cultures and more collective ones.

Such cultural differences can affect the level of comfort or anxiety that people feel when communicating. In collective societies, there is a higher degree of communication apprehension. For example, as a group, residents of China, South Korea, and Japan exhibit a significantly higher degree of anxiety about speaking out than do members of individualistic cultures.[51] But the high level of communication apprehension isn't a problem—just the opposite, in fact. In collectivistic societies, being quiet is valued. The goal is to *avoid* calling attention yourself. So while a self-concept that includes assertiveness might make a Westerner feel proud, it might cause shame in Asian countries.

The difference between individualism and collectivism shows up in everyday interaction. Communication researcher Stella Ting-Toomey has developed a theory that explains cultural differences in terms of honesty and directness.[52] She suggests that in individualistic Western cultures, where there is a strong "I" orientation, the norm of speaking directly is honoured; whereas in collectivistic cultures, where the desire is to build connections, then indirect approaches that maintain harmony are more desirable. While "I gotta be me" represents Western culture, "If I hurt you, I hurt myself" is more in keeping with the Asian approach.

Gender

Imagine that you were born as a member of another gender? Would you express your emotions, deal with conflict, or relate to friends and strangers in the same way? The answer is almost certainly no.

The Canadian Press/Aaron Harris

TABLE 2.3
The Self in Individualistic and Collectivistic Cultures

Individualistic Cultures

- Self is separate, unique individual; should be independent, self-sufficient.
- Individual should take care of him- or herself and immediate family.
- Many flexible group memberships; friends based on shared interests and activities.
- Individual achievement and initiative rewarded; individual decisions encouraged; individual credit and blame assigned.
- High value placed on autonomy, change, youth, individual security, equality.

Collectivistic Cultures

- People belong to extended families or in-groups; "we," or group, orientation.
- Person should take care of extended family before self.
- Emphasize belonging to a very few permanent in-groups that have a strong influence over the person.
- Contributing to group goals and well-being rewarded; cooperation with in-group members prioritized; group decisions valued; credit and blame shared.
- High value placed on duty, order, tradition, age, group security, status, and hierarchy.

Adapted from the *Nebraska Symposium on Motivation, Volume 37: Cross-Cultural Perspectives,* edited by John J. berman, by permission of the University of Nebraska Press. Copyright 1990 by the University of Nebraska Press.

Right from the beginning, we are socialized to think about males and females in very different ways and this can shape our sense of self. For example, people want to know the sex of a child as soon as, or even before, it is born. As the *Cathy* cartoon shows, only then do people know how to behave.[53] Comments about boys focus on size, strength, and activity; comments about girls address beauty, sweetness, and facial responsiveness. The underlying message is that some behaviours are masculine and others feminine. Little girls are often praised for acting "sweet." The same principle operates in adulthood: Even today, men who stand up for their beliefs are considered "tough" or "persistent," whereas women who do so are called "nags" or "bitches."[54]

It's not hard to see how gender roles and labels like these can have a profound effect on how women and men view themselves and on how they communicate.

Gender depictions are also associated with self-esteem. One study of 550 Canadian secondary school students showed that male adolescents have higher self-esteem than their female counterparts.[55] Researchers from the Department of Sociology at the University of Western Ontario found that women, across ages, had lower levels of self-esteem than men did.[56] These results may be linked to gender expectations in that competitiveness is valued more in men than in women. It isn't surprising that the self-esteem of adolescent young men is closely related to having abilities

cathy®   **by Cathy Guisewite**

Seiya Kawamoto/Getty Images

is referred to as *genderfuck*.[59] There's a point to be made here; why should anyone be a slave to outdated gender role expectations?

LO3
The Self-Fulfilling Prophecy and Communication

The self-concept not only determines how you see yourself in the present but it can actually influence your future behaviour and that of others. This is known as the **self-fulfilling prophecy**. It refers to the notion of making predictions about future behaviours and feelings and then acting according to these predictions.

The self-fulfilling prophecy has four stages:

1. You hold an expectation (for yourself or for others)
2. You behave in accordance with that expectation
3. The expectation comes to pass
4. This reinforces the original expectation

For example, imagine that you're scheduled for a job interview. You're nervous about how you'll do and aren't sure that you're really qualified for the position. You share your concerns with a professor who knows you well and a friend who works for the company. Both assure you that you're ideal for the job. Based on these comments, you arrive at the interview feeling good about yourself. You speak with authority and sell yourself with confidence. The employers are impressed and you receive the job offer. Your conclusion: "I can and will do this well."

Thanks to the assurances of your professor and friend, your expectations about the interview were upbeat (stage 1). Because of your optimistic attitude, you communicated confidently in the interview (stage 2). Your confident

Self-fulfilling prophecy
A prediction or expectation of an event that makes the outcome more likely to occur than would otherwise have been the case.

that are superior in some way to those of their peers, whereas teenage women's self-worth is tied more closely to the success of their social relationships and verbal skills.[57]

When it comes to self-concept, there are problems associated with this paradigm. It limits the "acceptable" behaviours for both females and males and the expectations typically place males in the dominate roles. There's something else as well. Everything you've read so far seems to be based on the notion that everyone is heterosexual, which is not the case. This way of categorizing behaviours has an impact on members of the LGBTQ community. For example, the approach can be oppressive when it comes to transgendered individuals. Their sense of gender is incongruent with the gender they were assigned at birth.[58] They would define their gender as the way they feel on the inside. And while some transgendered individuals (such as Caitlyn Jenner) opt to take on the traits and trappings of the "opposite" sex, others prefer to mix, match, and change up these external characteristics. Some are even confrontational about this practice and this

In her hit song "If I Were a Boy," pop star Beyoncé expresses her belief that male gender role expectations are more liberating than those imposed on women.

Jared Silber/National Hockey League/Getty Images

Kevin Winter/Getty Images

behaviour—along with your qualifications—led to a job offer (stage 3). Finally, the positive results reinforced your positive self-assessment and you'll be an excellent employee (stage 4).

Self-fulfilling prophecies have a tremendous influence in our lives and, to a great extent, we become what we believe. In this sense, we and those around us constantly create and recreate our self-concepts. There are two types of self-fulfilling prophecies: self-imposed and other-imposed.

Self-Imposed Prophecies

Self-imposed prophecies occur when your own expectations influence your behaviour. For instance, perhaps you've faced an audience at one time or another when you were fearful and forgotten your remarks, not because you were unprepared but because you said to yourself, "I know I'll blow it."

We have to watch our self-imposed prophecies.[60] Communicators who believe they are incompetent are less likely to pursue rewarding relationships and more likely to sabotage their existing relationships.[61] On the other hand, students who perceive themselves as capable do better academically.[62] In another study, subjects who were sensitive to social rejection tended to expect rejection, perceived it where it didn't exist, and overreacted in ways that jeopardized the quality of their relationships.[63] Finally, communicators who feel anxious about giving speeches seem to create self-fulfilling prophecies about doing poorly that cause them to perform less effectively.[64]

Self-imposed prophecies operate in many ways that affect everyday communication. Say you wake up in a sour mood and think to yourself, "This is going to be a bad day." After this declaration, you act in ways that make it come true. On the other hand, if you approached the same day thinking it can only get better, this expectation will probably be met. Researchers have found that putting a smile on your face, even if you're not happy, can lead to a more positive disposition.[65]

Other-Imposed Prophecies

The second category of self-fulfilling prophecies is **other-imposed prophecies**, where your actions are governed by the expectations that others have of you. The classic example was demonstrated by Robert Rosenthal and Lenore Jacobson in a study they described in their book *Pygmalion in the Classroom*.[66] The experimenters told teachers that 20 percent of the children in a certain elementary school showed unusual potential for intellectual growth. The names of these 20 percent were randomly selected, and eight months later these "gifted" children showed significantly greater gains in IQ than did the other students! What led to the actual change in the intellectual performance of these allegedly "special" students was a

"When you hold me like this, you make me feel I can do <u>anything</u>."

Edward Koren The New Yorker Collection/The Cartoon Bank

change in the teachers' expectations regarding their intellectual performance. Although the children were no more intelligent than their classmates, they had learned that their teachers—significant others—believed that they were and they performed accordingly.

Clearly, teachers affect students' self-concepts. When a teacher communicates to a child the message "I think you're bright," the child accepts that evaluation and changes her self-concept to include it. Unfortunately, the same principle holds for students whose teachers send the message "I think you're stupid."

This type of prophecy is also a powerful force for shaping the self-concept and thus the behaviour of people outside schools.[67] In psychotherapy, patients who believe they will benefit from treatment often do so regardless of the type of treatment they receive. In the same vein, when doctors believe that patients will improve, they often do so because of this expectation. If doctors think there is little hope, patients often fail to recover.[68] Apparently, a patient's self-concept as sick

Self-imposed prophecy
Occurs when your own expectations influence your behaviour.

Other-imposed prophecy
Occurs when your actions may be governed by the expectations that others have of you.

or well (as shaped by the doctor) plays an important role in determining the actual state of health.

It's important to note that you must do more than believe something about a person to shape his or her expectations; you must communicate that belief. If parents have faith in their children but the kids aren't aware of that confidence, they won't be affected by their parents' expectations. Therefore, self-fulfilling prophecies are both a communication and a psychological event.

LO4

Presenting the Self: Communication as Identity Management

So far we have described how communication shapes the way communicators view themselves. In the remainder of this chapter we will turn the tables and focus on the topic of **identity management**—the communication strategies that people use to influence how others view them.[69]

Public and Private Selves

Until now, we have referred to the "self" as if each of us had only one identity. In truth, however, each of us has several different selves, some private and others public.

The **perceived self** is a reflection of the self-concept. Your perceived self is the person you believe yourself to be in moments of honest self-examination. We can call the perceived self "private" because you are unlikely to reveal all of it to another person. You might, for example, be reluctant to share some feelings about your intelligence ("I'm not as smart as I wish I were"), your goals ("The most important thing to me is becoming rich"), your motives ("I care more about myself than about others"), or a host of other things.

The **presenting self** is a public image—the way we want others to view us. For example, a person would behave and even dress differently in class, at work as a sale representative at *The Bay*, on a sports team, or trying to attract a potential lover. Typically, the presenting self that we seek to create is a socially approved image: diligent student, loving partner, conscientious worker, loyal friend, and so on. Social norms often create a gap between perceived and presenting selves.

Identity management
The communication strategies people use to influence how others view them.

Perceived self
The person you believe yourself to be in moments of honest self-examination. It may be identical to or different from the presenting and ideal selves.

Presenting self
The image a person presents to others. It may be identical to or different from the perceived and ideal selves.

You can recognize the difference between public and private behaviours by recalling a time when you observed a driver, alone in the car, behaving in ways that would never be acceptable in public. Everyone does things when they are alone that they would never do in public…and, this is probably a good thing.

Characteristics of Identity Management

Now that you have a sense of what identity management is, we can look at some of its characteristics.

We Strive to Construct Multiple Identities

Most of us have more than one identity. In the course of a day, most people play a variety of roles: respectful student, joking friend, friendly neighbour, and helpful worker, to suggest just a few. The ability to construct multiple identities is one element of communication competence, and changing the language we use or our speaking style is one way to do this. A style of speaking, or even the language itself, can reflect a choice about how to construct one's identity. For example, a scholarly female biology professor plays on the faculty/staff hockey team against a student group. When asked how she manages her communication style, she responded that in the classroom she is dogmatic and authoritarian but also lively and enthusiastic. When delivering scientific papers, she minimizes the human element to appear serious and informative. To ensure she's taken seriously on the ice, however, she uses foul language as well as checking and light sticking. Players and spectators alike see a very different person on the ice than students see in the classroom.

We even strive to construct different identities with the same person. Think of the different roles you play in your family—from helpless child to dedicated family

Andrew Chin/Getty Images

Drake's presenting self seems to be very natural. This suggests that his identity management is unconscious. What do you think his perceived self is like?

member, from young rebel to responsible adult. Likewise, in romantic relationships, we switch from friend to lover to business partner to critic and so forth, depending on the context.

Identity Management Is Collaborative

Sociologist Erving Goffman used a drama metaphor to describe identity management, suggesting that each of us is a kind of playwright creating our own role in terms of how we want others to see us.[70] This identity-related communication can be viewed as a kind of theatre process where we collaborate with other actors to improvise scenes in which our characters mesh.

You can appreciate the collaborative nature of identity management by thinking about how you might handle a gripe with a friend who has not returned your repeated texts regarding important details of a surprise party. You decide to call her and play the role of "nice guy." You don't want to seem like a nag and you don't want to embarrass your friend so she feels like a "screw up." If your tactful bid is accepted, the dialogue might sound like this:

> **You:** By the way, I've sent you several texts and I'm not sure if you've gotten them. We need to talk about the invitations before they go out tomorrow.
>
> **Friend:** Oh, sorry. I've been meaning to get back to you. I've been so busy lately with papers and work.
>
> **You:** That's okay. Can we talk now?
>
> **Friend:** I'm just finishing up an assignment. Can I call you back in an hour?
>
> **You:** That sounds good.

In this upbeat conversation, both of you accepted one another's bids for identity as thoughtful, responsible friends. Therefore, the conversation ran smoothly. But, what if your friend didn't accept your presenting self? It might go something like this:

> **You:** By the way, I've sent you several texts and I'm not sure if you've gotten…
>
> **Friend:** (Interrupting defensively) Okay, so I forgot. It's not that big a deal. You're not so perfect yourself, you know.

Stocklite/Shutterstock.com

At this point, you have the choice to persist and play the nice role ("Hey, I'm not mad at you and I know I'm not perfect but…") or you might switch to the unjustly accused person (Excuse me. I never said I was perfect but we're not talking about me here."). If you stick to the latter, the issue could mushroom out of control and you both may settle into the roles of combatants which, in turn, will affect the friendship.

Identity Management Can Be Deliberate or Unconscious

Sometimes we are highly aware of managing impressions, such as during an employment interview, but in other cases we unconsciously act in ways that are really small public performances.[71] For example, experimental subjects expressed facial disgust in reaction to eating sandwiches laced with a supersaturated saltwater solution only when someone else was present. When they were alone, they made no faces while eating the same sandwiches.[72] Another study showed that communicators engage in facial mimicry, such as smiling or looking sympathetic in response to another's message in face-to-face settings only when their expressions can be seen by the other person. However, when they speak on the phone and their reactions cannot be seen, they do not make the same expressions.[73]

These studies suggest that most of our behaviour is aimed at sending messages to others—in other words, identity management. But the experimental subjects didn't consciously think, "Somebody is watching and I better act accordingly." Instead, their actions

Looking at Diversity

Looking In and Coming Out

When I was quite young, I loved to role play with friends. We would assume the lives of people with make-believe dramas and stories. It was our own little soap opera and we were the stars (in our own minds). One thing that I never questioned was the fact that I often wanted to be the girl or woman. I never thought that it was bad or wrong; it seemed completely innocent and it felt good. It was only after my family and friends began to criticize me for wanting to be a female character that I started to feel insecure. I was learning that this wasn't "proper" behaviour for a young boy. This was when I went into the closet. As human beings, it is very natural to want to feel safe and in our early developmental stages, family and friends heavily influence our behaviour and how we feel about our own unique identity. Therefore, they served as my intimate environment—they were my home, my tribe, my safety net.

As I grew up, I was exposed to the so-called typical societal norms and judged myself on the basis of these standards. Eventually, I came to realize that I was gay and that's when the real mental struggle started. I didn't want to be gay! I was angry and scared. Instead, I wanted to have a normal life with a wife and two kids. Most of all, I was afraid that my family wouldn't love me anymore. I thought that maybe I could change or perhaps I could marry a woman and lead that life. The people I cared about would be happy and everything would be okay...right? All of these thoughts were swirling around my head and I hadn't even told a single soul that I was gay.

We all have stuff, parts of us that just don't seem to fit into society's molds or expectations.

From that perspective, a heterosexual could be in the closet about something just as much as any member of the LGBTQI* community. It is not until we make peace with those parts of ourselves that we can begin to feel our way through and come out. We start by telling a few close friends or family members. It is like we are dipping a toe in a lake to test the water temperature. Is it too cold? No? Okay, let me put my whole leg in and go from there. It is only when we feel safe, with a solid foundation of support under us and a home base from which to grow, that we can transition to the next phase, whatever that may be.

Now, I am public about my sexual orientation and I live a good life. I have been blessed with an amazing family and great friends, some of whom I have known since early childhood. At the same time, I am aware of the bumps in the road and the prejudice that still exists in today's society. I may walk with a level of caution but, rest assured, I hold my head high because I love myself and know that I have a strong foundation under my feet.

As human beings, we are always coming out of something and our self-concept continues to evolve based on personal change and life experiences. If there is one thing that I have learned, it is that change is constant. How we feel about ourselves today isn't necessarily how we will feel tomorrow. But, we do not grow through complacency. We grow through challenge.

Tim Damon

*lesbian, gay, bisexual, transgender, queer, questioning, and intersex
By Tim Damon. Used with permission.

---

were instantaneous and outside of their conscious awareness. Therefore, it seems like an exaggeration to suggest that *all* behaviour is aimed at making impressions. However, most people consciously or unconsciously communicate in ways that help construct desired identities for themselves and others.

Identity Management Varies by Situation

The degree to which we consciously manage our identities varies from one situation to another. For instance, most of us work harder at creating a desired impression in the early stages of a relationship—especially when we're seeking the approval of people whose opinion we value. Again, think of how carefully you present yourself to a potential boss during the interview process.[74] The same principle operates in courtship situations. University men changed their self-presentation more when they were talking to women they found attractive than they did when talking to less attractive women.[75] In another study, researchers found that people are less concerned with identity management among familiar people of the same sex than with less familiar people of the same sex or people of the opposite sex, regardless of how well we know them.[76]

People Differ in Their Degree of Identity Management

Some people are much more aware of their identity management behaviour than others. High self-monitors pay attention to their own behaviour and others' reactions and adjust their communication to create the desired impression. By contrast, low self-monitors express what they think and feel without paying attention to the impression their behaviour creates.[77] Complete the "Self-Monitoring Inventory" in Chapter 1, p. 23 to gauge your self-monitoring behaviours.

High self-monitors have clear communication advantages.[78] They can usually create the identity they want, acting interested when bored or friendly when they really feel quite the opposite. This allows them to handle social situations smoothly, often putting others at ease. They are also good "people readers" who can adjust their behaviour to get the desired reaction from others. But there are some disadvantages to being an extremely high self-monitor. Sometimes they don't experience events completely because a portion of their attention will always be viewing the situation from a detached position. One study found that high self-monitors often feel less intimacy, satisfaction, and commitment in their romantic relationships, in part because they hide what they really think and feel.[79]

Low self-monitors have a simpler, more focused idea of who they are and typically act the same way regardless of the situation, and therefore they are easy to read—what you see is what you get. Although this lack of flexibility may make their social interaction less smooth in many situations, low self-monitors can be counted on to be straightforward communicators.

Neither extremely high nor low self-monitoring is the ideal. There are many situations when paying attention to yourself and adapting your behaviour can be useful and others when reacting without considering the effects is a better approach. This need for a range of behaviours demonstrates the notion of communicative competence. Flexibility is the key to successful relationships.

Phovoir/Shutterstock.com

LO5
The Role of Identity Management

Why Manage Identities?

Social scientists have identified several overlapping reasons for why we shape our identities.[80]

To Start and Manage Relationships

Have you ever consciously and carefully managed your approach when meeting someone you wanted to know better? Did you try to be charming and witty—or perhaps cool and suave? If so, you were trying to manage your identity to initiate a relationship. Once it was up and running, you probably still managed your identity, although not as much.

To Gain the Compliance of Others

Sometimes we manage our identity to get others to do what we want. You might dress up for a visit to traffic court in the hope that your image (responsible citizen) will convince the judge to treat you sympathetically. You might chat sociably with neighbours you don't find especially interesting so they'll lend you tools and garden equipment.

To Save Others' Face

We often modify ourselves to support the way other people want to be seen. For example, able-bodied people are often uncomfortable meeting someone with a disability and attempt to mask it by acting nonchalant or stressing the similarities they share.[81] Young children who haven't learned about the importance of face-saving often embarrass their parents by behaving inappropriately ("Mommy, why is that man so fat?"). By the time they enter school, this once excusable or even amusing behaviour just isn't acceptable.

To Explore New "Selves"

Sometimes we try on a new identity to see if it changes how others view us and how we view and feel about ourselves. For instance, teens might come out first to members of their Gay-Straight Alliance group or to a few trusted friends before they do so with others. Trying on new selves can also be a means to self-improvement. For example, teens who experimented with new identities online reached out more to people of different ages and cultural backgrounds than they did in their face-to-face lives. As a result, they actually increased their social competence.[82]

Alter Egos in a Virtual World

Time was that the word *avatar* meant the earthly manifestation of a god. You might have also used it to describe an archetype. But in the earliest days of the Internet—back in the 1980s, when no one was looking—an avatar became one's digital self.

If this is news to you, consider yourself extravagantly late to the costume party that is online role playing. Let's get you up to speed. Introducing 27-year-old wife and mother Becky Glasure, who complains of never being taken seriously.

"Maybe I just exude it, I don't know. But I feel like I'm this short person with this squeaky little Filipino voice and nobody wants to pay attention." Glasure's first online game was *Everquest* and her avatar was female. But all anyone noticed were her pixel breasts, and this despite her considerable gaming expertise.

Fed up, she switched digital identities. "And I picked the biggest guy I could find," she says. She called him Stygion Physic—Stygion from the River Styx, Physic for healing. That's the closest she could get to Bad Medicine in the game *City of Heroes*.

And with her change of avatar, her pleasure in the game changed. "When I play this big guy, everybody listens to me," she says. "Nobody argues with me. If there's a group of people standing around, I say, 'OK, everybody follow me!' And they do. No questions asked."

Cue the cyberanalysts and virtual ethnographers, including Tracy Spaight, who's been inquiring into human gaming behaviour for as long as there have been online games. "In the virtual world you can be anything you want to be . . . construct a persona that is wildly different from your real-world self."

Spaight's own fascination with role playing, avatars, and gaming has been realized in the book and travelling exhibit *Alter Ego: Avatars and Their Creators*. Cooper and Spaight travelled to China, Japan, South Korea, parts of Europe, and the United States to photograph and interview gamers, whittling down some 3000 applicants to the several dozen people featured in their book.

There is ample repetition. For one, quite a number of avatars are just younger, thinner, and prettier versions of their creators. For another, just as many avatars are polar opposites of their people.

Cooper's portrait of Jason Rowe, for instance, stops you dead. He stares straight at you out of startled blue eyes. But what takes you aback is his frail body, his clenched hands, and the ominous ventilator strapped to his face.

"My condition is called Duchenne muscular dystrophy," Rowe told Spaight. "It pretty much affects all the muscles in the body. They don't function." His avatar is a steely, robot-like character who rides Imperial speeder bikes and fights monsters, his head helmeted, his face unseen. "My character in the game is a lot different from what you see here in real life," Rowe says. "[It] pretty much gave me a window to the world."

In the four years since he created his avatar, this frail 32-year-old has had an unprecedented life experience: Online, he is treated as an equal among his peers. "Not disabled," he says. "Not in a wheelchair. In virtual worlds, everyone is on common ground."

Rowe didn't set out to overcome people's prejudice. And Glasure, whose male avatar became a leader, doesn't mean to lose patience when friends and family don't fall in line. But stay in costume long enough—whether a general in a Civil War reenactment or a wench at a Renaissance fair—and the lines may blur between who you are and who you're pretending to be.

Ketzel Levine

How Do We Manage Identities?

Now that we've examined why we might shape our identities, in this section we look at how we manage identities.

Face-to-Face Impression Management

Communicators manage their identity in three ways: manner, setting, and appearance.[83] **Manner** consists of a communicator's words and nonverbal actions. For example, some physicians are friendly and conversational, whereas others adopt a curt and impersonal approach. (Think of the earlier seasons of the popular TV show *Grey's Anatomy*, and the difference between brusque Dr. Yang and the caring Meredith Grey.) Much of a communicator's manner comes from what he or she says. A doctor who remembers details about your interests or hobbies is quite different from one who sticks to clinical questions. One who explains a medical procedure creates a different impression than one who reveals little to the patient.

Nonverbal behaviours also play a big role in creating impressions. A doctor who greets you with a smile and a handshake comes across differently than one who gives nothing more than a nod. Manner also varies widely in

Hill Street Studios/Blend Images/Getty Images

Physical settings also influence our identities. The physical setting we choose and the way we arrange it are other important ways to manage identities. While the colours, artwork, and music you choose for your apartment or room reflect your tastes, they also create an environment that presents a desired front to others.

Online Impression Management

In addition to face-to-face interaction, impression management is just as common and important in online contexts.

You might think that texting, e-mailing, and blogging limit the potential for impression management because they lack nonverbal messages (tone of voice, postures, gestures, or facial expressions). However, this may actually be an *advantage* for communicators who want to manage the impressions they make.[85] Communicating online, however, allows you to edit your messages until your create just the desired impression.[86] With e-mail, and to a lesser degree with text messaging, you can compose difficult messages without forcing the receiver to respond immediately, and you can ignore others' messages rather than give an unpleasant response. Perhaps most important, when communicating via text-based technology you don't have to worry about stammering or blushing, what you're wearing, or what you look like (Photos, video, and streaming may be involved in some mediated communication—but you have choices as well.)

Of course, communicating via social media also allows strangers to change their age, history, personality, appearance, and other matters that would be impossible to hide in person.[87] Among teens, a quarter have

other professions and settings—professors, salespeople, hairstylists, and so on—and the impressions they create shape how others view them.

A second dimension of identity management is **appearance**—the personal items that people use to shape an image. Sometimes appearance is part of creating a professional image. A physician's white lab coat, a tailored suit, and a rumpled outfit create very different impressions. Off the job, clothing selection sends messages about whether a person is trendy or traditional. Some people dress in ways that accent their sexuality; others hide it. Clothing can say, "I'm an athlete," "I'm wealthy," or "I'm an environmentalist." Makeup and hairstyle also send messages. Some people accessorize to indicate that they belong to particular ethnic groups, religious groups, or countries. It is not uncommon, for example, for Canadians travelling the globe to wear a small Maple Leaf pin so others won't think of them as Americans.

Tattoos also make a statement, and the design or the words chosen say even more. One fascinating study explored the communicative function of tattoos worn by some people to announce they were HIV-positive.[84] Beyond being a practical announcement, these tattoos can also be a vehicle for identity management. One wearer explained that his tattoo conveyed the refusal to internalize shame, a commitment to safer sex practices, a challenge to stereotypes about weak "AIDS victims," and an educational tool.

A final way to manage identities is through the choice of **setting**—physical items used to influence how others view us. The automobile is a major example, and this explains why many people lust after far more expensive and powerful cars than they need. A sporty convertible doesn't just get drivers from one place to another, it also makes statements about the kind of people they are. Vanity plates offer another opportunity for identity management. Owners typically display names and topics related to their work, hobbies, and interests. In most provinces, requests for vanity plates are scrutinized for cultural, religious, prejudicial, or sexual connotations. Family names such as *Too Long Dong* and *Giver*, for example, are rejected.

"On the Internet, nobody knows you're a dog."

Peter Steiner The New Yorker Collection/The Cartoon Bank

pretended to be a different person online and a third confess to having given false information about themselves while e-mailing and instant messaging. A survey of one online dating site's participants found that 86 percent felt others misrepresented their physical appearance in their posted descriptions.[88]

Blogs, personal web pages, and profiles on social networking websites all provide opportunities for communicators to construct an identity.[89] Even the simple choice of a screen name (lovemyporsche, fun2bewith, footballdude) says something about you and is likely to lead others to create impressions of you.[90] And interestingly, research shows that viewing your own Facebook page on a regular basis can enhance your self-esteem.[91] This makes sense: If you're managing your identity on that site, it can be an ego-booster to see what you look like "at your best."

Viewing your online presence from the perspective of a neutral third party can also be a valuable exercise. You may decide that it's time to engage in what researchers call *reputation management*. These days, "many users are changing privacy setting on profiles, customizing who can see certain updates and deleting unwanted information about them that appears online."[92]

> You're not fooling anyone when you become
> Somebody else
> Round everyone else
>
> —Avril Lavigne,
> "Complicated"*

Identity Management and Honesty

Some readers might think of identity management as an academic label for phoniness, and there certainly are situations where identity management is dishonest. Manipulative dates who pretend to be affectionate to gain sexual favours, job applicants who lie about their academic records to get hired, or salespeople who pretend to be dedicated to customer service when their real goal is to make a quick buck are all being dishonest.

AT THE MOVIES

Catch Me If You Can (2003), Rated 13+

The movie *Catch Me If You Can* is a good example of impression management. Frank Abagnale (Leonardo DiCaprio) learns to escape his family's financial and interpersonal woes by creating false identities. He impersonates a teacher, a pilot, a doctor, and a lawyer. These false fronts allow him to become rich, admired, and respected—and very lonely. The more faces and façades he constructs, the more he loses his sense of self. More significantly, his unwillingness to disclose his real identity isolates him from significant others—including his fiancée.

The person who knows Frank best is FBI agent Carl Hanratty (Tom Hanks), who is trying to capture and arrest him. By the film's end, Carl becomes something of a father figure to Frank, helping him reestablish a legitimate identity.

Based on a true story, this movie illustrates how identity management, when used unethically, can lead to strained relationships and a loss of self.

DreamWorks/courtesy Everett Collection/The Canadian Press

"Frank Abagnale," played by Leonardo DeCaprio in the movie *Catch Me if You Can* is a great example of identity management to deceive others. In fact, he is an impostor. (See the "At The Movies" box.) But, managing impressions doesn't make you a liar. In fact, it is almost impossible to imagine how we could communicate

On the Job

Self-Fulfilling Prophecies in the Workplace

An abundance of research shows how self-fulfilling prophecies can affect job performance. For example,

- A group of clerks was told they were expected to punch about 550 cards per day. They were also told that processing more cards might cause stress. A second group was not given any limits or warnings; they were told to punch as many cards as they could. The first group averaged 550 cards and indeed reported stress when they tried to do more. The second group averaged almost 2000 cards a day with no signs of stress.[93]
- Military personnel who were randomly labelled as having high potential performed up to the expectations of their superiors. They were also more likely to volunteer for dangerous special duty.[94]
- A group of welders with relatively equal aptitudes began training. Everyone, including the trainer, was told that five of the welders had higher scores on an aptitude test—even though they'd been chosen randomly. All five finished at the top of the class. They had fewer absences and significantly higher final test scores. Most impressively, they learned the skills of their trade twice as quickly as those who weren't identified as being so talented.[95]

Many more studies of self-fulfilling prophecies show how managers can help employees become more productive by communicating high expectations.[96]

While this is valuable information for supervisors, self-fulfilling prophecies can assist those in non-managerial positions as well. Having positive expectations and communicating them confidently is an asset in any field or position. The salesperson who approaches a client or customer with high expectations ("I can succeed here") and then behaves accordingly is more likely to be successful than someone with lower hopes. It may sound simple, but research confirms that positive expectations can lead to positive communication, which can lead to positive results.

---

effectively without making decisions about which front to present in one situation or another. Each of us has a repertoire of faces—a cast of characters—and part of being a competent communicator is choosing the best face for the situation. Consider a few examples:

- You offer to teach a friend a new skill: playing the guitar, operating a computer program, or sharpening up a tennis backhand. Your friend is making slow progress with the skill, and you find yourself growing impatient.
- At work you face a belligerent customer. You don't believe anyone has the right to treat you this way.
- A friend or family member makes a joke about your appearance that hurts your feelings. You aren't sure whether to make an issue of the joke or to pretend that it doesn't bother you.

In each of these situations, you have a choice about how to act, and it's an oversimplification to say that there's only one honest way to behave. Identity management involves deciding which part of you to reveal. When teaching a new skill, for example, you choose to be "patient" instead of "impatient." At work you have the option of acting defensive or nondefensive in difficult situations. Deciding which face to show to others is an important decision because you are sharing a real part of yourself.

Communication in the Workplace

Self and Identity

Self-Esteem

Just as in our everyday lives, self-esteem also plays a role in the workplace. For example, referring back to **Table 2.1**, it appears that individuals with high esteem might make better employees in that they perform well when they're being watched, they work harder for individuals who demand high standards, and they are comfortable around people who hold superior positions. In contrast, communicators with low self-esteem expect rejection, they perform poorly when being watched, and they feel threatened by people they view as superior.[97] Clearly, having high self-esteem can make your work life a little easier.

Identity Management

Another factor related to self-concept in the workplace is identity management. Most individuals manage their identity by communicating in ways that are appropriate in their line of work. An additional form of identity management in the workplace has to do with managing sexual identity and this can be an important issue for individuals in the LGBTQI (lesbian, gay, bisexual, transgender, queer or questioning, and intersex) community. While openness is associated with less stress, higher self-esteem, and occupational satisfaction,[98] the decision to come out is a complex one and, even today, it's not uncommon for individuals to keep their sexual identity secret. One study found that males used three strategies to help manage their sexual identity. They used counterfeiting where they created a false heterosexual identity. In a second strategy, they avoided offering any information whatsoever about their personal lives, and they didn't socialize with their co-workers—not even going to lunch with them. The third strategy was to integrate by openly revealing their sexual identity and then attempting to manage the consequences. Most individuals did this in direct ways although some used less explicit methods such as hinting or offering clues about their real sexual orientation.[99]

Self-Fulfilling Prophecies

Another influence in the workplace is self-fulfilling prophecies and they can have a surprising impact on our work performance. Check out the box "On the Job" to see just how powerful they can be.

READY TO STUDY?

IN THE BOOK, YOU CAN:

❏ Rip out the Chapter in Review card at the back of the book to have the key terms and Learning Objectives handy, and complete the quizzes provided (answers are at the bottom of the back page).

ONLINE YOU CAN:

❏ Stay organized and efficient with MindTap—a single destination with all the course material and study aids you need to succeed. Built-in apps leverage social media and the latest learning technology. For example:

  ❏ Listen to the text using ReadSpeaker.

  ❏ Use pre-populated Flashcards as a jump start for review—or you can create your own.

  ❏ You can highlight text and make notes in your MindTap Reader. Your notes will flow into Evernote, the electronic notebook app that you can access anywhere when it's time to study for the exam.

  ❏ Prepare for tests with a variety of quizzes and activities.

Go to **nelson.com/student** to access these digital resources

---

Endnotes

1. R. F. Baumeister (2005). *The Cultural Animal: Human Nature, Meaning, and Social Life.* New York: Oxford University Press; R. F. Baumeister, J. D. Campbell, J. I. Krueger, & K. D. Vohs (2003). "Does High Self-Esteem Cause Better Performance, Interpersonal Success, Happiness, or Healthier Lifestyles?" *Psychological Science in the Public Interest, 4,* 1–44.

2. K. D. Vohs & T. F. Heatherton (2004). "Ego Threats Elicit Different Social Comparison Process Among High and Low Self-Esteem People: Implications for Interpersonal Perceptions." *Social Cognition, 22,* 168–191.

3. W. Soldz & G. E. Vaillant (1999). "The Big Five Personality Traits and the Life Course: A 45-Year Longitudinal Study." *Journal of Research in Personality, 33,* 208–232.

4. For a summary of research on heritability of personality, see W. Wright (1998). *Born That Way: Genes, Behaviour, Personality.* New York: Knopf.

5. C. E. Schwartz, C. I. Wright, L. M. Shin, J. Kagan, & S. L. Rauch (June 20, 2003). "Inhibited and Uninhibited Infants 'Grown Up': Adult Amygdalar Response to Novelty." *Science,* 1952–1953.

6. J. G. Cole & J. C. McCroskey (2000). "Temperament and Socio-Communicative Orientation." *Communication Research Reports, 17,* 105–114.

7. A. D. Heisel, J. C. McCroskey, & V. P. Richmond (1999). "Testing Theoretical Relationships and Non-Relationships of Genetically-Based Predictors: Getting Started with Communibiology," *Communication Research Reports, 16,* 1–9.

8. Cole & McCroskey, op. cit.

9. C. J. Wigley (1998). "Vergal Aggressiveness." In J. C. McCroskey, J. A. Daly, M. M. Martin, & M. J. Beatty (Eds.). *Personality and Communication: Trait Perspectives.* New York: Hampton.

10. J. C. McCroskey, A.D. Heisel, & V. P. Richmond (2001). "Eysenck's Big Three and Communication Traits: Three Correlational Studies." *Communication Monographs, 68,* 360–366.

11. R. R. McCrae & P. T. Costa Jr. (1987). "Validation of the Five-Factor Model of Personality across Instruments and Observers," *Journal of Personality and Social Psychology, 52,* 81–90.

12. R. R. McCrae & P. T Costa. Jr. (1997). "Personality Trait Structure as a Human Universal." *American Psychologist, 52,* 509–516.

13. C. Dweck (2008). "Can Personality Be Changed? The Role of Beliefs in Personality and Change." *Current Directions in Psychological Science, 6,* 391–394.

14. S. Begney (2008, December 1). "When DNA Is Not Destiny." *Newsweek, 152,* 14.

15. C. H. Cooley (1912). *Human Nature and the Social Order.* New York: Scribner's.

16. C. Jaret, D. Reitzes, & N. Shapkina (2005). "Reflected Appraisals and Self-Esteem." *Sociological Perspectives, 48,* 403–419.

17. S. Salimi, S. Mirzamani, & M. Shahiri-Tabarestani (2005). "Association of Parental Self-Esteem and Expectations with Adolescents' Anxiety about Career and Education." *Psychological Reports, 96,* 569–578; A. L. Vangelisti & L. P. Crumley (1998). "Reactions to Messages that Hurt: The Influence of Relational Contexts." *Communication Monographs, 65,* 173–196.

18. L. Leets & Sunwolf (2004). "Being Left Out: Rejecting Outsiders and Communicating Group Boundaries in Childhood and Adolescent Peer Groups." *Journal of Applied Communication Research, 32,* 195–223.

19. A. Sillars, A. Koerner, & M.A. Fitzpatrick (2005). "Communication and Understanding in Parent-Adolescent Relationships." *Human Communication Research, 31,* 107–128.

20. T. Adler (October 1992). "Personality, Like Plaster, Is Pretty Stable over Time." *APA Monitor,* 18.

21. J. D. Brown, N. J. Novick, K. A. Lord, & J. M. Richards (1992). "When Gulliver Travels: Social Context, Psychological Closeness, and Self-Appraisals." *Journal of Personality and Social Psychology, 62,* 717–734.

22. M. Krcmar, S. Giles, & D. Helme (2008). "Understanding the Process: How Mediated and Peer Norms Affect Young Women's Body Esteem." *Communication Quarterly, 56,* 111–130.

23. P. N. Myers & F. A. Biocca (1992). "The Elastic Body Image: The Effect of Television Advertising and Programming on Body Image Distortions in Young Women." *Journal of Communication, 42,* 108–134.

24. C. M. Strong (2005). "The Role of Exposure to Media Idealized Male Physiques on Men's Body Image." *Dissertation Abstracts International, 65,* 4306.

25. K. N. Kubric & R. M. Chory (2007). "Exposure to Television Makeover Programs and Perceptions of Self." *Communication Research Reports, 24,* 283–291.

26. D. Grodin & T. R. Lindolf (1995). *Constructing the Self in a Mediated World.* Newbury Park, CA: Sage.

27. M. Han (2003). "Body Image Dissatisfaction and Eating Disturbance among Korean College Female Students: Relationships to Media Exposure, Upward Comparison, and Perceived Reality." *Communication Studies, 34,* 65–78; K. Harrison & J. Cantor (1997). "The Relationship Between Media Consumption and Eating Disorders." *Journal of Communication, 47,* 40–67.

28. L. J. Carrell & S. C. Willmington (1996). "A Comparison of Self-Report and Performance Data in Assessing Speaking and Listening Competence." *Communication Reports, 9,* 185–191.

29. D. Meyers (May 1980). "The Inflated Self." *Psychology Today, 14,* 16.

30. A. B. Canton & K. H. Teigen. "Better Than Average and Better With Time: Relative Evaluations of Self and Others in the Past, Present, and Future." *European Journal of Social Psychology, 38,* 343–353.

31. N. Ellison, R. Heino, & J. Gibbs (2006). "Managing Impressions Online: Self-Presentation Processes in the Online Dating Environment." *Journal of Computer-Mediated Communication, 11,* http://jcmc.indiana.edu/ vol11/issue2/ ellison.html, article 2. Accessed September 11, 2006.

32. E. D. Sturman & M. Mongrain (2008). "The Role of Personality in Defeat: A Revised Social Rank Model." *European Journal of Personality, 22,* 55–79; J. D. Brown & T. A. Mankowski (1993). "Self-Esteem, Mood, and Self-Evaluation: Changes in Mood and the Way You See You." *Journal of Personality and Social Psychology, 64,* 421–430.

33. M. A. Gara, R. L. Woolfolk, B. D. Cohen, & R. B. Goldston (1993). "Perception of Self and Other in Major Depression." *Journal of Abnormal Psychology, 102,* 93–100.

34. K. A. Martin Ginis, M. E. Jong, & L. Gauvin (2003). "To See or Not to See: The Effects of Exercising in Mirrored Environments on Sedentary Women's Feeling States and Self-Efficacy," *Health Psychology, 22,* 354–361.

35. L. C. Miller, L. L. Cooke, J. Tsang, & F. Morgan (1992). "Should I Brag? Nature and Impact of Positive and Boastful Disclosures for Women and Men." *Human Communication Research, 18,* 364–399.

36. B. Bower (August 15, 1992). "Truth Aches: People Who View Themselves Poorly May Seek the 'Truth' and Find Despair." *Science News,* 110–111; W. B. Swann (2005). "The Self and Identity Negotiation." *Interaction Studies, 6,* 69–83.

37. For a thorough discussion of this subject, see M. E. P. Seligman (1993). *What You Can Change and What You Can't.* New York: Knopf.

38. A. Przezdziecki, K. Sherman, A. Baillie, A. Taylor, E. Foley & K. Stalgis-Bilnski (2012). "My changed body: Breast cancer, body image, distress and self-compassion." *Wiley Online Library,* DOI 10.1002/pon.3230. (wileyonlinelibrary.com).

39. Immigration and Ethnocultural Diversity in Canada (2011). Statistics Canada. http://www12.statcan.gc.ca/ nhs-enm/2011/as-sa/99-010-x/99-010-x2011001-eng.cfm. Retrieved December 9, 2015.

40. Statistics Canada (2010, March 9). "Study: Projections of the Diversity of the Canadian Population." *The Daily.* http://www.statcan.gc.ca/daily-quotidien/100309/dq100309a-eng.htm. Retrieved November 12, 2012.

41. J. Oxman-Martinez & J. Handley (2005). "Health and Social Services for Canada's Multicultural Population: Challenges for Equity." Canadian Heritage, www.pch.gc.ca/mutli/canada2017/4_e.cfm. Accessed December 8, 2005.

42. H. Giles & P. Johnson (1987). "Ethnolinguistic Identity Theory: A Social Psychological Approach to Language Maintenance," *International Journal of Sociology of Languages, 68,* 69–99.

43. M. Vicaire (2010). Cultural identity, intelligence, and self-esteem: Towards enriching the understanding of academic outcomes of a community of First Nation students. (Unpublished thesis). McGill University, Montreal, Quebec.

44. J. Murphy (2015, December 8). "Canada launches inquiry into murdered and missing indigenous women." *The Guardian Online.* http://www.theguardian.com/world/2015/dec/08/canada-40m-inquiry-violence-indigenous-women-justin-trudeau. Retrieved December 9, 2015.

45. W. W. Wilmot (1995). *Relational Communication.* New York: McGraw-Hill, pp. 35–54.

46. J. Servaes (1989). "Cultural Identity and Modes of Communication." In J. A. Anderson (Ed.). *Communication Yearbook 12* (p. 396). Newbury Park, CA: Sage.

47. A. Bharti (1985). "The Self in Hindu Thought and Action." In A. J. Marsella, G. DeVos, & F. L. K. Hsu (Eds.). *Culture and Self: Asian and Western Perspectives* (pp. 185–320). New York: Tavistock.

48. S. Bochner (1994). "Cross-Cultural Differences in the Self Concept: A Test of Hofstede's Individualism/Collectivism Distinction." *Journal of Cross-Cultural Psychology, 25,* 273–283.

49. W. B. Gudykunst & S. Ting-Toomey 1988. *Culture and Interpersonal Communication.* Newbury Park, CA: Sage

50. L. A. Samovar & R. E. Porter (1991). *Communication between Cultures.* Belmont, CA: Wadsworth, p. 91

51. D. Klopf (1984). "Cross-Cultural Apprehension Research: A Summary of Pacific Basin Studies." In J. Daly & J. McCroskey (Eds.). *Avoiding Communication: Shyness, Reticence, and Communication Apprehension.* Beverly Hills, CA: Sage.

52. S. Ting-Toomey (1988). "A Face-Negotiation Theory." In Y. Kim & W. Gudykunst (Eds.). *Theory in Interpersonal Communication*[. Newbury Park, CA: Sage.

53. L. C. Lederman (1993). "Gender and the Self." In L. P. Arliss & D. J. Borisoff (Eds.). *Women and Men Communicating: Challenges and Changes* (pp. 41–42). Fort Worth, TX: Harcourt Brace.

54. For more examples of gender-related labels, see A. Wittels (1978). *I Wonder . . . A Satirical Study of Sexist Semantics.* Los Angeles: Price Stern Sloan.

55. N. Khanlou (2004). "Influences on Adolescent Self-Esteem in Multicultural Canadian Secondary Schools," *Public Health Nursing, 21,* 404–411.

56. J. A. MacMullin and J. Cairney (2004). "Self-Esteem and the Intersection of Age, Class, and Gender." *Journal of Aging Studies, 18,* 75–90.

57. M. Knox, J. Funk, R. Elliott, & E. G. Bush (2000). "Gender Differences in Adolescents' Possible Selves." *Youth and Society, 31,* 287–309.

58. B. J. Burge (2006). "Bending gender, ending gender: Theoretical foundations for social work practice with the transgender community." *Social Work, 52* (3), 243–250.

59. B. A. Parker (2007). "Orientations: LGBTQ." In M. Tepper & A. F. Owens (Eds.), *Sexual Health.* Westport, CT: Praeger.

60. C. S. Dweck (2006). *Mindset: The New Psychology of Success.* New York: Random House.

61. J. Kolligan Jr. (1990). "Perceived Fraudulence as a Dimension of Perceived Incompetence." In R. J. Sternberg & J. Kolligen Jr. (Eds.). *Competence Considered.* New Haven, CT: Yale University Press. See also A. L. Vangelisti, S. D. Corbin, A. E. Lucchetti, & R. J. Sprague (1999). "Couples' Concurrent Cognitions: The Influence of Relational Satisfaction on the Thoughts Couples Have as They Converse." *Human Communication Research, 25,* 370–398.

62. B. Zimmerman, A. Bandura, & M. Martinez-Pons (1992). "Self-Motivation for Academic Attainment: The Role of Self-Efficacy Beliefs and Personal Goal Setting." *American Educational Research Journal, 29,* 663–676.

63. G. Downey & S. I. Feldman (1996). "Implications of Rejection Sensitivity for Intimate Relationships." *Journal of Personality and Social Psychology, 70,* 1327–1343.

64. P. D. MacIntyre & K. A Thivierge (1995). "The Effects of Speaker Personality on Anticipated Reactions to Public Speaking." *Communication Research Reports, 12,* 125–133.

65. C. L. Kleinke, T. R. Peterson, & T. R. Rutledge (1998). "Effects of Self-Generated Facial Expressions on Mood." *Journal of Personality and Social Psychology, 74,* 272–279.

66. R. Rosenthal & L. Jacobson (1968). *Pygmalion in the Classroom.* New York: Holt, Rinehart, and Winston.

67. P. D. Blank (Ed.) (1993). *Interpersonal Expectations: Theory, Research, and Applications* Cambridge: Cambridge University Press.

68. R. M. Perloff, B. Bonder, G. B. Ray, E. B. Ray, & L. A. Siminoff (2006). "Doctor-Patient Communication, Cultural Competence, and Minority Health." *American Behavioral Scientist, 49,* 835–852.

69. B. R. Schlenker & M. F. Wiegold (2010). "Interpersonal processes involving impression regulation and management." In M. L. Knapp & J. A. Daly (Eds.), *Interpersonal Communication* (Vol. II, pp. 160–194). Thousand Oaks, CA: Sage.

70. E. Goffman (1959). *The Presentation of Self in Everyday Life.* Garden City, NY: Doubleday; and (1971) *Relations in Public.* New York: Basic Books.

71. M. R. Leary & R. M. Kowalski (1990). "Impression Management: A Literature Review and Two-Component Model." *Psychological Bulletin, 107,* 34–47.

72. V. Brightman, A. Segal, P. Werther, & J. Steiner (1975). "Ethological Study of Facial Expression in Response to Taste Stimuli." *Journal of Dental Research, 54,* 141.

73. N. Chovil (1991). "Social Determinants of Facial Displays." *Journal of Nonverbal Behaviour, 15,* 141–154.

74. See, for example, R. A. Giacalone & P. Rosenfeld (Eds.) (1991). *Applied Impression Management: How Image-Making Affects Managerial Decisions.* Newbury Park, CA: Sage.

75. D. Morier & C. Seroy (1994). "The Effect of Interpersonal Expectancies on Men's Self-Presentation of Gender Role Attitudes to Women." *Sex Roles, 31,* 493–504.

76. M. Leary, J. B. Nezlek, D. Downs, et al. (1994). "Self-Presentation in Everyday Interactions: Effects of Target Familiarity and Gender Composition." *Journal of Personality and Social Psychology 67,* 664–673.

77. M. Snyder (1987). *Public Appearances, Private Realities: The Psychology of Self-Monitoring.* New York: W. H. Freeman.

78. The following discussion is based on material in D. E. Hamachek (1992). *Encounters with the Self,* 3rd ed. Fort Worth, TX: Harcourt, pp. 24–26.

79. C. N. Wright, A. Holloway, & M. E. Roloff (2007). "The Dark Side of Self-Monitoring: How High Self-Monitors View Their Romantic Relationships." *Communication Reports, 20,* 101–114.

80. For a more detailed discussion of identity-related goals, see S. Metts & E. Grohskopf (2003). "Impression Management: Goals, Strategies, and Skills." In J. O. Greene and B. R. Burleson (Eds.). *Handbook of Communication and Social Skills.* Mahwah, NJ: Erlbaum.

81. L. M. Coleman & B. M. DePaulo (1991). "Uncovering the Human Spirit: Moving beyond Disability and 'Missed' Communications." In N. Coupland, H. Giles, & J. M. Wiemann (Eds.), *"Miscommunication" and Problematic Talk* (pp. 61–84). Newbury Park, CA: Sage.

82. P. M. Valkenburg & J. Peter (2008). "Adolescents' Identity Experiments on the Internet: Consequences for Social Competence and Self-Concept Unity." *Communication Research, 35,* 208–231.

83. J. W. Vander Zanden (1984). Social Psychology, 3rd ed. New York: Random House, pp. 235–237.

84. D. Brouwer (1998). "The Precarious Visibility Politics of Self-Stigmatization: The Case of HIV/AIDS Tattoos." *Text and Performance Quarterly, 18,* 114–136.

85. P. B. O'Sullivan (2000). "What You Don't Know Won't Hurt Me: Impression Management Functions of Communication Channels in Relationships." *Communication Monographs, 26,* 403–432. See also S. B. Barnes (2003). *Computer-Mediated Communication:*

Human-to-Human Communication across the Internet. Boston: Allyn and Bacon, pp. 136–162.

86. J. Sanderson (2008). "The Blog is Serving Its Purpose: Self-Presentation Strategies on 38Pitches.com." *Journal of Computer-Mediated Communication, 13,* 912–936.

87. J. R. Suler (2002). "Identity Management in Cyberspace." *Journal of Applied Psychoanalytic Studies 4,* 455–459.

88. J. L. Gibbs, N. B. Ellison, & R. D. Heino (2006). "Self-Presentation in Online Personals: The Role of Anticipated Future Interaction, Self-Disclosure, and Perceived Success in Internet Dating." *Communication Research, 33,* 1–26.

89. See, for example, D. Chandler (n.d.). "Personal Home Pages and the Construction of Identities on the Web," www.aber.ac.uk/~dgc/webident.html. Accessed May 8, 2006.

90. R. Bennett (April 4, 2008). "Revealed: Secrets of Chosing on Online Dating Name." *Times Online.*

91. A. L. Gonzales & J. T. Hancock (2011). "Mirror, mirror on my Facebook wall: Effects of exposure to Facebook on self-esteem." *Cyberpsychology, Behaviour, and Social Networking, 14,* 79–83.

92. M. Madden & A. Smith (2010, May 26). "Reputation management and social media." Pew Internet & American Life Project. http://www.pewinternet.org/Reports/2010/Reputation-Management.aspx.

93. P. D. Blank (Ed.) (1993). *Interpersonal Expectations: Theory, Research, and Applications.* Cambridge: Cambridge University Press.

94. C. E. Johnson (2006). *Ethics in the Workplace: Tools and Tactics for Organizational Transformation.* Thousand Oaks, Sage.

95. W. Turk (2009). "Let's Go For Self-Fulfilling Prophecies." *Defense AT&L, 38,* 56–59.

96. D. Eden (1990). *Pygmalion in Management: Productivity as a Self-Fulfilling Prophecy.* New York: Simon & Schuster; Eden, D. (1990). "Pygmalion Without Interpersonal Contrast Effects: Whole Groups Gain From Raising Manager Expectations." *Journal of Applied Psychology, 75,* 394–398.

97. D. E. Hamachek (1982). *Encounters with the Self* (pp. 3–5). New York: Holt, Rinehart, and Winston.

98. D. Chrobot-Mason, S. B. Button, & J. D. DiClementi (2001). "Sexual Identity Management Strategies: An Exploration of Antecedents and Consequences." *Sex Roles, 45* (5–6), 321–336.

99. J. D. Woods (with J. H. Lucas) (1993). *The Corporate Closet: The Professional Lives of Gay Men in America.* New York: The Free Press as cited in D. Chrobot-Mason, S. B. Button, & J. D. DiClementi (2001).

PERCEPTION
WHAT YOU SEE IS WHAT YOU GET

LEARNING OUTCOMES

LO1 Describe how the processes of selection, organization, interpretation, and negotiation shape communication in a given situation.

LO2 Explain how the influences on perception affect communication in a specific situation.

LO3 Analyze how the common tendencies in perception distort your perceptions of another person, and hence your communication. Use this information to present a more accurate alternative set of perceptions.

LO4 Demonstrate how you might use the skill of perception checking in a significant relationship.

LO5 Enhance your cognitive complexity by applying the "pillow method" in a significant disagreement. Explain how your expanded view of this situation might affect your communication with the other(s) involved.

LO1
The Perception Process

Take a look at the picture in **Figure 3.1**. When asked what they see, most students will say a rabbit. How about you; what do you see? Now if you look at the figure from different angles you'll see something entirely different . . . a duck. Perhaps you see both. We have a tendency to think that when we look at something we see what everyone else sees. But this isn't always the case as this, and other common perceptual images, demonstrate.

The fact is, each of us experiences reality differently, and failing to understand other people's point of view can lead to practical and relational problems. But perceptual differences can also enhance our relationships. By seeing the world through others' eyes we can gain insights that are different from—and often more valuable than—those arising out of our own experiences.

Perception can be described as the process whereby we assign meaning to the world around us. However, everybody tunes in to the world differently. Perhaps you've seen photos of sights invisible to the unaided eye—maybe an infrared photo of a familiar area or the vastly enlarged image of a minute object taken by an electron microscope—or you've noticed how animals can hear sounds and smell odours that are not apparent to humans. Experiences like these remind us that there is much more going on in the world than we are able to experience with our limited senses. Our idea of reality is only a partial one.

Perception
The process whereby we assign meaning to the world around us.

What do you **THINK?**

I tend to judge people by my first impressions of them.

1	2	3	4	5	6	7
strongly agree						strongly disagree

FIGURE 3.1

Source: Block and Yuker, 1992. From Fliegende Blatter, October 23, 1892, p. 147.

Sami Sarkis/Getty

On a personal level, for example, we've all failed to notice something unusual about a friend—perhaps a new hairstyle or a sad expression—until it's called to our attention.

We notice some events and fail to recognize others because we simply can't be aware of everything that's going on around us, no matter how attentive we are. As William James said, "To the infant world is just a big blooming, buzzing confusion." But as we grow, we learn to manage these data and make sense of the world. Perception is very important, because how we interpret events influences how we communicate with others.

Further, conflict can emerge when individuals perceive situations differently. For example, you may be excited about attending a weekend music festival. You see it as an opportunity to catch a lot of good acts and some of your favourite performers. Your parents, on the other hand, might view the festival as a drug and alcohol free-for-all and may not even recognize any of the musicians on the roster.

Our perceptions also change over time. Take sexting, for example. The young woman who sends provocative photographs to her girlfriend or boyfriend does so because she trusts and loves that individual. But what happens when the relationship sours? We've all heard the stories of disgruntled former partners posting such photos all over the Internet. Does this change the woman's perceptions of her former lover or the viewers' perceptions of the young woman? Absolutely.

Selection
The first stage in the perception process, in which some data are chosen to attend to and others to ignore.

Organization
The stage in the perception process that involves arranging data in a meaningful way.

Perceptual schemata
Cognitive frameworks that allow individuals to organize perceptual data that they have selected from the environment. These include physical, role, interaction, psychological, and membership constructs.

There are four steps in the perception process: selection, organization, interpretation, and negotiation.

Selection

Because we're exposed to more input than we can possibly manage, the first step in perception is **selection** of the data to which we will attend. It is the selection process that allows you to glace over a crowded area and spot someone that you "like that way" within a matter of seconds. However, there are several factors that make some things more noticeable than others.

Stimuli that are ***intense*** attract our attention. Something that is louder, larger, or brighter, although not always in a positive way, will stand out. Think of those loud infomercials. ***Repetitious stimuli*** also attract attention.[1] Just as a quiet but steadily dripping faucet can come to dominate our awareness, so do people to whom we're frequently exposed become noticeable. ***Contrast or change*** also invite attention. Put differently, unchanging people or things become less noticeable, and this may account for why we take wonderful people for granted. It's only when they go away or stop being so wonderful that we appreciate them.

Motives also influence what is selected from our environment. If you're late for an appointment, you'll notice whatever clocks may be around you, and if you're hungry, you'll spot any restaurants or billboards advertising food. Motives also determine how we perceive people. For example, people looking for romantic adventures will be aware of attractive potential partners. In emergency situations, however, police or medical personnel would be more important than potential partners!

Selection also involves ignoring cues. If, for example, you think someone is a terrific person, you'll overlook their serious flaws. Or if you are focused on examples

We know that a printed photograph can't move, but perceptions may tell us otherwise. What we see isn't always what we get.

© Tristan3D/Alamy

of unfair male bosses, you might not recognize unfair female supervisors.

Organization

Once we select information, we must arrange it in some meaningful way. You saw how the principle of **organization** works when you looked at **Figure 3.1**. The figure can be viewed as either a rabbit or duck. We make sense of stimuli by noticing data that stand out as a *figure* against a less striking *ground*. The drawing is interesting because it allows us to choose between two sets of figure–ground relationships.

This principle of figure–ground organization operates in nonvisual ways as well. Recall how certain speech can suddenly stand out from a babble of voices. Sometimes the words are noticeable because they include your name, whereas at other times they might be spoken by a familiar voice.

We also use **perceptual schemata**—cognitive frameworks that allow us to organize the raw data we have selected—to make sense of information about others. Further, we tend to make judgments about individuals based on these constructs. (1) **Physical constructs** allow us to classify people according to their appearance: gender, transgender,

Invitation to Insight

Your Perceptual Filters

1. Identify the perceptual schemata (Physical, Role, Interaction, Psychological, and Membership) that you would use to classify people in each of the following contexts:
   a. spending time with new acquaintances at a party
   b. socializing with workers on the job
   c. choosing teammates for an important class project
   d. offering help to a stranded motorist

   Describe both the general type of organizing scheme (e.g., "physical," "membership") and the specific category within each type (such as "attractive," "roughly the same age as me").

2. Consider
   a. other schemata you might use in each context
   b. the different consequences of using the schemata you originally chose and the alternative you identified in the preceding step
   c. how your relationships might change if you used different constructs

skin colour, attractiveness, size, or age. (2) ***Role constructs*** use social position—student, lawyer, husband—as a means of organization. (3) ***Interaction constructs*** focus on social behaviour: friendly, intense, helpful, outgoing, entertaining, or sarcastic. (4) ***Psychological constructs*** are used to organize people according to their apparent personalities, such as curious, nervous, insecure, and so on. Finally, (5) ***membership constructs*** help us identify others according to the group or groups they belong to: union rep, ethnic group, clergy, health care worker, etc.

Christopher Malcolm/The Image Bank/Getty Images

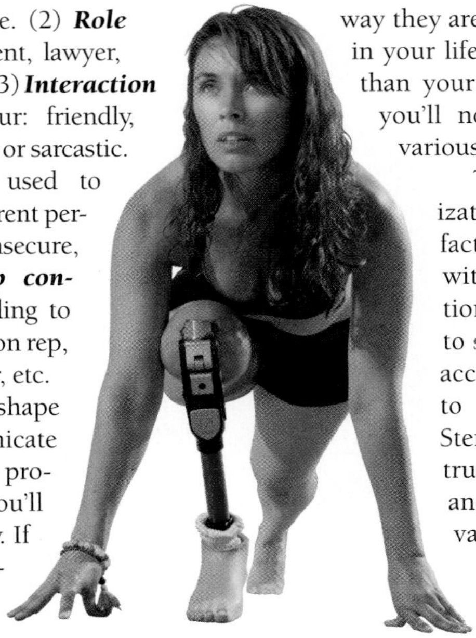

The perceptual schemata we use shape the way we think about and communicate with others. If you've classified a professor, for example, as "friendly," you'll handle questions or problems one way. If you've put the professor in the "pompous" category, your behaviour will probably be quite different. What constructs do you typically use to classify people? Consider how your relationship might change if you used different schemata.

Stereotyping

Once we select an organizing scheme to classify people, we use that scheme to make generalizations and predictions about members of the groups who fit the categories we use. For example, if you were especially aware of gender, you might be alert to the differences between the way women and men behave or the way they are treated. If sports play an important part in your life, you might think of athletes differently than your artist friend. If ethnicity is important, you'll notice differences between members of various ethnic groups.

Stereotyping
Categorizing individuals according to a set of characteristics assumed to belong to all members of a group.

There's nothing wrong with generalizations as long as they are accurate. In fact, it's impossible to get through life without them. But when generalizations lose touch with reality, they lead to **stereotyping**—categorizing individuals according to a set of characteristics assumed to belong to all members of a group.[2] Stereotypes may be based on a kernel of truth, but they go beyond the facts at hand and make claims that usually have no valid basis.

You can begin to get a sense of your tendency to make generalizations and to stereotype by completing the following sentences:

1. Politicians are ________________________
2. Children are ________________________
3. Inuit people are ________________________
4. Vegetarians are ________________________
5. Rap singers are ________________________
6. Seniors citizens are ________________________

You probably completed each sentence without much hesitation. Does this mean you were stereotyping? You can answer this question by deciding whether your generalizations fit the three characteristics of stereotypes described below. We'll use "senior citizens" as an example.

Win Initiative/Getty Images

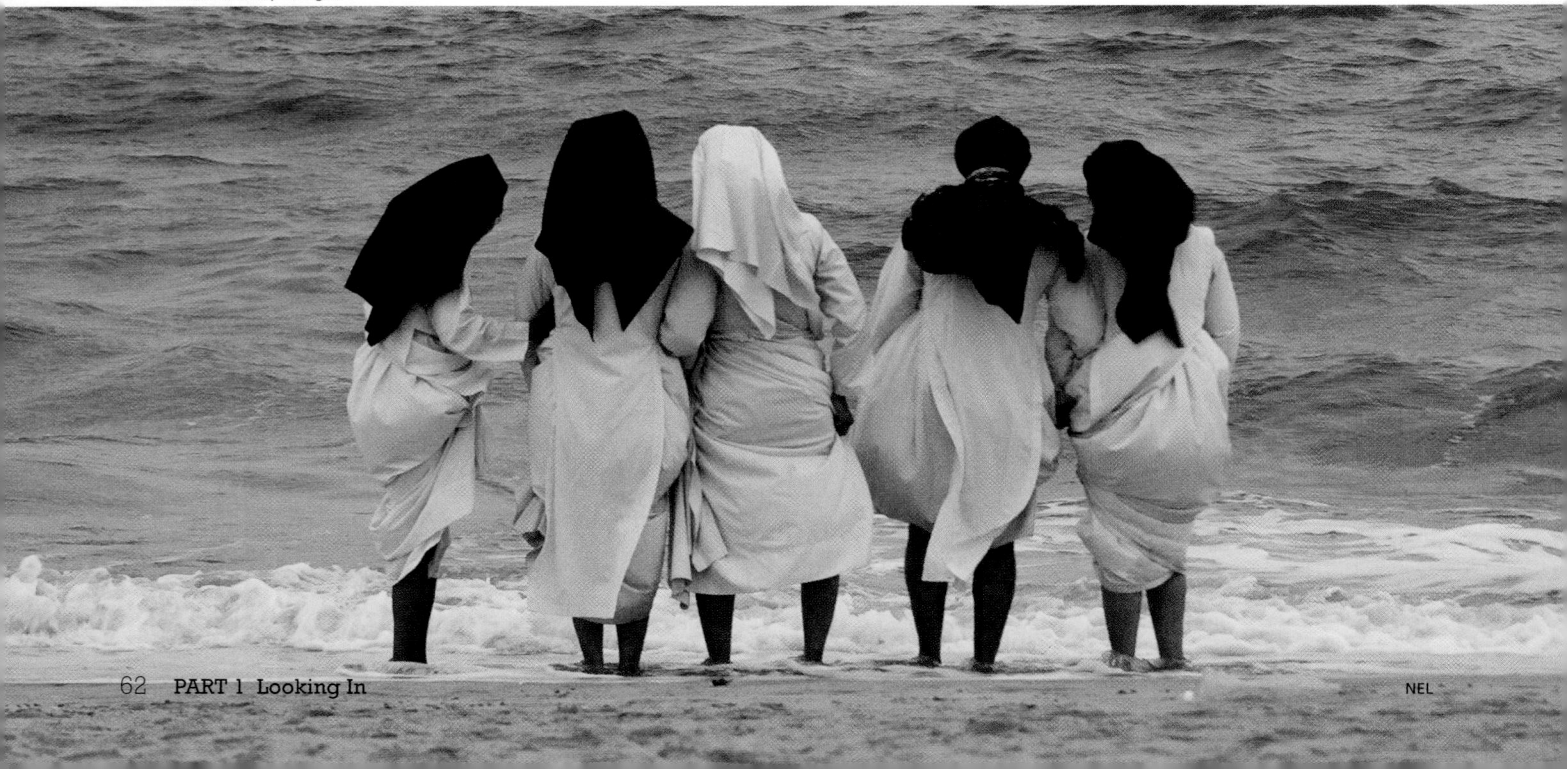

- **You often categorize people on the basis of an easily recognized characteristic**. Age is relatively simple to identify, so you might categorize someone who appears to be in her 80s as "elderly."
- **You ascribe a set of characteristics to most or all members of a category**. Based on your (limited) experiences with some senior relatives, you conclude that older people don't hear well and they're not mentally alert.
- **You apply the set of characteristics to every member of the group**. When you meet a senior citizen, you talk very loudly and slowly . . . which can be extremely annoying to fit, healthy older people who don't fit your stereotype.

It's hard to believe that the Rolling Stones, a rock band comprised of seniors, is still thrilling audiences (young and old) across the globe.

Reuters/Lucas Jackson

Once we buy into stereotypes, we often seek out isolated behaviours that support our inaccurate beliefs. But such stereotypes can have devastating effects for those being stereotyped. Canadian Muslims and Arabs are often targets of racial profiling. Rasha Mourtada writes of the obstacles Muslims face when attempting to fly out of Canada for business purposes. To combat these difficulties, companies are offering equivalent positions that do not require international travel and are working on regulations to have frequent-flier employees bypass discriminating procedures.[3] We recently saw an example of how it might feel to be stereotyped. Some students from Saudi Arabia were very uneasy following the shootings at the War Memorial and in the Parliament Buildings in Ottawa in 2014. They thought students were seeing them as terrorists and they were reluctant to attend a communication lab. However, after the lab co-ordinator facilitated a discussion among the domestic and foreign students, domestic students gained greater insight into the nuances of what the foreign students may experience and the Saudi students felt more accepted than ever by their group.

But racial profiling also occurs on Canadian streets. University of Toronto sociologists Scott Wortley and Julian Tanner note a Toronto survey that found that "black youth are much more likely to be stopped and searched by the police than youth from other racial backgrounds."[4] These examples, and a host of others that we see broadcast on television and social media, demonstrate the negative effects of stereotyping.

Stereotyping doesn't always arise from bad intentions, and careless generalizations can grow from good intentions. For example, knowing that people raised in collectivistic cultures tend to conform to group norms may lead you to mistakenly think that anyone from that background will be a selfless team player. But not all members of a group are equally collectivistic, or individualistic, for that matter. A close look at North Americans of European and Latin descent showed differences within each group.[5] Some Latinos were more independent than some Euro-Americans and vice versa. Moreover, teens in Japan, a traditionally collectivist culture, feel torn between individualism and collectivism; that is, between time-honoured traditions and contemporary trends.[6] As our "global village" becomes more connected, generalizations about specific cultures are likely to become less accurate.

Stereotypes don't always lead to communication problems. If a person fits the pattern in your mind, there may be no difficulties. But if your mental image and the person's characteristics don't match, problems can arise.

One way to avoid the communication problems that come from excessive stereotyping is to decategorize others and treat them as individuals instead of assuming that they possess the same characteristics as everyone else in that particular group. Consider how your communication might change if you moved some of their characteristics to the "background" and others to the "foreground."

Punctuation

The process of organizing goes beyond our generalized perceptions of people. We can also organize our interactions in terms of what communication theorists call **punctuation**: the tendency to determine the causal order of events.[7] In other words, how actions are interpreted depends on when the interpreter thinks they occurred. For example, visualize a running quarrel between a

Punctuation
The process of determining the causal order of events.

Looking at Diversity

Christa Kilvington: Socioeconomic Stereotyping

Courtesy of Christa Kilvington

What comes to mind when you hear the description "straight A student"? How about when you hear "single mom on social assistance"? Most likely you get two very different mental pictures. Did you think of both individuals as complete opposites? And yet, I am both: a college student with straight-A grades who is also a single mother on social assistance.

The stereotypes people use to classify me shape the way they communicate. People who only know me from school have no idea of my economic situation. They see me as intelligent and ambitious—an academic standout. They speak to me formally and respectfully. Those who know me only by my income level (caseworkers, health care workers) communicate in a very different way. When I go to the social assistance office, I am often treated as unintelligent, lazy, and dishonest. People speak to me in condescending and disrespectful tones.

Why do some people equate income level with intelligence or treat me and others differently because of our economic status? Why is it all right to treat people disrespectfully because they're poor? Stereotypes exist for a reason, but it's important to go beyond them to find out each person's unique story. When you open your mind to the possibility that there is more to a person than meets the eye, that is when you grow as a person yourself.

"Socioeconomic Stereotyping" by Christa Kilvington. Used with permission of author.

Interpretation
The process of attaching meaning to sense data; synonymous with *decode*.

husband and wife. The husband accuses the wife of being demanding, whereas she complains that he is withdrawing from her. Notice that the order in which each partner punctuates this cycle is different and that affects how the quarrel looks. The husband begins by blaming the wife: "I withdraw because you're so demanding." The wife organizes the situation differently, starting with the husband: "I demand because you withdraw." After the cycle gets rolling, it is impossible to say which accusation is accurate. **Figure 3.2** illustrates how this process operates.

Punctuating an event differently can lead to a variety of problems. Notice how the following situations seem different depending on how they're punctuated.

"I don't like your friend because he never has anything to say."
"He doesn't like to talk to you because you act like you don't like him."

"I keep talking because you interrupt me so much."
"I interrupt because you don't give me a chance to say what's on my mind."

The kind of finger-pointing that goes along with arguments over which punctuation is correct will probably make matters worse. It's more productive to move on and figure out how to make things better.

Interpretation

Once information has been selected and organized, it must be interpreted. **Interpretation**, the process of attaching meaning to sense data, plays a role in virtually every interpersonal act. Is the person who smiles at you across a crowded room interested in romance or simply being polite? Is a friend's kidding a sign of affection or irritation? Should you take an invitation to "drop by any time" literally or not? How you interpret these and other events depends on several factors.

Degree of involvement with the other person. Two coworkers offer you the same excuse for why they were late for work. One is a close friend; the other

FIGURE 3.2
The Same Event Can Be Punctuated in More than One Way

Punctuation #1

Demanding ⟶ Withdrawing ⟶ Demanding ⟶ Withdrawing

Punctuation #2

Withdrawing ⟶ Demanding ⟶ Withdrawing ⟶ Demanding

© Cengage Learning

you barely know. Chances are good that you will interpret your friend's excuse more charitably.

Personal experience. What meaning have similar events held? If, for example, you've been gouged by landlords in the past, you might be skeptical when a property manager insists that careful housekeeping will ensure that your cleaning deposit will be refunded.

Assumptions about human behaviour. How we interpret a person's behaviour depends on our assumptions. Believing that people do as little work as possible to get by, or that most do the best they can, shapes the way we interpret their actions.

Attitudes. Our attitudes shape the way we make sense of others' behaviours. For example, what would you think if you overheard one man say, "I love you," to another? In one study, people with a high degree of homophobia—the fear of or discrimination against homosexuals—assumed that the speaker was gay. Those with lower levels of homophobia regarded the affectionate statement as platonic rather than romantic.[8]

Expectations. Anticipation shapes perceptions.[9] As you read in Chapter 2, teachers who expect their students to do well will treat them and think about them differently. The same is true with our interpersonal transactions. Our expectations affect how we perceive and behave around others. If we think that we'll enjoy and be comfortable around a new group of people, we probably will be.

Knowledge. If you know that a friend has just been dropped by a lover or laid off from a job, you'll interpret his aloof behaviour differently than you would if you didn't know what had happened. If you know that a supervisor speaks sarcastically to everyone, you won't be as likely to take such remarks personally.

Self-concept. The world seems very different when you're feeling insecure. For example, when a person is being teased, the recipient's self-concept is the single greatest factor in determining whether the teaser's motives will be interpreted as friendly or hostile, and hence the recipient will respond with comfort or defensiveness.[10] The way we feel about ourselves strongly influences how we interpret others' behaviour.

Relational satisfaction. A behaviour that seems positive when you're happy with a partner might seem completely different when you're not. Couples in unsatisfying relationships tend to blame one another when things go wrong.[11] They

On *The Voice*, judges use blind auditions in the opening rounds. On other performance shows, judges view contestants' appearance and sometimes even know their back-stories before making an appraisal. Does knowing more affect the judges' perceptions of the performer and the performance? Are there times when you would be better off knowing less about someone when making an evaluation?

also tend to believe that their partners are selfish and have negative intentions.

Although we have talked about selection, organization, and interpretation separately, they can occur in differing sequences. For example, a parent or babysitter's past interpretations (such as "Jason is a troublemaker") can influence future selections (his behaviour becomes especially noticeable) and the organization of events (when there's a fight, the assumption is that Jason started it). Like all communication, perception is an ongoing process and it's hard to pin down beginnings and endings.

Before reading on, take a few moments to read Christa Kilvington's first-hand experience of being stereotyped in the Looking At Diversity box.

Negotiation

Thus far, perception has been discussed in terms of what occurs in each individual's mind. But perception isn't just a solitary activity: A big part of it occurs between and among people as they influence one another's perceptions and try to achieve a shared perspective. This process is known as **negotiation**.

Negotiation
What occurs between and among people as they influence one another's perceptions and try to achieve a shared perspective.

Think of negotiation as an exchange of stories. Scholars call the stories we use to describe our personal worlds **narratives**.[12] Virtually every interpersonal situation can be described by more than one narrative, and they often differ. You see this in courtrooms; they're filled with opponents who tell very different narratives about who the "villain" is and who the "hero" is. Even happy families have stories that place members in particular roles—the scatterbrain, the smart one, the athlete, and so on. In best-case scenarios, family storytelling enhances perspective taking and leads to family satisfaction and functioning.[13]

When our narratives clash, we can either hang on to our own point of view or negotiate a shared narrative that creates some common ground. Shared narratives make for smoother communication. For example, romantic partners who celebrate their successful struggles against relational obstacles are happier than those who don't have this shared appreciation.[14] Likewise, couples who agree on important turning points in their relationships are more satisfied than those who have different views of what incidents were most important.[15]

Shared narratives don't have to be accurate to be powerful. Couples who have been happily married for more than 50 years seem to collude in a relational narrative that doesn't jibe with the facts.[16] While they say they rarely have conflict, family members may say otherwise. Without overtly agreeing to do so, such couples blame outside forces for their problems instead of each other. They offer the most charitable interpretations of each other's behaviours, believing that their spouse acts with good intentions when things don't go well. They seem willing to forgive and forget. Communication researcher Judy Pearson evaluates these findings thus:

> Should we conclude that happy couples have a poor grip on reality? Perhaps they do, but is the

reality of one's marriage better known by outside onlookers than by the players themselves? The conclusion is evident. One key to a long happy marriage is to tell yourself and others that you have one and then to behave as though you do![17]

LO2
Influences on Perception

Now that we've explored how we process information, it's time to look at other influences that cause us to select, organize, interpret, and negotiate information.

Access to Information

We can only make sense of things from what we know and no one knows everything about even those who are closest to us. But when new information becomes available, your perceptions of others change. For example, you might perceive a professor differently if you learned that you shared a hobby or interest with that individual.

We often gain new information about others in situations where their roles overlap. Take an onsite staff party. A person's "work" roles and "party" roles can differ substantially but the "work" role will probably override in this situation. However, you might see very different and unexpected behaviours if you ran into the person at a friend's party. Similarly, you might see a different side of a romantic partner if you went home to meet his or her parents. You might see your partner playing a saucy sibling, a demanding daughter, or a devoted and caring grandchild. If you've ever said to someone, "I've seen a new side of you tonight," it's probably because you gained new information about the person.

SALLY FORTH   by Greg Howard

Social media also provides information that can shape perceptions. This is why job hunters are encouraged to clean up their Internet profiles and shape the impression they wish to create for potential employers. It may also account for why children and parents are often reluctant to become Facebook friends. Apparently, some roles are best kept quiet or at least played to a select audience.

Physiological Influences

Within the wide range of human similarities, each of us still perceives the world differently because of physiological factors. Consider the long list of physiological factors that shapes our views of the world. These include the senses, age, health and fatigue, hunger, biological cycles, and psychological challenges.

The Senses

Differences in how each of us sees, hears, tastes, touches, and smells stimuli can affect interpersonal relationships. Consider the following everyday situations:

> "Turn down that radio! It's going to drive me crazy!"
> "It's not too loud. If I turn it down, it will be impossible to hear it."

> "It's freezing in here."
> "Are you kidding? We'll suffocate if you turn up the heat!"

> "Why don't you pass? The highway is clear for miles."
> "Well, I can't see that far and I'm not about to get us killed."

These disputes aren't just over matters of opinion; the sensory data we receive are different. Differences in vision and hearing are the easiest to recognize, but there is also evidence that identical foods taste differently to different individuals.[18] Odours can please or repel. Recognizing these differences won't eliminate them, but it will help you remember that other people's preferences aren't crazy, just different.

Age

Besides the obvious physical changes, age also alters perspective. Consider, for instance, how you viewed your parents over the years. When you were a child, you probably thought they were all-knowing and flawless. As a teen, you may have considered them old-fashioned and mean. In adulthood, most people see their parents as helpful, wise, and trusting.

To get a sense of what it is like to be old, read "What Is It Really Like to Be Old." You might even like to give the experiment a try yourself.

Health and Fatigue

We've all had a cold, flu, or some other ailment that left us feeling tired, less sociable, or just not able to think straight. This affected how we related to others. Keep in mind how illness might affect the communication of others and don't be afraid to let others know when you feel ill. And just as being ill can affect your relationships, so can being overly tired. It's best not to deal with important issues at such times.

Hunger

People often get grumpy when they don't eat and sleepy after stuffing themselves. Sadly, teenagers who do not get enough food are almost three times as likely to be suspended from school, twice as likely to have difficulty getting along with others, and four times as likely to have no friends.[19]

Biological Cycles

Most of us identify ourselves as either early birds or night owls. This is because we all have a daily cycle wherein body temperature, sexual drive, alertness, tolerance to stress, and mood continually change.[20] These changes are mostly due to hormonal cycles. For instance, adrenal hormones, which affect feelings of stress, are secreted at higher rates during some hours. In the same manner, the male and female sex hormones enter our systems at variable rates. We often aren't conscious of these changes, but they surely influence the way we relate to one another. Once we are aware of how these cycles govern our own and others' feelings and behaviours, we can deal with important issues at the most effective times.

What Is It Really Like to Be Old?

Andersen Ross/Getty Images

For nearly two decades, I have listened as patients describe what it is like to live in a body that failed them. I have heard it all: the impact of strokes—which leave the body paralyzed and unwilling to do what the brain wants; arthritis—which makes every movement painful; the ominous terror of having heart disease and the potential of having a heart attack—will someone find them in time? I have also heard a number of stories about all of the common, weird and disturbing autoimmune diseases that seem to attack people for no reason. Most people express the wrenching questions, "Why does my body not work? Why is my body attacking me?"

Throughout all of these years and stories I am privileged to hear, I prided myself on being a good listener. I imagined what it must feel like to have a limited body with even more restricted function. I thought I got it.

Recently, as part of a course on working with geriatric patients..., I realized that I don't get it. My classmates and I had a number of experiential exercises, which were meant to simulate a variety of illnesses.... First, all of us were instructed to place earplugs in our ears. Following that, we were instructed to put popcorn kernels in our shoes. Right from the start, we were supposed to imagine being hearing impaired with simulated peripheral neuropathy in our feet. In case you are among the more rational in the world, you likely have not tried putting unpopped corn in your shoes. Walking with corn kernels in your shoes hurts—a lot. This was just the beginning.

We started with a mobility experience. In addition to not being able to hear much or walk well, we were instructed to wear gloves that would also simulate neuropathy (numbing), in our hands. We were given bands to place around our ankles, to mimic impaired walking. Finally, we were given glasses that simulate all of the various eye problems that can occur with aging and illness. My glasses seemed more benign than what my colleagues were wearing; I had no peripheral vision—a common problem of old age and elderly eyes. I thought to myself, "I can do this."

Then, given a cane, I was asked to walk down the hall. It was maybe 100 feet. I was pretending to be an elder with impaired hearing and vision, bad mobility and numbness in my hands and pain in my feet. I realized that I was not sure that I could actually complete the walk down the hall. Suddenly, my class exercise did not feel like a game. I started to panic. From the loss of peripheral vision, I could not see who was standing next to me, and I started to feel suspicious. As I walked, I had a lovely young woman at my side (I was lucky, she is a physical therapist in real life), who could help me if I needed it. I did not want help however; I wanted out of my body, which felt trapped, alone, and isolated. Weirdly, even though we were pretending, I felt mad at my companion, who had a body that worked so much better than mine....

Growing older scares us for a variety of reasons. Some of us can't imagine being dependent. Others just want to be able to exercise like we did when we were twenty. For me, pain and sensory impairment just seemed like it would take away everything that matters to me—connecting with people I love as well as my value on being independent....

We live in a manic culture in which we are supposed to embrace the victory of a long life. It is as if the world says, "Be Happy! You might live to be 100!" Yet, living to 100 might encompass a private, as well as public misery. Living a long life is rarely a guarantee of a life without pain and disability. Our elders, the people who are forging a new frontier in the vast experiment in longevity and increasing life spans deserve our support, now more than ever.

Tamara McLintock Greenberg

Discussion Starter

In what ways has this reading heightened your awareness of how many senior citizens experience life?

Tamara McClintock Greenberg, "What Is It Really Like to Be Old?" *Psychology Today*, November 15, 2013. https://www.psychologytoday.com/blog/21st-century-aging/201311/what-is-it-really-be-old. Reproduced by permission of the author.

Psychological Challenges

Some perceptual differences are rooted in neurology. People with ADHD (attention deficit hyperactivity disorder) are easily distracted and have difficulty delaying gratification. Those with ADHD might find a long lecture boring and tedious, while other audience members are fascinated by the same lecture. People with bipolar disorder experience significant mood swings that dramatically affect their perceptions of events, friends, and even family members. According to the Canadian Mental Health Association, about 4 percent of the population lives with ADHD and 2 percent of Canadians will be bipolar at some point in their lives.[21] Therefore, when others see and respond to the world differently, there may be causes beyond what we immediately recognize.

Cultural Differences

Another perceptual gap that often blocks communication is culture. Every culture has its own way of looking at the world and sometimes it's easy to forget this. The range of cultural differences is very wide. For instance, nonverbal behaviours have different meanings in different cultures. In many cultures, the OK sign, made by touching the thumb and forefinger, is an obscene gesture representing

Andersen Ross/Getty Images

the female genitalia. To a woman, it's a proposition for sex, and to a man, it suggests he's gay.[22] Imagine the problems that could result from just one innocent gesture.

In Middle Eastern countries, personal odours play an important role in interpersonal relationships. Arabs consistently breathe on people when they talk. As anthropologist Edward Hall explains:

> To smell one's friend is not only nice, but desirable, for to deny him your breath is to act ashamed. [North] Americans, on the other hand, trained as they are not to breathe in people's faces, automatically communicate shame in trying to be polite. Who would expect that when our highest diplomats are putting on their best manners they are also communicating shame? Yet this is what occurs constantly, because diplomacy is not only "eyeball to eyeball" but breath to breath.[23]

Even beliefs about the value of talk differ from one culture to another.[24] Western cultures view talk as desirable and silence is considered negative in that it suggests a lack of interest, unwillingness to communicate, hostility, anxiety, shyness, or a sign of interpersonal incompatibility. Westerners find silence embarrassing and awkward. In Asian cultures, silence is valued and expression of thoughts and feelings is discouraged. As Taoist sayings indicate, "In much talk there is great weariness," or "One who speaks does not know; one who knows does not speak." Unlike Westerners, Japanese and Chinese believe that remaining quiet is proper when there's nothing to say. To Asians, a talkative person is often considered a show-off or an insincere person.

Obviously, this intercultural feature can lead to communication problems. The talkative Westerner and the silent Asian are behaving in "proper" ways, yet each views the other with disapproval. This may require them to recognize and deal with their **ethnocentrism**—the attitude that one's own culture is superior to others. Ethnocentric people believe that anyone who does not belong to their in-group is somehow strange, wrong, or even inferior.

We see this in our own country. Take the notion of time, for instance. Aboriginal time is experiential in nature; that is, there is no particular time, only what is occurring at the moment. Non-Aboriginal Canadians—perceived as immigrants by

Ethnocentrism
The attitude that one's own culture is superior to others.

Ellen Cabot:
From My World to the Real World

I am a 25-year old Mi'kmaq woman from Eskasoni First Nation, the largest Mi'kmaq community in Nova Scotia. It's located in Cape Breton overlooking the beautiful Bras d'Or Lakes and consists of roughly 5000+ residents.

When you grow up on a First Nation reserve, you deal mostly with other native peoples merely because our community is located in the countryside, somewhat secluded from any non-native communities. We have our own schools that range from daycare to high school and that is where I was educated. For me, this reality represented my perception of the entire world. This was my world and I only knew what I saw on a daily basis. For instance, many members of my community speak our native tongue, Mi'kmaq, so naturally hearing the language spoken everyday was the norm. I too speak Mi'kmaq. And you hear a lot of Mi'Klish, a mixture of Mi'Kmaq and English. Further, we are a very tight knit community so everybody knows everyone else and is generally friendly.

Upon reflection, my perceptions of how we lived seemed adequate but only because, as a native people, we live with the resources we really need. We are not materialistic but I was beginning to learn that this was not the case in the "outside" world. As

I got older, I knew that I would have to go into that other "real world" which was filled with different cultures, different values, and most of all, different people. This was a scary thought.

After I graduated from high school, I went to university. On my first day at Cape Breton University, I was overwhelmed by how different things were from life on the reserve. For instance, one of the biggest differences was that English was spoken everywhere and all the time. And not only was I mixing with white people, but there were students from China, Saudi Arabia, Africa, and so forth. People weren't nearly as friendly as they were on the reserve and they seemed to keep to themselves. Initially, I felt awkward and worried that people were judging me on the basis of how I looked, acted, and spoke. All of these reflected my First Nations heritage. I always felt self-conscious about these things but these feelings were at an all time high at this point. However, after a couple of days, I realized that no one was judging me in the way that I thought. Rather, other students and professors were very accepting. Now, after having been introduced into the "real world," I no longer feel self-conscious about what people think of me. I've learned to adapt to a different way of life and I'm no longer shy. I've become integrated and involved. Finally, the "real world" has become "my world."

By Ellen Cabot. Used with permission.

Invitation to Insight

Role Reversal

Walk a mile in another person's shoes. Find a group that is foreign to you and try to become a member of it for a while.

- If you're down on the police, see if your local department has a ride-along program where you can spend several hours on patrol with one or two officers.

- If you think the present state of education is a mess, become a teacher yourself. Maybe an instructor will give you the chance to plan one or more classes.

- If you're adventuresome, become a homeless person for a day and see how you are treated.

- If you're a political conservative, try getting involved in a radical organization; if you're a radical, check out the conservatives.

Whatever group you join, try to become part of it as best you can. Don't just observe. Get into the philosophy of your new role and see how it feels. You may find that all those weird people aren't so weird after all.

Indigenous people—think of time as event-driven, moving in a linear fashion. Because of these perceptual differences, Aboriginal students arriving late for class may be pigeon-holed as apathetic, undependable, or irresponsible when in fact a momentary matter may have consumed their attention. One student related that if he was leaving for the university and his son wanted to play, that was more important than getting to a scheduled class. Failure to recognize such perceptual differences can lead to unfortunate and unnecessary misunderstandings.

The way we communicate with strangers also reflects ethnocentric thinking. Travel writer Rick Steves describes how an ethnocentric point of view can interfere with respect for other cultural practices:

Photo courtesy of Chris Greene

"For instance, we consider ourselves very clean, but when we take baths, we use the same water for soaking, cleaning, and rinsing. (We wouldn't wash our dishes that way.) The Japanese, who use clean water for every step of the bathing process, might find our ways strange or even disgusting. People in some cultures blow their nose right onto the street. They couldn't imagine doing that into a small cloth, called a hanky, and storing it in their pocket to be used again and again.

Once when I was having lunch at a cafeteria in Afghanistan, an older man joined me to make a point. He said, "I am a professor here in Afghanistan. In this world, one-third of the people use a spoon and fork like you, one-third use chopsticks, and one-third uses fingers—like me. And we are all civilized the same."*

Geography also influences perceptions. Sixty percent of Canadians define themselves according to the region they live in.[25] Our distinct climates, histories, and economics influence how we think about ourselves and others, and any one event might be viewed differently by individuals from the Prairies, downtown Toronto, or Nain in Northern Labrador.

Social Roles

Social roles can also cause communication breakdowns. From the time we're born, we're indirectly taught a set of roles we're expected to play. Prescribed roles help society function smoothly and help us know what's expected of us. But narrowly defined roles can lead to wide gaps in understanding. When roles become unquestioned and rigid,

---

*Rick Steves, "Culture Shock and Wiggle Room," Rick Steves' Europe. https://www.ricksteves.com/watch-read-listen/read/articles/culture-shock-and-wiggle-room. Reproduced by permission.

people tend to see the world from their own viewpoint, having no experiences that show them how other people see it. Naturally, communication suffers in such situations.

Gender Roles

Gender refers to the social and psychological expectations that are placed on females and males. You probably experienced this when you were a child and your mother told you that little boys weren't suppose to play with dolls or little girls weren't suppose to lift up their dresses to expose their panties. Transgender individuals view gender as how they feel on the inside and this can be incongruent with their external appearance. To date, most of the research in gender and communication focuses on males and females and it has been acknowledged that societal roles affect perception dramatically.[26] Today's parents are much more enlightened than the previous two generations. For instance, one new mother said her baby was a little girl but she really wouldn't be sure until she was four or five. That mother recognized that her newborn may transition to another gender at some point. In spite of this awareness on the part of many, sex role stereotyping is still prevalent and these socially approved behaviours are learned in several ways.

First, families play a major role in developing gender roles. You've probably noticed that baby girls are still dressed in pink and boys in blue, or that little boys are taught that it's inappropriate for them to cry but this behaviour

Purestock/Thinkstock

is acceptable for girls. Families even influence the types of communication characteristics that are appropriate. For instance, one study found that parents viewed assertiveness more favourably when it was displayed by boys than by girls.[27] Once children learn such gender expectations, violations are perceived as undesirable.

Gender researcher, Diana K. Ivy, writes that children also learn gender roles through toys, peers and schools, and the media.[28] Just check out the toy section in any retail catalogue and you'll find that, for the most part, little boys are shown with drum sets, train sets, action figures, toy trucks, and hands-on games such as hockey sets; little girls are featured with dolls, toy strollers, crafts, and kitchen appliances. Even though you'll find boys with the latter, the kitchen sets are housed in the female toy section. The overall message is that males are active and females are passive. When children, and even adults, look at these displays, they unconsciously learn the so-called gender "appropriate" toys.

Children also learn their gender roles through fairly tales where it is apparent that men seek action and serve as the heroes. Women, on the other hand, are assigned roles where they must wait for their Prince "Charming" to rescue them. Fortunately, Disney's popular movie "Frozen" offers viewers a much more progressive portrayal of young women.[29] But in school curriculum, girls will be exposed to text books that contain more pictures of males, more examples of male experiences, and more reference to male authors.[30] And, it doesn't get much better in secondary education. One research team found that, for instance, males are called upon more often and professors wait longer for them to answer. They also found that female students are interrupted more often, are asked lower-order questions, and are given less positive nonverbal feedback for their responses.[31] Such behaviours greatly affect the expectations and roles that females and males must play. Even though there has been pressure to offer more gender friendly educational experiences, equity in the classroom is still not the norm. Finally, children learn sex roles through the media where gendered stereotypes still abound. Girls are portrayed as pretty and cute and boys as active and verbal.

The problem with outdated gender roles is that they limit the behaviours of everyone. If you breach the expectations, you will be perceived differently. Further, they perpetuate the notion that males are in the one-up position and women are subordinate to men. Fortunately, things are changing and women are being encouraged to go into the sciences and other male dominated careers. In January 2013, six of the premiers of the thirteen Canadian provinces and territories were female. In January 2016, that number was reduced to four.[32] However, men are also changing and we see, for instance, more stay-at-home dads. (Even the

© King Features Syndicate. Reprinted with permission—Torstar Syndication Services

term "stay-at-home dads" suggests we still have a way to go.) Nor is it uncommon today to see fathers with infants and dads are no longer thought to be "babysitting" when they are at home with the children.

Transgendered individuals are also making their needs known and educational institutions are beginning to provide gender neutral bathrooms for people transitioning to another gender. One student who was transitioning from female to male had a difficult time using the women's facilities which he was legally bound to do. There was always uproar at every visit because he was perceived as a man in a woman's bathroom.[33]

LWA/Larry Williams/Blend Images/Getty Images

Occupational Roles

Even our jobs can influence our perception. For example, five people walk through a park—a botanist, a zoologist, a meteorologist, a communicologist, and a pickpocket. The botanist is fascinated by the trees and other plants. The zoologist looks for interesting animals. The meteorologist notices changes in the sky. The communicologist concentrates on the interactions among the people in the park. And, of course, the pickpocket takes advantage of the others' absorption to help himself. Can you recall when your perceptions may have been altered because of a job you had?

Relational Roles

Think back to the "Who am I?" list you made in Chapter 2. It's likely that your list included roles you play in relation to others: daughter, roommate, husband, friend, etc. These roles not only define you, they also affect your perception.

Take, for example, the role of parent. New mothers and fathers will attest that having a child alters how they see the world. They might perceive their baby's crying as a need for comfort, while nearby strangers have a less charitable appraisal. As the child grows, parents become more aware of the messages in the child's environment. One father said he never noticed how much football fans swore until he took his six-year-old to a game. In other words, his father role affected what he heard and how he interpreted it.

Your romantic roles—partner, spouse, boyfriend/girlfriend, sweetheart, etc.—also affect your perception. For example, you may see your sweetheart as more

attractive than other people do, and perhaps you overlook some noticeable faults.[34] Your romantic role can also change the way you view others. One study found that people in love view other romantic candidates as less attractive than they normally would.[35] But when the "love goggles" come off and partners break up, they often ask, "What did I ever *see* in that person?" The answer—in part—is what your relational role led you to see.

LO3
Common Tendencies in Perception

Social scientists use the term **attribution** to describe the process of attaching meaning to behaviour. We attribute meaning both to our own actions and to the actions of others, but we often use different yardsticks. Research has uncovered several perceptual tendencies that can lead to, what we refer to as, attribution errors.[36]

We Judge Ourselves More Charitably than Others

In an attempt to convince ourselves and others that the positive face we show to the world is accurate, we judge ourselves more generously, and this tendency is called the **self-serving bias**.[37] When others suffer, we somehow think it's their fault, but when we're the victims, there are always extenuating circumstances. Consider the following: When *others* botch a job, we think they weren't listening well or trying hard enough; when *we* botch a job, it was unclear directions or not enough time that caused the problem. When *friends* get caught speeding, we say they should have been more careful; when *we* get the ticket, we deny that we were driving too fast.[38]

Attribution
The process of attaching meaning to behaviour.

Self-serving bias
The tendency to interpret and explain information in a way that casts the perceiver in the most favourable manner.

Jayme Thornton/Stone/Getty Images

We Cling to First Impressions

We label people according to our first impressions in order to make some interpretations about them: "She seems cheerful." "He seems sincere." "They sound awfully conceited."

When first impressions are accurate, labels help us decide how to respond in the future. When labels are inaccurate, however, we still hang onto them, making conflicting information fit our positive, or negative, opinion of the person.

This tendency to form an overall positive impression on the basis of one positive characteristic is called the **halo effect**. Typically, positive impressions stem from physical attractiveness and leads people to attribute other unrelated virtues to the good-looking person.[39] For example, employment interviewers rate mediocre but attractive job applicants higher than their less attractive candidates.[40] When employers form positive impressions, they then ask questions that confirm their image.[41] Attractive applicants who moved from one job to another are thought to be industrious, go-getters, or ambitious. Less attractive candidates who made a negative impression and moved from job to job might be thought of as unreliable, and it may be impossible for them to dispel a phenomenon sometimes referred to as "the devil effect."[42]

The power of first impressions is also important in personal relationships. College roommates who had positive initial impressions of each other were likely to have positive subsequent interactions, manage their conflicts constructively, and continue living together.[43] Roommates who got off to a bad start tended to spiral negatively.

Halo effect
The tendency to form an overall positive impression on the basis of one positive characteristic.

We Assume that Others Are Similar to Us

We tend to think that others' views are similar to our own, and this applies in a wide range of situations:

- You've heard a slightly raunchy joke that you think is pretty funny. You assume that it won't offend a strait-laced friend. It does.
- An instructor has a tendency to get off the subject during lectures. If you were a professor, you'd want to know if anything you were doing was creating problems for your students. You decide your instructor will probably be grateful for some constructive criticism—you're wrong.

Examples like these show that others do not always think or feel the way we do and that assuming that similarities exist can lead to problems.[44] One way to find out the other person's real position is to engage in perception checking, which will be discussed shortly.

We Are Influenced by the Obvious

Being influenced by the obvious is understandable. The problem, however, is that the most obvious factor is not necessarily the only one—or the most significant one for an event. For example:

- When two children (or adults, for that matter) fight, it may be a mistake to blame the one who lashes out first. Perhaps the other was equally responsible by teasing or refusing to cooperate.
- You might complain about an acquaintance whose malicious gossip or arguing has become a bother, forgetting that by putting up with such behaviour in the past you have been at least partially responsible.
- You might blame an unhappy working situation on the boss, overlooking other factors beyond her control, such as a change in the economy, the policy of higher management, or the demands of customers or other workers.

What we need to do in situations like these, and others, is to look beyond the obvious to what else might be going on.

LO4
Perception Checking

Serious problems can arise when we treat our interpretations of a person's comments or behaviours as if they were actual facts. For example, your friend Lennon who is usually very chipper and always looking for the humour in life is very quiet when you meet for lunch. You begin to think, perhaps, that maybe it was something you said or did, or maybe her on-again off-again relationship with Caleigh is off. Rather than hint at what might be going on or decide that she no longer likes you, there's a very easy approach to find out what's happening. This simple strategy is called **perception checking** and it's a handy tool to confirm your perceptions.[45] Not only will it help you sort through a situation before it gets out of hand, the approach tends to put listeners at ease so that they are more likely to open up to you.

This approach is also helpful in professional or work situations. For example, James said he would text you an order by the end of the afternoon; by six o'clock you still hadn't received anything. You assume that he is no longer interested and you let it go at that—you figure you lost the sale. Here is where perception checking comes in and it consists of three elements, or parts.

Elements of Perception Checking

1. Provide a description of the behaviour you noticed.
2. Offer at least two possible interpretations of the behaviour.
3. Request clarification about how to interpret the behaviour.

Going back to the examples above, you could use perception checking with Lennon by saying something as simple as:

> "You seem pretty down today. I'm wondering if it's something I said or maybe you and Caleigh are on the outs again. Are you okay?"

As a result, she might reveal that a professor said something very insulting to her in class. She was actually thinking of going to see the dean about it. Or, she may tell you that she's feeling a lot of anxiety today and is barely hanging on.

Here's how you might address the client, James.

> "You said that you would text your order by late afternoon but I hadn't received anything by six. Did you forget about it or perhaps you're no longer interested? What happened?"

Using this approach, James might inform you that there was an emergency situation at work that needed immediate attention and that he was still very interested in the order. Or, he might give you any number of reasons why the order wasn't sent.

If you look closely at both of these perception checks, you can see that we included the three elements in the process: We stated the behaviour observed (without being judgmental), offered two possible explanations for the behaviour, and then asked for clarification. The examples below include both the perception check dialogues and the elements.

> "When you rushed out of the room and slammed the door," (*behaviour*) "I wasn't sure whether you were mad at me" (*first interpretation*) "or just in a hurry." (*second interpretation*) "How *did* you feel?" (*request for clarification*)

> "You haven't laughed much in the last couple of days." (*behaviour*) "It makes me wonder whether something's bothering you" (*first interpretation*) "or whether you're just feeling quiet." (*second interpretation*) "What's up?" (*request for clarification*)

> "You said you really liked the job I did." (*behaviour*) "On the other hand, there was something about your voice that made me think you may not like it." (*first interpretation*) "Maybe it's just my imagination, though." (*second interpretation*) "How do you really feel?" (*request for clarification*)

Because the goal of perception checking is mutual understanding, it is a cooperative approach to communication. Besides more accurate perceptions, it minimizes defensiveness. Instead of saying, in effect, "I know what you're thinking …" it takes the more respectful approach that implies, "I know I'm not qualified to judge you without some help."

To see more examples of how perception checking can work in real-life contexts, see the In Real Life box.

Perception checking
A three-part method for verifying the accuracy of interpretations, including a description of the behaviour, two possible interpretations, and a request for clarification of the interpretation.

SKILL BUILDER

Perception Checking Practice
Develop a three-part perception checking strategy for each of the situations below.

1. A neighbour has not responded to your "Good morning" for three days in a row. This person is usually friendly.
2. An old friend with whom you have shared your love life problems for years has recently changed. The formerly casual hugs and kisses have become longer and stronger, and you "accidentally" brush up against each other more often.

Perception Checking in Everyday Life

Perception checking only works if it is sincere and fits your personal style. The following examples show how perception checking sounds in everyday life and may help you find ways to use it when you are faced with ambiguous messages.

My Boss's Jokes

I get confused by my boss's sense of humour. Sometimes he jokes just to be funny, but other times he uses humour to make a point without coming right out and saying what's on his mind. Last week he was talking about the upcoming work schedule and he said with a laugh, "I own you all weekend!" I have a life besides work, so his comment left me worried.

I used a perception check to figure out what he meant: "Brad, when you told me, 'I own you all weekend,' I wasn't sure whether you were kidding or whether you really expect me to work Saturday and Sunday. Were you serious?"

He kind of smiled and said, "No, I was just kidding. You only have to work Saturday and Sunday."

I still couldn't be sure whether or not he was serious, so I checked again: "You're kidding, right?"

My boss replied, "Well, I do need you at least one day, and two would be better." Once I figured out what he really meant, we worked out a schedule that had me work Friday evening and Saturday morning, which gave me the time off I needed.

If I hadn't used the perception check, I would have wound up worrying about being tied up all weekend and getting mad at my boss for no good reason. I'm glad I spoke up.

My Dad's Affection

My father and I have a great relationship. A while back I picked him up at the airport after a week-long business trip and a long cross-country flight. On the way home, he was quiet—not his usual self. He said he was exhausted, which I understood. When we got home, he brightened up and started joking and playing with my younger brother. I thought to myself, "Why is he so happy to see my brother when he hardly said a word to me?" I didn't say anything at the time. The next day I felt resentful toward my dad, and it showed. He said, "What's up with you?" But I was too embarrassed to say anything.

After learning this approach in class, I tried a perception check. I said, "Dad—when you were quiet on the way home after your business trip and then you perked up when you got home and saw Jaime, I wasn't sure what was up. I thought maybe you were happier to see him than me, or that maybe I'm imagining things. How come you said you were tired with me and then you perked up with Jaime?"

My dad felt awful. He said he was tired in the car, but once he got back to the house he was glad to be home and felt like a new man. I was too wrapped up in my mind to consider this alternative.

Perception Checking Considerations

Like all communication skills, perception checking isn't a mechanical formula that works in every situation. The following factors must be considered when deciding when and how to use this approach.

Completeness

Sometimes a perception check won't need all the parts listed earlier to be effective:

"You haven't dropped by lately. Is anything the matter?" (*single interpretation combined with request for clarification*)

"I can't tell whether you're kidding me about being cheap or if you're serious." (*behaviour combined with interpretations*) "Are you mad at me?"

Sometimes even the most skimpy perception check—a simple question like "What's going on?"—will do the job. You might also rely on other people to help you make sense of confusing behaviour: "Rachelle has been awfully quiet lately. Do you know what's up?" A complete perception check is most necessary when the risk of sounding judgmental is highest.

Nonverbal Congruency

A perception check can succeed only if your nonverbal behaviour reflects the open-mindedness of your words. An accusing tone of voice or a hostile glare contradicts a sincerely worded request for clarification and suggests that you've already made up your mind about the other person's intentions.

Cultural Rules

The straightforward approach of perception checking works best in *low-context cultures* like Canada, where

Iakov Filimonov/Shutterstock.com

Daniel Goleman believes that cultivating this tendency is the essence of "social intelligence."[48] The ability to empathize exists in even the youngest children. Virtually from birth, infants become visibly upset when they hear another baby crying, and if one child hurts its finger, another baby might put its own finger into its mouth as if in pain. When children see their parents cry, they wipe their own eyes even though they're not crying.

Although children have a basic capacity to empathize, studies with twins suggest that the degree to which we are born with the ability to sense how others are feeling seems to vary according to genetic factors.[49] Further, environment also plays a role. Specifically, how parents communicate with their children affects their ability to understand others' emotional states.[50] When parents indicate to children how their misbehaviour makes others feel ("Look how sad Jessica is because you took her toy. Wouldn't you be sad if someone took away your toys?"), those children are more likely to learn that their acts have emotional consequences than when parents simply label behaviours as inappropriate ("That was a mean thing to do!"). Studies also show that allowing children to experience and manage frustrating events can help increase their empathic concern for others later in life.[51]

Culture also influences our ability to empathize. For example, people raised in individualist cultures, which value independence, are often less adept at perspective taking than those from collectivist cultures, which value interdependence.[52] In one study, Chinese and American subjects played a communication game that required

language is used as clearly and logically as possible. These groups appreciate the kind of straight talking that perception checking embodies. Members of *high-context cultures* (common in Latin America and Asia) value social harmony over clarity. They are likely to regard perception checking as potentially embarrassing, preferring less direct ways of understanding one another. Thus, a "let's get this straight" perception check that might work well in Canada would be a serious mistake in Mexico or Asia.

Empathy and Cognitive Complexity

While perception checking is a valuable tool for clarifying ambiguous messages, sometimes we just don't understand where people are coming from. This is where empathy can help.

Empathy

Empathy is the ability to recreate another person's perspective, and while it's impossible to completely understand a person's viewpoint, we can learn how the world appears to him or her. In other words, it means to "walk in another person's shoes." Used here, empathy involves three dimensions.[46] On one level, empathy involves ***perspective taking***—an attempt to understand the viewpoint of another person. To do this, you must set aside your own opinions. Empathy also has an ***emotional*** dimension that helps us get closer and gain a sense of the other person's fear, joy, sadness, and so on. A third dimension of empathy is a genuine ***concern*** for the welfare of the other person. When we empathize, we go beyond just thinking and feeling as others do and genuinely care about their well-being.

Humans are "hardwired" to empathize with others—it's built into our brains.[47] Bestselling author

Empathy
The ability to project oneself into another person's point of view so as to experience the other's thoughts and feelings.

Andy Cox/Stone/Getty Images

"How would you feel if the mouse did that to you?"

William Steig The New Yorker Collection/The Cartoon Bank

Sympathy
Compassion for another's situation.

Cognitive complexity
The ability to construct a variety of frameworks for viewing an issue.

Pillow method
A way of understanding an issue from several perspectives, rather than with an egocentric "I'm right and you're wrong" attitude.

participants to take on the perspective of their partners. In all measures, the collectivist Chinese participants had greater success than did their American counterparts. This suggests that culture shapes the way we perceive, understand, and empathize with others.

Sympathy

Many people confuse empathy with **sympathy**, but they differ in a couple of ways. First, sympathy means that you feel compassion for another person's predicament, whereas empathy means you have a personal sense of what the predicament is like. Consider the difference between sympathizing and empathizing with a homeless person. When you sympathize, it's the other person's confusion, joy, or pain. When you empathize, the experience becomes your own, at least for the moment. It's one thing to feel bad (or good) *for* someone—sympathy—but it's more profound to feel bad (or good) *with* someone—empathy.

LO5
Cognitive Complexity

Given how important empathy is in relationships, how can we become more empathetic? One way is to increase cognitive complexity.

Cognitive Complexity and Communication

Cognitive complexity is the ability to construct a variety of frameworks for viewing an issue. In other words, to look at an event or interaction and offer several explanations for what might be happening. Research shows that this can increase the chances of satisfying communication in various contexts, including marriage,[53] helping others who are feeling distressed,[54] persuading others,[55] and advancing your career.[56]

There is also a connection between cognitive complexity and empathy.[57] The more ways you have to understand others and interpret their behaviours, the greater the likelihood that you'll see the world from their perspective. Cognitive complexity can also help people describe situations more thoroughly and less simplistically.[58] Further, cognitively complex people are better at identifying and understanding sarcasm—an abstract form of communication that is sometimes lost on those with less mental acumen.[59] Fortunately, our cognitive complexity skills can be enhanced through training.[60]

Increasing Your Cognitive Complexity: The Pillow Method

Some issues are too complex and serious to be handled with perception checking. To enhance your empathy, writer Paul Reps describes a tool that will help you get insight into another's position—the **pillow method**.[61]

Developed by a group of Japanese school-children, it gets its name from the fact that problems have four sides and a middle, just like a pillow **(Figure 3.3)**. Viewing an issue from each of these perspectives leads to valuable insights—and in so doing enhances cognitive complexity.

FIGURE 3.3
The Pillow Method

POSITION 1:
I'm right;
you're wrong

POSITION 3:
Both right;
both wrong

POSITION 5:
There's truth in
all four perspectives

POSITION 4:
The issue isn't
important

POSITION 2:
You're right;
I'm wrong

© Cengage Learning

Position 1: I'm Right, You're Wrong

We usually take this perspective when viewing an issue. We see the virtues in our position and find fault with those who disagree with us.

Position 2: You're Right, I'm Wrong

In this position, you try to build the strongest possible arguments to explain your opponent's point of view. Besides identifying the strengths in the other's position, this is the time to play the devil's advocate and find flaws in your own. Most people find that switching perspectives reveals some merits in the other person's point of view.

While you may not be able to approve criminal behaviours or deceit, you may be able to find some way of comprehending how someone could behave in a way that you originally found impossible to defend.

Position 3: Both Right, Both Wrong

From this perspective, you acknowledge the merits and flaws of each of your arguments. Taking this more even-handed look at the issue can lead you to be less critical and more understanding of another's point of view. You will also find the commonalities between your position and the other's.

Position 4: The Issue Isn't as Important as It Seems

Although it is hard to think of some issues as unimportant, most concerns are less important than we make them out to be. The impact of even the most traumatic events—the

Library of Congress LC-USZC4-8702

It was six men of Indostan
To learning much inclined,
Who went to see the elephant
Though all of them were blind
That each by observation
Might satisfy his mind.

The first approached the elephant
And, happening to fall
Against the broad and sturdy side,
At once began to bawl:
"Why, bless me! But the elephant
Is very much like a wall!"

The second, feeling of the tusk,
Cried: "Ho! What have we here
So very round and smooth and sharp?
To me, 'tis very clear,
This wonder of an elephant
Is very like a spear!"

The third approached the animal,
And, happening to take
The squirming trunk within his hands
Thus boldly up he spake:
"I see," quoth he, "the elephant
Is very like a snake!"

The fourth reached out his hand
And felt about the knee:
"What most this wondrous beast is like
Is very plain," quoth he:
"Tis clear enough the elephant
Is very like a tree!"

The fifth, who chanced to touch the ear,
Said: "E'en the blindest man
Can tell what this resembles most—
Deny the fact who can:
This marvel of an elephant
Is very like a fan!"

The sixth no sooner had begun
About the beast to grope
Than, seizing on the swinging tail
That fell within his scope,
"I see," quoth he, "the elephant
Is very like a rope!"

And so these men of Indostan
Disputed loud and long,
Each in his own opinion
Exceeding stiff and strong;
Though each was partly in the right,
And all were in the wrong.

John G. Saxe

Source: John G. Saxe

In Real Life

The Pillow Method in Action

© David J. Green-Lifestyle themes/Alamy

Example: My Mother and Facebook

Background

My mother recently opened a Facebook account and sent me an invitation to become her friend. I ignored her request for a couple of weeks, until she finally asked why I hadn't responded. The talk turned into an argument. She couldn't understand why I didn't want her as a Facebook friend. I couldn't understand why she wanted to butt into my personal life.

Position 1: I'm Right, She's Wrong

Facebook was created for college students, not middle-aged parents. The fact that my mom wants access to my personal world feels like an invasion of privacy—like reading my diary or rummaging through my belongings. If she wants to keep up with her friends on Facebook, that's her business—but leave me out of it.

Position 2: She's Right, I'm Wrong

When I objected to my mom snooping, she said she'd stop looking at my page if it makes her uncomfortable. So she's right in saying that I don't need to worry about her judgments. When I told her I'd be embarrassed to have her commenting on my life, she promised not to write on my wall, tag embarrassing pictures of me, or do anything else visible.

Position 3: Both of Us Are Right and Both Are Wrong

I'm justified to be concerned about my mom being freaked out by some things on my Facebook page. She's justified in wanting to know more about my life and how my generation communicates. I'm probably overreacting when I worry about her reactions or demand that she keep her nose out of my business. She's wrong not to appreciate my desire for privacy.

Position 4: The Issue Isn't Important

I don't think anything I or my friends post on my Facebook page would change my relationship with my mom. Turning this into a major issue is probably not worth the hurt feelings that have resulted from this mini-crisis.

Conclusion

Viewing this issue from several angles calmed me down and made it easier for my mother and I to have a good talk. We decided that I would friend her for a trial period. If I decide her looking at my page has become a problem, she agreed to willingly remove herself from my friends list.

---

death of a loved one or the breakup of a relationship, for example—usually lessens over time. The effects may not disappear, but we learn to accept them and get on with life. The importance of a dispute can also fade when you realize that you've let it overshadow the importance of your relationship with the other person.

Conclusion: There Is Truth in All Four Perspectives

The final step is recognizing that each position has some merit. While it seems impossible for a position to be both right and wrong or important and unimportant, your own experience will show how there can be some truth in each position.

After you have looked at an issue from these five perspectives, it is almost certain that you will gain new insights. These can increase your tolerance for the other person's position and thus improve the communication climate.

Communication in the Workplace

The Pillow method is also pertinent in the workplace. If, for example, you disagreed with the future restructuring of a department or, say, a major change in customer service, you might give the Pillow Method a go. At the very least you'll recognize some positive outcomes. Afterwards, if you still disagree, you might come to the realization that, in the big scheme of things, it really doesn't matter. You may have more important things in your life to focus on.

Another application of perception in the workplace has to do with teamwork. One trend we're seeing is the use of teamwork in both in-house and in virtual teams where members live in different countries with different languages and cultures. Ultimately, teams make better decisions because of the range of information that exists

Digital Vision/Thinkstock

perceptions are similar. However, working with diverse members is not always easy. Leaders in global virtual teams noted that cultural diversity greatly enriched their teams but also created challenges in the areas of language, cultural values, and management styles.[65] And, unless individuals in virtual groups use Skype, or a similar device, they won't have access to nonverbal cues to help them interpret messages. It's easy to see how this can lead to misunderstandings.

In spite of all of this, many teams achieve super-team status! First, a team differs from a group in that they are a diverse group of individuals who share leadership responsibility. They still achieve tasks, but these are mutually defined goals that reflect the group as a whole and as individuals.[66] To achieve superteam status, individuals tend to be success-driven, committed to quality, flexible but consistent, leader valuing and people valuing. They are also vision-driven, creative and innovative, and analytical. Finally, they form formal and informal networks and they are committed to the team as a whole.[67]

Superteams are extremely successful because they share leadership, argue their diverse positions, and ultimately make top notch decisions. As a result, super-team members feel good about themselves and their accomplishments. Clearly, their success can be attributed in part to each member's different perceptions of issues and events.

among group members.[62] In addition, groups can gain synergy; that is, the group's output "exceeds the sum of individual contributions."[63] For instance, one study showed that teams outperformed their best member 97 percent of the time.[64]

Another factor that contributes to a team's effectiveness is diversity among its members. This can come in the form of gender, age, culture, areas of expertise, and so forth. Heterogeneous groups bring a breadth of perceptions and depth to their decision making that cannot be achieved by individuals whose experiences and

---

READY TO STUDY?

IN THE BOOK, YOU CAN:

❏ Rip out the Chapter in Review card at the back of the book to have the key terms and Learning Objectives handy, and complete the quizzes provided (answers are at the bottom of the back page).

ONLINE YOU CAN:

❏ Stay organized and efficient with MindTap—a single destination with all the course material and study aids you need to succeed. Built-in apps leverage social media and the latest learning technology. For example:

  ❏ Listen to the text using ReadSpeaker.

  ❏ Use pre-populated Flashcards as a jump start for review—or you can create your own.

  ❏ You can highlight text and make notes in your MindTap Reader. Your notes will flow into Evernote, the electronic notebook app that you can access anywhere when it's time to study for the exam.

  ❏ Prepare for tests with a variety of quizzes and activities.

Go to **nelson.com/student** to access these digital resources

Endnotes

1. The graphic demonstrations of factors influencing perception in this and the following paragraph are borrowed from D. Coon & J. Mitterer (2010). *Introduction to Psychology,* 12th ed. Belmont, CA: Wadsworth/Cengage.

2. G. W. Allport (1958). *The Nature of Prejudice.* New York: Doubleday Anchor, p. 85.

3. R. Mourtada (2004). "A Climate of Fear." *Canadian Business, 77,* 24–25.

4. See S. Wortley & J. Tanner (2005). "Inflammatory Rhetoric? Baseless Accusations? A Response to Gabor's Critique of Racial Profiling Research in Canada." *Canadian Journal of Criminology and Criminal Justice, 47,* 581–609; S. Wortley & J. Tanner (2003). "Data, Denials, and Confusion: The Racial Profiling Debate in Toronto." *Canadian Journal of Criminology and Criminal Justice, 45,* 367–389.

5. J. Oetzel (1998). "The Effects of Self-Construals and Ethnicity on Self-Reported Conflict Styles." *Communication Reports, 11,* 133–144.

6. N. Nishizawa (2004). "The 'Self' of Japanese Teenagers: Growing Up in the Flux of a Changing Culture and Society." *Dissertation Abstracts International, 65,* 2642.

7. P. Watzlawick, J. Beavin, & D. D. Jackson (1967). *Pragmatics of Human Communication.* New York: Norton, p. 65.

8. K. Floyd & M. T. Morman (2000). "Reacting to the Verbal Expression of Affection in Same-Sex Interaction." *Southern Communication Journal, 65,* 287–299.

9. R. Rosenthal & D. B. Rubin (2010). "Interpersonal expectancy effects: The first 345 studies." In M. L. Knapp & J. A. Daly (Eds.) *Interpersonal Communication* (pp. 297–338). Thousand Oaks, CA: Sage.

10. J. K. Alberts, U. Kellar-Guenther, & S. R. Corman (1996). "That's Not Funny: Understanding Recipients' Responses to Teasing." *Western Journal of Communication, 60,* 337–357. See also R. Edwards, R. Bello, F. Brandau-Brown, & D. Hollems (2001). "The Effects of Loneliness and Verbal Aggressiveness on Message Interpretation." *Southern Communication Journal, 66,* 139–150.

11. See T. N. Bradbury & F. D. Fincham (1990). "Attributions in Marriage: Review and Critique." *Psychological Bulletin, 107,* 3–33; V. Manusov (1990). "An Application of Attribution Principles to Nonverbal Behaviour in Romantic Dyads." *Communication Monographs, 57,* 104–118.

12. C. L. M. Shaw (1997). "Personal Narrative: Revealing Self and Reflecting Other." *Human Communication Research, 24,* 302–319.

13. J. K. Kellas (2005). "Family Ties: Communicating Identity through Jointly Told Family Stories." *Communication Monographs, 72,* 365–389.

14. J. Flora & C. Segrin (2000). "Relationship Development in Dating Couples: Implications for Relational Satisfaction and Loneliness." *Journal of Social and Personal Relationships, 17,* 811–825.

15. L. A. Baxter & G. Pittman (2001). "Communicatively Remembering Turning Points of Relational Development in Heterosexual Romantic Relationships." *Communication Reports, 14,* 1–17.

16. S. L. Murray, J. G. Holmes, & D. W. Griffin (2004). "The Benefits of Positive Illusions: Idealization and the Construction of Satisfaction in Close Relationships." In *Close Relationships: Key Readings* (pp. 317–338). Philadelphia: Taylor & Francis. See also J. M. Martz, J. Verette, X. B. Arriaga, L. F. Slovik, C. L. Cox, & C. E. Rosbult (1998). "Positive Illusion in Close Relationships." *Personal Relationships, 5,* 159–181.

17. J. C. Pearson (1996). "Positive Distortion: 'The Most Beautiful Woman in the World.'" In K. M. Galvin and P. Cooper (Eds.). *Making Connections: Readings in Interpersonal Communication* (p. 177). Beverly Hills, CA: Roxbury.

18. For a detailed description of how the senses affect perception, see N. Ackerman (1990). *A Natural History of the Senses.* New York: Random House.

19. K. Alaimo, C. M. Olson, & E. A. Frongillo (2001). "Food Insufficiency and American School-Aged Children's Cognitive, Academic, and Psychosocial Development." *Pediatrics, 108,* 44–53.

20. M. Maguire (2005). "Biological Cycles and Cognitive Performance." In A. Esgate et al., *An Introduction to Applied Cognitive Psychology* (pp. 137–161). New York: Psychology Press. See also C. Cooper & C. McConville (1990). "Interpreting Mood Scores: Clinical Implications of Individual Differences in Mood Variability." *British Journal of Medical Psychology, 63,* 215–225.

21. Canadian Mental Health Association (British Columbia Division) (2012). https://www.cmha.bc.ca/get-informed/mental-health-information/adult-adhd and https://www.cmha.bc.ca/get-informed/mental-health-information/bipolar-disorder. Retrieved January 31, 2015.

22. R. Harrison (1972). "Nonverbal Behaviour: An Approach to Human Communication." In R. Budd and B. Ruben (Eds.). *Approaches to Human Communication.* New York: Spartan Books.

23. E. T. Hall (1969). *The Hidden Dimension.* New York: Doubleday Anchor, p. 160.

24. H. Giles, N. Coupland, & J. M. Wiemann (1992). "Talk Is Cheap . . . But 'My Word Is My Bond': Beliefs about Talk." In K. Bolton & H. Kwok (Eds.). *Sociolinguistics Today: International Perspectives.* London: Routledge & Kegan Paul.

25. H. Hiller, *Canadian Society: A Macro Analysis.* Scarborough, ON: Prentice Hall, 1991, p. 36.

26. D. F. Halpern (2000). *Sex Differences in Cognitive Abilities,* 3rd ed. Mahwah, NJ: Erlbaum.

27. C. Leaper, K. Anderson, & P. Sanders (1998). "Moderators of Gender Effects on Parents' Talk to Their Children: A Meta-Analysis." *Developmental Psychology, 34,* 3–27.

28. D. K. Ivy (2012). *GenderSpeak: Personal Effectiveness in Gender Communication.* New York: Pearson.

29. M. Law (2014). "Sisters doin' it for themselves: Frozen and the evolution of the Disney heroine" [online]. *Screen Education, 74,* 16–25. http://search.informit.com.au /documentSummary;dn=436282205645360;res=IELHSS. Retrieved December 31, 2015.

30. C. J. Simonds & P. J. Cooper (2001). "Communication and Gender in the Classroom." In L. P. Arliss and D. J. Borisoff (Eds.), *Women and Men Communicating: Challenges and Changes* (pp. 232–253) Prospect Heights, IL: Waveland.

31. R. Hall, & B. Sandler (1982). "The Classroom Climate: A Chilly one for Women." Washington, DC: *Project on the Status and Education of Women, Association of American Colleges.*

32. Parliament of Canada (2015). Premiers Current List. http://www.lop.parl.gc.ca/ParlInfo/Compilations/ ProvinceTerritory/PremiersTerritorialLeaders.aspx. Retrieved December 31, 2015.

33. A. Sisney (November 5, 2010). "Transgender Student Pleads for Rights at Webster." *The Journal: Webster University.*

34. V. Swami & A. Furnham (2008). "Is Love Really So Blind?" *The Psychologist, 21,* 108–111.

35. G. C. Gonzaga, M. G. Haselton, J. Smurda, M. Davies, & J. C. Poore (2008). "Love, Desire, and the Suppression of Thoughts of Romantic Alternatives." *Evolution and Human Behaviour, 29,* 119–126.

36. D. Hamachek (1992). *Encounters with the Self,* 3rd ed. Fort Worth, TX: Harcourt Brace Jovanovich.

37. For a review of these perceptual biases, see Hamachek, *Encounters with the Self.* See also Bradbury & Fincham, op. cit. For an example of the self-serving bias in action, see R. Buttny (1997). "Reported Speech in Talking Race on Campus." *Human Communication Research, 23,* 477–506.

38. S. L. Young (2004). "What the _____ Is Your Problem? Attribution Theory and Perceived Reasons for Profanity Usage During Conflict." *Communication Research Reports, 21,* 338–347.

39. K. Dion, E. Berscheid, & E. Walster (1972). "What Is Beautiful Is Good." *Journal of Personality and Social Psychology, 24,* 285–290.

40. L. Watkins & L. Johnston (2000). "Screening Job Applicants: The Impact of Physical Attractiveness and Application Quality." *International Journal of Selection and Assessment, 8,* 76–84.

41. T. Dougherty, D. Turban, & J. Collander (1994). "Conforming First Impressions in the Employment Interview." *Journal of Applied Psychology, 79,* 659–665.

42. G. I. Cook, R. L. Marsh, & J. L. Hicks (2003). "Halo and Devil Effects Demonstrate Valenced-Based Influences on Source-Mentoring Decisions." *Consciousness and Cognition, 12,* 257–278.

43. C. I. Marek, M. B. Wanzer, & J. L. Knapp (2004). "An Exploratory Investigation of the Relationship between Roommates' First Impressions and Subsequent Communication Patterns." *Communication Research Reports, 21,* 210–220.

44. B. Keysar (2007). "Communication and Miscommunication: The Role of Egocentric Processes." *Intercultural Pragmatics, 4,* 71–84.

45. See, for example, A. Sillars, W. Shellen, A. McInto, & M. Pomegranate (1997). "Relational Characteristics of Language: Elaboration and Differentiation in Marital Conversations." *Western Journal of Communication, 61,* 403–422.

46. J. B. Stiff, J. P. Dillard, L. Somera, H. Kim, & C. Sleight (1988). "Empathy, Communication, and Prosocial Behaviour." *Communication Monographs, 55,* 198–213.

47. This research is described by D. Goleman (2006) in *Social Intelligence.* New York: Bantam. See also J. Decety, K. Michalska, & Y. Aktsuki (2008) "Who Caused the Pain? An fMRI Investigation of Empathy and Intentionality in Children." *Neuropsychologia, 46,* 2607–2614.

48. Goleman, op cit.

49. M. Davis (1994). "The Heritability of Characteristics Associated with Dispositional Empathy." *Journal of Personality, 62,* 369–391.

50. B. Burleson, J. Delia, & J. Applegate (1995). "The Socialization of Person-Centered Communication: Parental Contributions to the Social-Cognitive and Communication Skills of Their Children." In M. A. Fitzpatrick & Vangelisti (Eds.). *Perspectives in Family Communication.* Thousand Oaks, CA: Sage.

51. D. M. Tucker, P. Luu, & D. Derryberry (2005). "Love Hurts: The Evolution of Empathic Concern through the Encephalization of Nociceptive Capacity." *Development and Psychopathology, 17,* 699–713.

52. S. Wu & B. Keysar (2007). "Cultural Effects on Perspective Taking." *Psychological Science, 18,* 600–606.

53. R. Martin (1992). "Relational Cognition Complexity and Relational Communication in Personal Relationships." *Communication Monographs, 59,* 150–163. See also B. R. Burleson & S. E. Caplan (1998). "Cognitive Complexity." In J. C. McCroskey, J. A. Daly, M. M. Martin, and M. J. Beatty (Eds.). *Communication and Personality: Trait Perspectives* (pp. 233–286). Creskill, NY: Hampton Press.

54. Burleson & Caplan, op. cit., p. 22.

55. B. R. Burleson (1989). "The Constructivist Approach to Person-Centered Communication: Analysis of a Research Exemplar." In B. Dervin, L. Grossberg, B. J. O'Keefe, & E. Wartella (Eds.). *Rethinking Communication: Paradigm Exemplars* (pp. 33–72). Newbury Park, CA: Sage.

56. B. D. Sypher & T. Zorn (1986). "Communication-Related Abilities and Upward Mobility: A Longitudinal Investigation." *Human Communication Research, 12,* 420–431.

57. Joireman, J. (2004). "Relationships Between Attributional Complexity and Empathy." *Individual Differences Research, 2,* 197–202.

58. Medvene, L., Grosch, K., & Swink, N. (2006). "Interpersonal Complexity: A Cognitive Component of Person-Centered Care." *The Gerontologist, 46,* 220–226.

59. Rockwell, P. (2007). "The Effects of Cognitive Complexity and Communication Apprehension on the Expression

and Recognition of Sarcasm." In A. M. Columbus (Ed.). *Advances in Psychology Research, 49,* 185–196. Hauppauge, NY: Nova Science Publishers.

60. C. Little, J. Packman, M. H. Smaby, & C. D. Maddux (2005). "The Skilled Counselor Training Model: Skills Acquisition, Self-Assessment, and Cognitive Complexity." *Counselor Education & Supervision, 44,* 189–200.

61. P. Reps (1967). "Pillow Education in Rural Japan." *Square Sun, Square Moon.* New York: Tuttle.

62. G. Lumsden, D. Lumsden, & C. Wiethoff (2010). *Communicating in Groups and Teams: Sharing Leadership.* US: Wadsworth Cengage Learning.

63. A. J. DuBrin, & Terri Geerinck (2009). *Human Relations: Interpersonal, Job-Oriented Skills,* p. 74 (3rd Canadian Edition). Toronto: Pearson Prentice Hall.

64. L. K. Michaelson, W. E. Watson, & R. H. Black (1989). "A Realistic Test of Individual Versus Group Consensus Decision Making." *Journal of Applied Psychology, 74,* 834–839 as cited in Lumsden, Lumsden, Wiethoff (2010). Also see H. van Mierlo, C. G. Rutte, J. K. Vermunt, M. A. J. Kompier, & J. A. C. M. Doorewaard (2007). "A Multi-level Mediation Model of the Relationships Between Team Autonomy, Individual Task Design, and Psychological Well-being." *Journal of Occupational and Organizational Psychology, 88,* 647–664 as cited in Lumsden, Lumsden & Wiethoff (2010).

65. L. Dubé & G. Paré (2001). "Global Virtual Teams," *Communications of the ACM, 44,* 71–75.

66. Lumsen, Lumsden, & Wiethoff, op. cit., p. 14.

67. Lumsen, Lumsden, & Wiethoff, op. cit., pp. 84–85.

Learning like never before.

4LTR PRESS

nelson.com/student

CHAPTER 4

EMOTIONS
FEELING, THINKING, AND COMMUNICATING

LEARNING OUTCOMES

LO1 Describe how the four components of emotions affect the way you feel, and hence, how you communicate.

LO2 Describe how the influences on emotional expression have affected your communication in an important relationship.

LO3 Apply the guidelines for effectively communicating emotions in an important situation.

LO4 Identify and dispute the fallacies that are creating debilitative emotions in an important situation. Explain how more rational thinking can lead to more constructive communication.

LO1
What Are Emotions?

Suppose an extraterrestrial visitor asked you to explain emotions. How would you answer? According to social scientists, there are several components to what we label as feelings.[1]

The role of emotions in human affairs is apparent to social scientists and lay people alike. Daniel Goleman coined the term **emotional intelligence** to describe the ability to understand and manage one's own emotions and be sensitive to others' feelings.[2] Emotional intelligence is positively linked to self-esteem, life satisfaction, and self-acceptance,[3] as well as with healthy relationships and conflict management.[4] Clearly, emotional intelligence is vital to both personal and interpersonal success. Stop for a moment and think of an individual whom you would classify as emotionally intelligent. It might be a family member who's in touch with a wide range of feelings without being overwhelmed by them or a boss who makes wise and rational choices even under stress. Now, think of someone who might lack emotional intelligence. Perhaps it's a workmate who is uptight and dismissive about honest human feelings, or a friend who blows up at the smallest inconvenience. Finally, assess your own emotional intelligence. How well do you understand and manage your emotions, and how sensitive are you to the feelings or others?

Emotional intelligence
The ability to understand and manage one's own emotions and be sensitive to others' feelings.

What do you THINK?

I always express my emotions properly.

1	2	3	4	5	6	7
strongly agree						strongly disagree

Silvia Jansen/iStock/Getty Images

Because emotions play such an important role in the transactional communication that occurs in virtually all types of relationships, this chapter is devoted to the topic. If you would like to demonstrate a greater degree of emotional intelligence, you can do so by applying the suggestions in this chapter. We begin by examining the nature of emotions.

Physiological Factors

Strong emotions are generally accompanied by physiological changes. For example, fear increases heart rate, blood pressure, adrenaline secretions, and blood sugar level but slows digestion and pupil dilation.[5] Marriage researcher John Gottman notes that similar symptoms also occur when couples are in intense conflicts.[6] He calls the condition "flooding" and has found that it impedes effective problem solving.

Some physiological changes (a churning stomach or tense jaw) are recognizable to the person having them, and these internal cues can offer a significant clue to your emotions.

Nonverbal Reactions

While some physical changes that accompany emotions are external, observable ones such as blushing, sweating, or shaking, others involve behaviour: a distinctive facial expression, posture, or gestures; modification in vocal tone or rate; and so on. And research confirms what might be guessed: nonverbal expression of emotions become more pronounced under the influence of alcohol.[7] Alcohol serves as an emotional enhancer—sometimes for better, sometimes for worse.

Although it's reasonably easy to tell when someone is feeling a strong emotion, the ambiguity of nonverbal behaviour makes it difficult to know exactly just what emotion that might be. A slumped posture and sigh could signify sadness or fatigue. Likewise, trembling hands might indicate excitement or fear. Therefore, it's dangerous to assume we can "read" a person's emotions with great accuracy.

Nonverbal behaviour can also induce emotional states. In one study, experimental subjects were able to create various emotional states by altering their facial expressions.[8] When coached to move their facial muscles to look afraid, angry, disgusted, amused, sad, surprised, and contemptuous, the subjects' bodies responded as if they were actually having these feelings. In another experiment, subjects who were coached to smile actually reported feeling better, and when they altered their expressions to look unhappy, they felt worse than before.[9]

There's also a connection between nonverbal reactions and verbalizing emotions. One study showed that participants unconsciously stood taller when talking about pride and slumped when using words for disappointment.[10] This reminds us that verbal and nonverbal expressions of emotion are often interconnected.

Cognitive Interpretations

While there can be a direct connection between physical behaviour and emotional states, the mind and our self-talk play a major role in how we feel. For instance, it's interesting to note that the physiological components of fear—racing heart, perspiration, tense muscles, and elevated blood pressure—are similar to the physical changes that accompany excitement, joy, and other emotions. If we were to measure a person's physical condition during a strong emotion, we wouldn't know if the person was trembling with fear or quivering with excitement. The label an individual applies to these physical symptoms determines whether symptoms will be experienced or interpreted as fright, joy, or anger.[11]

Psychologist Philip Zimbardo offers an interesting example of this principle:

> I notice I'm perspiring while lecturing. From that I infer I am nervous. If it occurs often, I might even label myself a "nervous person." Once I

Fans of "EMO" artist Dallas Green, formerly of Alexisonfire, will likely agree that his music and lyrics have helped them get through difficult emotional times.

Suzi Pratt/FilmMagic/Getty Images

have the label, the next question I must answer is, "Why am I nervous?" Then I start to search for an appropriate explanation. I might notice some students leaving the room, or being inattentive. I am nervous because I'm not giving a good lecture. That makes me nervous. How do I know it's not good? Because I'm boring my audience. I am nervous because I am a boring lecturer and I want to be a good lecturer. I feel inadequate. Maybe I should open a delicatessen instead. Just then a student says, "It's hot in here, I'm perspiring, and it makes it tough to concentrate on your lecture." Instantly, I'm no longer "nervous" or "boring."[12]

Zimbardo found that changing his self-talk, or interpretation, of the event affected the way he felt about it. Social scientists refer to this process as **reappraisal**—rethinking the meaning of emotionally charged events in ways that alter their emotional impact.[13] Research shows that reappraisal is vastly superior to suppressing one's feelings: It often leads to lower stress, higher self-esteem, and increased productivity.[14] Here are two examples:

- You lost your job, while some less ambitious co-workers were not fired; hence your self-esteem is shattered. You lack confidence as you look for new employment. You could reappraise the event and interpret it as an opportunity to find a better position where hard work and contributions to the firm are appreciated and rewarded.
- A friend says malicious things about you behind your back. Even though you are hurt, you interpret her actions as statements about *her* character, not yours. You demonstrate your character by not speaking poorly about her to others.

Reappraisal is not about denying your feelings. Recognizing and acknowledging positive (happiness, relief, love)

J Walters/Shutterstock.com

and negative (hurt, anger, grief) emotions is vital to psychological and relational health.

Verbal Expression

While nonverbal actions are generally better at conveying emotions, sometimes it takes words to identify them. For example, whether your friend's uncharacteristically short temper is a sign of anger at you or something less personal, or if a lover's unenthusiastic response is a sign of boredom or the result of a long workday can be determined most accurately through verbal expression. In fact, perception checking would be useful in cases such as these.

Primary and Mixed Emotions

Some researchers believe there are several "basic," or **primary emotions**.[15] However, there isn't much agreement about what those emotions are or about what makes them "basic."[16] Further, primary emotions in one culture may not be primary in others, and some emotions have no direct equivalent in other cultures.[17] For example, shame is a central emotion in the Chinese experience, while it's much less relevant in Western cultures.[18] However, most scholars acknowledge that *anger, joy, fear,* and *sadness* are common human emotions.

Sometimes we experience conflicting primary emotions at the same time. These are referred to as **mixed emotions**. For instance, you expect your friend from another city to arrive around 6, give or take the traffic. When he waltzes in at 11:30 with a flippant, "Oh, I got a late start," you're angry that he didn't get in touch but relieved and happy that he's safe.

Intense and Mild Emotions

We also experience emotions with different degrees of intensity, as **Figure 4.1** illustrates. Some people understate their emotions, failing to let others know how strongly they feel. Saying that you're "annoyed" when a friend breaks an important promise would probably be an understatement. In other cases, people chronically overstate the strength of their feelings. To them, everything is "wonderful" or "terrible." The problem with this sort of exaggeration is that there are no words left to describe a truly intense emotion. If chocolate chip cookies are "fabulous," how does it feel to fall in love?

Reappraisal
Rethinking the meaning of emotionally charged events in ways that alter their emotional impact.

Primary emotions
Basic emotions such as anger, joy, fear, and sadness.

Mixed emotions
Feeling two or more conflicting emotions at the same time.

CHAPTER 4 Emotions: Feeling, Thinking, and Communicating

FIGURE 4.1
Intensity of Emotions

Annoyed	**Angry**	**Furious**
Pensive	**Sad**	**Grieving**
Content	**Happy**	**Ecstatic**
Anxious	**Afraid**	**Terrified**
Liking	**Loving**	**Adoring**

© Cengage Learning

For 43 years, Hank had successfully stuffed every feeling he'd ever had, until, of course, the morning when Fred asked if he could borrow a paper clip.

© www.CartoonStock.com

Intensity of Emotions

When people can't talk about their emotions constructively, it can result in social isolation, unsatisfying relationships, anxiety and depression, and misdirected aggression.[19] Check out the cartoon about "Hank". How parents talk to children about emotions also affects their development.[20] Two distinct parenting styles have been identified: emotion coaching, which gives children skills to communicate their emotions, and emotion dismissing, which does not. Unfortunately, children who grow up in families where parents dismiss emotions are at higher risk for behaviour problems than those who are raised in families that practise emotion coaching.[21] Clearly, emotions are very complex, and guidelines for communicating them are provided later in the chapter.

LO2
Influences on Emotional Expression

While most people are comfortable stating facts or expressing opinions, they rarely disclose how they feel. There are several reasons for this.

Invitation to Insight

Recognizing Your Emotions

Keep a three-day record of your feelings by taking a few minutes each evening to recall and record the emotions you felt that day, the people involved, and the circumstances surrounding the emotions that occurred. To help identify your emotions, refer to the common human emotions listed in **Table 4.1**.

At the end of the three-day period, you can understand the role that emotions play in your communication by answering the following questions:

1. How did you recognize the emotions you felt: through physiological stimuli, nonverbal behaviours, or cognitive processes?

2. Did you have any difficulty deciding which emotions you were feeling?

3. What emotions do you have most often? Are they mild or intense?

4. In what circumstances do you or do you not show your feelings? What factors influence your decision to show or not show your feelings? The type of feeling? The person or persons involved? The situation (time, place)? The subject that the feeling involves (money, sex, and so on)?

5. What are the consequences of the type of communicating you just described in step 4? Are you satisfied with these consequences? If not, what can you do to become more satisfied?

Personality

There is an increasingly clear relationship between personality and the way we experience and communicate emotions.[22] Extroverted people, for example, who tend to be upbeat, optimistic, and enjoy social contact, report more positive emotions than do less extroverted individuals.[23] Likewise, people with neurotic personalities, who tend to worry, feel anxious, or apprehensive, report more negative emotions. These personality traits are at least partially biological in nature.

But personality doesn't have to govern your communication satisfaction. Introverted people find ways to reach out to others. For example, the Internet has proven to be an effective tool for quiet individuals because it has been found to reduce social anxiety.[24] E-mail and computer dating services provide low-threat ways for reticent communicators to approach others and get acquainted.[25]

Culture

While people from different cultures generally experience the same emotions, similar events can generate different feelings.[26] Eating snails might bring a smile of delight to many Quebec residents, while other Canadians might grimace in disgust. Further, Asian Americans and Hong Kong Chinese value calmness, whereas European Americans tend to value excitement.[27] For example, some people see the United States as a "culture of cheerfulness." An author from Poland described American

expressiveness this way: "Wow! Great! How nice! That's fantastic! I had a terrific time! It was wonderful! Have a nice day! Americans. So damned cheerful."[28]

There are also differences in the degree to which people in various cultures display their feelings. For example, people from warmer climates are more emotionally expressive than those who live in cooler climates.[29] Even people from the southern part of their countries were more emotionally expressive than were northerners!

Whether a culture is individualistic or collectivistic is a major factor that influences emotional expression. Collectivistic cultures such as Japan's and India's prize harmony among members of their "in-group" and discourage expression of any negative emotions that might upset relationships among people who belong to it. Members of highly individualistic cultures like Canada's are comfortable revealing their feelings to people they trust.[30] It's easy to see how these differences could lead to communication problems. For example, individualistic North Americans might view collectivistic Asians as less than candid, while people raised in Asia could easily regard North Americans as overly demonstrative.[31]

The phrase "I love you" offers another interesting intercultural difference. North Americans say "I love you" more frequently (and to more people) than do members of most other cultures.[32] Further, there are significant cultural differences about when, where, how often, and with whom the phrase should be used. Middle Easterners believe that "I love you" should only be expressed between spouses. North American men using the phrase cavalierly with Middle Eastern women might find that they're making a marriage proposal. People in Eastern Europe, India, and Korea hold that the phrase be used sparingly so it won't lose its power and meaning. Interestingly, across cultures, women tend to say "I love you" more often than men. However, contrary to popular belief, men in heterosexual relationships are more likely to say "I love you" first.[33]

"I'm not in one of my moods. I'm in one of your moods."

CHAPTER 4 Emotions: Feeling, Thinking, and Communicating

Gender

Even within a culture, biological sex and gender roles shape how women and men experience and express their emotions.[34] In fact, biological sex is the best predictor of the ability to detect and interpret emotional expressions—better than academic background, amount of foreign travel, cultural similarity, or ethnicity.[35] For example, women are more attuned to emotions than men,[36] both within and across cultures.[37] Further, females were 10 to 15 percent more accurate than men when it came to remembering emotional images and their reactions to these emotion-producing stimuli. Further, women's reactions were significantly more intense than men's.

Research on emotional expression suggests that there is at least some truth in the stereotypical unexpressive male and the more expressive female.[38] Overall, women are more likely to express feelings of vulnerability such as fear or embarrassment while men are more likely than women to reveal their strengths.[39] As a result, they are more likely to be promoted to leadership positions.[40] In addition, men are more likely to express feelings, especially positive ones, to a woman as opposed to a man.[41] In face-to-face communication, one study showed that fathers mask their emotions more than mothers which makes it harder for children to read their father's emotional state.[42]

On the Internet, women were more likely than men to use emoticons (such as the smiley face symbol) and to express their feelings.[43] Women also express more affection on Facebook than do men.[44] Overall, while all human beings experience emotions, regardless of gender, there is evidence to suggest that women and men express them differently.[45]

"I've been thinking—it might be good for Andrew if he could see you cry once in a while."

Robert Weber The New Yorker Collection/The Cartoon Bank

Social Conventions

Social conventions refer to the notion of acting in ways that are acceptable within our society. For instance, while expressions of emotion are rare,[46] those that are shared are usually positive. Communicators are often reluctant to send messages that embarrass or threaten the "face" of others,[47] especially in the early stages of a new relationship.[48] They also attempt to suppress unpleasant emotions in contexts such as child rearing, the workplace, and personal relationships. One study of married couples revealed that partners often shared complimentary feelings ("I love you") or face-saving ones ("I'm sorry I yelled at you"). They also willingly disclosed both positive and negative feelings about absent third parties ("I like Jonathan," "I'm uncomfortable around

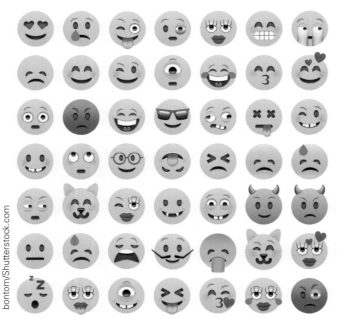

bontom/Shutterstock.com

Emoticons, from the words *emotion* and *icons,* are a way to express and clarify feelings in mediated messages.

Rick Eglinton/Toronto Star/Getty Images

Sarah"). On the other hand, the husbands and wives rarely verbalized face-threatening feelings ("I'm disappointed in you") or hostility ("I'm mad at you").[49]

Surprisingly, social rules even discourage too much expression of positive feelings.[50] While a hug and kiss for Mother is all right, a young man is more likely to shake hands with Dad. Canadians witnessed this when the media caught former Prime Minister Stephen Harper dropping his children at school. Instead of kissing them goodbye, he shook their hands. *The Globe and Mail* received more than 40 letters responding to the formal sendoff—more than for any other event it reported that day.[51]

Expression of emotions is also shaped by the requirements of many social roles. Researchers use the term **emotion labour** to describe situations in which managing and even suppressing emotions is both appropriate and necessary. For instance, you would suppress an urge to laugh during an important ceremony.

Fear of Self-Disclosure

In a society that discourages emotional expression, to do so seems risky.[52] Someone who maintains an image of confidence and certainty may find it frightening to say, "I'm scared my parents are going to break up." Someone who has never relied on others might have a hard time saying, "I'm lonesome. I want your friendship."

When people do muster up the courage to share feelings, they run the risk of being misunderstood. For instance, an expression of affection might be construed as a romantic invitation,[53] or a confession of uncertainty might look like a sign of weakness. Such expressions might make others feel uncomfortable or they may be used against you. Little wonder people are reluctant to express their emotions.

Emotional Contagion

Our emotions are also influenced by the feelings of those around us through **emotional contagion**: the process by which emotions are transferred from person to person.[54] As one commentator observed, "We catch feelings from one another as though they were some kind of social virus."[55] There is evidence that students "catch" the mood of their teachers,[56] that customers are affected by employees who serve them,[57] and that husbands and wives directly influence each other's emotions.[58] In fact, our happiness (or unhappiness) can actually be affected by neighbours, friends of friends, and even total strangers.[59]

Emotion labour
The notion that managing and even suppressing emotions is both appropriate and necessary

Emotional contagion
The process by which emotions are transferred from one person to another.

My First Flame

Ana Blazic Pavlovic/Shutterstock.com

To flame, according to *Que's Computer User's Dictionary*, is "to lose one's self-control and write a message that uses derogatory, obscene, or inappropriate language."

My flame arrived on a windy Friday morning. I got to work at 9, and, as usual, I checked my e-mail. I saw I had a message from a technology writer who I knew by name only. I had recently published a piece about Bill Gates and as I opened his e-mail I was expecting to get feedback from a colleague. Instead, I got:

Crave this, a**hole: Listen, you toadying dips**t scumbag . . . remove your head from your rectum long enough to look around and notice that real reporters don't fawn over their subjects, pretend that their subjects are making some sort of special contact with them, or, worse, curry favour by telling their subjects how great the a**-licking profile is going to turn out and then brag in print about doing it.

I felt cold. The insults, being premeditated, were more forceful than insults spoken in the heat of the moment.

No one had ever said something like this to me before. In any other medium, these words would be, literally, unspeakable. The guy couldn't have said this to me on the phone, because I would have hung up. He couldn't have said it to my face, because I wouldn't have let him finish. I suppose the guy could have written me a nasty letter but he would have thought twice while he was addressing the envelope. But the nature of e-mail is that you don't think twice. You write and send.

What would Emily Post advise me to do? Flame the dips**t scumbag right back? I did spend most of that

(Continued)

Friday in front of the screen composing the mostly vile insults I could dream up—words I have never spoken to another human being, and would never speak in any other medium, but which I found easy to type into the computer. I managed to restrain myself from sending my reply until I got home and asked my wife to look at it. She had the good sense to be horrified.

I asked [computer expert John Norstad] to look at it. He said, "My 13-year-old daughter is a Pearl Jam fan, and the other night she asked me if there might be some Pearl Jam stuff on the net. So we logged on and looked around, and we were able to download some Pearl Jam posters, some music, some song lyrics—really neat stuff. But then we came to the Pearl Jam newsgroup, and there was a really terrible flame war going on in there. People were saying really awful things to each other, things I was embarrassed to be sitting next to my daughter reading . . . Terrible things. After a while, my daughter looked over at me and asked, 'Daddy, do these people have a life?' And I said, 'No, darling, most of them don't have a life.'"

John Seabrook

Courtesy of the author. Originally published in *The New Yorker*.

Most of us recognize the degree to which emotions are "infectious." A calm person can leave us feeling peaceful and a grouch can ruin our sunny mood. This process occurs quickly and with very little apparent verbal communication.[60] In one study, two volunteers completed a survey that identified their moods. Afterward, they sat quietly, facing each other, for a two-minute period, supposedly waiting for the researcher to return. Then they completed another emotional survey which indicated that this brief exposure resulted in the less expressive partner's moods coming to resemble the moods of the more expressive one. Another study indicated that the emotional responses of dating couples and college roommates become dramatically similar in just a few minutes.[61] If an expressive communicator can shape another person's emotions with so little input in such a short time, it's easy to understand how "infectious" emotions can be with prolonged contact.

LO3
Guidelines for Expressing Emotions

People who know how to express their emotions are healthier, and underexpression of feelings can lead to serious health risks such as cancer, asthma, and heart disease.[62] However, *overly* expressive people also suffer physiologically. When people lash out verbally, their blood pressure jumps between 20 and 100 points.[63] The key to health, then, is to learn how to express emotions *constructively*.

Expressing emotions effectively can also improve relationships.[64] For instance, people who show their affection toward others tend to be happier, more self-assured, and comfortable with interpersonal closeness. While showing every feeling of boredom, fear, anger, or frustration could get you into trouble, withholding emotions can be personally frustrating and can keep relationships from growing and prospering. The following suggestions can help you decide when and how to express your emotions.

"Honey, let's play 'emoting.' It will give you an edge in business."

J.P. Rini The New Yorker Collection/The Cartoon Bank

Recognize Your Feelings

Some people are acutely aware of their emotional states and use that knowledge to make important decisions.[65] By contrast, people with a low affective orientation are usually unaware of their emotional states and tend to regard feelings as useless or unimportant information.

Beyond being *aware* of one's feelings, it's valuable to be able to *identify* them. College students who can pinpoint negative emotions such as nervousness, anger, sadness, shame, and guilt are better able to manage them.[66] This explains why the ability to distinguish and label emotions is a vital component of emotional intelligence.[67] You can tune in to your feelings by recognizing any physiological changes you may experience. You can also monitor your nonverbal behaviours, your thoughts, and the verbal messages you are sending to others. It's not far from the verbal statement "I hate this!" to the realization that you're angry (or bored, nervous, or embarrassed).

Discussions about Canada's former residential schools by Indigenous individuals still bring up strong emotions.

The Canadian Press/Sean Kilpatrick

Recognize the Difference Between Feeling, Talking, and Acting

Just because you feel a certain way doesn't mean you must always talk about it, and talking about a feeling doesn't mean you must act on it. In fact, people who act out angry feelings actually feel worse than those who experience anger without lashing out.[68]

Understanding the difference between having feelings and acting them out can help you express yourself constructively in tough situations. If, for instance, you recognize that you are upset with a friend, it's possible to explore why you feel so upset. Expressing your feeling ("Sometimes I get so mad at you that I could scream") might open the door to resolving whatever is bothering you. Pretending that nothing is the matter is unlikely to diminish your resentful feelings. Instead, they may contaminate the relationship.

"Any healthy relationship requires fundamental acting skills."

William Haefeli The New Yorker Collection/The Cartoon Bank

Expand Your Emotional Vocabulary

Most people think they're expressing feelings when in fact their statements are counterfeits of emotion. For example, it sounds emotionally revealing to say, "I feel like going to a show," or "I feel we've been seeing too much of each other." But neither statement has any emotional content. In the first sentence, the word *feel* really stands for an intention: "I *want* to go to a show." In the second sentence, the "feeling" is really a thought: "I *think* we've been seeing too much of each other." You can recognize the absence of emotion in each case by adding a genuine word of feeling to it. For instance, "I'm *bored* and I want to go to a show," or "I think we've been seeing too much of each other and I feel *confined*."

Relying on a small vocabulary is as limiting as using only a few terms to describe colours. To say that the ocean in all its moods and the sky with its daily variations are both "blue" tells only a fraction of the story. Likewise, it's overly broad to use a term like *good* or *great* to describe how you feel in situations as different as earning a high grade, finishing a marathon, and hearing the words "I love you" from a special person.

There are several ways to express a feeling verbally:[69]

- By using *single words*: "I'm angry" (or "excited," "depressed," "curious," and so on)
- By describing what's happening to you: "My stomach is tied in knots," "I'm on top of the world"
- By describing what you'd like *to do*: "I want to run away," "I'd like to give you a hug," "I feel like giving up"

Alex Malikov/Shutterstock.com

CHAPTER 4 Emotions: Feeling, Thinking, and Communicating

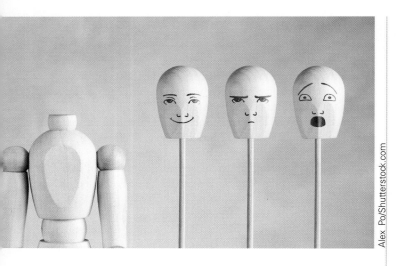
Alex Po/Shutterstock.com

their needs met. To help you express your feelings more precisely, refer to **Table 4.1**.

When expressing your feelings, make sure that both you and your partner understand that your feeling is centred on a specific set of circumstances, not the whole relationship. Instead of saying, "I resent you," say, "I resent it when you don't keep your promises." Rather than, "I'm bored with you," say, "I'm bored when you talk about the economy all the time."

Express Multiple Feelings

As humans, there's a tendency to express only one emotion, or feeling, when we might be experiencing multiple or mixed emotions. For example, you might express anger but overlook the confusion, disappointment, frustration, or embarrassment that preceded it. Recall the example earlier in the chapter where an out-of-town friend was supposed to arrive at a particular time but didn't show up until much later. Most of us would feel relieved to see the friend arrive safe but be angry at him or her for not getting in touch sooner. Thus, we would experience mixed emotions.

Despite the commonness of mixed emotions, we often communicate only one feeling—usually the most negative one. This leaves the other person with little idea of the full range of your feelings. Consider the different reactions you would get by showing all your emotions in, for instance, the example above.

Sometimes communicators inaccurately minimize the strength of their feelings—"I'm a *little* unhappy," or "I'm *pretty* excited." Not all feelings are strong ones—we feel degrees of sadness and joy—but some people tend to discount almost every feeling. Do you?

In other cases, communicators express feelings in a coded manner. Instead of saying, "I'm lonely," they may say something like, "I guess there isn't much happening this weekend, so if you're not busy, why don't you drop by?" This message is so indirect that any feeling may not be recognized. This is why people who send coded messages stand less chance of having their feelings understood and

TABLE 4.1
Common Human Emotions

afraid	concerned	exhausted	hurried	nervous	sexy
aggravated	confident	fearful	hurt	numb	shaky
amazed	confused	fed	hysterical	optimistic	shocked
ambivalent	content	fidgety	impatient	paranoid	shy
angry	crazy	flattered	impressed	passionate	sorry
annoyed	defeated	foolish	inhibited	peaceful	strong
anxious	defensive	forlorn	insecure	pessimistic	subdued
apathetic	delighted	free	interested	playful	surprised
ashamed	depressed	friendly	intimidated	pleased	suspicious
bashful	detached	frustrated	irritable	possessive	tender
bewildered	devastated	furious	jealous	pressured	tense
bitchy	disappointed	glad	joyful	protective	terrified
bitter	disgusted	glum	lazy	puzzled	tired
bored	disturbed	grateful	lonely	refreshed	trapped
brave	ecstatic	happy	loving	regretful	ugly
calm	edgy	harassed	lukewarm	relieved	uneasy
cantankerous	elated	helpless	mad	resentful	up
carefree	embarrassed	high	mean	restless	vulnerable
cheerful	empty	hopeful	miserable	ridiculous	warm
cocky	enthusiastic	horrible	mixed	romantic	weak
cold	envious	hostile	mortified	sad	wonderful
comfortable	excited	humiliated	neglected	sentimental	worried

Consider When and Where to Express Your Feelings

The first flush of a strong feeling isn't usually the best time to speak out. If a noisy neighbour wakes you, storming over to complain could result in saying things you'll regret later. It's probably wiser to wait until you have thought through exactly what you want to say and how you want to say it. "Imagining interactions" in advance of actual conversations enhances relationships by allowing communicators to rehearse the message and consider how others might respond.[70] Being rushed, tired, or distracted by another matter are good reasons to postpone the visit. Dealing with your emotions can sometimes take a great amount of time and effort, and fatigue or distraction will make it difficult to follow through in the manner you've stated. Further, it's important to ensure that the recipient of your message is ready to hear you out before you begin.

There are also cases where you may choose not to express your feelings verbally. In such cases, writing out your thoughts and feelings can have mental, physical, and emotional benefits.[71] One study found that writing about feelings of affection can actually reduce the writer's cholesterol level.[72]

Accept Responsibility for Your Feelings

It's important to ensure that your language reflects that you are responsible for your feelings.[73] Instead of saying, "You make me angry," say, "I'm getting

liannelin/iStock/Thinkstock

angry." Instead of saying, "You hurt my feelings," say, "I feel hurt when you do that." People don't make us like or dislike them, and believing that they do denies the responsibility that we have for our own emotions.

Be Mindful of the Communication Channel

The different channels we use to communicate make a difference in how others interpret our messages, especially when it comes to expressing emotions.

Given the number of communication channels available today, deciding when to use mediated channels—

In Real Life

Guidelines for Emotional Expression

After a long and frustrating search, Logan thinks he has found the ideal job that he wants and needs. The interview went well. As Logan was leaving, the interviewer said he was "very well qualified" and promised "You'll be hearing from us soon." That conversation took place almost two weeks ago, and Logan hasn't heard a word from the company.

The two transcripts below reflect very different ways of responding to this difficult situation. The first one ignores and the second one follows the Guidelines for Expressing Emotions described in this chapter. In each, Logan begins by *ruminating* about the employer's failure to get in touch as promised.

Ignoring Guidelines for Expressing Emotions

Logan doesn't explicitly recognize a single emotion he is experiencing, let alone any mixed emotions. Rather than accepting responsibility for his own feelings, he blames the employer for "driving me crazy."	"I can't believe those inconsiderate idiots! Who do they think they are, promising to call soon and then doing nothing? They're driving me crazy."
Logan jumps to the conclusion that a job offer isn't forthcoming, and lashes out without considering any alternatives.	"I give up. Since they aren't going to hire me, I'm going to call that interviewer and let her know what a screwed-up company they're running. I'll probably get her voice mail, but that's even better: That way I can say what's on my mind without getting nervous or being interrupted. They have no right to jerk me around like this, and I'm going to tell them just that." *(Angrily dials phone)*

Following Guidelines for Expressing Emotions

Logan identifies his mixture of feelings as a starting point for deciding what to do.	"I'm mad at the company for not keeping in touch like they promised. I'm also confused about whether I'm as qualified as I thought I was, and I'm starting to worry that maybe I didn't do as well in the interview as I thought. I'm also sorry I didn't ask her for a more specific time than 'soon.' And I'm really unsure about whether to give up, wait for them to call me, or reach out to the company and ask what's going on."
He recognizes the difference between what he would like to do (chew out the interviewer) and what is more appropriate and effective.	"If I'm not going to get the job, I'd like to chew out that interviewer for promising to call. But that would probably be a bad idea—burning my bridges, as my family would say."
Logan uses a perception check and considers sharing his feelings with the employer in a non-blaming way. He deliberately considers when and how to express himself, choosing e-mail as the best channel to achieve his goals.	"Maybe I'll call her and say something like 'I'm confused. You said at the interview that I'd hear from you soon, but it's been almost two weeks now with no word.' I could ask whether I misunderstood (although I doubt that), or whether they need some more information from me. Let me think about that overnight. If the idea still sounds good in the morning, I'll call them."
Having decided to e-mail the employer, Logan could use the face saving methods described in Chapter 9 to compose his message. He could begin by speaking positively about his continued interest in the company, then raise his concern about not having heard from them, and then close by saying that he's looking forward to hearing back from them.	"Actually, an e-mail would be better. I could edit my words until they're just right, and an e-mail wouldn't put the interviewer on the spot like a phone call would."

such as e-mail, instant messaging, cellphones, social media sites, PDAs, and blogging—calls for a level of analysis that wasn't required in the past.[74] For instance, is voice mail an appropriate way to end a relationship? Is it acceptable to use CAPITAL LETTERS in a blog to express displeasure? If you're excited about some good news, should you tell your family and friends in person before posting it on Facebook? When young couples have babies these days, there's a trend to ask friends and family not to put it on Facebook until the proud parents are ready to go public.

Most people recognize that channel selection depends in part on the kind of message they're sending. However, in one survey, students said they would have little trouble expressing positive messages in person but preferred mediated channels for negative messages.[75] So much for the face-to-face breakup.

"Flaming" is an extreme example of how social-mediated channels lend themselves to expressing negative emotions. The kind of civility that most people accept as appropriate in other communication channels doesn't seem to hold on the Internet. Before saying something you may later regret, it's worth remembering the principle that communication is irreversible. Once you hit the Send button, you cannot retract an emotional outburst.

LO4
Managing Difficult Emotions

Although feeling and expressing many emotions adds to the quality of interpersonal relationships, not all feelings are beneficial.

Facilitative and Debilitative Emotions

There are two types of emotions: **facilitative emotions** are positive and contribute to effective functioning. **Debilitative emotions** keep us from relating effectively

and thus, they can have a negative impact on us.

One major difference between the two types is their ***intensity***. For instance, a certain amount of anger or irritation can be constructive and provide that extra "oomph" to improve unsatisfying conditions. Rage, on the other hand, usually makes matters worse, as in the case of "road rage."[76] The same holds true for fear. A little nervousness before an important athletic contest or job interview energizes you and improves your performance (mellow athletes or prospective employees usually don't do well).[77] But total terror is something else.

Not surprisingly, debilitative emotions like communication apprehension can lead to a variety of problems in personal, business, educational, and even medical settings.[78] When people become anxious, they often speak less, and when they do manage to speak up, they're not as effective as their more confident counterparts.[79]

A second characteristic that distinguishes debilitative feelings from facilitative ones is ***duration***. Feeling depressed after a relationship breakup or the loss of a job is natural, but spending the rest of your life grieving your loss accomplishes nothing. In the same way, staying angry at someone

Facilitative emotions Emotions that contribute to effective functioning.

Debilitative emotions Emotions that prevent a person from functioning effectively.

Difficult emotions can spoil the quality of a relationship.

© Blend Images/Superstock

The lyrics of Dan Mangan's popular song "Basket" offer an array of relational emotions that span a lifetime from early adulthood into old age.

Redferns/Getty

CHAPTER 4 Emotions: Feeling, Thinking, and Communicating

for a long time is just as punishing to you as it is to the wrong-doer. Social scientists call this **rumination**: dwelling persistently on negative thoughts that, in turn, intensify negative feelings. Rumination can increase feelings of sadness, anxiety, and depression,[80] and "ruminaters" are more likely to lash out with displaced aggression at innocent bystanders.[81]

As you are probably aware, many debilitative emotions involve communication. Below are some examples.

> I left my boyfriend when I came to university. I was so lonesome and unhappy that I was a terrible roommate.
>
> I got so frustrated with my critical boss that I told him what a horrible manager he was and walked out. Now I'm afraid to list him as a reference and I'm scared that my tantrum will prevent me from getting a job.
>
> I've had ongoing problems with my family and sometimes I get so frustrated that I can't study or even sleep.

In the following pages you will learn a method for dealing with debilitative feelings in a way that will improve your effectiveness as a communicator.

Sources of Debilitative Emotions

For most people, feelings seem to have a life of their own. You wish you could feel calm when approaching strangers, yet your voice quivers. You try to appear confident when asking for a raise, yet your eye twitches nervously. Where do feelings and indications of feelings like these come from?

Rumination
Dwelling persistently on negative thoughts that, in turn, intensify negative feelings.

Self-talk
The process of thinking. On some level, self-talk occurs as a person interprets another's behaviour.

Physiology

Some debilitative feelings come from communication traits like shyness, aggressiveness, and assertiveness which are rooted in biology. But, as we noted in Chapter 2, biology isn't destiny. Other debilitative feelings like flight or fight are controlled by the amygdala (uh-MIG-duh-lah). It acts as a kind of sentinel and, in a split second, it can scan our every experience looking for threats. It can trigger a flood of physiological responses from a speeding heart to an elevated blood pressure to preparing the muscles to act.[82] While this is very useful when there are real physical dangers, it can be annoying in social situations where no threat exists. This is where clear thinking can prevent overacting.

Emotional Memory

Emotional memory kicks in when seemingly harmless events trigger a debilitative feeling if they bear even a slight resemblance to troublesome experiences from the past. For example:

> Ever since being teased when he moved to a new elementary school, Abdul has been uncomfortable in unfamiliar situations.
>
> Josh feels a wave of insecurity when he's around a woman who uses the same perfume as a lover who jilted him.

Self-Talk

Finally, some debilitative feelings come from how we label events and situations.

Cognitive psychologists argue that it is not *events* that cause people to feel bad, but rather the *beliefs they hold* about these events. As discussed earlier in the chapter, *reappraisal* involves changing our thoughts to help manage our emotions.

Albert Ellis, who developed an approach to reappraisal called *rational emotive therapy*, provides an example. If you were walking by a friend's house and that person stuck his head out the window and called you a string of vile names, you would probably feel hurt and upset. But if your friend was living in a mental health facility and did the same thing, your reactions or feelings would be different. Perhaps you would be sad for your friend. The

difference in your feelings has to do with your thinking. In the first instance, you might think that your friend is very angry with you or that you had done something terribly wrong. In the second case, you would probably assume that your friend was having a psychotic episode and you would be more apt to feel sympathetic.

This example illustrates that the way people *interpret* events during the process of self-talk determines their feelings.[83] Thus, the model for emotions looks like this:

Event	Thought (Self-talk)	Feeling
Being called names	"I've done something wrong."	hurt, upset
Being called names	"My friend must be sick."	concern, sympathy

The same principle applies in more common situations. The words "I love you" can be interpreted as a genuine expression of deep affection, or they might be decoded in a variety of other ways: for example, as an attempt at manipulation, a sincere but mistaken declaration uttered in a moment of passion, or a way to make the recipient feel better. One study revealed that women are more likely than men to regard expressions of love as genuine statements.[84] It's easy

Fallacies
Debilitative feelings that come from accepting irrational thoughts.

Fallacy of perfection
The irrational belief that a worthwhile communicator should be able to handle every situation with complete confidence and skill.

Carol and Mike Werner/Photolibrary/Getty Images

Most emotions come from the way we think. When thoughts are irrational, unwelcome emotions can interfere with effective communication.

to imagine how different interpretations of a statement like "I love you" can lead to different emotional reactions:

Event	Thought (Self-talk)	Feeling
Hearing "I love you"	"This is a genuine statement."	delight (perhaps)
Hearing "I love you"	"S/he's just saying this to manipulate me."	anger

---

Invitation to Insight

Talking to Yourself

You can better understand how your thoughts shape your feelings by completing the following steps:

1. Take a few minutes to listen to the inner voice you use when thinking. Close your eyes now and listen to it . . . Did you hear the voice? Perhaps it was saying, "What voice? I don't have any voice . . ." Try again, and pay attention to what the voice is saying.

2. Now think about the following situations and imagine how you would react in each. How would you interpret them with your inner voice? What feelings would follow from each interpretation?
   a. While sitting on a bus, in class, or on the street, you notice an attractive person sneaking glances at you.
   b. During a lecture, your professor asks the class, "What do you think about this?" and looks toward you.
   c. You are telling friends about your vacation, and one yawns.
   d. You run into a friend on the street and ask how things are going. "Fine," she replies and rushes off.

3. Now recall three recent times when you felt a strong emotion. For each one, recall the activating event and then the interpretation that led to your emotional reaction.

Irrational Thinking and Debilitative Emotions

We can understand debilitative emotions by examining our self-talk. Debilitative feelings that come from accepting irrational thoughts are called **fallacies**. These lead to illogical conclusions and, in turn, to debilitating feelings. They are so powerful because we are usually unaware of such thoughts.[85] However, when students discuss the following fallacies they come to realize just how widespread irrational thinking really is. As you read, try to select the three fallacies that are most common among your friends.

1. The Fallacy of Perfection

The **fallacy of perfection** is the irrational belief that worthwhile communicators should be able to handle every situation with complete confidence and skill.

If you accept this belief, you'll probably assume that people won't appreciate you unless you are perfect. Admitting mistakes, saying, "I don't know," and expressing feelings of uncertainty may seem like social defects, and therefore you may be tempted to try to *appear* perfect. But the costs of such deception are high. Such performances use so much psychological energy that the approval is less enjoyable.

Subscribing to the myth of perfection diminishes self-esteem. How can you act like yourself when you think that you don't measure up to the way you ought to be? Accepting the idea that you don't have to be perfect is very liberating. Then you can acknowledge that

Like everyone else, you sometimes have a hard time expressing yourself.
Like everyone else, you make mistakes from time to time, and there is no reason to hide this.
You are honestly doing the best you can to realize your potential, to become the best person you can be.

2. The Fallacy of Approval

The **fallacy of approval** is based on the notion that it is vital to get the approval of virtually everyone! Clearly, this is impossible. People who accept this belief go to incredible lengths to seek acceptance, even when they have to sacrifice their own principles and happiness to do so. This can lead to some ludicrous situations:

Feeling nervous because people you really don't like seem to disapprove of you.
Feeling apologetic when others are at fault.
Feeling embarrassed after behaving unnaturally to gain another's approval.

Besides denying your principles and needs, the fallacy of approval implies that others will only respect you if you go out of your way to please them, which simply isn't true. It's difficult to respect people who have compromised important values to gain acceptance or to think highly of people who repeatedly deny their own needs. Striving for universal approval is irrational because it's simply impossible and the price of abandoning your own needs and principles is too high.

3. The Fallacy of Shoulds

The **fallacy of shoulds** is the inability to distinguish between what is and what should be. You can see the difference by imagining a person who is full of complaints about the world:

"There shouldn't be rain on weekends."
"People ought to live forever."
"Money should grow on trees."

Insisting that the unchangeable be changed won't affect reality one bit, but many people engage in this sort of irrational thinking. They confuse *is* with *should*.

"My friend should be more understanding."
"They should be more friendly."
"You should work harder."

The message in each of these cases is that you would *prefer* people to behave differently. However, it's unreasonable to *insist* that the world operate the way you want it to or to feel cheated when things aren't ideal.

Imposing the fallacy of shoulds on yourself leads to misery. Aaron Beck points out some unrealistic self-imposed "shoulds":[86]

"I should be able to find a quick solution to every problem."
"I should never feel hurt; I should always be happy and serene."
"I should always demonstrate the utmost generosity, considerateness, dignity, courage, unselfishness."

Becoming obsessed with "shoulds" results in three consequences. First, such people are seldom satisfied with what they have or who they are. Second, complaining without acting does nothing to change unsatisfying conditions. Third, complaining can build a defensiveness in others, who resent being nagged. For example, it's more effective to say, "I wish you'd be more punctual," instead of "You should be on time."

Looking at Diversity

Keeping Emotions in Check

When a car accident left high school athlete Pam LeJean paralyzed from the chest down, she didn't let negative emotions drown her spirit. In fact, she went on to compete in the 2016 Paralympics in Rio de Janeiro. She shares her journey below.

My name is Pamela LeJean. I was born on a small island called Cape Breton in Northern Nova Scotia. I was an elementary, junior high, and high school athlete and very close to my family. In my senior year of high school I was hurt in a car accident and was told I would never walk again. That sucked. But I learned to drive again, I graduated from high school with my friends, on time, with honours, and went on to do the same in University. I started a grown-up life, I moved a few hours away to Halifax on my own, did motivation talks at schools, got a great dog. But I couldn't find that thing … that mystery thing that gave me passion that sport used to give me in my "walkin' days" as an adolescent. Before I really realized it, I'd been searching for 10 years, fruitlessly! The realization came when a child from a classroom I was talking to asked, outright "What do you do now that you like as much?" I thought, "I gotta shake this kid! He's onto me! Lie, bitch! Lie!" Kids aren't stupid and I didn't fool that one. Who knows how many I thought I'd fooled in the past. All of 'em, I guess. I still don't remember what I said to that kid, but the truth was much worse. It was nothing. I did nothing I liked as much as I used to. Not one thing. TV. Maybe? Kind of sad. "Ya know, that DVR is keen!" Ugh. Fix this! So my mission was pretty clear. I thought I was too high of an injury to play sports, my balance is terrible! It's like sitting on a basketball. But after that, I HAD to try! I went to a wheelchair basketball game and asked the coach if I could come by and get involved. I played and

Reprinted with permission from The Chronicle Herald.

practiced hard for a year, and it was the best year of my life! Until this year happened.

I wasn't able to keep training for basketball without activating previous shoulder injuries through pushing. It was a constant battle. My personal trainer, noticing my rather impressive wingspan and everyday struggle suggested we go into the gymnasium and throw some indoor discus, and it was an immediate game-changer. I love basketball, but switched to throwing and haven't looked back! It was a necessary step.

I've never trained this hard or have been so dedicated and focused in my entire life. Realizing that I am able to compete in a sport I love after thinking I couldn't for so long after my injury is like being given another second chance in my life! It's like when you think you've lost your favourite shirt but you find it again after searching for forever. But it's about a million times better than that feeling….

Source: Global Wheelchair Athletics, http://globalwheelchairathletics .com/athlete-bio/pamela-le-jean. Reproduced by permission of Ueli Albert and Pamela LeJean.

4. The Fallacy of Overgeneralization

The **fallacy of overgeneralization** consists of two types. The first is *generalizing* from a limited amount of evidence. For instance,

> "I'm so stupid! I can't even figure out how to install this new streaming device."
> "Some friend I am! I forgot my best friend's birthday."

In such cases, we focus on a small shortcoming as if it represented the entire situation and we ignore any positive attributes.

A second type of overgeneralization occurs when we *exaggerate* shortcomings:

> "You *never* listen to me."
> "You're *always* late."

Fallacy of overgeneralization
Irrational beliefs in which conclusions (usually negative) are based on limited evidence or exaggerated shortcomings.

Still Alice (2014), Rated PG13

Alice Howland (Julianne Moore) is a popular linguistics professor who has been diagnosed with early onset Alzheimer's disease. She encounters a whole realm of emotions as she struggles to stay in touch with who she once was for as long as she can. Of course, she is eventually forced to leave teaching as the disease becomes more evident to students and faculty alike. Not only does Alice grapple with terror, confusion, hurt, forlornness, impatience, helplessness, humiliation, and a host of other painful feelings, so too does her family suffer emotionally as they witness her decline.

© Sony Pictures Classics/courtesy Everett Collection/The Canadian Press

Absolute statements like these are almost always false and lead to discouragement or anger. It's better to replace overgeneralizations with more accurate messages such as:

"You often don't listen to me."
"You've been late three times this week."

5. The Fallacy of Causation

The **fallacy of causation** is based on the irrational belief that emotions are caused by others rather than by our own self-talk.

This fallacy causes trouble in two ways. The first is when people become overly cautious about communicating because they don't want to "cause" pain or inconvenience for others. For example,

Visiting friends or family out of a sense of obligation rather than a genuine desire to see them.
Keeping quiet when another person's behaviour is bothering you.
Pretending to be interested in a speaker when you're late for an appointment.

There's certainly no excuse for intentionally saying things to hurt someone, and sometimes you'll choose to inconvenience yourself to make life easier for someone. However, it's an overstatement to say that you cause others' feelings. More accurately, they *respond* to your behaviour with their own feelings. For example, you wouldn't say that you make others fall in love with you. But you could say that you act in a way that someone might fall in love with you. In the same way, it's incorrect to say that you *make* others angry, upset—or happy, for that matter. It's more fitting to say that others create their own responses to your behaviour.

The fallacy of causation also operates when we believe that others cause *our* emotions. While it can seem as if they do, the same actions that can make you happy or unhappy on one day have little effect at other times. The insult that affected your mood strongly yesterday leaves you unaffected today. Why? Because in the latter case you attached less importance to either. It's your reaction, not their actions, that determines how you feel.

6. The Fallacy of Helplessness

The **fallacy of helplessness** suggests that satisfaction in life is determined by forces beyond your control. People who see themselves as victims make statements like

"I was born with a shy personality. There's nothing I can do about that."
"I can't tell my boss that she's putting too many demands on me. I might lose my job."

These statements are mistaken in that there are many things you can do if you really want to. Most "can't" statements can be rephrased as "won't" statements ("I can't tell her what I think" becomes "I won't be honest with her") or as "don't know how" statements ("I can't have an interesting conversation" becomes "I don't know what to say"). Once these inaccurate "can'ts" are rephrased, it becomes clear that they're either a matter of choice or something that calls for your action, and thus different from saying you're helpless.

The self-fulfilling prophecy is also at work with this type of attitude. Believing that there is only one way to look at something will be followed by consistent behaviours. On the other hand, acknowledging that there is a way to change puts the responsibility for your predicament on *your* shoulders. Don't sell yourself short.

Fallacy of causation
The irrational belief that emotions are caused by others and not by the person who experiences them.

Fallacy of helplessness
The irrational belief that satisfaction in life is determined by forces beyond one's control.

7. The Fallacy of Catastrophic Expectations

Communicators who subscribe to the **fallacy of catastrophic expectations** assume that if something bad can possibly happen, it will. Typical catastrophic expectations include

> "If I invite them to the party, they probably won't come."
> "If I speak up to try to resolve a conflict, things will probably get worse."
> "If I apply for the job I want, I probably won't be hired."

After you start expecting catastrophic consequences, the self-fulfilling prophecy begins to build. One study revealed that people who believed that their romantic partners would not change for the better were more likely to behave in ways that contributed to the breakup.[87]

While it's naive to assume that all your interactions with others will meet with success, it's just as naive to assume that they won't. To escape the fallacy of catastrophic expectations, think about the consequences if you don't communicate successfully. It's not as bad as you think. So what if you don't get the response you want? Are these matters really *that* serious?

"So the prince and the princess lowered their expectations and lived reasonably contentedly forever after."

© 2013 Steve Delmonte

Imagining the worst possible outcome can create unnecessary debilitative feelings.

Finally, it's important to realize that thinking rationally won't completely eliminate debilitative emotions. Some debilitative emotions are very rational, such as grief over someone's death or euphoria over a new job. But thinking rationally can eliminate many debilitative emotions from your life.

> **Fallacy of catastrophic expectations**
> The irrational belief that the worst possible outcome will probably occur.

Minimizing Debilitative Emotions

Social scientists and therapists have developed several simple yet effective strategies to help you cut down on the self-defeating thinking that leads to debilitative emotions.[88]

1. ***Monitor your emotional reactions.*** The first step is to recognize your debilitative emotions. One way to recognize emotions is through your physiological stimuli: butterflies in the stomach, racing heart, etc. Although such stimuli might signify food poisoning, more likely they are symptoms of a strong emotion. Also look for behaviours that might suggest your feelings: stomping instead of walking normally, speaking in a sarcastic tone of voice, or just being unusually quiet, for example.

   While it may seem strange to look for emotions, we often suffer from debilitative emotions without even noticing them. For example, after a

Invitation to Insight

How Irrational Are You?

1. Return to the situations described in the exercise "Talking to Yourself." Examine each one to see whether your self-talk contains any irrational thoughts.

2. Keep a two- or three-day diary of your debilitative emotions. Are any of them based on irrational thinking? Examine your conclusions and see if you repeatedly use any of the fallacies described in the preceding section.

3. Take a class poll to see which fallacies are most "popular." Also discuss what subjects seem to stimulate most of this irrational thinking (e.g., schoolwork, dating, jobs, family).

emotions. Once you get in the habit of recognizing your internal monologue, you'll be able to identify your thoughts quickly and easily.

4. ***Reappraise your irrational beliefs.*** Reappraising your irrational beliefs means stepping back and trying to see the errors in your thinking process. Use the list of irrational fallacies discussed earlier to discover which of your internal statements are inaccurate.

trying day, you might find yourself frowning and realize that you've been wearing that mask without realizing it.

2. ***Note the activating event.*** Once you're aware of how you're feeling, the next step is to figure out what triggered your response. Sometimes it is obvious, like being accused unfairly (or fairly) of foolish behaviour or being rejected by someone. In other cases, however, the activating event isn't so apparent. Sometimes it's a series of incidents that triggers a debilitative emotion. The best way to identify activating events is to notice the circumstances in which you have debilitative feelings. You may find that they occur when you're around *specific* people or certain *types of individuals* or in certain *settings.*

3. ***Record your self-talk.*** This is the point at which you link the activating event to the feeling. To eliminate debilitative emotions, it's important to write down your self-talk. Putting your thoughts on paper helps you see whether they actually make any sense.

   While monitoring your self-talk might be difficult at first, you'll soon find that you will be able to identify the thoughts that lead to your debilitative

SKILL BUILDER

Rational Thinking

1. Return to the diary of irrational thoughts you recorded in this chapter's "Invitation to insight." Examine the self-talk in each case and write a more rational interpretation of the event.

2. Now try to think rationally on the spot by acting out the scenes listed in step 4 below. You'll need three players: a subject, the subject's "little voice"—his or her thoughts—and a second party.

3. Have the subject and second party interact while the "little voice" stands behind the subject and says what the subject is probably thinking. For example, in a scene where the subject asks an instructor to reconsider a low grade, the little voice might say, "I hope I haven't made things worse by bringing this up. Maybe he'll lower the grade after rereading the test. I'm an idiot! Why didn't I keep quiet?"

4. Whenever the little voice expresses an irrational thought, the observers who are watching the skit should call out, "Foul." Stop the action to discuss the irrational thought and suggests a more rational line of self-talk. Then, replay the scene with the little voice speaking in a more rational way.

   Here are some scenes. You can invent others as well.
   a. Two people are just beginning their first date.
   b. A potential employee has just begun a job interview.
   c. A teacher or boss criticizes the subject for being late.
   d. A student runs across an instructor in the market.

Replacing self-defeating self-talk with more constructive thinking improves self-confidence and relational communication.[89] Nonetheless, this approach has triggered several objections from some readers. For example

"The rational emotive approach sounds like nothing more than trying to talk yourself out of feeling bad." This accusation is totally correct. If we talk ourselves into feeling bad, why not talk ourselves out of feeling bad, especially when such feelings are based on irrational thoughts?

"The kind of reappraising we just read sounds phony and unnatural. I don't talk to myself in sentences and paragraphs." There's no need to dispute your irrational beliefs in any special literary style. The important thing is to understand what thoughts led you into your debilitative emotions so you can reappraise them clearly.

"This approach is too cold and impersonal. It seems to aim at turning people into cold-blooded, calculating, emotionless machines." This is simply not true. Rational thinkers can still dream, hope, and love—there's nothing necessarily irrational about feelings like these. Even basically rational people indulge in a bit of irrational thinking once in a while. But they usually know what they're doing.

This technique promises too much. There's no chance I could rid myself of all unpleasant feelings, however nice that might be." We can answer this by assuring you that rational emotive thinking probably won't totally solve your emotional problems. However, it can reduce their number, intensity, and duration. This method is not the answer to all your problems, but it can make a significant difference—which is not a bad accomplishment.

Finally, you may wish to talk to others about certain situations and emotions you encounter. Often the experience of "telling someone your story" or attempting to explain how and why you feel a certain way can actually give you insight into what is happening to you. Further, a trusted listener may also provide another perspective as well as some sound advice.

In Real Life

Rational Thinking in Action

The following scenarios demonstrate how the rational thinking method applies in everyday challenges. Notice that thinking rationally doesn't eliminate debilitative emotions. Instead, it helps keep them in control, making effective communication more possible.

Situation 1: Meeting My Girlfriend's Family

Activating Event

Tracy and I are talking about marriage—maybe not soon, but eventually. Her family is very close, and they want to meet me. I'm sure I'll like them, but I'm not sure what they will think about me. I was married once before, at a young age. It was a big mistake, and it didn't last. Furthermore, I was laid off two months ago, and I'm between jobs. The family is coming to town next week, and I am very nervous about what they will think of me.

Beliefs and Self-Talk

1. They've *got* to like me! This is a close family, and I'm doomed if they think I'm not right for Tracy.

2. No matter how sensibly I act, all they'll think about is my divorce and unemployment.

3. Maybe the family is right. Tracy deserves the best, and I'm certainly not that!

Reappraising Irrational Beliefs

1. The family's approval is definitely important. Still, my relationship with Tracy doesn't depend on it. She's already said that she's committed to me, no matter what they think. The sensible approach is to say I want their approval, but I don't need it.

2. I'm expecting the absolute worst if I think that I'm doomed no matter what happens when we meet. There is a chance that they will dislike me, but there's also a chance that things will work out fine. There's no point in dwelling on catastrophes.

3. Just because I've had an imperfect past doesn't mean I'm wrong for Tracy. I've learned from my past mistakes, and I am committed to living a good life. I know I can be the kind of husband she deserves, even though I'm not perfect.

(Continued)

Situation 2: Dealing with Annoying Customers

Activating Event

I work in a shopping mall that swarms with tourists and locals. Our company's reputation is based on service, but lately I've been losing my patience with the customers. The store is busy from the second we open until we close. Many of the customers are rude, pushy, and demanding. Others expect me to be a tour guide, restaurant reviewer, medical consultant, and even a babysitter. I feel like I'm ready to explode.

Beliefs and Self-Talk

1. I'm sick of working with the public. People are really obnoxious!

2. The customers should be more patient and polite instead of treating me like a servant.

3. This work is driving me crazy! If I keep working here, I'm going to become as rude as the customers.

4. I can't quit. I could never find another job that pays this well.

Reappraising Irrational Beliefs

1. It's an overgeneralization to say that *all* people are obnoxious. Actually, most of the customers are fine. Some are even very nice. About 10 percent of them cause most of the trouble. Recognizing that most people are OK leaves me feeling less bitter.

2. It's true that obnoxious customers *should* be more polite, but it's unrealistic to expect that everybody will behave the way they ought to. After all, it's not a perfect world.

3. By saying that the customers are driving me crazy, I suggest that I have no control over the situation. I'm an adult, and I am able to keep a grip on myself. I may not like the way some people behave, but it's my choice how to respond to them.

4. I'm not helpless. If the job is too unpleasant, I can quit. I probably wouldn't find another job that pays as well as this one, so I have to choose which is more important: money or peace of mind. It's my choice.

Communication in the Workplace

Emotional intelligence has particular application in the workplace and this may account for why employers today are looking to hire individuals who display emotional intelligence. Recruiters are quick to state that emotional intelligence skills are just as, if not more, important than job-related skills.[90] As Mariah DeLeon, vice president of a recruiting firm argues, degrees and on-paper qualifications are nothing if an employee can't work with others. Individuals who demonstrate emotional intelligence are able to work in teams, they adjust well to change, and they are very flexible.[91] They also earn more money![92] This makes sense because they would more likely be promoted.

According to Daniel Goleman, who first described this human attribute, emotional intelligence consists of five dimensions.[93] The first is **self-awareness** where people recognize their strengths and weaknesses and the effect these have on others. Second is **self-regulation** in that they know when (and when not) to reveal their emotions. Plus they are usually resilient and optimistic. The third dimension is **motivation** in that they are self-motivated. The fourth is **empathy** in that they understand others and relate to their concerns. Finally, emotionally intelligent individuals have **people skills** in that they can build rapport quickly and avoid debilitating behaviours such as backstabbing.[94] These characteristics are so important to a successful, happy workplace that both nonprofit organizations and government agencies encourage employees to become more emotionally intelligent. For instance, an article that describes and applies this concept is posted on the Treasury Board of Canada Secretariat website.[95]

Emotional intelligence is especially salient in the helping professions. In nursing, for example, it is vital to good patient care.[96] But it's not easy. Nurses are expected to manage their own emotions which may include

Glow Wellness/Getty Images

disgust, annoyance, or frustration and still recognize and respond to their clients' emotional needs. When nurses identify with or empathize with patients' suffering, those with higher emotional intelligence facilitate the best outcomes.[97] Another challenge is forming relationships and interacting with family members. Given the trend toward shorter hospital stays, nurses are called upon to develop rapport more quickly than in the past.[98]

Emotional intelligence also plays a role in teamwork. Groups that have high emotional intelligence tend to be more cohesive.[99] Canadian researchers at the University of Alberta report that emotionally intelligent nurse leaders have a positive influence on nurse retention, patient care, and patient outcomes.[100]

Masking emotions to promote best outcomes is an emotional intelligence that is used across disciplines. For example, if firefighters don't mask their fear, disgust, and stress, it will impede their ability to help the people whose lives they are trying to save. Emotion management training is therefore vital for new firefighters.[101] Correctional officers described the tension of needing to be "warm, nurturing, and respectful" to inmates while also being "suspicious, strong, and tough." The officers acknowledged that it's taxing to manage competing emotions and juggle conflicting demands.[102]

Finally, the contrast between managing emotions and allowing them to rage out of control is evident in the amount of bullying that goes on today. In fact, the Canada Safety Council (CSC) reports that it is more common than harassment and is encouraging employers to identify bullying as an unacceptable workplace behaviour.[103]

It's interesting that the attributes of emotional intelligence are also communication behaviours that can be learned. You can learn new approaches by considering, adapting, and adding the communication strategies discussed in this text to your communication competency list.

© iStockphoto.com/Stuart Freeman

READY TO STUDY?

IN THE BOOK, YOU CAN:

❏ Rip out the Chapter in Review card at the back of the book to have the key terms and Learning Objectives handy, and complete the quizzes provided (answers are at the bottom of the back page).

ONLINE YOU CAN:

❏ Stay organized and efficient with MindTap—a single destination with all the course material and study aids you need to succeed. Built-in apps leverage social media and the latest learning technology. For example:

    ❏ Listen to the text using ReadSpeaker.

    ❏ Use pre-populated Flashcards as a jump start for review—or you can create your own.

    ❏ You can highlight text and make notes in your MindTap Reader. Your notes will flow into Evernote, the electronic notebook app that you can access anywhere when it's time to study for the exam.

    ❏ Prepare for tests with a variety of quizzes and activities.

Go to **nelson.com/student** to access these digital resources

---

Endnotes

1. S. Planalp, J. Fitness, & B. Fehr (2006). "Emotion in Theories of Close Relationships." In A. L. Vangelisti & D. Perlman (Eds.). *The Cambridge Handbook of Personal Relationships* (pp. 369–384). New York: Cambridge University Press; R. F. Baumeister (2005). *The Human Animal*. New York: Oxford University Press.

2. D. Goleman (1995). *Emotional Intelligence: Why It Can Matter More Than I.Q.* New York: Bantam. See also D. Goleman (2006). *Social Intelligence: The New Science of Human Relationships*. New York: Bantam.

3. A. Carmeli, M. Yitzhak-Halevy, & J. Weisberg (2009). "The Relationship Between Emotional Intelligence and Psychological Wellbeing." *Journal of Managerial Psychology, 24,* 66–78.

4. L. Smith, P. C. Heaven, & J. Ciarrochi (2008). "Trait Emotional Intelligence, Conflict Communication Patterns, and Relationship Satisfaction." *Personality and Individual Differences, 44,* 1314–1325.

5. G. M. Rochman & G. M. Diamond (2008). "From Unresolved Anger to Sadness: Identifying Physiological Correlates." *Journal of Counseling Psychology, 55,* 96–105.

6. J. M. Gottman & N. Silver (1999). *The Seven Principles for Making Marriages Work*. New York: Three Rivers Press.

7. J. A. Stamp & J. I. Monahan (2009). "Alcohol-influenced nonverbal behaviours during discussions about a relationship problem." *Journal of Nonverbal Behaviour, 33,* 193–211.

8. P. Ekman, R. W. Levenson, & W. V. Friesen (September 16, 1983). "Autonomic Nervous System Activity Distinguishes among Emotions." *Science, 221,* 1208–1210.

9. C. L. Kleinke, T. R. Peterson, & T. R. Rutledge (1998). "Effects of Self-Generated Facial Expressions on Mood." *Journal of Personality and Social Psychology, 74,* 272–279.

10. S. Oosterwijk, M. Rotteveel, A. H. Fischer, & U. Hess (2009). "Embodied emotion concepts: How generating words about pride and disappointment influences posture." *European Journal of Social Psychology, 39,* 457–466.

11. S. Valins (1966). "Cognitive Effects of False Heart-Rate Feedback." *Journal of Personality and Social Psychology, 4,* 400–408.

12. P. Zimbardo (1977). *Shyness: What It Is, What to Do about It*. Reading, MA: Addison-Wesley, p. 53.

13. C. R. Berger & K. J. Lee (2011). "Second thoughts, second feelings: Attenuating the impact of threatening narratives through rational reappraisal." *Communication Research, 38,* 3–26.

14. J. C. Wallace, B. D. Edwards, A. Shull, & D. M. Finch (2009). "Examining the Consequences in the Tendency to Suppress and Reappraise Emotions on Task-Related Job Performance." *Human Performance, 22,* 23–43; S. A. Moore, L. A. Zoellner, & N. Mollenholt (2008). "Are Expressive Suppression and Cognitive Reappraisal Associated with Stress-Related Symptoms?" *Behaviour Research and Therapy, 46,* 993–1000; J. B. Nezlek & B. Kuppens (2008).

"Regulating Positive Negative Emotions in Daily Life." *Journal of Personality, 76,* 561–580.

15. R. Plutchik (1980). *Emotion: A Psychoevolutionary Synthesis*. New York: Harper & Row; P. R. Shaver, S. Wu, & J. C. Schwartz (1992). "Cross-Cultural Similarities and Differences in Emotion and its Representation: A Prototype Approach." In M. S. Clark (Ed.). *Emotion* (pp. 175–212). Newbury Park, CA: Sage.

16. P. Ekman (1999). "Basic Emotions." In T. Dalgleish & T. Power (Eds.). *The Handbook of Cognition and Emotion* (pp. 45–60). Sussex, UK: John Wiley & Sons; A. Ortony & T. J. Turner (1990). "What's Basic about Basic Emotions?" *Psychological Review, 97,* 315–331.

17. M. Ferrari & E. Koyama (2002). "Meta-Emotions about Anger and Amae: A Cross-Cultural Comparison." *Consciousness and Emotion, 3,* 197–211.

18. Shaver et al., op. cit.

19. Goleman, op. cit.

20. J. M. Gottman, L. F. Katz, & C. Hooven (1997). *Meta-Emotion: How Families Communicate Emotionally*. Mahwah, NJ: Erlbaum.

21. E. S. Lunkenheimer, A. M. Shields, & K. S. Kortina (2007). "Parental Emotion Coaching and Dismissing in Family Interaction." *Social Development, 16,* 232–248.

22. J. C. McCroskey, V. P. Richmond, A. D. Heisel, & J. L Hayhurst (2004). "Eysenck's Big Three and Communication Traits: Communication Traits as Manifestations of Temperament." *Communication Research Reports, 21,* 404–410; J. J. Gross, S. K. Sutton, & T. V. Ketelaar (1998). "Relations between Affect and Personality: Support for the Affect-Level and Affective-Reactivity Views." *Personality and Social Psychology Bulletin, 24,* 279–288.

23. P. T. Costa & R. R. McCrae (1980). "Influence of Extraversion and Neuroticism on Subjective Well-Being: Happy and Unhappy People." *Journal of Personality and Social Psychology, 38,* 668–678.

24. J. Yen, C. Yen, C. Chen, P. Wang, Y. Chang, & C. Ko (2012). "Social anxiety in online and real-life interaction and their associated factors." *Cyberpsychology, Behaviour, and Social Networking, 15,* 7–12.

25. L. Kelly, R. L. Duran, & J. J. Zolten (2001). "The Effect of Reticence on College Students' Use of Electronic Mail to Communicate with Faculty." *Communication Education, 50,* 170–176. See also B. W. Scharlott & W. G. Christ (2001). "Overcoming Relationship-Initiation Barriers: The Impact of a Computer-Dating System on Sex Role, Shyness, and Appearance Inhibitions." *Computers in Human Behaviour, 11,* 191–204.

26. C. Goddard (2002). "Explicating Emotions across Languages and Cultures: A Semantic Approach." In S. R. Fussell (Ed.). *The Verbal Communication of Emotions*. Mahwah, NJ: Erlbaum.

27. J. L. Tsai, B. Knutson, & H. H. Fung (2006). "Cultural Variation in Affect Valuation." *Journal of Personality and Social Psychology, 90,* 288–307.

28. C. Kotchemidova (2010). "Emotions culture and cognitive constructions of reality." *Communication Quarterly, 58,* 207–234.

29. J. W. Pennebaker, B. Rime, & V. E. Blankenship (1996). "Stereotypes of Emotional Expressiveness of Northerners and Southerners: A Cross-Cultural Test of Montesquieu's Hypotheses." *Journal of Personality and Social Psychology, 70,* 372–380.

30. Ibid., p. 176. See also Gallois, op. cit.

31. S. T. Mortenson (2009). "Interpersonal Trust and Social Skill in Seeking Social Support Among Chinese and Americans." *Communication Research, 36,* 32–53.

32. R. Wilkins & E. Gareis (2006). "Emotion Expression and the Locution 'I Love You': A Cross-Cultural Study." *International Journal of Intercultural Relations, 30,* 51–75.

33. A. Brantley, D. Knox, M. E. Zusman (2002). "When and Why: Gender Differences in Saying 'I Love You' Among College Students." *College Student Journal, 36,* 614–615.

34. L. K. Guerrero, S. M. Jones, & R. R. Boburka (2006). "Sex Differences in Emotional Communication." In K. Dindia & D. J. Canary (Eds.). *Sex Differences and Similarities in Communication,* 2nd ed. Mahweh, NJ: Erlbaum; S. R. Wester, D. L. Vogel, P. K. Pressly, & M. Heesacker (2002). "Sex Differences in Emotion: A Critical Review of the Literature and Implications for Counseling Psychology." *Counseling Psychologist, 30,* 630–652.

35. J. Swenson & F. L. Casmir (1998). "The Impact of Culture-Sameness, Gender, Foreign Travel, and Academic Background on the Ability to Interpret Facial Expression of Emotion in Others." *Communication Quarterly, 46,* 214–230.

36. T. Canli, J. E. Desmond, Z. Zhao, & J. D. E. Gabrieli (2002). "Sex Differences in the Neural Basis of Emotional Memories." *Proceedings of the National Academy of Sciences, 10,* 10,789–10,794.

37. J. Merten (2005). "Culture, Gender and the Recognition of the Basic Emotions." *Psychologia: An International Journal of Psychology in the Orient, 48,* 306–316.

38. See, for example, A. W. Kunkel & B. R. Burleson (1999). "Assessing Explanations for Sex Differences in Emotional Support: A Test of the Different Cultures and Skill Specialization Accounts." *Human Communication Research, 25,* 307–340.

39. D. J. Goldsmith & P. A. Fulfs (1999). "'You Just Don't Have the Evidence': An Analysis of Claims and Evidence in Deborah Tannen's You Just Don't Understand." In M. E. Roloff (Ed.). *Communication Yearbook 22* (pp. 1–49). Thousand Oaks, CA: Sage.

40. E. G. Reuben, R. Pedro, P. Sapienza, & L. Zingales (2012). "The Emergence of Male Leadership in Competitive Environments." *Journal of Economic Behaviour and Organization, 83,* 111–117.

41. K. Floyd (1997). "Communication Affection in Dyadic Relationships: An Assessment of Behaviour and Expectancies." *Communication Quarterly, 45,* 68–80.

42. J. Dunsmore, P. Her, A. Halberstadt, & M. Perez-Rivera (2009). "Parents' beliefs about emotions and children's recognition of parents' emotions." *Journal of Nonverbal Behaviour, 33,* 121–140.

43. D. F. Witmer & S. L. Katzman (1999). "On-Line Smiles: Does Gender Make a Difference in the Use of Graphic Accents?" *Journal of Computer-Mediated Communication, 2,* online. Domain name expired.

44. D. H. Mansson & S. A. Myers (2011). "An initial examination of college students' expressions of affection through Facebook." *Southern Communication Journal, 76,* 155–168.

45. L. R. Brody & J. A. Hall (2008). "Gender and emotion in context." In M. Lewis, J. M. Haviland-Jones, and L. E. Barrett (Eds.). *Handbook 24 emotions,* 3rd edn. (pp. 395–408). New York: Guildford.

46. S. B. Shimanoff (1984). "Commonly Named Emotions in Everyday Conversations." *Perceptual and Motor Skills, 58,* 514. See also J. M. Gottman (1982). "Emotional Responsiveness in Marital Conversations." *Journal of Communication, 32,* 108–120.

47. J. G. Haybe & S. Metts (2008). "Managing the Expression of Emotion." *Western Journal of Communication, 72,* 374–396; S. B. Shimanoff (1988). "Degree of Emotional Expressiveness as a Function of Face-Needs, Gender, and Interpersonal Relationship." *Communication Reports, 1,* 43–53.

48. C. E. Waugh & B. L. Fredericson (2006). "Nice to Know You: Positive Emotions, Self-Other Overlap, and Complex Understanding in the Formation of a New Relationship." *The Journal of Positive Psychology, 1,* 93–106.

49. S. B. Shimanoff (1985). "Rules Governing the Verbal Expression of Emotions between Married Couples." *Western Journal of Speech Communication, 49,* 149–165.

50. S. Duck (1992). "Social Emotions: Showing Our Feelings about Other People." *Human Relationships.* Newbury Park, CA: Sage. See also S. B. Shimanoff (1985). "Expressing Emotions in Words: Verbal Patterns of Interaction." *Journal of Communication, 35,* 16–31.

51. G. Galloway (January 28, 2006). "Smile Mr. Harper, You're Now on Candid Camera." *The Globe and Mail,* A8.

52. L. B. Rosenfeld (1979). "Self-Disclosure Avoidance: Why I Am Afraid To Tell You Who I Am." *Communication Monographs, 46,* 63–74.

53. L. A. Erbert & K. Floyd (2004). "Affectionate Expressions as Face-Threatening Act: Receiver Assessments." *Journal of Social and Personal Relationships, 17,* 230–246.

54. E. Hatfield, J. T. Cacioppo, R. L. Rapson, & K. Oatley (1984). *Emotional Contagion.* Cambridge: Cambridge University Press. See also S. Colino (May 30, 2006). "That Look — It's Catching." *Washington Post,* HE01.

55. Goleman, op. cit., p. 115.

56. A. B. Bakker (2005). "Flow Among Music Teachers and Their Students: The Crossover of Peak Experiences." *Journal of Vocational Behaviour, 66,* 822–833.

57. D. Jiangang, F. Xiucheng, & F. Tianjun (2011). "Multiple emotional contagions in service encounters." *Journal of the Academy of Marketing Science, 39,* 449–466.

58. C. R. Goodman & R. A. Shippy (2002). "Is it Contagious? Affect Similarity Among Spouses." *Aging and Mental Health, 6,* 266–274.

59. P. Belluck (December 5, 2008). "Strangers May Cheer You Up, Study Says." *New York Times,* A12.

60. E. S. Sullins (1991). "Emotional Contagion Revisited: Effects of Social Comparison and Expressive Style on Mood Convergence." *Personality and Social Psychology Bulletin, 17,* 166–174.

61. C. Anderson, D. Keltner, & O. P. John (May 2003). "Emotional Convergence between People over Time." *Journal of Personality and Social Psychology, 84,* 1054–1068.

62. T. DeAngelis (1992). "Illness Linked with Repressive Style of Coping." *APA Monitor, 23*(12), 14–15.

63. A. W. Seigman & T. W. Smith (1994). *Anger, Hostility, and the Heart.* Hillsdale, NJ: Erlbaum.

64. S. Graham, J. Y. Huang, M. S. Clark, & V. S. Helgeson (2008). "The Positives of Negative Emotions: Willingness to Express Negative Emotions Promotes Relationships." *Personality and Social Psychology Bulletin, 34,* 394–406; E. Kennedy-Moore & J. C. Watson (1999). *Expressing Emotion: Myths, Realities, and Therapeutic Strategies.* New York: Guilford.

65. M. Booth-Butterfield & S. Booth-Butterfield (1998). "Emotionality and Affective Orientation." In J. C. McCroskey, J. A. Daly, M. M. Martin, & M. J. Beatty (Eds.). *Communication and Personality: Trait Perspectives.* Creskill, NY: Hampton.

66. L. F. Barrett, J. Gross, T. Christensen, & M. Benvenuto (2001). "Knowing What You're Feeling and Knowing What to Do About It: Mapping the Relation Between Emotion Differentiation and Emotion Regulation." *Cognition and Emotion, 15,* 713–724.

67. D. Grewal & P. Salovey (2005). "Feeling Smart: The Science of Emotional Intelligence." *American Scientist, 93,* 330–339; S. H. Yoo, D. Matsumoto, & J. LeRoux (2006). "The Influence of Emotion Recognition and Emotion Regulation on Intercultural Adjustment." *International Journal of Intercultural Relations, 30,* 345–363.

68. B. J. Bushman, R. F. Baumeister, & A. D. Stack (1999). "Catharsis, Aggression, and Persuasive Influence: Self-Fulfilling or Self-Defeating Prophecies?" *Journal of Personality and Social Psychology, 76,* 367–376.

69. For an extensive discussion of ways to express emotions, see S. R. Fussell (2002). *The Verbal Communication of Emotions.* Mahwah, NJ: Erlbaum.

70. J. M. Honeycutt (2003). *Imagined Interactions: Daydreaming About Communication.* Cresskill, NJ: Hampton Press; J. M. Honeycutt & S. G. Ford (2001). "Mental Imagery and Intrapersonal Communication: A Review of Research on Imagined Interactions (IIs) and Current Developments." *Communication Yearbook, 25,* 315–338.

71. J. Pennebaker (2004). *Writing to Heal: A Guided Journal for Recovering from Trauma and Emotional Upheaval.* Oakland, CA: Harbinger.

72. K. Floyd, A. C. Mikkelson, C. Hesse, & P. M. Pauley (2007). "Affectionate Writing Reduces Total Cholesterol: Two Randomized, Controlled Studies." *Human Communication Research, 33,* 119–142.

73. S. Metts & B. Wood (2008). "Interpersonal Emotional Competence." In M. T. Motley (Ed.). *Studies in Applied Interpersonal Communication* (pp. 267–285). Thousand Oaks, CA: Sage.

74. B. H. Spitzberg (2006). "Preliminary Development of a Model and Measure of Computer-Mediated Communication (CMC) Competence." *Journal of Computer-Mediated Communcation, 11,* article 12, http://jcmc.indiana.edu/vol11/issue2/ spitzberg.html. Accessed September 11, 2006.

75. P. B. O'Sullivan (2000). "What You Don't Know Won't Hurt Me: Impression Management Functions of Communication Channels in Relationships." *Human Communication Research, 26,* 403–431.

76. T. E. Galovski, L. S. Malta, & E. B. Blanchard (2005). *Road Rage: Assessment and Treatment of the Angry, Aggressive Driver.* Washington, DC: American Psychological Association.

77. S. D. Mallalieu, S. Hanton, & G. Jones (2003). "Emotional Labeling and Competitive Anxiety in Preparation and Competition." *Sports Psychologist, 17,* 157–174.

78. J. Bourhis & M. Allen (1992). "Meta-Analysis of the Relationship between Communication Apprehension and Cognitive Performance." *Communication Education, 41,* 68–76.

79. M. L. Patterson & V. Ritts (1997). "Social and Communicative Anxiety: A Review and Meta-Analysis." In B. R. Burleson (Ed.). *Communication Yearbook 20.* Thousand Oaks, CA: Sage.

80. J. M. Smith & L. B. Alloy (2009). "A roadmap to rumination: A review of the definition, assessment, and conceptualization of this multifaceted construct." *Clinical Psychology Review, 29,* 116–128.

81. B. J. Bushman, A. M. Bonacci, W. C. Pedersen, E. A. Vasquez, & N. Miller (2005). "Chewing on It Can Chew You Up: Effects of Rumination on Triggered Displaced Aggression." *Journal of Personality and Social Psychology, 88,* 969–983.

82. J. E. LeDoux (1996). *The Emotional Brain.* New York: Simon and Schuster.

83. D. R. Vocate (1994). "Self-Talk and Inner Speech." In D. R. Vocate (Ed.). *Intrapersonal Communication: Different Voices, Different Minds.* Hillsdale, NJ: Erlbaum.

84. M. Booth-Butterfield & M. R. Trotta (1994). "Attributional Patterns for Expressions of Love." *Communication Reports, 7,* 119–129.

85. J. A. Bargh (1988). "Automatic Information Processing: Implications for Communication and Affect." In H. E. Sypher & E. T. Higgins (Eds.). *Communication, Social Cognition, and Affect.* Hillsdale, NJ: Erlbaum.

86. A. Beck (1976). *Cognitive Therapy and the Emotional Disorders.* New York: International Universities Press.

87. S. Metts & W. R. Cupach (1990). "The Influence of Relationship Beliefs and Problem-Solving Relationships

on Satisfaction in Romantic Relationships." *Human Communication Research, 17,* 170–185.

88. A. Meichenbaum (1977). *Cognitive Behaviour Modification.* New York: Plenum. See also A. Ellis & R. Greiger (1977). *Handbook for Rational-Emotive Therapy.* New York: Springer; M. Wirga & M. DeBernardi (March 2002). "The ABCs of Cognition, Emotion, and Action." *Archives of Psychiatry and Psychotherapy, 1,* 5–16.

89. A. Chatham-Carpenter & V. DeFrancisco (1997). "Pulling Yourself Up Again: Women's Choices and Strategies for Recovering and Maintaining Self-Esteem." *Western Journal of Communication, 61,* 164–187.

90. J.J. Liptak (2005). "Using Emotional Intelligence to Help College Students Succeed in the Workplace," *Journal of Employment Counseling, 42,* 171–187.

91. M. DeLeon (2015, May 8). "The importance of emotional intelligence at work." *Entrepreneur.* http://www .entrepreneur.com/article/245755. Retrieved January 9, 2016.

92. K. Quan (2015, February 15). "People with 'emotional intelligence' tend to make more money." *Canadian Business.* http://www.canadianbusiness.com/innovation/ emotional-intelligence-for-higher-income/. Retrieved January 9, 2016.

93. Goleman, op. cit.

94. DeLeon, op. cit.

95. The Treasury Board of Canada Secretariat (2015, March 31). *Emotional intelligence in the workplace.* http:// www.tbs-sct.gc.ca/chro-dprh/icms-sgic/eiw-iet-eng.asp. Retrieved January 9, 2016.

96. K. B. Smith, J. Profetto-McGrath, & G. G. Cummings (2009). "Emotional Intelligence and Nursing: An Integrative Literature Review." *International Journal of Nursing Studies, 46,* 1624–1636.

97. A. C. H. MacQueen (2004). "Emotional Intelligence in Nursing Work." *Journal of Advanced Nursing, 47,* 101–108.

98. Ibid.

99. J. Quoidbach & M. Hansenne (2009). "The Impact of Trait Emotional Intelligence on Nursing Team Performance and Cohesiveness." *Journal of Professional Nursing, 25,* 23–29.

100. Smith, Profetto-McGrath, & G. G. Cummings, op. cit.

101. C. Scott & K. K. Myers (2005). "The Socialization of Emotion: Learning Emotion Management at the Fire Station." *Journal of Applied Communication Research, 33,* 67–92.

102. K. I. Miller & J. Koesten (2008). "Financial Feeling: An Investigation of Emotion and Communication in the Workplace." *Journal of Applied Communication Research, 36,* 8–32.

103. Canada Safety Council. "Bullying in the Workplace," http://www.safety-council.org/info/OSH/bullies.html. Accessed February 21, 2006.

LANGUAGE
BARRIER AND BRIDGE

LEARNING OUTCOMES

LO1 Analyze a real or potential misunderstanding in terms of semantic or pragmatic rules.

LO2 Describe how principles in the section titled "The Impact of Language" operate in your life.

LO3 Rephrase disruptive statements in less inflammatory terms.

LO4 Recast "it" statements, "but" statements, and "you" statements into statements that reflect your responsibility for the message.

LO5 Analyze how gender and/or cultural differences may affect the quality of interaction.

LO1
Understandings and Misunderstandings

Most people vastly overestimate how well others understand them and how well they understand others.[1] Therefore, we'll begin by looking at the rules we use to understand—and misunderstand—one another's speech.

Communication is an amazing tool that allows us to exchange ideas or abstract thoughts, talk about the past, or just play with one another. Sometimes, however, even simple messages that are clear to you can prove confusing to others. You ask the hairstylist to "take a little off the sides," only to find that her definition of "a little" was equivalent to your description of "a lot." Or you and a friend argue the merits of "feminism" without realizing that you're both working from entirely different definitions. Misunderstandings like these remind us that meanings come from people, not words. It's people's interpretation of words that give them meaning.

These aspects of communication occur because language is *symbolic*—words stand for things, events, etc. The problem lies in the fact that the connection between words and what they represent is arbitrary. For example, there is nothing particularly "fivelike" about the word *five*. It represents the number of fingers on your hand only because English speakers agree that it does. French speakers use *cinq*, German speakers use *fünf*, Inuktitut speakers use *tallimat*, and computer programmers use 00110101 to represent the same concept.

What do you THINK?

I think that men and women use language differently.

1	2	3	4	5	6	7
strongly agree						strongly disagree

Calvin and Hobbes

by Bill Watterson

Even sign language, the nonverbal system used by individuals with hearing loss, is symbolic and not the pantomime it might seem. There are actually hundreds of different sign languages:[2] American Sign Language, British Sign Language, French Sign Language, Danish Sign Language, Chinese Sign Language—even Australian Aboriginal and Mayan sign languages.

We get into trouble with words, or symbols, when we and our conversational partners have different connotations for them. If that were not true, the hairstylist would know exactly what you had meant.

Understanding Words: Semantic Rules

Semantic rules govern the meaning that is assigned to words. You could think of it as the dictionary meaning of words. They make it possible for us to agree that bikes are for riding and books are for reading. Without semantic rules, communication would be impossible because everyone would use symbols in unique ways and there would be no shared meaning.

Semantic misunderstandings arise when people assign different meanings to the same words or use different words to describe the same thing. In the next few pages, we will look at some of the reasons for these common misunderstandings.

Semantic rules
Rules that govern the meaning of language, as opposed to its structure.

Equivocal language
Words, word orders, phrases, or expressions that have more than one commonly accepted definition.

Equivocal Language

Equivocal language consists of words that have more than one commonly accepted definition. For example, a tube could refer to a test tube, a tube of toothpaste, a TV, and so forth. Equivocal language also refers to word orders, or phrases as the following newspaper headlines illustrate:

Family Catches Fire Just in Time
Man Stuck on Toilet; Stool Suspected
20-Year Friendship Ends at the Altar

OH GREAT, THIS BOOK'S IN COW.

© www.CartoonStock.com

© Guy & Rodd/Distributed by Universal Uclick via CartoonStock.com

Some equivocal misunderstandings can be embarrassing. One woman recalled that when she was in Grade 4, the teacher asked the class what a period was. She shared everything she had learned about girls getting their period! Of course, the teacher was referring to the dot at the end of sentences.[3]

Other examples of equivocal statements are more serious. A nurse gave a client a scare when she told him that he "wouldn't be needing" his robe, books, and shaving materials anymore. The patient became exceptionally

"Let me get this straight now. Is what you want to build a jean factory or a gene factory?"

Bob Schochet/Artizans.com

quiet, and when she inquired about his behaviour, the nurse discovered that the poor man thought he was going to die. Instead, the nurse meant he was going home. In another example, Snoop Dogg got into trouble during a CBC interview when he referred to the camera operator as "thick."[4] You probably have several meanings for this word, but Snoop Dogg meant it as a compliment, although it was sexist in nature. According to Urban Dictionary, *thick* refers to "... nice legs, not skinny, with meat on your bones."[5] The camera operator was embarrassed and offended; clearly, she understood the meaning of the term.

The seemingly simple phrase of "I love you" illustrates the various ways in which three simple words can be interpreted. Imagine the troubles that can—and do—arise when people express their love to one another without really knowing what their notion of *love* means. Check out the reading, *A Philosopher's View of Love*.

Because it's difficult to catch and clarify every equivocal statement while speaking, the responsibility for interpreting statements accurately rests in large part with the receiver.

Relative Language

Relative words gain their meaning through comparison. For example, whether or not you attend a large or small institution depends on what the others are like. Alongside a campus like the University of British Columbia with over 30,000 students, your university or college may seem small. But compared with even smaller institutions, it could be quite large. Relative words such as *fast, slow, smart, stupid, short,* or *long* can only be defined through comparison.

Some relative terms are so common that we mistakenly assume they have a clear meaning. But if you try to turn them into something measurable, they become clearer. Health care practitioners have learned that patients often use vague descriptions to describe their pain: "It hurts a little," or "I'm pretty sore." Using a numeric pain scale can give a more precise response—and lead to a better diagnosis.[6] When patients rank their pain from 1 to 10, with 10 being the most severe pain they've ever experienced, the number 7 becomes more concrete and specific than "It aches a bit." This technique can be used to rate anything from the movies to job satisfaction.

When factual and inferential statements are set side by side like this, the difference between them is clear. In everyday conversation, however, we often present our inferences as if they were facts, and in doing so we invite an unnecessary argument. We'll come back to this topic later on in the chapter.

> **Relative words**
> Words that gain their meaning through comparison.

Static Evaluation

"Matt is a nervous guy." "Grace is short-tempered." "You can always count on Jonathan." Statements that contain or imply the word *is* lead to the mistaken assumption that people are consistent and unchanging—an incorrect belief known as **static evaluation**. Instead of labelling Matt as

permanently nervous, it's more accurate to indicate the situations in which he behaves nervously. The same goes for Grace, Jonathan, and the rest of us: We are much more changeable than static.

Abstraction

When it comes to describing problems, goals, appreciation, and requests, we can choose three types of language. We can use **abstract language** that is vague and unclear; we can use **behavioural language** which refers specifically to things that people do or say, or, we could chose a style that is somewhere between abstract and behavioural. **Figure 5.1** illustrates how an event or situation can be described at various levels of specificity and abstraction along an **abstraction ladder**. The ladder's bottom-rung description

Static evaluation
The tendency to view people or relationships as unchanging.

Abstract language
Language that is vague and unclear.

Behavioural language
Language that refers to specific things that people do or say.

Abstraction ladder
A range of more to less abstract terms describing an event or object.

A Philosopher's View of Love

Shakespeare famously said that "love is a many splendored thing." It is also a many 'meaning-ed' thing because we don't always know what someone means when they say they love something. We say we love all sorts of things—ice cream, a car, a favorite singer, God, siblings, parents, or a romantic partner, but do these expressions of love have anything in common?

Plato suggested that they do. They all express a desire for something we don't possess but are moved to do so. Therefore, whether it's a shirt or a person you love, you want them to be yours, or to continue possessing them if they're already yours.

But what makes you love someone or something and hence desire to possess it? Here, we find a wide variety of answers. Some scholars say that your love of something is based on the object's qualities (we love a house because of its location or a person because of his or her looks). Others say that this is shallow love, only applicable to things. We don't, after all, trade in our partners whenever a newer, more striking version comes along. Some argue that love is more like a gift, modeled after God's love of humans—He loves us in spite of, not because of our qualities. This position also misses something because we fall in love with people because of their qualities. Perhaps both views should be combined. We start by falling in love with the person's qualities but that love transcends those qualities so, e.g., it's her particular sense of humor we love, and not humor in general.

While all uses of the word *love* have something in common, our love of things and people differ substantially. Perhaps we don't recognize this because we don't attend to the various meanings of love.

Robert Scott Stewart
Cape Breton University

Courtesy of Scott Stewart

FIGURE 5.1
Abstraction Ladder

More abstract

You need to have a better attitude.

↑ ↓

You need to be more positive.

↑ ↓

You need to complain less.

↑ ↓

You need to complain less about working too hard.

↑ ↓

You need to complain less about working overtime on weekends.

More specific

blue jean images/Getty Images

is concrete and behavioural, and thus is probably clearer than the top-rung's abstract injunction to develop a "better attitude."

We often use higher-level abstractions as verbal shorthand. For instance, we say, "Thanks for helping," instead of using more specific language, such as, "Thanks for washing the dishes, vacuuming the rug, and making the bed." Sometimes politicians use high-level abstraction so they can make speeches without making any specific commitments that may be held against them later.

Although such verbal short-hand can be useful, highly abstract language can also lead to blanket judgments and stereotyping: "Marriage counsellors are worthless," "Mounties are rude," or "Skateboarders are delinquents." Overly abstract expressions like these can cause people to *think* in generalities, ignoring uniqueness. Such stereotyping can injure interpersonal relationships by categorizing and evaluating people in ways that may not be accurate.

To ensure clarity on your part, try to begin with a general statement and follow it with specific examples—in other words, work from high- to low-level abstraction. A boss might say to employees, "While I was away, you did a great job. You dealt with some difficult customers, you got the orders out on time, and you got the interns lined up with their mentors."

cathy
by Cathy Guisewite

SKILL BUILDER

Down-to-Earth Language

You can appreciate the value of non-abstract language by translating the following into behavioural terms.

In each case, describe the person or persons involved, the circumstances in which the behaviour occurs, and the precise behaviours involved. What differences can you expect when you use behavioural descriptions like the ones you have created here?

1. An abstract goal for improving your interpersonal communication (e.g., be more assertive or stop being so sarcastic)
2. A complaint you have about another person (e.g., that he or she is "selfish" or "insensitive")
3. A request for someone to change (e.g., "I wish you'd be more punctual," or "Try to be more positive")
4. An appreciation you could share with another person (e.g., "Thanks for being so helpful," or "I appreciate your patience")

Understanding Structure: Syntactic Rules

Syntactic rules govern the grammar of a language. You can appreciate how syntax contributes to the meaning of a statement by considering two versions of a letter:

Version 1

Dear John:

I want a man who knows what love is all about. You are generous, kind, thoughtful. People who are not like you admit to being useless and inferior. You have ruined me for other men. I yearn for you. I have no feelings whatsoever when we're apart. I can be forever happy—will you let me be yours?

Mary

Syntactic rules
Rules that govern the way symbols can be arranged, as opposed to the meanings of those symbols.

Version 2

Dear John:

I want a man who knows what love is. All about you are generous, kind, thoughtful people, who

are not like you. Admit to being useless and inferior. You have ruined me. For other men, I yearn. For you, I have no feelings whatsoever. When we're apart, I can be forever happy. Will you let me be?

Yours,

Mary

"Be honest with me, Roger. By 'mid-course correction' you mean divorce, don't you."

Leo Cullum The New Yorker Collection/The Cartoon Bank

When Syntactic Rules Are Broken

Sometimes, seemingly ungrammatical speech is simply following a different set of syntactic rules. The English spoken by some members of the black community—a form of speech recently termed by some as Ebonics—treats forms of the verb *to be* differently than does standard English.[1] An ungrammatical expression like "I be angry" is perfectly correct in Ebonics and means "I've been angry for a while." Ebonics might loosely be referred to as pidgin, a speech variety that blends two or more languages in a simplified syntactic structure.

In southeast New Brunswick, many francophones speak a linguistic variation called *chiac*, a combination of French and English. *Chiac* speakers, however,

"experience disparaging remarks concerning their vernacular, and many experience significant hardships in learning 'standard' French in school."[2] Cooperative education placement officers note that *chiac*-speaking students have difficulty securing employment in private and government offices where standard English and/or French is the norm.

1.   M. L. Hecht, M.J. Collier, & S.A. Ribeau (1993). *African American Communication: Ethnic Identity and Cultural Interpretation.* Newbury Park, CA: Sage, pp. 84–89.
2.   R. Allard & R. Landry (1998). "French in New Brunswick." In J. Edwards (Ed.). *Language in Canada.* Cambridge: Cambridge University Press, pp. 202–225.

Semantic rules don't explain why these letters send virtually opposite messages; the different meanings come from the syntax.

Although most of us aren't able to describe the syntactic rules that govern our language, we recognize when they are violated. A humorous example is the way the character Yoda speaks in the *Star Wars* movies. Phrases such as "the dark side are they" or "your father he is" often elicit a chuckle because they bend syntactical norms. Sometimes, however, apparently ungrammatical speech is simply following a different set of syntactic rules, reflecting regional or co-cultural dialects. Linguists believe it is crucial to view such dialects as *different* rather than *deficient* forms of English.[7]

Understanding Context: Pragmatic Rules

Semantic and syntactic problems don't account for all misunderstandings.[8] **Pragmatic rules** help us understand how a message is to be interpreted within a context. To appreciate a different type of communication challenge, imagine a young female's response to her older male boss's statement "You look nice today." She would understand the meaning of the words, and the syntax is clear. The message, however, could have several interpretations: a simple compliment, a come-on, or a suggestion that she didn't normally look nice. If the boss and employee share the same interpretation, their communication would be smooth. If

they interpret the statement differently, potential problems and tensions could arise. This example might also be explained by using the terms *denotative meaning* and *connotative meaning*. Denotative refers to the dictionary meaning of a word; connotative refers to what a particular word or phrase means to you. While the dictionary meaning of the word *nice* might be *pleasant, pleasing, and agreeable,* in the context described

Pragmatic rules
Rules that help communicators understand how messages may be used and interpreted in a given context.

Invitation to Insight

Your Linguistic Rules

To what extent do linguistic rules affect your understanding of and relationships with others? Explore this question by following these steps:

1.   Recall a time when you encountered someone whose speech violated the syntactic rules that you're used to. What was your impression of this person? To what degree was this impression influenced by her or his failure to follow familiar linguistic rules? Consider whether this impression was or was not valid.

2.   Recall at least one misunderstanding that arose when you and another person followed different semantic rules. Use hindsight to consider whether this misunderstanding (and others like it) could be avoided. If semantic misunderstandings can be minimized, explain what approaches might be useful.

3.   Identify at least two pragmatic rules that govern the use of language in one of your relationships. Share these rules with other students. Do they use language in the same way as you and your relational partner?

Double Double, Please: The Language of Tim Hortons

Imagine landing in Canada and going to Tim Hortons for the first time. Upon arriving at "Tim's," "Timmy's," or "Horton's," you notice a peculiar ordering ritual. You hear words like "medium double double," "large triple single," "small French vanilla," "large with milk," "double cup it," "medium tea with milk, bag in," etc. It's almost as if you have to learn a new language just to order a coffee! Here's a quick lesson in this precise, built-for-speed Hortons dialogue.

If you want a large coffee with two creams and two sugars, plus a Boston cream doughnut, you say, "Large double double and a Boston cream." You don't say "coffee," "cappuccino," or "doughnut," just the size and type will do. Note that the cream always comes first, the sugar second. If you want milk, however, you must state that outright, and this holds for Sugar Twin as well. So if you want a small coffee with two milks and one Sugar Twin, you will order "small double single with milk and twin."

It's expected that patrons know how to order in Tim Hortonese, and employees can become frustrated with customers who don't know the language. So don't make any mistakes. For instance, do not order a "medium regular with one cream and one sugar" because a "medium regular" is a coffee with one cream and one sugar. All you need to say is, "medium regular."

A typical order from a patron may be: a large cup of coffee with milk, a large cup of French vanilla cappuccino, and two sour cream–glazed doughnuts. With the Tim Hortons "no muss, no fuss, that's us" language style, all the customer has to say is, "a large with milk, a large French vanilla, and two sour cream–glazed," and they're on their way!

Dawn White

Dawn White

---

here, you can see how the young woman is trying to determine what her boss's connotative meaning is.

In situations like this, we rely on pragmatic rules to decide how to interpret messages. Pragmatic rules govern the way speech operates in everyday interaction, and there are no pragmatic rules in any dictionary. They're typically unstated, but they're just as important as semantic and syntactic rules when trying to make sense of others' messages.

To appreciate how pragmatic rules operate, think of communication as a kind of cooperative game where success depends on everyone understanding and following the same rules. This is why communication scholars use the term *coordination* to describe the way conversation operates when everyone involved uses the same set of pragmatic rules.[9] For example, if someone says to you, "What's up?" you wouldn't look upwards to see. You know that the phrase is a way of asking what was new. You'd also know not to give a lengthy response, so you might say, "Not too much. How's it going with you?" As English speakers, we understand the unspoken pragmatic rules. However, a person with a limited knowledge of English might be confused by the question "What's up?"

Interestingly, people in individual relationships also create their own sets of pragmatic rules. Consider the use of humour. The teasing and joking you exchange with one friend might be considered tasteless or offensive in another relationship.[10] For instance, imagine an e-mail message typed in CAPITAL LETTERS and filled with CURSE WORDS, INSULTS, NAME-CALLING, and EXCLAMATION MARKS!!! How would you interpret such a message? An observer may consider this an example of "flaming" and be appalled, when in fact the

message might be a fun-loving case of "verbal jousting" between buddies.[11]

If you have a good friend you call by a less-than-tasteful nickname as a term of endearment, then you understand the concept. However, those who aren't privy to your relationship's pragmatic rules are likely to misunderstand you, so you'll want to be wise about when and where to use these "personal codes."

LO2
The Impact of Language

In addition to helping communicators understand one another, language also shapes our perceptions and reflects the attitudes we hold toward one another.

Naming and Identity

"What's in a name?" Juliet asked rhetorically. If Romeo had been a social scientist, he would have answered, "A great deal."

Research has demonstrated that names shape the way others think of us, the way we view ourselves, and the way we act. Early studies of the impact of naming claimed that people with unusual names suffered everything from psychological and emotional disturbance to failure in college.[12] This may account for why international students anglicize their names—Yingqi becomes Christy and Quin becomes Becky. More recent studies show that people even have negative appraisals of unusual name spellings.[13] This is interesting, given that BabyCenter indicated that Canadian parents tend to give popular names different spellings. For instance, they found the popular name Kaitlyn was spelled at least nine different ways: Kaitlyn, Kaitlin, Katelynn, Katelyn, Caitlyn, Caitlin, Caitlynn, Katelyn, and Kaitlyn.[14]

Of course, what makes a name (and its spelling) unusual changes with time. In 1900, Bertha, Mildred, and Ethel were among the most popular baby names. In 2013, names like Sophia, Olivia, and Isabella for baby girls and Liam, Noah, and Mason for boys were among the most popular.[15] However, predictions for popular names in 2016 have a more old-fashioned ring to them, such as Effie, Beryl, and Nora for girls and Hector, Nelson, and Otto for boys.[16] Were these predictions accurate where you live?

> ## I also have to thank my wife, Mrs. Hank Snow.
>
> —Hank Snow, accepting a country-and-western music award in the fall of 1979

Recognizing how names affect one's identity, many women wonder how they should label themselves after marriage. Should they take their husband's last name, hyphenate their own and their husband's name, or keep their birth name? One study found that women who took their husband's names placed the most importance on relationships and issues of self were the least important. Women keeping their names put their personal concerns ahead of the relationship and social expectations. Women who hyphenated their names fell somewhere between the groups, valuing self and relationships equally.[17] While most women in Canada have a choice regarding their "married" names, both spouses in Quebec are required by law to retain their birth names, even if they were married outside of the province.[18]

Lopolo/Shutterstock.com

Then there's the question of how to address women. Men are always addressed as *Mr.* which does not identify their marital status. Women, on the other hand, may be called Ms., Miss, or Mrs. To remedy this unbalanced situation, many women are opting to be referred to as *Ms.* This term is equivalent to *Mr.* in that it does not indicate marital status. Therefore, Ms. Abenaki could be married, single, divorced, separated, or otherwise.

Language and Sensitivity

The power of naming extends beyond individuals. The terms used to label groups affect the way they regard themselves and the way others view them. For instance, people with disabilities prefer to be called just that, people with disabilities, rather than disabled.[19] If you stop and think for a moment, referring to individuals as disabled automatically excludes other possibilities and reduces their personhood to that of disability. Referring instead to a person with a disability suggests that the disability is simply one attribute of many that the individual possesses. The same notion holds when referring to individuals by their race, ethnicity, or national origin. To label someone from that one perspective is very narrowing.

We also see this phenomenon when lesbian and gay individuals are referred to by their sexual orientation. We probably would not refer to an individual as heterosexual ("My friend Mary is bringing lobster to the potluck. She's straight, you know."), yet there seems to be some compulsion to announce a lesbian's sexual orientation. Further, there is a more inclusive term that's used today—lesbian, gay, bisexual, transgender, queer or questioning, and intersex (LGBTQI). Today, communities support Gay Pride Parades and local chapters of Parents, Families and Friends of Lesbians and Gays (PFLAG). We're also learning appropriate terminology from the trans community. A woman who transitions to a man would be referred to as a *transman*. A man who transitions to woman is referred to as a *transwoman*.

We're using more sensitive language in other areas as well. For instance, 20 years ago it was not uncommon to refer to men and women in their 70s, 80s or 90s as *aged*, *elderly*, or even as *old geezers*. However, today the more appropriate terms *senior* or *senior citizen* are used. These words reflect a person who is a valued member of a community. Of course, there is also gender and language but that will be discussed later in the chapter.

Affiliation

How we speak can also build and demonstrate solidarity with others. For instance, communicators are attracted to others whose style of speaking is similar to theirs.[20] Likewise, communicators who want to affiliate with someone

Convergence
The process of adapting one's speech style to match that of others with whom the communicator wants to identify.

Divergence
Speech mannerisms that emphasize a communicator's differences from others.

Deferential language
A language style in which speakers defer to listeners by using hedges, hesitations, intensifiers, polite forms, tag questions, and disclaimers.

adapt their speech by altering their vocabulary choice, rate, number and placement of pauses, and level of politeness.[21] Adolescents who all adopt the same vocabulary of slang words and speech mannerisms illustrate the principle of linguistic solidarity. The same process works among members of street gangs or military personnel. One study even showed that adopting the swearing patterns of bosses and co-workers can help people feel connected on the job.[22] The notion of modifying your speech (rate, word selection, accent, grammar, and so forth) in a particular situation is referred to as accommodation theory. When you adapt your speech so that it matches that of others, as in the examples above, it is referred to as **convergence**.[23] We also see convergence in cyberspace. Members of online communities develop a shared language or conversational style, and their affiliation is evident through the use of the word *we*.[24]

Communicators also adapt their speech to gain acceptance. For instance, immigrants strive to master the host language in hopes of gaining material success. And employees seeking advancement speak more like their superiors.

But accommodation theory also works in reverse. Communicators who want to distance themselves from others adopt the strategy of **divergence** — speaking in a way that emphasizes their differences. For example, a lawyer or physician who wants to establish credibility with a client might use more professional jargon to demonstrate their knowledge and show how different they are. You also see this with teens who adopt the slang of particular subcultures to show divergence from adults and convergence with their peers.[25]

Of course, it's important to recognize when and when not to use convergence or divergence. Using ethnic or racial epithets when you're not a member of that in-group can be inappropriate and offensive. One of the pragmatic goals of divergence is the creation of norms about who has the "right" to use certain words and who does not.

Power

There are also language patterns that add to or detract from a speaker's perceived power to influence others. Notice the difference between these two statements:

"Excuse me, Professor. I hate to say this, but I ... uh ... I guess I won't be able to turn in the

AT THE MOVIES

Mean Girls (2004), Rated 13+

To see linguistic convergence in action, you might want to watch *Mean Girls*. Cady Heron (Lindsay Lohan) was raised in African bush country by her zoologist parents and has her first formal schooling experience at North Shore High in the US. She soon learns that social life there is as vicious as anything she witnessed in the wild.

At the urging of her unpopular friends, Cady infiltrates the popular Plastics clique, and part of fitting in is learning their slang, which includes terms like "fetch" (cool), "word vomit" (babbling), and the self-explanatory "fugly." But the more Cady uses the Plastics slang, the more her values and behaviours become like theirs. By the movie's end, she makes some important decisions about herself and her friends.

assignment on time. I had a personal emergency, and ... well ... it was just impossible to finish it by today. I'll have it on your desk Monday, OK?"

"I won't be able to turn in the assignment on time. I had a personal emergency, and it was impossible to finish it by today. I'll have it on Monday morning."

Whether or not the professor finds the excuse acceptable, it's clear that the second message sounds more confident, whereas the first is apologetic and uncertain. **Table 5.1** identifies several language markers that are illustrated in the statements you just read. This speaking style is referred to as powerless language, ingratiating language, or **deferential language**[26] where the speaker includes hedges, hesitations, intensifiers, polite forms, tag questions, and disclaimers in their message. Speakers whose talk is free of these mannerisms are rated as more competent, dynamic, and attractive than speakers who defer to the listener.[27] Nondeferential language (the absence of the markers noted above) can help candidates in job interviews in that applicants using a nondeferential style are thought to be more competent and employable than candidates who speak less forcefully.[28] Even using a single type of powerlessness marker can make you appear less authoritative or socially attractive.[29]

However, there are many interpersonal situations where using a nondeferential language style does not benefit us. For example, in Japan, where saving face for others is important,[30] communicators tend to speak in ambiguous terms and use hedge words and qualifiers. In Mexico, to prevent others from feeling ill at ease, people use the deferential markers

TABLE 5.1
Examples of Deferential Language

Hedges	"I'm *kinda* disappointed ..." "I *think* we should ..." "I *guess* I'd like to ..."
Hesitations	"*Uh*, can I have a minute of your time?" "*Well*, we could try this idea ..." "I wish you would—*er*—try to be on time."
Intensifiers	"I'm *really* glad to see you." "I'm not *very* hungry."
Polite forms	"Excuse me, *sir* ..."
Tag questions	"It's about time we got started, *isn't it?*" "*Don't you think* we should give it another try?"
Disclaimers	"*I probably shouldn't say this, but* ..." "*I'm not really sure, but* ..."
Rising inflections	"But I left a message for you last night?" "I understand that this issue is complicated?"

described here, and in Korea, indirect language (e.g., "perhaps," "could be") is preferred over "direct" speech.

Even in cultures that value assertiveness, language that is *too* powerful may intimidate or annoy others. Consider these two different approaches to handling a common situation:

Powerful speech is one way—but not the only way—to get what you want.

Mark Bowden/iStock/Getty Images

"Excuse me. My baby is having a little trouble getting to sleep. Would you mind turning down the music just a little?"

"My baby can't sleep because your music is too loud. Please turn it down."

The more polite, if less powerful, approach would probably produce better results. If you come across as too powerful, you may get what you're seeking in the short term but make your relationship more difficult in the long term. Furthermore, statements that are too powerful can convey disrespect and superiority and are likely to antagonize rather than gain compliance.

In some situations, polite, deferential language can even enhance a speaker's effectiveness.[31] For example, an administrator might say to an assistant, "Would you mind redoing these figures?" In truth, both know that this is an order, not a request, but the questioning form is more considerate and leaves the assistant feeling better about the boss.[32] The importance of achieving both content and relational goals helps explain why a mixture of powerful speech and polite speech is usually most effective.[33]

> **Inferences**
> Conclusions that are arrived at from an interpretation of evidence.

LO3
Disruptive Language

Sometimes people understand one another perfectly and still wind up in a conflict. While not all disagreements can or should be avoided, you can minimize the kinds of clashes that don't need to happen by being aware of the following linguistic habits.

Fact–Inference Confusion

Inferences are conclusions based on a speaker's beliefs while facts, on the other hand, can be verified as true or false. Fact–inference confusion occurs when inferences, or assumptions we make about something, are presented as if they were facts. You can see the differences in the examples below.

Facts	Inferences
I didn't get a card from you on my birthday.	You don't care about me.
You keep interrupting me.	You're a control freak.
It rains more in Vancouver than it does in Kamloops.	The climate is better in Kamloops than in Vancouver.

When factual and inferential statements are set side by side, the difference between them is clear. In everyday conversation, however, we often present opinions as if they were facts, and this can invite unnecessary argument. For example:

"Spending that much on a pair of shoes is a waste of money!"

"*Raised by Wolves* is the funniest show on TV."

It would be less antagonistic if you prefaced the sentences by saying things like "I believe … ," "In my opinion … ," or "It seems to me …"

Arguments can also arise when we confuse factual statements with inferential statements. The statements below demonstrate how easily this can happen.

A: Why are you mad at me?
B: I'm not mad at you. Why have you been so insecure lately?
A: I'm not insecure. It's just that you've been so critical.
B: What do you mean, "critical"? I haven't been critical …

Rather than argue with someone, a better approach is to use perception checking. Recall from Chapter 3 that you identify the observable behaviours (facts), offer two possible interpretations (inferences), and then ask the person to comment on what you've said.

"You've been asking me whether I still love you a lot lately (*fact*), and that makes me think you're feeling insecure (*1st inference*). Or maybe I'm behaving differently (*2nd inference*). What's on your mind?" (*question*)

Finally, presenting inferences as if they were facts is problematic in that we may not be presenting the truth when listeners believe we are. For example, people sometimes make faulty inferences about others and spread these to their friends even though they are not conveying the truth. This is how rumours get started. If you listen carefully, you'll be amazed how many inferences your family, friends, and coworkers make. To determine how well you

SKILL BUILDER

Fact–Inference Confusion

In small groups or alone, read the following story and then indicate whether the statements are true, false, or questionable.

A couple decided to go boating on a sunny summer day. He packed the fishing rods in the speedboat, then asked his wife if the petrol tank was full. She said, "Yes, it's full." They drove down to the jetty, launched the boat, and then sped out to sea. After about 10 minutes, the boat's motor spluttered, then stopped. They arrived back at the shore several hours later.

Statements about the Story

1. The couple went boating.
   ❑ T ❑ F ❑ ?
2. The couple intended to go fishing.
   ❑ T ❑ F ❑ ?
3. They didn't catch any fish because the motor stopped.
   ❑ T ❑ F ❑ ?
4. The motor stopped because they ran out of petrol.
   ❑ T ❑ F ❑ ?
5. They couldn't have run out of petrol because the wife had looked in the tank and had seen that it was full.
   ❑ T ❑ F ❑ ?
6. She said that the petrol tank was full.
   ❑ T ❑ F ❑ ?
7. He believed that what she said about the petrol was true.
   ❑ T ❑ F ❑ ?
8. The outboard motor stopped after 10 minutes.
   ❑ T ❑ F ❑ ?
9. The boat sped out to sea on a sunny summer day.
   ❑ T ❑ F ❑ ?
10. Because the motor broke down, they had to row back to shore.
    ❑ T ❑ F ❑ ?
11. The car they used to tow the boat had a full tank of petrol.
    ❑ T ❑ F ❑ ?
12. The water was calm.
    ❑ T ❑ F ❑ ?

For further explanation of these results, go to http://www.dh.id.au/ InfTest1.htm.
Answers: 1.T 2.? 3.? 4.? 5.? 6.T 7.? 8.? 9.F 10.? 11.? 12.?

distinguish inferences from facts, read the story in the **Skill Builder** and then take the test below it.

Emotive Language

Emotive language appears to describe something but really announces the speaker's positive or negative attitude toward it. Emotive language might also have a nonverbal component in that the speaker's feelings are usually evident through their facial expressions, vocal expressions, and gestures. If you approve of a friend's roundabout approach to difficult subjects, you'll call her "tactful"; if you disapprove, you'll accuse her of "beating around the bush." Or, if you want to warn international travellers about the importance of possessing car insurance, you might say, "If you don't have the proper coverage and you're in an accident, they'll throw you in jail" as opposed to "… you may find yourself in jail." You can appreciate how emotive words can be editorial statements when you consider these examples:

If you approve, you say	If you disapprove, you say
thrifty	cheap
traditional	old-fashioned
extrovert	loudmouth
cautious	cowardly
progressive	radical
information	propaganda
eccentric	crazy

Allen Russell/Photolibrary/Getty Images

Emotive labels can also result in ugly consequences, as Canadian researcher Colleen Reid's work shows. She found that women living in poverty were often referred to as "welfare cases," "welfare bums," "lazy," and "bad mothers."[34]

To avoid arguments involving emotive words, it's better to describe the person, thing, or idea in neutral terms and to label your opinions as such. Instead of saying, "Quit

Emotive language
Language that conveys the speaker's attitude rather than simply offering an objective description.

Bitching It Out (Out with Bitching)

Different words hold different taboos for different people. I personally don't care when people swear or reference things I've only read about on Urban Dictionary. I don't feel much remorse when I use the word *lame* when referring to that Friday night I spent watching *High School Musical* by myself. But I abhor "the B word." Let me explain why.

Some say that *bitch* is an insult for both genders. That's actually what makes the word so chauvinist. The most frequently used version of *bitch* directed at women makes us think of a boss who is abrasive or a girl who always gets what she wants. The term takes on new meaning when it's used to describe men. While a woman who is a bitch is generally at the top of some social or economic hierarchy, the same term applied to a man means he is weak or subordinate (i.e., "a little bitch"). Even the height of power for a woman is a low place for men. At least, that's what the word implies.

The word *bitch* has attached itself to empowered women. If you disagree, think of the biggest, well, bitch you know. Consider describing her to someone else. What other term could you use? The word automatically comes with a superficial gender-biased archetype of power. To phase out its usage would be to help phase out the idea that women in power have different leadership capabilities than men.

Of course, *bitch* is used in other ways. For example, one can bitch about something. I find that the verb tags along with the noun's oppressive meaning. Bitching is nagging. For women it's expected; for men it shows weakness. Again, the word reinforces the gender divide. It's also a popularized term—especially visible in hip-hop and rap music—for women in general. To say that this slang definition is harmless is ridiculous. I like to think my sex is composed of more than "hoes and tricks." But that's another discussion.

The only usage I don't find fault with seems to be *bitchin'*, as in cool. That doesn't refer to any one sex. If we all try to make a conscious effort to let go of such troublesome vocabulary choices, we can make an impact in escaping their disappointing societal implications. And that's pretty bitchin'.

Alice Stanley

Euphemisms
Pleasant terms or phrases substituted for blunt ones in order to soften the impact of unpleasant information.

"It" statements
Statements that replace the personal pronoun *I* with the less immediate word *it*, often with the effect of reducing the speaker's acceptance of responsibility for the statements.

"I" language
A statement that describes the speaker's reaction to another person's behaviour without making judgments about the behaviour's worth.

making sexist remarks," say, "I really don't like it when you call us girls instead of women." Not only is this more accurate, but it will be better received by others.

Euphemisms

Euphemisms are pleasant terms or phrases used to substitute for blunt ones in order to soften the impact of unpleasant information. For example, rather than saying that a person has cancer, you may say that he is sick. Or, rather than the obscene language you might use with your friends, you may say "freaking," or "shoot" in more formal settings or with older people. You hear euphemisms when small children use the word "pee pee" instead of penis, or that someone has passed away rather than died, or your friend is going to the "little girl's room" as opposed to the bathroom.

Euphemisms can also obscure the accuracy of a message. For instance, when companies want to fire or lay off people, terms like downsizing or rightsizing are used. To obscure the number of people killed in combat, the term casualties is used. When companies want to reduce customer services in order to save money, they say, "In order to serve you better, we are . . . ."

When deciding how to broach difficult subjects, the challenge is to be as kind as possible without sacrificing the clarity of the message.

LO4
The Language of Responsibility

It is through language that we can learn if speakers are willing to take responsibility for their beliefs and feelings. Such a responsibility says a great deal about a person and can shape the tone of a relationship. To see how, read on.

Cultura RM Exclusive/Howard Kingsnorth/Getty Images

1. "It" Statements

As the name implies, **"it" statements** replace the personal pronoun *I* with the less immediate word "it." By contrast, **"I" language** clearly identifies the speaker as the source of a message. Notice the difference between the sentences in each set:

"It bothers me when you're late."
"I'm worried when you're late."

By using "I" language, the person reveals her or his emotions to the listener.

Invitation to Insight

Conjugating "Irregular Verbs"

To demonstrate emotive language, try this simple technique. Take an action or personality trait and show how it can be viewed either favourably or unfavourably, according to the label it's given. For example:

> I'm casual.
> You're a little careless.
> He's a slob.
> **Or try this one:**
> I'm thrifty.
> You're money conscious.
> She's a tightwad.

1. Try a few conjugations yourself, using the following statements:
   a. I'm tactful.
   b. I'm creative.
   c. I'm quiet.
   d. I'm relaxed.
   e. My child is high-spirited.
   f. I have high self-esteem.

2. Now recall at least two situations in which you used emotive language as if it was a description of fact and not an opinion. A good way to recall these situations is to think of a recent disagreement and imagine how the other people involved might have described it differently than you.

"It's nice to see you."
"I'm glad to see you."

Again, the speaker reveals his or her feelings.

"It's a boring class."
"I'm bored in the class."

This time, the "I" language indicates that the student is bored as opposed to stating that the class, course, or teacher is boring in general. Further, while one person may find a class exciting, it might be dreadfully dull for another.

As you can see from these examples, communicators who use "it" statements attribute ownership to some unidentified source. This habit isn't just imprecise, it's an unconscious way to avoid taking a position and conveying that to another individual.

2. "But" Statements

Most of us have had the experience where someone told us three or four nice things about ourselves and then offered one criticism. (Maybe it was a performance at work, for example, or how a particular situation was handled.) When this happens, however, there's a tendency to focus on that one negative comment and to ignore completely the positives ones. That's because **"But" statements** cancel out the thought that precedes it:

> "You're really a great person, but I think we ought to stop seeing each other."
> "You've done good work for us, but we're going to have to let you go."
> "This paper has some good ideas, but because it's late, it gets a D."

This approach can be a face-saving strategy but when the goal is to be absolutely clear, it's better just to state the central idea without the distraction of the "but" statement.

3. Questions

Some questions are sincere requests for information, while others are just a way to avoid making a declaration. "How many textbooks are assigned in that class?" may hide the statement, "I'm afraid to get into a class with too much reading." Or "Are you doing anything tonight?" can be a less risky way of saying, "I want to go out with you tonight."

Sometimes being indirect can be a tactful way to approach a difficult topic, but when used unnecessarily, it can be a way to avoid saying what you mean.

4. "I" and "You" Language

Although there's a tendency to think that using *I* is egotistical ("I did this" and "I did that," etc.), it's also a way to take responsibility for what you say, just like it is with the use of "It" language. For example, the statement "Doug did a good job" makes it sound as if it is a fact. However, the job may not seem good to others, only to that individual. A more responsible statement would be, "*I think* Doug did a good job," or "*In my view*, Doug did a good job and we should hire him again." "I" language can also have a disarming effect on others and enables them to be vulnerable, if need be.

"You" language is quite different in that it judges the other person. Notice how the following statements imply that the subject of the complaint is doing something wrong:

> "You left this place a mess!"
> "You didn't keep your promise!"
> "You're really crude sometimes!"

"But" statements
Statements in which the word *but* cancels out the expression that preceded it.

"You" language
A statement that expresses or implies a judgment of the other person.

SKILL BUILDER

Practising "I" Language
You can develop your skill at delivering "I" messages by following these steps:

1. Visualize situations in your life when you might have sent each of the following messages:
   You're not telling me the truth!
   You think only of yourself!
   Don't be so touchy!
   Quit fooling around!
   You don't understand a word I'm saying!

2. Write alternatives to each statement using "I" language.

3. Think of three "you" statements you might make to people in your life. Transform each of these statements into "I" language and rehearse them with a classmate.

I'm afraid they'll think I'm stupid [*interpretation*]. That's why I got so worked up last night [*consequence*]."

"When you didn't pick me up on time this morning [*behaviour*], I was late for class, and I wound up getting chewed out by the professor [*consequence*]. It seemed to me that my being on time didn't seem important [*interpretation*]. That's why I got so mad [*feeling*]."

"I haven't been very affectionate [*consequence*] because you've hardly spent any time with me in the past few weeks [*behaviour*]. I'm not sure if you're avoiding me or if you're just busy [*interpretation*]. I'm confused [*feeling*] about how you feel about me."

For "I" statements to work, however, they must be delivered with the right tone of voice, facial expressions, and posture to be accepted. Otherwise, the listener is likely to become defensive. To make your actions match your words, remind yourself before speaking that your goal is to explain how the other person's behaviour affects you, not to act like a judge and jury.

Other forms of "you" language don't even contain the pronoun *you*, but it is implied rather than stated outright:

"That was a stupid joke!" ["Your jokes are stupid."]
"Don't be so critical!" ["You're too negative."]
"Mind your own business!" ["You're too nosy."]

Whether stated outright or implied, "you" language arouses defensiveness in others. A less provocative and more accurate way to express a complaint is with "I" language.[35] "I" language shows that speakers take responsibility for the gripe by describing their reaction to a behaviour rather than making any judgments about its worth.

To make a complete "I" statement, it needs to have four parts, although they can appear in any order. They describe:

1. The other person's behaviour
2. Your interpretation
3. Your feelings
4. The consequences the other's behaviour has for you

For example, in everyday conversations, they may sound something like this:

"I get embarrassed [*feeling*] when you talk about my bad grades in front of our friends [*behaviour*].

"I" and "You" Language on the Job

Rebecca is frustrated by Tom's absences from work. She's kept quiet because she likes Tom and doesn't want to sound like a complainer. However, today was the final straw. Rebecca confronted him with "you" language.

imtmphoto/Shutterstock.com

Rebecca Where have you been? You're almost an hour late!

Tom (*Surprised by Rebecca's angry tone*) I had a few errands to run. What's the problem?

Rebecca We all have errands to run, but you shouldn't do them on company time.

Tom (*Feeling defensive*) Why are you worried? The boss hasn't complained.

Rebecca That's because we all cover for you—making excuses when you're late or leave early.

Tom (*Now too defensive to consider Rebecca's concerns*) I thought we all covered for each other. I worked late for a week last year so you could go to a wedding.

Rebecca Nobody was lying then. We have to make up stories all the time about where you are. You're putting me in a difficult spot, Tom, and I can't keep covering for you.

Tom (*Feeling too guilty and angry from Rebecca's judgments to acknowledge his mistakes*) Fine. Sorry to put you out.

Now let's look at this same scenario using "I" language to describe the problem.

Rebecca Tom, I need to talk to you about a problem. (*Rebecca identifies the problem as hers instead of attacking Tom.*)

Tom What's up?

Rebecca You know how you come to work late or take long lunch hours?

Tom (*Sensing trouble ahead*) Yeah?

Rebecca Well, it's putting me in a tight spot. (*Rebecca describes the problem in behavioural terms and then expresses her feeling.*) When the boss asks where you are, I make excuses or even lie for you. But he's starting to get suspicious and I'm worried about that.

Tom (*Feeling defensive because he knows he's guilty but also sympathetic to Rebecca's position*) I don't want to get you in trouble. It's just that I've got a lot of personal stuff going on.

Rebecca I know. I just want you to understand that it's getting impossible to cover for you any longer.

Tom Yeah, OK. I appreciate what you've done. Thanks.

The "I" language helped Rebecca confront Tom without blaming or attacking him. Even if Tom doesn't change, Rebecca's got the problem off her chest, and she did so in a respectful way.

Despite its obvious advantages, even the best-constructed and delivered "I" messages won't always succeed. As author Thomas Gordon points out, "I" statements can leave the recipient feeling "hurt, sorry, surprised, embarrassed, defensive, argumentative, or even tearful."[36] Furthermore, "I" language in large doses can sound egotistical. Research shows that self-absorbed people, also known as "conversational narcissists," are identified by their constant use of *I*.[37] For this reason, "I" language works best in moderation.

5. "We" Language

One way to avoid overuse of "I" language is to consider the pronoun *we*. **"We" statements** imply that the issue is a concern for both parties. Consider a few examples:

"We need to figure out a budget that doesn't bankrupt us."

"I think we have a problem. We can't seem to talk about money without fighting."

"We aren't doing a very good job of keeping the place clean, are we?"

"We" language builds a constructive climate, a kind of "we're in this together" orientation that reflects the transactional nature of communication. It also signals closeness, commonality, and cohesiveness with others.[38]

> **"We" statement**
> A statement that implies that the issue is the concern and responsibility of both the sender and receiver of a message.

TABLE 5.2
Pronoun Use and Its Effects

	Advantages	Disadvantages	Tips
"I" language	Takes responsibility for personal thoughts, feelings, and wants. Less defence-provoking than evaluative "you" language.	Can be perceived as egotistical, narcissistic, and self-absorbed.	Use "I" messages when other person doesn't perceive a problem. Combine "I" with "we" language.
"We" language	Signals inclusion, immediacy, cohesiveness, and commitment.	Can speak improperly for others.	Combine with "I" language. Use in group settings to enhance unity. Avoid when expressing personal thoughts, feelings, and wants.
"You" language	Signals other orientation, particularly when the topic is positive.	Can sound evaluative and judgmental, particularly during confrontations.	Use "I" language during confrontations. Use "you" language when praising or including others.

But "we" statements aren't always appropriate. Some listeners will think that you're quite presumptuous to be speaking for them. You could get a response like, "We have a problem! Maybe *you* have a problem, but don't tell me *I* do!"

Because too much of any pronoun comes across as inappropriate, combining pronouns is a good idea. Researchers have found that I/we combinations (e.g., "I think that we …" or "I would like to see us …") have a good chance of being received favourably.[39] **Table 5.2** summarizes the advantages and disadvantages of each type of language and offers suggestions for approaches that have a good chance of success.

LO5
Gender and Language

The big question when it comes to gender and language is: How different are males and females? Communication scholars are finding that while there are some major differences in the ways that females and males use language,

"Talk to me, Alice. I speak woman."

Mick Stevens The New Yorker Collection/The Cartoon Bank

many differences are not so large.[40] In fact, researcher Janet Hyde developed the Gender Similarities Hypothesis which holds that, overall, females and males are more similar than different.[41] In addition to the unsubstantiated research found in many self-help books on the topic, British language researcher Deborah Cameron takes exception with the so-called "scientific" literature which attributes any sex differences to nature. Not only is this stance inaccurate, it also serves to reinforce and perpetuate sexual stereotypes for females and males and does a disservice to both.[42]

So, having said that, what are some of the differences in the ways the females and males communicate? Let's begin with why we communicate.

Reasons for Communicating

Regardless of their sex, most people communicate to maintain social relationships, and they do so by being friendly, showing interest, and talking about topics that interest the other person.[43] But *how* men and women accomplish this is often different. For instance, while both women and men reject hostile humour and value humour in everyday life,[44] men tend to make their conversation more enjoyable by telling jokes and using good-natured teasing. However, women don't enjoy teasing.

Their discussions commonly involve feelings, relationships, and personal problems.[45] In fact, communication researcher Julia Wood flatly states that "for women, talk *is* the essence of relationships."[46] They gain a sense of satisfaction and empathy by talking with their friends in that they "know they're not alone" in their feelings and perceptions.[47] In other words, while men *like* same-sex conversations, women *need* them. For example, wives spend more time than husbands communicating in ways that help maintain their relationship.[48]

Conversational Style

While women and men behave differently in conversations, the differences aren't as dramatic as you might imagine.[49] For instance, who do you think talks more, men or women? The stereotypical belief is that women talk more than men. However, some researchers have found that they both speak about the same number of words per day.[50] Others have found that men talk longer than women, particularly in public forum.[51] But in mixed-sex conversations, women ask more questions, while men interrupt more and are more likely to use judgmental adjectives ("Reading can be a drag"), directives ("Think of some more"), and "I" references ("I have a lot to do").[52] When it comes to the use of deferential (tentative, less powerful) and nondeferential language styles, researchers report over and over again that women typically use deferential language and men use nondeferential language. In fact, early researchers referred to deferential language as "women's language."[53]

However, other communication scholars examined language use in the courtroom and found that when women and men were on the witness stand, they both spoke in the tentative, deferential style.[54] They concluded that the language style was a function context, not sex. In that situation, both males and females were in the less powerful role. This suggests that the situation, as opposed to the gender of the speaker, has an influence on which style is used. In other words, factors other than gender influence language use.[55] For example, social philosophy plays a role. One study found that feminist wives talk longer than their partners, whereas non-feminist wives speak less than their partners. In addition, cooperative or competitive orientations of the speakers have more influence on speaking style than gender.[56] So does occupation; for example, male daycare teachers' speech to their students resembles the language of female teachers more closely than it resembles the language of fathers at home.

The use of deferential language by women may also have to do with building and maintaining relationships.[57] Women are also more likely to show support, demonstrate equality, and make an effort to keep the conversation going.[58] In all, it's not surprising that female speech often contains statements of sympathy and empathy: "I've felt like that

myself." Women are also inclined to invite the other person to share information: "How did you feel about that?" Because of its focus on nurturing relationships, female speech is often somewhat tentative. Saying "This is just my opinion …" is less likely to put off a conversational partner than a more definite "Here's what I think …" This deferential, accommodating style can actually make women more persuasive than men who use a more powerful language style.[59] But the style can be less effective when persuading women. Overall, women who are willing and able to be flexible in their approach can persuade both other women and men. It seems that, given their concern for developing harmonious relationships, women may also use a deferential style to build rapport.[60]

A final reason why women may use deferential language has to do with gender roles. Gender roles can influence a communicator's style more than his or her biological sex. For example, one study revealed that masculine subjects used significantly more dominance language than did either feminine or androgynous subjects.[61] Feminine subjects expressed slightly more submissive behaviours and more equivalence behaviours than did the androgynous subjects, and their submissiveness and equivalence were much greater than those of the masculine subjects, regardless of their biological sex. In gay and lesbian relationships, conversational styles reflect power differences in the relationship more than the biological sex of the communicators.[62]

Gender and the English Language

One aspect of gender and language that has received considerable attention is the sexist nature of the English language which seems to erase women.[63] We see this in several forms and will look at three of them here:

the use of the generic pronoun "he" to refer to females and males, the use of maleness as the "standard," and the use of exclusive language, or man-linked language. Many readers may already be familiar with the problems associated with each of these.

The Generic Pronoun

The generic pronoun problem refers to the use of *he, his,* and *himself* to refer to both men and women. This can be tricky because in some situations *he, his,* or *himself* is used to refer to a male (Jack won't be back from the library until he finishes his communication paper.). In others, it is supposed to include both males and females (A good student hands in his papers on time.). However, when you read the latter statement, I'll bet that you didn't think of females. Given that our language affects our perception and how we understand the world, avoiding the pronoun when you mean to refer to men and women, or boys and girls, is important. So, what do you do? One of the easiest ways to handle it is to speak in the plural.[64] So, instead of saying, "A good student hands in his papers on time," say "Good *students* hand in *their* papers on time."

Maleness as Standard

In the English language, maleness is set up as the standard. For example, one of the text's authors saw a promo for a television show titled *Women Explorers.* As the title implied, the program featured women who were, or had been, explorers. If male explorers were to be highlighted, the title would have been *Explorers,* not *Male Explorers.* Other examples include *lady doctor, female lawyer,* or *woman minister.* Such language sends a message that it's odd when women hold such positions when in fact, 57.7 percent of medical students in Canada are women![65]

Man-Linked Language

Finally, man-linked language refers only to men and essentially excludes women. Some common examples heard on a daily basis include mailman, fireman, policeman, chairman, weather man, and so forth. Such

Marian Henley The New Yorker Collection/The Cartoon Bank

language perpetuates the myth that these positions are more suited to men than to women. Other words also exclude women: mankind, man-made, men working, man the phones, self-made man, etc.

So, why should you use inclusive language? Gender researcher Dianna Ivy argues that it demonstrates sensitivity, reflects nonsexist attitudes, strengthens expression, and is considered appropriate in today's workplace.[66] Further, people who use inclusive language are considered more current in their thinking. To help you incorporate inclusive language into your vocabulary, here are some examples to get you started. They may sound strange at first, but they will become a habit if you use them regularly.

Current Nonsexist Terms	Outdated Sexist Terms
Chairperson or Chair	Chairman
Letter Carrier	Postman
Business Executive	Businessman
Guard	Watchman
Camera Operator	Cameraman
Fire Fighter	Fireman
Police Officer	Policeman
Meteorologist	Weatherman
Draftsperson	Draftsman
Self-made person/Entrepreneur	Self-made man
Fisher	Fisherman
Humanity	Mankind
Astronaut	Spaceman
Synthetic	Manmade
People working/Workers ahead	Men working
Sewer/Utilityhole	Manhole
Rough up	Manhandle
Answer the phones	Man the phones

Culture and Language

Translating ideas from one language to another isn't always easy,[67] and the sometimes bungled results can be amusing. For example, an American firm unknowingly introduced its product, Pet milk, to French-speaking markets without realizing that the word *pet* in French means "to break wind."[68] Likewise, the English-speaking representative of a soft drink manufacturer naively drew laughs from Mexican customers when she offered free samples of Fresca. In Mexican slang, the word *fresca* means "lesbian."

> **Language is a steed that carries one into a far country.**
>
> —Arab proverb

Difficult as it may be, translation is only a small part of the problem. You must understand the connotations for the language within the culture. For example, Japanese insurance companies warn their policyholders who are visiting North America to avoid saying "I'm sorry" if they are involved in a traffic accident.[69] While interpreted in Japan as a sign of good will, it is perceived as an admission of guilt in North America, especially in the United States.

Language Sensitivity

Language to Avoid

Sexist Language
Avoid man-linked language such as *chairman*, *weatherman*, etc., the generic *he* to refer to a male or female, and terms like *lady doctor*. Instead, use *chairperson*, *meteorologist*, *they*, or *doctor*.

Heterosexist Language
Avoid the derogatory terms used to describe gays and lesbians and labelling someone by their sexual orientation.

Race, Ethnicity, and National Origin
Avoid referring to individuals by their race, ethnicity, or origin. Ask individuals how they wish to be named.

Disabilities
Avoid saying someone is *disabled*, *handicapped*, or *crippled*. Instead, use the term *person with a disability*. Don't say that someone is a *polio victim*, for instance; instead, say the person *has [or had] polio*.

Age
Don't refer to people as *old*, *elderly*, or *geriatric*. Instead, call them *seniors* or *senior citizens*.

Differences in the way language is used can make communicating across cultures a challenging task. We see this in our own country. For instance, rather than say a dollar or two dollars, we use the terms *Loonies* and *Toonies* which may be misunderstood by tourists coming to Canada. In Newfoundland, many people speak Newfoundland English—a dialect consisting of words and lexical items unique to Newfoundland or to specific areas of the island. For instance, *drite* refers to dryness in the air, *dwall* to a short, light sleep, *joog* to a drop of liquid, and *quoit* to skipping flat stones over the water. You may also hear individuals use certain past-time constructions, such as "How many times am I after telling you?" as opposed to "How many times have I told you?" These and other phonological features might be very confusing to someone who is unfamiliar with the culture and the language.[70]

Of course, the issue of language and culture is particularly salient here in Canada with its two national languages—English and French. While Canada's population still consists mainly of English and French speakers, the number of allophones—those having a mother tongue other than French or English—has been increasingly on the rise.[71] For example, there are over 60 different Aboriginal languages spoken throughout Canada and the most commonly used is the Algonquian family languages—Cree, Inuktitut, and Ojibway. Also, about one in five individuals who has an Aboriginal mother tongue lives

Robert Nickelsberg/Getty Images

in Quebec.[72] However Chinese is ranked the third-most-spoken mother tongue in Canada.[73]

Verbal Communication Styles

The role of culture and language is also related to verbal styles. For example, when a communicator tries to use the verbal style from one culture in a different one, problems are likely to arise.[74] These can include matters related to formality and informality, precision or vagueness, and brevity or detail, and directness.

In terms of ***directness***, anthropologist Edward Hall identified two distinct cultural ways of using language.[75] **Low-context cultures** use language to express thoughts, feelings, and ideas as clearly and logically as possible. Low-context communicators look for the meaning of a statement in the words spoken. Canada, overall, would be considered a low-context culture. By contrast, **high-context cultures** use language to maintain social harmony. Rather than upset others by speaking clearly, high-context communicators learn to discover meaning from the context in which a message is delivered: the speaker's nonverbal behaviours, the relationship's history, and the general social rules that govern the interaction. **Table 5.3** summarizes some key language differences in low- and high-context cultures.

In low-context cultures like Canada, we value straight talk and grow impatient with "beating around the bush." Most Asian and Middle Eastern cultures fit the high-context patterns that focus on harmony. They avoid speaking clearly so

Low-context cultures
Cultures that use language primarily to express thoughts, feelings, and ideas as clearly and logically as possible.

High-context cultures
Cultures that avoid direct use of language, relying instead on the context of a message to convey meaning.

Invitation to Insight

O Canada, Our Dah Dah Dah Dah Dum

In 2002, in a movement to make the lyrics of our national anthem gender-inclusive, one Canadian senator argued that the line "all thy sons command" should be changed. Some people agreed; others did not. Then in 2010 it came up again. But given the climate when Parliament reconvened after the controversial prorogation, the issue was considered a diversion from several other controversial issues. So for the second time the move to include gender-inclusive lyrics in Canada's national anthem was dropped. The issue arose again in the fall of 2013. The bill was once again reintroduced by Mauril Belanger as a private member's bill in January 2016 and on June 15, 2016 it was finally passed by a vote of 255 to 74. So, from now on, instead of singing "... in all thy sons command ..." we'll be shouting out, "in all of us command."

Adapted from C. Cosh, "O Canada, Our Dah Dah Dah Dah Dum," *Report/Newsmagazine (Alberta Edition)*, March 18, 2002, p. 3; T. Haig. CBC, June, 2016. MP Mauril Belanger gets dying wish in Commons. Retrieved July 13 from http://www.rcinet.ca/en/2016/06/16/mp-mauril-belanger-gets-dying-wish-in-commons/.

TABLE 5.3

Low- and High-Context Communication Styles

Low Context	High Context
Majority of information carried in explicit verbal messages, with less focus on the situational context.	Important information carried in contextual cues (time, place, relationship). Less reliance on explicit verbal messages.
Self-expression valued. Communicators state opinions and desires directly and strive to persuade others to accept their own viewpoint.	Relational harmony valued and maintained by indirect expression of opinions. Communicators abstain from saying no directly.
Clear, eloquent speech considered praiseworthy. Verbal fluency admired.	Communicators talk "around" the point, allowing the other to fill in the missing pieces. Ambiguity and use of silence admired.

as not to threaten another person's "face." That is, they try not to make others look bad. Further, they are less likely to offer a clear *no* to an undesirable request. Instead, they will probably use roundabout expressions like "I agree with you in principle, but ..." or "I sympathize with you ..." For example, Dr. Dejun Liu, a former Chinese colleague, explained that when he is at home, he speaks Chinese. He focuses on the listener and says things in an unclear fashion on purpose. He explained that one doesn't always want to be clear because understanding would emerge from the context. At the university, however, Dr. Liu's speech style was more direct and succinct. He also noted that cultural differences don't fade when we speak another language. He told the story of an Asian colleague who wasn't being promoted. She, in the Asian tradition, was waiting for her superior to tell her to apply. In Canadian universities this is not the custom; she was expected to initiate the process.

Language styles also vary in terms of *elaboration* and *succinctness*. Arabic speakers, for instance, have a much richer and more expressive style than English-speaking communicators. Strong assertions and exaggerations that would sound ridiculous in English are common in Arabic. This contrast can lead to misunderstandings.

As one observer put it, first, Arabs feel compelled to overassert in almost all types of communication because others expect them to. If Arabs say exactly what they mean without the expected assertion, other Arabs may still think that they mean the opposite. For example, a simple no by guests to the host's requests to eat more or drink more will not suffice. To convey the meaning

that they are actually full, guests must keep repeating no several times, coupling it with an oath such as "By God" or "I swear to God." Second, Arabs tend not to recognize that others, particularly foreigners, may mean exactly what they say even though their language is simple. To the Arabs, a simple no may be interpreted as an indirectly expressed consent. On the other hand, a simple consent may mean the rejection of a hypocritical politician.[76]

Succinctness is most extreme in cultures where silence is valued. In many First Nations cultures, for example, the favoured way to handle ambiguous social situations is to remain quiet.[77] Contrasting this silent style to the talkativeness in mainstream North American cultures when people first meet, it's easy to imagine how the first encounter between an Inuktitut speaker and an English speaker might feel uncomfortable to both people.

Languages also differ in terms of their *formality* and *informality*. When one of the authors was studying conversational French, she had to gain a sense of when to use *vous*, the formal form of the word *you*, and *tu*, the more familiar usage, which was not only acceptable but expected. In Asia and Africa, formality isn't so much a matter of using correct grammar as of defining social position. The Korean language reflects the Confucian system of relational hierarchies[78] and has special vocabularies for each sex, for different levels of social status, for different degrees of intimacy, and for different types of social occasions. There are different degrees of formality for speaking with old friends, non-acquaintances whose background one knows, and complete strangers. A sign of a learned person is using language that recognizes these relational distinctions.

These explanations make it clear that if we want to be successful in our pursuit of global connectedness, we must have a strong knowledge of the culture and language of those with whom we wish to communicate. Little wonder international companies are providing intercultural communication training for their personnel. They cannot succeed without such information.

Language and Worldview

For almost 150 years, theorists have put forth the notion of **linguistic relativism**: that the worldview of a culture is shaped and reflected by the language its members speak.[79] A well-known example refers to the notion that the Inuit have many different words, somewhere between 17 and 100, for snow and for various snow conditions. Basic survival in the Arctic led the Inuit to make distinctions that would be unimportant to residents of warmer environments. And once these distinctions were made, speakers are more likely to see the world in ways that match the broader vocabulary.

Linguistic relativism
The notion that the worldview of a culture is shaped and reflected by the language its members speak.

Language and Heritage

Junial Enterprises/Shutterstock.com

"Mi'ja, it's me. Call me when you wake up." It was a message left on my phone machine from a friend. But when I heard that word *mi'ja*, a pain squeezed my heart. My father was the only one who ever called me this. Because his death is so recent, the word overwhelmed me and filled me with grief.

Mi'ja (MEE-ha), from *mi hija* (me ee-HA). The words translate as "my daughter." Daughter, my daughter, daughter of mine: They're all stiff and clumsy, and have nothing of the intimacy and warmth of the word *mi'ja*—"daughter of my heart," maybe. Perhaps a more accurate translation of *mi'ja* is "I love you." Sometimes a word can be translated into more than a meaning. In it is the translation of a worldview, a way of looking at things, and, yes, even a way of accepting what others might not perceive as beautiful. *Urraca*, for example, instead of "grackle." Two ways of looking at a black bird. One sings; the other cackles. Or *tocayola*, your name-twin and therefore your friend. Or the beautiful *estrenar*, which means to wear something for the first time. There is no word in English for the thrill and pride of wearing something new.

Spanish gives me a way of looking at myself and the world in a new way. For those of us living between worlds, our job in the universe is to help others see with more than their eyes during this period of chaotic transition.

Sandra Cisneros

From *A House of My Own: Stories from My Life*, by Sandra Cisneros

---

Even though there is some doubt as to whether there really are so many words for snow,[80] other examples support this principle.[81] For instance, bilingual speakers seem to think differently when they change languages. When French speakers were asked to interpret a series of pictures, their descriptions were more romantic and emotional than when they described the pictures in English. Likewise, when students in Hong Kong completed a values test, they expressed more traditional Chinese values when they answered in Cantonese than when they answered in English. Such examples demonstrate how powerful language is in shaping cultural identity.

Sapir–Whorf hypothesis
This hypothesis suggests that the language we speak affects how we interact with the world around us.

The best-known declaration of linguistic relativism is the **Sapir–Whorf hypothesis**, formulated by Edward Sapir and Benjamin Whorf.[82] This hypothesis suggests that the language we speak affects how we interact with the world around us. Whorf observed that the language spoken by Hopi Native Americans represents a view of reality that is dramatically different from more familiar tongues. The Hopi language makes no distinction between nouns and verbs! Therefore, people speaking Hopi see the entire world as a constant process. In English, nouns characterize people or objects as being fixed (recall the idea of static evaluation), while Hopi view people and objects as constantly changing. You might say that English represents the world like a snapshot, whereas Hopi represents it more like a motion picture.

Another way in which we see linguistic relativism is that fact that some languages contain terms that have no English equivalents.[83] Here are a few examples:

> *nemawashi* (Japanese): The process of informally feeling out all the people involved with an issue before making a decision

monkeybusinessimages/iStock/Thinkstock

lagniappe (French/Creole): An extra gift given in a transaction that wasn't expected by the terms of a contract

lao (Mandarin): A respectful term used for older people, showing their importance in the family and in society

dharma (Sanskrit): Each person's unique, ideal path in life and knowledge of how to find it

koyaanisquatsi (Hopi): Nature out of balance; a way of life so crazy it calls for a new way of living

Once words like these exist, then the ideas that they represent are easier to recognize. But even without such words, each of the ideas just listed is still possible to imagine. Thus, speakers of a language that includes the notion of *lao* would probably treat its older members respectfully, and those who are familiar with *lagniappe* might be more generous.

Although language may shape thoughts and behaviour, it doesn't dominate them absolutely.

Language in the Workplace

Language also plays a significant role in the workplace and one concern is the use of inclusive language. Researchers and practitioners alike hold that "the elimination of sexist language can improve the quality of work life and heighten employee satisfaction within the workplace."[84] You can do several things to eliminate sexist language practices. For instance, in the last number of years, names of government agencies, organizations, and businesses have been changed

to reflect inclusive language. One example would be Worker's Compensation which used to be called *Workman's Compensation*. Further, the language in organizational documentation has also been updated. It seems that the most difficult part is getting individuals to adopt inclusive language.

Another issue related to language in the workplace has to do with diversity and language. Managing language diversity can be challenging but it can also be viewed as a competitive edge.[85] Of course, the issue is complicated by Canada's *Official Languages* Act which states that Canadians have the freedom to speak their preferred official language (French or English).[86] However, the act also ensures us the ability to understand and be understood. Therefore, it is not uncommon to have translators at meetings.

"Gads. I've forgotten today's buzzword."

A third aspect of language that is relevant to the workplace is the notion of abstraction. Recall that high-level abstract language is fuzzy, unclear, and very general. When people hear this type of language they interpret it in many different ways. More appropriate for the workplace would be low level, clear language that leaves very little to the imagination. For example, you could say something vague like:

> "We have a large time sensitive order to fill and I need you on deck. You'll be rewarded if you do a good job."

To be clearer, you could use lower level abstraction language by saying:

> "As you know, we have to get this order out by Friday. Therefore, we'll need to start an hour earlier, take shorter breaks and lunches, and work overtime for at least an hour. If we meet this deadline, everyone will receive a $500.00 bonus."

Not only is the second message clearer, it's more motivating. Related to this is jargon. Sometimes, even people within an organization don't understand it. However, while users may feel well informed or "on top of things," they may sacrifice meaning to feel that way.

Finally, language formality can be an issue in the workplace. As you are aware, language has become less formal over the years and this has seeped into the workplace; we're hearing more vulgar, lewd, and provocative language. There's also more swearing which is considered the most impolite behaviour at work.[87] This talk may be acceptable in some interpersonal situations, but it is inappropriate and unprofessional at work. To help you find the fitting formality level for any situation, check out the **Language Style and Formality** box. It was developed to help customer service personnel use more professional language when working with both customers and colleagues.[88]

Language Style and Formality

Tuxedo
This type of communication is used in public forums and various cultural and religious rites. The language is conventional, prim, reserved, formal, stately, proper, and even decorous.

Casual/Dress Code
Relationships in this category centre on acquaintances or individuals we do not know. Casual/dress code style is used in professional contexts. The talk is polite, tasteful, appropriate, and correct.

Blue Jeans
Blue jeans communication occurs with our good friends and family—people we know well and with whom we are very comfortable. The talk is unceremonious, unpretentious, candid, straightforward, earthy, and sometimes obscene, ribald, or lewd.

Bathrobe
This style of talk is reserved for people with whom we have very private, close relationships, such as lovers and life partners. Bathrobe talk is intimate, private, exclusive, personal, and sometimes vulgar or suggestive.

READY TO STUDY?

IN THE BOOK, YOU CAN:

❏ Rip out the Chapter in Review card at the back of the book to have the key terms and Learning Objectives handy, and complete the quizzes provided (answers are at the bottom of the back page).

ONLINE YOU CAN:

❏ Stay organized and efficient with MindTap—a single destination with all the course material and study aids you need to succeed. Built-in apps leverage social media and the latest learning technology. For example:

    ❏ Listen to the text using ReadSpeaker.

    ❏ Use pre-populated Flashcards as a jump start for review—or you can create your own.

    ❏ You can highlight text and make notes in your MindTap Reader. Your notes will flow into Evernote, the electronic notebook app that you can access anywhere when it's time to study for the exam.

    ❏ Prepare for tests with a variety of quizzes and activities.

Go to **nelson.com/student** to access these digital resources

Endnotes

1. B. Keysar & A. S. Henly (2002). "Speakers' Overestimation of Their Effectiveness." *Psychological Science, 13*, 207–212. See also R. S. Wyer & R. Adava (2003). "Message Reception Skills in Social Communication." In J. O. Greene & B. R. Burleson (Eds.). *Handbook of Communication and Social Interaction Skills* (pp. 291–355). Mahwah, NJ: Erlbaum.

2. O. W. Sacks (1989). *Seeing Voices: A Journey into the World of the Deaf*. Berkeley: University of California Press, p. 17.

3. T. L. Scott (November 27, 2000). "Teens before Their Time." *Time,* 22.

4. The Canadian Press (2015, June 8). "Snoop Dogg under fire for comments to CBC staffer." *The Chronicle Herald,* p. C4.

5. Thick [Def. 1]. (n.d.). In *Urban Dictionary*. http://www.urbandictionary.com/define.php?term=thick. Retrieved January 16, 2016.

6. W. E. Prentice (2005). *Therapeutic Modalities in Rehabilitation*. New York: McGraw-Hill.

7. W. Wolfram & N. Schilling-Estes (2005). *American English: Dialects and Variation*, 2nd ed. Malden, MA: Blackwell.

8. N. Coupland, J. M. Wiemann, & H. Giles (1991). "Talk as 'Problem' and Communication as 'Miscommunication': An Integrative Analysis." In N. Coupland, J. M. Wiemann, & H. Giles (Eds.). *"Miscommunication" and Problematic Talk*. Newbury Park, CA: Sage.

9. W. B. Pearce & V. Cronen (1980). *Communication, Action, and Meaning*. New York: Praeger. See also V. Cronen, V. Chen, & W. B. Pearce (1988). "Coordinated Management of Meaning: A Critical Theory." In Y. Y. Kim & W. B. Gudykunst (Eds.). *Theories in Intercultural Communication*. Newbury Park, CA: Sage.

10. E. K. E. Graham, M. Papa, & G. P. Brooks (1992). "Functions of Humour in Conversation: Conceptualization and Measurement." *Western Journal of Communication, 56*, 161–183.

11. P. B. O'Sullivan & A. Flanagin (2003). "Reconceptualizing 'Flaming' and Other Problematic Communication." *New Media and Society, 5*, 67–93.

12. N. Christenfeld & B. Larsen, B. (2008). "The Name Game." *The Psychologist, 21*, 210–213.

13. A. Mehrabian (2001). "Characteristics Attributed to Individuals on the Basis of Their First Names." *Genetic, Social, and General Psychology Monographs, 127*, 59–88.

14. BabyCenter. (2010). "Canada's Top Baby Names for 2009," www.babycenter.ca/pregnancy/naming/top2009. Accessed March 14, 2010.

15. BabyCentre. (2013). "Popular Baby Names for 2013," http://www.babycenter.com/popularBabyNames.htm?year=2013. Accessed February 7, 2013.

16. K. Khoo (2015, November 5). "Baby names 2016: Top predictions for the New Year." *The Huffington Post Canada*. http://www.huffingtonpost.ca/2015/11/05/baby-names-2016_n_8479244.html. Retrieved January 17, 2016.

17. K. Foss & B. Edson (1989). "What's in a Name? Accounts of Married Women's Name Choices," *Western Journal of Speech Communication, 53*, 356–373.

18. Justice Quebec. (2003). Marriage. http://www.justice.gouv.qc.ca/english/publications/generale/maria-a.htm. Retrieved January 17, 2016.

19. Interview with Marie Westhaver by Judith A. Rolls (January, 25, 2003).

20. See, for example, R. K. Aune & Toshiyuki Kikuchi (1993). "Effects of Language Intensity Similarity on Perceptions of Credibility, Relational Attributions, and Persuasion." *Journal of Language and Social Psychology, 12*, 224–238.

21. H. Giles, J. Coupland, & N. Coupland (Eds.) (1991). *Contexts of Accommodation: Developments in Applied Sociolinguistics*. Cambridge: Cambridge University Press.

22. Y. Baruch & S. Jenkins (2006). "Swearing at Work and Permissive Leadership Culture: When Anti-Social Becomes Social and Incivility Is Acceptable." *Leadership & Organization Development Journal, 28*, 492–507.

23. H. Giles, J. Coupland, & N. Coupland (1991). "Accommodation Theory: Communication, Context, and Consequence." In H. Giles, J. Coupland, & N. Coupland (Eds.). *Contexts of Accommodation: Studies in Emotion and Social Interaction*. New York: Cambridge University Press.

24. J. Cassell & D. Tversky (2005). "The Language of Online Intercultural Community Formation." *Journal of Computer-Mediated Communication, 10*, article 2.

25. A. Reyes (2005). "Appropriation of African American Slang by Asian American Youth." *Journal of Sociolinguistics, 9*, 509–532.

26. J. A. Rolls (1998). "The Influence of Language Style and Gender on Leadership Potential: A Review of Relevant Literature." US Educational Resources Information Centre (ERIC Document) Ed 352–686.

27. S. H. Ng & J. J. Bradac (1993). *Power in Language: Verbal Communication and Social Influence*. Newbury Park, CA: Sage, p. 27. See also A. El-Alayli, C. J. Myers, T. L. Petersen, & A. L. Lystad (2008). "I Don't Mean to Sound Arrogant, But …": The Effects of Using Disclaimers on Person Perception." *Personality and Social Psychology Bulletin, 34*, 130–143.

28. S. Parton, S. A. Siltanen, L. A. Hosman, & J. Langenderfer (2002). "Employment Interview Outcomes and Speech Style Effects." *Journal of Language and Social Psychology, 21*, 144–161.

29. L. A. Hosman (1989). "The Evaluative Consequences of Hedges, Hesitations, and Intensifiers: Powerful and Powerless Speech Styles." *Human Communication Research, 15*, 383–406.

30. L. A. Samovar & R. E. Porter (2001). *Communication between Cultures*, 4th ed. Belmont, CA: Wadsworth, pp. 58–59.

31. J. Bradac & A. Mulac (1984). "Attributional Consequences of Powerful and Powerless Speech Styles in a Crisis-Intervention Context." *Journal of Language and Social Psychology, 3*, 1–19.

32. J. J. Bradac (1983). "The Language of Lovers, Flovers [sic], and Friends: Communicating in Social and Personal Relationships." *Journal of Language and Social Psychology, 2*, 141–162.

33. D. Geddes (1992). "Sex Roles in Management: The Impact of Varying Power and Speech Style on Union Members' Perception of Satisfaction and Effectiveness." *Journal of Psychology, 126*, 589–607.

34. C. Reid (2004). *The Woulds of Exclusion: Poverty, Women's Health, and Social Justice.* Edmonton, AB: Qual Institute Press.

35. E. S. Kubany, D. C. Richard, G. B. Bauer, & M. Y. Muraoka (1992). "Impact of Assertive and Accusatory Communication of Distress and Anger: A Verbal Component Analysis." *Aggressive Behaviour, 18*, 337–347.

36. T. Gordon. (1974). *T.E.T.: Teacher Effectiveness Training.* New York: Wyden, p. 74.

37. R. Raskin & R. Shaw (1988). "Narcissism and the Use of Personal Pronouns." *Journal of Personality, 56*, 393–404; A. L. Vangelisti, M. L. Knapp, & J. A. Daly (1990). "Conversational Narcissism." *Communication Monographs, 57*, 251–274.

38. A. S. Dreyer, C. A. Dreyer, & J. E. Davis (1987). "Individuality and Mutuality in the Language of Families of Field-Dependent and Field-Independent Children." *Journal of Genetic Psychology, 148*, 105–117.

39. R. F. Proctor & J. R. Wilcox (1993). "An Exploratory Analysis of Responses to Owned Messages in Interpersonal Communication." *ETC: A Review of General Semantics, 50*, 201–220; Vangelisti et al., *Conversational Narcissism*, op. cit.

40. K. Dindia (2006). "Men Are from North Dakota, Women Are from South Dakota." In K. Dindia and D. J. Canary (Eds.). *Sex Differences and Similarities in Communication: Critical Essays and Empirical Investigations of Sex and Gender in Interaction*, 2nd ed. Mahwah, NJ: Erlbaum; D. J. Goldsmith & P. A. Fulfs (1999). "'You Just Don't Have the Evidence': An Analysis of Claims and Evidence in Deborah Tannen's *You Just Don't Understand*." In M. E. Roloff (Ed.). *Communication Yearbook 22*. Thousand Oaks, CA: Sage.

41. J. Hyde (2006). "Epilogue." In K. Dindia and D. J. Canary (Eds.). *Sex Differences and Similarities in Communication: Critical Essays and Empirical Investigations of Sex and Gender in Interaction*, 2nd ed. Mahwah, NJ: Erlbaum.

42. D. Cameron (2007). *The Myth of Venus and Mars: Do Men and Women Really Speak Different Languages?* UK: Cambridge University Press.

43. R. A. Clark (1998). "A Comparison of Topics and Objectives in a Cross Section of Young Men's and Women's Everyday Conversations." In D. J. Canary & K. Dindia, (Eds.). *Sex Differences and Similarities in Communication: Critical Essays and Empirical Investigations of Sex and Gender in Interaction.* Mahwah, NJ: Erlbaum.

44. J. Gallivan (1999). "Gender and Humour: What Makes a Difference?" *North American Journal of Psychology, 1* (2), 307–318.

45. A. DeCapua, D. Berkowitz, & D. Boxer (2006). "Women Talk Revisited: Personal Disclosures and Alignment Development." *Multilingua, 25*, 393–412.

46. J. T. Wood (2011). *Gendered Lives: Communication, Gender, and Culture.* Boston: Wadsworth.

47. M. A. Sherman & A. Haas (June 1984). "Man to Man, Woman to Woman." *Psychology Today, 17*, 72–73.

48. J. D. Ragsdale (1996). "Gender, Satisfaction Level, and the Use of Relational Maintenance Strategies in Marriage." *Communication Monographs, 63*, 354–371.

49. See D. Cameron (2007). *The Myth of Venus and Mars: Do Men and Women Really Speak Different Languages?* UK: Cambridge University Press. Also see M. Swacker (1975). "The Sex of the Speaker as a Sociolinguistic Variable." In B. Thorne & N. Henley (Eds.), *Language and Sex: Differences and Dominance.* Massachusettes: Newbury House. For a summary of research on differences between male and female conversational behaviors, see H. Giles & R. L. Street Jr. (1985). "Communication Characteristics and Behavior." In M. L. Knapp & G. R. Miller (Eds.). *Handbook of Interpersonal Communication* (pp. 205–261). Beverly Hills, CA: Sage; A. Kohn (February 1988). "Girl Talk, Guy Talk." *Psychology Today, 22,* 65–66.

50. M. R. Mehl, S. Vazire, N. Ramírez-Esparza, R. B. Slatcher, & J. W. Pennebaker (2007). "Are Women Really More Talkative Than Men?" *Science, 317,* 82.

51. See D. Cameron (2007). *The Myth of Venus and Mars: Do Men and Women Really Speak Different Languages?* UK: Cambridge University Press. Also see M. Swacker (1975). "The Sex of the Speaker as a Sociolinguistic Variable." In B. Thorne & N. Henley (Eds.), *Language and Sex: Differences and Dominance.* Massachusettes: Newbury House.

52. A. Mulac (2006). "The Gender-Linked Language Effect: Do Language Differences Really Make a Difference?" In K. Dindia & D. J. Canary (Eds.). *Sex Differences and Similarities in Communication: Critical Essays and Empirical Investigations of Sex and Gender in Interaction*, 2nd ed. Mahwah, NJ: Erlbaum.

53. R. Lakoff (1975). *Language and Women's Place.* New York: Harper and Row.

54. B. Erickson, A. E. Lind, B. C. Johnson, & W. N. O'Barr (1974). "Speech Style and Impression Formation in a Court Setting: The Effects of 'Powerful' and 'Powerless' Speech." *Journal of Experimental Social Psychology, 14*, 266–279.

55. Clark, op. cit.

56. L. L. Carli (1990). "Gender, Language, and Influence." *Journal of Personality and Social Psychology, 59*, 941–951.

57. See, for example, D. Tannen (1994). *Talking from 9 to 5: Women and Men in the Workplace: Language, Sex and Power.* New York: William Morrow; Wood, op. cit.

58. D. G. Ellis & L. McCallister (1980). "Relational Control Sequences in Sex-Typed and Androgynous Groups." *Western Journal of Speech Communication, 44,* 35–49.

59. S. Steen & P. Schwarz (1995). "Communication, Gender, and Power: Homosexual Couples as a Case Study." In M. A. Fitzpatrick & A. L. Vangelisti (Eds.). *Explaining Family Interactions* (pp. 310–343). Thousand Oaks, CA: Sage.

60. Wood, op. cit.

61. J. A. Rolls (2007). *Public Speaking Made Easy.* Toronto: Nelson Education.

62. M. C. Sheppard (May 7, 2011). "Women are Changing the Face of Medicine: But are Underrepresented in Upper Level Positions." *CBC News: Health.* http://www.cbc.ca/news/health/story/2011/03/07/f-women-medicine-iwf.htm Accessed February 10, 2013.

63. C. J. Zahn (1989). "The Bases for Differing Evaluations of Male and Female Speech: Evidence from Ratings of Transcribed Conversation." *Communication Monographs, 56,* 59–74.

64. B. A. Fisher (1983). "Differential Effects of Sexual Composition and Interactional Content on Interaction Patterns in Dyads." *Human Communication Research, 9,* 225–238.

65. Wood, op. cit.

66. D. K. Ivy (2012). *GenderSpeak: Personal Effectiveness in Gender Communication,* 5th edn. Boston: Pearson.

67. For a thorough discussion of the challenges involved in translation from one language to another, see L. A. Samovar & R. E. Porter (1991). *Communication between Cultures.* Dubuque, IA: W. C. Brown, pp. 165–169.

68. The examples in this paragraph are taken from D. Ricks (1983). *Big Business Blunders: Mistakes in International Marketing.* Homewood, IL: Dow Jones-Irwin, p. 41.

69. N. Sugimoto (March 1991) *"Excuse Me" and "I'm Sorry": Apologetic Behaviours of Americans and Japanese.* Paper presented at the Conference on Communication in Japan and the United States, California State University, Fullerton, CA.

70. For a thorough discussion, see W. O'Grady & M. Dobrovolsky (1996). *Contemporary Linguistic Analysis: An Introduction,* 3rd ed. (pp. 427–528). Toronto: Copp.

71. The Daily Online, Statistics Canada (December 2002). "Census of Population: Language, Mobility and Migration," www.statcan.ca/Daily/English/02210/do21210a.htm. Accessed July 12, 2006.

72. Statistics Canada (2011). "Aboriginal languages in Canada." *Census in Brief.* http://www.statcan.gc.ca/bsolc/olc-cel/olc-cel?catno=98-314-X2011003&lang=eng. Retrieved January 22, 2016.

73. The Daily Online, Statistics Canada (Dec. 2007). "2006 Census: Immigration, Citizenship, Language, Mobility and Migration," www.statcan.gc.ca/daily-quotidien/071204/dq071204a-eng.htm. Accessed March 21, 2010.

74. A summary of how verbal style varies across cultures can be found in Chapter 5 of W. B. Gudykunst & S. Ting-Toomey (1988). *Culture and Interpersonal Communication.* Newbury Park, CA: Sage.

75. E. Hall (1959). *Beyond Culture.* New York: Doubleday.

76. A. Almaney & A. Alwan (1982). *Communicating with the Arabs.* Prospect Heights, IL: Waveland.

77. K. Basso (1970). "To Give Up on Words: Silence in Western Apache Culture." *Southern Journal of Anthropology, 26,* 213–230.

78. J. Yum (1987). "The Practice of Uye-ri in Interpersonal Relationships in Korea." In D. Kincaid (Ed.). *Communication Theory from Eastern and Western Perspectives.* New York: Academic Press.

79. T. Seinfatt (1989). "Linguistic Relativity: Toward a Broader View." In S. Ting-Toomey and F. Korzenny (Eds.). *Language, Communication, and Culture: Current Directions.* Newbury Park, CA: Sage.

80. L. Martin & G. Pullum (1991). *The Great Eskimo Vocabulary Hoax.* Chicago: University of Chicago Press.

81. H. Giles & A. Franklyn-Stokes (1989). "Communicator Characteristics." In M. K. Asante & W. B. Gudykunst (Eds.). *Handbook of International and Intercultural Communication.* Newbury Park, CA: Sage.

82. B. Whorf (1956). "The Relation of Habitual Thought and Behaviour to Language." In J. B. Carrol (Ed.). *Language, Thought, and Reality.* Cambridge, MA: MIT Press.

83. H. Rheingold (1988). *They Have a Word for It.* Los Angeles: Jeremy P. Tarcher.

84. B. Daily & M. Finch (1993). "Benefiting from Nonsexist Language in the Workplace" *Business Horizons, 36,* 30–34.

85. B. Kreissl (January 7, 2011). "Language in the Workplace." *HR Reporter.* http://www.hrreporter.com/blog/hr-policies-practices/archive/2011/06/07/language-in-the-workplace. Accessed February 11, 2013.

86. (December 1, 2011). "Creating a Workplace That Respects the Language Rights of Its Employees." *Archives: Office of the Commissioner of Official Languages.* http://www.ocol-clo.gc.ca/html/stu_etu_042005_16_e.php. Accessed February 11, 2013.

87. I. N. Engleberg & J. A. Daly (2009). *Presentations in Everyday Life,* 3rd edn (p. 56). Boston: Pearson/Allyn and Bacon.

88. Rolls, op. cit. p. 179.

CHAPTER 6

NONVERBAL COMMUNICATION
MESSAGES BEYOND WORDS

LEARNING OUTCOMES

LO1 Explain the defining characteristics of nonverbal communication.

LO2 List and offer examples of each type of nonverbal message introduced in this chapter.

LO3 Recognize how individual factors such as voice, touch, and physical attractiveness are related to nonverbal communication.

LO4 Become more aware of how external factors such as distance, environment, and time are related to nonverbal communication.

LO5 Improve your nonverbal communication in the workplace.

LO1
Characteristics of Nonverbal Communication

In the following pages, we'll look at characteristics that are true in all the forms and functions of nonverbal communication.

What's going on in the photo of the couple? You don't have to be a mind reader to recognize that there are several unspoken messages being expressed here. Some social scientists argue that 93 percent of the emotional impact of a message comes from nonverbal sources, while others suggest a more conservative estimate of 65 percent.[1] Regardless of the precise figure, nonverbal communication plays a vital role in human interaction.

Nonverbal communication is defined as messages expressed by other than linguistic means. This includes messages transmitted by vocal cues that don't involve language such as sighs, laughs, and other assorted noises as well as the nonlinguistic dimensions of the spoken word such as volume, rate, pitch, and so on. Of course, it also includes the features most people think of when they consider nonverbal communication: body language, gestures, facial expressions, posture, and so forth. Most communication scholars wouldn't define sign languages as nonverbal, however, because they are symbolic in nature, like words. (See **Table 6.1**.)

Nonverbal communication Messages expressed by other than linguistic means.

What do you THINK?

Nonverbal communication isn't as effective as verbal.

1	2	3	4	5	6	7
strongly agree						strongly disagree

TABLE 6.1
The Intersection between Verbal and Nonverbal Communication

	Verbal	**Nonverbal**
Vocal	spoken language	signs, snorts, grunts, laughter tone, pitch, rate, laughter
Nonvocal	sign language, emblems	illustrators, adaptors, facial expressions, body orientation

Gawrav Sinha/E+/Getty Images

By examining the characteristics of nonverbal communication, you can begin to gain insight into just how rich and powerful it can be.

Nonverbal Skills Are Vital

It's hard to overemphasize the importance of effective nonverbal communication and the ability to read and respond to others' nonverbal behaviour.[2] Some people even think that nonverbal communication is more important than verbal communication. Nonverbal encoding and decoding skills are a strong predictor of popularity, attractiveness, and socioemotional well-being.[3] Good nonverbal communicators are more persuasive and have greater success in settings ranging from careers to playing poker to romance. Sensitivity to nonverbal communication is a

Paramount/Allstar Picture Library

major part of "emotional intelligence," and researchers recognize that it's impossible to study spoken language without paying attention to its nonverbal dimensions.[4]

All Behaviour Has Communicative Value

In reality, we cannot stop communicating. The impossibility of not communicating is extremely important to understand because it means that each of us is a kind of transmitter that can't be shut off.[5] No matter what we do, we give off information about ourselves through our posture, clothing, facial expressions, eyes, and so forth.[6] Of course, we don't always intend to send nonverbal messages. Unintentional nonverbal behaviours differ from deliberate ones.[7] For example, we stammer, blush, frown, and sweat without meaning to do so. But even if our nonverbal behaviour is unintentional, others still pick up on it and make interpretations about it.

Some theorists argue that unintentional behaviours provide information but it shouldn't count as communication.[8] We believe, however, that even unconscious and unintentional behaviours convey messages and are thus worth studying.

> **What you are speaks so loudly I cannot hear what you say.**
>
> — Ralph Waldo Emerson

Nonverbal Communication Is Primarily Relational

While some nonverbal messages serve utilitarian functions (police officers direct the traffic or surveyors use hand motions to coordinate their work), nonverbal

"Is your knee still bothering you?"

Reprinted with permission from LaughingStock Licensing Inc.

communication more commonly expresses relational and identity messages.[9]

Take identity management, for example. What do you do when you attend a party and meet new people who you'd like to get to know better? Instead of going up to someone and saying, "Hi! I'm attractive, friendly, and easygoing," you behave in ways that present your identity through nonverbal means.[10] You might smile and try to look relaxed. There's also a good likelihood that you dressed carefully—even if the image you've chosen looks as though you hadn't given a lot of attention to your appearance.

Along with identity management, nonverbal communication defines the kind of relationships we have with others. Greeting another person with a wave, a handshake, a nod, a smile, a clap on the back, or a big hug sends messages about the nature of your relationship with that person. Within romantic relationships, displays of affection such as sitting close together, holding hands, or exchanging affectionate gazes are strongly connected to satisfaction and commitment.[11]

Nonverbal communication performs a third valuable social function: conveying emotions that we may be unwilling or unable to express—or we aren't even aware of. In fact, nonverbal communication is much better suited to expressing attitudes and feelings (you're tired or you're attracted to a person in the group). It is much more limited when used to express simple facts (the book was written in 2017), past or future tenses (I was stressed yesterday), an imaginary idea (what if . . .), or conditional statements (If you don't get the job, we'll have to find a smaller place).

Nonverbal Communication Occurs in Mediated Messages

As technology develops, more Internet and phone messages are including visual and vocal dimensions, making communication richer and enhancing understanding.[12] For example, we see this with Skype and FaceTime. However, with text messaging or e-mails, we are forced to rely on a few emoticons or emoji to relay emotional expression.[13] But these too can sometimes be ambiguous and confusing.[14] For example, a smiley face could have several meanings such as, "I'm happy," "I'm kidding," or "I just zinged you." Clearly, while such symbols can be helpful, they cannot possibly substitute for the rich mixture of nonverbal messages that flow in face-to-face and telephone exchanges.

Not only does the content of the nonverbal message matter, when it was sent is equally important.[15] If you have ever been upset because a friend didn't get back to you soon enough, then you understand the role that time (chronemics) plays in online interactions. Communicators have expectations about when others should reply to their posts, emails, or text messages and delays are perceived negatively.

Nonverbal Communication Serves Many Functions

You may be getting the idea that words and actions are unrelated. However, nonverbal behaviours often operate in tandem with verbal ones, as you'll see in this section. But first, take a look at **Table 6.2** to see some of the differences between verbal and nonverbal communication.

COMMUNICATION
COMPETENCE

Nonverbal Communication in Everyday Life

Seinfeld **(TV series, 1989–1998, available on CraveTV, DVD, and reruns)**

In this popular television series, familiar characters Jerry, George, Elaine, and Kramer regularly monitor, discuss, and poke fun at people's nonverbal communication traits. Fans of the show remember the "Close Talker," who infringes on others' personal and intimate space, the "Low Talker," who whispers everything she says, the "High Talker," whose vocal pitch is far higher than normal for a man, and the woman with the "man hands." Other antics occur over George's unintentional winking, the size of Elaine's head, Jerry's puffy shirt, and Kramer's body tan. The writers of the show clearly understood that people pay a great deal of attention to nonverbal communication cues.

TABLE 6.2
Some Differences between Verbal and Nonverbal Communication

	Verbal Communication	Nonverbal Communication
Complexity	One dimension (words only)	Multiple dimensions (voice, posture, gestures, distance, etc.)
Flow	Intermittent (speaking and silence alternate)	Continuous (it's impossible to not communicate nonverbally)
Clarity	Less subject to misinterpretation	More ambiguous
Impact	Has less impact when verbal and nonverbal cues are contradictory	Has stronger impact when verbal and nonverbal cues are contradictory
Intentionality	Usually deliberate	Often unintentional

Repeating
Nonverbal behaviours that duplicate the content of a verbal message.

Complementing
Nonverbal behaviour that reinforces a verbal message.

Substituting
Nonverbal behaviour that takes the place of a verbal message.

Accenting
Nonverbal behaviours that emphasize part of a verbal message.

Regulating
A function of nonverbal communication in which nonverbal cues control the flow of verbal communication between and among individuals.

Repeating

The first function of nonverbal communication is **repeating**. If someone asked for directions to the nearest drugstore, you might say, "North of here about two blocks," repeating your instructions nonverbally by pointing north. This sort of repetition isn't just decorative: People remember comments accompanied by gestures more than those made with words alone.[16]

Complementing

Even when it doesn't repeat language, nonverbal behaviour reinforces what's been said. **Complementing** nonverbal behaviours match the thoughts and emotions that the communicator is expressing verbally. For example, imagine the difference between saying "thank you" with a sincere facial expression and tone of voice, and saying the same words in a deadpan manner and with a monotone voice.

Substituting

When a friend asks, "What's up?" you might shrug your shoulders or make a face instead of actually answering the question. It's easy to recognize expressions that function like verbal interjections and say, "Gosh," "Really?" "Oh, please!" and so on.[17] Nonverbal **substituting** is sometimes used when communicators are reluctant to express their feelings—instead, they sigh, roll their eyes, or yawn. Likewise, parents just need to glare at their children and they know to behave accordingly. Or a woman might flick her hair and tilt her head to convey to a person that she is "interested."

Accenting

Just as we use italics to emphasize an idea in print, so do we use nonverbal devices to emphasize oral messages. Pointing an accusing finger adds emphasis to criticism. Other examples of **accenting** include emphasizing certain words with the voice ("It was *your* idea!") or adding a bit of sarcasm.

Regulating

Nonverbal behaviours serve to **regulate** the flow of verbal communication.[18]

Felix Behnke/Cultura/Getty Images

The Canadian Press/Darren Calabrese

Conversations are regulated by nodding ("I understand" or "keep going"), looking away (lack of attention), or moving toward the door (ending the conversation). Of course, such nonverbal signals don't guarantee that the other party will pay attention, interpret, or respond in the ways we hope.

> **Beware of the man whose belly does not move when he laughs.**
>
> — Chinese proverb

Contradicting

People often simultaneously express different and even **contradicting** messages in their verbal and nonverbal behaviours. A common example of this sort of **mixed message** is the experience we've all had of hearing someone with a red face and bulging veins yelling, "Angry? No, I'm not angry!" In situations like these, we tend to believe the nonverbal message instead of the words.[19]

Nonverbal Communication Offers Deception Cues

When message senders are telling lies, their nonverbal behaviour sometimes gives them away. This is known as **leakage** and it can come through a number of nonverbal channels. For example, while facial expressions offer important information,[20] deceivers are more likely to monitor these **deception cues** and maintain a "poker face." More reliable indicators of lying are pupil dilation[21] and vocal cues.[22] In one experiment, subjects who tried to be deceitful made more speech errors, spoke for shorter periods of time, and had a lower speech rate. Another experiment revealed that liars' voices were more high-pitched than those of truth tellers. See **Table 6.3** to learn some of the conditions under which leakage is more likely.

While self-help books and seminars claim that liars can be easily identified, the scientific research doesn't support that notion. Communication scholars Judee Burgoon and Tim Levine, who have studied deception detection for years, have found three consistent results:[23]

- We are accurate in detecting deception only slightly more than half the time—in other words, only a shade better than leaving it to chance.
- We overestimate our abilities to detect others' lies—in other words, we're not as good at catching deception as we think we are.
- We have a strong tendency to judge others' messages as truthful—in other words, we want to believe people wouldn't lie to us, which biases our ability to detect deceit.

As one writer put it, "There is no unique telltale signal for a fib. Pinocchio's nose just doesn't exist, and that makes liars difficult to spot."[24] For example, people erroneously believe that liars don't make eye contact

TABLE 6.3

Leakage of Nonverbal Cues to Deception

Deception Cues Are More Likely When the Deceiver

Wants to hide emotions being felt at the moment

Feels strongly about the information being hidden

Feels apprehensive or guilty about the deception

Gets little enjoyment from being deceptive

Has not had time to rehearse the lie in advance

Knows there are severe punishments for being caught

Based on P. Ekman (2001). *Telling Lies.* New York: Norton.

Contradicting
Nonverbal behaviour that is inconsistent with a verbal message.

Mixed message
Situations in which a person's words are incongruent with his or her nonverbal behaviour.

Leakage
Nonverbal behaviours that reveal information a communicator does not disclose verbally.

Deception cues
Nonverbal behaviours that signal the untruthfulness of a verbal message.

Phovoir/Shutterstock.com

"Be honest—how much are you exercising?"

Charles Barsotti The New Yorker Collection/The Cartoon Bank

and fidget. In reality, liars often sustain *more* eye contact and fidget *less*, in part because they believe that to do otherwise might look deceitful.[25] While it's possible to make some generalizations about nonverbal tendencies of liars, caution should be exercised in making such evaluations based on limited and ambiguous nonverbal cues.[26]

Nonverbal Communication Is Ambiguous

Nonverbal messages are even more ambiguous than verbal ones. For example, consider the photo of the man and woman at the grocery store checkout. What do you think the relationship between them is? Can you be sure? Even something as simple as a wink can be interpreted by college students, for instance, as an expression of thanks, a sign of friendliness, a measure of insecurity, a sexual come-on, or an eye problem.[27]

The ambiguous nature of nonverbal behaviours becomes clear in the area of courtship and sexuality. Does a kiss mean "I like you a lot" or "I want to have sex"? According to one survey, college students saw kissing as an indicator of desire to have sex.[28] However, kissing is often considered a willingness to have sex, which is quite different. Intentions are far less likely to be misunderstood if they are accompanied by verbal cues. For example, does playing with hair or jewellery mean that you're a little stressed about something or does it mean you're attracted to a person? A group of Safeway workers in the United States was asked to smile and make eye contact with their customers. But the group had to file a grievance because their nonverbal gestures were continually interpreted as flirting.[29]

Because of the ambiguous nature of nonverbal communication, it is important not to read, or interpret, one cue but to look at the whole picture. Further, you must consider context, culture, and the nature of the relationship you have with the person. Keeping an open mind and not jumping to conclusions is essential.

Dreamworks SKG/Allstar Picture Library
Image source/Getty Images

"What is it, boy? Want to go outside?"

© www.CartoonStock.com

It's more difficult for some people to decode nonverbal signals than it is for others. Young boys often miss nonverbal emotional messages like when teachers express displeasure through arched eyebrows.[30]

People with nonverbal learning disorder (NVLD) find it dramatically more difficult to read facial expressions, tone of voice, and other cues than the average person.[31] Humour or sarcasm can be especially hard to understand. Thus, they are unable to examine nonverbal cues to ensure that what is said is what is intended. Even for those who don't suffer from NVLD, the ambiguity of nonverbal behaviour can be confusing and frustrating. Using the perception-checking tool you learned in Chapter 3 can help you decipher the meanings that communicators are actually trying to convey.

Influences on Nonverbal Communication

The way we communicate nonverbally is influenced to a certain degree by how we are socialized in terms of gender and culture.

Gender

Although few of us act like stereotypical feminine or masculine movie characters, there are many gender differences when it comes to nonverbal communication. For example, women are more expressive and better at recognizing others' nonverbal behaviour.[32] More specifically, compared to men, women:

- smile more;
- use more facial expressions;
- use more head, hand, and arm gestures (but less expansive gestures);
- touch others more;
- stand closer to others;
- are more vocally expressive; and
- make more eye contact.[33]

Men's and women's nonverbal communication differs in other ways, too.[34] Women are more vocally expressive. Men are more likely to lean forward in conversations, and they require and are given more personal space. Women face conversational partners head on, while men typically stand at an angle. However, male-female nonverbal differences are less pronounced in conversations involving gay and lesbian participants.[35] Gender certainly

Looking at Diversity

Let's Get Together – LGBTQ Preening Gestures

Jessie Rose MacDonald interviewed people in the LGBTQI (Lesbian, gay, bisexual, transexual, queer or questioning, and intersex) community to better understand their courtship behaviours.

We often hear about the preening gestures (or courtship behaviours) used by heterosexuals to attract one another, but what signals do individuals in the LGBTQI community use? I interviewed several individuals to see what I could learn. This is what they told me.

"The difference between flirting with girls and flirting with guys," one woman said "is that you need to rely on certain cues before you can even start to flirt; cues like hair, clothing, etc. — gaydar! And even then, there's no guarantee. It's the worst." She explains that she uses eye contact to determine whether or not someone is interested. As she says, "You wait for someone to keep eye contact for just a few seconds longer than is socially acceptable and then it's game on." She says that she usually flirts with both men and women in the same way, but that, "there is that extra difference of figuring out if flirting would even be welcome."

Once the women establish that their potential partner is receptive, then the behaviours appear to be similar to those used by heterosexuals. For instance, one woman said she tries to make herself look good and attempts to get the person's attention by laughing and smiling to show that she is a fun person. "I'd make eye contact and when I got theirs back, I would try to lock eyes." Another woman told me she wasn't interested in the more obvious forms of preening gestures. Instead, she preferred to flirt with women in intimate settings. She explained that one of the most attractive things to her was when a woman gently grazed her arm or played with her hair. She also noted that she was drawn in by intense eye contact, but only in intimate environments. In more public settings, she said, intense eye contact would probably be "creepy."

The men also talked about the importance of attracting attention. One man said that when he is trying to gain someone's attention (a man or a woman), he showcases his best features, his "eyes, ass, and lips." And, while he generally maintains a hostile attitude, his entire demeanour changes when he flirts — he assumes a friendly, open, approachable body posture. Another man shared that, "If I see a guy that I find attractive, I usually try to catch his eye and smile. To be sure they know I'm flirting, I try to give them a once over and I make sure they see me doing it. If they're a passerby, I will do a double-take, hoping they notice." His goal is to have the individual make the first move. He goes on to say, "As proud and confident as I am with my sexuality, I still don't want to make a straight guy uncomfortable by hitting on him so openly or so aggressively. My courting abilities are better suited for one-on-one conversation. That's where I have the most success."

Another male interviewee talked about confidence. Not only did he attempt to look confident, he was attracted by confidence in others. He described it as,

> . . . things such as good posture, a positive facial expression (happiness, a smile), and a well put-together and trendy outfit. Clothing is a pretty important part of a person's appearance for me. Knowing how to wear a good outfit shows me that you take pride in your appearance and how you present yourself. Oh, and hair! Add hair. People who don't style their hair just look lazy.

Noting that he was not entirely shallow, he added other things he found attractive:

> Being funny is more important to me than anything else. If you're beautiful with no personality then you're not going to get very far. I always try to be witty and clever when I'm talking to a guy I'm interested in. Touch is also great. A light touch on the knee or arm feels nice and personal, even when the intention is non-sexual.

Finally, one man brought up the notion of sex roles within the relationship: "I think a lot of gays (if they want to be the 'man' in the relationship) will do things to affirm their masculinity. I will lower my voice, try to sound manly, stand tall, etc." This is very interesting, because in most heterosexual relationships, the stereotypical male and female roles are already established. Individuals in the LGBTQI community (or at least gay men), however, need to negotiate these when the relationship begins.

The information above offers just a small peek into the LGBTQI community courting behaviours. However, it's important to note that the interviews include the experiences of a select few individuals and may not be representative of the entire community. Even so, it is interesting to scratch the surface of this branch of communication that has not yet been explored in depth.

has an influence on nonverbal style, but the differences are often a matter of degree as opposed to the type of nonverbal communication.

Culture

Cultures have different nonverbal languages as well as verbal ones.[36] In a Canadian study, for example, anglophones and francophones were asked to rate the gestures of bilingual speakers who each spoke one language and then the other. The results support the stereotype that francophones speak with their hands. Francophones, regardless of which language they spoke, gestured more than anglophones.[37] Some anglophones actually gesture more when they speak French. One English speaker related that when she spoke French, her whole body spoke.

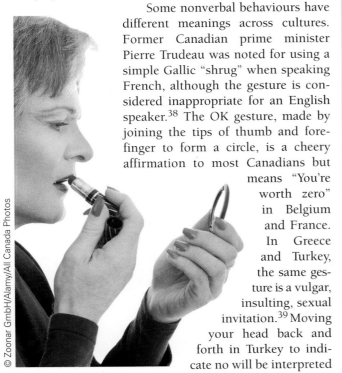

Some nonverbal behaviours have different meanings across cultures. Former Canadian prime minister Pierre Trudeau was noted for using a simple Gallic "shrug" when speaking French, although the gesture is considered inappropriate for an English speaker.[38] The OK gesture, made by joining the tips of thumb and forefinger to form a circle, is a cheery affirmation to most Canadians but means "You're worth zero" in Belgium and France. In Greece and Turkey, the same gesture is a vulgar, insulting, sexual invitation.[39] Moving your head back and forth in Turkey to indicate no will be interpreted as "I don't understand," and showing the sole of your shoe to someone in Egypt is a grave insult.[40] Given this sort of cross-cultural ambiguity, you can see how an innocent tourist can generate nonverbal misunderstandings.

Other differences can damage relationships without the parties ever recognizing what went wrong. According to Edward Hall, North Americans conduct business at a distance of roughly 1.2 metres; people from the Middle East stand much closer.[41] You can visualize the awkward advance-and-retreat pattern that might occur when people from these cultures meet. One author experienced this at a party. While talking to a Middle Eastern man, she noticed that he kept moving closer to her. Feeling that her personal space was being invaded, she kept moving backward. She later learned, however, that he couldn't understand why she was being so rude.

CHAPTER 6 Nonverbal Communication: Messages beyond Words 153

Clearly, it can be difficult for foreign students studying in Canada. Male students from Saudi Arabia, for instance, talk about having to "learn the rules." For instance, they were surprised that heterosexual men in Canada typically don't kiss when they meet, don't sit close together, and don't hold hands, and that these actions might suggest a gay relationship. They learned that it's professional for men and women to shake hands in Canada. They also told us that while they would be offended if someone in Saudi Arabia sat with the sole of his or her foot facing them, they were not offended in Canada because no negative connotations were intended. Once they understand the new "rules" they adapt quickly.

Eye contact patterns also vary around the world.[42] A direct gaze is considered appropriate for speakers seeking power in Latin America, the Arab world, and southern Europe. On the other hand, Asians, Indians, Pakistanis, and northern Europeans gaze at a listener peripherally or not at all out of respect for the other person.[43] In either case, deviations from the norm are likely to make a listener uncomfortable.

The use of time also depends greatly on culture.[44] North Americans, Germans, and the Swiss tend to be *monochronic* in that they emphasize punctuality, schedules, and completing one task at a time. In South America and in Mediterranean cultures, they are more *polychronic*, with flexible schedules and multitasking.[45] For example, a psychologist teaching at a university in Brazil found that some students arrived halfway through a two-hour class but stayed put asking questions when the class was scheduled to end.[46] This flexibility is very different from what occurs in our Canadian classrooms. As **Table 6.4** shows, differences in cultural rules can lead to misunderstandings.

TABLE 6.4
Cultural Differences in Nonverbal Communication Can Lead to Misunderstandings

Behaviours that have one meaning for members of the same culture or co-culture can be interpreted differently by members of other groups.

Behaviour	Probable In-Group Perception	Possible Out-Group Perception
Avoidance of direct eye contact (First Nations)	Used to communicate attentiveness or respect	A sign of inattentiveness; direct eye contact is preferred
Aggressively challenging a point with which one disagrees (African Canadian)	Acceptable means of dialogue; not regarded as verbal abuse or a precursor to violence	Arguments are viewed as inappropriate and a sign of potential imminent violence
Use of finger gestures to beckon others (Asian)	Appropriate if used by adults for children, but highly offensive if directed at adults	Appropriate gesture to use with both children and adults
Silence (First Nations)	Sign of respect, thoughtfulness, and/or uncertainty/ambiguity	Interpreted as boredom, disagreement, or refusal to participate
Touch (Spanish, Italian)	Normal and appropriate for interpersonal interactions	Deemed appropriate for some intimate or friendly interactions; otherwise perceived as a violation of personal space
Public display of intense emotions (African Canadian)	Accepted and valued as measure of expressiveness; appropriate in most settings	Violates expectations for self-controlled public behaviours; inappropriate in most public settings
Touching or holding hands of same-sex friends (Asian)	Acceptable in behaviour that signifies closeness in platonic relationships	Perceived as a sign of homosexuality when displayed by two men.

Observing What You See

As a grad student, I often had my morning tea and bagel between classes at the student union cafeteria and entertained myself by watching the goings-on. As most people-watchers do, I selected a table with a good view that included the cash register, where most of the "action" occurred. From my carefully selected position, I watched and made inferences about people.

On several occasions, I happened to notice an attractive, dark-haired male student who appeared to be in his junior or senior year. He had strong white teeth that contrasted with his tanned complexion. About six feet tall, he had a trendy haircut and wore blue jeans and hiking boots. Under what looked like a ski jacket (I believe I saw a lift tag), he wore a light-coloured turtleneck and a wool sweater. He had a strong but not overpowering body, and it was clear that he exercised regularly. In fact, he looked like he had just walked out of an L.L. Bean or Eddie Bauer catalogue.

One day he greeted a tall, well-dressed woman in her 50s with a polite hug. They looked surprised but not unhappy to see one another and they chatted. Their relationship seemed to fall somewhere between professional and informal — as though they had known each other at one time. After three or four minutes, both smiled, said goodbye to one another, and looked for seats in different parts of the cafeteria.

I had observed this student's behaviour for a week and a half when our eyes met. Because I was a married woman and seven years his senior, I quickly looked away, not wanting to communicate interest. But shortly after this encounter, we met at a university function. When introduced, we both acknowledged having seen each other in the cafeteria. He noted that when he smiled at me, I hadn't returned it, and as a result, he concluded that I wasn't very friendly. This surprised me — I had no idea my nonverbal response relayed such aloofness.

However, his comments gave me an opportunity to offer my interpretation of him. Based on my observations, I told him that I guessed that he was from an upper-middle-class background — his parents might be doctors or lawyers. He conceded that his father was a doctor, his mother a lawyer, and was quite amazed that I should have guessed this. It was a guess, but based on his appearance — expensive clothing, expensive teeth, and a refined manner. Clearly, he wanted for nothing. I continued by saying that he was probably in the sciences (he was an engineering student), that he skied (he did), and that he lived in a fraternity house (right again). I was correct on all three counts. Again, my predictions were educated guesses, although the lift tag helped a lot. I probably guessed he was in engineering because I thought I had seen him one day with an engineering friend of mine. Regarding the fraternity, most of the guys on campus who looked like him lived in frat houses.

By now, he was becoming uncomfortable. The final straw came when I mentioned his recent interaction with the older woman. I told him that, based on his friendly but polite and distant interaction style, the woman was probably not a professor but rather the mother of a friend. It looked like she had asked how he was, how his courses were going, and he had responded in kind. I took another guess and suggested that perhaps she was the mother of a former girlfriend.

Correct. He was dumbfounded!

Am I a witch with special powers? No, but I do possess the power of observation. And you will have this same power once you hone your sensitivity to nonverbal messages and look beyond what you see. It's easier than you think.

Now, I wonder if anyone was observing me as I enjoyed my tea and bagel.

Judith A. Rolls

Despite differences like these, some nonverbal behaviours are universal. Smiles and laughter are signals of positive emotions, for example, while sour expressions convey displeasure in every culture.[47] Charles Darwin believed that expressions like these are the result of evolution, functioning as survival mechanisms that allowed early humans to convey emotional states before the development of language.

LO2
Types of Nonverbal Communication

One way to enhance your ability to pick up on and decode nonverbal communication is to recognize its many different types.

Body Movement

The first type of nonverbal communication to be discussed is **kinesics**, the study of body position and motion. This includes body orientation, posture, gestures, facial expressions, and eye movements.

Body Orientation

We'll start with **body orientation**—the degree to which we face toward or away from someone with our body, feet, and head. Facing someone directly generally signals your interest and facing away signals a desire to avoid involvement. When two friends are in deep conversation with one another, they face one another. Should a third party attempt to join them at this inappropriate time, the friends will likely turn their bodies slightly away from the intruder, thus making it known that they do not wish to be interrupted.

You can learn a good deal about how people feel by observing the way they position themselves. The next time you're in a crowded place where people can choose who they face directly, try noticing who seems to be included in the action and who seems to be subtly left out. And, in the same way, pay attention to your own body orientation, especially when you're doing group work. You may be surprised at what you learn.

> I could hear every word
> that he wasn't saying.
>
> — Jo-Anne Rolls
> "Every Word"

"Say what's on your mind, Harris—the language of dance has always eluded me."

Robert Mankoff The New Yorker Collection/The Cartoon Bank

Posture may be the least ambiguous type of nonverbal behaviour. In one study, observers were asked to assign emotions to 176 computer-generated mannequin figures. The raters had over 90 percent success with postures related to anger, sadness, and happiness.[48] Disgust, on the other hand, was the hardest to identify from body posture, and some raters thought that surprise and happiness had similar postural configurations.

Tension and relaxation also offer clues about feelings. We assume relaxed postures in nonthreatening situations and tighten up in threatening situations.[49] Based on this observation, we can learn how others feel simply by watching how tense or loose they seem to be. Tenseness also denotes status: The lower-status person is generally the more rigid, tense-appearing one, whereas the higher-status person is more relaxed. Research shows that adopting a high status pose—such as putting your feet up on the desk with your hands behind your head—can actually lead to increased feelings of power[50] provided, or course, that a woman is wearing pants as opposed to a skirt or dress!

Gestures

Gestures—movements of the hands and arms—are an important type of nonverbal communication. In fact, they are so fundamental that people who are sight-impaired from birth use them.[51] Some social scientists claim that a language of gestures was the first form of human communication, preceding speech by tens of thousands of years.[52] Canadian parents seem to agree in that many are teaching their wee children, as young as five months old, how to use sign language.[53] For example, the word "milk" is indicated by opening and closing your hand as if you were milking a cow.[54] By learning sign language, babies are able to express their needs long before they have the verbal skills to do so.

The most common forms of gestures are called **illustrators**—movements that accompany speech but don't stand on their own.[55] For instance, if someone asked you how to get to a restaurant across town, you might offer street names and addresses, but as you do so, you'll

Kinesics
The study of body position and motion.

Body orientation
The degree to which we face toward or away from someone with our body, feet, and head.

Posture
The way people carry themselves.

Gestures
Motions of the body, usually hands or arms, that have communicative value.

Illustrators
Nonverbal behaviours that accompany and support verbal messages.

Posture

Another way we communicate nonverbally is through our **posture**—the way we carry ourselves. The importance of posture is demonstrated in the number of expressions we have that link emotional states to body postures:

I won't take this lying down! (Nor will I stand for it!)

I feel the weight of the world on my shoulders.

I can stand on my own two feet.

They've been sitting on that project for weeks.

also point your fingers and gesture with your hands to illustrate how to get there. Remove the words from your directions and it's unlikely that the person would find the restaurant. Think also of people who like to "talk with their hands," even when they're on the phone and can't be seen by the other party. We tend to use illustrators more often when we are emotionally aroused—trying to explain difficult ideas when we're furious, horrified, agitated, distressed, or excited.[56] Studies also show that it is easier to comprehend and learn a second language when it is accompanied by illustrators and other nonverbal cues.[57]

A second type of gestures is **emblems**—deliberate nonverbal behaviours that have a precise meaning, known to virtually everyone within a cultural group. Unlike illustrators, emblems can stand on their own and often function as replacements for words. For example, we all know that a head nod means yes, a head shake means no, a wave means hello or goodbye, and a hand to the ear means "I can't hear you." And almost everyone over the age of five knows the meaning of a raised middle finger. But while the thumbs up sign means "good" to us, it is considered an obscene gesture in Iraq and several other countries.[58] Another example of emblems would be the sign language that babies are taught. Mothers quickly teach them the sign for milk by moving their hands as if it were milking a cow. The sign for "more" or "again" by making two fists and knocking the knuckles together.[59]

A third type of gestures is **adaptors**, also known as **manipulators**, consist of unconscious bodily movements in response to the environment. These would include fiddling with your hands, clicking a pen, or even shivering. But not *all* fidgeting signals uneasiness.[60] People are also likely to engage in self-touching when relaxed. When they let down their guard, either alone or with friends, they will be more likely to fiddle with an earlobe, twirl a strand of hair, or play with their jewellery. But these

Huntstock/Getty Images

same gestures could also be considered *preening gestures* or *courtship behaviours* that suggest an "interest" in someone. Clearly, it's important not to jump to conclusions about the meaning of adaptors.

Actually, *too few* gestures may be as significant an indicator of mixed messages as *too many*.[61] Lack of gesturing may signal a lack of interest, sadness, boredom, or low enthusiasm. Illustrators also decrease whenever someone is cautious about speaking. For these reasons, a careful observer will look for either an increase or a decrease in the usual level of gestures.

Face and Eyes

While the face and eyes are the most noticed parts of the body, their nonverbal messages are not the easiest to read. The face is a tremendously complicated

Emblems
Deliberate nonverbal behaviours with precise meanings known to virtually all members of a cultural group.

Adaptors
Movements in which one part of the body grooms, massages, rubs, holds, fidgets, pinches, picks, or otherwise manipulates another part. Also known as *manipulators*.

A commonly used emblem.

Gabi Moisa/Shutterstock.com

Microexpression
Brief facial expression.

channel of expression for several reasons. First, there are at least eight distinguishable positions of the eyebrows and forehead, eight of the eyes and lids, and ten for the lower face.[62] When you multiply this complexity by the number of emotions we feel, you can see why it's almost impossible to compile a dictionary of facial expressions and their corresponding emotions.

Second, there's the speed at which facial expressions can change. For example, slow-motion films show **microexpressions**, those brief expressions that flit across a subject's face in as short a time as it takes to blink an eye.[63] Without being aware, liars may leak their feelings though brief furrows in the brow, pursing of the lips, or crinkling around the eyes.[64] These microexpressions are more likely to occur during "high stakes" lying such as when there are severe punishments for being caught.[65] Keep in mind, however, that you would have to be a trained professional using slow-motion recordings to spot these brief deceptive cues.

In spite of the complex way in which the face shows emotions, you can still pick up clues by watching it carefully. Look for expressions that seem exaggerated. When people try to fool themselves or others, they tend to exaggerate the point, while genuine facial expressions usually last no longer than five seconds. After that, we start to doubt they are real.[66] You can also watch people when they aren't thinking about their appearance, because they're more likely to express emotions that they wouldn't show in more guarded moments.

The eyes themselves can send several kinds of messages—they can provide clues to interest in something, they can establish relationships and reflect intimacy, and they can promote credibility and manage impressions.[67] Distinguishing among these goals can sometimes be difficult. Meeting someone's glance with your eyes is usually a sign of involvement, whereas looking away is often a sign of a desire to avoid contact. This principle has a practical application in commerce: Customers leave larger tips when their servers, whether male or female,

The Look of a Victim

© iStockphoto.com/Sasa Dinic

Little Red Riding Hood set herself up to be mugged. Her first mistake was skipping through the forest to grandma's house. Her second mistake was stopping to pick flowers. At this point, as you might remember in the story, the mean, heavy wolf comes along and begins to check her out. He observes, quite perceptively, that she is happy, outgoing, and basically unaware of any dangers in her surrounding environment. The big bad wolf catches these nonverbal clues and splits to grandma's house. He knows that Red is an easy mark. From this point we all know what happens.

Body movements and gestures reveal a lot of information about a person. Like Little Red Riding Hood, pedestrians may signal to criminals that they are easy targets for mugging by the way they walk. When was the last time you assessed your "muggability rating"? In a recent study two psychologists set out to identify

those body movements that characterized easy victims. They assembled "muggability ratings" of 60 New York pedestrians from the people who may have been the most qualified to judge — prison inmates who had been convicted of assault.

The researchers unobtrusively videotaped pedestrians on weekdays between 10 a.m. and 12 p.m. Each pedestrian was taped for six to eight seconds, the approximate time it takes for a mugger to size up an approaching person. The judges (prison inmates) rated the "assault potential" of the 60 pedestrians on a 10-point scale. A rating of 1 indicated someone was "a very easy rip-off," of 2, "an easy dude to corner." Toward the other end of the scale, 9 meant a person "would be heavy; would give you a hard time," and 10 indicated that the mugger "would avoid it, too big a situation, too heavy." The results revealed several body movements that characterized easy victims: "Their strides were either very long or very short; they moved awkwardly, raising their left legs with their left arms (instead of alternating them); on each step they tended to lift their whole foot up and then place it down (less muggable sorts took steps in which their feet rocked from heel to toe). Overall, the people rated most muggable walked as if they were in conflict with themselves; they seemed to make each move in the most difficult way possible."

Loretta Malandro and Larry Barker

Excerpt from Loretta Malandro and Larry Barker, *Nonverbal Communication*, 2nd edition. New York, Random House, 1989.

Looking at Diversity

Annie Donnellon: Blindness and Nonverbal Cues

Courtesy of Annie Donnellon

I have been blind since birth, so I've never had access to many of the nonverbal cues that sighted people use. In fact, I think that "sightlings" (a pet name for my friends who are sighted) take for granted how much of their meaning comes through nonverbal channels. When I recently took an interpersonal communication course, the material on nonverbal communication was in some ways a foreign language to me.

For instance, I felt a bit left out when the class discussed things like body movement, eye contact, and facial expressions. I understand how these cues work, but I haven't experienced many of them myself. I have never "stared someone down" or "shot a look" at anyone (at least not intentionally!). While I know that some people "talk with their hands," that's something I've never witnessed and rarely do.

When the subject turned to paralanguage, I was back on familiar territory. I listen very carefully to the way people speak to figure out what they're thinking and feeling. My family and friends tell me I'm more tuned in to these issues than most sightlings are. It's typical for me to ask, "Are you okay today?" when friends send messages that seem mixed. They may say everything's fine, but their voice often tells a different story.

I'm a singer and performer, and some of my biggest frustrations have come from well-meaning teachers who coach me on my nonverbals. I remember one acting instructor asking me, "How do you think your character would express herself nonverbally in this scene?" and I thought to myself, "I have no idea." People who are sighted may think that anger cues like clenched fists, rigid posture, or shrugged shoulders are "natural" expressions, but I think that many of them are learned by watching others.

Let me pass along some key hints that can help make communication smoother and more effective. It's important to mention your name when starting a conversation with people who are blind: Don't assume they can figure out who you are from your voice. At the end of a conversation, please say that you're leaving. I often feel embarrassed when I'm talking to someone, only to find out that they walked away mid-sentence.

Most important: Clue in visually-impaired people when something is going on that they can't see. Often at my sorority meetings, something will happen that everyone is laughing about, but I'm left out of the loop because I can't see the nonverbal cues. Over the years my friends and family have learned that whispering a quick description of the events helps me feel more a part of the interaction.

Annie Donnellon

---

maintain eye contact with them,[68] and communicators who make direct eye contact are more likely to get others to comply with their requests.[69] This is why panhandlers, salespeople, and petitioners try to catch our eye. Eye contact is even responsible for selling cereal! Researchers found that cereal boxes with cartoon characters making direct eye contact with consumers sold better than those with an averted gaze.[70]

The eyes can also communicate positive or negative attitudes,[71] like when someone is seeking to demonstrate interest; hence the expression "making eyes." When our long glances toward someone else are avoided, we get the idea that they are not interested. (Of course, there are all sorts of courtship games where the receiver of a glance pretends not to notice.) The eyes can also communicate both dominance and submission.[72] We've all played the game of trying to stare down somebody, and there are times when downcast eyes are a sign of giving in.

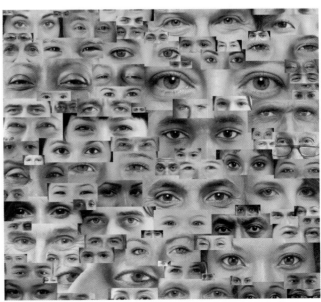

John Lund/Stephanie Roeser/Blend Images/Getty Images

Paralanguage
Nonlinguistic means of vocal expression: rate, pitch, tone, and so on.

Vocal filler
A nonlinguistic verbalization; for example, stammering or saying "um," "er," or "ah."

Even the pupils of our eyes communicate. Researchers have found that pupils dilate during the decision making process and they grow larger if the decision involves a "yes" response than they would if the decision was going to be a "no" response.[73]

LO3
Individual Factors

In addition to the types of nonverbal communication, individual factors such as voice, touch, and physical attractiveness are also related to nonverbal communication.

Voice

People are often surprised to find voice included in a chapter on nonverbal communication, but social scientists use the term **paralanguage** to describe nonverbal vocal messages. The way a message is spoken can give the same word or words many meanings. For example, note how many meanings come from a single sentence just by shifting the emphasis from one word to another:

This is a fantastic communication book. (Not just any book, but *this* one in particular.)

This is a *fantastic* communication book. (This book is superior, exciting.)

This is a fantastic *communication* book. (The book is good as far as communication goes; it may not be so great as literature or drama.)

This is a fantastic communication *book*. (It's not a play or a movie; it's a book.)

We communicate paralinguistically through tone, rate, pitch, volume—even through pauses. For example, two types of pauses can lead to communication snags. The first is the **unintentional pause**—when people collect their thoughts before deciding how best to proceed with their verbal message. Liars tend to have more unintentional pauses because they often make up stories on the fly.[74] A second type of pause is the **vocalized pause**, which includes the use of **vocal fillers** such as "um," "er," and "uh" or vocal filler words such as "like," "okay," and "ya know." Research shows that vocalized

pauses reduce a person's perceived credibility[75] and negatively affect perceptions of candidates in job interviews.[76]

Researchers have identified the power of paralanguage through the use of content-free speech—ordinary speech that has been electronically manipulated so that the words are unintelligible but the paralanguage remains unaffected. (Hearing a foreign language has the same effect.) Subjects who hear content-free speech can consistently recognize the emotion that's being expressed, and its strength.[77] Young children respond to the paralanguage of adults, warming up to those who speak warmly and shying away from those who speak in a less friendly manner.[78]

Paralanguage can affect behaviour in some surprising ways. For example, communicators are most likely to comply with requests that are delivered by speakers whose rate is similar to their own. One study showed that people who spoke rapidly responded most favourably to rapid talkers, whereas slow speakers

By Ruben Bolling, from the weekly comic strip "Tom the Dancing Bug."

preferred those whose rate was also slow.[79] Further, listeners feel more positively about people who speak at their own rate.

Sarcasm is created through the use of both emphasis and tone of voice to change a statement's meaning to the opposite of its verbal message. Experience this reversal yourself with the following three statements. First say them literally, and then say them sarcastically.

"Thanks a lot!"

"I really had a wonderful time on my blind date."

"There's nothing I like better than lima beans."

As they do with other nonverbal messages, people often ignore or misinterpret the vocal nuances of sarcasm. Children, people with weak intellectual skills, and poor listeners are more likely to misunderstand sarcastic messages,[80] and children under 10 lack the linguistic sophistication to tell when a message is sarcastic.[81]

Besides reinforcing or contradicting messages, some vocal factors influence the way speakers are perceived by others. For instance, communicators who speak loudly and without hesitations are viewed as more confident than those who pause and speak quietly.[82] People with more attractive voices are rated more highly than those with less attractive voices.[83] Further, there's a gender difference when it comes to paralanguage. Women have a tendency to raise the pitch of their voices at the end of statements, thus turning them into questions. For example, "I can meet with you at three this afternoon?" or "I submitted the report on Tuesday?" These tonal patterns reduce credibility and make the women using them sound unsure of themselves.

Finally, vocal features can be used for fun. Inuit throat songs, for instance, are essentially vocal games with the low-pitched sounds representing birds and animals. Typically created by two females standing face to face, the goal of the exercise is for one person to set a pattern and for the other to imitate the sounds and rhythms. This creates a wonderfully odd sound, produced by inhaling in the throat and varying the pitch while exhaling. "Inuit throat singing is a skill that has to be taught and developed. Inuit throat singers try to show their vocal abilities in a fun competitive manner, and the first one to either run out of breath, stop, or laugh is declared the loser of the game."[84] You can check out Inuit throat singers on Internet sites such as YouTube.

Touch

Social scientists use the word **haptics** to describe the study of touching. Touch can communicate many messages and signify a variety of relationships:[85]

- functional/professional (dental exam, haircut)
- social/polite (handshake)
- friendship/warmth (clap on back)
- sexual arousal (some kisses, strokes)
- aggression (shoves, slaps)

Because of the ambiguous nature of communication, however, touch is often misunderstood. Is a hug playful or suggestive of stronger feelings? Is a touch on the shoulder a friendly gesture or an attempt at domination? And a kiss can mean anything from a polite but superficial

Haptics
The study of touching.

greeting to the most intense arousal. What makes touch more or less intense depends on a number of factors:

- the part of the body doing the touching
- the part of the body being touched
- the length of the touch
- the pressure of the touch
- whether there is movement after contact
- whether anyone else is present
- the situation in which the touch occurs
- the relationship between the persons involved[86]

Further, touch plays a powerful role in our responses to others. For instance, in a laboratory task, subjects evaluated partners more positively when they were touched (appropriately, of course) by them.[87] Besides increasing liking, touch also increases compliance. In one study, subjects were asked by a male and female confederate to sign a petition or complete a rating scale. Subjects were more likely to cooperate when they were touched lightly on the arm. In fact, 70 percent of those who were touched complied, whereas only 40 percent of the untouched subjects were willing to cooperate.[88]

An additional power of touch is its on-the-job utility: A restaurant server's fleeting touches on the hand and shoulder result in larger tips,[89] as does squatting down to make eye contact with customers.[90] Further, touching consumers in stores increases their shopping time, their overall evaluation of the store, and the amount of money they spend.[91] And, National Basketball Association (NBA) teams with the most amount of member touching had more wins than teams with the least amount of member touching.[92] Clearly, touch can have a positive persuasive influence on individuals.

Touching is also essential for healthy development. Today we know that premature babies grow faster and gain more weight when massaged.[93] Massage also helps colicky children sleep better, improves the mood of depressed adolescents, and boosts the immune function of cancer and HIV patients. Research shows that touch between therapists and clients encourages self-disclosure, client self-acceptance, and more positive client–therapist relationships.[94] And, patients are more likely to take their medicines if touched slightly by their medical practitioners.[95]

Of course, touch must be culturally appropriate and touch by itself is no guarantee of success. As you know, too much contact can be bothersome, annoying, or downright creepy. But, research does confirm that appropriate touch can enhance your interpersonal success.

Appearance

Whether or not we're aware of the fact, how we look sends messages to others. There are two dimensions to appearance: physical attractiveness and clothing.

Physical Attractiveness

There is little dispute that people who are deemed physically attractive receive many social benefits.[96] For example, women who are perceived as attractive have more dates, receive higher grades in university or college, persuade

MANDY GODBEHEAR/Shutterstock.com

males with greater ease, and receive lighter court sentences. Both men and women whom others find attractive are rated as being more sensitive, kind, strong, sociable, and interesting than their less fortunate brothers and sisters.

The influence of physical attractiveness begins early in life.[97] When preschoolers were shown photographs of children their own age and asked to choose potential friends and enemies, children as young as three agreed about who was attractive and unattractive. Furthermore, the children valued their attractive counterparts—of both the same and the opposite sex—more highly. Teachers also are affected by students' attractiveness. Physically attractive students are usually judged more favourably—as being more intelligent, friendly, and popular—than their less attractive counterparts.[98] And teacher–student assessments work in both directions—physically attractive professors receive higher evaluations from their students.[99]

"I was just flippin' through your yearbook and couldn't help noticing that you used to be a dude."

C. Covert Darbyshire/The New Yorker Collection/The Cartoon Bank

Physical attractiveness is also helpful in the professional world, impacting hiring, promotion, and evaluation decisions.[100] However, this "lookism" can have the same prejudice as racism or sexism.[101] For example, above-average looking women gain an eight percent wage bonus while below-average appearance receives a four percent penalty. For men, the attractiveness wage bonus is only four percent but below-average looks receive a 13 percent penalty. Sometimes, though, physical attractiveness has negative effects in that interviewers might see an attractive person as a threat.[102] While attractiveness generally gets rewarded, glamorous beauty can have intimidating effects.[103]

Fortunately, attractiveness is controllable. Beauty isn't just based on the "original equipment." Evidence suggests that, as we get to know more about people and like them, we start viewing them as better-looking.[104] Further, posture, gestures, facial expressions, and other behaviours all add to our physical attractiveness.

Beauty is also culturally defined in that what may be considered beautiful in one country might not be so in another. Further, beauty is a product of what advertisers tell us is it. Today's culturally defined notion of beauty is a narrow one where women and men are supposed to be extremely thin and fit.

Clothing

Clothing is also a means of nonverbal communication that can convey 10 types of messages to others:[105]

- economic level
- economic background
- educational level
- social background
- trustworthiness
- educational background
- social position
- level of success
- level of sophistication
- moral character

Research shows that we do make assumptions about people based on their clothing.[106] Uniforms and formal attire, for example, carry influence. Researchers dressed in uniforms resembling police officers were more successful than researchers dressed in civilian clothing in requesting pedestrians to pick up litter and persuading them to lend a dime to an overparked motorist. Likewise, solicitors wearing sheriff's and nurse's uniforms increased the level of contributions to law enforcement and health care campaigns.

We're also more likely to follow the lead of high-status dressers, even when it violates social rules. In one study, 83 percent of the pedestrians followed a well-dressed jaywalker who violated a "wait" crossing signal, whereas only 48 percent followed a confederate dressed in lower-status clothing.

CHAPTER 6 Nonverbal Communication: Messages beyond Words

XiXinXing/Shutterstock.com

personal space. We think of the areas inside this bubble as our private territory—almost as much a part of us as our own bodies. When someone invades it, we feel uncomfortable—both physically and emotionally. We then move or adjust ourselves according to the person we're with and the situation we're in. It is precisely the distance that we voluntarily put between ourselves and others and that gives a nonverbal clue about our feelings and the nature of the relationship.

As you read earlier in this chapter, appropriate proxemic distances differ from culture to culture. Anthropologist Edward T. Hall described four distances that we use in our everyday lives,[108] and we choose a particular distance depending on how we feel toward the other person according to the time, the context, and our interpersonal goals.

- The first of Hall's four spatial zones begins with skin contact and ranges out to about 45 centimetres. We usually use **intimate distance** with people who are emotionally very close to us, and then mostly in private situations—making love, caressing, comforting, protecting.

- The second spatial zone, **personal distance**, ranges from 45 centimetres at its closest point to 1.2 metres at its farthest. Its closer range is the distance at which most couples stand in public. The far range runs from about 75 centimetres to 1.2 metres. As Hall puts it, at this distance we can keep someone "at arm's length." This choice of words suggests the type of communication that goes on at this range: The contacts are still reasonably close, but they're much less personal than the ones that occur a foot or so closer.

LO4
External Factors

External factors such as distance, environment, and time are also related to nonverbal communication.

Proxemics
The study of how people and animals use space.

Intimate distance
One of anthropologist Edward Hall's four distance zones, ranging from skin contact to 45 centimetres.

Personal distance
One of Hall's four distance zones, ranging from 45 centimetres to 1.2 metres.

Physical Space

Proxemics is the study of how people and animals use space. There are at least two dimensions of proxemics: distance and territoriality.

Distance

You can often tell how people feel about one another by noting the distance between them.[107] This is because each of us carries around a sort of invisible bubble of

Leo Cullum/The New Yorker Collection/The Cartoon Bank

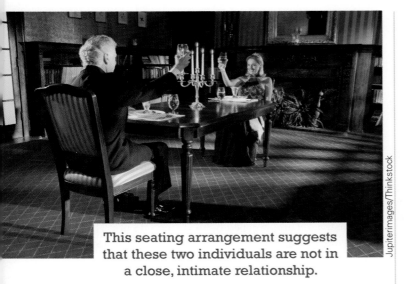

This seating arrangement suggests that these two individuals are not in a close, intimate relationship.

Jupiterimages/Thinkstock

- The third spatial zone, **social distance**, ranges from 1.2 to 3.6 metres. Within it are the kinds of communication that usually occur in business. Its closer range, from 1.2 to 2.1 metres, is the distance at which conversations usually occur between salespeople and customers and between people who work together. We use the far range of social distance—2.1 to 3.6 metres—for more formal and impersonal situations. Sitting at this distance signals a far different and less relaxed type of conversation than would pulling a chair around to the boss's side of the desk and sitting 90 centimetres away.
- **Public distance** is Hall's term for the farthest zone, running outward from 3.6 metres. The closer range of public distance is the one that most teachers use in the classroom. In the farther ranges of public space—7.5 metres and beyond—two-way communication is almost impossible. In some cases, it's necessary for speakers to use public distance because of the size of their audience, but we can assume that anyone who voluntarily chooses to use it when he or she could be closer is not interested in communication.

Choosing the optimal distance can have a powerful effect on how we regard and respond to others. For example, students are more satisfied with teachers who reduce the distance between themselves and their classes. They are also more satisfied with the course itself, and they are more likely to follow a teacher's instructions.[109] Medical patients are more satisfied with physicians who operate at the closer end of the social distance zone.[110]

Social distance
One of Hall's four distance zones, ranging from 1.2 to 3.6 metres.

Public distance
One of Hall's four distance zones, extending outward from 3.6 metres.

Territoriality
The notion that an area is claimed by an individual or a group of individuals.

Territoriality

Although personal space is the invisible bubble we carry around as an extension of our physical being, territory remains stationary. Any geographical area, such as a work station, room, house, or other physical space, to which we assume some kind of "rights" is our territory. Even though there's no real basis for these proprietary rights, the feeling of ownership exists nonetheless. You see this on the first day of class when students select a seat that typically remains "theirs" for the duration of the course,[111] or in different student groups' hanging out in particular areas of the campus. This exemplifies the notion of **territoriality**.

How people use space communicates a good deal about power and status.[112] Generally, we grant people with higher status more personal territory and greater privacy. We knock before entering a boss's office, whereas the boss can usually walk into our workspace area without hesitating. In traditional colleges and universities, professors have offices and dining rooms that are private, whereas students, with presumably less status, have no such sanctuaries.

Physical Environment

Physical settings, architecture, and interior design also affect our communication. The impressions that home designs communicate can be remarkably accurate. Researchers showed students exterior and interior slides of 12 upper-middle-class homes and then asked them to infer the owner's personality from their impressions.[113] The students were especially

Invitation to Insight

Distance Makes a Difference

1. Choose a partner and go to opposite sides of the room and face each other.
2. Very slowly begin walking toward each other while carrying on a conversation. You might simply talk about how you feel as you conduct the exercise. As you move closer, try to be aware of any change in your feelings. Continue moving slowly toward each other until you are only an inch or so apart. Remember how you feel at this point.
3. Now, while still facing each other, back up until you're at a comfortable distance for carrying on your conversation.
4. Share your feelings with each other and/or the whole group.

accurate after glancing at interior photos. The decorating schemes communicated homeowners' intellectualism, politeness, maturity, optimism, tenseness, willingness for adventures, and family orientations. The home exteriors also gave viewers accurate perceptions of the owners' artistic interests, graciousness, privacy, and quietness.

Environment can also shape the kind of interaction that takes place in it. In one experiment, subjects working in a "beautiful" room were more positive and energetic than those working in "average" or "ugly" spaces.[114] In another experiment, students perceived professors who occupied well-decorated offices as being more credible than those occupying less attractive offices,[115] and when doctors remove their desk, patients feel almost five times more at ease during

Chronemics
The study of how humans use and structure time.

office visits.[116] Further, when chairs were removed from the edge of a convalescence ward and placed around small tables, the number of conversations among patients doubled. In office cubicles, those occupants who face out rather than in send the message that they're open to communication—and it also allows them to better protect their work's confidentiality.[117]

Smell

The study of smell, known as **olfactics**, is another dimension of nonverbal communication. Smell is related to attractiveness. For instance, buyers looking at new homes are influenced by how they smell, just as we're attracted to people who smell good and repelled by those who do not. Having a sense of smell is related to a positive quality of life and[118] those suffering from smell disorders lose interest in sex and feel depressed.[119] Smell is also associated with memory in that it helps us form and recall events and information. Perhaps you've had the experience where a smell can bring you right back to an experience you have had.

> Time is a beautiful thing. It's like when you meet an old lover on the street six years later and they don't look so ugly anymore.
>
> — Sarah McLachlan

Time

Chronemics is the study of how humans use and structure time. The way we handle time can express both intentional and unintentional messages.[120] For instance,

"Men find this shampoo irresistible.
It's called 'Gee, Your Hair Smells Like A New Car'."
© www.CartoonStock.com

© The Weinstein Company/courtesy Everett Collection/The Canadian Press

and valued in mediated communication. Studies show that the length of time it takes for someone to respond to e-mail messages or to postings in virtual groups has a strong correlation with perceptions of that person.[123] As you might guess, quick responses get positive appraisals, while tardy or neglected replies can have an adverse effect on trust and effectiveness in virtual groups.[124]

LO5
Communication in the Workplace

Nonverbal Communication in the Workplace

Nonverbal communication has many applications in the workplace. In fact, it may account for why you have a job! Researchers have shown that successful interview candidates had good eye contact and communicated in a dynamic, enthusiastic, professional, and assertive manner. They also smiled and nodded more than unsuccessful interviewees.[125] (See **Table 6.5** for some suggested nonverbal behaviours that will increase your chances of getting hired.) Regardless of whether we work in healthcare, education, government, the service industry, or construction, nonverbal communication will play a large part in our professional life.

In the education field, for instance, what differentiates good teachers from bad teachers is immediacy—the

AT THE MOVIES

The Artist (2011), Rated PG 13
To see the dimensions of nonverbal communication acting in concert with one another, watch the romantic comedy The Artist, written and directed by Michael Hazanavicius. It tells the story of a 1920's silent movie idol, George Valentin (Jean Dujardin), who doesn't make the transition to talkies while his new girlfriend, Peppy Miller (Bérénice Bejo), does. Shot as an actual silent movie, it won an Oscar for Best Picture in 2012. Living in a text-based world, you may think that a movie without dialogue would be boring. However, after seeing it, you'll be amazed at the powerful role that nonverbal communication can play in the distribution of meanings.

waiting can be an indicator of status. "Important" people, whose time is supposedly more valuable than that of others, may be seen by appointment only, while it is acceptable to intrude without notice on lesser beings. Relatedly, low-status people don't make high-status people wait. It would be a serious mistake to show up late for a job interview, whereas the interviewer might keep you cooling your heels in the lobby. Important people are often whisked to the head of a restaurant or airport line, while presumably less exalted masses are forced to wait their turn.

Time also serves as a relationship marker. Research shows that the amount of time spent with a relational partner sends important messages about valuing that person.[121] In one study analyzing 20 nonverbal behaviours, "spending time together" was the most powerful predictor of both relational satisfaction and perceived interpersonal understanding.[122] Time is also measured

TABLE 6.5

Tips for Using Nonverbal Communication to Land the Job

Dress appropriately.
Walk in with confidence, but not cockiness.
Shake hands with the interviewer/s.
Sit after you have been invited to do so.
Lean forward as you speak.
Use your posture to indicate interest.
Establish and maintain eye contact, but don't stare.
Use appropriate facial expressions.
Smile when it is appropriate.
Use appropriate gestures.
Avoid adaptors.
Show your enthusiasm through your body and voice.
Avoid using vocal fillers.
Maintain a good rate.
Match your interviewer's volume.
Be attentive.

From ADLER/TOWNE/ROLLS. *Looking Out Looking In*, 1E. © 2009 Nelson Education Ltd. Reproduced by permission. www.cengage.com/permissions

Klaus Vedfelt/DigitalVision/Getty Images

degree to which individuals feel physically and psychologically close.[126] Much of immediacy is conveyed through nonverbal cues. In a review of literature, researchers write that students learn more from teachers who use gestures, who move around the classroom, who lean toward their students, and who look at them most of the time. College students report that they learn more from teachers who appropriately touch them. The authors also found that students learn more from teachers who demonstrate vocal variety.[127] The authors feel so strongly about the role that nonverbal communication plays in the teaching process that they state: "In our opinion, certification of teachers without substantial instruction in nonverbal communication concepts and skills would be pure folly. The success of teachers at all levels depends on how they communicate nonverbally."[128] What do you think? Did your favourite teachers express themselves nonverbally?

Nonverbal communication is also integral to effective healthcare. Patient-directed eye gaze, affirmative head nodding, smiling, forward leaning, and affective touch are all important behaviours to nurses wishing to establish good relationships with seniors still living in their homes or living in homes for continuous care.[129] More attention is also being placed on the use of physicians' nonverbal communication. The two major dimensions of doctor-patient communication are the medical-technical aspect and the affective-relational (interpersonal) aspect. Doctors who demonstrate more affective-relational behaviours tend to be more highly rated; we might say that they have good bedside manner. In a review of literature, one researcher found that when doctors make direct eye contact, patients are more willing to self-disclose. When it comes to nodding, patients feel more positively about doctors who do so. Further, female doctors nod more than their male counterparts and female doctors nod more to their female patients than to their male patients. Patients tend to feel more satisfied and retain more information when doctors stand in close proximity and lean in toward them.[130]

Clearly, no matter what we do in life, having an understanding of how nonverbal communication works can help us to do it better.

READY TO STUDY?

IN THE BOOK, YOU CAN:

❑ Rip out the Chapter in Review card at the back of the book to have the key terms and Learning Objectives handy, and complete the quizzes provided (answers are at the bottom of the back page).

ONLINE YOU CAN:

 MINDTAP

❑ Stay organized and efficient with MindTap—a single destination with all the course material and study aids you need to succeed. Built-in apps leverage social media and the latest learning technology. For example:

  ❑ Listen to the text using ReadSpeaker.

  ❑ Use pre-populated Flashcards as a jump start for review—or you can create your own.

  ❑ You can highlight text and make notes in your MindTap Reader. Your notes will flow into Evernote, the electronic notebook app that you can access anywhere when it's time to study for the exam.

  ❑ Prepare for tests with a variety of quizzes and activities.

Go to **nelson.com/student** to access these digital resources

Endnotes

1. Research summarized by J. K. Burgoon (1994). "Nonverbal Signals." In M. L. Knapp & G. R. Miller (Eds.). *Handbook of Interpersonal Communication* (p. 235). Newbury Park, CA: Sage.

2. R. E. Riggio (2006). "Nonverbal Skills and Abilities." In V. Manusov & M. L. Patterson (Eds.). *The Sage Handbook of Nonverbal Communication* (pp. 79–86). Thousand Oaks, CA: Sage.

3. J. K. Burgoon & G. D. Hoobler (2002). "Nonverbal Signals." In M. L. Knapp & J. A. Daly (Eds.), *Handbook of Interpersonal Communication*, 3rd ed. Thousand Oaks, CA: Sage.

4. S. E. Jones & C. D. LeBaron (2002). "Research on the Relationship between Verbal and Nonverbal Communication: Emerging Interactions." *Journal of Communication, 52*, 499–521.

5. B. M. DePaulo (1994). "Spotting Lies: Can Humans Learn to Do Better?" *Current Directions in Psychological Science, 3*, 83–86.

6. J. K. Burgoon (1994). "Nonverbal signals." In M. L. Knapp & G. R. Miller (Eds.), *Handbook of Interpersonal Communication* (pp. 229–232.). Newbury Park, CA: Sage.

7. F. Manusov (Summer 1991). "Perceiving Nonverbal Messages: Effects of Immediacy and Encoded Intent on Receiver Judgments." *Western Journal of Speech Communication, 55*, 235–253. See also R. Buck and C. A. VanLear (2002). "Verbal and Nonverbal Communication: Distinguishing Symbolic, Spontaneous, and Pseudo-Spontaneous Nonverbal Behaviour." *Journal of Communication, 52*, 522–541.

8. T. Clevenger Jr. (1991). "Can One Not Communicate? A Conflict of Models." *Communication Studies, 42*, 340–353.

9. J. K. Burgoon & B. A. LePoire (1999). "Nonverbal Cues and Interpersonal Judgments: Participant and Observer Perceptions of Intimacy, Dominance, Composure, and Formality." *Communication Monographs, 66*, 105–124. See also Burgoon & Hoobler, op. cit.

10. C. F. Keating (2006). "Why and How the Silent Self Speaks Volumes: Functional Approaches to Nonverbal Impression Management." In V. Manusov & M. L. Patterson (Eds.). *The Sage Handbook of Nonverbal Communication* (pp. 321–340). Thousand Oaks, CA: Sage.

11. S. M. Horan & M. Booth-Butterfield (2010). "Investing in affection: An investigation of affection exchange theory and relational qualities." *Communication Quarterly*, 58, 394–413.

12. A. Ramirez & J. K. Burgoon (2004). "The Effect of Interactivity on Initial Interactions: The Influence of Information Valence and Modality and Information Richness on Computer-Mediated Interaction." *Communication Monographs, 71*, 442–447.

13. K. Byron & D. Baldridge, D. (2007). "E-Mail Recipients' Impressions of Senders' Likeability: The Interactive Effect of Nonverbal Cues and Recipients' Personality." *Journal of Business Communication, 44*, 137.

14. E. Dresner & S. C. Herring (2010). "Functions of the nonverbal in CMC: Emoticons and illocutionary force." *Communication Theory*, 20, 249–268.

15. I. Vandergiff (2013). "Emotive communication online: A contextual analysis of computer-mediated communication cues." *Journal of Pragmatics*, 51, 1–12.

16. E. S. Cross & E. A. Franz (April 2003). *Talking Hands: Observation of Bimanual Gestures as a Facilitative Working Memory Mechanism*. Cognitive Neuroscience Society 10th Annual Meeting, New York.

17. M. T. Motley (1993). "Facial Affect and Verbal Context in Conversation: Facial Expression as Interjection." *Human Communication Research, 20*, 3–40.

18. J. N. Capella & D. M. Schreiber (2006). "The Interaction Management Function of Nonverbal Cues." In V. Manusov & M. L. Patterson (Eds.). *The Sage Handbook of Nonverbal Communication* (pp. 361–379). Thousand Oaks, CA: Sage.

19. H. Giles & B. A. LePoire (2006). "The Ubiquity of Social Meaningfulness of Nonverbal Communication." In V. Manusov & M. L. Patterson (Eds.). *The Sage Handbook of Nonverbal Communication* (pp. xv–xxvii). Thousand Oaks, CA: Sage.

20. P. Ekman (2003). *Emotions Revealed: Recognizing Faces and Feelings to Improve Communication and Emotional Life*. New York: Holt.

21. A. Vrig (2006). "Nonverbal Communication and Deception." In V. Manusov & M. L. Patterson (Eds.). *The Sage Handbook of Nonverbal Communication* (pp. 341–360). Thousand Oaks, CA: Sage.

22. Summarized in L. K. Guerrero and K. Floyd (2006). *Nonverbal Communication in Close Relationships*. Mahweh, NJ: Erlbaum. See also B. M. DePaulo (1980). "Detecting Deception Modality Effects." In L. Wheeler (Ed.). *Review of Personality and Social Psychology*, vol. 1. Beverly Hills, CA: Sage; J. Greene, D. O'Hair, M. Cody, & C. Yen (1985). "Planning and Control of Behaviour during Deception." *Human Communication Research, 11*, 335–364.

23. J. K. Burgoon & T. R. Levine (2010). "Advances in Deception Detection." In S. W. Smith & S. R. Wilson (Eds.). *New Directions in Interpersonal Communication Research* (pp. 201–220). Thousand Oaks, CA: Sage.

24. C. Lock (2004). "Deception Detection: Psychologists Try to Learn How to Spot a Liar." *Science News Online, 166*, 72.

25. S. Mann, S. Ewens, D. Shaw, A. Vrij, S. Leal, & J. Hillman (2013). "Lying eyes: Why liars seek deliberate eye contact." *Psychiatry, Psychology, and Law, 20*, 452–461.

26. M. Harwig & C. E. Bond (2011). "Why do lie-catchers fail? A lens model meta-analysis of human lie judgements." *Psychological Bulletin*, 137, 643–659.

27. A. E. Lindsey & V. Vigil (1999). "The Interpretation and Evaluation of Winking in Stranger Dyads." *Communication Research Reports, 16*, 256–265.

28. G. Y. Lim & M. E. Roloff (1989). "Attributing sexual consent." *Journal of Applied Communication Research, 27*, 1–23.

29. S. Synmanovich (September 11,1998). "Safeway's Perky Rules Yield Plastic Smiles." *San Francisco Business Times.*

30. J. Amos (September 8. 2005). "How Boys Miss Teacher's Reprimand." BBC News, http://news.bbc.co.uk/1/hi/sci/tech/ 4227296.stm. Accessed September 11, 2006.

31. B. P. Rourke (1989). *Nonverbal Learning Disabilities: The Syndrome and the Model.* New York: Guilford. Also see E. S. Fudge (n.d.). "Nonverbal Learning Disorder Syndrome?" www.nldontheweb.org/fudge.htm. Accessed September 11, 2006.

32. J. C. Rosip & J. A. Hall (2004). "Knowledge of Nonverbal Cues, Gender, and Nonverbal Decoding Accuracy." *Journal of Nonverbal Behaviour, 28,* 267–286; J. A. Hall (1985). "Male and Female Nonverbal Behaviour." In A. W. Siegman & S. Feldstein (Eds.). *Multichannel Integrations of Nonverbal Behaviour.* Hillsdale, NJ: Erlbaum.

33. J. A. Hall (2006). "Women and Men's Nonverbal Communication." In V. Manusov & M. L. Patterson (Eds.). *The Sage Handbook of Nonverbal Communication* (pp. 201–218). Thousand Oaks, CA: Sage.

34. For a comprehensive summary of female/male nonverbal communication differences and similarities, see P.A. Anderson (1999). *Nonverbal Communication: Forms and Functions.* Mountain View, CA: Mayfield; D. J. Canary & T. M. Emmers-Sommer (1997). *Sex and Gender Differences in Personal Relationships.* New York: Guilford.

35. T. Knofler & M. Imhof (2007). "Does sexual orientation have an impact on nonverbal behaviour in interpersonal communication?" *Journal of Nonverbal Behaviour,* 31, 189–204.

36. D. Matsumoto & S. H. Yoo (2005). "Culture and Applied Nonverbal Communication." In R. S. Feldman & R. E. Riggio (Eds.). *Applications of Nonverbal Communication* (pp. 255–277). Mahweh, NJ: Erlbaum.

37. J. M. Lacroix & Y. Rious. (1978). "La Communication Nonverbal Chez Bilingue." *Canadian Journal of Behavioural Science, 10,* 130–140.

38. For further discussion, see J. E. Alcock, D. W. Carmet, & W. W. Sadava (1996). *A Textbook of Social Psychology.* Scarborough, ON: Prentice Hall.

39. P. Ekman, W. V. Friesen, & J. Baer (May 1984). "The International Language of Gestures." *Psychology Today, 18,* 64–69.

40. M. W. Lustig & J. Koester (1996). *Intercultural Competence:Interpersonal Communication across Cultures.* New York: HarperCollins College.

41. E. Hall (1969). *The Hidden Dimension.* Garden City, NY: Anchor Books.

42. D. Matsumoto (2006). "Culture and Nonverbal Behaviour." In V. Manusov & M. L. Patterson (Eds.). *The Sage Handbook of Nonverbal Communication* (pp. 219–235). Thousand Oaks, CA: Sage.

43. J. B. Bavelas, L. Coates, & T. Johnson (2002). "Listener Responses as a Collaborative Process: The Role of Gaze." *Journal of Communication, 52,* 566–579.

44. R. Levine (1988). "The Pace of Life across Cultures." In J. E. McGrath (Ed.). *The Social Psychology of Time.* Newbury Park, CA: Sage.

45. E. T. Hall & M. R. Hall (1987). *Hidden Differences: Doing Business with the Japanese.* Garden City, NY: Anchor Press.

46. R. Levine & E. Wolff (March 1985). "Social Time: The Heartbeat of Culture." *Psychology Today, 19,* 28–35.

47. P. Eckman (2003). *Emotions Revealed.* New York: Holt.

48. M. Coulson (2004). "Attributing Emotion to Static Body Postures: Recognition Accuracy, Confusions, and Viewpoint Dependence." *Journal of Nonverbal Behaviour, 28,* 117–139.

49. A. Mehrabian (1981). *Silent Messages,* 2nd ed. Belmont, CA: Wadsworth. pp. 47–48, 61–62.

50. D. R. Carney, A. J. Cuddy & A. J. Yap (2010). "Power posing: Brief nonverbal displays affect neuroendrocrine levels and risk tolerance." *Psychological Science,* 21, 1363–1368.

51. J. M. Iverson (1999). "How to Get to the Cafeteria: Gesture and Speech in Blind and Sighted Children's Spatial Descriptions." *Developmental Psychology, 35,* 1132–1142.

52. M. C. Corballis (2002). *From Hand to Mouth: The Origins of Language.* Princeton, NJ: Princeton University Press.

53. Baby Signs Canada (2006). "The Original Baby Signs Program,"www.babysigns.ca/information.htm#1_2. Accessed April 2, 2010.

54. L. Berg (2012). *The Baby Signing Bible.* New York: Avery.

55. P. A. Andersen (2008). *Nonverbal Communication: Forms and Functions,* 2nd ed. Long Grove, IL: Waveland Press, p. 37.

56. P. Ekman & W. V. Friesen (1969). "The Repertoire of Nonverbal Behaviour: Categories, Origins, Usage, and Coding." *Semiotica, 1,* 49–98.

57. A. Sueyoshi & D. M. Hardison (2005). "The Role of Gestures and Facial Cues in Second Language Listening Comprehension." *Language Learning, 55,* 661–699.

58. B. I. Koerner (March 28, 2003). "What Does a 'Thumbs Up' Mean in Iraq?" Slate, www.slate.com/id/2080812. Accessed September 11, 2006.

59. My Smart Hands: Educating Young Minds. http://mysmarthands.com/babysigningbible. Accessed April 16, 2013.

60. P. Ekman & W. V. Friesen (1974). "Nonverbal Behaviour and Psychopathology." In R. J. Friedman & M. N. Katz (Eds.). *The Psychology of Depression: Contemporary Theory and Research.* Washington, DC: J. Winston.

61. P. Ekman (2009). *Telling Lies: Clues to Deceit in the Marketplace, Politics, and Marriage,* 4th ed. New York: W. W. Norton.

62. P. Ekman & W. V. Friesen (1975). *Unmasking the Face: A Guide to Recognizing Emotions from Facial Clues.* Englewood Cliffs, NJ: Prentice Hall.

63. W. Yan, Q. Wu, J. Liang, Y. Chen, & X. Fu (2013). "How fast are the leaked facial expressions: The duration of microexpressions." *Journal of Nonverbal Behaviour,* 37, 217–230.

64. S. Porter, L. Brinke, & B. Wallace (2012). "Secrets and lies: Involuntary leakage in deceptive facial expressions as a function of emotional intensity." *Journal of Nonverbal Behaviour, 36,* 23–37.

65. P. Ekman (2009). *Telling Lies: Clues to Deceit in the Marketplace, Politics, and marriage,* 4th ed. New York: W. W. Norton.

66. E. Krumhuber & A. Kappas (2005). "Moving Smiles: The Role of Dynamic Components for the Perception of the Genuineness of Smiles." *Journal of Nonverbal Behaviour, 29,* 3–24.

67. T. Gregerson, & P. D. MacIntyre (Forthcoming). *Optimizing Language Learners' Nonverbal Communication: From Tenet to Technique.* Bristol, UK: Multilingual Matters.

68. S. F. Davis & J. C. Kieffer (1998). "Restaurant Servers Influence Tipping Behaviour." *Psychological Reports, 83,* 223–226.

69. N. Gueguen & C. Jacob (2002). "Direct Look versus Evasive Glance and Compliance with a Request." *Journal of Social Psychology, 142,* 393–396.

70. T. Aner, M. Aviva, & B. Wansink (2015). "Eyes in the aisles: Why is Cap'n Crunch looking down at my child?" *Journal of Environment and Behaviour, 47,* 715–733.

71. P. A. Andersen, L. K. Guerrero, & S. M. Jones (2006). "Nonverbal Behaviour in Intimate Interactions and Intimate Relationships." In V. Manusov & M. L. Patterson (Eds.). *The Sage Handbook of Nonverbal Communication* (pp. 259–278). Thousand Oaks, CA: Sage.

72. J. K. Burgoon & N. E. Dunbar (2006). "Nonverbal Skills and Abilities." In V. Manusov & M. L. Patterson (Eds.). *The Sage Handbook of Nonverbal Communication* (pp. 279–298). Thousand Oaks, CA: Sage.

73. J. W. deGee, T. Knapen, & T. H. Donner (2014). "Decision-related pupil dilation reflects upcoming choice and individual bias." *PNAS Proceedings of the National Academy of Sciences of the United States of America,* 111, 5, pp. E618–E625.

74. L. K. Guerrero & K. Floyd (2006). *Nonverbal Communication in Close Relationships.* Mahweh, NJ: Erlbaum.

75. M. Davis, K. A. Markus, & S. B. Walters (2006). "Judging the Credibility of Criminal Suspect Statements: Does Mode of Presentation Matter?" *Journal of Nonverbal Behaviour, 30,* 181–198.

76. L. J. Einhorn (1981). "An Inner View of the Job Interview: An Investigation of Successful Communicative Behaviours. *Communication Education, 30,* 217–228.

77. For a summary, see M. L. Knapp & J. A. Hall (2010). *Nonverbal Communication in Human Interaction,* 7th ed. (pp. 344–346). Boston: Cengage; Hall, op. cit., pp. 344–346.

78. A. R. Trees (2000). "Nonverbal Communication and the Support Process: Interactional Sensitivity in Interactions between Mothers and Young Adult Children." *Communication Monographs, 67,* 239–261.

79. D. Buller & K. Aune (1992). "The Effects of Speech Rate Similarity on Compliance: Application of Communication Accommodation Theory." *Western Journal of Communication, 56,* 37–53. See also D. Buller, B. A. LePoire, K. Aune, & S. V. Eloy (1992). "Social Perceptions as Mediators of the Effect of Speech Rate Similarity on Compliance." *Human Communication Research, 19,* 286–311; D. B. Buller & R. K. Aune (1988). "The Effects of Vocalics and Nonverbal Sensitivity on Compliance: A Speech Accommodation Theory Explanation." *Human Communication Research, 14,* 301–332.

80. P. A. Andersen (1984). "Nonverbal Communication in the Small Group." In R. S. Cathcart & L. A. Samovar (Eds.). *Small Group Communication: A Reader,* 4th ed. Dubuque, IA: W. C. Brown.

81. M. Harris, S. Ivanko, S. Jungen, S. Hala, & P. Pexman (October. 2001). *You're Really Nice: Children's Understanding of Sarcasm and Personality Traits.* Poster presented at the 2nd Biennial Meeting of the Cognitive Development Society, Virginia Beach, VA.

82. K. J. Tusing & J. P. Dillard (2000). "The Sounds of Dominance: Vocal Precursors of Perceived Dominance during Interpersonal Influence." *Human Communication Research, 26,* 148–171.

83. M. Zuckerman & R. E. Driver (1989). "What Sounds Beautiful Is Good: The Vocal Attractiveness Stereotype." *Journal of Nonverbal Behaviour, 13,* 67–82.

84. Free Spirit Gallery (2009). "Throat Singing Music in Inuit Culture," www.freespiritgallery.ca/inuitthroatsinging.htm. Accessed April 3, 2010.

85. R. Heslin & T. Alper (1983). "Touch: A Bonding Gesture." In J. M. Wiemann & R. P. Harrison (Eds.). *Nonverbal Interaction* (pp. 47–75). Beverly Hills, CA: Sage.

86. R. Heslin & T. Alper (1983). "Touch: A bonding gesture." In J. M. Wiemann & R. P. Harrison (Eds.), *Nonverbal Interaction* (pp. 47–75). Beverly Hills, CA: Sage.

87. J. Burgoon, J. Walther, & E. Baesler (1992). "Interpretations, Evaluations, and Consequences of Interpersonal Touch." *Human Communication Research, 19,* 237–263.

88. F. N. Willis & H. K. Hamm (1980). "The Use of Interpersonal Touch in Securing Compliance." *Journal of Nonverbal Behaviour, 5,* 49–55.

89. A. H. Crusco & C. G. Wetzel (1984). "The Midas Touch: Effects of Interpersonal Touch on Restaurant Tipping." *Personality and Social Psychology Bulletin, 10,* 512–517.

90. M. Lynn & K. Mynier (1993). " Effect of Server Posture on Restaurant Tipping." *Journal of Applied Social Psychology, 23,* 678–685.

91. J. Hornik (1992). "Effects of physical contact on consumers' shopping time and behaviour." *Marketing Letters, 2,* 49–55.

92. M.W. Kraus, C. Huang, & D. Keltner (2010). "Tactile communication, cooperation, and performance: An ethological study of the NBA." *Emotion, 10,* 745–749.

93. T. Adler (February 1993). "Congressional Staffers Witness Miracle of Touch." *APA Monitor,* 12–13.

94. M. S. Driscoll, D. L. Newman, & J. M. Seal (1988). "The Effect of Touch on the Perception of Counsellors."

Counsellor Education and Supervision, 27, 344–354; J. M. Wilson (1982). "The Value of Touch in Psychotherapy." *American Journal of Orthopsychiatry, 52,* 65–72.

95. N. Gueguen & M. Vion (2009). "The effect of a practitioner's touch on a patient's medication compliance." *Psychology, Health & Medicine, 14,* 689–694.

96. G. Patzer (2008). *Looks: What They Matter More Than You Ever Imagined.* New York: Amacom.

97. K. K. Dion (1973). "Young Children's Stereotyping of Facial Attractiveness." *Developmental Psychology, 9,* 183–188.

98. V. Ritts, M. L. Patterson, & M. E. Tubbs (1992). "Expectations, Impressions, and Judgments of Physically Attractive Students: A Review." *Review of Educational Research, 62,* 413–426.

99. T. C. Riniolo, K. C. Johnson, & T. R. Sherman (2006). "Hot or Not: Do Professors Perceived as Physically Attractive Receive Higher Student Evaluations?" *Journal of General Psychology, 133,* 19–35.

100. M. Hosoda, E. F. Stone-Romero, & G. Goats (2003). "The effects of physical attractiveness on job-related outcomes: A meta-analysis of experimental studies." *Personnel Psychology, 56,* 431–462.

101. A. Furnhan (2014, April 29). "Lookism at work." Psychology Today; R. Gordon, R. Crosnoe, & X. Wang (2013). "Physical attractiveness and the accumulation of social and human capital in adolescence and young adulthood." *Monographs of the Society for Research in Child Development, 78,* 1–137.

102. M. Agthe, M. Sporrle, & J. K. Maner (2011). "Does being attractive always help? Positive and negative effects of attractiveness on social decision making." *Personality and Social Psychology Bulletin, 37,* 1042–1054.

103. T. K. Fervert & L. S. Walker (2014). "Physical attractiveness and social status." *Sociology Compass, 8,* 313–323.

104. K. F. Albada, M. L. Knapp, & K. E. Theune (2002). "Interaction Appearance Theory: Changing Perceptions of Physical Attractiveness Through Social Interaction." *Communication Theory, 12,* 8–40.

105. W. Thourlby (1978). *You Are What You Wear.* New York: New American Library, p. 1.

106. M. L. Knapp & J. A. Hall (2010). *Nonverbal Communication in Human Interaction* 7th ed. (pp. 201–207). Boston: Wadsworth.

107. P. A. Andersen, L. K. Guerrero, & S. M. Jones (2006). "Nonverbal Behaviour in Intimate Interactions and Intimate Relationships." In V. Manusov & M. L. Patterson (Eds.). *The Sage Handbook of Nonverbal Communication* (pp. 259–278). Thousand Oaks, CA: Sage.

108. E. Hall (1969). *The Hidden Dimension.* Garden City, NY: Anchor Books.

109. M. Hackman & K. Walker (1990). "Instructional Communication in the Televised Classroom: The Effects of System Design and Teacher Immediacy." *Communication Education, 39,* 196–206. See also

110. J. C. McCroskey & V. P. Richmond (1992). "Increasing Teacher Influence through Immediacy." In V. P. Richmond & J. C. McCroskey (Eds.). *Power in the Classroom: Communication, Control, and Concern.* Hillsdale, NJ: Erlbaum.

110. C. Conlee, J. Olvera, & N. Vagim (1993). "The Relationships among Physician Nonverbal Immediacy and Measures of Patient Satisfaction with Physician Care." *Communication Reports, 6,* 25–33.

111. N. Kaya & B. Burgess (2007). "Territoriality: Seat preferences in different types of classroom arrangements." *Environment and Behaviour, 39,* 859–876.

112. G. Brown, T. B. Lawrence, & S. L. Robinson, (2005). "Territoriality in Organizations." *Academy of Management Review, 30,* 577–594.

113. E. Sadalla (1987). "Identity and Symbolism in Housing." *Environment and Behaviour, 19,* 569–587.

114. A. Maslow & N. Mintz (1956). "Effects of Aesthetic Surroundings: Initial Effects of Those Aesthetic Surroundings upon Perceiving 'Energy' and 'Well-Being' in Faces." *Journal of Psychology, 41,* 247–254.

115. J. J. Teven & M. E. Comadena (1996). "The Effects of Office Aesthetic Quality on Students' Perceptions of Teacher Credibility and Communicator Style." *Communication Research Reports, 13,* 101–108.

116. R. Sommer (1969). *Personal Space: The Behavioural Basis of Design.* Englewood Cliffs, NJ: Prentice Hall.

117. R. Sommer & S. Augustin (2007). "Spatial Orientation in the Cubicle." *Journal of Facilities Management, 5,* 205–214.

118. M. Smeets, M.G. Veldhuizen, S. Galle, J. Gouweloos, A. de Haan, J. Vernooij, F. Visscher, & J. Kroeze (2009). "Sense of Smell Disorder and Health-Related Quality of Life." *Rehabilitation Psychology, 54,* 404–412.

119. V. P. Richmond & J. C. McCroskey (1995). *Nonverbal Behavior in Interpersonal Relations.* Boston: Allyn and Bacon.

120. D. I. Ballard & D. R. Seibold (2000). "Time Orientation and Temporal Variation across Work Groups: Implications for Group and Organizational Communication." *Western Journal of Communication, 64,* 218–242.

121. P. A. Andersen, L. K. Guerrero, & S. M. Jones (2006). "Nonverbal Behaviour in Intimate Interactions and Intimate Relationships." In V. Manusov & M. L. Patterson (Eds.). *The Sage Handbook of Nonverbal Communication* (pp. 259–278). Thousand Oaks, CA: Sage.

122. K. I. Egland, M. A. Stelzner, P. A. Andersen, & B. S. Spitzberg (1997). "Perceived Understanding, Nonverbal Communication, and Relational Satisfaction." In J. E. Aitken & L. J. Shedletsky (Eds.). *Intrapersonal Communication Processes* (pp. 386–396). Annandale, VA: Speech Communication Association.

123. J. B. Walther (2006). "Nonverbal Dynamics in Computer-Mediated Communication." In V. Manusov & M. L. Patterson (Eds.). *The Sage Handbook of Nonverbal Communication* (pp. 461–479). Thousand Oaks, CA: Sage.

124. J. B. Walther & U. Bunz (2005). "The Rules of Virtual Groups: Trust, Liking, and Performance in Computer-Mediated Communication." *Journal of Communication, 55,* 828–846.

125. R. Anderson & G. Killenberg (1999). *Interviewing: Speaking, Listening, and Learning for Professional Life.* Mountain View, CA: Mayfield.

126. A. Mehrabian (1970). *Silent Messages.* Belmont, CA: Wadsworth.

127. J. C. McCroskey, V. P. Richmond, L. L. McCroskey (2006). "Nonverbal Communication in Instructional Contexts." In V. Manusov & M. L. Patterson (Eds.). *The Sage Handbook of Nonverbal Communication* (pp. 421–436). Thousand Oaks, CA: Sage.

128. J. C. McCroskey & L. L. McCroskey (2006). "Nonverbal communication in instructional contexts." In B. Manusov & M. L. Patterson, (Eds.). *The Save Handbook of Nonverbal Communication* (p. 434). Thousand Oaks, CA: Sage.

129. W. M Caris-Verhallen, A. Kerkstra, & J. M. Bensing (1999). "Non-verbal Behaviour in Nurse-Elderly Patient Communication." *Journal of Advanced Nursing, 29,* 808–818.

130. J. D. Robinson (2006). "Nonverbal Communication and Physician-Patient Interaction." In V. Manusov & M. L. Patterson (Eds.). *The Sage Handbook of Nonverbal Communication* (pp. 437–479). Thousand Oaks, CA: Sage.

Rebecca Drobis/Blend Images/Getty Images

LISTENING
MORE THAN MEETS THE EAR

LO1
Listening Defined

There's a lot more to listening than nodding your head and gazing politely at a speaker. Listening is actually a very demanding activity—and one that is just as important as speaking.

If frequency is a measure of importance, then listening easily qualifies as the most important kind of communication. We spend more time listening than in any other type of communication. One study, summarized in **Figure 7.1**, revealed that post-secondary students spend about 11 percent of their communicating time writing, 16 percent speaking, 17 percent reading, but more than 55 percent listening.[1] On the job, studies show that most employees of major corporations in North America spend about 60 percent of each workday listening to others.[2]

Listening is also important in terms of making relationships work. In committed relationships, listening to personal information in everyday conversations is considered a vital ingredient of satisfaction.[3] Marital counsellors identified "failing to take the other's perspective when listening" as one of the most frequent communication problems in the couples they see.[4] When a group of adults was asked what communication skills were most important in family and social settings, listening was ranked first.[5] In fact, the *International Journal of Listening* devoted an entire issue to exploring various

FIGURE 7.1
Time Devoted to Communication Activities

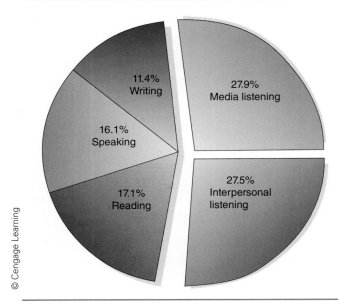

- 11.4% Writing
- 27.9% Media listening
- 16.1% Speaking
- 17.1% Reading
- 27.5% Interpersonal listening

© Cengage Learning

"I'm sorry, dear. I wasn't listening. Could you repeat what you've said since we've been married?"

Robert Mankoff The New Yorker Collection/The Cartoon Bank

contexts in which listening skills are crucial. These included education,[6] health care,[7] religion,[8] and the business world.[9] The vital role that listening plays in the workplace is further discussed later in the chapter.

So far we've used the term *listening* as if it needs no explanation but there's more to this concept than you might think. Interpersonal **listening** is defined as the process of making sense of others' spoken messages. However, we've broadened our definition to include messages of all sorts because much of today's listening takes place through mediated channels that involve the written word. For examples, perhaps you've said, "I was talking Rebekah the other day and she told me . . ." but the conversation actually took place

Listening
Making sense of others' spoken messages.

via texting, emailing, or instant messaging. We'll still focus on spoken messages in this chapter, but "listening" in contemporary society involves more than meets the ear.

Hearing versus Listening

People often think of hearing and listening as the same thing, but they are quite different. Hearing is the process in which sound waves strike the eardrum and cause vibrations that are transmitted to the brain. Listening occurs when the brain reconstructs these electrochemical impulses into a representation of the original sound and then gives them meaning. Barring illness, injury, or earplugs, you can't stop hearing.[10] Your ears pick up sound waves and transmit them to your brain whether you want them to or not. Listening, on the other hand, isn't automatic; you have to work at it.

As the cartoon about the married couple shows, people hear all the time without listening. We automatically and unconsciously block out irritating sounds or stop listening when we find a subject unimportant or uninteresting. TV commercials and nagging complaints are common examples of messages we may tune out.

© King Features Syndicate. Reprinted with permission – Torstar Syndication Services

Passive Listening

Passive listening is "superficial" listening. It can be described as mindless and occurs when we react to others' messages automatically and routinely, without much mental investment.

While passive listening may sound negative, this type of processing allows us to focus on messages that require careful attention.[11] Plus, it's impossible to listen to everything. The only realistic way to manage this onslaught of messages is to be "lazy" at times. If you think about the messages you heard today, most of them have probably been processed mindlessly.

Active Listening

By contrast, **active listening** involves paraphrasing what an individual has said and then providing a thoughtful and careful response. You'll read more about active listening later in the chapter.

Once we become accustomed to listening attentively to others, we can then engage in different types of listening. For example, we might listen critically. Critical listening involves evaluating and judging messages.[12] Being able to listen critically is an important skill. For example, if you listen critically, you can discern whether or not speakers are telling the truth, whether or not you're getting a good deal, if a new policy really has your best interests in mind, or if the attack ads you see during political campaigns are true or not.

Another type of listening that is essential in interpersonal relationships is listening empathically. Empathic listening involves mutual understanding and trust.[13] You learned in Chapter 3 that perspective taking, emotion, and concern are key elements in empathy. For example, Isabella is straight and her best friend, Chloe, is gay. Chloe hasn't come out to her parents or the wider community yet but she is thinking about doing so. She and Isabella have had many conversations about this. In order to listen empathically, Isabella needs to put herself in Chloe's situation—to try and imagine the types of fears and concerns that Chloe might have.

Sometimes we respond passively to information that deserves mindful attention. For instance, Ellen Langer's determination to study the listening process began when her grandmother complained about headaches coming from a "snake crawling around" beneath her skull. Diagnosed with senility, she actually had a brain tumor that eventually took her life. The event made a deep impression on Langer:

> For years afterward I kept thinking about the doctors' reactions to my grandmother's complaints, and about our reactions to the doctors. They went through the motions of diagnosis, but were not open to what they were hearing. Mindsets about senility interfered. We did not question the doctors; mindsets about experts interfered.[14]

Clearly, there are times when we need to listen consciously and carefully to what others are telling us.

Passive listening
Reacting to others' messages automatically, without much mental investment.

Active listening
Giving careful and thoughtful attention and responses to the messages we receive.

EAR

EYES

UNDIVIDED ATTENTION

HEART

The Chinese characters that make up the verb *to listen* tell us something significant about this skill.

Photographee.eu/Shutterstock.com

Teaching Doctors to Listen

Comstock/Thinkstock

As she looks up at the young faces in the auditorium, Cathy Chovaz's voice wavers slightly. "I could be you," she tells the audience. "You could be me. I went through university like every other student, and when I graduated, the whole world was there waiting for me. Then, bang—that whole reality changed drastically for me and my family." Her hands never stop gesturing, a habit cultivated after losing her hearing nine years ago. Chovaz has RED-M syndrome, a rare condition associated with constrictions of the small arteries in the brain, eyes, and ears that can result in small strokes, deafness, blindness, and brain dysfunction. "It wasn't just me lying there in the hospital," Chovaz tells the

medical students. "With a patient come her dreams, hopes, and ambitions. When you admit a patient, you admit all of that."

Chovaz, 35, is telling her story to first-year medical students at the University of Western Ontario in a unique program where patients become teachers and medical students learn about the human side of medicine. Developed by Dr. John Howard, it was designed as part of a shift toward patient-centred medicine. "Sometimes doctors need to be encouraged to listen to what the patient wants, rather than simply dispensing treatment," says Dr. Howard.

Dr. Wayne Weston sees the need to create doctors who are good advocates, gatekeepers, collaborators, and, most importantly, communicators. Patients' number one beef about doctors is their poor listening skills, and according to Weston, "It's one of the most common complaints to the College of Physicians and Surgeons of Ontario and a leading cause of lawsuits." It's also one of the chief reasons why women switch doctors.

On the first day of UWO's clinical methods course, students listen to the stories of several patients and develop a mission statement that describes the qualities that make good physicians. That mission becomes a focal point of the class's undergraduate medical education for students and instructors alike and helps students determine the kind of doctors they want to become. The day is an invaluable one for students, and the first-year students really listen to the patients' stories.

For Chovaz, her experience with doctors ranged from those who truly acknowledged the power of her spirit to those who treated her as a fascinating collection of symptoms. Her advice to students: "Approach your patients as whole people. People who come to you need to be in partnership with you. Keep your minds and hearts open." An improved doctor-patient relationship is long overdue.

Dahlia Reich

Dahlia Reich, Health Writer. Reprinted with permission.

Elements in the Listening Process

You may be surprised to learn that listening is a process consisting of five specific elements: hearing, attending, understanding, responding, and remembering.[15]

Hearing

Hearing is the physiological dimension of listening when sound waves strike the ear at a certain frequency and loudness. Hearing can be influenced by background noises, especially if they are loud or at the same frequency. For many people, the challenge of hearing is even more difficult

due to physiological problems. According to a survey conducted by the Canadian Hearing Society, some 23 percent of Canadians suffer from some degree of hearing loss.[16] Interestingly, males are more likely to have hearing loss than females and five percent of Canadian children ages 6–18 suffer hearing loss, but typically only in one ear.[17]

The major cause of hearing loss is exposure to noise. Marshall Chasin, an audiologist at the University of Toronto, notes that prolonged exposure to sounds above 85 decibels—equivalent of the sound of a dial tone—can cause permanent hearing loss. Little wonder individuals experience temporary hearing loss after a rock concert, which registers about 110 decibels. Chasin recommends that we preserve our hearing by reducing the volume when we listen to music.[18]

Attending

Although hearing is a physiological process, **attending** is a psychological part of the selection process. We would go crazy if we attended to everything we hear, so we filter out some messages. We tend to focus on needs, wants, desires, and interests and we attend most carefully to messages when there's a payoff for doing so.[19] For example, if you want to get better acquainted with others, you'll pay careful attention to almost anything they say, in hopes of improving the relationship.

Surprisingly, attending also helps the speaker. Participants in one study viewed brief movie segments and then described them to listeners who varied in their degree of attentiveness. Later, when the speakers' long-term recall was tested, speakers who had recounted the movie to attentive listeners remembered more details of the film.[20]

Understanding

Understanding occurs when we make sense of a message. But it is possible to hear and attend to a message without understanding it at all. And, of course, it's

possible to misunderstand a message. Communication researchers use the term **listening fidelity** to describe the degree of congruence between what a listener understands and what the message sender attempted to communicate.[21]

Responding

Responding to a message consists of giving observable feedback to the speaker, and while we don't always respond visibly to a speaker, research suggests we should. One study of 195 critical incidents in banking and medical settings showed that a major difference between effective and ineffective listening was the type of feedback offered.[22] Good listeners kept eye contact and reacted with appropriate facial expressions—which was of particular importance to children in one study who were asked to evaluate "good" versus "bad" listeners.[23] Verbal feedback such as answering questions and exchanging ideas also demonstrate attentive behaviour.[24] It's easy to imagine how a slumped posture, bored expression, or focusing on a cell phone can signal less effective listening.

Because interpersonal communication is *transactional* in nature, remember that as we are receiving messages, we are also responding to them.

Remembering

Remembering is the ability to recall information. Unfortunately, we remember only 50 percent of what we hear *immediately* after hearing it, even if we work hard

Attending
The process of filtering out some messages and focusing on others.

Understanding
Occurs when sense is made of a message.

Listening fidelity
The degree of congruence between what a listener understands and what the message sender intended to convey.

Responding
Giving observable feedback to a speaker.

Remembering
The ability to recall information.

Do you think these two figures are experiencing listening fidelity?

Types of Ineffective Listening

Although a certain amount of ineffective listening is inevitable, and sometimes even understandable, most of us have some bad listening habits. As you read through these, pick out the ones that pertain to you.

Pseudolistening

Pseudolistening is an imitation of the real thing. Pseudolisteners give the appearance of being attentive, but their thoughts are elsewhere. They look you in the eye, nod and smile at the right times, and occasionally they even respond with an "uh huh." Pseudolistening is like counterfeit communication—it's not real.

Stage-hogging

Stage-hogs (sometimes called "conversational narcissists") try to turn the topic of conversations to themselves instead of showing interest in the speaker.[26] One **stage-hogging** strategy is a "shift-response"—changing the focus of the conversation from the speaker to the narcissist: "You think *your* persuasion class is tough? You ought to try my communication theory class!"

Interruptions are another hallmark of stage-hogging. Interrupting prevents listeners from learning potentially valuable information and can damage their relationship with the speaker. Applicants who interrupt the questions in an employment interview, for example, are likely to be rated less favourably than job seekers who wait until the interviewer finishes speaking before they respond.[27]

Pseudolistening
An imitation of true listening in which the receiver's mind is elsewhere.

Stage-hogging
A listening style in which the receiver is more concerned with making a point than with understanding the speaker.

Selective listening
A listening style in which receivers respond only to the messages that interest them.

to listen.[25] Within eight hours, that 50 percent drops to about 35 percent. After two months, the average recall is only about 25 percent of the original message. Given the amount of information we process daily—from teachers, friends, the radio, movies, cell phones, and other sources—the *residual message* (what we remember) is a small fraction of what we hear. To get a sense of how tough it is to listen effectively, answer the questions in the Invitation to Insight below.

LO2
The Challenge of Listening

Being a good listener is very difficult and there are several factors that can prevent us from improving. One way to become a better listener is to recognize what can get in our way.

Invitation to Insight

Listening Breakdowns

Try to recall some specific instances when

1. You heard another person's message but did not attend to it.
2. You attended to a message but forgot it almost immediately.
3. You attended to and remembered a message but did not understand it accurately.
4. You understood a message but did not respond sufficiently to convey your understanding to the sender.
5. You failed to remember some or all of an important message.

Did this exercise change how you perceive yourself as a listener?

> Listening, not imitation, may be the sincerest form of flattery.
>
> —Dr. Joyce Brothers

Selective Listening

Selective listeners respond only to the parts of your remarks that interest them and reject everything else. While **selective listening** can be legitimate (e.g., screening out commercials, background noises), it is less appropriate in personal settings where your inattention can be insulting and

NOT REALLY LISTENING

© Mark Stivers

hurtful. Consider how you feel when speakers only perk up when the conversation shifts to something that interests them.

Insulated Listening

Insulated listening is a style of listening in which receivers ignore undesirable information. If a topic arises that listeners would rather not deal with, they simply fail to hear or acknowledge it. If reminded about an unfinished job or poor grades, they may nod and answer, but then promptly forget what you've just said.

Defensive Listening

Defensive listening means taking others' remarks as personal attacks. An example is when teenagers take their parents' questions about their friends and activities as distrustful snooping. Many defensive listeners suffer from shaky

Dean Drobot/Shutterstock.com

presenting images and avoid admitting it by projecting their own insecurities onto others.

Ambushing

Ambushers listen carefully to you, but only because they're collecting information to pounce on you. The cross-examining prosecution lawyer is a good example of **ambushing.** Using this kind of strategy will justifiably initiate defensiveness in the other person.

Insensitive Listening

Those who use **insensitive listening** respond to superficial content but fail to recognize important emotional information because they don't, or can't, read the nonverbal messages. An example would be if you asked someone, "How's it going?" The person answers by saying, "Oh, okay, I guess" in a dejected, depressed tone. You respond by saying, "Well, great! Catch you later."

Insulated listening
A style in which the receiver ignores undesirable information.

Defensive listening
A response style in which the receiver perceives a speaker's comments as an attack.

Ambushing
A style in which the receiver listens carefully to gather information to use in an attack on the speaker.

Insensitive listening
Failure to recognize the thoughts or feelings that are not directly expressed by a speaker.

Why We Don't Listen Better

In addition to our bad listening habits, there are several other reasons that make it impossible for us to listen well *all* the time. Some of these are outlined in this section.

Message Overload

Clearly, we live in a message overloaded society. We have face-to-face messages and personal media messages (text messages, phone calls, e-mails, and instant messages), all competing for our attention. This deluge of communication has made the challenge of attending tougher than at any time in human history,[28] and it's little wonder that listening can be difficult.

Preoccupation

Another reason we don't always listen carefully is that we're often preoccupied with personal concerns. It's hard to pay attention when you're worrying about an upcoming exam, getting a decent summer job, or thinking what you're going to do with your life.

© Claudia Dewald/iStockphoto

Rapid Thought

Listening carefully is also difficult for physiological reasons. The average person speaks between 100 to 150 words per minute,[29] but we can process information at rates up to 600 words per minute. Thus, we have "spare time" in our minds, which we ultimately fill by thinking about personal interests, daydreaming, planning a rebuttal, and so on. The trick is to use this spare time to understand the speaker's ideas.

Effort

Listening effectively is hard work—so hard that physical changes actually occur during careful listening: The heart rate quickens, respiration increases, and body temperature rises.[30] These changes are similar to the body's reaction to physical effort. This is no coincidence—listening carefully can be just as taxing as a workout.[31] If you've come home exhausted after an evening of listening intently to a friend in need, you know how draining the process can be.

External Noise

The physical world in which we live often presents distractions that make it hard to pay attention to others. Consider, for example, how the efficiency of your listening decreases when you are seated in a crowded, hot, stuffy room, surrounded by others talking next to you and with the roar of traffic noises outside. And, you're probably not surprised that classroom noise makes it difficult for some students to learn.[32] Even the best intentions aren't enough to ensure clear understanding in such circumstances.

Faulty Assumptions

We often make faulty assumptions that lead us to believe we're listening attentively when quite the opposite is true. For instance, we are less likely to listen when the subject is a familiar one, when we assume the speaker's thoughts are too simple or too complex, or when we think the topic is unimportant. In such circumstances, we should try to pay close attention to compensate for our assumptions.

Lack of Apparent Advantages

It often seems that there's more to gain by speaking than by listening. When business consultant Nancy Kline asked some of her clients why they interrupted their colleagues, these are the reasons she heard:

> My idea is better than theirs.
>
> If I don't interrupt them, I'll never get to say my idea.
>
> I know what they are about to say.
>
> They don't need to finish their thoughts since mine are better.
>
> Nothing about their idea will improve with further development.
>
> It is more important for me to get recognized than it is to hear their idea.
>
> I am more important than they are.[33]

dotshock/Shutterstock.com

One of the most common forms of noise today is the intrusion caused by the use of mediated communication. It clearly affects how we listen to others.

Even if some of these thoughts are true, the egotism behind them is stunning. Furthermore, nonlisteners are likely to find that the people they cut off are less likely to treat their ideas with respect. Like defensiveness, listening is often reciprocal: You get what you give.

Lack of Training

A common but mistaken belief is that listening, like breathing, is natural. In truth, listening is a skill that few people do well. However, there is no connection between how competently most communicators *think* they listen and how competent they really are in their ability to understand others.[34] The good news is that listening can be improved through instruction and training.[35] Unfortunately, more time is spent teaching other types of communication than is spent teaching listening. **Table 7.1** reflects this lopsided arrangement.

Hearing Problems

Sometimes a person's listening ability suffers from a physiological hearing problem. In such cases, both the person with the problem and others can become frustrated

TABLE 7.1
Comparison of Communication Activities

	Listening	Speaking	Reading	Writing
Learned	First	Second	Third	Fourth
Used	Most	Next to most	Next to least	Least
Taught	Least	Next to least	Next to most	Most

© Cengage Learning

How to Communicate with Someone with a Hearing Disability

Bruce C. Anderson has some useful advice

I grew up with a mild hearing disability. The word "mild" doesn't begin to describe how this affected my life. I couldn't hear many of the sounds or tones that are part of most people's voices. You can get an idea what this is like by imagining how hard it would be to listen to a muffled, quiet voice that is being drowned out by loud TV and radio playing at the same time, or trying to understand somebody whispering words while your ears are covered and your head is turned away.

If you're communicating with someone who has a hearing disability, here are a few tips. Have patience when asked to repeat something once, twice, or even three times. Remember, people with a hearing disability are doing the best they can. Help is very hard to ask for, and it is very difficult to draw attention to yourself by asking others what was said. If this still has not solved the problem, try another avenue, such as using different words or moving to a more quiet location to talk. Even writing something down may be necessary. Hard of hearing and deaf people listen with our eyes, so make sure you're standing or sitting so that the other person can see your face and your gestures.

If you make efforts like these, you will help people with hearing disabilities. And you might also get a new appreciation and respect for their world.

From ADLER/TOWNE. *Activities Manual/Student Guide for Adler/Towne's Looking Out, Looking In, Media Edition (with InfoTrac and CD-ROM)*, 10E. © 2002 Wadsworth, a part of Cengage Learning, Inc. Reproduced by permission. www.cengage.com/permissions

---

at the ineffective communication that results. One survey explored the feelings of adults who have spouses with hearing loss. Nearly two-thirds of the respondents said they feel annoyed when their partner can't hear them clearly. Almost a quarter said that beyond just being annoyed, they felt ignored, hurt, or sad. Many respondents believe their spouses are in denial about their condition, which makes the problem even more frustrating.[36] If you suspect that you or someone you know suffers from a hearing loss, it's wise to consult a physician or audiologist.

Meeting the Challenge of Listening Better

After reading the preceeding few pages, you might decide that listening well is impossible. However, here are some simple ways to help you improve.

> Learn to listen. Opportunity could be knocking at your door very softly.
>
> —Frank Tyger

Talk Less

Zeno of Citium put it most succinctly: "We have been given two ears and but a single mouth, in order that we may hear more and talk less." If you truly want to understand the speaker, don't stage-hog and shift the conversation to your ideas. Talking less doesn't mean you must remain completely silent. Using feedback to clarify your understanding and seeking new information promotes understanding. Nonetheless, most of us talk too much. Other cultures, including many First Nations people, value listening as much as talking.[37] You can appreciate the value of this approach by trying the "Invitation to insight" exercise.

To be heard, there are times you must be silent.
—Chinese proverb

Stockbyte/Thinkstock

Face Time: Phones Down, Eyes Up

iStockphoto/Thinkstock

At first cell phones seemed like a great way to stay connected to everyone. But recently, I got pretty tired of getting together socially with friends only to watch them spend most of the visit with their faces in their phones. Don't get me wrong: I was just as guilty of "quickly checking" my text messages or posting an online personal update "out with friends for dinner." But I soon realized that my online connections were distracting me from real connections with the very friends who were sitting right in front of me. Once, at a party, a friend was telling us about her week. I was distracted (again) and texting someone who wasn't even at the party. At a pause in the conversation, I looked up and responded "uh huh" to something she'd just said, even though I wasn't really listening. Turns out, my friend was sharing her news about some recent health issues and the potential need for surgery that really frightened her. My response to that was "uh huh"?! I decided then and there to put down my phone when I was out and start to really pay attention to the people I was with.

Turns out I'm not the only one tired of competing with virtual friends at real social engagements. Recently, bloggers have been talking about "the phone stack." When you meet with friends for a meal, everyone puts their phones down. Let the emails, texts, tweets, and updates ring in and avoid the temptation to check your phone. The person who simply can't resist does more than just check messages, he or she picks up the cheque for the whole table!

Courtney Thorne

Courtney Thorne

Get Rid of Distractions

Some distractions are external: ringing telephones, radio or television programs, friends dropping in, and so on. Other distractions are internal: preoccupation with your problems, being hungry, dealing with a cold, etc.

One of the greatest distractions these days is the cell phone. Most people have one in their hand, or within reach, all the time. Researchers are now finding that these phones are having a negative effect on the quality of interpersonal communication. For example, one study found that when people checked their phones regularly during conversations, they demonstrated little empathy. Those who had interactions and conversations without the presence of mobile devices showed much higher levels of empathic concern.[38] For an example of this, read Courtney Thorne's Face Time: Phones Down, Eyes Up.

Don't Judge Prematurely

Most people agree that it's essential to understand ideas before judging them. However, we often make snap judgments before we hear the entire idea, especially when it conflicts with one of our own. Conversations meant to be exchanges of ideas turn into verbal battles. Not all premature judgments are negative, though. We sometimes jump to overly favourable conclusions. It's also tempting to counterattack when we're being criticized, even when those criticisms are true. The lesson contained in these examples is clear: Listen first. Make sure you understand. *Then* evaluate.

Look for Key Ideas

It's easy to lose patience with long-winded speakers who don't get to the point—or don't *have* a point, for that matter. Nonetheless, most people do have a central idea. Using your ability to think more quickly than the speaker can talk, you may be able to extract the central idea from the surrounding mass of words. If you can't figure out

© iStockphoto.com/piranka

what the speaker is driving at, try some of the response skills which we will examine now.

LO3
Types of Listening Responses

Of the five elements of listening, it's responding that lets us know how well others are tuned in to what we're saying. Think for a moment of someone you consider a good listener. Why did you choose that person? It's probably because of the way she or he responds while you're speaking: making eye contact and nodding, staying attentive, reacting with an exclamation when you say something startling, expressing empathy and support when you're hurting, and offering another perspective or advice when you ask for it.[39]

In the rest of this chapter, a variety of response styles will be described.

Prompting

Sometimes the best response a listener can give is a small nudge to keep the speaker talking. **Prompting** involves using silences and brief statements of encouragement to draw out others. Besides helping you better understand the speaker, prompting can help listeners clarify their thoughts and feelings. Consider this example:

Katie: Julie's dad is selling his 2012 Subaru for only $5000. It's loaded—sunroof, BlueTooth, and a great sound system but I have to buy it now. Someone else is interested. It's a great deal, but it would wipe out my savings. At the rate I spend money, it would take me a while to save up this much again.

Logan: Uh-huh.

Katie: I wouldn't be able to take that ski trip to Whistler but I need a car to get back and forth to work, to the university, oh, and to the mall.

Logan: That's true.

Katie: Do you think I should buy it?

Logan: I don't know. What do *you* think?

Katie: I just can't decide.

Logan: *(silence)*

Katie: I'm going to do it. I'll never get a deal like this again.

In cases like this, prompting can be a catalyst to help others find their own answers. Prompting works best when it's sincere. Your eye contact, posture, facial expression, and tone of voice must show your concern as well. Mechanical prompting will just irritate the person.

Questioning

It's easy to understand why questioning has been called "the most popular piece of language."[40] **Questioning** can help both the person doing

Prompting
Using silences and brief statements of encouragement to draw out a speaker.

Questioning
A style of helping in which the receiver seeks additional information from the sender to be sure the speaker's thoughts and feelings are being received accurately.

Katarzyna Bialasiewicz/iStock/Thinkstock

Closed questions
Questions that call for a specific or yes/no response.

Open questions
Questions that allow the respondent to answer in a variety of ways and to include a great deal of description and detail.

Sincere questions
Questions aimed at soliciting information that enables the asker to understand the other person.

Counterfeit questions
Questions aimed at sending rather than receiving a message.

the asking and the person answering the question.[41] It can also help the asker fill in facts and details, learn what others are thinking and feeling, and find out what the other person may want. For the person answering the questions, they can serve as a tool for self-discovery. While playing counsellor can be dangerous, some questions can encourage others to explore their thoughts and feelings.

Questions are often described as open or closed. **Closed questions** seek a specific or short answer ("What is your name?" "Where do you live?") and are good for gathering facts, but not for drawing out individuals. **Open questions** allow speakers to respond in a variety of ways and to express how they think or feel about something ("Describe how you felt and what you went through when Pat left you." or "Explain your philosophical take on war."). While closed questions ask for specifics, open ones can actually be statements.

Despite their apparent benefits, not all questions are equally helpful. While, **sincere questions** are aimed at understanding others, **counterfeit questions** are aimed at sending a message, not receiving one. Counterfeit questions come in several varieties:

- **Questions that trap the speaker.** When your friend says, "You didn't like that movie, did you?" it's clear that your friend disapproves. The question leaves you with two choices: disagree and defend your position, or devalue your reaction by lying or

OLJ Studio/Shutterstock.com

equivocating—"I guess it wasn't perfect." It would be so much easier to respond to a sincere question, such as, "What did you think of the movie?"

- **A tag question.** Phrases like "did you?" or "isn't that right?" at the end of a question can be a tip-off that the asker is looking for agreement, not information. Although some tag questions are genuine requests for confirmation, counterfeit ones are used to coerce agreement: "Don't you think he would make a good boss?" directs you toward a desired response. As a simple solution, changing "Don't you?" to "Do you?" makes the question less leading.

- **Questions that make statements.** "Are you *finally* off the phone?" is more of a statement than a question, and emphasizing certain words can also turn a question into a statement: "You lent money to *Tony?*" We also use questions to offer advice. The person who asks, "Are you going to stand up to him and give him what he deserves?" clearly has stated an opinion about what should be done.

- **Questions that carry hidden agendas.** "Are you busy Friday night?" is a dangerous question to answer. If you say no, you'll be hearing, "Good, because I need some help moving out of my appartment." Obviously, such questions are not designed to enhance understanding; they're setups for the proposal that follows. Other examples include, "Will you do me a favour?" or "If I tell you what happened, will you promise not

Michelangelo Gratton/Stockbyte/Getty Images

to get mad?" Wise communicators learn to answer such questions with responses like "It depends" or "Let me hear what you have in mind before I answer."

- **Questions that seek "correct" answers.** Most of us have been victims of a questioner who seeks a particular response. "Which shoes do you think I should wear?" can be a sincere question—unless the asker has a predetermined preference. When this happens, the asker isn't interested in listening to contrary opinions and "incorrect" responses get shot down. Some of these questions may venture into delicate territory: "Do these jeans make me look fat?"

- **Questions based on unchecked assumptions.** "Why aren't you listening to me?" assumes that the other person isn't paying attention. "What's the matter?" assumes that something is wrong. Perception checking is a better way to confirm your assumptions. A perception check offers a description and two interpretations, followed by a sincere request for clarification: "When you didn't show up for class today, I thought maybe you'd slept in or you were sick. What happened?"

Paraphrasing

However valuable, questioning won't always help you understand or help others, because questions can sometimes lead to even greater confusion. Therefore, you might want to consider another kind of feedback that tells you if you've understood what's been said before you ask more questions. This type of feedback, called **paraphrasing** or active listening, involves restating the message you thought you heard in your own words and without adding anything new. Sometimes a paraphrase will reflect the ideas you think a speaker has expressed:

(*To a direction-giver*) "You're telling me to drive down to the traffic light by the high school and turn toward the mountains, is that it?"

(*To the boss*) "So you need me both this Saturday *and* next Saturday—right?"

Although paraphrasing is typically used to clarify facts or information, it can also be used to learn whether your perception of a person's feelings is accurate:

"I get the sense that you're in a hurry and would prefer to talk later on. Am I correct in my assumption?"

"Although you said, 'Forget it,' I get the feeling you're angry. Is this right?"

The key to successful paraphrasing is to restate the other person's comments in your own words as a way of cross-checking the information. But don't simply repeat

BURGER/PHANIE/First Light

the person's comments verbatim—it will sound foolish, and you still might not understand what was actually said. Notice the difference between simply parroting a statement and true paraphrasing:

Paraphrasing
Repeating a speaker's thoughts and/or feelings in the listener's own words. Also known as *active listening*.

Speaker: I'd like to go, but I can't afford it.

Parroting: You'd like to go, but you can't afford it.

Paraphrasing: So if we could find a way to cover your costs, you'd be willing to come? Is that right?

Speaker: You look awful!

Parroting: You think I look terrible.

Paraphrasing: Sounds like you think I need to shower and put on some clean clothes.

Paraphrasing personal information can also be a tool for helping others. Reflecting the speaker's thoughts and feelings (instead of judging or analyzing, for example) shows your involvement and concern. The nonevaluative nature of paraphrasing encourages the problem-holder to discuss the matter and unload some of the concerns he or she may have been carrying around. This catharsis often leads to relief. Finally, paraphrasing helps the problem-holder sort through the issue and find solutions that weren't apparent before. Such features make paraphrasing a vital skill for those in human services professions, leadership training, and even hostage negotiation.[42]

Effective paraphrasing is a skill that takes time to develop. You can make your paraphrasing sound more natural by taking any of these three approaches, depending on the situation:

1. Change the speaker's wording.

   Speaker: "Social assistance is just another way for Canadians to feel like we're doing the right thing."

How Good Are Your Listening Skills?

Assess your listening skills by taking the listening test below.

Instructions

The following statements reflect various habits we use when listening to others. For each statement, indicate the extent to which you agree or disagree by selecting one number from the scale provided. Circle your response for each statement. Remember, there are no right or wrong answers.

Listening Skills Survey

1 = Strongly disagree
2 = Disagree
3 = Neither agree or disagree
4 = Agree
5 = Strongly agree

1. I daydream or think about other things when listening to others.
   1   2   3   4   5
2. I do not summarize the ideas being communicated by a speaker.
   1   2   3   4   5
3. I do not use a speaker's tone of voice or body language to help interpret what he or she is saying.
   1   2   3   4   5
4. I listen more for facts than overall ideas during classroom lectures.
   1   2   3   4   5
5. I tune out dry speakers.
   1   2   3   4   5
6. I have a hard time paying attention to boring people.
   1   2   3   4   5
7. I can tell whether someone has anything useful to say before he or she finishes communicating a message.
   1   2   3   4   5
8. I quit listening to a speaker when I think he or she has nothing interesting to say.
   1   2   3   4   5
9. I get emotional or upset when speakers make jokes about issues or things that are important to me.
   1   2   3   4   5
10. I get angry or offensive when speakers use offensive words.
   1   2   3   4   5
11. I do not expend a lot of energy when listening to others.
   1   2   3   4   5
12. I pretend to listen to others even when I'm not really listening.
   1   2   3   4   5
13. I get distracted when listening to others.
   1   2   3   4   5
14. I deny or ignore information and comments that go against my thoughts and feelings.
   1   2   3   4   5
15. I do not seek opportunities to challenge my listening skills.
   1   2   3   4   5
16. I do not pay attention to the visual aids used during lectures.
   1   2   3   4   5
17. I do not take notes on handouts when they are provided.
   1   2   3   4   5

Now add up your total score for the 17 items and record it in the space provided. Refer to the norms below to evaluate your listening skills.

Total Score = _____

Norms

Use the following norms to evaluate your listening skills:

17–34 = Good listening skills
35–53 = Moderately good listening skills
54–85 = Poor listening skills

How would you evaluate your listening skills?

Paraphrase: "Let me see if I've got this right. You're upset because you think the amount of social assistance received isn't enough for people to live on, but if recipients work, then those earnings are deducted. There's just no way for them to get ahead."

2. Offer an example of what you think the speaker is talking about.

   Speaker: "Lee is such a jerk. I can't believe the way he acted last night."

   Paraphrase: "You think those jokes were pretty offensive, huh?"

3. Reflect the underlying theme of the speaker's remarks.

   Paraphrase: "You keep reminding me to be careful. Sounds like you're worried that something might happen to me. Am I right?"

Paraphrasing won't always be accurate, but even if your restatement is off-base, your response gives the other person a chance to make a correction. (Note how the examples end with questions in an attempt to confirm if the paraphrase was accurate.)

Because it's an unfamiliar way of responding, paraphrasing may feel awkward at first, but if you start by paraphrasing occasionally and then gradually increase the frequency of such responses, you can begin to learn the benefits of this method.

There are several factors to consider before you decide to paraphrase:

1. ***Is the issue complex enough?*** If you're fixing dinner, and someone wants to know when it will be ready, it would be exasperating to hear, "You're interested in knowing when we'll be eating."

2. ***Do you have the necessary time and concern?*** Paraphrasing can take a good deal of time. Therefore, if you're in a hurry, don't start a conversation you won't be able to finish. Even more important than time is concern: Paraphrasing that comes across as mechanical or as insincere reflecting can do more harm than good.[43]

3. ***Can you withhold judgment?*** Use paraphrasing only if you are willing to focus on the speaker's message without injecting your own judgments. It can be tempting to rephrase others' comments in a way that leads them toward the position you think is best without ever clearly stating your intentions.

4. ***Is your paraphrasing in proportion to other responses?*** Paraphrasing can become annoying when it's overused. This is especially true if you suddenly add this approach to your style. It's better to introduce paraphrasing gradually.

SKILL BUILDER

Paraphrasing Practice

This exercise will help you see that it is possible to understand someone who disagrees with you, without arguing or sacrificing your point of view.

1. Find a partner. Designate one person as *A* and the other as *B*.

2. Find a subject on which you and your partner apparently disagree—a current events topic, a philosophical or moral issue, or perhaps simply a matter of personal taste.

3. Person *A* begins by making a statement on the subject. Person *B*'s job is then to paraphrase the statement. *B*'s job is simply to understand here, and doing so in no way should signify agreement or disagreement with *A*'s remarks.

4. *A* then responds by telling *B* whether her response was accurate. If there was some misunderstanding, *A* should make the correction and *B* should feed back her new understanding of the statement. Continue this process until you're both sure that *B* understands *A*'s statement.

5. Now it's *B*'s turn to respond to *A*'s statement and for *A* to help the process of understanding by correcting *B*.

6. Continue this process until each partner is satisfied that she has explained herself fully and has been understood by the other person.

7. Now discuss the following questions:
   a. How did your understanding of the speaker's statement change after you used active listening?
   b. Did you find that the gap between your position and that of your partner narrowed as a result of active listening?
   c. How did you feel at the end of your conversation? How does this feeling compare to your usual feeling after discussing controversial issues?
   d. How might your life change if you used paraphrasing at home? At work? With friends?

"Listen, Mom, I'm not your little girl anymore."

Bruce Eric Kaplan The New Yorker Collection/The Cartoon Bank

Supporting

Supporting
A helping response that reveals a listener's solidarity with the speaker's situation.

There are times when people want to hear more than a reflection of how *they* feel—they want to know how *you* feel. **Supportive responses** reveal a listener's solidarity with the speaker's situation and come in the form of "expressions of care, concern, affection, and interest, especially during times of stress or upset."[44]

There are several types of support:

Empathizing	"I can understand why you'd be upset about this"
	"Yeah, that class was tough for me, too."
Agreement	"You're right—the landlord is being unfair."
	"Sounds like the job is a perfect match for you."
Offers to help	"I'm here if you need me."
	"I'd be happy to study with you for the next test if you'd like."
Praise	"Wow—you did a fantastic job!"
	"You're a terrific person, and if she doesn't recognize it, that's her problem!"
Reassurance	"The worst part seems to be over. It will probably get easier from here."
	"I'm sure you'll do a great job."

It's easy to identify what effective support *doesn't* sound like. Some scholars refer to these messages as "cold comfort."[45] (See **Table 7.2** to read cold comfort messages found in online discussions.) As the following examples suggest, you're not being supportive if you:

- **Deny others the right to their feelings.** For example, when you say, "Don't worry about it," the underlying message is that you want the person to feel differently, but people cannot just stop worrying just because you tell them to do so.[46] According to the research, "Messages that explicitly acknowledge, elaborate, and legitimize the feelings and perspective of a distressed person are perceived as more helpful than messages which only implicitly recognize or deny the feelings and perspective of the other."[47]
- **Minimize the significance of the situation.** Consider the times you've been told, "Hey, it's only _____." Fill in the blank with words like "a job," "her opinion," "a test," "a party." To a victim of verbal abuse, the hurtful message isn't "just words," or to a child who didn't get an invitation, it isn't "just a party."

TABLE 7.2
Cold Comfort: Messages That Don't Help When You've Just Been Dumped

Don't take it so hard. S/he was a slut/prick anyway.

That's nothing! Want to hear how I got dumped?

I don't know what you ever saw in him/her anyway. S/he's ugly. You can do much better.

You know you had this coming—you were due for payback.

S/he was way too young (old) for you.

You can't have everything you want in this life.

Now that it's finally over, I can tell you s/he's been cheating on you.

S/he was just using you for sex.

S/he was always a jerk about you behind your back. Who needs that?

Now we'll have more time to hang out together, just like we used to!

Photos.com/Thinkstock

Analyzing
A helping style in which the listener offers an interpretation of a speaker's message.

and you disagree with the decision. You could still be supportive by saying, "I know you've given this a lot of thought and you're doing what you think is best." Responses like this can provide face-saving support without compromising your principles.[50]

2. ***Monitor the other person's reaction to your support.*** If it doesn't seem to help, consider other types of responses that let him or her explore the issue.

3. ***Realize that support isn't always welcome.*** In one survey, some people reported occasions when social support wasn't necessary because they felt they could handle the problem themselves.[51] Many regarded uninvited support as an intrusion, while others said it left them feeling more nervous. Most respondents preferred to control whether their distressing situations were discussed, even with the most helpful friend.

4. ***Make sure you're ready for the consequences.*** Talking about a difficult event may reduce distress for the speaker but may increase distress for the listener.[52] Recognize that supporting another person is a worthwhile, but potentially taxing, venture.

Analyzing

In an **analyzing** response, listeners offer an interpretation of a speaker's message. Analyses like these are probably familiar to you:

> "I think what's really bothering you is . . ."
>
> "She's doing it because . . ."
>
> "Maybe the problem started when he . . ."

Interpretations can help people consider alternative meanings—things they wouldn't have thought of without your help. Sometimes an analysis can clarify a confusing problem so that a solution emerges. In other cases, an analysis can create more problems than it solves.

There are two potential problems with analyzing. First, your interpretation may not be correct, in which case the speaker may become even more confused. Second, even if your analysis is correct, telling it to the problemholder might not be useful. It could arouse defensiveness, because analysis implies superiority. Even if it doesn't, the person may not be able to understand your view of the problem without working it out personally.

To know when it's helpful to offer an analysis, follow the guidelines below:

- ***Offer your interpretation as tentative rather than as absolute fact.*** There's a big difference between saying, "Maybe the reason is . . ." or "The way it looks to me . . ." and insisting, "This is what's happening here."

- ***Focus on "then and there" rather than "here and now."*** Although it is sometimes true that "you'll feel better tomorrow," sometimes you won't. Even if the prediction that "in ten years you won't remember her/his name" proves correct, it provides little comfort today.

- ***Cast judgment.*** "It's your own fault—you really shouldn't have done that" is not very encouraging to hear, and it can make people defensive.

- ***Focus on yourself.*** While it's tempting to share a similar experience you've encountered ("I know exactly how you feel. When something like that happened to me . . ."), such messages aren't perceived as helpful because they draw attention away from the distressed person.[48]

- ***Defend yourself.*** When your response to others' concerns is to defend yourself ("Don't blame me; I've done my part"), it's clear that you are more concerned about yourself than with supporting the other person.

People often fail to provide appropriate supportive responses. Mourners, for example, report that 80 percent of the statements made to them were unhelpful.[49] Statements such as, "You've got to get out more," "Don't question God's will," "She's out of pain now," were helpful only three percent of the time. Expressions that acknowledged the mourner's feelings were more useful. To help you offer more effective support, see the following guidelines.

1. ***Recognize that you can support another person's struggles without approving of his or her decisions.*** Suppose, for instance, that a friend decides to quit a job

Let Mourners Grieve

© iStockphoto.com/Rich Legg

After a recent death in my family, I received a number of condolence cards that tried to talk me out of my grief. "You should be happy you have your memories," wrote one friend. "You should feel lucky you got to be with your father in the hospital." Lucky? Happy? You've got to be kidding!

Condolences are some of the most difficult words to write or say. So it's natural that we freeze with writer's block when faced with such an immense task. Here are my basic guidelines for mastering the Art of the Condolence:

- Always begin directly and simply. "I am so sorry about your mother's death."
- It's better to ask, "How are you?" or "How are you feeling?" instead of telling someone how she should feel.
- Never give advice about how someone should get through the loss. Some mourners go to parties; others stay home with the shades drawn. Be open to the mourner's individual needs. Be open to the possibility that these needs will change day by day.
- If you want to offer something upbeat, share a funny anecdote or memory about the deceased that might bring a smile to the mourner's face.

Grieving is private, but it can be public, too. We need to stop being afraid of public mourning. We need to be open to mourners. We need to look each other in the eye, and say, "I am so sorry."

Jess Decourcy Hinds

- ***Make sure that the person is receptive to your analysis.*** Even if you're completely accurate, your thoughts won't help if the problem-holder isn't ready to consider them.
- ***Be sure that your motive for offering an analysis is truly to help the other person.*** It can be tempting to offer an analysis to show how brilliant you are or even to make the other person feel bad for not having thought of the right answer in the first place. Needless to say, an analysis offered under such conditions isn't helpful.

Advising

When approached with another's problem, a common tendency is to give an **advising** response: to help by offering a solution.[53] Advice can be helpful if it's given in a respectful, caring way,[54] but research shows that it is actually *unhelpful* at least as often as it's helpful.[55] Studies on advice-giving offer the following considerations when trying to help others:[56]

Advising
A helping response in which the receiver offers suggestions about how the speaker should deal with a problem.

monkeybusinessimages/iStock/Thinkstock

NEL

- **Is the advice needed?** If the person has already taken a course of action, advice is rarely appreciated.
- **Is the advice wanted?** People generally don't value unsolicited advice. It's better to ask if the person is interested in hearing your counsel. Sometimes people just want a listening ear, not solutions.
- **Is the advice given in the right sequence?** Advice is more likely to be received if the listener first offers supporting, paraphrasing, and questioning responses to better understand the situation.
- **Is the advice coming from an expert?** It's important to have experience and success in the topic on which you are advising. If not, then offer the speaker supportive responses, then encourage that person to seek expert counsel.
- **Is the advisor a close and trusted person?** In most cases, we value advice from individuals with whom we have a close and ongoing interpersonal relationship.
- **Is the advice offered in a sensitive, face-saving manner?** Remember that messages have both content and relational dimensions, and sometimes the unstated relational messages ("I'm smarter than you," or "You're not bright enough to figure this out yourself") will keep people from hearing your counsel.[57]

In all, while advice is great when solicited, one study of womens' comments on an online breast cancer support group found that only 40 percent of the posts sought advice.[58] Instead, women sought out narratives of those who were in similar situations or those consisting of "this is what worked for me."

Judging

A **judging** response evaluates the sender's thoughts or behaviours in some way. The judgment may be

favourable — "That's a good idea," or "You're on the right track now" — or unfavourable — "An attitude like that won't get you anywhere." But in either case, it implies that the person doing the judging is in some way qualified to pass judgment on the speaker's thoughts or actions.

Sometimes negative judgments are purely critical. How many times have you heard a response like "Well, you asked for it!" or "I *told* you so!" Although comments like these sometimes serve as a verbal slap that brings problem-holders to their senses, they usually make matters worse.

In other cases, negative judgments are less critical. These involve *constructive criticism* that is intended to help the person in the future. This is the sort of response given by friends

> **Judging**
> A response in which the receiver evaluates the sender's message either favourably or unfavourably

about everything from the choice of clothing to jobs to friends. Constructive criticism occurs in school, where instructors evaluate students' work to help them master concepts and skills. Whether it's justified or not, constructive criticism can run the risk of arousing defensiveness because it may threaten the person's self-concept.

Judgments have the best chance of being received when two conditions exist:

1. ***The person with the problem requested an evaluation from you.*** Occasionally an unsolicited evaluation may bring someone to his or her senses, but more often unsolicited evaluation triggers a defensive response.

2. ***The intent of your judgment is genuinely constructive and not designed as a put-down.*** If you are tempted to use judgments as a weapon, don't fool yourself into thinking that you're being helpful. Often the statement "I'm telling you this for your own good . . ." simply isn't true.

Now that you're aware of all the possible listening responses, try the "Invitation to Insight" exercise to see how you might use them in everyday situations.

LO4
Choosing the Best Listening Response

As you can see, there are many ways to respond as a listener. In the right circumstances, *all* response styles can help others accept their situation, feel better, and have a sense of control over their problems.[59] But there is enormous variability in which style will work with a given person.[60] This explains why communicators who use a wide variety of response styles are usually more effective than those who use just one or two styles.[61] However, there are other factors to consider as well.

Gender

Research shows that men and women differ in the way they listen and respond to others.[62] Women are more likely to give supportive responses,[63] are more skilful at

"There you go again — trying to solve my problems. I am not asking you to do that. I just want you to listen to me."

composing such messages,[64] and are more likely to seek out such responses from listeners.[65] Men are less skilful at providing emotional support and tend to respond to others' problems by offering advice or diverting the topic.[66] In a study of helping styles in sororities and fraternities, researchers found that sorority women frequently respond with emotional support when asked to help. Sorority sisters were also rated better at listening nonjudgmentally, comforting, and showing concern. Fraternity men, on the other hand, fit

Invitation to Insight

When Advising Does — and Doesn't — Work

To see why advising can be tricky business, follow these steps:

1. Recall an instance when someone gave you advice that proved helpful. See how closely that advising communication followed the guidelines in the bulleted list.

2. Now recall an instance when someone gave you advice that wasn't helpful. See whether that person violated any of the guidelines for giving advice.

3. Based on your insights here, describe how you can advise (or not advise) others in a way that is truly helpful.

the stereotypical pattern of offering help by challenging their brothers to evaluate their attitudes and values.[67]

Based on the previous facts, you might assume that women want support and men want advice at difficult times, but research doesn't bear that out. Numerous studies show that both men and women prefer and want supportive, endorsing messages in difficult situations.[68] The fact that women are more adept at creating and delivering such messages and they make more eye contact when they listen[69] may explain why both males and females tend to seek out women listeners when they want emotional support.

The Situation

Competent communicators need to analyze the situation and develop an appropriate response for the individual.[70] As a rule of thumb, begin by seeking an understanding of the situation by using prompting, questioning, paraphrasing, and supporting responses. Then the speaker will be more receptive to and perhaps even ask for your analyzing, advising, and evaluating responses.[71]

The Other Person

Besides the situation, sophisticated listeners choose a style that fits the person. Some listeners will consider advice thoughtfully, while others will use it to avoid making their own decisions. Some may become defensive or are not capable of receiving analysis or judgments without lashing out. Still others are not equipped to think through problems clearly enough to profit from paraphrasing and probing. One way to determine the appropriate response is to ask the person what she or he wants from you. A simple question such as, "Are you looking for my advice, or do you just want a listening ear right now?" can help you give others the kinds of responses that they want and need at the time.

Your Personal Style

Most of us reflexively use one or two response styles. Perhaps you're best at listening quietly and prompting from time to time. Or maybe you're especially insightful and can offer a truly useful analysis. Of course, it's also possible to rely on a response style that is *unhelpful*. You may be overly judgmental or too eager to advise, even when your suggestions aren't invited or productive. As you think about how to respond to another's messages, consider both your strengths and weaknesses and adapt accordingly.

Listening in the Workplace

Listening is just as important on the job as in personal relationships. A study examining the link between listening and career success revealed that better listeners rose to higher levels in their organizations.[72] When 1000 human resource executives were asked to identify skills of the ideal manager, the ability to listen effectively ranked at the top of the list.[73] In problem-solving groups, effective listeners are judged as having the most leadership skills.[74]

John Joyner, in an article in *Computing Canada*, says, "Effective listening saves time and money, and people who listen well make fewer mistakes, create fewer interpersonal misunderstandings, and are more likely to make positive first impressions. Good listening skills result in happier customers and less employee

---

Invitation to Insight

What Would You Say?

1. In each situation below, write out what you would say in response to the problem being shared:
   a. My family doesn't understand me. Everything I like seems to go against their values, and they just won't accept my feelings as being right for me. It's not that they don't love me—they do. But they don't accept me.
   b. I've been pretty discouraged lately. I just can't get a good relationship going with any guys. I've got plenty of male friends, but that's always as far as it goes. I'm tired of being just a pal . . . I want to be more than that.
   c. *(Child to parents)* I hate you guys! You always go out and leave me with some stupid sitter. Why don't you like me?
   d. I don't know what I want to do with my life. I'm tired of school, but there aren't any good jobs around. I could just drop out for a while, but that doesn't really sound very good either.
   e. Things really seem to be kind of lousy in my marriage lately. It's not that we fight much, but all the excitement seems to be gone. We're in a rut, and it keeps getting worse . . .
   f. I keep getting the idea that my boss is angry at me. It seems as if lately he hasn't been joking around very much, and he hasn't said anything at all about my work for about three weeks now. I wonder what I should do.

2. After you've written your response to each of these messages, imagine the probable outcome of the conversation that would have followed. If you've tried this exercise in class, you might have two group members role-play each response. Based on your idea of how the conversation might have gone, decide which responses were productive and which were unproductive.

TABLE 7.3

Tips to Keep Listening on Track

1. **Eliminate poor listening habits** such as pseudolistening, insulated listening, insensitive listening, and so forth.

2. **Take the basic steps to effective listening** by talking less and getting rid of distractions,

3. **Send encouraging nonverbal cues** by leaning forward, making eye contact, nodding, and responding with appropriate facial expressions.

4. **Be patient when listening to non-native language speakers** by not judging accents, finishing sentences, correcting grammar and pronunciation, and pretending to understand when you don't.[75]

5. **Paraphrase** whenever the opportunity presents itself.

6. **Monitor your input and the length of your comments.** Keep them brief and don't repeat what others have said.

7. **Encourage quiet individuals to provide their input** by drawing out their thoughts.

8. **Keep in mind that listening is hard** work and takes substantial effort.

---

turnover."[76] See **Table 7.3** for some tips to keep listening on track.

Today, much of our workplace listening can take place via mediated meetings. Keeping track of what's going on can sometimes be difficult, particularly in meetings with several individuals and no video to help identify who is speaking. There are several things you can do to remedy these and other issues.[77] For example, before the meeting, ensure that participants have the agenda and any documents to be discussed. During phone conversations, identify yourself to avoid confusion ("Nicole, this is Sarah. I'm wondering if . . .") and try not to leave out people just because you can't see them ("We haven't heard from Ross yet. What do you think?"). Having a participate list can help with this. Finally, keep distractions to a minimum (interruptions, background noise, and so forth) and use the best equipment possible.

Listening is particularly important in the helping professions. Vancouver researchers found that women living with breast cancer identified active listening as the most helpful characteristic their physicians displayed during diagnosis. They noted that the most important quality for their physicians to have was listening. They valued doctors who looked at them when speaking and who listened and acted on their concerns. They also valued doctors who avoided interruptions and paraphrased what they had said.[78]

Not only is listening important on the job, we're expected to listen more often than we would in our interpersonal relationships. For example, given the amount of time spent working in teams, we could actually pass 90 percent of our day listening to others.[79] The exhaustion alone from this might cause us to fall into those bad listening habits discussed earlier in the chapter—pseudolistening, selective listening, insensitive listening, etc.

One way to combat this possibility is to use *interactive questioning*. Small group researchers say that, "Interactive questioning clarifies, probes, analyzes, and follows up on information your teammate has expressed."[80] This type of questioning can have a positive effect on groups—information can be clarified and further explained and other team members are encouraged to think more critically which can lead to more sound decisions. Interactive questioning may egg on quiet team members to share their thoughts and feelings. All this interaction

COMMUNICATION COMPETENCE

CSI and *Law & Order* (TV Shows, 2000–2015 and 1990–2010, also available on DVD)

In the crime shows *CSI* and *Law and Order*, the main characters must engage in active listening to do their jobs effectively. Sometimes a lawyer uses prompting and support to draw out a difficult confession. Other times a private investigator asks probing questions and offers analyzing responses to arrive at important conclusions. In other instances, a police officer carefully attends to and remembers specific details during a testimony, which later helps solve a case. And in a variety of situations, the characters offer advising and judging responses to their clients, colleagues, and co-workers. Watch an episode of one of these programs and see how many of the listening responses you can observe. Chances are, you'll find quite a few.

demonstrates to the teammate who produced the information that his or her work is appreciated.

So, how do you ask interactive questions? Small group researchers Lumsden, Lumsden, and Wiethoff suggest that you ask the kinds of questions that probe what members think about the issues and why they think that. You can also probe for further information. Second, you can ask questions that help the speaker answer objectively and honestly. Do this by being clear about what you want to ask, being specific, asking one question at a time, avoiding loaded questions, not attacking the speaker, and offering your questions in a nonverbally supportive way.[81] Asking questions will not only help groups do better work, it makes listening easier and helps keep everyone involved. It leaves less room for daydreaming.

Another area where we see the use of listening and questioning at work is in the interview process. More and more companies are now using behavioural questions—questions that ask candidates how they performed in the past. For instance, you might ask interviewees to describe a conflict situation and how it was dealt with. You could ask how they handled a stressful situation, a delicate situation, or how they use humour at work. Regarding the latter, if the candidate tells a sexist, racist joke, you've learned a lot. Asking probing questions about each topic area can garner useful information about a candidate's work ethic, interactional style, values, and so forth.

READY TO STUDY?

 MINDTAP

IN THE BOOK, YOU CAN:

❏ Rip out the Chapter in Review card at the back of the book to have the key terms and Learning Objectives handy, and complete the quizzes provided (answers are at the bottom of the back page).

ONLINE YOU CAN:

❏ Stay organized and efficient with MindTap—a single destination with all the course material and study aids you need to succeed. Built-in apps leverage social media and the latest learning technology. For example:

❏ Listen to the text using ReadSpeaker.

❏ Use pre-populated Flashcards as a jump start for review—or you can create your own.

❏ You can highlight text and make notes in your MindTap Reader. Your notes will flow into Evernote, the electronic notebook app that you can access anywhere when it's time to study for the exam.

❏ Prepare for tests with a variety of quizzes and activities.

Go to **nelson.com/student** to access these digital resources

Endnotes

1. R. Emanuel, J. Adams, K. Baker, E. K. Daufin, C. Ellington, E. Fitts, J. Himsel, L. Holladay, & D. Okeowo (2008). "How College Students Spend Their Time Communicating." *International Journal of Listening, 22,* 13–28. See also L. Barker, R. Edwards, C. Gaines, K. Gladney, & R. Holley (1981). "An Investigation of Proportional Time Spent in Various Communication Activities by College Students." *Journal of Applied Communication Research, 8,* 101–109.

2. A. D. Wovin & C. G. Coakley (1981). "A survey of the status of listening training in Fortune 500 corporations." *Communication Education, 40,* 152–164.

3. K. J. Prager & D. Buhrmester (1998). "Intimacy and Need Fulfillment in Couple Relationships." *Journal of Social and Personal Relationships, 15,* 435–469.

4. A. L. Vangelisti (1994). "Couples' Communication Problems: The Counsellor's Perspective." *Journal of Applied Communication Research, 22,* 106–126.

5. A. D. Wolvin (1984). "Meeting the Communication Needs of the Adult Learners." *Communication Education, 33,* 267–271.

6. M. L. Beall, J. Gill-Rosier, J. Tate, & A. Matten (2008). "State of the Context: Listening in Education." *International Journal of Listening, 22,* 123–132.

7. J. Davis, A. Foley, N. Crigger, & M. C. Brannigan (2008). "Healthcare and Listening: A Relationship for Caring." *International Journal of Listening, 22,* 168–175; J. Davis, C. R. Thompson, A. Foley, C. D. Bond, & J. DeWitt (2008). "An Examination of Listening Concepts in the Healthcare Context: Differences Among Nurses, Physicians, and Administrators." *International Journal of Listening, 22,* 152–167.

8. D. C. Schnapp (2008). "Listening in Context: Religion and Spirituality." *International Journal of Listening, 22,* 133–140.

9. J. Flynn, T. Valikoski, J. Grau (2008). "Listening in the Business Context: Reviewing the State of Research." *International Journal of Listening, 22,* 141–151.

10. A. Fernald (2001). "Hearing, Listening, and Understanding: Auditory Development in Infancy." In G. Bemner & A. Fogel (Eds.). *Blackwell Handbook of Infant Development* (pp. 35–70). Malden, MA: Blackwell.

11. J. K. Burgoon, C. R. Berger, & V. R. Waldron (2000). "Mindfulness and Interpersonal Communication." *Journal of Social Issues, 56,* 105–127.

12. A. Wolvin (2009). "Listening, Understanding, and Misunderstanding." In *21st Century Communication: A Reference Handbook* (pp. 137–147). Thousand Oaks, CA: SAGE.

13. R. Salem (2003). "Empathic Listening." Beyond Intractability. In G. Burgess & H. Burgess (Eds). Conflict Information Consortium, University of Colorado, Boulder. <http://www.beyondintractability.org/bi-essay/empathic-listening>. Accessed April 20, 2013.

14. E. Langer (1990). *Mindfulness.* Reading, MA: Addison-Wesley, p. 90.

15. L. O. Cooper & T. Buchanan (2010). "Listening competency on campus: A Psychometric analysis of student listening." *The International Journal of Listening, 24,* 141–163.

16. Canadian Hearing Society (April 30, 2002). *The Canadian Hearing Society Awareness Survey,* www.canadianhearingsociety.com/survey/deck20402.ppt.pdf. Accessed April 19, 2010.

17. Statistics Canada (2015, November 27). "Hearing Loss of Canadians, 2012 and 2013." http://www.statcan.gc.ca/pub/82-625-x/2015001/article/14156-eng.htm. Retrieved on March 11, 2016.

18. M. Chasin (July 1997). "Fast Facts on Noise, Loud Music and Hearing Loss," www.chs.ca/resources/vibes/1997/july/noise.htm; M. Chasin (Oct. 1995). "Musicians and Hearing Loss." Accessed July 12, 2006.

19. L. R. Smeltzer & K. W. Watson (1984). "Listening: An Empirical Comparison of Discussion Length and Level of Incentive." *Central States Speech Journal, 35,* 166–170.

20. M. Pasupathi, L. M. Stallworth, & K. Murdoch (1998). "How What We Tell Becomes What We Know: Listener Effects on Speakers' Long-Term Memory for Events." *Discourse Processes, 26,* 1–25.

21. W. G. Powers & P. L. Witt (2008). "Expanding the Theoretical Framework of Communication Fidelity." *Communication Quarterly, 56,* 247–267; M. Fitch-Hauser, W. G. Powers, K. O'Brien, & S. Hanson (2007). "Extending the Conceptualization of Listening Fidelity." *International Journal of Listening, 21,* 81–91; W. G. Powers & G. D. Bodie (2003). "Listening Fidelity: Seeking Congruence Between Cognitions of the Listener and the Sender." *International Journal of Listening, 17,* 19–31.

22. M. H. Lewis & N. L. Reinsch Jr. (1988). "Listening in Organizational Environments." *Journal of Business Communication, 23,* 49–67.

23. M. Imhof (2002). "In The Eye of the Beholder: Children's Perception of Good and Poor Listening Behavior." *International Journal of Listening, 16,* 40–57.

24. H. Weger, G. C. Bell, E. M. Minei, & M. C. Robinson (2014). "The relative effectiveness of active listening in initial interactions." *International Journal of Listening, 28,* 13–31.

25. L. L. Barker (1971). *Listening Behavior.* Englewood Cliffs, NJ: Prentice Hall.

26. A. L. Vangelisti, M. L. Knapp, & J. A. Daly (1990). "Conversational Narcissism." *Communication Monographs, 57,* 251–274. See also J. C. McCroskey & V. P. Richmond (1993). "Identifying Compulsive Communicators: The Talkaholic Scale." *Communication Research Reports, 10,* 107–114.

27. K. B. McComb & F. M. Jablin (1984). "Verbal Correlates of Interviewer Empathic Listening and Employment Interview Outcomes." *Communication Monographs, 51,* 367.

28. J. Hansen (2007). *24/7: How Cell Phones and the Internet Change the Way We Live, Work, and Play.* New York: Praeger. See also J. W. Turner & N. L. Reinsch (2007).

"The Business Communicator as Presence Allocator: Multicommunicating, Equivocality, and Status at Work." *Journal of Business Communication, 44*, 36–58.

29. A. Wolvin & C. G. Coakley (1988). *Listening*, 3rd ed. Dubuque, IA: W.C. Brown, p. 208.

30. R. Nichols (September 1987). "Listening Is a Ten-Part Skill." *Nation's Business, 75*, 40.

31. S. Golen (1990). "A Factor Analysis of Barriers to Effective Listening," *Journal of Business Communication, 27*, 25–36.

32. P. Nelson, K. Kohnert, S. Sabur, & D. Shaw (2005). "Noise and children learning a second language: Double jeopardy?" *Language, Speech, & Hearing Services in Schools, 36*, 219–229.

33. N. Kline (1999). *Time to Think: Listening to Ignite the Human Mind.* London: Ward Lock, p. 21.

34. L. J. Carrell & S. C. Willmington (1996). "A Comparison of Self-Report and Performance Data in Assessing Speaking and Listening Competence." *Communication Reports, 9*, 185–191.

35. R. G. Nichols, J. I. Brown, & R. J. Keller (2006). "Measurement of Communication Skills." *International Journal of Listening, 20*, 13–17; N. Spinks & B. Wells (1991). "Improving Listening Power: The Payoff." *Bulletin of the Association for Business Communication, 54*, 75–32.

36. "Listen to This: Hearing Problems Can Stress Relationships." (2008). Available at www.energizer.com/livehealthy/#listentothis. See also D. N. Shafer (2007). "Hearing Loss Hinders Relationships." *ASHA Leader, 12*, 5–7.

37. D. Carbaugh (1999). "'Just Listen': 'Listening' and Landscape among the Blackfeet." *Western Journal of Communication, 63*, 250–270.

38. Misra, S., Cheng, L., Genevie, J., & Yuan, Miao. (2016). The iPhone effect: The quality of in-person social interactions in the presence of mobile devices. *Environment and Behaviour, 48*, 275–298.

39. Bodie, G. D., St. Cyr, K., Pence, M., Rold, M., & Honeycutt, J. (2012). Listening competence in initial interactions 1: Distinguishing between what listening is and what listeners do. *International Journal of Listening, 26*, 1–28. A. M. Bippus (2001). "Recipients' Criteria for Evaluating the Skillfulness of Comforting Communication and the Outcomes of Comforting Interactions." *Communication Monographs, 68*, 301–313.

40. G. Goodman & G. Easterly (1990). "Questions: The most popular piece of language." In J. Stewart (Ed.), *Bridges not walls*, 5th edn (pp. 69–77). New York: McGraw-Hill.

41. F. S. Chen, J. A. Minson, & Z. L. Tormala (2010). "Tell me more: The effects of expressed interest on receptiveness during dialogue." *Journal of Experimental Social Psychology, 46*, 850–853.

42. S. Myers (2000). "Empathic Listening: Reports on the Experience of Being Heard." *Journal of Humanistic Psychology, 40*, 148–173; S. G. Grant (1998). "A Principal's Active Listening Skills and Teachers' Perceptions of the Principal's Leader Behaviors." *Dissertation Abstracts International Section A: Humanities and Social Sciences,*

58, 2933; V. B. Van Hasselt, M. T. Baker, & S. J. Romano (2006). "Crisis (Hostage) Negotiation Training: A Preliminary Evaluation of Program Efficacy." *Criminal Justice and Behavior, 33*, 56–69.

43. See T. Bruneau (1989). "Empathy and Listening: A Conceptual Review and Theoretical Directions," *Journal of the International Listening Association, 3*, 1–20; K. N. Cissna & R. Anderson (1990). "The Contributions of Carl R. Rogers to a Philosophical Praxis of Dialogue." *Western Journal of Speech Communication, 54*, 137–147.

44. B. R. Burleson (2003). "Emotional Support Skills." In J. O. Greene and B. R. Burleson (Eds.). *Handbook of Communication and Social Interaction Skills* (p. 552). Mahwah, NJ: Erlbaum.

45. "D. Hample (2006). "Anti-Comforting Messages." In K. M. Galvin & P. J. Cooper (Eds.). *Making Connections: Readings in Relational Communication*, 4th ed. (pp. 222–227). Los Angeles: Roxbury. See also B. R. Burleson & E. L. MacGeorge (2002). "Supportive Communication." In M. L. Knapp & J. A. Daly (Eds.). *Handbook of Interpersonal Communication*, 3rd ed. Thousand Oaks, CA: Sage.

46. J. Singal (2014, June 25). "Stop telling your depressed friends to cheer up." *New York Magazine.*

47. W. Samter, B. R. Burleson, & L. B. Murphy (1987). "Comforting Conversations: The Effects of Strategy Type on Evaluations of Messages and Message Producers." *Southern Speech Communication Journal, 52*, 263–284.

48. B. Burleson (2008). "What Counts as Effective Emotional Support?" In M. T. Motley (Ed.). *Studies in Applied Interpersonal Communication* (pp. 207–227). Thousand Oaks, CA: Sage.

49. M. Davidowitz & R. D. Myrick (1984). "Responding to the Bereaved: An Analysis of 'Helping' Statements." *Death Education, 8*, 1–10. See also H. L. Servaty-Seib & B. R. Burleson (2007). "Bereaved Adolescents Evaluations of the Helpfulness of Support-Intended Statements." *Journal of Social and Personal Relationships, 24*, 207–223.

50. N. Miczo & J. K. Burgoon (2008). "Facework and Nonverbal Behaviour in Social Support Interactions Within Romantic Dyads." In M. T. Motley (Ed.). *Studies in Applied Interpersonal Communication* (pp. 245–266). Thousand Oaks, CA: Sage.

51. R. A. Clark & J. G. Delia (1997). "Individuals' Preferences for Friends' Approaches to Providing Support in Distressing Situations." *Communication Reports, 10*, 115–121.

52. T. Lewis & B. Manusov (2009). "Listening to another's distress in everyday relationships." *Communication Quarterly, 57*, 282–301.

53. E. L. MacGeorge, B. Feng, & E. R. Thompson (2008). "'Good' and 'Bad' Advice: How to Advise More Effectively." In M. T. Motley (Ed.). *Studies in Applied Interpersonal Communication* (pp. 145–164). Thousand Oaks, CA: Sage. See also C. J. Notarius & L. R. Herrick (1988). "Listener Response Strategies to a Distressed Other." *Journal of Social and Personal Relationships, 5*, 97–108.

54. S. J. Messman, D. J. Canary, & K. S. Hause (2000). "Motives to Remain Platonic, Equity, and the Use of

Maintenance Strategies in Opposite-Sex Friendships." *Journal of Social and Personal Relationships, 17,* 67–94.

55. D. J. Goldsmith & K. Fitch (1997). "The Normative Context of Advice as Social Support." *Human Communication Research, 23,* 454–476. See also D. J. Goldsmith & E. L. MacGeorge (2000). "The Impact of Politeness and Relationship on Perceived Quality of Advice about a Problem." *Human Communication Research, 26,* 234–263; B. R. Burleson (1992). "Social Support." In M. L. Knapp & J. A. Daly (Eds.). *Handbook of Interpersonal Communication,* 3rd ed. Thousand Oaks, CA: Sage.

56. E. L. MacGeorge, B. Feng, & E. R. Thompson (2008). "'Good'" and 'bad' advice: How to advise more effectively." In M. T. Motley (Ed.), *Studies in Applied Interpersonal Communication* (pp. 145–164). Thousand Oaks, CA: Sage.

57. N. Miczo & J. K. Burgoon (2008). "Facework and Nonverbal Behaviour in Social Support Interactions within Romantic Dyads." In M. T. Motley (Ed.). *Studies in Applied Interpersonal Communication* (pp. 245–266). Thousand Oaks, CA: Sage.

58. E. Sillence (2013). "Giving and receiving peer advice in an online breast cancer support group." *Cyberpsychology, Behaviour, and Social Networking, 16,* 480–485.

59. See, for example, R. Silver & C. Wortman (1981). "Coping with Undesirable Life Events." In J. Garber & M. Seligman (Eds.). *Human Helplessness: Theory and Applications* (pp. 279–340). New York: Academic Press; C. R. Young, D. E. Giles, & M. C. Plantz (1982). "Natural Networks: Help-Giving and Help-Seeking in Two Rural Communities." *American Journal of Community Psychology, 10,* 457–469.

60. Clark & Delia, op. cit.

61. See research cited in B. Burleson (1990). "Comforting Messages: Their Significance and Effects." In J. A. Daly & J. M. Wiemann (Eds.). *Communicating Strategically: Strategies in Interpersonal Communication.* Hillside, NJ: Erlbaum. See also J. L. Chesbro (1999). "The Relationship between Listening Styles and Conversational Sensitivity." *Communication Research Reports, 16,* 233–238.

62. S. L. Sargent & J. B. Weaver (2003). "Listening Styles: Sex Differences in Perceptions of Self and Others." *International Journal of Listening, 17,* 5–18. See also M. Johnston, M. Kirtley, J. B. Weaver, K. Watson, & L. Barker (2000). "Listening Styles: Biological or Psychological Differences?" *International Journal of Listening, 14,* 32–47.

63. W. Samter (2002). "How Gender and Cognitive Complexity Influence the Provision of Emotional Support: A Study of Indirect Effects." *Communication Reports, 15,* 5–17; J. L. Hale, M. R. Tighe, & P. A. Mongeau (1997). "Effects of Event Type and Sex on Comforting Messages." *Communication Research Reports, 14,* 214–220.

64. B. R. Burleson (1982). "The Development of Comforting Communication Skills in Childhood and Adolescence." *Child Development, 53,* 1578–1588.

65. R. Lemieux & M. R. Tighe (2004). "Attachment Styles and the Evaluation of Comforting Responses: A Receiver Perspective." *Communication Research Reports, 21,* 144–153.

66. B. R. Burleson, A. J. Holmstrom, & C. M. Gilstrap (2005). "'Guys Can't Say That to Guys: Four Experiments Assessing the Normative Motivation Account for Deficiencies in the Emotional Support Provided by Men." *Communication Monographs, 72,* 468–501.

67. M. S. Woodward, L. B. Rosenfeld, & S. K. May (1996). "Sex Differences in Social Support in Sororities and Fraternities." *Journal of Applied Communication Research, 24,* 260–272.

68. B. R. Burleson & A. Kunkel (2006). "Revisiting the Different Cultures Thesis: An Assessment of Sex Differences and Similarities in Supportive Communication." In K. Dindia & D. J. Canary (Eds.). *Sex Differences and Similarities in Communication,* 2nd ed. (pp. 137–159). Mawah, NJ: Erlbaum.

69. Brownell, J. (2010). *Listening, principles, and skills,* 4th ed. Boston, MA: Allyn & Bacon.

70. L. M. Horowitz, E. N. Krasnoperova, & D. G. Tatar (2001). "The Way to Console May Depend on the Goal: Experimental Studies of Social Support." *Journal of Experimental Social Psychology, 37,* 49–61.

71. E. L. MacGeorge, B. Feng, & E. R. Thompson (2008), op cit. See also R. W. Young & C. M. Cates (2004). "Emotional and Directive Listening in Peer Mentoring." *International Journal of Listening, 18,* 21–33.

72. B. D. Sypher, R. N. Bostrom, & J. H. Seibert (1989). "Listening Communication Abilities and Success at Work." *Journal of Business Communication, 26,* 293–303. See also E. R. Alexander, L. E. Penley, & I. E. Jernigan (1992). "The Relationship of Basic Decoding Skills to Managerial Effectiveness." *Management Communication Quarterly, 6,* 58–73.

73. J. L. Winsor, D. B. Curtis, & R. D. Stephens (1999). "National Preferences in Business and Communication Education: An Update." *Journal of the Association for Communication Administration, 3,* 170–179.

74. S. Johnson & C. Bechler (1998). "Examining the Relationship between Listening Effectiveness and Leadership Emergence: Perceptions, Behaviours, and Recall." *Small Group Research, 29,* 452–471.

75. M. E. Guffey, K. Rhodes, & P. Rogin (2005). *Business Communication: Process and Product,* 4th Canadian edn (p. 79). Toronto: Thomson Nelson.

76. J. Joyner (2001). "Listening Increases Support from Co-Workers." *Computing Canada, 27,* 31.

77. D. S. Collins (2003). *Communication in a virtual organization.* Cincinnati: Thomson Learning.

78. S. R. Harris & E. Templeton (2001). "Who's Listening: Experiences of Women with Breast Cancer in Communicating with Physicians." *Breast Journal, 7,* 444–449.

79. J. A. Kolb & W. J. Rothwell (2002). "Competencies of Small Group Facilitators: What Practitioners View as Important." *Journal of European Training, 26,* 200–203.

80. G. Lumsden, D. Lumsden, & C. Wiethoff (2010). *Communicating in Groups and Teams: Sharing Leadership* (p. 239). Boston: Wadsworth.

81. G. Lumsden, D. L. Lumsden, & C. Weithoff (2010). *Communicating in Groups and Teams: Sharing Leadership* (p. 239). Boston: Wadsworth.

MINDTAP

MindTap empowers students.
Personalized content in an easy-to-use interface
helps you achieve better grades.

The new **MindTap Mobile App** allows
for learning anytime, anywhere with
flashcards, quizzes and notifications.

The **MindTap Reader** lets you highlight
and take notes online, right within the
pages, and easily reference them later.

nelson.com/mindtap

NELSON

COMMUNICATION AND RELATIONAL DYNAMICS

LEARNING OUTCOMES

LO1 Identify factors that have influenced your choice of relational partners.

LO2 Use Knapp's model to describe the nature of communication in the various stages of a relationship.

LO3 Describe the dialectical tensions in a given relationship, how they influence communication, and the most effective strategies for managing them.

LO4 Describe the possible strategies for repairing a given relational transgression.

LO5 Identify the dimensions of intimacy and how they are expressed in a specific relationship.

LO6 Use the social penetration and Johari Window models to identify the nature of self-disclosing communication in one of your relationships.

LO7 Outline the potential benefits and risks of disclosing in a selected situation.

LO8 Assess the most competent mixture of candour and equivocation in a given situation.

LO1
Why We Form Relationships

When we think of relationships, we tend to think in romantic terms. But we also have relationships with friends, family members, acquaintances, co-workers, and, in some cases, with people merely because we have to. **Interpersonal relationships** involve the way people deal with one another socially. This chapter will give you a better sense of how communication both defines and reflects our important relationships. We form relationships with others for a variety of reasons. These include appearance, similarity and complementarity, reciprocal attraction, competence, disclosure, and proximity.[1]

Appearance

While most people know that we shouldn't judge others by their appearance, the reality is quite the opposite.[2] In one study, more than 700 men and women were matched as blind dates for a "computer dance." Afterward, they were asked whether they would like to date their partners again. The result? The more physically attractive

> **Interpersonal relationship**
> An association in which the parties meet each other's social needs to a greater or lesser degree.

What do you THINK?

Real lovers share all their thoughts and feelings with each other.

1	2	3	4	5	6	7
strongly agree						strongly disagree

© Wavebreak Media ltd/Alamy Stock Photo

the person, as judged in advance by independent raters, the more likely that person was seen as desirable. Factors like social skills or intelligence didn't seem to affect the decision.[3]

In a more contemporary example, physical appearance is the primary attraction in speed dates.[4] This may be why online daters enhance their photographs and "adapt" their height or weight a little.[5] Online profiles are even rated more highly when there are attractive individuals on their site. It's as if they are as attractive as the company they keep.[6] And, the opposite is also true: Attractive faces are rated as less attractive when they are in the middle of average or unattractive faces.[7]

However, after initial impressions pass, ordinary-looking people with pleasing personalities are likely to be judged as attractive,[8] and physical factors become less important as a relationship progresses.[9] Interestingly, as romantic relationships develop, partners view one another as more attractive with time.[10] As one social scientist put it, "Attractive features may open doors, but apparently it takes more than physical beauty to keep them open."[11]

Similarity

We generally like people who are similar to us.[12] For example, the more similar a married couple's personalities are, the more likely that they will be happy and satisfied in the marriage.[13] Junior and high school friends also report being similar in terms of mutual friends, enjoying the same sports, liking similar social activities, and using (or not using) alcohol and cigarettes to the same degree.[14] Friendships can last decades when the friends are similar to one another,[15] regardless of whether or not they have high or low levels of communication skills.[16]

Similarity plays an important role in initial attraction. People are more likely to accept a Facebook friend request from strangers who they perceive to be similar.[17] Given that half of Canadians access Facebook daily,[18] this might be something to consider because the operative concept here is perception. We are more attracted to similarities *we believe exist* than we are to actual similarities.[19] In fact, perceived similarities often create attraction in that once we decide that we like someone, it leads to perceptions of similarity rather

than the other way around.[20] Accounting for this attraction might be the fact that if we find people like ourselves attractive, then we too must be attractive. In fact, the results of one study showed that people are disproportionately likely to marry others whose first or last names resemble their own, and they are also attracted to those with similar birthdays or even jersey numbers![21] On a more substantive note, similar values about politics and religion were found, in one study, to be the best predictors of mate choice—significantly more than physical attraction or personality traits.[22]

When we're similar to others in a high percentage of important areas such as career goals, friends, and beliefs about human rights, attraction is greatest. With enough similarity in key areas, couples can survive disputes in a number of areas, but if the number and content of disagreements become too great, the relationship may be threatened.

Attraction turns to dislike, however, when the other person behaves in a strange or socially offensive manner.[23] In such cases, these individuals threaten our self-esteem in that we fear that we may be as unappealing as they are. When that happens, we'll distance ourselves from them to protect our ideal self-image.

Complementarity

The familiar saying that "opposites attract" is also valid. Differences strengthen a relationship when they are complementary—when each partner's characteristics satisfy the other's needs. Research suggests that attraction to partners who have complementary temperaments might be rooted in biology.[24] For instance, a dominant person may be attracted to a passive one.[25] Relationships also work well when the partners agree that one will exercise control in certain areas ("You make financial decisions") and the

Zade Rosenthal/© Paramount Pictures/courtesy Everett Collection/The Canadian Press

In the *Star Trek* sagas, hotheaded Kirk and emotionless Spock find that their differing styles complement each other, leading to a strong personal and professional friendship.

other will exercise control in different areas ("I'll decide how to decorate the place"). Strains occur when control issues are disputed.

When successful and unsuccessful couples are compared over a 20-year period, partners in successful marriages tend to be similar enough to satisfy each other physically and mentally but different enough to keep the relationship interesting. Successful couples find ways to balance their similarities and differences by adjusting to the changes that occur over the years.

Reciprocal Attraction

We usually like people who like us, and conversely, we don't care much for people who seem indifferent or attack us in some way.[26]

It's no mystery why reciprocal liking builds attractiveness—people who approve of us bolster self-esteem. But we don't like people when we think they're insincere and just trying to get something from us. Or the liking may not fit with our own self-concept. For example, if someone says you're good-looking and intelligent but you think you're ugly and stupid, then you may disregard the flattery.

Competence

We also like talented, competent people, but not if they're too competent—this makes us look bad by comparison. People are generally attracted to those who are talented but have some visible flaws. This shows that they are human, like us.[27] Moreover, we're attracted to people whose competence is paired with interpersonal warmth. "Competent but cool" is generally not seen as an attractive mix.[28]

Self-Disclosure

Revealing important information about yourself can also build liking.[29] Sometimes the basis of this liking comes from learning about how we are similar, either in experiences ("I broke off an engagement myself") or in attitudes ("I feel nervous with strangers, too"). Self-disclosure is also a sign of regard. When people share private information, it suggests that they respect and trust you. Disclosure plays an even more important role as relationships develop. This is the case in both online and face-to-face communication and relationships.[30]

But not all disclosure leads to liking. The key to satisfying self-disclosure is reciprocity: getting back the amount and kind of information equivalent to that which you reveal.[31] Further, the timing must be right, and it's important not to disclose intimate information when you first meet someone. Finally, for your own protection, only reveal personal information to people you know are trustworthy.[32] You'll read more about self-disclosure later in the chapter.

Proximity

The more often we interact with someone, the more likely we will form a relationship with that person.[33] For instance, we develop friendships with neighbours, classmates, co-workers, members of organizations we belong to, and so forth. Proximity allows us to get more information about other people and benefit from a relationship with them. The Internet provides a new means for creating closeness, as users are able to experience "virtual proximity" in cyberspace.[34]

Rewards

Some social scientists say that relationships—both impersonal and personal—are based on a socioeconomic model called **social exchange theory**.[35] This model suggests that we seek out people who can give us tangible or emotional rewards that are greater than or equal to the costs we encounter in dealing with them. According to social exchange theory, relationships suffer when one partner feels "underbenefited."[36]

Tangible rewards might be a nice place to live or a high-paying job, while intangible ones might include prestige, emotional support, or companionship. Costs refer to undesirable outcomes: unpleasant work, emotional pain, and so on. A simple formula captures the social exchange theory of why we form and maintain relationships:

$$Rewards - Costs = Outcome$$

Social exchange theory
A socioeconomic theory of relational development that suggests people seek relationships in which the rewards they receive from others are equal to or greater than the costs they encounter.

While exchange theory seems cold and calculating, it seems quite appropriate in business relationships and in some friendships: "I don't mind listening to the ups and downs of your love life because you rescue me when the house needs repairs." Even close relationships have an element of

AT THE MOVIES

Waitress (2007), Rated 13+

Jenna (Keri Russell) is a small-town waitress who creates delicious pies for the customers at Joe's Diner. Unfortunately, she feels stuck in an unhappy marriage to a controlling and abusive husband. Social exchange theory explains why Jenna stays in the relationship—and it also describes why she wants to get out. She isn't alone: Virtually every character in the film makes relational choices based on rewards, costs, and comparisons with alternatives. For the folks who frequent Joe's Diner, social exchange is as much a part of their everyday lives as Jenna's scrumptious pies.

exchange. Friends and lovers tolerate each other's quirks because the comfort they get overrides them. When the costs outweigh the rewards, some people feel that the relationship is not worth the effort. Others choose to be in a bad relationship as opposed to no relationship at all.

LO2
Models of Relational Development and Maintenance

So far we have looked at some factors that influence why we are attracted to certain people. In the following pages we'll examine the kinds of communication that we use to start, maintain, and end relationships.

Developmental Models

One well-known model of relational stages was developed by Mark Knapp. He divided the rise and fall of relationships into 10 stages consisting of two broad phases: "coming together" and "coming apart."[37] Other researchers suggest that models of relational communication should have a third area—**relational maintenance**—communication aimed at keeping relationships operating smoothly and satisfactorily. **Figure 8.1** shows how Knapp's 10 stages fit this three-phase view of relational communication.

Keep in mind that initiating is the opening stage in *all* relationships, not just romantic ones. Friendships start here,[38] as do business partnerships. In fact, some have compared interviews to first dates because they have similar properties.[39] As you read through this section, consider how each stage plays out in your long-term friendships, romantic relationships, or work/business partnerships.

Initiating

In the **initiating** stage, we make contact. Communication is usually brief and follows conventional formulas: handshakes, innocuous remarks about the weather, and friendly expressions. These seemingly superficial and meaningless behaviours signal interest in building a relationship.

Initiating relationships—especially romantic ones—can be hard for shy people, and here's where the Internet comes into play. One study of an online dating service found that participants who identified themselves as shy expressed a greater appreciation for the system's anonymous, nonthreatening environment than did non-shy users.[40] Shy people used the service to help overcome their inhibitions about initiating relationships in face-to-face settings. This may explain why so many young people—shy or not—use Facebook and other sites to initiate relationships.[41]

> **Relational maintenance**
> Communication aimed at keeping relationships operating smoothly and satisfactorily.
>
> **Initiating**
> The first stage in relational development, in which the parties express interest in one another.

FIGURE 8.1
Stages of Relational Development

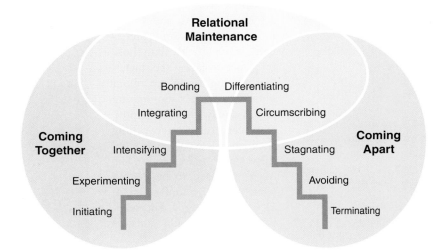

Adapted from Mark L. Knapp & Anita L. Vangelisti (1992). *Interpersonal Communication and Human Relationships*, 2nd ed. (Boston, MA: Allyn and Bacon).

Experimenting

Once we've made contact, the next step is deciding whether we're interested in pursuing the relationship. This involves **uncertainty reduction**—the process of getting to know others by gaining more information about them.[42] Typically, people search for common ground with conversational basics such as, "Where are you from?" or "What's your major?" and then move on to similarities: "You're a runner, too? How many klicks do you do a week?"

The hallmark of the **experimenting** stage is small talk. It enables us to learn what interests we have in common and to "audition" the other person—to help us decide whether a relationship is worth pursuing. This is when the "crush" starts.

The move from initiating to experimenting seems to occur even more rapidly in cyberspace. One study found that people who develop relationships via e-mail begin asking questions about attitudes, opinions, and preferences more quickly than those in face-to-face contact.[43] Not having to worry about blushing and stammering is probably very helpful. However, social networking sites are also changing how this stage plays out. The big thing used to be getting someone's telephone number. Now it's getting a Facebook friend request.[44] Once access is given, communicators can pour over the site, allowing them to "chug" rather than "sip" information in a less face-threatening way. Photos and mutual friends also influence whether or not someone will take the relationship to the next level.

Uncertainty reduction
The process of getting to know others by gaining more information about them.

Experimenting
An early stage in relational development, consisting of a search for common ground. If the experimentation is successful, the relationship will progress to *intensifying*. If not, it may go no further.

Intensifying
A stage of relational development, preceding *integrating*, in which the parties move toward integration by increasing the amount of contact and the breadth and depth of self-disclosure.

Integrating
A stage of relational development in which the parties begin to take on a single identity.

Intensifying

In the **intensifying** stage, the parties increase both contact time and the breadth and depth of their self-disclosure. Dating couples use a wide range of communication strategies to describe their feelings of attraction.[45] About a quarter of the time they express feelings directly, using metacommunication to openly discuss the state of the relationship. More often they use less direct methods of communication: spending an increasing amount of time together, doing favours for each other, giving tokens of affection, hinting and flirting, expressing feelings nonverbally, getting to know the partner's friends and family, and trying to look more physically attractive. In developing friendships, partners might share activities, hang out with mutual friends, or take trips together.[46]

The intensifying stage is the most exciting and even euphoric stage. For romantic partners, it's often filled with starstruck gazes, goosebumps, and daydreaming. It's the stage most often depicted in movies[47] and romance novels. But, as you know, this stage doesn't last.

Integrating

At the **integrating** stage, the parties take on an identity as a social unit—invitations come addressed to the couple. Partners also begin to take on each other's commitments: "Sure, we'll spend Christmas with your family." Common property may begin to be designated our apartment, our car, our song.[48] Partners develop unique, ritualistic ways of behaving[49] and begin to speak alike.[50] In the integrating stage, individuals give up some characteristics of their old selves and develop shared identities.

In contemporary relationships, integrating may include going "Facebook Official" (FBO) by declaring that the couple is in a relationship.[51] Of course, problems

"Good game." "Good game." "Nice game." "Good game."
"I'm in love with you." "Good game." "Nice game."

Harry Bliss The New Yorker Collection/The Cartoon Bank

Bonding is marked by public expressions of commitment.

arise when one partner wants to be "FBO" and the other doesn't.[52] And the meaning of FBO can be different for each partner. In heterosexual relationships, women tend to perceive FBO declarations as involving more intensity and commitment then did their male counterparts.[53] As a result, women may connect FBO status with the rights and restrictions normally associated with bonding—a stage we'll look at now.

Bonding

During the **bonding** stage, parties make symbolic public gestures to show the world that their relationship exists. Bonding is the peak of what Knapp calls the "coming together" phase of relational development. What constitutes a bonded, committed relationship isn't easily defined.[54] For our purposes, we'll define bonded relationships as those involving a significant measure to make the relationship "official." These include getting married, moving in together, having a public ceremony, making a written or verbal pledge, and so forth. It's the declaration of exclusivity that makes this a distinct stage in the relationship.

Relationships don't have to be romantic to achieve bonding. We see it with contracts that formalize a business partnership or initiation ceremonies into a fraternity or sorority.

Differentiating

In the **differentiating** stage, couples begin to re-assert their individual identities. Previously agreed upon issues ("You work and I'll look after the children") may now become points of contention: "Why am I stuck at home when I have better career potential?"

Bonding
A stage of relational development in which the parties make symbolic public gestures to show that their relationship exists.

Differentiating
A stage of relational development in which the parties reestablish their individual identities after having bonded together.

© King Features Syndicate. Reprinted with permission — Torstar Syndication Services

Looking at Diversity

The Identification That Needs an Explanation

It's been four years since the first time I publicly identified as a gay woman and you'd think that, by now, it would be easy to say, "I'm a lesbian." But, it isn't. For example, when I'm in friendly conversations with people I've just met, they eventually ask about a boyfriend and I respond by saying, "I don't have a boyfriend, I'm gay." That's when I sense an uncomfortable tension that seems to fill the room and they start to stumble over their words saying things like, "Oh, ah, I'm so sorry, its just that . . . you don't look gay." They hardly ever say, "Do you have a girlfriend? What's her name?" It's as if I have confused *them* and then the conversation dies or fades into a less "awkward" topic. This makes me feel as if being Gay is wrong and that's why others feel awkward. Some of my friends will even say, "Don't tell my parents you're uhhhh . . . gay because I don't think they would like it."

All this only gets worse when I disclose to men who are attracted to me. They'll say things like, "Prove it" or "I could change that!" This suggests that I have to justify my sexual orientation and fight to be respected. Just imagine that if every time you were asked your name, you were told to prove it. Pretty soon, you'd become exhausted with the question. Yet, you didn't choose your name, just like I didn't choose my sexual identity. It's not something I can change; it's just the way I am.

As if identifying as lesbian in a heterosexist society isn't enough of a sore thumb, the year I came out was 2013—the same year I was taken out of my home and placed in foster care! I became a ward of the court because Social Services had been notified that I was being sexually abused. When people learn that I come from foster care and that I identify as a lesbian, they jump to one conclusion— the traumas I experienced explain why I am gay. . .

"You're only *that way* because of what happened to you" . . . or, "You'll grow out of it once you heal" . . . or, "You'll go back into the closet in a few years" . . . or, "It must be easier to have lesbian sex with all you've been through." When people say these things they don't realize the damage their words cause. They use my trauma to define who I am as a person. The language around my identity makes me feel ashamed to be who I am, even though I'm proud of myself and my accomplishments.

These comments also infuriate me because the damage caused by the sexual abuse prevents me from letting anyone get too close, especially when it comes to intimate relationships. So often a good relationship with a female suffers as I push her away. Eventually, the romance fades into memories of the horrible things that were done to me. Regardless of the sex of the person I'm seeing, the trauma still exists. But, it's not why I'm a lesbian. Even though the sexual abuse was primarily caused by a male, I still struggle with its effects in intimate same-sex relationships.

Having to prove or justify my sexual orientation is an overbearing reality for many gay women. From personal experience, I believe the only way to change this is to educate people about what it's like to identify under the LGBTQI umbrella. I've come to realize that I can have an impact on changing the stigma around being gay, I can help people understand that there's no reason someone is attracted to the same sex. It just happens. I can do this by proudly telling people that I am a lesbian and talking about it more frequently. I can correct people when they make comments like, "You don't look gay," or "You're only a lesbian because of what happened to you." I can inform them that my trauma does not define me or explain why I am attracted to the same sex. I do not need to explain why I identify as a gay woman because . . . love is love.

Rebekah Naomi Mifflin

Rebekah Naomi Mifflin

But the need for individuality needn't be a negative experience. For instance, young adults forge their own unique lives and identity, even while maintaining their relationships with their parents.[55] The key to successful differentiating is maintaining a commitment to the relationship while you create your individual "spaces."

Circumscribing
A stage of relational development in which parties begin to reduce the scope of their contact and commitment to one another.

Circumscribing

While most long-term relationships reach a plateau of development, others pass through several stages of decline and dissolution. In the **circumscribing** stage, communication between members decreases in quantity and quality, and the stage is characterized by restrictions and restraints. Rather than discuss a disagreement, members withdraw mentally or physically. Circumscribing doesn't involve total avoidance, but interest and commitment begin to wane. To maintain a healthy relationship at this time, partners need to balance the need for togetherness (connecting) with the need for independence (autonomy), which is discussed later in the chapter.

Ana Blazic Pavlovic/Shutterstock.com

©2008 Harry Bliss. Distributed by Tribune Media Services, Inc.   10/9

www.harrybliss.com

"We'll always have Facebook"

Stagnating

If circumscribing continues, the relationship enters the **stagnating** stage, where there's little feeling for one another. Couples in this stage unenthusiastically have the same conversations, see the same people, and follow the same routines without any sense of joy or novelty. In all, there is no growth in this stage and relational boredom sets in.[56]

Avoiding

In the **avoiding** stage, partners create physical distance between each other, either indirectly by using a guise of excuses ("I've been sick lately") or directly ("Don't call me; I don't want to see you now"). The prognosis for the relationship is not good at this stage.

But deterioration is not inevitable. A key difference between marriages that end in separation and those that are restored is the type of communication that occurs when partners are unsatisfied.[57] Unsuccessful couples deal with problems by avoidance, indirectness, and less involvement with each other. Couples who "repair" their

relationship confront each other with their concerns and negotiate solutions to their problems.

Terminating

While not all relationships end, many do reach the **terminating** stage. Nor do all relationships move toward termination in a straight line. Some go back and forth toward dissolution.[58] But termination need not be negative. Understanding each other's needs for personal growth may dilute hard feelings. The best predictor of whether romantic parties will remain friends is whether they were friends beforehand.[59]

Technology also plays a role in relational termination. For example, in one study, thousands of respondents admitted to having broken up with someone via text message and men were far more likely than women to use this method.[60] Obviously, this approach runs the risk of hurting and/or infuriating the former partner and reduces the likelihood of maintaining any kind of a friendship. In fact, in another study, those on the

iStockphoto/Thinkstock

Stagnating
A stage of relational development characterized by declining enthusiasm and standardized forms of behaviour.

Avoiding
A stage of relational development, immediately prior to *terminating*, in which the parties minimize contact with one another.

Terminating
The concluding stage of relational development, characterized by the acknowledgment of one or both parties that the relationship is over.

receiving end of a "technology" breakup tended to have high levels of attachment anxiety—which may account for why partners were reluctant to deliver the news in person.[61]

While Knapp's model offers insights into relational stages, it doesn't describe the ebb and flow of communication that occurs in every relationships or that other patterns of development and deterioration have been identified. Further, not all relationships follow the same linear fashion. In real life, elements of other stages are usually present. For example, two lovers deep in the throes of integrating may still do their share of experimenting ("Wow, I never knew that about you!") or differentiating ("Nothing personal, but I need a weekend to myself").

Dialectical tensions
Inherent conflicts that arise when two opposing or incompatible forces exist simultaneously.

Connection–autonomy dialectic
The dialectical tension between a desire for connection and a need for independence in a relationship.

LO3
Dialectical Perspectives

Rather than see relationships in stages, others see them in terms of balancing the scale between being a couple and maintaining individuality. This is referred to as a dialectical tension—when two opposing forces come together. Three types of **dialectical tensions** are described below.

Connection versus Autonomy (Independence)

Needing both connection and independence within relationships results in the **connection–autonomy dialectic**. Couples who can't find ways to manage these personal needs break up.[63] Some research suggests that men value independence while women tend to value connection and commitment.[64]

In marriages, the "hold me tight" bonds of the first year are often followed by a need for autonomy. This desire can manifest itself in wanting to make new friends, engage

Tales from Broken Hearts – Women and Recovery from Romantic Relationships

While Mark Knapp's model looks at the rise and fall of relationships in general, Judith Rolls studied what happens to women as their romantic relationships fell apart. She asked women to share their break-up stories and found that they went through six sequential stages from the decline to the full recovery.[62] What happens in each stage is outlined below.

Decline – There were three types of decline. First was an immediate one that happened to women in abusive relationships. As soon as the relationships were formalized in some way (like Knapp's bonding stage), the abuse started. The women felt that the relationship was in decline before it really got started. The second type of decline was a gradual one and this was the most common. In the third type, the women were all breakees and had no idea that their romantic relationship was in trouble. They were completely blind to what was going on with their partners. Hence, the blind decline.

Pivotal Moment – The pivotal moment came when the women knew "in their hearts" that the relationship as they knew it was over. Breakers decided to leave their partner while breakees learned that their partner was breaking up with them. The breakees used language such as "shock, panic, terror, hurt, disbelieve, and a host of other unnerving descriptions to recount their feelings."

Interim Phase – What was interesting was that whether the women were breakers or breakees, the relationships didn't end right away. Instead, they went through an interim period. For breakees, the stage was characterized by "emotional withdrawal, absence, dishonesty, struggle, lonliness, tension, anger, fighting, crying, and awkwardness." Breakers spent this stage preparing emotionally and economically to leave.

The Termination – At this point, one of the partners leaves the home. The women reacted in a couple of ways. Some breakees were quite devastated, especially if they were blind to the decline. Other breakees had got used to the idea during the interim. For some of the breakers, it was a time of celebration.

The Recovery Phase – There were two dimensions to the recovery. First, the women had to recovery from the romantic aspect of the relationship. This was easier for the breakers. Breakees cried, rearranged their furniture, read self-help and spiritually books, cut up their wedding dresses, sought counselling and so forth. The second dimension focused on issues that emerged as a result of the breakup: poor finances, ill health, a drop in self-esteem, needing to help their children deal with the change, dealing with old sex-role stereotypes ("Oh, stay with him, dear. Men are like that sometimes."), and so forth. It's the emergent issues that prolong the recovery phase.

The Enlightenment – This occurred when the women got over the relationship and dealt with the emergent themes. Every woman said that she felt more confident, skilled, happy, strong, and contented. In all, they felt they had reached a new level of self-actualization.

commitment, conflict, disengagement, and reconciliation. When it comes to technology, studies have found that satisfied couples negotiate and adhere to rules about cell phone usage as a way to balance connection and independence.[66] For example, cell phones allow people to stay connected, but rules help manage expectations about how often couples will (or won't) talk to or text each other. This can establish a measure of autonomy if partners want and need it.

Openness–privacy dialectic
The dialectical tension between a desire for open communication and the need for privacy in a relationship.

in activities without the spouse, or to make a career move that might disrupt the relationship. This movement from connection to independence may lead to a breakup or it can also be part of a cycle that redefines it in new and interesting ways that can recapture or even surpass the intimacy that existed in the past.

Both women and men in heterosexual romantic pairs cite the connection–autonomy balance as one of the most significant factors affecting their relationship.[65] Managing this tension is crucial in negotiating turning points related to

> "Love passes" . . . men say (and women sigh), but it isn't true. Infatuation passes, but not a love that has become one's life!
>
> —Henriette Dessaulles,
> *Hopes and Dreams: The Diary of Henriette Dessaulles, 1874–1881*

Openness versus Privacy

While we need disclosure in our relationships, we also need privacy. We may wish to keep certain thoughts, feelings, and behaviours to ourselves. These conflicting drives create the **openness–privacy dialectic**. Partners use a variety of strategies to gain privacy.[67] They may explain that they don't want to continue a discussion, offer indirect nonverbal cues, change the topic, or leave the room.

While long-term couples learn that it's best not to disclose all their thoughts and feelings, they still go through periods of much sharing and times of relative withdrawal. Likewise, they experience periods of passion and times of little physical contact.

Another challenge to privacy management is social media. Although it's easy to share personal information, it's not always wise—especially if it involves someone else. It's important to know how to use privacy controls and to negotiate with your partner what you will and will not share about each other.[68]

Invitation to Insight

Your Relational Stage

You can gain a clearer appreciation of the accuracy and value of relational stages by answering the following questions:

1. Describe the present stage of your relationship and the behaviours that characterize your communication at this stage. Give specific examples to support your assessment.

2. Discuss the trend of the communication in terms of Mark Knapp's relational stages. Are you likely to remain in the present stage, or do you anticipate movement to another stage? Which one? Explain your answer.

3. Describe your level of satisfaction with the answer to question 2. If you are satisfied, describe what you can do to increase the likelihood that the relationship will operate at the stage you described. If you are not satisfied, discuss what you can do to move the relationship toward a more satisfying stage.

4. Because both parties define a relationship, define your partner's perspective. Would she or he say the relationship is at the same stage as you describe it? If not, explain how your partner would describe it. What does your partner do to determine the stage at which your relationship operates? (Give specific examples.) How would you like your partner to behave in order to move the relationship to or maintain it at the stage you desire? What can you do to encourage your partner to behave in the way you desire?

"And do you, Rebecca, promise to make love only to Richard, month after month, year after year, and decade after decade, until one of you is dead?"

Tom Cheney The New Yorker Collection/The Cartoon Bank

Predictability versus Novelty

While stability is important in relationships, too much can lead to staleness. The **predictability–novelty dialectic** reflects this tension. For instance, long-term couples can predict exactly how their partners will react in certain situations. This can be tiresome. On the other hand, nobody wants a completely unpredictable partner who, for example, invites dinner guests without informing you or tells you at the last minute that he or she can't attend a social function. Too many surprises can threaten the foundations upon which the relationship is based.

Managing Dialectical Tensions

Managing these dialectical tensions can be challenging, and couples go about it differently. However, there are three strategies that seem to have the best results.[69]

- **Integration**. Communicators accept opposing forces without trying to diminish them. In terms of novelty and prediction, a couple might decide that once a week they'll do something different together that they've never done before.[70] Some stepfamilies manage the tension between the "old family" and the "new family" by adapting and blending their family rituals.[71]

- **Recalibration**. Dialectical challenges are reframed so the contradiction disappears; for example, changing an attitude from loving someone in spite of the differences to loving her or him because of those differences.[72] Instead of thinking of someone's unwillingness to share parts of their past as secret keeping, think of it as mysterious.

- **Reaffirmation**. Recognizing and then embracing the notion that dialectical tensions will always be there.

Predictability–novelty dialectic
The dialectical tension between a desire for stability and the need for novelty in a relationship.

Characteristics of Relationships

Regardless of how you analyze relationships, they change constantly, are affected by culture, and require maintenance and commitment.

Relationships and Change

As you've previously read, the dialectical tensions that are inherent in long-term relationships result in constant change. In addition, communication theorist Richard Conville describes the constantly changing, evolving nature of relationships as a cycle in which partners move through a series of stages, returning to ones they previously encountered, although at a new level.[73] (See **Figure 8.2**). In terms of Knapp's model of relational development, partners might move from integration to differentiating to intensifying to a new level of security. It's the changing nature of relationships that keep them together.

Relationships Are Affected by Culture

Many qualities that shape relationships are universal in nature.[74] For example, communication in all cultures has both a task and relational dimension, and similar facial expressions signal the same emotions. All cultures have a distribution of power, and males are more competitive and tend to invest less emotionally in sexual relationships.

While generalities do exist, particulars can differ across cultures. In Western nations, romance and marriage reflect Knapp's model of relational stages.[75] In other cultures, the bride and groom may meet only weeks, days, or

FIGURE 8.2
A Helical Model Of Relational Cycles

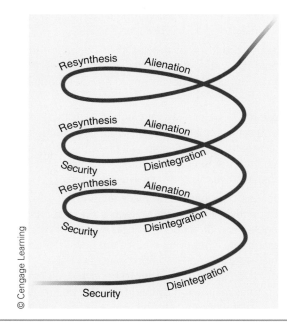

© Cengage Learning

even minutes before the marriage. Yet these relationships can be successful and satisfying.[76] And being in an intercultural relationship can be challenging.[77] For instance, deciding how much to disclose can be tricky. Low-context cultures such as Canada's value directness, while high-context ones like Japan's consider tact far more important. The titles of two self-help books reveal the mindset of these approaches. An American self-help book is titled *How to Say No Without Feeling Guilty,*[78] while its Japanese counterpart is called *16 Ways to Avoid Saying No.*[79] You can see how these differences can lead to interpersonal challenges. Possessing a level of intercultural competence is useful when couples from different cultures come together.

Relationships Require Maintenance

Just as gardens need tending, so too do relationships need work.[80] Researchers have identified five maintenance strategies that couples use to keep their interaction satisfying:[81]

- *Positivity.* Keeping the relational climate polite and upbeat, and avoiding criticism.
- *Openness.* Talking directly about the nature of the relationship and disclosing personal needs and concerns.
- *Assurances.* Letting the other person know that he or she matters to you.
- *Social networks.* Having communication with friends, family, co-workers to provide companionship to take pressure off the relationship to satisfy all the partners' needs.
- *Sharing tasks.* Helping one another take care of life's chores and obligations.

These maintenance strategies aren't only for romantic relationships.[82] One study found that college students depended on two strategies with family and friends: openness ("Things have been a little crazy for me lately") and

social networks ("How are you and Sam? Hopefully good"). With romantic partners, however, assurances ("This is just a little e-mail to say I love you") were used most.

Gay and lesbian partners seem to be better at maintaining a positive tone by using some of the maintenance strategies outlined above.[83] Further, they are more upbeat in the face of conflict. They tend to take disagreements less personally; use fewer controlling, hostile tactics; and get less emotionally aroused when problems arise.

> I won't leave you lonely tonight,
> I want you to hold me all night,
> It's gonna be alright won't leave
> you lonely tonight
>
> —Shania Twain*

Invitation to Insight

Your Dialectical Tensions

Describe how dialectical tensions operate in your life. Which incompatible goals do you and your relational partner(s) seek? Which strategies do you use to manage tensions? Are you satisfied with the strategies, or can you suggest better ones?

Technology and Indian Marriage: A Match Made in Heaven

Ken Seet/Corbis/VCG/Getty Images

Some 18 months ago in southern India, the parents of a software engineer working in Chennai began to despair of finding him a suitable bride. They were, truth to tell, rather picky: "Our requirement is a suitable Hindu Nadar girl of Sivakasi/Madurai side origin, preferably employed as a software engineer in Chennai, age between 21 to 24, height 5 feet 2 inches to 5 feet 6 inches and sufficiently good-looking." She also had to speak Tamil.

There was, however, a happy ending. They ventured online, to a website called Bharatmatrimony.com, which now flaunts their story. They identified a girl, received a message from her father, matched horoscopes, and having introduced the happy couple to each other, will celebrate the wedding next month.

Online marriage-broking is one of the successes of Indian e-business, used by the single looking for "love matches" as well as by their parents and siblings. So complex are the requirements of Indians seeking a partner that the Internet might have been designed to meet their needs. Bharatmatrimony's boss, Janakiram Murugavel, says that language is the biggest criterion. His site is divided into 15 linguistic sections. Then comes status and caste, which divides Indians at birth into thousands of groups. About 70 percent of his customers want to marry within their caste. Most still also use astrology. Bharatmatrimony offers an online horoscope service.

Relationships Require Commitment

Commitment is important in every type of interpersonal relationship—friendship, ("Friends for life!"), family ("We're always here for you"), a work team ("I've got you covered"), or a romantic relationship ("Till death do us part"). **Relational commitment** involves a promise to remain and make a relationship successful. Social media play a role in relational maintenance.[84] For example, tools such as Facebook allow loved ones to view status updates or post comments on each other's walls.[85] E-mails and the old fashioned phone call for more intimate topics can also help.[86] Even swapping photo-messages is a means to maintain a relationship.[87] One study found that women use social media for relational maintenance more than men, regardless of the type of relationship.[88] This is consistent with research that women expect and receive more maintenance communication with their female friends than men do with other males.[89]

Social media is also helping long distance relationships to be as stable as geographically close ones[90] and this holds true for romantic, family, and friendship relationships.[91] The key is commitment to relational maintenance. In terms of romantic relationships, female college students in one study said that openness and mutual problem solving were key strategies in maintaining such relationships.[92] And, in another study, both women and men noted self-disclosure as the most important factor. Sharing tasks and giving practical help were less relevant in long-distance relationships.[93]

Relational commitment
An implied or explicit promise to remain and make a relationship successful.

Social Support

While relational maintenance is about keeping a relationship thriving, social support is about providing emotion, informational, and instrumental support during challenging time.[94] It's through communication that we provide such aid.[95]

1. *Emotional support:* Fewer things are more helpful during times of stress, hurt, or grief than having someone who listens with empathy and responds in caring ways.[96] Therefore, it's important to keep messages person centred—that is, focused on the emotions of the speaker. For example, saying "This must be difficult for you," as opposed to, "It's not the end of the world" which minimizes those feelings. Another example of what not to say would be, "Don't worry, the sun will come up tomorrow," because it draws attention away from the individual.[97]

2. *Informational support:* Sometimes it's important for us to find information for loved ones. Perhaps they're just not in the right frame of mind to do so, or we may have access to information that can be helpful to them.

3. *Instrumental support:* Finally, sometimes our friends and family need us to do things for them. It could be as simple as giving someone a ride to the airport to something more complicated such as providing care during an illness. We count on romantic partners and family members to assist us in times of need, and instrumental support is a primary marker of a close relationship.[98]

Many partners in romantic relationships feel that they don't receive enough support while a few think that they receive too much—usually in the form of unsolicited advice or information.[99] Because partners and loved ones aren't always the mind readers we wish they were, it's vital for us to state outright how we're feeling and how that person can help us.[100] Sometimes such support can come through social media from people we don't even know.[101]

LO4
Repairing Damaged Relationships

Sooner or later, all relationships hit bumpy patches and these are referred to as **relational transgressions**.[102] For example, we see this in lack of commitment, physical and psychological distancing, disrespect, problematic emotions (jealousy, rage, unjustified suspicion), and aggression.[103] Each of these share several dimensions.

Minor versus Significant

A little distance can make the heart grow fonder and a little jealousy can be a sign of affection. But in large and regular doses, they will seriously damage personal relationships.

Social versus Relational

Some transgressions violate social rules shared by society at large. For example, most people agree that ridiculing or humiliating a friend in public is rude. Other rules are uniquely constructed by the parties involved. For instance, some families have a rule stating, "If you're going to be late, call so we won't worry." Failure to honour this accepted procedure feels like a violation.

Deliberate versus Unintentional

An unintentional transgression would be inadvertently revealing something about a friend's past. An intentional transgression might be purposely making a cruel comment because you know it will hurt the person's feelings.

One-Time versus Incremental

The most obvious transgressions occur in a single episode: an act of betrayal, a verbal assault, or stalking out in anger. But subtle transgressions, such as emotional withdrawal, can occur over time. If the withdrawal is pervasive, however, it violates the fundamental nature of relationships in that partners are unavailable to one another.

Strategies for Relational Repair

The first step in repairing a transgression is to talk about the violation.[104]

© Queerstock, Inc./Alamy Stock Photo

In cases where you're responsible for the transgression, raise the issue by asking, in an appropriate tone of voice, "What did I do that you found so hurtful?" "Why was my behaviour a problem for you?"

The best way to right a wrong is to take responsibility for your transgression.[105] Even though apologizing doesn't come easy in Western cultures,[106] not offering an apology can be worse. Participants in one study reported that they felt more remorse over apologies they didn't offer than those they did.[107] Further, transgressors who have been forgiven are less likely to repeat their offences.[108]

To repair damaged relationships, your apology requires three elements:

1. An explicit acknowledgment that the transgression was wrong: "I acted like a selfish jerk."

Invitation to Insight

Maintaining Your Relationships

How well are you maintaining your important relationships? Choose one relationship that matters to you: with family members, friends, or a romantic partner. Analyze the degree to which you and the other person use the maintenance strategies listed above to keep the relationship strong and satisfying. What steps could you take to improve matters?

---

2. A sincere apology: "I'm really sorry. I feel awful for letting you down."

3. Some type of compensation: "If I act that way again, you can call me on it."[109]

Again, make sure your nonverbal behaviours match your words when you apologize. Even then, it may be unrealistic to expect immediate forgiveness. With severe transgressions, expressions of regret and promises of new behaviour need to be acted on before the aggrieved party accepts them as genuine.[110]

Forgiving Transgressions

Forgiveness has both personal and relational benefits. On a personal level, forgiveness can reduce emotional distress and aggression[111] and improve cardiovascular functioning.[112] Interpersonally, it can restore damaged relationships.[113] In a study of how women recover from romantic relationships, forgiving their former partner was a turning point in their recovery process.[114]

While an apology should contain certain elements, so too must forgiveness:

1. An explicit statement: "I can't forget what you did, but I believe your apology and I accept it."

2. A discussion of the implications of the transgression and the future of the relationship: "I have to be honest. It's going to take time before I can trust you again."[115]

Of course, some transgressions are harder to forgive than others—sexual infidelity and breaking up with the partner are the two least forgivable offences,[116] but being emotionally unfaithful—like when you're having an online affair with someone—can be as distressing as sexual infidelity.[117]

Intimacy
A state of personal sharing arising from physical, intellectual, emotional, and/or contact.

"I said I'm sorry."

Mick Stevens The New Yorker Collection/The Cartoon Bank

While forgiveness may be very difficult, Douglas Kelley encourages us to remember these words from R. P. Walters: "When we have been hurt we have two alternatives: be destroyed by resentment, or forgive. Resentment is death; forgiving leads to healing and life."[118]

LO5
Intimacy in Relationships

How important are close, intimate relationships? Apparently, they are extremely important. When researchers interviewed dying people, 90 percent said that what mattered most in life was having relationships. One mother of three who was dying of cancer said, "You need not wait until you are in my condition to know that nothing in life is as important as loving relationships."[119] Another researcher concluded that close relationships "may be the single most important source of life satisfaction and emotional well-being, across different ages and cultures."[120] With this in mind, let's take a closer look at intimate relationships.

Dimensions of Intimacy

Intimacy, that state of close contact with another, occurs in a variety of relationships. Forty-seven percent of college students reported that they had their "closest, deepest" intimate relationship with a romantic partner, 36 percent said it was with a close friend, and 14 percent cited a family member.[121] There are several dimensions of intimacy: physical, intellectual, emotional, and shared activities.

Physical intimacy begins before birth, when the fetus experiences a physical closeness with its mother that will never happen again.[122] Some physical intimacy is sexual, but sex is not always connected with a close relationship. One study of sexually active teens reported that half of them were not dating, nor did they want to date their sexual partner.[123]

Intellectual intimacy occurs when we share important ideas. This can result in an exciting closeness. Emotional intimacy comes from exchanging important feelings in both face-to-face and online interactions. Shared activities is the fourth dimension. When partners do things together, they develop in ways that can transform the relationship. For example, couples "play" by inventing private codes, acting like other people, teasing one another, and so forth.[124] Companions who have endured physical challenges together—in athletics or emergencies, for example—also form lifetime bonds.

Some intimate relationships exhibit all four dimensions, while others display only one or two. Although no relationship is always intimate, living without any sort of intimacy is hardly desirable. Research shows that people who have a fear of intimacy experience problems in both creating and then sustaining relationships.[125]

Masculine and Feminine Intimacy Styles

Researchers once thought that women were better at developing and maintaining relationships than men[126] because of the link between intimacy and women's propensity to self-disclose.[127] However, emotional expression isn't the

Kelvin Murray/Stone/Getty Images

Most teammates agree that working together can create bonds of intimacy unlike any other.

The Canadian Press/AP/Hussein Malla

only way to develop close relationships. Men develop meaningful relationships through shared activities.[128] By doing things together, they "grow on one another," develop feelings of interdependence, show appreciation for one another, and demonstrate mutual liking. Men also think of help as a measure of caring; a friend does things for you and with you.

Because women and men express caring differently, this can lead to misunderstandings. Women who look for emotional disclosure as a measure of affection may overlook an "inexpressive" man's efforts to show he cares by helping her. A man who fixes a leaky faucet may do so as a bid for intimacy. Further, while women think of sex as a way to express intimacy that has already developed, men see it as a way to create that intimacy.[129] When men want sex early in a relationship or after a fight, they see it as a way to build closeness. By contrast, women may resist physical closeness until the emotional side of the relationship is resolved.

However, what constitutes appropriate male behaviour is changing.[130] Male characters who disclose personal information receive favourable responses from other characters on prime-time sitcoms,[131] and fathers are becoming more affectionate with their sons, although some of that affection is still expressed through shared activities.[132]

Cultural Influences on Intimacy

The notion of intimacy varies across cultures. For instance, people in the United States disclose the most.[133] This contrasts with individuals from collectivistic countries such as Taiwan and Japan. They don't reach out to strangers; rather, they wait to be introduced before joining a conversation. Outsiders are addressed formally and unfavourable information about in-group members is hidden—they don't air their dirty laundry in public.[134] In individualistic cultures (Canada, the United States, and Australia), there is less distinction between personal and casual relationships. People are "familiar" with strangers and readily disclose information. But the large differences that once existed between Western and Eastern cultures is fast disappearing.[135]

Invitation to Insight

Hooking Up

Hooking up, a trend that started in the 1990s, is a norm in most places in Canada. Basically, hooking up refers to no-strings-attached sex— anything from a kiss to petting to oral sex or even intercourse. Hooking up is acceptable for females and males.

Respond to the following questions and then meet in small groups to share your answers. Discuss any different definitions of hooking up that you might have. In some parts of Labrador, for instance, hooking up refers to the initial getting together sexually, but dragging off refers to having sexual intercourse.

- How does hooking up relate to the old double standard for women and men? Do young women who hook up with lots of different people develop reputations? What about the men who do so?

- Are there ethical issues associated with hooking up? For instance, is it more acceptable to hook up with a "friend with benefits" than with a stranger?

- How does hooking up relate to intimacy and relationship development?

Intimacy in Mediated Communication

Intimacy also occurs via mediated sources. In fact, intimacy develops more quickly through mediated channels than in face-to-face communication.[136] Further, blogging, Facebooking, etc., enhance verbal, emotional, and social intimacy in interpersonal relationships.[137] The relative anonymity of chat rooms, blogs, and online dating services provides a freedom of expression that might not occur in face-to-face meetings.[138] In addition, instant messaging, e-mailing, and text messaging offer more constant contact with people than might otherwise be possible.[139] As one Internet punster put it, "I've never clicked this much with anyone in my life."[140]

However, intimacy in cyberspace can be problematic at times. For example, some people are virtually unfaithful while in committed face-to-face relationships but this online infidelity is considered as much as, or even more of, a betrayal than cheating in person.[141] Another type of Internet intimacy is sexting. Many adult partners who are separated geographically send sexy pictures to one another. This can help keep a romantic relationship alive. On the other hand, teens are also sexting. In one survey of students across Canada, 15 percent of the grade 11 students said they had sexted and 36 reported that they had received a sext.[142] This can be cause for concern because, depending on the age of the sender and receiver, it may be

> In the age of the text message, the power of the thumb has outgrown the power of the tongue.
>
> — Brent D. Wolfe and Colbey Penton Sparkman

Invitation to Insight

Your IQ (Intimacy Quotient)

What is the level of intimacy in your important relationships? Find out by following these directions.

1. Identify the point on each scale below that best describes one of your important relationships.

   a. Your level of physical intimacy

1	2	3	4	5
low				high

   b. Your amount of emotional intimacy

1	2	3	4	5
low				high

   c. The extent of your intellectual intimacy

1	2	3	4	5
low				high

   d. The degree of shared activities in your relationship

1	2	3	4	5
low				high

2. Now answer the following questions:

   a. What responses to each dimension of intimacy seem most significant to you?

   b. Are you satisfied with the intimacy profile outlined by your responses?

   c. If you are not satisfied, what steps can you take to change your degree of intimacy?

nito/Shutterstock.com

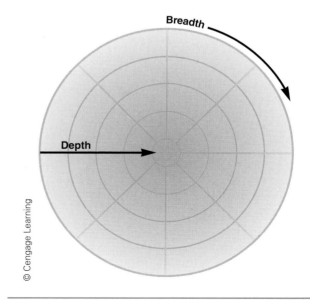
corepics/Shutterstock.com

considered child pornography. Further, teens can suffer extreme humiliation or be subjected to bullying when sexts are distributed without the sender's consent. This is such a problem that Planned Parenthood Ottawa offers risk-reduction approach workshops so teens can learn more about sexting.[143]

The Limits of Intimacy

It's impossible to have a close relationship with everyone you know—nor is that necessarily desirable. Most people want four to six close relationships in their lives at any given time.[144] Scholars have pointed out that an obsession with intimacy actually leads to less satisfying relationships.[145] When you consider the pleasure that comes from polite but distant communication, the limitations of intimacy become clear. Intimacy is rewarding, but it's not the only way to relate to others.

Self-disclosure
The process of deliberately revealing information about oneself that is significant and not normally known by others.

Social penetration
A model that describes relationships in terms of their breadth and depth.

Breadth
The first dimension of self-disclosure, involving the range of subjects being discussed.

Depth
A dimension of self-disclosure involving a shift from relatively nonrevealing messages to more personal ones.

LO6
Self-Disclosure in Relationships

Self-disclosure is the process of deliberately revealing significant information about oneself that is not normally known by others. In self-disclosure, the sharing is deliberate, significant, and previously unknown to the listener. If you accidentally tell a friend something, that information wouldn't qualify because it isn't deliberate. Other characteristics are that self-disclosure typically occurs in one-on-one situations, it is incremental, it doesn't happen all that often, and it is best in contexts of positive relationships.

Degrees of Self-Disclosure

Have you ever been on a train or plane or somewhere and a stranger tells you the gory, intimate details of a sordid relationship breakup? You know nothing about the individual except that dimension of his or her life? If you have had this, or a similar experience, then you have some insight into the **social penetration** model of self-disclosure. This model suggests that there are two dimensions of self-disclosure: depth and breadth.[146] **Breadth** refers to the range of subjects discussed and **depth** refers to the shift from impersonal topics to more personal ones. In the example above, the disclosure had little breadth but a large degree of depth. If you look at the most intimate relationships you have, you'll notice that there is both depth and breadth. (See **Figure 8.3**).

FIGURE 8.3
Social Penetration Model

Breadth

Depth

© Cengage Learning

The disclosure in the development of a relationship progresses from the periphery of the model to it's centre and this occurs over time.

Depending on the breadth and depth of information shared, a relationship will be casual or intimate. In casual relationships, the breadth may be great but not the depth. In the opening example, there was great depth in one area but nothing in terms of breadth. However, in intimate relationships, there is both breadth and depth. Each of your personal relationships probably has a different combination of breadth of subjects and depth of disclosure. **Figure 8.4** pictures a student's self-disclosure in one relationship.

What makes the disclosure in some messages deeper than others depends on its significance or its privacy level. You can also measure the depth of disclosure by looking at the levels of information.

FIGURE 8.4
Sample Model of Social Penetration

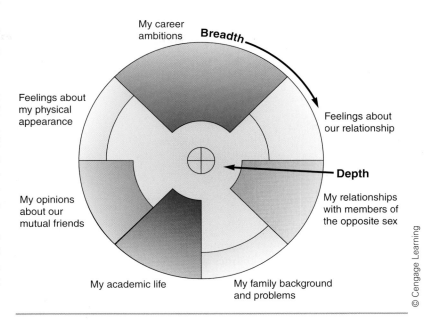

© Cengage Learning

A Model of Self-Disclosure

One way to look at the role of self-disclosure in interpersonal communication is by means of a device called the **Johari Window**, created by Joseph Luft and Harry Ingham.[147] Imagine a frame like **Figure 8.5** that contains everything about you: your likes, dislikes, goals, secrets, needs—everything. To understand the model, look at the four parts.

- Part 1, the open area, represents the information that you and others know about you. It would include things like your address, your interests, all the things that you might post on Facebook.
- Part 2, the blind area, represents information that you are unaware of but others know. For example, you may not know that your professors think very highly of you or that your behaviour changes when you're around a certain person.
- Part 3, your hidden area, represents information that you don't share with others. Perhaps you have an addiction or you did something in your youth that

Invitation to Insight

Building a Johari Window

You can use the Johari Window model to examine the level of self-disclosure in your own relationships.

1. Use the format described in the preceding section to draw two Johari Windows representing the relationship between you and one other person.

2. Describe which parts of yourself you keep in the hidden area. Explain your reasons for doing so. Describe the advantages or disadvantages or both of not disclosing these parts of yourself.

3. Look at the blind area of your model. Is this area large or small because of the amount of feedback (much or little) that you get from your partner or because of your willingness to receive the feedback that is offered?

4. Explain whether you are satisfied with the results illustrated by your answers. If you are not satisfied, explain what you can do to remedy the problem.

you're ashamed of now. You're likely to keep things like this to yourself.
- Part 4, the unknown area, represents information unknown to both you and others. This would include future honours or awards or your "hidden" talents that have yet to emerge because the

FIGURE 8.5

	Known to self	Not known to self
Known to others	1 OPEN	2 BLIND
Not known to others	3 HIDDEN	4 UNKNOWN

© Cengage Learning

Marynchenko Oleksandr/Shutterstock.com

opportunity has not yet presented itself. Maybe your bravery and swimming abilities will enable you to save someone's life in the future.

How the model works is that if you begin to self-disclose more of your hidden area, then others will provide information about you that you don't know. For instance, perhaps you see yourself as a very apprehensive public speaker. You share this with a classmate. She indicates her surprise and tells you that you don't look the least bit nervous and, in fact, you're one of the best speakers in

Privacy management
The choices people make to reveal or conceal information about themselves.

the class! Up until your disclosure, you had been blind to this fact about yourself. In addition to learning about yourself, self-disclosure has several other benefits which you will read about in the next section.

LO7
Benefits and Risks of Self-Disclosure

Like most things in life, there are benefits and risks of self-disclosing. The choices people make to reveal or conceal information about themselves is referred to as **privacy management**.[148] People disclose for a variety of reasons—which ones apply to you?

Benefits of Self-Disclosure
Catharsis

Sometimes we disclose just to "get it off our chest," like when you reveal your regrets about behaving badly in the past. This catharsis can provide mental and emotional relief.[149]

Reciprocity

Self-disclosure usually begets more of the same.[150] While your own self-disclosures won't guarantee self-disclosure by others, your honesty will create a climate that makes others feel safe or even obligated to reciprocate. Sometimes reciprocity occurs later; you tell a friend something today, and she or he opens up at a later date.

Self-Clarification

Sometimes we clarify our beliefs, opinions, thoughts, attitudes, and

---

Invitation to Insight

Examining Your Self-Disclosure

Here's a chance to explore the levels of self-disclosure you use with some important people in your life.

   Choose a "significant other" as the subject of this exercise.

   Over a three-day period, record the number of statements you make in each category: clichés, facts, opinions, and feelings. Try to be aware of the topics you discuss on each level, along with the number of statements in each category.

   Based on your findings, answer these questions:

a. Which topics of self-disclosure do you engage in most frequently? Least often?

b. What type of disclosure (cliché, fact, opinion, or feeling) do you use in each topic area?

c. Explain the reason for omitting topical categories (e.g., conflicts, the future) or levels of disclosure (e.g., feelings), or both.

d. Explain the consequences of any omissions described in part c.

feelings merely by talking about them out loud. This "talking the problem out" occurs with psychotherapists, or even good friends, bartenders, and hairdressers.

Self-Validation

When you disclose with the hope of obtaining a listener's agreement ("I think I did the right thing when . . ."), you are disclosing for self-validation, a confirmation of something about you. This occurs, for example, in the "coming out" process when gay individuals choose to integrate their sexual orientation into their personal, family, and social lives.[151]

Relationship Maintenance and Enhancement

Self-disclosure also plays a role in relational success.[152] For example, there's a strong relationship between the

quality of self-disclosure and marital satisfaction.[153] The same principle applies in other personal relationships.

Social Influence

Revealing personal information can sometimes increase your control over a person and the situation. An employee who tells the boss that another firm is making overtures will likely have a greater chance of getting a raise or other perks.

Risks of Self-Disclosure

While disclosing has it merits, it can be risky when topics are difficult or painful.[154] There are several categories of

Secrets Website Gets a Million Hits a Week

When Tina Malament was 17, she felt isolated and alone. Suffering from anorexia, depression, and suicidal thoughts, she lashed out at everyone close to her.

It took an intervention from family and friends for her to realize starving herself to be thin wasn't worth it. Over the next few years, she became serious about her recovery, and she took heart from a blog called PostSecret, where strangers mail in postcards to be posted online every Sunday. On the postcards, people anonymously share their secrets—funny secrets, happy secrets, and secrets filled with anguish, remorse, and pain. It is a place where people can release the secrets that suffocate them. About 1 million people visit the site each week.

The secrets posted on the site vary widely. One reads, "My mom won't tell me who my real father is. I wonder if she told him about me." Another reads, "I am so much bigger than the life I am leading."

Malament, now 21 and living in Colorado, sent in her own secret as well. She took a picture of herself standing in front of another postcard, which had a cupcake crossed out on it. She put her hands across the postcard and wrote across the picture that she was going to win her fight with anorexia. Although her secret wasn't posted, she found the process of making and sending it therapeutic, and the idea that someone else might read it and get something out of it encouraging.

PostSecret's ability to help people inspired Malament to start her own project. When she was a freshman at American University she made a T-shirt with a message about anorexia. On the front was a statistic about anorexics who die from the disorder. The back read: "I refuse to become a statistic." She wore the shirt around campus and eventually to a PostSecret event. At the end she stood up and told her story. Afterward six girls approached her crying and told her how much her story had affected them. They also asked her to make them T-shirts.

Courtney R. Brooks

Courtney R. Brooks, "Secret Website Gets a Million Hits a Week," *Boston Globe*, October 23, 2007. Reproduced by permission of the author.

risks: rejection, negative impression, decrease in relational satisfaction, loss of influence, and hurting the other person.[155] Deciding when and how much information to disclose can be complicated. Therefore, the following guidelines can help match the level to the situation.

Guidelines for Self-Disclosure

Do You Have a Moral Obligation to Disclose?

Sometimes we are morally obliged to disclose. For example, if someone tells you that a child is being sexually abused, you are required by law to report it to the proper authorities. Or, most HIV-positive patients believe it's their "duty" to reveal their status to healthcare providers and partners.[156] Yet 40 percent didn't reveal this information to their sexual partners.[157]

Are the Amount and Types of Disclosure Appropriate?

Some people have problems with "TMI"—sharing too much information,[158] particularly in university classrooms. One study found that while some disclosure (such as a student describing her heart condition in a physiology class) helped the learning process, other comments seemed to cross a line. Participants objected to disclosure that was too frequent, negative, irrelevant to course materials, and unexpected.[159] It's generally not wise to divulge personal secrets in class, with strangers, on public Facebook postings, and so forth.[160]

Is the Risk of Disclosing Reasonable?

There is always risk involved in disclosure, especially on the job.[161] However, if the person is trustworthy and supportive, the prospect of disclosing may be more reasonable. Further, some relationships are well worth the risk.

Will the Effect Be Constructive?

Self-disclosure can be a vicious tool if it's not used carefully, so consider the effects of your candour before opening up. Comments such as, "Last year I slept with your partner," may resolve your guilt but devastate the listener.

SKILL BUILDER

Appropriate Self-Disclosure

Develop a scenario in which you might reveal a self-disclosing message to someone who is important to you. This person could be a family member, a friend, a romantic interest, a work colleague, a club member, and so forth. To help you construct your message, consider the following:

- The benefits of disclosing
- The risks of self-disclosing
- Whether you have a moral obligation to disclose
- The importance of the other person to you
- The amount and type of disclosure that would be appropriate
- If the person will understand the disclosure
- If the disclosure is relevant to the situation at hand
- If the disclosure will be constructive
- If the disclosure will be reciprocated

Is the Self-Disclosure Reciprocated?

The amount of personal information you share usually depends on how much the other person reveals. Typically, disclosure is a two-way street and couples are happiest when their levels of openness are roughly equal.[162] One-way disclosure does have a role in therapeutic relationships, like when clients disclose to a trained professional. But you wouldn't expect or be receptive to your doctor's disclosing personal problems or ailments.[163]

LO8
Alternatives to Self-Disclosure

Although self-disclosure plays an important role in interpersonal relationships, complete honesty isn't always an easy or ideal choice. Consider the following:

> You're attracted to your best friend's mate, who has confessed that s/he is attracted to you. You agreed not to act on your feelings but now your friend asks if you're attracted to his or her mate. Would you tell the truth?

> A relative who visits often gives you large, ugly paintings and asks, "Where will you put this one?" What do you say?

ayzek/Shutterstock.com

Bertrand Demee/Getty

Although total honesty is desirable in principle, it can result in unpleasant and uncomfortable consequences. Research shows that in such situations, communicators aren't always honest[164] and resort to four alternatives: silence, lying, equivocating, and hinting.

Silence

Silence—withholding thoughts and feelings—need not be dishonourable, especially when total candour is likely to cause pain. People make distinctions between "lies of omission" and "lies of commission"—and saying nothing (omission) is usually judged less harshly than telling an outright lie (commission).[165] One study showed that, in the workplace, withholding information is often seen as a better alternative than lying or engaging in intentional deception.[166]

Lying

Although lying to gain unfair advantage is wrong, the "benevolent lie" isn't so easy to dismiss. A **benevolent lie** is defined as unmalicious or even helpful to the person to whom it is told, and they are quite common in face-to-face and mediated relationships.[167] Most people believe that there are times when lying is justified,[168] and one study found that only 38.5 percent of the subjects' statements were totally honest.[169] Another showed that people lie at a rate of three fibs per 10 minutes of conversation![170] Apparently our world is not such an honest one.

Most people think that benevolent lies are told for the benefit of the recipient. However, one study showed that two out of every three lies told are for selfish reasons.[171] (See **Table 8.1** to identify other reasons why people lie.)

> **Benevolent lie**
> A lie defined by the teller as unmalicious or even helpful to the person to whom it is told.

TABLE 8.1
Some Reasons for Lying

Reason	Example
Save face for others	"Don't worry—I'm sure nobody noticed that stain on your shirt."
Save face for self	"I wasn't looking at the files—I was accidentally in the wrong drawer."
Acquire resources	"Oh, *please* let me add this class. If I don't get in, I'll never graduate on time!"
Protect resources	"I'd like to lend you the money, but I'm short myself."
Initiate interaction	"Excuse me, I'm lost. Do you live around here?"
Be socially gracious	"No, I'm not bored—tell me more about your vacation."
Avoid conflict	"It's not a big deal. We can do it your way. Really."
Avoid interaction	"That sounds like fun, but I'm busy Saturday night."
Leave taking	"Oh, look what time it is! I've got to run!"

© Cengage Learning

Sam Urdank/© Warner Bros./Courtesy Everett Collection/The Canadian Press

AT THE MOVIES

The Invention of Lying (2009), Rated 13+

This entertaining and humorous movie portrays self-disclosure at its best. In a world where lying does not exist, deep and broad self-disclosure occurs continuously and the role played by benevolent lies in our society is well illustrated. Characters never resort to alternatives such as silence, lying, equivocating, and hinting—that is, until Mark (played by Ricky Gervais) stumbles upon the notion of lying. His world changes as he lies himself to success and power, but he is no happier. None of this can bring him the woman he loves.

However, other research shows that deception threatens relationships,[172] but not all lies are equally devastating. The liar's motives can influence whether the deception is acceptable or not.[173] Self-serving and exploitive lies are treated as a relational transgression, while lies aimed at sparing another's feelings are generally forgiven. But lying about major parts of your relationship can have the gravest consequences.

Equivocating

When faced with the choice of telling an unpleasant truth, communicators often equivocate—responding in language that has two plausible meanings.[174] If a friend asks what you think of an awful outfit, you could say, "It's really unusual—one of a kind!" The value of equivocation becomes clear when you consider the dilemma of what to say when you've been given an unwanted present—that ugly painting mentioned earlier, for example—and the giver asks what you think of it. Do you lie or tell the truth? You could choose to give a vague response, but equivocating is positive in that it spares the receiver embarrassment, it can save face for both the sender and the receiver,[175] and it provides a viable alternative to lying.[176]

Given these advantages, it's not surprising that people equivocate. They say they prefer truth-telling to equivocating, but given the choice, people prefer to finesse the truth.[177]

Hinting

Hints are more direct than equivocal statements. Although equivocal statements aren't aimed at changing others' behaviour, hints seek to get a desired response from others.[178]

Direct Statement	Face-Saving Hint
I'm too busy to continue with this conversation.	I know you're busy; I better let you go.

The face-saving value of hints explains why communicators are more likely to be indirect than fully disclosing when they deliver a potentially embarrassing message.[179] Hints are only as successful as the other person's ability to pick up on them. Subtle remarks might go right over the head of insensitive receivers, or they may chose not to respond.

The Ethics of Evasion

People use hints, equivocations, and benevolent lies because they help manage difficult situations. But are they ethical? Most people accept lies when the speaker's motives and the effects of the lie are positive. In some circumstances, lies are judged as more appropriate than the undiluted truth.[180] In light of these facts, perhaps it's better to ask whether an indirect message is truly in the interests of the receiver and whether this sort of evasion is the only, or the best, way to behave in a given situation.

Communication in the Workplace

Given the amount of time we spend in the workplace, developing and maintaining both interpersonal and professional relationships is very important. One way to promote this is to get off to a good start.

Scholars use the terms *assimilation* and *socialization* to describe how employees are integrated into their organizations. Not surprisingly, communication plays a major role in the socialization process. When helpful information is plentiful, new employees grow more satisfied with and committed to their jobs in the long run.[181]

In one study, researchers explored the nature of socialization messages.[182] While orientation sessions, handbooks, e-mails, and memos were useful, new employees reported that the most valuable messages often come via informal conversations—over 90 percent of which took place in face-to-face settings.

Many of the helpful messages were about professional behaviour and office rules ("It's crucial to be punctual," "Be careful when you challenge the boss"). Office politics also came into play ("Always be nice to the administrative assistant, Nadine, because she's the gateway to the supervisor"). Not all the messages were warnings; some were warm and welcoming ("It's one big family here," "We're glad they hired you"). Regardless of the specific content, virtually all of the messages were perceived as positive, supportive, and designed to help the recipient, the company, or both.

It's important to remember the power of messages—both large and small, deliberate and offhand—in building a happy, effective work team. As a newcomer, it's wise to seek the counsel and support of your colleagues. As a veteran, it's important to help rookies get off to a good start.

"I just worry that it's affecting our work."

Paul Noth The New Yorker Collection/The Cartoon Bank

READY TO STUDY?

IN THE BOOK, YOU CAN:

❏ Rip out the Chapter in Review card at the back of the book to have the key terms and Learning Objectives handy, and complete the quizzes provided (answers are at the bottom of the back page).

ONLINE YOU CAN:

❏ Stay organized and efficient with MindTap—a single destination with all the course material and study aids you need to succeed. Built-in apps leverage social media and the latest learning technology. For example:

   ❏ Listen to the text using ReadSpeaker.

   ❏ Use pre-populated Flashcards as a jump start for review—or you can create your own.

   ❏ You can highlight text and make notes in your MindTap Reader. Your notes will flow into Evernote, the electronic notebook app that you can access anywhere when it's time to study for the exam.

   ❏ Prepare for tests with a variety of quizzes and activities.

Go to **nelson.com/student** to access these digital resources

---

Endnotes

1. D. Byrne (1997). "An Overview (and Underview) of Research and Theory within the Attraction Paradigm." *Journal of Social and Personal Relationships, 17,* 417–431.

2. E. Hatfield & S. Sprecher (1986). *Mirror, Mirror: The Importance of Looks in Everyday Life.* Albany: State University of New York Press.

3. E. Walster, E. Aronson, D. Abrahams, & L. Rottmann (1966). "Importance of Physical Attractiveness in Dating Behaviour." *Journal of Personality and Social Psychology, 4,* 508–516.

4. S. Luo & G. Zang (2009). "What leads to romantic attraction: Similarity, reciprocity, security, or beauty? Evidence from a speed-dating study." *Journal of Personality, 7,* 933–964.

5. J. T. Hancock & C. L. Toma (2011). "Putting your best face forward: The accuracy of online dating profile photographs." *Journal of Communication, 59,* 367–386.

6. M. L. Antheunis & A. P. Schouten (2011). "The effects of other-generated and system-created cues on adolescents' perceived attractiveness on social network sites." *Journal of Computer-Mediated Communication, 16,* 391–406; C. Jaschinski & P. Kommers (2012). "Does beauty matter? The role of friends' attractiveness and gender on social

attractiveness of individuals on Facebook." *International Journal of Web-Based Communities, 8,* 389–401.

7. P. Rodway, A. Schepman & J. Lambert (2013). "The influence of position and context on facial attractiveness." *Acta Psychologica, 144,* 522–529.

8. G. W. Lewandowski, A. Aron, & J. Gee (2007). "Personality Goes a Long Way: The Malleability of Opposite-Sex Physical Attractiveness." *Personal Relationships, 14,* 571–585.

9. K. F. Albada (2002). "Interaction Appearance Theory: Changing Perceptions of Physical Attractiveness through Social Interaction." *Communication Theory, 12,* 8–41.

10. D. Barelds & P. Dijkstra (2009). "Positive Illusions about a Partner's Physical Attractiveness and Relationship Quality." *Personal Relationships, 16,* 263–283.

11. D. Hamachek (1982). *Encounters with Others: Interpersonal Relationships and You.* New York: Holt, Rinehart and Winston.

12. K.A.Yun (2002). "Similarity and Attraction." In M. Allen, N. Burrell, B. M. Eayle, & R. W. Preiss (Eds.). *Interpersonal Communication Research: Advances Through Meta-analysis* (pp. 145–168). Mahwah, NJ: Erlbaum.

13. S. Luo & E. Klohnen (2005). "Assortative Mating and Marital Quality in Newlyweds: A Couple-Centered Approach." *Journal of Personality and Social Psychology, 88,* 304–326. See also D. M. Amodio & C. J. Showers (2005). "Similarity Breeds Liking Revisited: The Moderating Role of Commitment." *Journal of Social and Personal Relationships, 22,* 817–836.

14. F. E. Aboud & M. J. Mendelson (1998). "Determinants of Friendship Selection and Quality: Developmental Perspectives." In W. M. Bukowski & A. F. Newcomb (Eds.). *The Company They Keep: Friendship in Childhood and Adolescence.* New York: Cambridge University Press.

15. A. M. Ledbetter, E. Griffin, & G. G. Sparks (2007). "Forecasting Friends Forever: A Longitudinal Investigation of Sustained Closeness Between Best Friends." *Personal Relationships, 14,* 343–350.

16. B. R. Burleson & W. Samter (1996). "Similarity in the Communication Skills of Young Adults: Foundations of Attraction, Friendship, and Relationship Satisfaction." *Communication Reports, 9,* 127–139.

17. A. Martin, C. Jacob, & N. Gueguen (2013). "Similarity facilitates relationships on social networks: A field experiment on Facebook." *Psychological Reports, 113,* 217–220.

18. M. Oliveira (2014, February 19). "Ten million Canadians use Facebook on mobile daily." *The Globe and Mail.* http://www.theglobeandmail.com/technology/10-million-canadians-use-facebook-on-mobile-daily/article16976434/. Retrieved March 25, 2016.

19. N. D. Tidwell, P. Eastwick, & E. J. Finkel (2013). "Perceived, not actual, similarity predicts initial attraction in a live romantic context: Evidence from the speed-dating paradigm." *Personal Relationships, 20,* 199–215.

20. S. Sprecher (2014). "Effects of actual (manipulated) and perceived similarity on liking in get-acquainted interactions: The role of communication." *Communication Monographs, 81,* 4–27.

21. J. T. Jones, B. W. Pelham, & M. Carvallo (2004) "How Do I Love Thee? Let Me Count the J's: Implicit Egotism and Interpersonal Attraction." *Journal of Personality and Social Psychology, 87,* 665–683.

22. J. R. Alford, P. K. Hatemi, J. R. Hibbing, N. G. Martin, & L. J. Eaves, (2011). The politics of mate choice. *The Journal of Politics, 73,* 362–379.

23. D. Mette & S. Taylor (1971). "When Similarity Breeds Contempt." *Journal of Personality and Social Psychology, 20,* 75–81.

24. H. Fisher (May/June 2007). "The Laws of Chemistry." *Psychology Today, 40,* 76–81.

25. L. Heatherington, V. Escudero, & M. L. Friedlander (2005). "Couple Interaction During Problem Discussions: Toward an Integrative Methodology." *Journal of Family Communication, 5,* 191–207.

26. S. Specher (1998). "Insiders' Perspectives on Reasons for Attraction to a Close Other." *Social Psychology Quarterly, 61,* 287–300.

27. E. Aronson (2004). *The Social Animal,* 9th ed. New York: Bedford, Freeman, & Worth. See Chapter 9.

28. S. T. Fish, A. J. C. Cuddy, & P. Glick (2007). "Universal dimensions of social cognition: Warmth and competence." *Trends in Cognitive Sciences, 11,* 77–83.

29. K. Dindia (2002). "Self-Disclosure Research: Knowledge Through Meta-Analysis." In M. Allen & R. W. Preiss (Eds.). *Interpersonal Communication Research: Advances Through Meta-Analysis* (pp. 169–185). Mahwah, NJ: Erlbaum.

30. A. M. Ledbetter, J. P. Mazer, J. M. DeGroot, & K. R. Meyer (2011). "Attitudes toward online social connection and self-disclosure as predictors of Facebook communication and relational closeness." *Communication Research, 38,* 27–53; P. Sheldon (2009). "I'll poke you. You'll poke me! Self-disclosure, social attraction, predictability and trust as important predictors of Facebook relationships." *Cyberpsychology: Journal of Psychosocial Research on Cyberspace, 3* (2), article 1.

31. K. Dindia (2004). "Self-disclosure research: Knowledge through meta-analysis." In M. Allen & W. Preiss, (Eds.). *Interpersonal Communication Research: Advances Through Meta-Analysis* (pp. 169–185). Mahwah, NJ: Erlbaum.

32. J. A. Shirley, W. G. Powers, & C. R. Sawyer (2007). "Psychologically Abusive Relationships and Self-Disclosure Orientations." *Human Communication, 10,* 289–301.

33. C. Flora (January/February 2004). "Close Quarters." *Psychology Today, 37,* 15–16.

34. C. Haythornthwaite, M. M. Kazmer, & J. Robbins (2000). "Community Development Among Distance Learners: Temporal and Technological Dimensions." *Journal of Computer- Mediated Communication, 6(1),* article 2, http://jcmc.indiana.edu/vol6/ issue1/haythornthwaite.html. Accessed September 11, 2006.

35. L. Stafford (2008). "Social exchange theories." In L. A. Baxter & D. O. Braithewaite (Eds.), *Engaging Theories in Interpersonal Communication: Multiple Perspectives* (pp. 377–389). Thousand Oaks, CA: Sage.

36. A. DeMaris (2007). "The Role Of Relationship Inequity in Marital Disruption." *Journal of Social and Personal Relationships, 24,* 177–195.

37. M. L. Knapp & A. L. Vangelisti (2006). *Interpersonal Communication and Human Relationships,* 6th ed. Boston: Allyn and Bacon. See also T. A. Avtgis, D. V. West, & T. L. Anderson (1998). "Relationship Stages: An Inductive Analysis Identifying Cognitive, Affective, and Behavioural Dimensions of Knapp fs Relational Stages Model." *Communication Research Reports 15,* 280–287; S. A. Welch & R. B. Rubin (2002). "Development of Relationship Stage Measures." *Communication Quarterly, 50,* 34–40.

38. A. J. Johnson, E. Wittenberg, M. Haigh, S. Wigley, J. Becker, K. Brown, & E. Craig (2004). "The Process of Relationship Development and Deterioration: Turning Points in Friendships That Have Terminated." *Communication Quarterly, 52,* 54–67.

39 A. Sobel (2009, July 27). "Interview etiquette: Lessons from a first date." *The Ladders.*

40. B. W. Scharlott & W. G. Christ (1995). "Overcoming Relationship-Initiation Barriers: The Impact of a Computer-Dating System on Sex Role, Shyness, and Appearance Inhibitions." *Computers in Human Behaviour, 11,* 191–204.

41. M. A. Urista, Q. Dong, & K. D. Day (2009). "Explaining why young adults use MySpace and Facebook through uses and gratifications theory." *Human Communication, 12,* 215–230.

42. C. R. Berger (1987). "Communicating under Uncertainty." In M. E. Roloff & G. R. Miller (Eds.). *Interpersonal Processes: New Directions in Communication Research.* Newbury Park, CA: Sage. See also C. R. Berger & R. J. Calabrese (1975). "Some Explorations in Initial Interaction and Beyond: Toward a Developmental Theory of Interpersonal Communication." *Human Communication Research, 1,* 99–112.

43. L. Pratt, R. L. Wiseman, M. J. Cody, & P. F. Wendt (1999). "Interrogative Strategies and Information Exchange in Computer-Mediated Communication." *Communication Quarterly, 47,* 46–66.

44. J. Fox, K. M. Warber, & D. C. Makstaller (2013). "The role of Facebook in romantic relationship development: An exploration of Knapp's relational stage model." *Journal of Social and Personal Relationships, 30,* 771–794.

45. T. R. Levine, K. Aune, & H. Park (2006). "Love styles and communication in relationships: Partner preferences, initiation, and intensification." *Communication Quarterly, 54,* 465–486; J. H. Tolhuizen (1989). "Communication Strategies for Intensifying Dating Relationships: Identification, Use and Structure." *Journal of Social and Personal Relationships, 6,* 413–434.

46. Johnson et al., op. cit.

47. K. R. Johnson & B. M. Holmes (2009). "Contradictory messages: A content analysis of Hollywood-produced romantic comedy feature films." *Communication Quarterly, 57,* 352–373.

48. L. A. Baxter (1987). "Symbols of Relationship Identity in Relationship Culture." *Journal of Social and Personal Relationships, 4,* 261–280.

49. C. J. S. Buress & J. C. Pearson (1997). "Interpersonal Rituals in Marriage and Adult Friendship," *Communication Monographs, 64,* 25–46.

50. K. N. Dunleavy & M. Booth-Butterfield (2009). "Idiomatic communication in the stages of coming together and falling apart." *Communication Quarterly, 57,* 416–432; R. A. Bell & J. G. Healey (1992) "Idiomatic Communication and Interpersonal Solidarity in Friends' Relational Cultures." Human Communication Research, 18, 307–335.

51. J. Fox, K. M. Warber, & D. C. Makstaller (2013). "The role of Facebook in romantic relationship development: An exploration of Knapp's relational stage model." *Journal of Social and Personal Relationships, 30,* 771–794.

52. L. M. Papp, J. Danielewicz, & C. Cayemberg (2012). "Are we Facebook official? Implications of dating partners' Facebook use and profiles for intimate relationship satisfaction." *Cyberpsychology, Behaviour, & Social Networking, 15,* 85–90.

53. J. Fox & K. M. Warber (2013). "Romantic relationship development in the age of Facebook: An exploratory study of emerging adults' perceptions, motives, and behaviours." *Cyberpsychology, Behaviour, & Social Networking, 16,* 3–7.

54. E. Foster (2008). "Commitment, Communication, and Contending with Heteronormativity: An Invitation to Greater Reflexivity in Interpersonal Research." *Southern Communication Journal, 73,* 84–101.

55. L. G. Ferdinand (2005). "The Influence of Differentiation of Self and Family of Origin on Individual and Relationship Functioning in Young Adults." *Dissertation Abstracts International: Section B: The Sciences and Engineering, 66,* 1715.

56. C. Harasymchuk & B. Fehr (2013). "A prototype analysis of relational boredom." *Journal of Personal and Social Relationships, 30,* 627–646.

57. J. A. Courtright, F. E. Miller, L. E. Rogers, & D. Bagarozzi (1990). "Interaction Dynamics of Relational Negotiation: Reconciliation versus Termination of Distressed Relationships." *Western Journal of Speech Communication, 54,* 429–453.

58. D. M. Battaglia, F. D. Richard, D. L. Datteri, & C. G. Lord (1998). "Breaking Up Is (Relatively) Easy to Do: A Script for the Dissolution of Close Relationships." *Journal of Social and Personal Relationships, 15,* 829–845.

59. S. Metts, W. R. Cupach, & R. A. Bejllovec (1989). "'I Love You Too Much to Ever Start Liking You': Redefining Romantic Relationships." *Journal of Social and Personal Relationships, 6,* 259–274.

60. A. Chatel (2013, July 12). "You'll Probably be Dumped Via Text More than Once in Your Life." *The Gloss.*

61. R. S. Weisskirch & R. Delevi (2013). "Attachment style and conflict resolution skills predicting technology use in relationship dissolution." *Computers in Human Behaviour, 29,* 2530–2534.

62. J. A. Rolls (2010). "Tales From Broken Hearts: Women and Recover from Romantic Relationships." *Storytelling, Self, Society: An International Journal of Storytelling Studies, 6,* 107–121.

63. Summarized by L. A. Baxter (1994). "A Dialogic Approach to Relationship Maintenance." In D. J. Canary & L. Stafford (Eds.). *Communication and Relational Maintenance.* San Diego, CA: Academic Press. See also E. Sahlstein & T. Dun (2008). "'I Wanted Time to Myself and He Wanted to be Together All the Time': Constructing Breakups and Managing Autonomy-Connection." *Qualitative Research Reports in Communication, 9,* 37–45.

64. A. P. Buunk (2005). "How Do People Respond to Others with High Commitment or Autonomy in their Relationships?" *Journal of Social and Personal Relationships, 22,* 653–672. See also E. Sahlstein & T. Dun (2008), op cit.

65. L. A. Baxter & L. A. Erbert (1999). "Perceptions of dialectical contradictions in turning points of development in heterosexual relationships." *Journal of Social and Personal Relationships, 16,* 547–569.

66. A. E. Miller-Ott, L. Kelly, & R. L. Duran (2012). "The effects of cell phone usage rules on satisfaction in romantic relationships." *Communication Quarterly, 60,* 17–34; R. L. Duran, L. Kelly, & T. Rotaru (2011). "Mobile phones in romantic relationships and the dialectic of autonomy versus connection." *Communication Quarterly, 59,* 19–36.

67. S. Petronio (2000). "The Boundaries of Privacy: Praxis of Everyday Life." In S. Petronio (Ed.). *Balancing the Secrets of Private Disclosures* (pp. 37–49). Mahwah, NJ: Erlbaum.

68. B. Debatin, J. P. Lovejoy, A. Horn, & B. N. Hughes (2009). "Facebook and online privacy: Attitudes, behaviours, and unintended consequences." *Journal of Computer Mediated Communication, 15,* 83–108.

69. L. A. Baxter & D. O. Braithwaite (2006). "Social dialectics: The contradictions of relating." In B. Whaley & W. Samter (Eds.). *Explaining Communication: Contemporary Communication Theories and Exemplars* (pp. 305–324). Mahwah, NJ: Erlbaum.

70. B. M. Montgomery (1993). "Relationship Maintenance versus Relationship Change: A Dialectical Dilemma." *Journal of Social and Personal Relationships, 10,* 205–223.

71. D. O. Braithwaite, L. A. Baxter, & A. M. Harper (1998). "The Role of Rituals in the Management of the Dialectical Tension of 'Old' and 'New' in Blended Families." *Communication Studies, 49,* 101–120.

72. See A. Christensen & J. Jacobson (2000). *Reconcilable Differences.* New York: Guilford.

73. R. L. Conville (1991). *Relational Transitions: The Evolution of Personal Relationships* (p. 80). New York: Praeger.

74. For a discussion of similarities across cultures, see D. E. Brown (1991). *Human Universals.* New York: McGraw-Hill.

75. R. R. Hamon & B. B. Ingoldsby (Eds.) (2003). *Mate Selection Across Cultures.* Thousand Oaks, CA: Sage.

76. J. E. Myers, J. Madathil, & L. R. Tingle (2005). "Marriage Satisfaction and Wellness in India and the United States: A Preliminary Comparison of Arranged Marriages and Marriages of Choice." *Journal of Counselling & Development,*

83, 183–190; P. Yelsma & K. Athappilly (1988). "Marriage Satisfaction and Communication Practices: Comparisons Among Indian and American Couples." *Journal of Comparative Family Studies, 19,* 37–54.

77. For a detailed discussion of cultural differences that affect relationships, see M. Sun Kim (2002). *Non-Western Perspectives on Human Communication: Implications for Theory and Practice.* Thousand Oaks, CA: Sage.

78. P. Breitman & C. Hatch (2000). *How To Say No Without Feeling Guilty.* New York: Broadway Books.

79. M. Imami (1981). *16 Ways to Avoid Saying No.* Tokyo: The Nihon Keizai Shimbun.

80. J. E. Lydon & S. K. Quinn (2013). "Relationship maintenance processes." In J. A. Simpson & L. Campbell (Eds.), *The Oxford Handbook of Close Relationships* (pp. 573–588). New York: Oxford.

81. L. Stafford & D. J. Canary (1991). "Maintenance Strategies and Romantic Relationship Type, Gender, and Relational Characteristics." *Journal of Personality and Social Psychology, 7,* 217–242.

82. A. J. Johnson, M. M. Haigh, J. A. H. Becker, E. A. Craig, & S. Wigley (2008). "College Students' Use of Relational Management Strategies in Email in Long-Distance and Geographically Close Relationships." *Journal of Computer-Mediated Communication, 13,* 381–404.

83. For a description of this ongoing research program, see The Gottman Institute. "Twelve-Year Study of Gay and Lesbian Couples," *www.gottman.com/research.* Accessed July 28, 2006.

84. A. M. Ledbetter (2010). "Assessing the measurement invariance of relational maintenance behaviour when face-to-face and online." *Communication Research Reports, 27,* 30–37.

85. E. Craig & B. Wright (2012). "Computer-mediated relational development and maintenance on Facebook." *Communication Research Reports, 29,* 119–129; M. Dainton (2013). "Relational maintenance on Facebook: Development of a measure, relationship to general maintenance, and relationship satisfaction." *College Student Journal, 47,* 112–121.

86. S. Utz (2007). "Media use in long-distance friendships." *Information, Communication & Society, 10,* 694–713.

87. D. S. Hunt, C. A. Lin, & D. J. Atkin (2014). "Communicating social relationships via the use of photo-messaging." *Journal of Broadcasting and Electronic Media, 58,* 234–252.

88. M. L. Houser, C. Fleuriet, & D. Estrada (2012). "The cyber factor: An analysis of relational maintenance through the use of computer-mediated communication." *Communication Reports, 29,* 34–43.

89. J. A. Hall, K. A. Larson, & A. Watts (2011). "Satisfying friendship maintenance expectations: The role of friendship standards and biological sex." *Human Communication Research, 37,* 529–552.

90. A. J. Merolla (2010). "Relational maintenance and noncopresence reconsidered: Conceptualizing geographic separation in close relationships." *Communication Theory, 20,* 169–193; L. Stafford (2005). *Maintaining long-distance and cross residential relationships.* Mahwah, NJ: Erlbaum.

91. A. J. Johnson, J. A. H. Becker, E. A. Craig, E. S. Gilchrist, & M. M. Haigh (2009). "Changes in friendship commitment: Comparing geographically close and long-distance young-adult friendships." *Communication Quarterly, 57,* 395–415.

92. K. C. McGuire & T. A. Kinnery (2010). "When distance is problematic: Communication, coping, and relational satisfaction in female college students' long-distance dating relationships." *Journal of Applied Communication Research, 38,* 27–46.

93. A. J. Johnson, M. M. Haigh, E. A. Craig, & J. A. H. Becker (2009). "Relational closeness: comparing undergraduate college students' geographically close and long-distance friendships." *Personal Relationships, 16,* 631–646.

94. B. Lakey (2013). "Social support processes in relationships." In J. A. Simpson & L. Campbell (Eds.), *The Oxford Handbook of Close Relationships* (pp. 711–730). New York: Oxford.

95. E. L. MacGeorge, B. Feng, & B. R. Burleson (2011). "Supportive communication." In M. L. Knapp & J. A. Daly (Eds.), *The Sage Handbook of Interpersonal Communication,* 4th edn (pp. 317–354). Thousand Oaks, CA: Sage.

96. H. T. Reis & M. S. Cark (2013). "Responsiveness." In J. A. Simpson & L. Campbell (Eds.), The *Oxford Handbook of Close Relationships* (pp. 400–426). New York: Oxford.

97. A. C. High & J. P. Dillard (2012). "A review and meta-analysis of person-centered messages and social support outcomes." *Communication Studies, 53,* 99–118.

98. N. K. Semmer, A. Elfering, N. Jacobshagen, T. Perrot, T. A. Beehr, & N. Boos (2008). "The emotional meanings of instrumental support." *International Journal of Stress Management, 15,* 285–251.

99. R. A. Barry, M. Bundle, R. L. Brock, & E. Lawrence (2009). "Validity and utility of a multidimensional model of received support in intimate relationships." *Journal of Family Psychology, 29,* 48–57.

100. R. Nauert (2010, February 1). *Support Your Partner, but Not Too Much.* PsychCentral.

101. H. J. Oh, E. Ozkaya, & R. LaRose (2014). "How does online social networking enhance life satisfaction? The perceived relationships among online support interaction, affect, perceived social support, sense of community, and life satisfaction." *Computers in Human Behaviour, 30,* 69-78.

102. T. M. Emmers-Sommer (2003). "When Partners Falter: Repair After a Transgression." In D. J. Canary & M. Dainton (Eds.). *Maintaining Relationships through Communication* (pp. 185–205). Mahwah, NJ: Erlbaum.

103. For an overview of this topic, see C. E. Rusbult, P. A. Hannon, S. L. Stocker, & E. J. Finkel (2005). "Forgiveness and Relational Repair." In E.L. Worthington (Ed.). *Handbook of Forgiveness* (pp. 185–206). New York: Routledge.

104. K. Dindia & L. A. Baxter (1987). "Strategies for Maintaining and Repairing Marital Relationships." *Journal of Social and Personal Relationships, 4,* 143–158.

105. V. R. Waldron, D. L. Kelley, & J. Harvey (2008). "Forgiving Communication and Relational Consequence." In M. T. Motley (Ed.). *Studies in Applied Interpersonal Communication* (pp. 165–184). Thousand Oaks, CA: Sage.

106. H. S. Park (2009). "Cross-Cultural Comparison of Verbal and Nonverbal Strategies of Apologizing." *Journal of International and Intercultural Communication, 2,* 66–87. See also H. S. Park & X. Guan (2006). "Effects of National Culture and Face Concerns on Intention to Apologize: A Comparison of U.S. and China." *Journal of Intercultural Communication Research, 35,* 183–204.

107. J. J. Exline, L. Deshea, & V. T. Holeman (2007). "Is Apology Worth the Risk? Predictors, Outcomes, and Ways to Avoid Regret." *Journal of Social & Clinical Psychology, 26,* 479–504.

108. H. M. Wallace, J. J. Exline, & R. F. Baumeister (2008). "Interpersonal Consequences of Forgiveness: Does Forgiveness Deter or Encourage Repeat Offenses?" *Journal of Experimental Social Psychology, 44,* 453–460.

109. D. L. Kelley & V. R. Waldron (2005). "An Investigation of Forgiveness-Seeking Communication and Relational Outcomes." *Communication Quarterly, 53,* 339–358.

110. A. J. Merolla (2008). "Communicating Forgiveness in Friendships and Dating Relationships." *Communication Studies, 59,* 114–131.

111. H. K. Orcutt (2006). "The Prospective Relationship of Interpersonal Forgiveness and Psychological Distress Symptoms Among College Women." *Journal of Counselling Psychology, 53,* 350–361; J. Eaton & C. W. Struthers (2006). "The Reduction of Psychological Aggression Across Varied Interpersonal Contexts Through Repentance and Forgiveness." *Aggressive Behaviour, 32,* 195–206.

112. K. A. Lawler, J. W. Younger, R. L. Piferi, et al. (2003). "A Change of Heart: Cardiovascular Correlates of Forgiveness in Response to Interpersonal Conflict." *Journal of Behavioural Medicine, 26,* 373–393.

113. F. D. Fincham & S. R. H. Beach (2013). "Gratitude and forgiveness in relationships." In J. A. Simpson & L. Campbell (Eds.), *The Oxford Handbook of Close Relationships* (pp. 638–663). New York: Oxford.

114. J. A. Rolls (2010). "Tales from Broken Hearts: Women and Recovery from Romantic Relationships." *Storytelling, Self, Society: An Interdisciplinary Journal of Storytelling Studies, 6,* 107–121.

115. V. R. Waldron & D. L. Kelley (2008). *Communicating Forgiveness.* Thousand Oaks, CA: Sage.

116. F. Bachman & L. K. Guerrero (2006). "Forgiveness, Apology, and Communicative Responses to Hurtful Events." *Communication Reports, 19,* 45–56.

117. Henline, B. H., L. K. Lamke, & M. D. Howard (2007). "Exploring Perceptions of Online Infidelity." *Personal Relationships, 14,* 113–128.

118. D. L. Kelley (1998). "The Communication of Forgiveness." *Communication Studies, 49,* 255–272.

119. C. E. Crowther & G. Stone (1986). *Intimacy: Strategies for Successful Relationships.* Santa Barbara, CA: Capra Press, p. 13.

120. C. Peterson (2006). *A Primer in Positive Psychology.* New York: Oxford.

121. E. Berscheid, M. Schneider, & A. M. Omoto (1989). "Issues in Studying Close Relationships: Conceptualizing

and Measuring Closeness." In C. Hendrick (Ed.). *Close Relationships* (pp. 63–91).Newbury Park, CA: Sage.

122. D. Morris (1973). *Intimate Behaviour.* New York: Bantam, p. 7.

123. W. D. Manning, P. C. Giordano, & M. A. Longmore (2006). "Hooking Up: The Relationship Contexts of 'Nonrelationship' Sex." *Journal of Adolescent Research, 21,* 459–483.

124. L. A. Baxter (1994). "A Dialogic Approach to Relationship Maintenance." In D. Canary & L. Stafford (Eds.). *Communication and Relational Maintenance.* San Diego, CA: Academic Press.

125. A. L. Vangelisti & G. Beck (2007). "Intimacy and the fear of intimacy." In L. L'Abate (Ed.), *Low-cost Approaches to Promote Physical and Mental Health: Theory , Research, and Practice.* (pp. 395–414). New York: Springer.

126. J. T. Wood & C. C. Inman (1993). "In a Different Mode: Masculine Styles of Communicating Closeness." *Applied Communication Research, 21,* 279–295; K. Floyd (1995). "Gender and Closeness among Friends and Siblings." *Journal of Psychology, 129,* 193–202.

127. See, for example, K. Dindia (2000). "Sex Differences in Self-Disclosure, Reciprocity of Self-Disclosure, and Self-Disclosure and Liking: Three Meta-Analyses Reviewed." In S. Petronio (Ed.). *Balancing Disclosure, Privacy and Secrecy.* Mahwah, NJ: Erlbaum.

128. S. Swain (1989). "Covert Intimacy in Men's Friendships: Closeness in Men's Friendships." In B. J. Risman & P. Schwartz (Eds.). *Gender in Intimate Relationships: A Microstructural Approach.* Belmont, CA: Wadsworth.

129. C. K. Reissman (1990). *Divorce Talk: Women and Men Make Sense of Personal Relationships.* New Brunswick, NJ: Rutgers University Press.

130. J. M. Bowman (2008). "Gender Role Orientation and Relational Closeness: Self-Disclosive Behaviour in Same-Sex Male Friendships." *Journal of Men's Studies, 16,* 316–330.

131. G. E. Good, M. J. Porter, & M. G. Dillon (2002). "When Men Divulge: Men's Self-Disclosure on Prime Time Situation Comedies." *Sex Roles, 46,* 419–427.

132. M. T. Morman & K. Floyd (2002). "A 'Changing Culture of Fatherhood': Effects of Affectionate Communication, Closeness, and Satisfaction in Men's Relationships With Their Fathers and Their Sons." *Western Journal of Communication, 66,* 395–411.

133. W. B. Gudykunst & S. Ting-Toomey (1988). *Culture and Interpersonal Communication.* Newbury Park, CA: Sage, pp. 197–198.

134. H. C. Triandis (1994). *Culture and Social Behaviour.* New York: McGraw-Hill, p. 230.

135. E. Hatfield & R. L. Rapson (2006). "Passionate Love, Sexual Desire, and Mate Selection: Cross-Cultural and Historical Perspectives." In P. Noller & J. A. Feeney (Eds.). *Close Relationships: Functions, Forms and Processes* (pp. 227–243). Hove, England: Psychology Press/Taylor & Francis.

136. E. J. Finkel, P. W. Eastwick, B. R. Karney, H. T. Reis, & S. Sprecher (2012). "Online dating: A critical analysis from the perspective of psychological science." *Psychological Science in the Public Interest, 3,* 3–66; L. B. Hian, S. L. Chuan, T. M. K. Trevor, & B. H. Detenber (2004). "Getting to Know You: Exploring the Development of Relational Intimacy in Computer-Mediated Communication." *Journal of Computer-Mediated Communication, 9,* Issue 3.

137. P. Valkenberg & J. Peter (2009). "The Effects of Instant Messaging on the Quality of Adolescents' Existing Friendships: A Longitudinal Study." *Journal of Communication, 59,* 79–97; H. Ko & F. Kuo (2009). "Can Blogging Enhance Subjective Well-Being Through Self-Disclosure?" *CyberPsychology & Behaviour, 12,* 75–79; J. P. Mazer, R. E. Murphy, & C. J. Simonds (2008). "The Effects of Teacher Self-Disclosure via 'Facebook' on Teacher Credibility." RCA Vestnik (*Russian Communication Association*), 30–37; Y. Hu, J. F. Wood, V. Smith, & N. Westbrook (2004). Friendships Through IM: Examining the Relationship Between Instant Messaging and Intimacy." *Journal of Computer-Mediated Communication, 10,* Issue 1.

138. L. D. Rosen et al. (2008). "The Impact of Emotionality and Self-Disclosure on Online Dating versus Traditional Dating." *Computers in Human Behaviour, 24,* 2124–2157; A. Ben-Ze fev (2003). Privacy, Emotional Closeness, and Openness in Cyberspace." *Computers in Human Behaviour, 19,* 451–467.

139. J. Boase, J. B. Horrigan, B. Wellman, & L Rainie (2006). *The Strength of Internet Ties.* Pew Internet & American Life Project, *www.pewinternet.org/pdfs/PIP_Internet_ties .pdf.* Accessed September 11, 2006.

140. S. Henderson & M. Gilding (2004). "'I've Never Clicked This Much with Anyone in My Life': Trust and Hyperpersonal Communication in Online Friendships." *New Media & Society, 6,* 487–506.

141. B. H. Henline, L. K. Lamke, & M. D. Howard (2007). "Exploring perceptions of online infidelity." *Personal Relationships, 14,* 113-128; M. T. Whitty (2005). "The realness of cybercheating: Men's and women's representations of unfaithful Internet relationships." *Social Science Computer Review, 23,* 57–67.

142. V. Steeves (2014). *Young Canadians in a Wired World, Phase III: Sexuality and Romantic Relationships in the Digital Age.* Ottawa: MediaSmarts.

143. R. Browne (2015, February 16). "Is sexting safe?" *MacLean's Magazine.*

144. R. F. Baumeister (2005). *The Cultural Animal: Human Nature, Meaning, and Social Life.* New York: Oxford.

145. See, for example, R. Bellah, W. M. Madsen, A. Sullivan, & S. M. Tipton (1985). *Habits of the Heart: Individualism and Commitment in American Life.* Berkeley: University of California Press; R. Sennett (1974). *The Fall of Public Man: On the Social Psychology of Capitalism.* New York: Random House; S. Trenholm & A. Jensen (1990). *The Guarded Self: Toward a Social History of Interpersonal Styles.* Paper presented at the Speech Communication Association meeting, San Juan, PR.

146. I. Altman & D. A. Taylor (1973). *Social Penetration: The Development of Interpersonal Relationships*. New York: Holt, Rinehart and Winston. See also D. A. Taylor & I. Altman (1987). "Communication in Interpersonal Relationships: Social Penetration Processes." In M. E. Roloff & G. R. Miller (Eds.). *Interpersonal Processes: New Directions in Communication Research*. Newbury Park, CA: Sage.

147. J. Luft (1969). *Of Human Interaction*. Palo Alto, CA: National Press Books.

148. S. Petronio (2007). "Translational Research Endeavors and the Practices of Communication Privacy Management." *Journal of Applied Communication Research, 35*, 218–22.

149. T. D. Affifi & K. Steuber (2009). "The Revelation Risk Model (RRM): Factors that Predict the Revelation of Secrets and the Strategies Used to Reveal Them." *Communication Monographs, 76*, 144–176. See also T. D. Affifi & K. Steuber (2009). Keeping and Revealing Secrets." *Communication Currents, 4*, 1–2.

150. K. Dindia (2002). "Self-Disclosure Research: Advances Through Meta-Analysis." In M. Allen & R. W. Preiss (Eds.). *Interpersonal Communication Research: Advances Through Meta-Analysis* (pp. 169–185). Mahwah, NJ: Erlbaum; V. J. Derlega & A. L. Chaikin (1975). *Sharing Intimacy: What We Reveal to Others and Why*. Englewood Cliffs, NJ: Prentice Hall.

151. R. C. Savin-Williams (2001). *Mom, Dad. I'm Gay: How Families Negotiate Coming Out*. Washington, DC: American Psychological Association.

152. J. A. Hess, A. D. Fannin, & L. H. Pollom (2007). "Creating Closeness: Discerning and Measuring Strategies for Fostering Closer Relationships. *Personal Relationships, 14*, 25–44; A. E. Mitchell et al. (2008). "Predictors of Intimacy in Couples' Discussions of Relationship Injuries: An Observational Study." *Journal of Family Psychology, 22*, 21–29.

153. S. MacNeil & E. S. Byers (2009). "Role of Sexual Self-Disclosure in the Sexual Satisfaction of Long-Term Heterosexual Couples." *Journal of Sex Research, 46*, 3–14; F. D. Fincham & T. N. Bradbury (1989). "The Impact of Attributions in Marriage: An Individual Difference Analysis." *Journal of Social and Personal Relationships, 6*, 69–85.

154. V. Derlega, B. A. Winstead, A. Mathews, & A. L. Braitman (2008). "Why Does Someone Reveal Highly Personal Information? Attributions for and against Self-Disclosure in Close Relationships." *Communication Research Reports, 25*, 115–130; K. G. Niederhoffer & J. W. Pennebaker (2002). "Sharing One fs Story: On the Benefits of Writing or Talking About Emotional Experience." In C. R. Snyder & S. J. Lopez (Eds.). *Handbook of Positive Psychology* (pp. 573–583). London: Oxford University Press.

155. K. Greene, V. J. Derlega, & A. Mathews (2006). "Self-Disclosure in Personal Relationships." In A. Vangelisti & D. Perlman (Eds.). *The Cambridge Handbook of Personal Relationships*. New York: Cambridge University Press; L. B. Rosenfeld (2000). "Overview of the Ways Privacy, Secrecy, and Disclosure are Balanced in Today's Society." In S. Petronio (Ed.). *Balancing the Secrets of Private Disclosures* (pp. 3–17). Mahweh, NJ: Erlbaum.

156. R. Agne, T. L. Thompson, & L. P. Cusella (2000). "Stigma in the Line of Face: Self-Disclosure of Patients' HIV Status to Health Care Providers." *Journal of Applied Communication Research, 28*, 235–261; V. J. Derlega, B. A. Winstead, & L. Folk-Barron (2000). "Reasons For and Against Disclosing HIV-Seropositive Test Results to an Intimate Partner: A Functional Perspective." In S. Petronio (Ed.). *Balancing the Secrets of Private Disclosures* (pp. 71–82). Mahwah, NJ: Erlbaum. See also J P. Caughlin et al. 2009). "Do Message Features Influence Reactions to HIV Disclosures? A Multiple-Goals Perspective." *Health Communication, 24*, 270–283.

157. M. Allen et al. (2008). "Persons Living with HIV: Disclosure to Sexual Partners." *Communication Research Reports, 25*, 192–199.

158. A. L. Alter & D. M. Oppenheimer (2009). "Suppressing secrecy through metacognitive ease: Cognitive fluency encourages self-disclosure." *Psychological Science, 20*, 1414–1420.

159. B. N. Frisby & R. J. Sidelinger (2013). "Violating student expectations: Student disclosures and student reactions in the college classroom." *Communication Studies, 64*, 241–258.

160. S. Myers & M. Brann (2009). "College students' perceptions of how instructors establish and enhance credibility through self-disclosure." *Qualitative Research Reports in Communication, 10*, 9–16.

161. E. M. Eisenbery & M. B. Witten (1987) "Reconsidering Openess in Organizational Communication." *Academy of Management Review, 12*, 418–428.

162. L. B. Rosenfeld & G. I. Bowen (1991). "Marital Disclosure and Marital Satisfaction: Direct-Effect versus Interaction- Effect Models." *Western Journal of Speech Communication, 55*, 69–84.

163. S. H. McDaniel et al. (2007). "Physician Self-Disclosure in Primary Care Visits: Enough About You, What About Me?" *Archives of Internal Medicine, 167*, 1321–1326.

164. D. O'Hair & M. J. Cody (1993). "Interpersonal Deception: The Dark Side of Interpersonal Communication?" In B. H. Spitzberg & W. R. Cupach (Eds.). *The Dark Side of Interpersonal Communication*. Hillsdale, NJ: Erlbaum.

165. M. Spranca, E. Minsk, & J. Baron (1991). "Omission and Commission in Judgement and Choice." *Journal of Experimental Social Psychology, 27*, 76–105.

166. K. N. Dunleavy, R. M. Chory, & A. K. Goodboy (2010). "Responses to deception in the workplace: Perceptions of credibility, power, and trustworthiness." *Communication Studies, 61*, 239–255.

167. J. F. George and A. Robb (2008). "Deception and Computer-Mediated Communication in Daily Life." *Communication Reports, http://mail.cbu.ca/Owner/Local Settings/Temporary Internet Files/OLK1B/title~content =t714592826~db=all~tab=issueslist~branches=21 - v2121*, 92–103. Accesssed July 13, 2008.

168. M. L. Knapp (2006). "Lying and Deception in Close Relationships." In A. Vangelisti & D. Perlman (Eds.). *The Cambridge Handbook of Personal Relationships.* New York: Cambridge University Press.

169. R. E. Turner, C. Edgely, & G. Olmstead (1975). "Information Control in Conversation: Honesty Is Not Always the Best Policy." *Kansas Journal of Sociology, 11,* 69–89.

170. R. S. Feldman, J. A. Forrest, & B. R. Happ (2002). "Self-Presentation and Verbal Deception: Do Self-Presenters Lie More?" *Basic and Applied Social Psychology, 24,* 163–170.

171. D. Hample (1980). "Purposes and Effects of Lying." *Southern Speech Communication Journal, 46,* 33–47.

172. S. A. McCornack & T. R. Levine (1990). "When Lies Are Uncovered: Emotional and Relational Outcomes of Discovered Deception." *Communication Monographs, 57,* 119–138.

173. J. S. Seiter, J. Bruschke, & C. Bai (2002). "The Acceptability of Deception as a Function of Perceivers' Culture, Deceiver's Intention, and Deceiver-Deceived Relationship." *Western Journal of Communication, 66,* 158–181.

174. J. B. Bavelas, A. Black, N. Chovil, & J. Mullett (2010). "Truth, lies, and equivocations: The effects of conflicting goals on discourse." In M. L. Knapp & J. A. Daly (Eds.), *Interpersonal Communication* (Vol II, pp. 379–408). Thousand Oaks, CA: Sage.

175. S. Metts, W. R. Cupach, & T. T. Imahori (1992). "Perceptions of Sexual Compliance-Resisting Messages in Three Types of Cross-Sex Relationships." *Western Journal of Communication, 56,* 1–17.

176. J. B. Bavelas, A. Black, N. Chovil, & J. Mullett (1990). *Equivocal Communication.* Newbury Park, CA: Sage, p. 171.

177. W. P. Robinson, A. Shepherd, & J. Heywood (1998). "Truth, Equivocation/Concealment, & Lies in Job Applications & Doctor-Patient Communication." *Journal of Language & Social Psychology, 17,* 149–164.

178. M. T. Motley (1992). "Mindfulness in Solving Communicators' Dilemmas." *Communication Monographs, 59,* 306–314.

179. S. B. Shimanoff (1988). "Degree of Emotional Expressiveness as a Function of Face-Needs, Gender, & Interpersonal Relationship." *Communication Reports, 1,* 43–53.

180. A. P. Hubbell (May 1999). *"I Love Your Family — They Are Just Like You": Lies We Tell to Lovers and Perceptions of Their Honesty and Appropriateness.* Paper presented at the annual meeting of the International Communication Association, San Francisco. See also S. A. McCornack (1992). "Information Manipulation Theory." *Communication Monographs, 59,* 1–16.

181. J. H. Waldeck & K. K. Myers (2007). "Organizational Assimilation Theory, Research, and Implications for Multiple Areas of the Discipline: A State of the Art Review." *Communication Yearbook, 31,* 322–367; Z. P. Hart & V. D. Miller (2005). "Context and Message Content During Organizational Socialization: A Research Note." *Human Communication Research, 31,* 295–309; P. E. Madlock & S. M. Horan (2009). "Predicted Outcome Value of Organizational Commitment." *Communication Research Reports, 26,* 40–49.

182. Barge, J. K., & Schlueter, D. W. (2004). "Memorable Messages and Newcomer Socialization." *Western Journal of Communication, 68,* 233–256.

MINDTAP

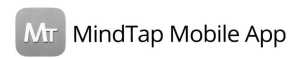

MindTap Mobile App

Empower 92% of Your Students to Read Anyplace, Anytime.

In 2015, smartphone ownership on campus grew
to 92%, surpassing laptop ownership[*].

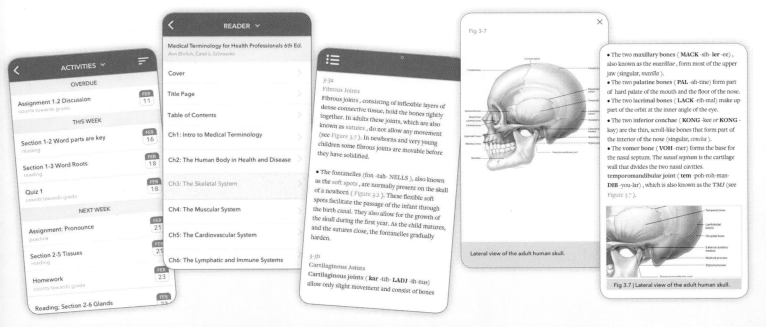

The MindTap Mobile App now contains the entire book in electronic form, delivering ultimate flexibility.

With the newly updated MindTap Mobile App, students who have registered in MindTap can download the MindTap Mobile App for free to their smartphone and access the entire eBook at all times — online or offline.

Instructors can still keep students on track with instant due date notifications and messaging, and the additional support of flashcards and low-stakes quizzing.

*ECAR Study of Undergraduate Students and Information Technology, 2015
https://library.educause.edu/~/media/files/library/2015/8/ers1510ss.pdf?la=en

Source Code: M16020099

nelson.com/mindtap

NELSON

NEL

IMPROVING COMMUNICATION CLIMATES

LEARNING OUTCOMES

LO1 Identify confirming, disagreeing, and disconfirming messages and patterns in your important relationships and describe their consequences.

LO2 Describe how communication climates develop through positive or negative reciprocal communication patterns.

LO3 Use Gibb's categories and the assertive message format to create messages that are likely to build supportive rather than defensive communication climates.

LO4 Create appropriate nondefensive responses to real or hypothetical criticisms.

Communication Climate: The Key to Positive Relationships

Personal relationships are a lot like the weather. Some are cool and formal, some are hot and steamy, some are polluted, and so forth. Some relationships have stable climates, whereas others change dramatically—calm one moment and turbulent the next. Every relationship has a feeling, a pervasive mood that shapes the interactions of the participants.

Although we can't change the external weather, we *can* improve our interpersonal climate. This chapter explains the forces that make some relationships pleasant and others unpleasant.

Communication climate refers to the emotional tone of a relationship—the way people feel about each other. The role of climate in families and friendships is obvious. So is the impact of climate in the workplace. Have you ever worked in a climate where backbiting, criticism, and suspicion were the norm? Or have you been lucky enough to be employed in an atmosphere that was positive and supportive? If you've experienced both, you know what a difference the climate makes.

The importance of relational climate cannot be overstated. For example, couples who create and maintain an emotionally healthy, positive climate have happy, enduring relationships.[1] Couples who are unsupported—whether straight or gay, rich or poor, parents or childless—are likely to break up or endure

Communication climate
The emotional tone of a relationship between two or more individuals.

What do you THINK?

I become defensive when I think I am being attacked.

1	2	3	4	5	6	7
strongly agree						strongly disagree

joyless lives together.[2] Positive, confirming messages are just as important in families, and the climate parents create affects how their children interact.[3] Children who feel confirmed (valued and loved) have more open communication with parents, higher self-esteem, and lower stress levels. Unconfirmed children suffer a broad range of emotional and behavioural problems.[4] The satisfaction that siblings feel with one another drops sharply as aggressive, disconfirming messages increase.[5]

Communication climates are shared climates, and it's rare to find one person describing a relationship as open and positive while another characterizes it as cold and hostile. But, like their meteorological counterparts, communication climates can change over time, and people can greatly influence that change.

LO1
Levels of Message Confirmation

What makes a communication climate positive or negative is surprisingly simple. It's basically the degree to which the people believe themselves to be valued by one another. Social scientists use the term **confirming communication** to describe messages that convey value and contribute to supportive communication climates. On the other hand, **disconfirming communication** describes behaviours that show a lack of regard and make listeners feel defensive. It is obvious that confirming messages are more desirable than disconfirming ones. But what characteristics or behaviours distinguish the two types?

Like beauty, whether a message is confirming or disconfirming is up to the beholder.[6] Consider times when you used a comment as a sign of affection, but to an outsider it sounded like insulting or disconfirming ("You turkey!"). Likewise, a comment that the sender might have meant to be helpful ("I'm telling you this for your own good…") could easily disconfirm and put the receiver on the defensive.

What makes some messages more confirming than others? **Table 9.1** outlines the levels of message confirmation that are described in the following pages.

Confirming communication
A message that expresses caring or respect for another person.

Disconfirming communication
A message that expresses a lack of caring or respect for another person.

Disconfirming Messages

Disconfirming communication shows a lack of regard for the other person, either by disputing or ignoring some important part of that person's message.[7] Communication researchers have identified seven types of disconfirming messages.[8]

TABLE 9.1
Levels of Message Confirmation and Disconfirmation

Disconfirming (Least Valuing)	Disagreeing	Confirming (Most Valuing)
Impervious	Aggressiveness	Recognition
Interrupting	Complaining	Acknowledgment
Irrelevant	Argumentativeness	Endorsement
Tangential		
Impersonal		
Ambiguous		
Incongruous		

© Cengage Learning

Impervious Responses

An *impervious response* doesn't acknowledge the other person's message. It is very disconcerting when there's no reaction from a person with whom you're attempting to communicate. It can be even more disconfirming than being dismissed or attacked. Research shows that employees sometimes nudge unwanted co-workers toward quitting by not interacting with them.[9] And stonewalling in marriage is a strong predictor of divorce.[10]

Interrupting

While an occasional *interrupting response* is not likely to be taken as a disconfirmation, repeatedly interrupting a speaker can be both discouraging and irritating.

Irrelevant Responses

A comment unrelated to what the other person has just said is an *irrelevant response*:

A: What a day! The car overheated, I had to call a tow truck, and the computer at work broke down.

B: Oh yeah, but listen, we have to talk about Ami's birthday present. I only have tomorrow to shop for it.

A: I'm beat. Let's talk later. This day was something else.

B: I can't figure out what to get. She's got everything…

In the TV show *Modern Family*, members exchange messages ranging from highly confirming to highly disconfirming.

Peter 'Hopper' Stone/© ABC/Courtesy: Everett Collection/The Canadian Press

Tangential Responses

Conversational "take-aways," where listeners don't entirely ignore the speaker's remarks but use them as a starting point for a shift to a different topic, are called *tangential responses*:

A: I'd like to know soon if you're interested in a skiing vacation. Otherwise, it'll be impossible to get reservations anywhere.

B: Yeah. And if I don't finish this communication paper, I won't want to go anywhere. Could you proofread this for me?

Impersonal Responses

Impersonal responses refer to clichés and other statements that don't truly respond to the speaker:

A: I'm having some personal problems, and I need to leave early a couple of afternoons this week.

B: Ah, yes. We've all got problems, Jane.

Ambiguous Responses

Ambiguous responses have more than one meaning and leave the other party unsure of the responder's position:

A: I'd like to get together soon. How about Tuesday?
B: Uh, maybe.
A: Well, how about it? Can we talk Tuesday?
B: Probably.

Incongruous Responses

An ***incongruous response*** contains two contradictory messages, one of which is nonverbal:

A: Darling, I love you.
B: I love you, too. (*said in a monotone while watching TV*)

Disagreeing Messages

Between disconfirming and confirming communication lie **disagreeing messages**—messages that say "you're wrong" in one way or another. Some disagreements are quite hostile, but others aren't as disconfirming as they may first seem. There are three types of disagreeing messages: aggressiveness, complaining, and argumentativeness.

Disconfirming messages can pollute a communication climate. Read on to learn ways to disagree without being disagreeable.

Aggressiveness

Aggressiveness is the most destructive way to disagree because it attacks the self-concepts of other people to inflict psychological pain.[11] Aggressiveness demeans the worth of others through the use of name calling, put-downs, sarcasm, taunting, yelling, and badgering. "You idiot. Get that report to me by three or you'll be looking for a new job." Bullies typically use aggressive behaviours.

Unfortunately, aggressiveness isn't just limited to face-to-face encounters—cyberbullying is disturbingly common. A study of Canadian students of grades 6, 7, 10, and 11 reported that 15 percent of the students had abused someone online and twice as many report having been victims.[12] Apathy, cheating in school, substance abuse, violence and self-destructive behaviours (even suicide in the most severe cases) are the results of such abuse. Another study found that 73 percent of adult internet users have seen someone being harassed online and 40 percent have personally experienced it.[13]

Complaining

When communicators aren't prepared to argue, but want to register dissatisfaction, they *complain*. Some ways of complaining are better than others. Satisfied couples tend to offer behavioural complaints ("You always throw your socks on the floor"), while unsatisfied couples make personal attacks ("You're a slob").[14] Personal complaints are more likely to result in an episode of escalated conflict because they attack a more fundamental part of the presenting self.[15] Talking about socks deals with a change of habits; calling someone a slob is a character assault that is unlikely to be forgotten. While complaining isn't necessarily a sign of a

Disagreeing messages
Messages that say "you're wrong" in one way or another.

troubled relationship, the complaint should be coached in behavioural language rather than as a personal criticism.[16]

Argumentativeness

Calling someone *argumentative* is an unfavourable evaluation, yet we value the ability to create and deliver a sound argument in lawyers, talk-show participants, letters to the editor, and political debates. Communication researchers define argumentativeness as presenting and defending positions on issues while attacking positions taken by others.[17] Argumentativeness is associated with positive attributes such as an enhanced self-concept and communicative competence.

To maintain a positive climate while arguing, make sure to attack issues, not people. Also, arguments are better received when they're delivered in a supportive, affirming manner.[18]

Confirming Messages

Research shows that three increasingly positive types of messages tend to be the most confirming: recognition, acknowledgment, and endorsement.[19]

Recognition

The most fundamental way to confirm someone is to *recognize* the person. Recognition seems easy, yet there are times when we don't even respond to others on this basic level. Failing to return an e-mail or phone message is one of the common examples. Even if it's an oversight, the message has a disconfirming effect on the sender.

Acknowledgment

Acknowledging another's ideas and feelings is a stronger form of confirmation. Listening is probably the most common form of acknowledgment, but counterfeit listening—stage-hogging, pseudolistening, and so on—has the opposite effect. Acknowledgment includes asking questions, paraphrasing, and reflecting. Managers who solicit opinions—even when they're not accepted—are rated highly by employees.[20] Reflecting a speaker's thoughts and feelings can be a powerful way to offer support.

Spiral
A reciprocal communication pattern in which each person's message reinforces the other's.

Escalatory conflict spiral
A communication spiral in which one attack leads to another until the initial skirmish escalates into a full-fledged battle.

Endorsement

Endorsement means that you agree with another's ideas or find them important. Endorsement is the strongest type of confirming message because it communicates valuing. But you don't have to agree completely with another person to endorse a message; you just need to find something that you can

© iStockphoto.com/Marcus Clackson

endorse. "I can see why you were so angry," you might say, even if you don't approve of the outburst. Outright praise is a strong form of endorsement, and one that can be used surprisingly often.

LO2
How Communication Climates Develop

Relational climates begin to develop as soon as two people start to communicate. If the messages are confirming, the climate will be positive. If not, it will be hostile or defensive. Many climate-shaping messages are nonverbal[21]—smiles or frowns, the presence or absence of eye contact, tone of voice, or the use of personal space all send messages about how the parties feel about one another.

Once climates are formed, they take on lives of their own and grow in self-perpetuating **spirals**: reciprocating communication patterns in which each person's message reinforces the other's.[22] In positive spirals, one partner's confirming message leads to a similar message from the other, which leads the first person to be even more confirming. Negative spirals are just as powerful, though they leave the partners feeling worse about themselves and each other. See **Table 9.2** for examples of how reciprocal communication patterns occur.

Escalatory conflict spirals are the most visible way that disconfirming messages reinforce one another.[23] One attack leads to another until a skirmish escalates into a full-fledged battle:

A: (*mildly irritated*) Where were you? We were supposed to meet a half-hour ago.

B: (*defensively*) I'm sorry. I got hung up at the library. I don't have as much free time as you do, you know.

TABLE 9.2
Positive and Negative Reciprocal Communication Patterns

Negative Reciprocal Patterns

Pattern	Example
Complaint—counter complaint	A: I wish you weren't so self-centered. B: Well, I wish you weren't so critical.
Disagreement—disagreement	A: Why are you so hard on Marta? She's a great boss. B: Are you kidding? She's the biggest phony I've ever seen. A: You wouldn't know a good boss if you saw one. B: Neither would you.
Mutual indifference	A: I don't care if you want to stay. I'm exhausted, and I'm getting out of here. B: Go ahead if you want, but find your own way home.
Arguments involving punctuation	A: How can I talk when you won't listen? B: How can I listen when you won't talk?

Positive Reciprocal Patterns

Pattern	Example
Validation of other's perspective	A: This assignment is really confusing. Nobody can figure out what we're supposed to do. B: I can understand how it might be unclear. Let me try to explain…
Recognizing similarities	A: I can't believe you want to take an expensive vacation! We should be saving money, not spending more! B: I agree we should be saving. But I think we can take this trip and still save some money. Let me show you what I've figured out…
Supportiveness	A: I'm going crazy with this job. It was supposed to be temporary. I have to do something different, and soon. B: I can see how much you hate it. Let's figure out how we can get the project finished soon, so you can get back to your regular work.

© Wavebreakmedia Ltd UC10/Alamy Stock Photo

A: I wasn't *blaming* you, so don't be so touchy. I do resent what you just said, though. I'm plenty busy. And I've got lots of better things to do than wait around for you!

B: Who's getting touchy? I just made a simple comment. You've sure been defensive lately. What's the matter with you?

Although they are less obvious, **de-escalatory conflict spirals** can also be destructive.[24] Rather than fighting, parties decrease their dependence on each other, withdraw, and become less invested in the relationship. But spirals can also be positive. A word of praise can lead to a returned compliment, which can lead to an

> **De-escalatory conflict spiral**
> A communication spiral in which the parties slowly lessen their dependence on one another, withdraw, and become less invested in the relationship.

act of kindness, and can result in an improved relational climate. The ability to rebound from negative spirals and turn them around in a positive direction is a hallmark of successful relationships.[25]

AT THE MOVIES

Communication Spirals

Changing Lanes (2002), Rated R

Gavin Banek (Ben Affleck) and Doyle Gipson (Samuel L. Jackson) are strangers who literally meet by accident. Both are running late for court appointments when their cars collide. Gipson wants to exchange insurance information and file an accident report; Banek only cares about getting to court on time. Banek hands Gipson a blank cheque and drives away yelling, "Better luck next time"—leaving Gipson stranded in the middle of the road with a disabled car.

This event begins a negative spiral that quickly spins out of control. Gipson sends Banek a fax with the phrase "Better luck next time" scrawled on an important document that Banek accidentally left with Gipson. Banek retaliates by finding ways to ruin Gipson's credit rating. Gipson counterattacks and so does Banek—and in one day's time, these two men wreak havoc on each other's lives. *Changing Lanes* offers a sobering look at how the ineffective handling of a communication episode between strangers can lead to a destructive communication spiral.

LO3

Defensiveness: Causes and Remedies

No type of communication pollutes an interpersonal climate more than **defensiveness**. The word suggests protecting oneself from physical harm. In this case, however, we are most likely protecting our presenting self—our face—which you will read about in the next section.

Face-Threatening Acts

The notion of face originates in Chinese cultures and refers to how we attempt to present ourselves to the world.[26] It's kind of like the image we hope to project. And, we try to project different faces to different people. You might, for example, want an employer to see you as serious but your friends to see you as witty and outrageous.

We don't feel defensive when others accept and acknowledge important parts of our presenting image. But when confronted with **face-threatening acts**—messages that challenge the image we want to project—we are likely to resist. Defensiveness, then, is the process of protecting our presenting self, our face. While responding defensively to a face-threatening attack may seem logical, over time defensiveness erodes relationship stability.[27]

For example, we may feel threatened and act defensively if a boss criticizes a job we have done, especially if the supervisor was correct! In fact, we tend to feel most defensive when criticism is on target.[28] The drive to defend a presenting image—even when it is false—leads some people to act in destructive ways, such as being sarcastic or verbally abusive.[29]

Defensiveness is not only the responsibility of the person who feels threatened. If that were so, all you would need to do is grow a thick skin. In fact, competent communicators protect others' face needs as well as their own.[30] For instance, skilled instructors try to support their students' presenting faces, especially when offering constructive criticism. This facework leads to less defensive responses from their students.[31] Likewise, effective supervisors use face-saving statements such as, "You're on the right track and your work has potential" to buffer corrections.[32]

> **Defensiveness**
> The attempt to protect a presenting image a person believes is being attacked.
>
> **Face-threatening act**
> Behaviour by another that is perceived as attacking an individual's presenting image, or face.

Invitation to Insight

Evaluating Communication Climates

It doesn't take much analysis to recognize the communication climate in each of your relationships. Taking the following steps will help explain why these climates exist and may also suggest how to improve negative climates.

1. Identify the communication climate of an important interpersonal relationship. Using weather metaphors (sunny, gloomy, calm) may help.

2. List the confirming or disconfirming communication that created and now maintain this climate. Be sure to list both verbal and nonverbal messages.

3. Describe what you can do either to maintain the existing climate (if positive) or to change it (if negative). Again, list both verbal and nonverbal messages.

"I didn't get where I am by trying to please."

Mike Twohy The New Yorker Collection/The Cartoon Bank

TABLE 9.3

The Gibb Categories of Defensive and Supportive Behaviours

Defensive Behaviours	Supportive Behaviours
1. Evaluation	1. Description
2. Control	2. Problem orientation
3. Strategy	3. Spontaneity
4. Neutrality	4. Empathy
5. Superiority	5. Equality
6. Certainty	6. Provisionalism

Republished with permission of Blackwell Publishing, Inc., from "Defensive Communications" by Jack R. Gibb © 1961 in the *Journal of Communication*, Vol. 11(3): 141–148; permission conveyed through Copyright Clearance Center, Inc.

Evaluation: "Those jokes are sick and depraved!"
Description: "When you tell off-colour jokes, I get embarrassed."

Note how the descriptive statements focus on the speaker's thoughts and feelings without judging the person. But effectiveness also depends on when, where, and how the language is used. If the preceding descriptive statements were delivered in front of a room full of bystanders or in a whining tone of voice, they may not work. Nonetheless, describing how the other person's behaviour affects you is likely to produce better results than judgmentally attacking the person.

Evaluative communication Messages in which the sender judges the receiver in some way, usually resulting in a defensive response.

Control versus Problem Orientation

Controlling communication occurs when senders impose solutions on receivers with little regard for the receivers' needs or interests. Control can involve almost anything:

Descriptive communication Messages that describe the speaker's position without evaluating others. Synonymous with "I" language.

Preventing Defensiveness in Others

Researcher Jack Gibb offers some useful tools for reducing defensiveness.[33] He isolated six types of defence-arousing communication and six contrasting behaviours that reduce the level of threat and defensiveness by conveying face-honouring relational messages of respect **(see Table 9.3)**.

Evaluation versus Description

The first type of defence-arousing behaviour is **evaluation**. Most people become irritated at judgmental statements, which they are likely to interpret as a lack of regard. One form of evaluation is "you" language that judges a person.

Unlike evaluative "you" language, **description** focuses on the *speaker's* thoughts and feelings. Descriptive messages are often expressed in "I" language, which provokes less defensiveness.[34] Contrast the following evaluative "you" claims with their descriptive "I" counterparts:

Evaluation: "This place is a *#$%&*@ mess!"
Description: "When you don't clean up, I have to either do it or live in squalor. That's why I'm mad!"

Controlling communication

Messages in which the sender tries to impose some sort of outcome on the receiver, usually resulting in a defensive reaction.

Problem orientation

A supportive style of communication described by Jack Gibb in which the communicators focus on working together to solve their problems instead of trying to impose their own solutions on one another.

Strategy

A defence-arousing style of communication described by Jack Gibb in which the sender tries to manipulate or deceive a receiver.

Spontaneity

A supportive communication behaviour described by Jack Gibb in which the sender expresses a message without any attempt to manipulate the receiver.

Neutrality

A defence-arousing behaviour described by Jack Gibb in which the sender expresses indifference toward a receiver.

where to eat dinner, what TV program to watch, or how to spend a large sum of money. When people act in controlling ways, it creates a defensive climate. No one likes to feel that their ideas are worthless or that nothing they say will change other people's determination to have their way. Individuals who physically or mentally abuse their partners use controlling communication. Whether with words, gestures, tone of voice, or status, the unspoken message is, "I know what's best for you, and we'll get along if you do as I say."

In **problem orientation**, communicators seek a solution that satisfies everyone's needs so that everyone wins. Problem orientation is often typified by "we" language which suggests that the speaker is making decision *with* rather than *for* people.[35] For example, university chairpersons who adopted a problem orientation approach were thought to be more effective than those who did not.[36]

Here are some examples of how some controlling and problem-orientation messages might sound:

Controlling:	"You need to stay off the phone for the next two hours."
Problem orientation:	"I'm expecting some important calls. Can we work out a way to keep the line open?"
Controlling:	"There's only one way to handle this problem…"
Problem orientation:	"Looks like we have a problem. Let's work out a solution we can both live with."

Strategy versus Spontaneity

Gibb uses the word **strategy** to characterize defence-arousing messages where speakers hide their ulterior motives. *Dishonesty* and *manipulation* characterize this strategy. Even if the intentions of strategic communication are honourable, victims feel defensive when they discover they were played for a naive sucker.

In contrast to this behaviour is **spontaneity**, which simply means being honest with others. It doesn't mean blurting out every idea that comes into your head, though. You would undoubtedly threaten others' presenting selves if you were "spontaneous" about every opinion that crossed your mind. Gibb's notion of spontaneity involves setting aside hidden agendas that others both sense and resist. These examples illustrate the difference:

Strategy:	"What are you doing Friday after work?"
Spontaneity:	"I have a piano I need to move Friday after work. Can you give me a hand?"
Strategy:	"Pat and Jen go out to dinner every week."
Spontaneity:	"I'd like to go out to dinner more often."

Spontaneity doesn't mean indiscriminately saying whatever you're thinking and feeling. That's *blurting*, which is detrimental to interpersonal relationships.[37] Blurters tend to be high in aggressiveness and neuroticism and low in empathy and perspective taking—they are unconcerned about the harm their comments might cause.

Neutrality versus Empathy

Gibb uses the term **neutrality** to describe *indifference*—a lack of concern for the welfare of another that implies that the person isn't important to you. Such perceived indifference promotes defensiveness because people don't like to think of themselves as worthless and they'll fight a self-concept that portrays them as such. Notice the difference between neutral and empathetic statements:

Neutral:	"That's what happens when you don't plan properly."
Empathetic:	"Ouch—looks like this didn't turn out the way you expected."
Neutral:	"Sometimes things just don't work out. That's the way it goes."
Empathetic:	"I know you put a lot of time and effort into this project."

Gibb found that *empathy* helps rid communication of the quality of indifference. **Empathy** means accepting another's feelings by putting yourself in another's place. This doesn't mean that you need to agree with that person—you simply convey your care and respect in a supportive way. Gibb also noted the nonverbal expressions of concern were just as, if not more, important to the receiver than the words used.

Superiority versus Equality

The fifth defence-creating behaviour is **superiority**. Any message that suggests, "I'm better than you," is likely to arouse feelings of defensiveness in the recipients. In Western cultures, both young people and senior citizens are irritated when people patronize them.[38] Consider, for example, how using simplified grammar and vocabulary, talking loudly and slowly, not listening, and varying speaking pitch convey a patronizing attitude.

FARCUS®
© LaughingStock International Inc.

WAISGLASS/COULTHART

"We need to improve morale ... any of you boneheads have a good idea?"

Reprinted with permission from LaughingStock Licensing Inc.

Here are two examples of the difference between superiority and equality:

Superior:	"You don't know what you're talking about."
Equal:	"I see it a different way."
Superior:	"No, that's not the right way to do it!"
Equal:	"If you want, I can show you a way that has worked for me."

Gibb found ample evidence that many people who have superior skills and talents are capable of projecting feelings of **equality** rather than superiority. Such people convey that, although they may have greater talent in certain areas, they see others as having just as much worth as human beings.

Certainty versus Provisionalism

People who are positive they're right, who think theirs is the only way of doing something, or who insist that they have all the facts project the defence-arousing behaviour that Gibb calls **certainty**. Communicators who regard their own opinions with sureness while disregarding those of others demonstrate a lack of regard for what others hold to be important. It's likely that the receiver will take the certainty as a personal affront and react defensively.

Empathy
The ability to project oneself onto another person's point of view so as to experience the other's thoughts and feelings.

Superiority
A defence-arousing style of communication described by Jack Gibb in which the sender states or implies that the receiver is not worthy of respect.

Equality
A type of supportive communication described by Jack Gibb suggesting that the sender regards the receiver as worthy of respect.

Certainty
An attitude behind messages that dogmatically implies that the speaker's position is correct and the other person's ideas are not worth considering. Likely to generate a defensive response.

In contrast, there is **provisionalism**. This occurs when people with strong opinions are willing to acknowledge that they don't have a corner on the truth and will change their stand if another position seems more reasonable. Consider the contrasting examples below:

Certain: "That won't work!"
Provisional: "I think you'll run into problems with that approach."

Certain: "You don't know what you're talking about!"
Provisional: "Wow, I didn't know this. Perhaps we should look into it."

As these examples suggest, provisionalism often surfaces in word choice. Instead of words like *can't, never, always, must* and *have to,* provisional speakers say *perhaps, maybe, possibly,* and *could.* They seem to have an understanding of what research confirms: People respond better to open-minded messages.[39]

> # The need to be right—the sign of a vulgar mind.
> —Albert Camus

There is no guarantee that using Gibb's supportive, confirming approach to communication will build a positive climate. However, the chances for a constructive relationship will be greatest when communication consists of the supportive approach described here. Besides boosting the odds of getting a positive response from others, supportive communication can leave you feeling more comfortable and more positive toward others.

Saving Face

Gibb's categories of supportive communication offer useful guidelines for reducing defensiveness and saving face. In the following pages, you will learn some specific ways to use these approaches when delivering challenging messages.

Provisionalism
A supportive style of communication described by Jack Gibb in which the sender expresses a willingness to consider the other person's position.

Behavioural description
An account that refers only to observable phenomena.

The Assertive Message Format

As you've already seen, building a supportive climate requires that you avoid attacking others to preserve their face. However, there are times when you need to share your legitimate concerns. The assertive format is a method that allows you to speak your mind in a clear yet respectful, assertive way without judging or dictating to others. It can be used on a variety of messages: your hopes, problems, complaints, and appreciations.[40] A complete assertive message has five parts: behaviour, interpretation, feeling, consequences, and intent.

Behaviour

As you read in Chapter 5, a **behavioural description** is objective and only describes the raw material to which you react. It does not involve interpretation.

Two examples of behavioural descriptions might look like the following:

Example 1
"A week ago Liam promised me that he would ask my permission to smoke if I was in the room. Just a moment ago, he lit a cigarette without asking."

Example 2
"Sophie is acting differently this week. She didn't text me, she didn't drop by like she usually does, and she didn't return my phone calls."

CATHY © 1983 Cathy Guisewaite. Reprinted with permission of UNIVERSAL UCLICK. All rights reserved.

Interpretation statement
A statement that describes a speaker's interpretation of the meaning of another person's behaviour.

Feeling statement
An expression of a sender's emotions that results from interpretation of sense data.

Notice that, in both cases, the descriptive statement included only data that are available through the senses. The observer hasn't attached any judgment or evaluation.

Interpretation

An **interpretation statement** describes the meaning you've attached to the other person's behaviour. The important thing to realize is that interpretations are *subjective* and that we can attach more than one interpretation to any behaviour. For example, look at these two different interpretations of each of the preceding descriptions:

© iStockphoto.com/Timur Nisametdinov

Example 1
Interpretation A: "Liam must have forgotten that he wouldn't smoke without asking me first. I'm sure he's too considerate to go back on his word."

Interpretation B: "Liam is rude and inconsiderate. After promising not to smoke around me without asking, he's just deliberately done so. He's just doing this to drive me crazy!"

Example 2
Interpretation A: "Sophie must be worried about her family. She'll probably just feel worse if I keep pestering her."

Interpretation B: "Sophie is probably mad at me because I gave her a hard time about the tennis match. I'd better leave her alone until she cools down."

Once you're aware of the difference between observable behaviour and interpretation, you'll see how many communication problems occur when senders fail to describe the behaviour on which an interpretation is based. For instance, imagine the difference between hearing a friend say, "You're a tightwad!" (*no behavioural description*) versus explaining, "When you never offer to pay me back for the coffee and snacks I often buy you, I think you're a tightwad" (*behaviour plus interpretation*).

Feeling

While reporting behaviour and sharing your interpretations are important, **feeling statements** add a new dimension to a message.

Invitation to Insight

Defensive and Supportive Language
The following exercise will help you recognize the difference between the Gibb's categories of defensive and supportive language.

1. For each of the situations below, write out two messages—one using a defence-arousing statement and the other using a supportive statement—that a speaker might make.

2. After each message, label the Gibb's categories of language that your words represent.

> Example
>
> A neighbour's late-night music is keeping you awake.
> *Defence-arousing statement:* Why don't you show a little consideration and turn that damn thing down? If I hear any more noise, I'm going to call the police.
> *Type(s) of defensive language:* evaluation, control
> *Supportive statement:* When I hear your music late at night, I can't sleep, which leaves me more and more tired. I'd like to figure out some way you can listen and I can sleep.
> *Type(s) of supportive language:* description, problem orientation

1. You're an adult who has moved back in with your parents. They say they expect you to follow the "rules of the house."

2. You're attempting to tell your roommate he is trying to be "somebody he's not."

3. You find that a co-worker talks to you in a disrespectful manner and you wish to address the situation.

4. A boss criticizes a worker for taking so long to complete a project.

For example, consider the difference between saying, "When you laugh at me (*behaviour*), I think you find my comments foolish (*interpretation*)," versus, "When you laugh at me, I think you find my comments foolish, and *I feel angry*."

It's important to recognize that some statements *seem* as if they're expressing feelings but are actually interpretations or statements of intention. For instance, it's not accurate to say, "I feel like leaving," (really an intention) or "I feel you're wrong," (an interpretation). Statements like these obscure the true expression of feelings.

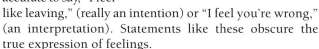

Consequence

A **consequence statement** explains the results of the situation you've described so far. There are three types of consequences:

- **What happens to you, the speaker**
  "When I didn't get the phone message yesterday (*behaviour*) that my doctor's appointment was delayed, I ended up waiting for an hour when I could have been studying (*consequences*). It seems to me that you don't care how busy I am, not even to write a simple note (*interpretation*), and that's why I'm so mad (*feeling*)."

- **What happens to the person you're addressing**
  "When you have seven or eight beers at a party (*behaviour*), you change. You make crude jokes that offend everybody and you become argumentative (*consequences*). For instance, last night you almost got into a fistfight (*more behaviour*). I don't think you realize how differently you act (*interpretation*), and I'm worried (*feeling*) about what will happen if you keep drinking like this.

- **What happens to others**
  "You probably don't know because you couldn't hear her cry (*interpretation*), but when you rehearse your lines for the play without closing the doors (*behaviour*), the baby can't sleep (*consequence*). I'm worried (*feeling*) about her because she's had a cold lately."

Communication Climate and Partner Abuse

Eileen Smith-Piovesan

Speaking from experience, I could have saved myself much psychological and physical pain had I been aware of the warning signs of abuse. At the beginning of my relationship with my first husband, I mistook his "wanting me all to himself" and making all the decisions as indications of his love for me. How wrong I was. They were efforts to control me and keep me away from my friends and family. He married me and during our seven-year relationship he eroded my sense of self-worth as I lived in constant fear of physical harm.

Upon reflection, I see that people with abusive personalities give off verbal clues and this is what you need to know. First, know the difference between communication that is caring and communication that is designed to control you. For example, if your partner says, "I don't want you to see Sally/Ben. I don't like her/him," that's controlling! If a partner says something like, "Just because I don't enjoy hanging out with Sally/Ben doesn't mean that you can't send time with her/him," that demonstrates sensitivity to your needs and wants. That's caring communication.

You should also know that in positive relationships, your partner does not diminish your self-worth, he/she enhances your self-worth. For example, take a situation where you tell your partner that you want to take some university classes, and your partner replies, "Why are you even thinking of going back to school—you're setting yourself up for failure!" This doesn't do much for your self-concept. In contrast, a response like, "You are such an inquisitive person; I think it's great that you decided to take some classes. I know you'll do well" gives you added confidence.

Finally, physical abuse often starts with verbal abuse where you're subjected to rage, outbursts, and name calling. If this happens, walk away. It's easier to leave at the first signs than to wait until you are so psychologically torn that your options are limited. Know that you cannot change a person and abusers do not change. If you are in such a relationship, tell a trusted friend or find information about assistance available for abused women in your local area.

By Eileen Smith-Piovesan. Used with permission.

Consequence statements are valuable because they help you understand why you are bothered or pleased by another's behaviour. Also, telling others about the consequences of their actions clarifies the results of their behaviour. As with interpretations, we often think that others *should* be aware of consequences without being told, but that's not necessarily the case. Explicitly stating consequences can ensure that you — or your message — leave nothing to the listener's imagination.

Intention

Intention statements make up the final element of the assertive message format. They can communicate three kinds of messages:

- **Where you stand on an issue**
  "When you call us 'girls' after I've told you we want to be called 'women' (*behaviour*), I get the idea you don't appreciate how important the difference is to us (*interpretation*) and how demeaning it feels (*feeling*). Now I'm in an awkward spot: Either I have to keep bringing up the subject or else drop it and feel bad (*consequence*). I want you to know how much this bothers me (*intention*)."
- **Requests of others**
  "When I didn't hear from you last night (*behaviour*), I thought you were mad at me (*interpretation*). I've been thinking about it ever since (*consequence*), and I'm still worried (*feeling*). I'd like to know if you're angry (*intention*)."
- **Descriptions of how you plan to act in the future**
  "I've asked you to repay the $25 you owe me (*behaviour*). I'm getting the idea that you're avoiding me (*interpretation*), and I'm pretty angry (*feeling*). Unless we clear this up now, don't expect me to lend you anything ever again (*intention*)."

As in the preceding cases, we're often motivated by a single intention. Sometimes, however, we act from a combination of intentions, which may even be in conflict with each other. When this happens, our conflicting intentions often make it difficult for us to reach decisions:

"I want to be truthful with you, but I don't want to violate my friend's privacy."
"I want to continue to enjoy your friendship and company, but I don't want to get too attached right now."

SKILL BUILDER

Behaviours and Interpretations

1. Select a partner and share several interpretations that you have recently made about other people in your life. For each interpretation, describe the behaviour on which you based your interpretations.
2. With your partner's help, consider some alternate interpretations of the behaviour that might be as plausible as your original one.
3. After considering the alternate interpretations, decide
   a. which one was most reasonable
   b. how you might share that interpretation (along with the behaviour) with the other person involved in a tentative, provisional way.

"I want to have time to study and get good grades, but I also want to have a job with some money coming in."

Using the Assertive Message Format

Before you try to deliver messages by using the assertive message format, there are a few points to remember:

1. **The elements may be delivered in mixed order.** As the examples on the preceding pages show, sometimes it's best to begin by stating your feelings, and at other times sharing your intentions or interpretations or describing consequences works better.

2. **Word the message to suit your personal style.** Instead of saying, "I interpret your behaviour to mean…" you might want to say, "I think…"

Consequence statement
An explanation of the results that follow either from the behaviour of the person to whom the message is addressed or from the speaker's interpretation of and feelings about the addressee's behaviour. Consequence statements can describe what happens to the speaker, the addressee, or others.

Intention statement
A description of where the speaker stands on an issue, what he or she wants, or how he or she plans to act in the future.

The Assertive Message Format

While the elements of the assertive message format don't vary, the way they sound depends on the situation and your personal style. Here are some examples to show how this approach can operate in real life.

To a neighbour

I had an awful scare just now *(feeling)*. I was backing out of the driveway, and Angela *(neighbour's toddler)* wandered right behind my car *(behaviour)*. Thank God I saw her, but she's so small that it would have been easy to miss her. I can't bear to think what might have happened if I hadn't seen her *(consequences for others)*. I know how toddlers can run off *(interpretation)*, but I really hope you can keep the door locked so she won't get outside without you knowing it *(intention)*.

To a friend

I just checked my Facebook account and saw that you tagged me in your photos from the party last weekend *(behaviour)*. I'm afraid those kinds of pictures could blow my chance of getting a good job *(consequence for you)*. You may think that I'm overreacting *(interpretation)*, but this is a big deal for me, so I need you to remember not to post any embarrassing pictures of me. If you aren't sure about a photo, just ask me *(intention)*.

To a boss

I've got a favour to ask *(intention)*. Last month I told you I wanted to work extra hours, and I know

Westend61/Getty Images

you're doing me a favour by giving me more shifts *(interpretation)*. But it would really help if you could give me a couple of days' advance notice instead of telling me the night before you want me to work *(clarifies intention)*. That way I can say yes to the extra shifts *(consequence for boss)*. It would also cause a lot less stress for me *(feeling)*.

To an auto mechanic

I need to tell you that I'm pretty unhappy *(feeling)*. When I dropped the car off yesterday, you told me it would definitely be ready today by noon. Now it's 12:30 and it isn't ready *(behaviour)*. I'm going to be late for an important meeting *(consequence for you)*. I know you aim to please *(interpretation)*, but you have to understand that I can't bring my car to you unless I can count on it being ready when you promise *(consequence for other)*.

---

or "It seems to me…" or perhaps "I get the idea…" In the same way, you can express your intentions by saying, "I hope you'll understand (or do)…" or perhaps "I wish you would…" The words that you choose should sound authentic in order to reinforce the genuineness of your statement.

3. **When appropriate, combine two elements in a single phrase.**
   The statement ". . . and ever since then I've been wanting to talk to you" expresses both a consequence and an intention. In the same way, saying, ". . . and after you said that, I felt confused" expresses a consequence and a feeling. Whether you combine elements or state them separately, the important point is to be sure that each one is present in your statement.

4. **Take your time delivering the message.**
   It isn't always possible to deliver all these messages at once, wrapped up in neat paragraphs. Most likely you have to repeat or restate one part before the other person understands what you're saying. As you've

already read, there are many types of psychological and physical noise that make it difficult for us to understand each other. In communication, as in many other activities, patience and persistence are essential.

Now try your hand at combining all these elements in the "Behaviours and Interpretations" Skill Builder.

LO4
Responding Nondefensively to Criticism

You can see how easy it might be to respond to a thoughtful, assertive message, but how can you respond nondefensively when you receive an aggressive message that doesn't match the prescriptions outlined in this chapter? Despite your best intentions, it's hard to be reasonable when you're being attacked, and even harder when the criticism is on target. There's a tendency either to counterattack or to withdraw nonassertively.

Because neither of these is likely to resolve a dispute, we need alternative ways of behaving. There are two such ways. Despite their apparent simplicity, they have proven to be among the most valuable skills many communicators have learned.[41]

> I was at a stop light, behind a car with a bumper sticker that said, "Honk if you love Jesus." I honked. The driver leaned out his window, flipped me the bird, and yelled, "Can't you see the light is still red, you moron?"
>
> —Dilbert Newsletter

Seek More Information

Seeking more information makes sense when you realize that it's foolish to respond to a critical attack until you understand what the other person has said. Even attacks that appear unjustified or foolish at first often contain some truth, if not much more.

Many readers object to asking for details, and their resistance stems from confusing the act of *listening open-mindedly* with *accepting* the comments. You can listen to, understand, and even acknowledge the most hostile comments without necessarily accepting them. If you disagree with a person's criticism, you'll be able to explain yourself better after you understand the criticism. On the other

© moodboard/CORBIS

Tyler Olson/Shutterstock.com

hand, you might see that it's valid, in which case you have learned some valuable information about yourself. In either case, you have everything to gain and nothing to lose by listening to the critic.

After spending years of instinctively resisting criticism, learning to listen to the other person will take some practice. Here are several ways to seek additional information from your critics.

Ask for Specifics

Vague attacks, such as, "You're being unfair," or "You never help out," can be difficult to understand, even if you sincerely want to change. In such cases, ask the critic for specific information. "What do I *do* that's unfair?" is an important question to ask before you can judge whether the attack is correct. You might ask, "When haven't I helped out?" before agreeing with or disagreeing with the attack.

If you are still accused of reacting defensively after you've asked for specifics, the problem may be in the *way* you ask. Your tone of voice and other nonverbal clues can give the same words radically different connotations. For example, think of how the words "Exactly what are you talking about?" can communicate a genuine desire to know or your belief that the speaker is crazy. Only request specific information if you genuinely want to learn more from the speaker; otherwise, it will only make matters worse.

Guess about Specifics

When your sincere and well-phrased requests for specific information aren't successful because your critics aren't able to define precisely the behaviour they find offensive, offer a guess! In a sense, you become both detective and suspect, the goal being to figure out exactly what "crime" you've committed. Like the technique of asking for specifics, guessing must be done with goodwill and the appropriate nonverbal cues if it's to produce satisfying results. You need to convey to the critic that for

both of your sakes, you're truly interested in finding out what is the matter. Here are some typical questions you might hear from someone guessing about the specifics of another's criticism:

- "So you object to the language I used in writing the paper. Was my language too formal?"
- "OK, I understand that you think the outfit looks funny. What's so bad about it? The colour? Does it have something to do with the fit? The fabric?"

Paraphrase the Speaker's Ideas

Paraphrasing, which involves active listening skills, is another strategy to understand a critic. It is especially important when critics think your behaviour has created a problem for them. By clarifying or amplifying what you understand critics to be saying, you'll learn more about their objections. A brief dialogue between a disgruntled customer and an especially talented store manager using paraphrasing might sound like this:

Customer: The way you people run this store is disgusting! I just want to tell you that I'll never shop here again.

Manager: (*reflecting the customer's feeling*) You seem to be upset. Can you tell me your problem?

Customer: It isn't *my* problem; it's the problem your salespeople have. They seem to think it's an inconvenience to help a customer find something.

Manager: So you didn't get enough help locating the items you were looking for, is that it?

Customer: Help? I spent 20 minutes looking around before I even talked to someone. It's a hell of a way to run a store.

Manager: So what you're saying is that the clerks seemed to be ignoring the customers?

Customer: No. They were all busy with other people. It just seems to me that you ought to have enough staff to handle the crowds that come in at this time of day.

Manager: I understand now. What frustrated you most was the fact that we didn't have enough staff to serve you promptly.

Customer: That's right. I have no complaint with the service I get after I'm waited on, and I've always thought you had a good selection here. It's just that I'm too busy to wait so long for help.

Manager: Well, I'm glad you brought this to my attention. We certainly don't want loyal customers going away mad. I'll try to see that it doesn't happen again.

This conversation illustrates two advantages of paraphrasing. First, the critic often reduces the intensity of the attack after he or she realizes that the complaint is being heard. Criticism generally grows from the frustration of unmet needs—which in this case was partly a lack of attention. Once the manager showed an interest in the customer, the customer began to feel better and was able to leave the store relatively calm. Of course, this sort of reflective listening won't always mollify a critic, but even when it doesn't, there's still another benefit that makes the strategy worthwhile. For example, the manager learned some valuable information by taking time to understand the customer—that a lack of staff might lose the store business. Had the manager reacted defensively to the customer, this information wouldn't have emerged.

Ask What the Critic Wants

Sometimes your critic's demand will be obvious: "Turn down that music!" or "I wish you'd remember to tell me about phone messages." In other cases, some investigation will be needed to learn what the critic wants:

Anna:	I can't believe you invited all those people over without asking me first!
Dejun:	Are you saying you want me to cancel the party?
Anna:	No, I just wish you'd ask me before you make plans.
Erica:	You're so critical! It sounds like you don't like anything about this paper.
Maria:	But you asked for my opinion. What do you expect me to do when you ask?
Erica:	I want to know what's wrong, but I don't *just* want to hear criticism. If you think there's anything good about my work, I wish you'd tell me that, too.

This last example illustrates the importance of accompanying your questions with the right nonverbal

behaviour. It's easy to imagine two ways in which Maria could have nonverbally supported her response "What do you expect me to do when you ask?" One tone of voice would show a genuine desire to clarify what Erica wanted, whereas the other would be clearly hostile and defensive. As with all the styles in this section, your responses to criticism must be sincere to work.

Ask about the Consequences of Your Behaviour

Generally, people criticize when some need is not being met. You can respond to this kind of criticism by learning what consequences your behaviour has for them. Actions that seem perfectly legitimate to you may cause difficulties for your critics. Once you understood this, criticisms that previously sounded foolish take on new meanings:

Worker A:	Why do you care whether I'm late for work?
Worker B:	Because when the boss asks, I feel obligated to make up some story so you won't get in trouble, and I don't like to lie.
Husband:	Why does it bother you when I lose money at poker? You know I never gamble more than I can afford.
Wife:	It's not the cash itself. It's that when you lose, you're cranky for two or three days, and that's no fun for me or the children.

Ask What Else Is Wrong

It might seem crazy to invite more criticism, but sometimes asking about other complaints can uncover the real problem:

Raul:	Are you mad at me?
Tina:	No. Why are you asking?
Raul:	Because you hardly spent any time talking to me at the picnic. In fact, it seemed like whenever I came over to talk, you went somewhere else.

AL ACCARDO/Masterfile

Alon Brik/Shutterstock.com

Tina: Is anything else wrong?

Raul: Well, I've been wondering lately if you're tired of me.

Asking if anything else bothers your critic isn't just an exercise in masochism. If you keep your defensiveness in check, further probing can lead to the real source of the critic's dissatisfaction.

Before soliciting more information from a critic, you may wish to role-play the scenario with someone. Not only will you gain another perspective, but you'll be able to practise and hone your nondefensive response skills.

Sometimes, however, soliciting more information isn't enough. What if you fully understand the other person's criticism and still feel defensive? You know that if you try to defend yourself, you'll get into an argument; on the other hand, you simply can't accept what the other person is saying about you. The solution to such a dilemma is outrageously simple: Agree with the critic!

Agree with the Critic

While you can't honestly agree with criticisms that you don't believe are true, you can agree with either the facts or the critic's perception of the problem. Here's how you do it.

Agree with the Facts

Agreeing with the critic restores the critic's damaged reputation.[42] Agree with your critic when the accusation is factually correct:

> "You're right, I am angry."
> "I suppose I was being defensive."
> "Now that you mention it, I did get pretty sarcastic."

Agreeing with the facts seems sensible when you realize that certain facts are indisputable. If you agree to meet at four and don't show up until five, there's no question, you're late. If you've broken a borrowed object, run out of gas, or failed to finish a job you started, there's no point in denying it. In the same way, if you're honest, you may have to agree with many interpretations of your behaviour even when they're not flattering. You do get

pathdoc/Shutterstock.com

"When will he be able to sit up and take criticism?"

Chon Day The New Yorker Collection/The Cartoon Bank

angry, act foolishly, fail to listen, and behave inconsiderately. But once you rid yourself of the myth of perfection, it's much easier to acknowledge these truths.

But why is it so difficult to accept these accurate criticisms without getting defensive? The answer lies in the confusion between agreeing with the *facts* and accepting the *judgment* that so often accompanies them. Most critics don't merely describe the action that offends them; they also evaluate it, and it's this evaluation that we resist:

> "It's silly to be angry."
> "You have no reason for being defensive."
> "You were wrong to be so sarcastic."

It's judgments like these that we resent. By realizing that you can agree with—and even learn from—the descriptive part of many criticisms and still not accept the accompanying evaluations, you'll find that you'll have a response that is both honest and nondefensive.

Of course, to reduce defensiveness, you must honestly agree with the facts. It's humiliating to accept descriptions that aren't accurate, and pretending to agree leads to trouble. You can imagine how unproductive the previously examined conversation between the store manager and disgruntled customer would have been if the manager had spoken the same words in a sarcastic tone. Only agree with the facts when you can do so sincerely. Though this won't always be possible, you'll be surprised at how often you can use this simple response.

Agree with the Critic's Perception

Agreeing with your critics may be fine when you think the criticisms are justified, but how can you confess when they are completely unjustified? You've listened and asked questions to understand the criticisms, but the more you listen, the more positive you are that the critic is totally out of line. Even in these cases, there is a way of agreeing—this time with the critic's right to see things a particular way.

Co-worker A: I want to let you know right from the start that I was against hiring you for the job. I think you got it because you're a woman.

Co-worker B: I can understand why you'd believe that, with the equal opportunities laws. I hope that after I've been here for a while, you'll change your mind.

Roommate A: I don't think you're being totally honest about your reason for wanting to stay home. You say it's because you have a headache, but I think you're avoiding Mary.

Roommate B: I can see why that would make sense to you, because Mary and I got into an argument the last time we were together. All I can say is that I do have a headache.

You may feel more comfortable agreeing with and acknowledging accurate criticism when you understand that you're not necessarily obliged to *apologize*. If you're not responsible for the behaviour that your critic finds objectionable, an explanation might be more appropriate than an apology:

"I know I'm late. There was an accident downtown, and the streets are jammed." (*spoken in an explanatory, nondefensive tone*)

In other cases, your behaviour might be understandable, if not perfect. When this happens, you can acknowledge the validity of the criticism without apologizing:

"You're right. I *did* lose my temper. I've had to remind you three or four times, and I guess I finally used up all my patience." (*again, delivered as an explanation, not a defence or counterattack*)

In still other cases, you can acknowledge your critic's right to see things differently than you without backing off from your position:

"I can understand why you think I'm overreacting. I know this doesn't seem as important to you as it does to me. I hope you can understand why I think this is such a big deal."

Apologizing is fine if you can do so sincerely; but you will be able to agree with critics more often if you

SKILL BUILDER

Coping with Criticism
Take turns practising nondefensive responses with a partner.

1. Choose one of the following criticisms and brief your partner on how it might be directed at you:
   a. You're so selfish sometimes. You think only of yourself.
   b. Don't be so touchy!
   c. You say you understand me, but you don't really.
   d. I wish you'd do your share around here.
   e. You're so critical!

2. As your partner criticizes you, answer with an appropriate response from the preceding pages. As you do so, try to adopt an attitude of genuinely wanting to understand the criticism and finding parts that you can sincerely agree with.

3. Ask your partner to evaluate your response. Does it follow the forms described in the previous pages? Does it sound sincere?

4. Replay the same scene, trying to improve your response.

understand that doing so doesn't require you to grovel. Some critics don't seem to deserve the kinds of respectful responses outlined here. They seem more interested in attacking you than explaining themselves. Before you counterattack these hostile critics, ask yourself whether a defensive response will be worth the consequences.

Communication in the Workplace

During your career, you are likely to spend more waking hours on the job than in any other setting. This means the emotional climate of the workplace can be just as important as salary or working conditions in shaping the quality of your life. In fact, positive communication climates lead to increased job satisfaction.[43] And two factors are consistently connected to supportive workplace environments.[44]

The first is **praise and encouragement**. Employees feel valued when their work is recognized. As researcher Daniel Goleman notes, "Small exchanges—a compliment on work well done, a word of support after a setback—add up to how we feel on the job."[45]

The second climate-boosting practice is **open communication**. Employees appreciate managers and co-workers with "open-door policies" allowing them opportunities to get and give feedback, make suggestions, and voice concerns.

Climate is equally important in virtual organizations as in face-to-face communication.[46] When most contact is text-based, taking time to treat co-workers cordially can make a real difference. One study revealed that morale and trust were higher in companies where e-mail correspondence opened with friendly greetings (even a simple "Hi") and closed with a friendly farewell ("Thanks" "Have a nice day") than in messages that lacked these elements.[47] Further, students in our small group classes say that they build and maintain a positive climate within their individual groups by posting positive comments on their group Facebook page. They might say something like, "We did a great job on our presentation today. Our hard work paid off! Great group."

By now, it is clear that communication can influence and change a climate. One climate that is not always positive in the workplace has to do with mental health. Twenty percent of Canadians suffer from some form of mental health issue such as depression, bipolar disorder, anxiety, and so forth.[48] The sad thing is that these same individuals are also discriminated again, bullied, ridiculed, devalued, and excluded in the workplace.[49] Accounting for this might be the many myths surrounding mental illness. For example, individuals erroneously buy into the notion that people with mental illness are "both socially and professionally incapable; that such people are dangerous; that a mental illness is not a legitimate illness; that mental illness is caused by work; and that employers should not be required to support those with mental illness, as companies are not charitable organizations."[50] Clearly, none of these is true.

In an effort to erase the stigma of mental illness and to get it "out of the closet," the Canadian Mental Health Commission is promoting workplace mental health literacy. As communicators, conveying a positive attitude toward mental health and those who suffer from mental illness can make a big difference in the communication climate, and hence, to all the employees who work within it.

Another factor that can influence communication climate is leadership style. The three traditional leadership styles are described as authoritarian (controlling), democratic (works with subordinates), and laissez-faire ("hands off," nonleadership).[51] Matching the right style with the task is important. For instance, an authoritarian manager wouldn't create the right climate in jobs that require creativity for success. Nor would a laissez-faire leader create the appropriate climate in military settings. But there are other ways of looking at leadership. Two more modern approaches are known as transactional leadership and transformational leadership.[52] "Transactional leaders set goals, clarify desired outcomes, provide feedback, and give subordinates rewards for good work."[53] There are many employment situations where such a style would pro-

What does this photo say about communication climate and teamwork?

specialists offer advice that is very much in keeping with this chapter. For instance, Amanda Augustine suggests that you select an appropriate time, and private space, to provide the feedback. She also recommends seeking permission by using words like, "Can I share some observations I'm made?" and using positive, as opposed to negative language to change behaviour. For example, instead of using discouraging words like "You shouldn't …." or "I don't think …" use more upbeat language such as, "What if we tried …?" or "Have you considered doing …?"[55] Including what the person does well is equally important. This approach saves face for the listener and reduces the likelihood that the receiver will become defensive. If the session is handled well, the employee will leave with a sense of his or her strengths as well as some goals to work on in the future.

But, what if you're on the receiving end? If so, here is an opportunity to practise what you've learned about responding nondefensively to criticism such as seeking more information and agreeing with the critic. Hazel Morley with Canadian Immigration offers other suggestions such as: listen without interrupting, try to avoid making negative assumptions, paraphrase what you're hearing, take notes, ask for a little time to process the information, and thank the person for the feedback.[56] This type of communication goes a long way to create and maintain a positive work climate.

duce very positive outcomes. Employees would know what was expected of them. The second "newer" leadership style is the transformational leader whose focus is on creating a vision for the future and then motivating people to buy into and work toward it. In so doing, they develop leadership in others as well. They do this through the use of charisma, inspiration, intellectual stimulation, and individualized consideration.[54] It appears that the transformational leadership style is most in keeping with the notion of creating a positive communication climate in the workplace.

Finally, communication climate is very important when it comes to giving (and receiving) feedback. Career

Bob Oliver/Moment/Getty Images

READY TO STUDY?

IN THE BOOK, YOU CAN:

❏ Rip out the Chapter in Review card at the back of the book to have the key terms and Learning Objectives handy, and complete the quizzes provided (answers are at the bottom of the back page).

ONLINE YOU CAN:

❏ Stay organized and efficient with MindTap—a single destination with all the course material and study aids you need to succeed. Built-in apps leverage social media and the latest learning technology. For example:

    ❏ Listen to the text using ReadSpeaker.

    ❏ Use pre-populated Flashcards as a jump start for review—or you can create your own.

    ❏ You can highlight text and make notes in your MindTap Reader. Your notes will flow into Evernote, the electronic notebook app that you can access anywhere when it's time to study for the exam.

    ❏ Prepare for tests with a variety of quizzes and activities.

Go to **nelson.com/student** to access these digital resources

Endnotes

1. J. Fitness (2006). "The emotionally intelligent marriage." In J. Ciarrochi, J. P. Forgas, & J. D. Mayer (Eds.), *Emotional Intelligence in everyday life* (pp. 129–139). New York: Psychology Press.

2. E. E. Smith (2014, June 12). "Masters of love." The Atlantic.

3. C. A. Barbato, E. E. Graham, & E. E. Perse (2003). "Communicating in the Family: An Examination of the Relationship of Family Communication Climate & Interpersonal Communication Motives." *Journal of Family Communication, 3*, 123–148.

4. R. M. Dailey (2006). "Confirmation in Parent-Adolescent Relationships and Adolescent Openness: Toward Extending Confirmation Theory." *Communication Monographs, 73*, 434–458.

5. J. J. Teven, M. M. Martin, & N. C. Neupauer (1998). "Sibling Relationships: Verbally Aggressive Messages & Their Effect on Relational Satisfaction." *Communication Reports, 11*, 179–186.

6. A. L. Vangelisti & S. L. Young (2000). "When Words Hurt: The Effects of Perceived Intentionality on Interpersonal Relationships." *Journal of Social & Personal Relationship, 17*, 393–424.

7. E. Seiberg (1976). "Confirming & Disconfirming Communication in an Organizational Setting." In J. Owen, P. Page, & G. Zimmerman (Eds.), *Communication in Organizations* (pp. 129–149). St. Paul, MN: West.

8. E. Sieberg & C. Larson (1971). *Dimensions of Interpersonal Response*. Paper presented at the meeting of the International Communication Association, Phoenix, AZ.

9. S. A. Cox (1999). "Group Communication & Employee Turnover: How Coworkers Encourage Peers to Voluntarily Exit." *Southern Communication Journal, 64*, 181–192.

10. J. M. Gottman & R. W. Levenson (2000). "The Timing of Divorce: Predicting When a Couple Will Divorce over a 14-Year Period." *Journal of Marriage and the Family, 62*, 737–745.

11. A. S. Rancer & T. A. Avtgis (2006). *Argumentative and Aggressive Communication: Theory, Research, and Application*. Thousand Oaks, CA: Sage.

12. A. Wade & T. Beran (2011). "Cyberbullying: The new era of bullying." *Canadian Journal of School Psychology, 26*, 44–61; A. G. Dempsey, M. L. Sulkowski, J. Dempsey, & E. A. Storch (2011). "Has cyber technology produced a new group of peer aggressors?" *Cyberpsychology, Behaviour, and Social Networking, 14*, 297–302.

13. M. Duggan (2014, October 22). "Online harassment." *Pew Research Internet Project*.

14. J. K. Alberts (1988). "An Analysis of Couples' Conversational Complaints." *Communication Monographs, 55*, 184–197.

15. J. K. Alberts & G. Driscoll (1992). "Containment versus Escalation: The Trajectory of Couples' Conversational Complaints." *Western Journal of Communication, 56*, 394–412.

16. J. M. Gottman & N. Silver (1999). *The Seven Principles for Making Marriage Work*. New York: Random House.

17. A. J. Johnson, D. Hample, & I. A. Cionea (2014). "Understanding argumentation in interpersonal communication." *Communication Yearbook, 38*, 145–173;

18. F. F. Jordan-Jackson, Y. Lin, A. S. Rancer, & D. A. Infante (2008). "Perceptions of Males and Females' Use of Aggressive Affirming and Nonaffirming Messages in an Interpersonal Dispute: You've Come a Long Way Baby?" *Western Journal of Communication, 72*, 239–258.

19. K. Cissna & E. Seiberg (1995). "Patterns of Interactional Confirmation & Disconfirmation." In M. V. Redmond (Ed.), *Interpersonal Communication: Readings in Theory & Research*. Fort Worth: Harcourt Brace.

20. M. W. Allen (1995). "Communication Concepts Related to Perceived Organizational Support." *Western Journal of Communication, 59*, 326–346.

21. See, for example, R. M. Dailey (2008). "Assessing the Contribution of Nonverbal Behaviours in Displays of Confirmation During Parent-Adolescent Interactions: An Actor-Partner Interdependence Model." *Journal of Family Communication, 8*, 62–91.

22. W. W. Wilmot, *Dyadic Communication* (New York: Random House, 1987), pp. 149–158.

23. J. L. Hocker & W. W. Wilmot (1995). *Interpersonal Conflict*, 4th ed. (p. 34). Dubuque, IA: Brown & Benchmark.

24. Ibid., p. 36.

25. J. M. Gottman & R. W. Levinson (1999). "Rebound from marital conflict and divorce prediction." *Family Process, 38*, 387–292.

26. K. Domenici & S. Littlejohn (2006): *Facework: Bridging Theory and Practice*. Thousand Oaks, CA: Sage; M. K. Lapinski & F. J. Boster (2001). "Modeling the Ego-Defensive Function of Attitudes." *Communication Monographs, 68*, 314–324.

27. D. G. Lannin, K. E. Bittner, & F. O. Lorenz (2013). "Longitudinal effect of defensive denial on relationship instability." *Journal of Family Psychology, 27*, 968–977.

28. J. A. H. Becker, B. Ellevold, & G. H. Stamp (2008). "The Creation of Defensiveness in Social Interaction II: A Model of Defensive Communication Among Romantic Couples." *Communication Monographs, 75*, 86–110; G. H. Stamp, A. L. Vangelisti, & J. A. Daly (1992). "The Creation of Defensiveness in Social Interaction." *Communication Quarterly, 40*, 177–190.

29. D. R. Turk & J. L. Monahan (1999). "'Here I Go Again': An Examination of Repetitive Behaviours during Interpersonal Conflicts." *Southern Communication Journal, 64*, 232–244.

30. W. R. Cupach & S. J. Messman (1999). "Face predictions and friendship solidarity." *Communication Reports, 12*, 117–124.

31. A. R. Trees, J. Kerssen-Griefp, & J. A. Hess (2009). "Earning influence by communicating respect: Facework's contributions to effective instructional feedback." *Communication Education, 58*, 379–416.

32. C. Y. Kingsley Westerman & D. Westerman (2010). "Supervisor impression management: Message content and

channel effects on impressions." *Communication Studies, 61,* 585–601.

33. J. Gibb (September 1961). "Defensive Communication." *Journal of Communication, 11,* 141–148. See also E. Robertson (2005). "Placing Leaders at the Heart of Organizational Communication." *Communication Management, 9,* 34–37.

34. R. F. Proctor & J. R. Wilcox (1993). "An Exploratory Analysis of Responses to Owned Messages in Interpersonal Communication." *ETC: A Review of General Semantics, 50,* 201–220.

35. B. H. Seider, G. Hirschberger, K. L. Nelson, & R. W. Levenson (2009). "We can work it out: Age differences in relational pronouns, physiology, and behaviour in marital conflict." *Psychology and Aging, 24,* 604–613.

36. K. Czeck & G. L. Forward (2010). "Leader communication: Faculty perceptions of the department chair." *Communication Quarterly, 58,* 431–457.

37. A. S. Hample, D. Richards & C. Skubisz (2013). "Blurting." Communication Monographs, 80, 503–532.

38. Research summarized in J. Harwood, E. B. Ryan, H. Giles, & S. Tysoski (1997). "Evaluations of Patronizing Speech & Three Response Styles in a Non-Service-Providing Context." *Journal of Applied Communication Research, 25,* 170–195.

39. J. A. Katt & S. J. Collins (2013). "The power of provisional/immediate language revisited: Adding student personality traits to the mix." *Communication Research Reports, 30,* 85–95.

40. Adapted from S. Miller, E. W. Nunnally, & D. B. Wackman (1975). *Alive & Aware: How to Improve Your Relationships through Better Communication.* Minneapolis, MN: International Communication Programs. See also R. Remer & P. deMesquita (1990). "Teaching & Learning the Skills of Interpersonal Confrontation." In D. D. Cahn (Ed.), *Intimates in Conflict: A Communication Perspective.* Hillsdale, NJ: Erlbaum.

41. Adapted from M. Smith (1975). *When I Say No, I Feel Guilty* (pp. 93–110). New York: Dial Press.

42. W. L. Benoit & S. Drew (1997). "Appropriateness & Effectiveness of Image Repair Strategies." *Communication Reports, 10,* 153–163. See also Stamp et al., "Creation of Defensiveness."

43. B. Cooil, L. Aksoy, T. L. Keiningham, & K. M. Maryott (2009). "The Relationship of Employee Perceptions of Organizational Climate to Business-Unit Outcomes: An MPLS Approach." *Journal of Service Research, 11,* 277–294; D. Pincus (1986). "Communication Satisfaction, Job Satisfaction, & Job Performance." *Human Communication Research, 12,* 395–419.

44. E. Sopow (2008). "The Communication Climate Change at RCMP." *Strategic Communication Management, 12,* 20–23; J. W. Kassing (2008). "Consider This: A Comparison of Factors Contributing to Employees' Expressions of Dissent." *Communication Quarterly, 56,* 342–355; D. Saunders (2008). "Create an Open Climate for Communication." *Supervision, 69,* 6–8; C. E. Beck & E. A. Beck (1996). "The Manager's Open Door and the Communication Climate." In K. M. Galving & P Cooper (Eds.), *Making Connections: Readings in Relational Communication* (pp. 286–290). Los Angeles: Roxbury.

45. D. Goleman (2006). *Social Intelligence.* New York: Random House, p. 279.

46. A. D. Akkirman & D. L. Harris (2005). "Organizational Communication Satisfaction in the Virtual Workplace." *Journal of Management Development, 24,* 397–409.

47. J. Waldvogel (2007). "Greetings and Closings in Workplace Email." *Journal of Computer-Mediated Communication, 12,* 456–477.

48. Changing Directions: Changing Lives (2012). "The first mental health strategy for Canada." *Mental Health Commission of Canada.* http://strategy.mentalhealth commission.ca/strategy/summary/. Retrieved April 9, 2016.

49. Workplace Mental Health Promotion: A How-To Guide. (2010). "Works well: Healthy minds, healthy business." Canadian Mental Health Association. http://wmhp .cmhaontario.ca/wordpress/wp-content/uploads/2010/03/ WMHP-Guide-Final1.pdf. Retrieved April 11, 2016.

50. Minds Together Against Stigma (2012). Changing how we see mental illness: A report on the 5th International Stigma Conference (June 4–6, 2012) (p. 64). Ottawa, ON: Mental Health Commission of Canada, the Canadian Human Rights Commission, the World Psychiatric Association Scientific Section on Stigma and Mental Health and the Public Health Agency of Canada. http://www .mentalhealthcommission.ca/English/system/files/private/ document/Stigma_Opening_Minds_Together_Against _Stigma_ENG.pdf.

51. P. G. Northouse (2012). *Introduction to Leadership: Concepts and Practice* (2nd ed.). Los Angeles: Sage.

52. B. M. Bass (1990, Winter). "From Transactional to Transformational Leadership: Learning to Share the Vision." *Organizational Dynamics,* 19–31.

53. G. Lumsden, D. Lumsden, & C. Wiethoff (2010). *Communicating in Groups and Teams: Sharing Leadership* (5th ed.), p. 260. Belmont, CA: Wadsworth Cengage Learning.

54. Ibid.

55. A. Augustine (2014, June 5). Tips for Giving Feedback in the Workplace. http://info.theladders.com/career-advice/ 6-tips-for-giving-feedback-in-the-workplace.

56. H. Morley (2014, April 22). "How to give and take feedback in the workplace." *Canadian Immigration.* http:// canadianimmigrant.ca/slider/how-to-give-and-take-negative -feedback-in-the-workplace. Retrieved April 11, 2016.

10

MANAGING INTERPERSONAL CONFLICTS

LO1
The Nature of Conflict

For most people, conflict has about the same appeal as a trip to the dentist; it is something to be avoided.[1] With connotations such as *battle, brawl, fight, strife, struggle* and *trouble,* it is little wonder that conflict is seen in such a negative light. But, conflict can actually be positive and constructive. With the right set of communication skills, conflict can be less like a competition and more like a kind of dance in which partners work together to create something that would be impossible without their cooperation. One study revealed that college students in close romantic relationships who believed that conflicts were destructive were most likely to neglect or quit the relationship and less likely to seek a solution than couples who had less negative attitudes.[2] The kinds of skills outlined in this chapter can help well-intentioned partners handle their disagreements constructively.

Before focusing on how to solve interpersonal problems, we need to take a brief look at the nature of conflict.

Conflict Defined

Whatever form they may take, all interpersonal conflicts share certain characteristics. William Wilmot and Joyce Hocker provide a thorough definition when they define **conflict** as "an

Conflict
An expressed struggle between at least two interdependent parties who perceive incompatible goals, scarce resources, and interference from the other party in achieving their goals.

LEARNING OUTCOMES

LO1 Identify the conflicts in your important relationships and how satisfied you are with the way they have been handled.

LO2 Describe your personal conflict styles, evaluate their effectiveness, and suggest alternatives as appropriate.

LO3 Identify the relational conflict styles, patterns of behaviour, and conflict rituals that define a given relationship.

LO4 Demonstrate how you could use the win–win approach in a given conflict.

What do you THINK?

Conflict should be avoided at all costs.

1	2	3	4	5	6	7
strongly agree						strongly disagree

Personal experience may suggest otherwise, but with skill and the right attitude, conflicts can be constructive.

Patrick Sheandell O'Carroll/PhotoAlto Agency RF Collections/Getty Images

expressed struggle between at least two interdependent parties who perceive incompatible goals, scarce resources, and interference from the other party in achieving their goals."[3] A closer look at this definition will help you recognize how conflict operates in your life.

Expressed Struggle

Conflict can exist only when both parties are aware of a disagreement. You may be upset for months about a neighbour's noisy music, but no conflict exists until the neighbour learns about the problem. You can show your displeasure nonverbally through a dirty look or the silent treatment. One way or another, however, both parties must know that a problem exists before they're in conflict. Up until that point, you're in a fight "with yourself."

Perceived Incompatible Goals

All conflicts appear as if one party's gain is another's loss. If the neighbour turns down the music, she loses the enjoyment of hearing it at full volume, but if she keeps the volume up, you're subjected to unwanted music.

The goals in this situation really aren't completely incompatible—there are solutions that allow both parties to get what they want. For instance, you could close your windows or the neighbour could close hers. You might use earplugs and she could use earphones. If these solutions prove workable, the conflict disappears. Unfortunately, people often fail to see mutually satisfying solutions to their problems. As long as they *perceive* their goals to be mutually exclusive, conflict will continue to exist.

Perceived Scarce Resources

Conflicts also exist when people believe there isn't enough of something to go around. Money is an obvious example. If a worker asks for a raise and the boss prefers to use extra profit to expand the business, the two parties are in conflict.

Time is another scarce commodity. Many people struggle to meet the demands of school, work, family, and friends. "If only there were more hours in the day," is a common refrain and making time for the people in your life—as well as yourself—can be a constant source of conflict.

Interdependence

Parties in conflict are usually interdependent: The welfare and satisfaction of one depends on the actions of the other. Interdependence exists between conflicting nations, social groups, organizations, friends, and lovers. If the parties didn't need each other to solve the problem, they would go their separate ways. The first step toward resolving a conflict is adapting the attitude that "we're all in this together."

Interference from the Other Party

No matter how much one person's position may differ from another's, a full-fledged conflict won't occur until the participants act in ways that prevent one another from reaching their goals. For example, you might let some friends know that you object to their driving after drinking, but the conflict won't escalate until you try to take away their keys.

Conflict Is Natural

Every relationship of any depth at all has conflict.[4] No matter how close, how understanding, and how compatible you are, there will be times when your ideas or actions or needs or goals won't match. You like rap music, but your partner likes country; you want to see other people, but your partner wants to keep the relationship exclusive; you think a paper you've written is fine, but your instructor wants it changed. There's no end to the number and kinds of disagreements possible.

University students have an average of seven arguments per week, and most have argued with the other person before, often about the same topic.[5] In another survey, 81 percent of the respondents acknowledged that they had conflicts with friends.[6] Conflict can be even more frequent in families. Researchers recorded dinner conversations for 52 families and found an average of 3.3 "conflict episodes" per meal.[7]

At first this might seem depressing. But it's not the conflict that's bad, it's how the conflict is handled. Conflict is a natural part of meaningful relationships, and you can change the way you approach it.

Conflict Can Be Beneficial

Because we can't avoid conflicts, the challenge is to handle them well. Effective communication during conflicts can actually keep good relationships strong. People who use constructive problem-solving strategies are more satisfied with their relationships[8] and with the outcomes of their conflicts.[9]

The best evidence of how constructive conflict skills can benefit a relationship focuses on spousal communication. More than 20 years of research shows that both happy and unhappy marriages have conflicts, but they manage it differently.[10] Another study revealed that unhappy couples argue in ways that are considered destructive.[11] They focus on defending themselves rather than being problem-oriented, they don't listen to each other, they don't empathize with each other, they use evaluative "you" language, and they ignore each other's nonverbal messages.

Satisfied couples see disagreement as healthy and recognize that conflicts need to be faced.[12] Although they may argue vigorously, they use perception checking and let each other know that they understand the other side of the dispute.[13] They willingly admit mistakes and try to solve the problem at hand.

Before reviewing the communication skills that make conflicts constructive, we need to examine how individuals handle conflict.

LO2
Conflict Styles

Most people have "default" styles of handing conflict (see **Figure 10.1**). These habitual styles work sometimes but they won't work in all situations. For example, check out how Jess and Marie manage a problem.

For more than a year, running partners Jess and Marie have run three times a week and spent an hour working out. Equally matched, they challenge one another to cover longer distances at quicker rates. Over the year,

their friendship has grown to include personal matters that they don't share with anyone else.

Recently, Marie invited less athletic friends to join them and Jess finds the workouts less satisfying and fears losing his one-on-one time with Marie. When he shared his concerns with her, she said, "I don't see the problem. We still get plenty of time on the road, and you said you like my friends." "But it isn't the same," replied Jess.

This situation has all the elements of a conflict: expressed struggle, perceived incompatible goals, apparently scarce resources (they only have so much time for running), and interdependence (They enjoy one another's company and run better together than apart.).

They could approach the conflict in one of five ways:

1. They could say, "Let's forget it," and stop running together.

2. Jess could give in, sacrificing his desire for one-on-one conversations and challenging runs. Or Marie could give in, sacrificing her friendships to maintain her friendship with Jess.

3. One or the other could issue an ultimatum: "Either we do it my way, or we stop running together."

4. They could compromise, inviting friends along on some runs but excluding them on other days.

5. Marie and Jess could brainstorm ways they could run with her friends and still get their workouts and one-on-one time with each other.

These approaches represent the five styles depicted in **Figure 10.1**, each of which is described in the following paragraphs.

FIGURE 10.1
Conflict Styles

Adapted from W.W. Wilmot & J. L. Hocker (2010). *Interpersonal Conflict* (8th ed.). New York: McGraw-Hill.

x

Avoiding (Lose–Lose)

Avoiding occurs when people nonassertively stay away from conflict. You can avoid someone physically or conversationally (changing the topic, joking, denying that a problem exists), but this approach has its costs. It is much more difficult for partners of "self-silencers" to deal with conflict constructively.[14]

Avoidance reflects the attitude that there's no good way to resolve an issue, and some avoiders figure that it's just easier to put up with the problem. In all, avoiding generally results in *lose–lose* outcomes where neither party gets what it wants.

In Jess and Marie's case, avoiding means that, rather than struggling with their disagreement, they would stop running together. Although it wouldn't seem like fighting, they would lose their running partner and good friend. This "solution" shows how avoidance can produce lose–lose results.

Although avoiding may keep the peace, it typically leads to unsatisfying relationships.[15] As misunderstandings, resentments, and disappointments pile up, the communication climate becomes contaminated. It seems that avoiders have a low concern both for their own needs as well as the other person's needs (see **Figure 10.1**).

But avoiding isn't always a bad idea.[16] You might avoid certain topics or situations when the risk of speaking up is too great or if the relationship isn't worth the effort. In close relationships, avoidance is logical if the issue is temporary or minor. This explains why communication between happily married couples is characterized by "selectively ignoring" the other person's minor flaws.[17] This doesn't mean that you should avoid *all* conflicts, but rather that you should conserve energy for the important ones.

Avoiding
A lose–lose conflict style in which the parties ignore the problem at hand.

Accommodating
A win–lose conflict style in which the communicator submits to a situation rather than attempting to have his or her needs met.

Accommodating (Lose–Win)

Accommodating occurs when you give in to others rather than asserting your own point of view. **Figure 10.1** depicts accommodators as having low concern for themselves and high concern for others, resulting in *lose–win,* "we'll do it your way" outcomes. For example, Jess could accommodate Marie by letting her friends join their runs, even though it reduced the physical challenge and the quality time with Marie—or Marie could accommodate Jess by running with just him.

The accommodator's motive plays a significant role in this style's effectiveness. If accommodation is genuine, then chances are it will enhance the relationship. Most people appreciate those who "take one for the team" or "lose the battle to win the war." However, people are less appreciative of those who habitually play the "martyr."[18]

> ### The best of us must sometimes eat our words.
>
> —J.K. Rowling

It's important to mention that culture can affect perceptions of conflict styles. People from high-context, collectivistic backgrounds, such as many Asian cultures, are likely to regard avoidance and accommodation as face-saving and noble ways to handle conflict.[19] In low-context, individualistic cultures, such as Canada, avoidance and accommodation are perceived less positively and people who give up or give in during conflicts are considered "pushovers" or "doormats." The point is that all conflict styles have value in certain situations and culture influences how each style is valued.

Competing (Win–Lose)

The flip side of accommodating is **competing**. This *win–lose* approach involves high concern for self and low concern for others. As **Figure 10.1** shows, competition seeks to resolve conflicts "my way." If Marie and Jess tried to force the other to concede, one would prevail—but at the other's expense.

People compete when they see a situation as an "either-or" one: Either I get what I want or you get what you want. You see this in most conflicts that require a winner and a loser. Some interpersonal issues also fit into this win–lose framework, such as two co-workers seeking a promotion to the same job. Only one can be promoted.

Sometimes competition can enhance relationships. For example, men and women in satisfying dating relationships use competition to enrich their interaction.[20] They compete in play (who's the better racquetball player?), in achievement (who gets the better job offer?), and in altruism (who's more romantic?). They develop a shared narrative that defines competition in altruistic terms. But these arrangements can backfire if one partner becomes a gloating winner or a sore loser. If one person tries to get even, it can create a downward competitive spiral that turns into a *lose–lose* relationship.[21]

Power is the distinguishing characteristic in win–lose problem solving because it is necessary to defeat an opponent. There are different types of power, the most obvious of which is physical. There is also real and enforced power. For example, parents threaten children ("Stop misbehaving or I'll send you to your room."), adults threaten each other, ("If you do that one more time, you'll be sorry."), and the legal system threatens those who use physical power: "Follow the rules, or we'll lock you up."

Then there are people who rely on authority of various types to engage in win–lose methods without ever threatening physical coercion. For example, supervisors have authority over assigned working hours, job promotions, and distribution of desirable or undesirable tasks. Teachers can use the power of grades to coerce students to act in desired ways.

The dark side of competition is that it often breeds aggression.[22] Sometimes aggression is obvious, but at other times it can be more subtle. To understand how, read on.

Direct Aggression

Direct aggression occurs when a communicator expresses a criticism or demand that threatens the face of the person at whom it is directed. There are several types of direct aggression: character attacks, competence attacks, physical appearance attacks, maledictions (wishing the other ill fortune), teasing, ridicule, threats, swearing, and nonverbal emblems.[23]

Direct aggression can have a severe impact on the target, making a recipient feel embarrassed, inadequate, humiliated, hopeless, desperate, or depressed.[24] This can result in decreased effectiveness in personal relationships, on the job, and in families.[25] There is also a significant connection between verbal aggression and physical aggression,[26] but even if the attacks never lead to blows, the psychological effects can be devastating. For example, siblings who were teased by a sibling report less satisfaction and trust than those whose relationships are free of such aggression.[27] And high school teams with aggressive coaches lose more games than teams with less aggressive coaches.[28]

Passive Aggression

Passive aggression occurs when a communicator expresses hostility in an obscure

> **Competing**
> A win–lose approach to conflicts that seeks to resolve them in one's own way.
>
> **Direct aggression**
> A criticism or demand that threatens the face of the person at whom it is directed.
>
> **Passive aggression**
> An indirect expression of aggression that occurs when a communicator expresses hostility in an obscure or manipulative way.

or manipulative way. This behaviour has been termed "crazymaking," and it occurs when people have feelings of resentment, anger, or rage that they are unable or unwilling to express directly. Instead of keeping them to themselves, crazymakers send aggressive messages in subtle, indirect ways, thus maintaining the front of kindness. But the façade eventually crumbles, and crazymaker's victims feel confused and angry for having been fooled. In response, they either react with aggressive behaviour or retreat to nurse their hurt feelings.

Passive aggression seldom has anything but harmful effects on a relationship.[29] If Marie took a passive-aggressive approach toward Jess, she might show up late just to annoy him. Jess could become passive-aggressive by agreeing to include Marie's friends, then pouring on the speed and leaving them behind.

Dirty Fighting with Crazymakers

Psychologist George Bach uses the term *crazymakers* to describe passive-aggressive behaviour. His term reflects the insidious nature of indirect aggression, which can confuse and anger a victim who may not even be aware of being victimized. Although a case can be made for using all the other approaches to conflict described in this chapter, it is difficult to find a justification for passive-aggressive crazymaking.

The following categories represent a nonexhaustive list of crazymaking. They are presented here as a warning for potential victims, who might choose to use perception checking, "I" language, assertion, or other communication strategies to explore whether the user has a complaint that can be addressed in a more constructive manner.

The Avoider Avoiders refuse to fight. When a conflict arises, they leave, fall asleep, pretend to be busy at work, or keep from facing the problem in some other way. Because avoiders won't fight back, this strategy can frustrate the person who wants to address an issue.

The Pseudoaccommodator Pseudoaccommodators pretend to give in and then continue to act in the same way.

The Guiltmaker Instead of expressing dissatisfaction directly, guiltmakers try to make others feel responsible for causing pain. A guiltmaker's favourite line is, "It's OK; don't worry about me . . ." accompanied by a big sigh.

The Mind Reader Instead of allowing their partners to express feelings honestly, mind readers go into character analysis, explaining what the partner really means or what's wrong with the partner. By behaving this way, mind readers refuse to handle their own feelings and leave no room for their partners to express themselves.

The Trapper Trappers play an especially dirty trick by setting up a desired behaviour for their partners and then, when it's met, attacking the very behaviour they requested. An example of this technique is for the trapper to say, "Let's be totally honest with each other," and then attack the partner's self-disclosure.

The Crisis Tickler Crisis ticklers almost bring what's bothering them to the surface but never quite come out and express themselves. Instead of admitting concern about finances, they innocently ask, "Gee, how much did that cost?" dropping a rather obvious hint but never really dealing with the crisis.

The Gunnysacker These people don't share complaints as they arise. Instead, they put their resentments into a psychological gunnysack, which after a while begins to bulge with both large and small gripes. Then, when the sack is about to burst, the gunnysacker pours out all the pent-up aggressions on the overwhelmed and unsuspecting victim.

The Trivial Tyrannizer Instead of honestly sharing their resentments, trivial tyrannizers do things they know will get their partners' goat—leaving dirty dishes in the sink, clipping fingernails in bed, belching out loud, turning up the television too loud, and so on.

The Beltliner Everyone has a psychological "beltline," and below it are subjects too sensitive to be approached without damaging the relationship. Beltlines may have to do with physical characteristics, intelligence, past behaviour, or deeply ingrained personality traits that a person is trying to overcome. In an attempt to "get even" or hurt their partners, beltliners will use intimate knowledge to hit below the belt, where they know it will hurt.

The Joker Because they are afraid to face conflicts squarely, jokers kid around when their partners want to be serious, thus blocking the expression of important feelings.

The Withholder Instead of expressing their anger honestly and directly, withholders punish their partners by keeping back something—courtesy, affection, good cooking, humour, sex. As you can imagine, this is likely to build up even greater resentments in the relationship.

The Benedict Arnold These characters get back at their partners by sabotage, by failing to defend them from attackers, and even by encouraging ridicule or disregard from outside the relationship.

For more information about crazymaking, see G. Bach & Peter Wyden (1968). *The Intimate Enemy.* New York: Avon; and G. Bach (1971). *Aggression Lab: The Fair Fight Manual.* Dubuque, IA: Kendall-Hunt.

Compromising (Partial Lose–Lose)

A **compromise** gives both people some of what they want and is used when it seems that partial satisfaction is the best they can hope for. For example, Jess and Marie could strike a "halfway" deal to alternate workouts with and without her friends. Unlike avoidance, where both parties lose because they don't address their problem, in a compromise "you win some, you lose some" in the negotiation.

Compromising is sometimes touted as an effective way to handle conflicts because it's better than losing everything.[30] Although compromises may be the best obtainable result in some conflicts, it's important to realize that if both parties worked harder, they could obtain even better solutions.

Some compromises are bad. Consider the conflict between one person's desire to smoke and another's need for clean air. The win–lose outcomes of this issue are obvious: Either the smoker abstains or the nonsmoker gets polluted lungs. But a compromise in which the smoker gets to enjoy a rare cigarette and the nonsmoker must inhale some fumes is hardly better. The costs involved in other compromises are even greater. If a divorced couple compromises on child care by haggling over custody and then grudgingly agrees to split the time with their children, it's hard to say that anybody has won.

However, some compromises can satisfy both parties. If you and a friend want to see a movie but neither agrees with the other's first choice, you could compromise if both of you had the same second choice and decided on that one. Or, you may pay a little more for a car than you wanted but much less than the salesperson asked originally. That would be a good outcome for you. Compromising is an effective way to resolve a conflict if everyone is happy with the solution.

> Cooperation is not a
> one-way street.
>
> —Maurice Duplessis,
> favourite phrase used in speeches as
> premier of Quebec, 1936–39, 1944–59

Collaborating (Win–Win)

Collaborating seeks win–win solutions and collaborators demonstrate a high degree of concern for themselves and others. They try to find solutions that meet everyone's needs. If Marie and Jess collaborate, they might come around to seeing that they can continue their one-on-one workouts but invite Marie's friends to join at the end of each run. They might have some less challenging workouts that include the friends, or they could to get together with Marie's friends at other times.

"My parents have decided to homeschool me, but they haven't decided which home."

Peter C. Vey/The New Yorker Collection/The Cartoon Bank

Not only do the partners avoid trying to win at the other's expense, but they also try to find solutions that go beyond a mere compromise. Here are some examples:

- Jason and Jennifer of Barrie, Ontario, were planning their first vacation. Jason, a golf enthusiast, wanted to head for Banff, while Jennifer, who had never seen the ocean, was thinking of Vancouver. Neither was interested in the other's vacation plans. After checking online together, they realized that both of their needs could be met on Prince Edward Island. With several golf courses and plenty of warm, sandy beaches, they opted for Cavendish Beach. And, as a bonus, they would be within walking distance of the popular Anne of Green Gables site.
- Celine, a store manager, hated rescheduling employee work shifts to accommodate their social and family needs. She and her staff developed an arrangement where employees organized schedule swaps on their own and then notified her in writing.

The point is not that these solutions are the correct ones for everybody with similar problems. The win–win method is an approach to help you find just the right answer for your unique problem. By generating win–win solutions, you can tailor-make a way of resolving your conflicts that everyone can live with comfortably.

Which Style to Use?

Collaborating might seem like the ideal approach to solving problems, but it's an oversimplification to imagine that there is a single "best" way.[31] Generally speaking, win–win approaches are preferable to

Compromising
An approach to conflict resolution in which both parties attain at least part of what they wanted through self-sacrifice.

Collaborating
A conflict management style that seeks win–win solutions.

TABLE 10.1

Factors to Consider When Choosing the Most Appropriate Conflict Style

Avoiding (lose–lose)	Accommodating (lose–win)	Competing (win–lose)	Compromising (partial lose–lose)	Collaborating (win–win)
When the issue is of little importance	When you discover you are wrong	When there is not enough time to seek a win–win outcome	When you want quick, temporary solutions to complex problems	When the issue is too important for a compromise
When the costs of confrontation outweigh the benefits	When the issue is more important to the other person than it is to you	When the issue is not important enough to negotiate at length	When opponents are strongly committed to mutually exclusive goals	When a long-term relationship between you and the other person is important
When you want to cool down and gain perspective	When the long-term cost of winning isn't worth the short-term gain	When the other person is not willing to cooperate	When the issues are moderately important but not enough for a stalemate	When you want to merge insights with someone who has a different perspective on the problem
	When you want to build up credits for later conflicts	When you are convinced that your position is right and necessary	When collaboration doesn't work	When you want to show commitment to the concerns of both parties
	When you want to let others learn from their own mistakes	When you want to protect yourself against those who take advantage of noncompetitive people		When you want to create unique solutions to problems

Adapted from W.W. Wilmot & J. L. Hocker (2010). *Interpersonal Conflict* (8th ed). New York: McGraw-Hill.

win–lose and lose–lose solutions, but there are times when avoiding, accommodating, and so forth are appropriate (see **Table 10.1**). To decide which approach to use, consider several factors:

1. **The relationship.** Accommodation is the best approach when someone else has more power than you. If the boss tells you to fill that order "*Now!*" a more assertive response ("I'm still tied up with yesterday's work.") might be reasonable but may cost you your job.

2. **The situation.** Different situations call for different conflict styles. After haggling over the price of a car for hours, it might be best to compromise and split the difference. In other cases, it may be a matter of sticking to your principle and attempting to get what you believe is right.

3. **The other person.** In some cases, the other person is unwilling or can't collaborate. Some people are so competitive that they put winning ahead of everything else. In such cases, your efforts to collaborate may have little chance of success.

4. **Your goals.** Sometimes your concern may be to calm an enraged person. Accommodating an outburst from your crotchety sick neighbour, for example, is probably better than shouting back and triggering a stroke. In still other cases, your moral principles might compel an aggressive statement even though it might not get you what you originally sought: "I've had enough of your racist jokes. I've tried to explain why they're so offensive, but you obviously haven't listened. I'm leaving!"

LO3
Conflict in Relational Systems

The style you choose isn't the only factor that determines how conflicts unfold. In reality, conflict is relational: Its character is usually determined by the way the parties interact with each other.[32] You may, for example, plan to hint to a professor that you are bothered by her apparent indifference but wind up discussing the matter in an open, assertive way

Jupiterimages/Stockbyte/Thinkstock

in reaction to her constructive response. This example suggests that conflict also depends on how the partners interact.

When two or more people are in a long-term relationship they develop a **relational conflict style**—a pattern of managing disagreements that repeats itself over time. The mutual influence that parties have on one another is so powerful that it can overcome a disposition to handle conflicts in a particular way.[33] Some relational conflict styles are constructive, while others can make life miserable.

Complementary, Symmetrical, and Parallel Styles

Partners in interpersonal and impersonal relationships can use one of three styles to manage their conflicts. In a **complementary conflict style**, partners use different but mutually reinforcing behaviours. In a **symmetrical conflict style**, both partners use the same tactics. In a **parallel conflict style**, the style shifts between complementary and symmetrical. **Table 10.2** illustrates how the same conflict could unfold in very different ways, depending on the style used to deal with it.

Research shows that a complementary "fight–flight" style is common in many unhappy marriages. One partner—most commonly the wife—addresses the conflict directly, whereas the other—usually the husband—withdraws.[34] This pattern can lead to a cycle of increasing hostility and isolation because each partner punctuates the conflict differently. "I withdraw because she's so critical," a husband might say, while the wife organizes it as "I criticize because he withdraws."

Some distressed marriages suffer from destructively symmetrical communication. If both partners treat each other with matching hostility, one threat or insult leads to another in an escalatory spiral. If the partners withdraw instead of facing their problems, a de-escalatory spiral results, leaving neither partner satisfied with the relationship.

Relational conflict style
A pattern of managing disagreements that repeats itself over time in a relationship.

Complementary conflict style
A relational conflict style in which partners use different but mutually reinforcing behaviours.

Symmetrical conflict style
A relational conflict style in which both partners use the same tactics.

Parallel conflict style
A relational conflict style in which the approach of the partners varies from one situation to another.

TABLE 10.2
Complementary and Symmetrical Conflict Styles

Situation	Complementary Styles	Symmetrical Styles
Example 1 Wife upset because husband is spending little time at home.	Wife complains; husband withdraws, spending even less time at home. (Destructive)	Wife complains. Husband responds angrily and defensively. (Destructive)
Example 2 Female employee offended when male boss calls her "sweetie."	Employee objects to boss, explaining her reasons for being offended. Boss apologizes for his unintentional insult. (Constructive)	Employee maliciously "jokes" about boss at company party. (Destructive)
Example 3 Parents uncomfortable with teenager's new friends.	Parents express concerns. Teen dismisses them, saying, "There's nothing to worry about." (Destructive)	Teen expresses discomfort with parents' protectiveness. Parents and teen negotiate a mutually agreeable solution. (Constructive)

As **Table 10.2** shows, both complementary and symmetrical behaviours can produce "good" results as well as "bad" results. If the complementary behaviours are positive, then a positive spiral results and the conflict stands a good chance of being resolved. This is the case in Example 2 in **Table 10.2**, where the boss is open to hearing the employee's concerns. Here, a complementary talk–listen pattern works well.

Symmetrical styles can also be beneficial. The clearest example of constructive symmetry occurs when both parties communicate assertively, listen to each other's concerns, and work together to resolve them. The potential for this sort of solution occurs in Example 3, in the parent–teenager conflict. With enough mutual respect and careful listening, both the parents and their teenager can understand one another's concerns and very possibly find a way to give both parties what they want.

Destructive Conflict Patterns

The uses of some conflict styles are so caustic that they almost guarantee relationship failure. John Gottman spent decades gathering data on recently wed couples and found four such destructive patterns.[35] Here are the four signs to watch for.

1. **Criticism.** These are attacks on a person's character. There's a distinctive difference in pointing out a behaviour you dislike and presenting it as an assault on the person's character. For example, it's one thing to say, "I don't like it when you leave your dirty laundry all over the bathroom because sometimes my friends see it and that embarrasses me," as opposed to, "You're such a pig to live with. You're disgusting!"

2. **Defensiveness.** Recall that defensiveness is a reaction that aims to protect one's presenting self by denying responsibility ("You're crazy; I never do that.") or counterattacking ("You're more of a slob than I am.") While some self-protection is necessary, never acknowledging another's complaints leads to real problems.

3. **Contempt.** Contemptuous communication belittles and demeans and it occurs verbally (name calling, putdowns) and nonverbally (eye rolling, disgusted sighs). Doing both simultaneously can be truly dismissive.

4. **Stonewalling.** This occurs when one person withdraws from the interaction and shuts down the dialogue which, in turn, makes resolving the problem impossible.

Conflict ritual
An unacknowledged repeating pattern of interlocking behaviour used by participants in a conflict.

Here is a brief exchange that shows how using these styles can lead to a destructive spiral of aggression:

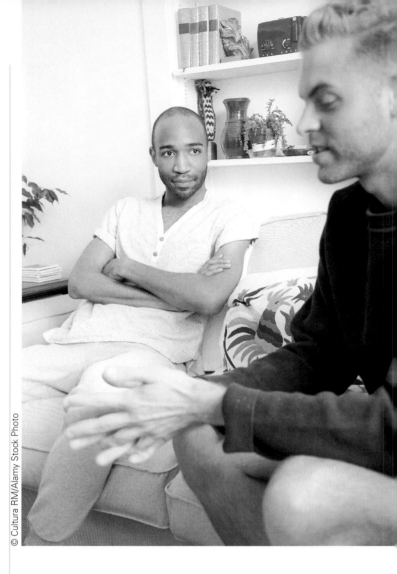

© Cultura RM/Alamy Stock Photo

"You overdrew on our account again—can't you do anything right? (*Criticism*)

"Hey, don't blame me—you're the one who spends most of the money." (*Defensiveness*)

"At least I have better math skills than a first grader. Way to go, Einstein." (*Contempt*)

"Whatever." (said while walking out of the room) (*Stonewalling*)

Using these styles not only poisons relationships, but they also lead to destructive conflict rituals, which are discussed next.

Conflict Rituals

When people have been in a relationship for some time, their communication often develops into **conflict rituals**—usually unacknowledged but very real patterns of interlocking behaviour.[36] Consider a few common rituals:

- A young child interrupts her parents, demanding to be included in their conversation. The parents tell the child to wait, but she whines and cries so much that they listen rather than ignore the fussing.

- A couple fights. One partner leaves. The other accepts the blame for the problem and begs forgiveness. When the partner returns, they have a happy reunion. Soon they fight again.
- A boss flies into rage when the pressure builds at work. Recognizing this, employees avoid him as much as possible. When the crisis is over, the boss compensates by being especially receptive to employee requests.

There's nothing inherently wrong with the interaction in many rituals, especially when those involved accept them as ways of managing conflict.[37] Consider the preceding examples. The little girl's whining may be the only way to get the parents' attention. In the second, both partners might use fighting to blow off steam, viewing the grief of separation as worth the joy of a reunion. The third ritual might help the boss release pressure and the employees to get their requests met.

Rituals cause problems when they are the *only* means used to handle conflicts. Competent communicators have a large repertoire of behaviours and select the most effective response for a given situation. Relying on one ritual pattern to handle all conflicts is no more effective than putting the same seasoning in every dish you cook. Although some rituals may be familiar and comfortable, they're not likely to resolve the various conflicts you will encounter.

Variables in Conflict Styles

Along with the differences that arise in individual relationships, there are two powerful variables that affect the way people manage conflict: gender and culture.

Frank Gaertner/Shutterstock.com

Gender

A look at the entire body of research on gender and conflict suggests that the differences in how individuals who identify as female, male, or otherwise handle conflict are relatively small, and sometimes different from the stereotypical picture of aggressive men and passive women.[38] People *think* there are more differences in male and female ways of handling conflicts than there actually are.[39] Having said that, however, you may be interested in learning some of the differences that have been found.

Studies of children from preschool to early adolescence show that boys try to get their way by ordering one another around ("Gimme your arm"), while girls will begin proposals with the word *let's* ("Let's go find some").[40] Although boys tell each other what role to take in pretend play ("Come on, be a doctor"), girls either ask what one each person wants or make a joint proposal ("We can both be doctors"). Furthermore, boys often make demands without offering an explanation, whereas girls provide reasons for their suggestions ("We gotta clean 'em first . . . 'cause they got germs.").

But some adolescent girls also use aggression in conflicts, although their methods are less direct. While verbal showdowns and physical fights are common in teenage boys, girls resort to gossip, backbiting, and social exclusion,[41] which can be just as destructive as the tactics boys use. The film *Mean Girls,* based on the book *Queen Bees and Wannabes,*[42] offers a vivid depiction of just how injurious these indirect assaults can be. However, as one reviewer so aptly noted, "Not all teenage girls are like this!"

Invitation to Insight

Your Conflict Rituals

Describe two conflict rituals in one of your important relationships. One of your examples should consist of a positive ritual and the other of a negative ritual. For each example, explain

1. A subject that is likely to trigger the conflict (money, leisure time, affection)
2. The behaviour of one partner that initiates the ritual
3. The series of responses by both partners that follow the initiating event
4. How the ritual ends

Based on your description, explain an alternative to the unsatifying ritual and describe how you could change the way you manage the conflict to a more satisfying way.

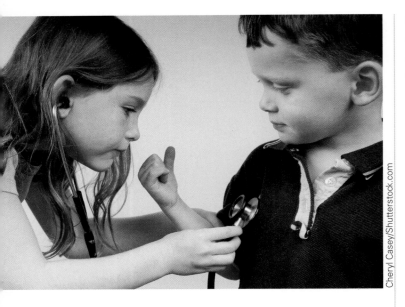

Cheryl Casey/Shutterstock.com

Another gender study found that female and male college students view conflicts in contrasting ways.[43] Regardless of their cultural background, female students saw men as more concerned with power and content than relational issues. By contrast, women were described as more concerned with maintaining the relationship during a conflict. When the conflict behaviours of both sexes are observed, women are more assertive about expressing their ideas and feelings, and men are more likely to withdraw from discussing issues.[44] Women tend to view withdrawal from conflict as more injurious to a relationship than do men (which is why it is more common for women to say, "We *have* to talk about this").[45] When it comes to breaking up a romantic relationship, women are more likely to see that a breakup is coming[46] and they are more likely than men to terminate a romantic relationship.[47]

© iStockphoto.com/urbancow

Culture

The way people manage conflict also depends on their cultural background. For instance, the straight-talking, assertive approach that is common across North America is not the universal norm.[48]

An orientation toward individualism or collectivism is the most important cultural influence on conflict.[49] In individualistic cultures like Canada's, the goals, rights, and needs of each person are considered important and individuals have the right to stand up for themselves. In collectivistic cultures—more common in Latin America and Asia—the group's concerns are more important than the individual's needs. The assertive behaviour that might seem perfectly appropriate in North America would be considered rude and insensitive in collectivistic cultures.

Another factor is the difference between high- and low-context cultural styles.[50] Low-context cultures like Canada's place a premium on being direct and literal. By contrast, high-context cultures like Japan's avoid confrontation and value self-restraint. Communicators in these cultures derive meaning from the context, social conventions, and hints. Preserving and honouring the other's person's face is a prime goal, and communicators go to great lengths to avoid embarrassing a conversational partner. In Japan, for example, even a simple request like "Close the door" would be too straightforward.[51] Instead, an indirect statement like "It is somewhat cold today" would be used. People in Japan are also reluctant to say no to a request. They would be likely to say, "Let me think about it for a while," which would be recognized as a refusal in Japan.

When people from different cultures face a conflict, their habitual communication patterns may not mesh smoothly. The challenge faced by a Canadian husband and his Taiwanese wife illustrates this sort of problem. The husband would try to confront his wife verbally and directly (as is typical in the Canada), leading her to either become defensive or withdraw completely from the discussion. She, on the other hand, would attempt to indicate her displeasure by changes in mood and eye contact (typical of Chinese culture) that were either not noticed (or uninterpretable) by her husband. Thus, neither "his way" nor "her way" was working and they could not see any realistic way to "compromise."[52]

Other cultural differences also influence conflict. Canadians visiting Greece, for example, often think they are witnessing an argument when they're overhearing a friendly conversation.[53] A comparative study of North American and Italian nursery school children showed that one of the Italian children's favourite pastimes was a kind of heated debating that Italians call *discussione* but what we would regard as arguing. Within Canada, the ethnic background of communicators also plays a role. Dolores Francis, a Mi'kmaq student, explained how there was really no need to adopt the communication patterns offered in this text because conflict is rare in her culture. When children say or do inappropriate things, for

Cultural Style

I work with clients from a variety of cultures. At one recent workshop in Dubai, we hosted attendees from countries including Sweden, India, Brazil, Germany, China, Iraq, Iran, Israel, South Africa, Poland, Japan, and Canada.

People all around the world have the same powerful emotions: pride, concern, fear, and anger. But the way they *deal* with those emotions is often shaped by their background. For example, some cultures deal with conflict head on, while others handle it much more indirectly. Some cultures are open to change, while others resist changing communication patterns that have been practiced for centuries.

When working with people from a different background, a lot of behaviour can seem odd, disturbing, or even offensive. "Why won't she speak up?" one person might think. "Why is he so loud and aggressive?" the other might wonder.

A major part of my training is to help people from different cultural backgrounds slow down when they encounter others with different conflict styles so they don't overreact. Instead of responding before you understand the other person's personal style and cultural background, it's better to adopt an attitude of curiosity. Be an observer and a listener: Try to find out how that stranger feels, and why. Get in the habit of saying, "Please help me understand ...." Being genuinely interested in the other person is a sign of respect, and that's very disarming. Once you understand why people are behaving as they do, their "strange" actions usually make more sense.

Techniques like these won't resolve every conflict, but they can make working together more smooth, satisfying, and productive.

Courtesy of Marilynn Jorgensen, Master Trainer/ICF Coach, Six Seconds, www.6seconds.org.

example, adults don't reprimand them because it would shame them. Instead, parents talk to the child in private about appropriate behaviour. Out of respect for their parents, the children wouldn't engage in the disorderly behaviour again. When Delores has a conflict with a First Nations person, she would describe the problem using one word, but she would have to use several with a non-Aboriginal person. In her words, "They would go on and on." To adapt to the non-Aboriginal approach, she must exaggerate, which runs contrary to her cultural norms. It's easy to imagine how two friends, lovers, or co-workers from different cultural backgrounds might have trouble finding a compatible conflict style.

Despite cultural differences, it's important to realize that our approach to conflict may be biological.[54]

Furthermore, scholarship suggests that the self-concept is more powerful than culture in determining conflict style.[55] For example, assertive individuals raised in environments that downplay conflict are likely to be more aggressive than unassertive persons growing up in cultures where conflict is common. You might handle conflicts calmly at work, where civility is the norm, but shriek like a banshee at home if that's how your family deals with conflict.

LO4
Constructive Conflict Skills

Although the win–win conflict style described earlier has many advantages over win–lose and lose–lose approaches, it is rarely used. There are three reasons for this. The first is lack of awareness. Some people are so used to competition that they mistakenly think that they have to win at all costs. Second, because conflict is accompanied by emotion, people don't stop to think of better alternatives. Therefore, it's often necessary to stop yourself from speaking out aggressively and starting an escalating spiral of defensiveness. The time-honoured advice of "counting to 10" applies here. This provides time to *act* constructively instead of *reacting* in a way that's likely to produce a lose–lose outcome.

A third reason win–win solutions are rare is that they require the other person's cooperation. It's difficult to negotiate constructively when someone insists on defeating you. In this case, use your best persuasive skills to explain that by working together you can find a solution that satisfies both of you.

Collaborative Problem Solving

Despite the challenges of the win–win approach, you can get better at resolving conflicts by trying the method below. It will increase your chances of being able to handle your conflicts in a collaborative, win–win manner.

1. Identify Your Problem and Unmet Needs

The first part of this step is to recognize that *you* have the problem because you're the one who's dissatisfied. Whether you want to return an unsatisfactory piece of merchandise or request a change in working conditions, the problem is yours because you paid for the defective article while the merchant has had the use of your good money, or you are the one who is unhappy with your working conditions, not your employer.

Realizing this will make a big difference when the time comes to approach the other party. Instead of feeling and acting in an evaluative way, you'll be more likely to state your problem in a descriptive way. This will reduce the chance of a defensive reaction.

After you realize that the problem is yours, the next step is to identify the unmet needs that make you dissatisfied. This isn't as simple as it seems. Behind the apparent content of an issue is often a relational need. Consider this example:

> A friend hasn't returned some money you lent long ago. Your apparent need is to get the cash back, but even if you were rolling in money, your unmet need might be *to avoid feeling victimized by your friend's taking advantage of you.*

As you'll soon see, the ability to identify your real needs plays a key role in resolving interpersonal problems. Before you voice your problem to your partner, or your employer, you ought to be clear about which of your needs aren't being met.

2. Make a Date

Destructive fights often start because the initiator confronts a partner who isn't ready. The person might be fatigued, in a hurry, upset over another problem, or not feeling well. At such times, it's unfair to "jump" a person without notice and expect to get their full attention. Instead, you'll probably have a row.

After you clarify the problem, approach your partner with a request to try to solve it. For example, "Something's been bothering me. Can we talk?" If the answer is yes, you're ready to go further. If it isn't the right time to confront your partner, find a time that's suitable for both of you.

3. Describe Your Problem and Needs

Your partner can't possibly meet your needs without knowing why you're upset or what you want. Therefore, describe your problem as specifically as possible. The best way to deliver a complete, accurate message is to use the assertive message format discussed in Chapter 9. Notice how well this approach works in the following examples:

Example 1

"I have a problem. It's about you leaving dirty clothes around the house after I've told you how much it bothers me (*behaviour*). It's a problem because I have to run around like crazy and pick things up whenever guests come (*consequence*). I'm starting to think that either you're not paying attention to my requests or you're trying to drive me crazy (*thoughts*), and either way I'm getting more and more resentful (*feeling*). I'd like to find some way to have a neat place without my having to be a maid or a nag."

Example 2

"Something is bothering me. When you tell me you love me and yet spend almost all your free time with your other friends (*behaviour*), I wonder whether you mean it (*thought*). I get insecure (*feeling*), and then I start getting moody (*consequence*). I need some way to find how you really feel about me (*intention*)."

After stating your problem and describing what you need, it's important to make sure that your partner has understood what you've said. As you can remember from the discussion of listening in Chapter 7, there's a good chance—especially in a stressful conflict—that your words will be misinterpreted. Therefore, you might try saying, "I'm not sure I expressed myself very well just now. Maybe you should tell what you heard me say so I can be sure I got it right." In any case, be sure that your

"Is this a good time to have a big fight?"

David Sipress/The New Yorker Collection/The Cartoon Bank

racorn/Shutterstock.com

partner understands your whole message before going any further. Legitimate arguments are tough enough without getting upset about a conflict that doesn't even exist.

4. Consider Your Partner's Point of View

The next step is to find out what your partner needs to feel satisfied. This is important because the other person has just as much right as you to feel satisfied. If you expect help in meeting your needs, it's reasonable that you behave in the same way. But in addition to fairness, an unhappy partner will make it hard for you to become satisfied and a happy partner will be more likely to cooperate in letting you reach your goals. Thus, it's in your own self-interest to discover and meet your partner's needs.

You can learn your partner's needs simply by asking: "Now I've told you what I want and why. Tell me what you need to feel OK about this." Once your partner begins to talk, use your listening skills to make sure that you understand.

5. Negotiate a Solution

Now that you and your partner understand each other's needs, the goal becomes finding a way to meet them. The next step is to negotiate a solution by using a modification of Thomas Gordon's approach as outlined in *Parent Effectiveness Training*.[56]

1. ***Identify and define the conflict.*** This consists of discovering each person's problem and needs, thus setting the stage for meeting all of them.

2. ***Generate a number of possible solutions.*** You and your partner generate but do not evaluate a list of possible solutions (the key is quantity). Nothing is too crazy or stupid. Sometimes a far-fetched idea will lead to a more workable one.

3. ***Evaluate the alternative solutions.*** Talk about which solutions will work and which ones won't—and be honest. If a solution is going to work, everyone involved has to support it.

4. ***Decide on the best solution.*** Select the solution that looks the best to everyone. Your decision doesn't have to be final, but it should look potentially successful.

6. Follow Up the Solution

After you've tested the solution for a while, take time to discuss its progress. It may need some adjustments, or you may need to rethink the whole problem. The idea is to keep on top of the problem, to keep using creativity to solve it.

To apply this method properly, it's important to follow every step. This prevents misunderstandings and the possibility of degenerating into a negative spiral. Second, realize that in real life this method is not likely to flow smoothly from one step to another. Expect and prepare for a certain amount of resistance from the other person. When a step doesn't meet with success, simply move back and repeat the preceding ones as necessary.

Win–win solutions aren't always possible. There will be times when even the best-intentioned people simply won't be able to find a way of meeting all their needs. In times like these, the process of negotiation has to include some compromises.

Constructive Conflict: Questions and Answers

People often express doubts about how well win–win negotiating works. Four questions typically arise, and they deserve an answer.

Isn't the Win–Win Approach Too Good to Be True?

Research shows that seeking mutual benefit is not only desirable—it works. In a series of experiments, subjects were presented with a bargaining situation called the "prisoner's dilemma" in which they could choose either to cooperate or betray a confederate.[57] There are three outcomes: One partner can win big by betraying a confederate, both can win by cooperating, or both can lose by betraying each other. Although cynics might assume that the most effective strategy is to betray a partner (a win–lose approach), researchers found that cooperation is actually the best hard-nosed strategy. Players who demonstrated their willingness to support their partner and not hold grudges did better than those who took a competitive approach. However, it is impossible to reach a win–win solution when your partner refuses to cooperate.

In Real Life

Win–Win Problem Solving

It is 7:15 a.m. on a typical school day. Chris enters the kitchen and finds the sink full of dirty dishes. It was her roommate Terry's turn to do them. She sighs in disgust and begins to clean up, slamming pots and pans.

Terry Can't you be a little more quiet? I don't have a class till 10:00, and I want to catch up on sleep.

Chris *(Expressing her aggression indirectly in a sarcastic tone of voice)* Sorry to bother you. I was cleaning up last night's dinner dishes.

Terry *(Misses the message)* Well, I wish you'd do it a little more quietly. I was up late studying last night, and I'm beat.

Chris *(Decides to communicate her irritation more directly, if aggressively)* Well, if you'd done the dishes last night, I wouldn't have had to wash them now.

Terry *(Finally realizes that Chris is mad at her, responds defensively)* I was going to do them when I got up. I've got two midterms this week, and I was studying until two last night. What's more important, grades or a spotless kitchen?

Chris *(Perpetuating the growing defensive spiral)* I've got classes too, you know. But that doesn't mean we have to live like pigs!

Terry *(Angrily)* Forget it. If it's such a big deal, I'll never leave another dirty dish!

> Chris and Terry avoid each other as they get ready for school. During the day, Chris realizes that attacking Terry will only make matters worse. She decides on a more constructive approach that evening.

Chris That wasn't much fun this morning. Want to talk about it?

Terry I suppose so. But I'm going out to study with Kim and Alisa in a few minutes.

Chris *(Realizing that it's important to talk at a good time)* If you have to leave soon, let's not get into it now. How about talking when you get back?

Terry OK, if I'm not too tired.

Chris Or we could talk tomorrow before class.

Terry OK.

Later that evening, Terry and Chris continue their conversation.

Chris *(Defines the issue as her problem by using the assertive clear message format)* I hated to start the day with a fight. But I also hate having to do the dishes when it's not my turn *(behaviour)*. It doesn't seem fair for me to do my job and yours *(interpretation)*, and that's why I got so mad *(feeling)* and nagged at you *(consequence)*.

Terry But I was studying! You know how much I have to do. It's not like I was partying.

Chris *(Avoids attacking Terry by sincerely agreeing with the facts and explaining further why she was upset)* I know. It wasn't just doing the dishes that got me upset. It seems like there have been a lot of times when I've done your jobs and mine too.

Terry *(Defensively)* Like when?

Chris *(Gives specific descriptions of Terry's behaviour)* Well, this was the third time this week that I've done the dishes when it's your turn, and I can think of a couple of times lately when I've had to clean up your stuff before people came over.

Terry I don't see why it's such a big deal. If you just leave the stuff there, I'll clean it up.

Chris *(Still trying to explain herself, she continues to use "I" language)* I know you would. I guess it's harder for me to put up with a messy place than it is for you.

Terry Yeah. If you'd just relax, living together would be a lot easier!

Chris *(Resenting Terry's judgmental accusation that the problem is all hers)* Hey, wait a second! Don't blame the whole thing on me. It's just that we have different standards. It looks to you like I'm too hung up on keeping the place clean . . .

Terry Right.

Chris . . . and if we do it your way, then I'd be giving up. I'd have to either live with the place messier than I like it or clean everything up myself. Then I'd get mad at you, and things would be pretty tense around here. *(Describes the unpleasant consequences of not solving the problem in a mutually satisfactory way)*

Terry I suppose so.

Chris We need to figure out how to take care of the apartment in a way we can both live with. *(Describes the broad outline of a win–win solution)*

Terry Yeah.

Chris So what could we do?

Terry *(Sounding resigned)* Look, from now on I'll just do the dishes right away. It isn't worth arguing about.

Chris Sure it is. If you're sore, the apartment may be clean, but it won't be worth it.

Terry *(Skeptically)* OK; what do you suggest?

Chris Well, I'm not sure. You don't want the pressure of having to clean up right away, and I don't want to have to do my jobs and yours, too. Right?

Terry Yeah. *(Still sounding skeptical)* So what are we going to do—hire a housekeeper to clean up?

Chris *(Refusing to let Terry sidetrack the discussion)* That would be great if we could afford it. How about using paper plates? That would make cleaning up from meals easier.

Terry Yeah, but there would still be pots and pans.

Chris Well, it's not a perfect fix, but it might help a little. *(Goes on to suggest other ideas)* How about cooking meals that don't take a lot of work to clean up—maybe more salads and less fried stuff that sticks to pans. That would be a better diet too.

Terry Yeah. I do hate to scrub crusty frying pans. But that doesn't do anything about your wanting the living room picked up all the time, and I bet I still wouldn't keep the kitchen as clean as you like it. Keeping the place super clean just isn't as big a deal to me as it is for you.

Chris That's true, and I don't want to have to nag you! *(Clarifies the end she's seeking)* You know, it's not really cleaning up that bothers me. It's doing more than my share of work. I wonder if there's a way I could be responsible for keeping the kitchen clean and picking up if you could do something else to keep the workload even.

Terry Are you serious? I'd love to get out of doing the dishes! You mean you'd do them . . . and keep the place picked up . . . if I did something else?

Chris As long as the work was equal and you really did your jobs without me having to remind you.

Terry What kind of work would you want me to do?

Chris How about cleaning up the bathroom?

Terry Forget it. That's worse than doing the dishes.

Chris OK. How about cooking?

Terry That might work, but then we'd have to eat together all the time. It's nice to do our own cooking when we want to. It's more flexible that way.

Chris OK. But what about shopping? I hate the time it takes, and you don't mind it that much, do you?

Terry You mean shop for groceries? You'd trade that for cleaning the kitchen?

Chris Sure. And picking up the living room. It takes an hour every time we shop, and we make two trips a week. Doing the dishes would be much quicker.

Terry All right!

The plan didn't work perfectly: At first Terry put off shopping until all the food was gone and Chris took advantage by asking Terry to run other errands during her shopping trips. But their new arrangement proved much more successful than the old arrangement. The apartment was cleaner and the workload more even, which satisfied Chris. Terry was less the object of Chris's nagging and she had no kitchen chores, which made her happier. Just as important, the relationship between Chris and Terry was more comfortable—thanks to win–win problem solving.

Isn't the Win–Win Approach Too Elaborate?

Not really. Once you are familiar with and skilled at using the steps, you can select what you need in a given situation. For important issues, you'll find that every step of the win–win approach is important. If this process seems time-consuming, consider the time and energy that not solving the issue will take.

Isn't Win–Win Negotiating Too Rational?

Some *LOOK* readers say, "Sometimes I'm so angry that I don't care about being supportive or empathetic or anything. I just want to blow my top!" When this occurs, remove yourself from the scene, confide in a third party, or blow off steam through physical exercise. An understanding partner may even allow you to have a

"We're fighting like—well, we're fighting."

Leo Cullum The New Yorker Collection/The Cartoon Bank

"Vesuvius" — an uncontrollable outburst. Let your partner know that you want to find a solution but that you might behave emotionally on occasion.

Is It Possible to Change Others?

Although you won't always be able to gain your partner's cooperation, a good attempt can do the trick most of the time. Showing that it's in the individual's self-interest to work together is key. "Look, if we can't settle this, we'll both feel miserable. But if we can find an answer, think how much better off we'll be." You can boost the odds of getting your partner's cooperation by modelling the communication skills described in this book. And even if this doesn't succeed, you'll gain self-respect by knowing that you behaved honourably and constructively.

Communication in the Workplace

Today's workplace is team-oriented, which means that we encounter conflict. Conflict can be dysfunctional or functional. **Dysfunctional conflict** creates animosity among group members and hinders a group's progress—and it can result in sleep loss. Stephen Mill suggests that if information technology professionals could address interpersonal conflict in the workplace, it would reduce their likelihood of burnout.[58] **Functional conflict**, however, is positive and focuses on issues rather than personalities. For example, a group in charge of developing a workplace behaviour policy might argue over content, implementation, or how to govern it. The more argument there is, the better their final decisions will be, because they will have considered a variety of ideas and potential paths.[59]

To create work environments where functional arguments are encouraged and dysfunctional arguments frowned upon, be mindful of group norms—those unwritten expectations that we have of one another. Negative norms might be using put-down humour or accepting rudeness. Both can have a negative effect. In fact, one study on rudeness in the workplace concluded that it reduced the quality of work, people lost work time trying to avoid people, some people considered leaving, and others actually left their jobs because of rudeness.[60]

Knowing how different cultures handle conflict can help us avoid dysfunctional conflict. For instance, when individuals from individualistic and collectivistic cultures have a sense of where each is coming from, they might develop alternative ways to resolve conflict. The same is true with the notion of saving face. Further, some dysfunctional conflicts can be reduced by recognizing *immigrant syndrome,* caused by struggles with a different language, customs, the adaptations of family members, changes in cultural values, and loss of identity.[61]

Dysfunctional conflict
Conflict that creates animosity, causes interpersonal stress, and hinders a group's progress.

Functional conflict
Positive conflict that focuses on issues rather than personalities.

Another issue, somewhat related to conflict, must also be addressed—bullying. The most obvious form of bullying is direct aggression: abusive language, threats, and even physical displays of anger. Less obvious, but equally damaging bully comes in the form of criticism—nitpicking, unreasonable demands for work, impossible deadlines, and expecting perfection from workers. An even more insidious form of bullying involves sabotage, in which the bully criticizes the victims behind their back. Bosses can also bully by controlling resources such as money, staffing, and time in order to keep employees from being successful.[62]

There was a time, and to a certain extent this still holds true, when bullying was overlooked. Individuals were bullied and witnesses, afraid to get involved and so thankful that they weren't victims, allowed such behaviours to continue. The onus was on the target to deal with the bully. However, this is changing. The new take on bullying is that it's not one person's problem, it's everybody's problem.

As a result, bullying is also being taken seriously in the workplace. For example, the Canadian Union of Public Employees (CUPE) has taken a very active role in eradicating bullying. Each year CUPE locals across the country promote and celebrate the *Day of Pink* to end bullying, discrimination, homophobia, and transphobia. They also support anti-bullying radio ads, support anti-bulling legislation, and encourage respectful schools and workplaces.[63] Such a philosophy, coupled with effective communication skills, is what it is going to take to rid society of bullying.

Picking Your Workplace Battles

Conflicts are a fact of life, even in the best of jobs. Issues are bound to arise with your boss, coworkers, subordinates, and people outside the organization. Your career success and peace of mind will depend on when and how you deal with those conflicts—and when you choose to keep quiet. Deciding when to speak up is the first step in managing conflicts successfully. Staying silent about important issues can damage your career and leave you feeling like a doormat. But asserting yourself too often or in the wrong way can earn you a reputation as a whiner or a hothead. Management consultants offer guidelines to help you choose when to speak up and when to let go of an issue.[64]

Consider a retreat when

- The issue isn't important to your organization or your ability to work.
- You can't offer a constructive approach to solve the problem.
- The issue is outside your area of responsibility.
- The others involved are much more powerful than you

Before speaking up, be prepared to

- Test support for your position informally with trusted colleagues.
- Speak with the person who has the power to do something about the problem.
- Describe the problem clearly and objectively.
- Control your emotions during discussions.
- Deal with criticism that may be directed back at you.

READY TO STUDY?

 MINDTAP

IN THE BOOK, YOU CAN:

❏ Rip out the Chapter in Review card at the back of the book to have the key terms and Learning Objectives handy, and complete the quizzes provided (answers are at the bottom of the back page).

ONLINE YOU CAN:

❏ Stay organized and efficient with MindTap—a single destination with all the course material and study aids you need to succeed. Built-in apps leverage social media and the latest learning technology. For example:

  ❏ Listen to the text using ReadSpeaker.

  ❏ Use pre-populated Flashcards as a jump start for review—or you can create your own.

  ❏ You can highlight text and make notes in your MindTap Reader. Your notes will flow into Evernote, the electronic notebook app that you can access anywhere when it's time to study for the exam.

  ❏ Prepare for tests with a variety of quizzes and activities.

Go to **nelson.com/student** to access these digital resources

Endnotes

1. W. Wilmot & J. L. Hocker (2010). *Interpersonal Conflict*, 8th ed. (pp. 44–56). New York: McGraw-Hill. See also P. M. Buzzanell & N. A. Burrell (1997). "Family & Workplace Conflict: Examining Metaphorical Conflict Schemas & Expressions across Context & Sex." *Human Communication Research*, 24, 109–146.

2. T. Kaur & G. Sokhey (2010). "Conflict resolution and marital satisfaction." *Indian Journal of Community Psychology*, 6, 90–104.

3. Wilmot & Hocker, op cit.. 11–19.

4. For a summary of research detailing the prevalence of conflict in relationships, see W. R. Cupach & D. J. Canary (1997). *Competence in Interpersonal Conflict* (pp. 5–6). New York: McGraw-Hill.

5. W. L. Benoit & P. J. Benoit (1987). "Everyday Argument Practices of Naive Social Actors." In J. Wenzel (Ed.). *Argument and Critical Practices*. Annandale, VA: Speech Communication Association.

6. W. Samter & W. R. Cupach (1998). "Friendly Fire: Topical Variations in Conflict among Same- & Cross-Sex Friends." *Communication Studies*, 49, 121–138.

7. S. Vuchinich (1987). "Starting & Stopping Spontaneous Family Conflicts." *Journal of Marriage and the Family 49*, 591–601.

8. J. M. Gottman (1982). "Emotional Responsiveness in Marital Conversations." *Journal of Communication, 32*, 108–120. See also W. R. Cupach (1982, May). *Communication Satisfaction and Interpersonal Solidarity as Outcomes of Conflict Message Strategy Use.* Paper presented at the International Communication Association conference, Boston.

9. P. Koren, K. Carlton, & D. Shaw (1980). "Marital Conflict: Relations among Behaviours, Outcomes, and Distress." *Journal of Consulting and Clinical Psychology, 48*, 460–468.

10. W. Wilmot & J. L. Hocker (2010). *Interpersonal Conflict*, 8th edn (p. 37). New York: McGraw-Hill.

11. J. M. Gottman (1979). *Marital Interaction: Experimental Investigations.* New York: Academic Press. See also D. A. Infante, S. A. Myers, & R. A. Buerkel (1994). "Argument and Verbal Aggression in Constructive and Destructive Family and Organizational Disagreements." *Western Journal of Communication, 58*, 73–84.

12. S. E. Crohan (1992). "Marital Happiness & Spousal Consensus on Beliefs about Marital Conflict: A Longitudinal Investigation." *Journal of Science and Personal Relationships, 9*, 89–102.

13. D. J. Canary, H. Weger, Jr., & L. Stafford (1991). "Couples' Argument Sequences and Their Associations with Relational Characteristics." *Western Journal of Speech Communication, 55*, 159–179.

14. M. S. Harper and D.P. Welsh (2007). "Keeping Quiet: Self-Silencing and Its Association with Relational and Individual Functioning among Adolescent Romantic Couples." *Journal of Social & Personal Relationships, 24*, 99–116.

15. T. D. Afifi, T. McManus, K. Steuber, & A. Coho (2009). "Verbal avoidance and dissatisfaction in intimate conflict situations." *Human Communication Research, 35*, 357–383; J. P. Caughlin & T. D. Golish (2002). "An Analysis of the Association between Topic Avoidance and Dissatisfcation: Comparing Perceptual and Interpersonal Explanations." *Communication Monographs, 69*, 275–295.

16. J. P. Caughlin & T. D. Arr (2004). "When is Topic Avoidance Unsatisfying? Examining Moderators of the Association between Avoidance and Dissatisfaction." *Human Communication Research, 30*, 479–513.

17. D. D. Cahn (1992). *Conflict in Intimate Relationships.* New York: Guilford, p. 100.

18. Wilmot & Hocker, op cit., p. 159.

19. J. G. Oetzel & S. Ting-Toomey (2003). "Face Concerns in Interpersonal Conflict: A Cross-Cultural Empirical Test of the Face Negotiation Theory." *Communication Research, 30*, 599–625; M. U. Dsilva & L. O. Whyte (1998). "Cultural Differences in Conflict Styles: Vietnamese Refugees and Established Residents." *Howard Journal of Communication, 9*, 57–68.

20. S. J. Messman & R. L. Mikesell (2000). "Competition and Interpersonal Conflict in Dating Relationships." *Communication Reports, 13*, 21–34.

21. L. N. Olson & D. O. Braithwaite (2004). "'If You Hit Me Again, I'll Hit You Back': Conflict Management Strategies of Individuals Experiencing Aggression During Conflicts." *Communication Studies, 55*, 271–285.

22. K. Warren, S. Schoppelrey, & D. Moberg (2005). "'A Model of Contagion Through Competition in the Aggressive Behaviours of Elementary School Students." *Journal of Abnormal Child Psychology, 33*, 283–292.

23. D. A. Infante (1987). "Aggressiveness." In J. C. McCroskey & J. A. Daly (Eds.). *Personality & Interpersonal Communication.* Newbury Park, CA: Sage.

24. M. E. Roloff & R. M. Reznick (2008). "Communication During Serial Arguments: Connections with Individuals' Mental and Physical Well-Being." In M. T. Motley (Ed.). *Studies in Applied Interpersonal Communication* (pp. 97–120). Thousand Oaks, CA: Sage.

25. D. A. Infante, A. S. Rancer, & F. F. Jordan (1996). "Affirming & Nonaffirming Style, Dyad Sex, and the Perception of Argumentation and Verbal Aggression in an Interpersonal Dispute." *Human Communication Research, 22*, 315–334.

26. D. A. Infante, T. A. Chandler, & J. E. Rudd (1989). "Test of an Argumentative Skill Deficiency Model of Interspousal Violence." *Communication Monographs, 56*, 163–177.

27. M. M. Martin, C. M. Anderson, P. A. Burant, & K. Weber (1997). "Verbal Aggression in Sibling Relationships." *Communication Quarterly, 45*, 304–317.

28. J. W. Kassing & D. A. Infante (1999). "Aggressive Communication in the Coach-Athlete Relationship." *Communication Research Reports, 16*, 110–120.

29. M. J. Beatty, K. M. Valencic, J. E. Rudd, & J. A. Dobos (1999). "A 'Dark Side' of Communication Avoidance: Indirect Interpersonal Aggressiveness." *Communication Research Reports, 16*, 103–109.

30. A. C. Filley (1975). *Interpersonal Conflict Resolutions* (p. 23). Glenview, IL: Scott, Foresman.

31. D. Canary (2003). "Managing Interpersonal Conflict: A Model of Events Related to Strategic Choices." In J. O. Greene & B. R. Burleson (Eds.). *Handbook of Communication and Social Interaction Skills* (pp. 515–549). Mahwah, NJ: Erlbaum.

32. W. Wilmot & J. L. Hocker(2010). *Interpersonal Conflict*, 8th edn (pp. 13–16). New York: McGraw-Hill; M. L. Knapp, L. L. Putman, & L. J. Davis (1988). "Measuring interpersonal conflict in organizations: Where do we go from here?" *Management Communication Quarterly, 1*, 414–429.

33. C. S. Burggraf & A. L. Sillars (1987). "A Critical Examination of Sex Differences in Marital Communication." *Communication Monographs, 53*, 276–294.

34. M. M. McGinn, P. T. McFarland, & A. Christensen (2009). "Antecedents and consequences of demand/withdraw." *Journal of Family Psychology, 23*, 794–757.

35. J. Gottman (1994). *Why Marriages Succeed Or Fail.* New York: Simon & Schuster; C. Fowler & M. R. Dillon (2011). "Detachment dimensions and the Four Horsemen of the Apocalypse." *Communication Research Reports, 28*, 16–26; T. B. Holman & M. O. Jarvis (2003). "Hostile, volatile,

avoiding, and validating couple-conflict types: An investigation of Gottman's couple-conflict types." *Personal Relationships, 10,* 267–282.

36. J. Rossel & R. Collins (2006). "Conflict theory and inter-action rituals: The microfoundations of conflict theory." In J. H. Turner (Ed.), *Handbook of Sociological Theory* (pp. 506–532.). New York: Springer.

37. W. R. Cupach & D. J. Canary (1997). *Competence in Interpersonal Conflict* (p. 109). New York: McGraw-Hill.

38. B. M. Gayle, R. W. Preiss, & M. A. Allen (2001). "A Meta-Analytic Interpretation of Intimate and Non-Intimate Interpersonal Conflict." In M. A. Allen, R. W. Preiss, B. M. Gayle, & N. Burrell (Eds.). *Interpersonal Communication: Advances through Meta-Analysis.* New York: Erlbaum.

39. M. Allen (1998). "Methodological Considerations When Examining a Gendered World." In D. Canary & K. Dindia (Eds.). *Handbook of Sex Differences and Similarities in Communication.* Mahwah, NJ: Erlbaum.

40. Research summarized by D. Tannen (1989). *You Just Don't Understand: Women and Men in Conversation.* New York: William Morrow, pp. 152–157, 162–165.

41. N. H. Hess & E. H. Hagen (2006). *Evolution and Human Behaviour, 27,* 231–245; M. K. Underwood (2003). *Social Aggression Among Girls.* New York: Guilford.

42. R. Wiseman (2003). *Queen Bees & Wannabes: Helping Your Daughter Survive Cliques, Gossip, Boyfriends, and Other Realities of Adolescence.* New York: Three Rivers Press.

43. M. J. Collier (1991). "Conflict Competence within African, Mexican, and Anglo-American Friendships." In S. Ting-Toomey & F. Korzenny (Eds.). *Cross-Cultural Interpersonal Communication.* Newbury Park, CA: Sage.

44. D. J. Canary, W. R. Cupach, & S. J. Messman (1995). *Relationship Conflict.* Newbury Park, CA: Sage.

45. T. D. Afifi, A. Joseph & D. Aldeis (2012). "The 'standards for openness hypothesis': Why women find (conflict) avoidance more dissatisfying than men." *Journal of Social and Personal Relationships, 29,* 102–125; B. M. Gayle, R. W. Preiss, & M. A. Allen (2001). "A meta-analytic interpretation of intimate and non-intimate interpersonal conflict." In M. A. Allen, R. W. Preiss, B. M Gayle, & N. Burrell (Eds.), *Interpersonal Communication: Advances Through Meta-analysis* (pp. 345–368). New York: Erlbaum.

46. J. Koenig Kellas & S. Sato (2011). "'The Worst Part Is, We Don't Even Talk Anymore': Post-Dissolutional Communication in Break-up Stories." In K. M. Galvin (Ed.). *Making Connections: Readings in Relational Communication.* New York: Oxford University Press.

47. D. Cullington (2008). *Breaking Up Blues: A Guide to Survival.* New York: Routledge.

48. For a more detailed discussion of culture, conflict, and context, see W. B. Gudykunst & S. Ting-Toomey (1988). *Culture and Interpersonal Communication.* Newbury Park, CA: Sage, pp. 153–160.

49. See, for example, J. L. Holt & C. J. DeVore (2005). "Culture, Gender, Organizational Role, and Styles of Conflict Resolution: A Meta-Analysis." *International Journal of Intercultural Relations, 29,* 165–196.

50. See, for example, S. Ting-Toomey (1988). "Rhetorical Sensitivity Style in Three Cultures: France, Japan, and the United States." *Central States Speech Journal, 39,* 28–36.

51. K. Okabe (1987). "Indirect Speech Acts of the Japanese." In L. Kincaid (Ed.), *Communication Theory: Eastern and Western Perspectives* (pp. 127–136). San Diego, CA: Academic Press.

52. G. Fontaine (1991). "Cultural Diversity in Intimate Intercultural Relationships." In D. D. Cahn, *Intimates in Conflict: A Communication Perspective.* Hillsdale, NJ: Erlbaum.

53. Summarized in Tannen, *You Just Don't Understand,* p. 160.

54. See, for example, K. J. Beatty & J. C. McCroskey (1997). "It's in Our Nature: Verbal Aggressiveness as Temperamental Expression." *Communication Quarterly, 45,* 466–460.

55. J. G. Oetzel (1998). "Explaining Individual Communication Processes in Homogeneous and Heterogeneous Groups through Individualism-Collectivism and Self-Construal." *Human Communication Research, 25,* 202–224.

56. T. Gordon (1970). *Parent Effectiveness Training.* New York: Wyden, pp. 236–264.

57. R. Axelrod (1984). *The Evolution of Cooperation.* New York: Basic Books.

58. S. Mill (2004). "Addressing Stress Helps Minimize Potential of Burnout." *Computing Canada, 30,* 27.

59. S. M. Heathfield. "Personal Courage and Conflict Resolution at Work," http://humanresources.about.com/cs/conflictresolves/a/conflictcourage.htm. Accessed July 10, 2007.

60. See "The Cost of Rudeness," *Motivational Manager* (November 1998), p. 9, as cited in P. H. Andrews and J. E. Baird Jr. (2000). *Communication for Business and the Professions,* Boston: McGraw-Hill, p. 230.

61. J. Suderman (2007). *Understanding Intercultural Communication.* Toronto, ON: Thomson Nelson, p. 288.

62. G. Namie & R. Namie (2009). *The Bully At Work: What You Can Do To Stop The Hurt And Reclaim Your Dignity On The Job.* Naperville, IL: Sourcebooks.

63. CUPE. Canadian Union of Public Employees. http://search.cupe.ca/?search=bullying&x=14&y=6&ie=&restrict=cupe&site=happycog&output=xml_no_dtd&client=happycog&hq=site%3Acupe.ca&proxystylesheet=happycog. Retrieved May 29, 2013.

64. S. Shellenbarger (2014, December 16). "To fight or not to fight? How to pick your battles in the workplace." *The Wall Street Journal.*

Index

Note: Page references followed by *f* and *t* refer to figures and tables respectively.

D

Damon, Tim, 48
Day of Pink, 280
debilitative emotions, 99–100
    approval, fallacy of, 102
    catastrophic expectations, fallacy of, 105
    causation, fallacy of, 104
    emotional memory, 100
    emotions checking, 103
    helplessness, fallacy of, 104
    irrational thinking and, 101
    minimizing debilitative emotions, 105–107
    overgeneralization, fallacy of, 103–104
    perfection, fallacy of, 101–102
    physiology, 100
    rational thinking in action, 107–108
    self-talk, 100–101
    shoulds, fallacy of, 102
    sources of debilitative emotions, 100
deception clues, 149–150
decode, 6
de-escalatory conflict spiral, 243
"default" styles, 265
defensive listening, 181
defensiveness, 244
    certainty *vs.* provisionalism, 247–248
    control *vs.* problem orientation, 245–246
    evaluation *vs.* description communication, 245
    face-threatening acts, 244
    Gibb categories of defensive and supportive
      behaviours, 245*t*
    neutrality *vs.* empathy, 246–247
    preventing, 245
    strategy *vs.* spontaneity, 246
    superiority *vs.* equality, 247
deferential language, 124, 125*t*
degrees of self-disclosure, 222–223
deliberate transgression, 217
denotative meaning, 121
depth, 222
descriptive communication, 245
destructive conflict patterns, 272
developmental models, 207
    avoiding, 211
    bonding, 209
    circumscribing, 210
    differentiating, 209–210
    experimenting, 208
    initiating stage, 207
    integrating, 208–209
    intensifying, 208
    stagnating, 211
    terminating, 211–212
"devil effect," 74
dharma, 139
dialectical perspectives, 212
    connection *vs.* autonomy, 212–213
    managing dialectical tensions, 214
    openness *vs.* privacy, 213–214
    predictability *vs.* novelty, 214

dialectical tension, 212, 214
differentiating stage, 209–210
Dillon, Matt, 61
dimensions of intimacy, 218–219
direct aggression, 267, 280
directness, 136
dirty fighting with crazymakers, 268
disagreeing messages, 241
    aggressiveness, 241
    argumentativeness, 242
    complaining, 241–242
disconfirming communication, 240, 240*t*
    ambiguous responses, 241
    impersonal responses, 241
    impervious responses, 240
    incongruous responses, 241
    interrupting response, 240
    irrelevant responses, 240
    tangential responses, 241
disinhibition, 17
disruptive language, 125–128
    emotive language, 127–128
    euphemisms, 128
    fact–inference confusion, 125–127
distance, 164–165
distorted feedback, 38
distractions, 184
divergence, 124
diversity, 40–42
Donnellon, Annie, 159
"doormats," 266
down-to-earth language, 120
dyad, 11
dyadic communication, 11
dysfunctional conflict, 280

E

effective communication, 18, 19, 22, 183
effective communicator, 18
    characteristics of competent communicators, 19–22
    communication competence, 18–19
    communication in the workplace, 24
    competence in intercultural communication,
      22–23
elaboration, 137
elements in listening process, 178
    attending, 179
    hearing, 178–179
    remembering, 179–180
    responding, 179
    understanding, 179
e-mail, 16–18, 51, 91
emblems, 157
emotions, 87
    accepting responsibility for feelings, 97
    cognitive interpretations, 88–89
    communication channel, 97–99
    communication in the workplace, 108–109
    contagion, 93–94
    culture, 91

preoccupation, 181
presenting self, 46
primary emotions, 89
prisoner's dilemma, 277
privacy management, 224
problem orientation, 246
prompting, 185
provisionalism, 247–248
proxemics, 164
proximity, 205
pseudoaccommodator, 268
pseudolistening, 180
psychological effects, 267
psychological noise, 8
public distance, 165
Pursuit of Happyness, The, 40
"pushovers," 266
Pygmalion in the Classroom, 45

Q

qualitative interpersonal relationships, 11–12
quantitative communication, 11
questioning, 185–187
questions
    closed, 186
    counterfeit, 186
    open, 186
    sincere, 186, 187

R

rational emotive therapy, 100
rational thinking, 106, 107
reaffirmation, 214
reappraisal, 89
recalibration, 214
receiver, 6
reciprocal attraction, 205
reciprocating, self-disclosure, 226
reciprocity, 224
recognition, 242
reference groups, 36
reflected appraisal, 35–36
regulating, 148–149
Reich, Dahlia, 178
relational, 217
relational commitment. *See* commitment
relational communication. *See also* relationships
    characteristics of relationships, 214–216
    deliberate *vs.* unintentional, 217
    developmental models, 207–212
    dialectical perspectives, 212–214
    forgiving transgressions, 218
    intimacy in relationships, 218–222
    minor *vs.* significant, 217
    models of relational development and maintenance, 207
    one-time *vs.* incremental, 217
    repairing damaged relationships, 217
    self-disclosure in relationships, 222–228
    social support, 216–217
    social *vs.* relational, 217

strategies for relational repair, 217–218
    in the workplace, 228–229
relational conflict style, 270
relational dimension, 9–10
relational maintenance, 207
relational messages, 9, 13–14
relational repair, strategies for, 217–218
relational systems
    complementary, symmetrical, and parallel styles, 271–272
    conflict in, 270
    conflict rituals, 272–273
    destructive conflict patterns, 272
relational transgressions, 217
relationship maintenance and enhancement, 225
relationships, 203, 214, 270
    affected by culture, 214–215
    appearance, 203–204
    and change, 214
    competence, 205
    complementarity, 204
    proximity, 205
    reciprocal attraction, 205
    requiring commitment, 216
    requiring maintenance, 215
    rewards, 206–207
    self-disclosure, 205
    similarity, 204
relative language, 117–118
relative words, 117
relying, 273
remembering, 179–180
repetitious stimuli, 60
residual message, 180
respect, 13
responding, 179
rewards, 206–207
risk of disclosing reasonable, 226
risks of self-disclosure, 225–226
Rolls, Judith A., 155, 212
Rosenthal, Robert, 45
rumination, 100

S

safety needs, 6
Sapir, Edward, 138
Sapir–Whorf hypothesis, 138
sarcasm, 15, 78, 148, 161
saving face, 248
    assertive message format, 248–252
"scientific" literature, 133
Seinfeld, 147
selection process, 60
selective listening, 180–181
"selectively ignoring," 266
self, 31
    "big five" personality traits, 34*t*
    and identity, 53–54
    in individualistic and collectivistic cultures, 43*t*
    self-concept, 32
    self-esteem, 32–33

Learning like never before.

4LTR PRESS

nelson.com/student

1 A First Look at Interpersonal Communication

Chapter in Review

LO1 Assess the needs (physical, identity, social, and practical) that communicators are attempting to satisfy in a given situation or relationship.

It turns out that interpersonal communication is more than haphazard interaction. We communicate to satisfy physical needs (e.g., touch is therapeutic and comforting). Communication also helps us discover what we're like as individuals (our identity needs) and to attain the pleasure, affection, and relaxation that come when our social needs are met. Finally, communication helps us achieve instrumental goals such as getting a deal, meeting someone special, or finding the nearest Tim Horton's.

LO2 Apply the transactional communication model to a specific situation.

Before reading this chapter, you might have thought of interpersonal communication as two people sending messages back and forth (the linear model). But communication is more complicated than that. In transactional communication, communicators send and receive messages simultaneously, and their individual interpretations of messages are influenced by the degree to which they share an *environment* or by the external, physiological, or psychological noise they are experiencing.

LO3 Describe how communication principles and misconceptions are evident in a specific situation.

Regardless of our situation, several communication principles hold true: Communication can be intentional or unintentional; it is both irreversible and unrepeatable; we cannot stop communicating because we continually send nonverbal cues, and finally, all communication events have content and relational dimensions. Communication misconceptions are rampant: We tend to think that more communication is always better, that meanings are in words, that successful communication always involves shared understanding, that people or events cause our reactions, or that communication solves all problems.

LO4 Describe the degree to which communication is qualitatively impersonal or interpersonal, as well as the consequences of these levels of interaction.

You can look at interpersonal communication from both a quantitative and a qualitative perspective. A quantitative definition involves two individuals (a dyad) in impersonal communication, like that between a clerk and a customer. A qualitative view entails much more. Communication is more personal, with the people involved treating one another as unique and irreplaceable. This view of communication is also characterized by interdependence (the other's joy is our joy) and the disclosure of thoughts and feelings. Finally, individuals in qualitatively interpersonal relationships communicate for intrinsic rewards—that is, for the joy of it.

Instrumental goals Goals aimed at getting things done. (Page 6)

Linear communication model A characterization of communication as a one-way event in which a message flows from sender to receiver. (Page 6)

Sender The creator of a message. (Page 6)

Encode The process of putting thoughts into symbols, most commonly words. (Page 6)

Message Information sent from a sender to a receiver. (Page 6)

Channel The medium through which a message passes from sender to receiver. (Page 6)

Receiver One who notices and attends to a message. (Page 6)

Decode The process in which a receiver attaches meaning to a message. Synonymous with *interpretation*. (Page 6)

Noise External, physiological, or psychological distractions that interfere with the accurate transmission and reception of a message. (Page 6)

Transactional communication model A characterization of communication as the simultaneous sending and receiving of messages in an ongoing, irreversible process. (Page 7)

Environment The field of experiences that lead a person to make sense of another's behaviour. (Page 7)

Interpersonal communication A continuous transactional process involving participants who occupy different but overlapping environments and create relationships through the exchange of messages, many of which are affected by external, physiological, and psychological noise. (Page 8)

Content message A message that communicates information about the subject being discussed. (Page 9)

Relational message A message that expresses the social relationship between two or more individuals. (Page 9)

Quantitative definition of interpersonal communication Impersonal communication, usually face to face, between two individuals. (Page 11)

Dyad Two people interacting. (Page 11)

Impersonal communication Behaviour that treats others as objects rather than as individuals. (Page 11)

Qualitative definition of interpersonal communication Communication in which the parties consider one another as unique individuals rather than as objects. Such communication is characterized by minimal use of stereotyped labels; by unique, idiosyncratic rules; and by a high degree of information exchange. (Page 11)

Content message A message that communicates information about the subject being discussed. (Page 13)

Affinity The degree to which people like or appreciate one another. (Page 13)

Immediacy The degree of interest and attention that we feel toward and communicate to others. (Page 13)

Respect The social need to be held in esteem by others. (Page 13)

Control The degree to which the parties in a relationship have the power to influence one another. (Page 13)

Metacommunication Messages that people exchange, verbally or nonverbally, about their relationship—communication about communication. (Page 14)

Social Media The various channels that make remote personal communication possible. (Page 14)

Disinhibition The tendency to transmit messages without considering their consequences. (Page 17)

Communication competence The ability to accomplish one's personal goals in a manner that maintains or enhances the relationship in which it occurs. (Page 18)

Cognitive complexity The ability to construct a variety of frameworks for viewing an issue. (Page 21)

Empathy The ability to project oneself into another person's point of view so as to experience the other's thoughts and feelings. (Page 21)

Self-monitoring The process of attending to your own behaviour and using these observations to shape the way you behave. (Page 21)

LO5 Identify the content and relational dimensions of communication in a given transaction and describe how metacommunication can be used to improve relationships.

The content dimension refers to the information you wish to convey (e.g., why you selected a particular holiday destination). The relational dimension refers to your feelings about the individual, commonly expressed nonverbally. Four categories of relational messages are affinity (the degree to which individuals like or appreciate one another), immediacy (the amount of attention given to one another), respect (the esteem felt for one another), and control (the degree to which the parties have power over one another). Metacommunication is communication about communication, and it can be used to resolve conflict because it shifts emphasis from the content to the relational dimension of the relationship. It reinforces the satisfying aspects of a relationship and boosts the odds that positive behaviour will continue.

LO6 Diagnose the effectiveness of various communication channels in a specific situation.

Communicating through text messages, e-mails, tweets, or by using social networking sites such as Facebook can be as effective as face-to-face communication. New technologies allow us to connect with people with similar interests or to interact with individuals anywhere in the world. They also help us to enhance our present relationships and to make new friends. But there are challenges: These messages are generally leaner than face-to-face communication in that they lack nonverbal cues, often making them difficult to interpret. We also tend to send messages without considering the consequences (disinhibition) and to forget about the permanent nature of the Internet. Those weekend photos might not appeal to a potential employer.

LO7 Describe your level of communication competence in a specific instance or relationship.

Just as you learn new computer applications, so too can you learn new communication skills. For instance, communication competence depends on the situation and your relationship with the other person; thus, there's no "proper" way to communicate. But competent communicators do share some similarities. They possess a wide range of behaviours and choose the most appropriate depending on the context, the goal, and the other person. They also demonstrate empathy, cognitive complexity, and self-monitoring and have an understanding of intercultural communication. These strengths allow them to fare well in the workplace.

Chapter 1 Quiz Questions

1. What view of communication suggests that communicators simultaneously send and receive messages?
   a. linear
   b. transactional
   c. qualitative
   d. quantitative
2. How Jack feels about Lucy comes through in his tone of voice and his nonverbal communication. What type of message is this?
   a. relational
   b. situational
   c. content
   d. quantitative
3. What view of communication suggests that interpersonal communication is defined by the worth, value, and uniqueness of the individuals?
   a. linear
   b. transactional
   c. qualitative
   d. quantitative
4. What is another term for "decoding"?
   a. cognitive complexity
   b. commitment
   c. interpretation
   d. encoding
5. Caitlyn always seems to know what to say and how to act. She can walk into a room, and within minutes she knows how to behave. Which statement best describes Caitlyn?
   a. She is a high self-monitor.
   b. She has the ability to choose the most appropriate behaviour.
   c. She demonstrates cognitive complexity.
   d. She demonstrates empathy.
6. You were checking out a classmate's Facebook page, and she posts more information about herself than anyone you know. She talks about her sex life, her arguments with parents and co-workers, even how she shortchanges people at work. Which term best describes this type of communication?
   a. mediated communication
   b. content messages
   c. transactional communication
   d. disinhibition
7. Kristen enjoys meeting and interacting with people from other cultures. She finds it entertaining when she does something "wrong" because the gesture, norm, or behaviour tends to mean something very different than it does in her culture. Which attribute of intercultural communication competence does this example best demonstrate?
   a. motivation
   b. tolerance for ambiguity
   c. open-mindedness
   d. knowledge and skill

8. Why is Maslow's hierarchy of needs important to the study of interpersonal communication?
   a. We all have needs.
   b. We can't understand our needs without communication.
   c. Communication can help us meet each need.
   d. The need for communication is the sixth, "hidden" need.
9. Which statement best describes how integrated communicators express themselves in skilful ways?
   a. Their communication is a self-conscious act.
   b. They have more experience.
   c. Skills are basic to communication.
   d. They have internalized effective behaviour.
10. Which statement is the most accurate regarding communication in the workplace?
    a. While effective communication can help you get a job, it's not so important afterward.
    b. There's no relationship between communication and employee satisfaction.
    c. Engineers don't have a need for effective communication because of the nature of their work.
    d. Communicating on the job can be challenging these days because four generations with four different value systems work side by side

Chapter 1 Questions for Thought and Discussion

1. Provide examples from your own life that explain how communication was used to satisfy your physical, identity, and social needs and to meet an instrumental goal.
2. Explain why the transactional model of interpersonal communication more accurately explains what happens when individuals communicate than does the linear model.
3. "Using social media is great for developing and maintaining relationships, but it is not so effective for communication." Do you agree or disagree with this statement? Provide support for your answer.
4. Your two friends will be teaching English as a second language in Japan next semester. What advice would you give them about intercultural communication?

Answers

1. b; 2. a; 3. c; 4. c; 5. a; 6. d; 7. c; 8. c; 9. d; 10. d

Notes

Chapter in Review

Chris Cheadle/All Canada Photos/Getty Images

LO1 Describe the relationship among self-concept, self-esteem, and communication.

Communication, self-concept, and self-esteem are interrelated in that self-concept is formed from the comments and evaluations that others make about you (reflected appraisal) and also from the comparisons you make between yourself and others (social comparison). Further, diversity, culture, and gender affect your identity. Once you have a sense of your basic characteristics, they, in turn, influence your self-esteem. Evaluating your qualities positively results in high self-esteem while negative evaluations result in low self-esteem. Self-esteem, regardless of its level, affects how you communicate with others. Fortunately, we have the power to change how we feel about ourselves.

LO2 Understand how to change your self-concept.

You're not stuck with your self-concept, and changing it could help you feel better. But you'll need the will to change (the self-concept resists change, so it's going to require work), and you'll need to have realistic expectations of yourself. You'll also need to develop the skills to change, which you can learn by understanding how communication works and by watching how competent communicators act. It's worth the effort. Changing your self-concept can make you feel more positive about yourself, which will affect your communication with others and also make them feel more positively about you.

LO3 Explain how self-fulfilling prophecies shape the self-concept and influence communication.

Self-imposed and other-imposed self-fulfilling prophecies greatly influence self-concept and, hence, communication. It works like this: Once you have an expectation of yourself ("I'm not smart enough to get this job"), you behave accordingly (you act uninterested and timid during the interview), which makes that expectation come to pass (you don't get the job). When the expected event occurs, it not only influences yourself-concept but reinforces the original notion ("I knew I couldn't do it—I'm such a loser").

LO4 Compare and contrast the perceived self and the presenting self as they relate to identity management.

We typically show others a public self in order to enhance relationships, gain compliance, save face, or explore new areas of ourselves. We do this by creating multiple identities (e.g., student, worker, sibling, musician) and managing those identities. Identity management can be deliberate or unconscious, but it must also be collaborative in that we need others to support us in it. It also varies according to the situation. However, not everyone manages identity to the same degree. High self-monitors engage in identity management more often than do low self-monitors.

Self-concept The relatively stable set of perceptions individuals hold about themselves. (Page 32)

Self-esteem The part of the self-concept that involves evaluations of self-worth. (Page 32)

Personality Characteristic ways that you think and behave across a variety of situations. (Page 34)

Reflected appraisal The theory that a person's self concept matches the way the person believes others regard him or her. (Page 35)

Significant other A person whose opinion is important enough to affect one's self-concept strongly. (Page 35)

Social comparison Evaluation of oneself in terms of or by comparison to others. (Page 36)

Reference groups Groups against which we compare ourselves, thereby influencing our self-concept and self-esteem. (Page 36)

Cognitive conservatism The tendency to seek and attend to information that conforms to an existing self-concept. (Page 38)

Self-fulfilling prophecy A prediction or expectation of an event that makes the outcome more likely to occur than would otherwise have been the case. (Page 44)

Self-imposed prophecy Occurs when your own expectations influence your behaviour. (Page 45)

Other-imposed prophecy Occurs when your actions may be governed by the expectations that others have of you. (Page 45)

Identity management The communication strategies people use to influence how others view them. (Page 46)

Perceived self The person you believe yourself to be in moments of honest self-examination. It may be identical to or different from the presenting and ideal selves. (Page 46)

Presenting self The image a person presents to others. It may be identical to or different from the perceived and ideal selves. (Page 46)

LO5 Describe the role that identity management plays in both face-to-face and mediated relationships.

In face-to-face communication, you manage your identity through your manner, nonverbal gestures, and appearance (e.g., clothing, hairstyle, body art). Even the car you drive or how your room or office cubicle looks influences your identity. Identity management is even more prominent on the Internet. Many people change their appearance, personality, age, or interests, and some take on entirely new personas. It is important to be aware of what your social networking sites convey about you.

Chapter 2 Quiz Questions

1. What occurs when we base our self-concept on messages that significant others may have given us?
   a. social comparison
   b. self-matching
   c. reflected appraisal
   d. distorted feedback
2. According to the text, which term describes a person who is always putting you down?
   a. a psychological influence
   b. an ego buster
   c. a high self-monitor
   d. an ego booster
3. Tingting is a woman in good physical shape. She sees herself as unfit, but she hangs out with university athletes. What is this an example of?
   a. social comparison
   b. self-matching
   c. reflected appraisal
   d. distorted feedback
4. What does the article titled, "Old Wisdom Finds Home in New Nunavut Schools" tell us about communication and self-concept?
   a. It's important to manage our identities.
   b. There is no connection between culture and self-concept.
   c. The perceived self and the presenting self can sometimes be similar.
   d. Our culture has a major influence on our self-concept and our identities.
5. In North American society, we are generally taught to be successful at all costs, to stand out from the crowd, and to make our "mark." What type of culture is this typical of?
   a. collectivistic
   b. high context
   c. low context
   d. individualistic
6. What concept refers to the relatively stable set of perceptions you hold about yourself?
   a. reflected appraisal
   b. cognitive complexity
   c. self-concept
   d. subjectivity

7. Which of the following methods is NOT used to make your self-concept more realistic?
   a. sharing your perception of yourself with a friend
   b. trying to engage in more accurate self-talk
   c. making an effort to recognize more "ego-buster" messages
   d. paying less attention to your past and more attention to your present behaviours
8. Which statement describes someone who pays attention to his or her behaviour in relationships?
   a. He or she is unlikely to pay attention to others.
   b. He or she is too uptight.
   c. He or she is probably ego-driven.
   d. He or she is self-monitoring.
9. What is the relationship between identity management and self-monitoring?
   a. Identity management makes people more aware of themselves so that they can be more effective self-monitors.
   b. Self-monitoring makes people more aware of their identity management.
   c. Identity management reduces the need for self-monitoring.
   d. Identity management and self-monitoring are not connected.
10. Many students travelling abroad display the Canadian maple leaf on their backpacks or jackets. What type of identity management is this an example of?
   a. appearance
   b. manner
   c. setting
   d. symbol

Chapter 2 Questions for Thought and Discussion

1. Describe two recent changes that took place in your self-concept and explain the role that communication played in these changes.
2. Explain the obvious and more subtle ways in which you manage your identity on social networking sites. Why do you do this?
3. Provide examples of how a person's private and public selves become blended on the Internet and discuss how social media in general can violate a person's privacy.
4. Explain the role that identity management plays in today's politicians. Provide lots of examples.
5. Describe how identity management could be an effective tool in the workplace. Offer several examples.

Answers

1. c; 2. b; 3. a; 4. d; 5. d; 6. c; 7. c; 8. d; 9. b; 10. a

Zachary Scott/Stone/Getty Images

LO1 Describe how the processes of selection, organization, interpretation, and negotiation shape communication in a given situation.

Your communication depends on how you "size up" a situation, or what you perceive. First, you select or tune in to something, typically things that are intense, repetitious, or related to your motives (I'm late, so I notice a cab on a crowded, busy city street). Then the stimuli are organized based on perceptual schemata such as physical, role, interaction, psychological, or membership constructs. This brings you to interpretation, and finally, you negotiate your story with others so that your narrative jives with theirs.

LO2 Explain how the influences on perception affect communication in a specific situation.

Several factors influence how any situation is perceived. One of these is access to information. If you learn something new about a person, that may change how you see that individual. Physiological influences include the senses, age, health, fatigue, and hunger. Anyone of these can greatly affect how you "see" a situation. So too can psychological challenges such as having ADHD. Perception and communication are also affected by culture, diversity, and social roles. For instance, gender, occupation, and your relational roles all shape your interpretation of any event. It's not hard to see how and why two individuals might see a situation differently.

LO3 Analyze how the common tendencies in perception distort your perceptions of another person and, hence, your communication. Use this information to present a more accurate alternative set of perceptions.

While we perceive the world differently, we share some common perceptual tendencies. For instance, we tend to judge ourselves more charitably than we judge others (self-serving bias). We also cling to first impressions and assume that others are similar to us. Finally, we are influenced by the obvious: If it's not right in front of us, we tend to overlook it. Once we are aware of these tendencies, we can rethink any situation to uncover a more realistic sense of what's really happening. This can only enhance our communication with others.

LO4 Demonstrate how you might use the skill of perception checking in a significant relationship.

Perception checking allows you to check interpretations. It has three phases: State the other person's behaviour, offer two possible interpretations, and ask for clarification. If a good friend rushes out of the room, later on you could say, "When you left the room this afternoon (state behaviour), I didn't know if you were sick or if I had said something that bothered you (offer two possible interpretations). What

Perception The process whereby we assign meaning to the world around us. (Page 59)

Selection The first stage in the perception process, in which some data are chosen to attend to and others to ignore. (Page 60)

Organization The stage in the perception process that involves arranging data in a meaningful way. (Page 60)

Perceptual schemata Cognitive frameworks that allow individuals to organize perceptual data that they have selected from the environment. These include physical, role, interaction, psychological, and membership constructs. (Page 60)

Stereotyping Categorizing individuals according to a set of characteristics assumed to belong to all members of a group. (Page 62)

Punctuation The process of determining the causal order of events. (Page 63)

Interpretation The process of attaching meaning to sense data; synonymous with *decode*. (Page 64)

Negotiation What occurs between and among people as they influence one another's perceptions and try to achieve a shared perspective. (Page 65)

Narratives The stories we use to describe our personal worlds. (Page 66)

Ethnocentrism The attitude that one's own culture is superior to others. (Page 69)

Attribution The process of attaching meaning to behaviour. (Page 73)

Self-serving bias The tendency to interpret and explain information in a way that casts the perceiver in the most favourable manner. (Page 73)

Halo effect The tendency to form an overall positive impression on the basis of one positive characteristic. (Page 74)

Perception checking A three-part method for verifying the accuracy of interpretations, including a description of the behaviour, two possible interpretations, and a request for clarification of the interpretation. (Page 75)

Empathy The ability to project oneself into another person's point of view so as to experience the other's thoughts and feelings. (Page 77)

Sympathy Compassion for another's situation. (Page 78)

Cognitive complexity The ability to construct a variety of frameworks for viewing an issue. (Page 78)

Pillow method A way of understanding an issue from several perspectives, rather than with an egocentric "I'm right and you're wrong" attitude. (Page 78)

happened (request clarification)?" Offered with the appropriate nonverbal communication and sensitivity to cultural rules, the other person won't get defensive, and you'll learn what's going on.

LO5 Enhance your cognitive complexity by applying the "pillow method" in a significant disagreement. Explain how your expanded view of this situation might affect your communication with the other(s) involved.

Cognitive complexity is the ability to construct a variety of frameworks for viewing an issue. People who demonstrate cognitive complexity often see situations from several perspectives. It can also help individuals to be more empathic. The pillow method can be used to foster empathy when we disagree with someone. Using a real-life disagreement with a roommate, review the problem from the following five positions: position 1: "I'm right and my roommate is wrong"; position 2: "My roommate's right and I'm wrong"; position 3: "We are both right and both wrong"; position 4:"The issue isn't important"; and position 5: "There is truth in all perspectives." Expanding your view of the problem will positively affect your communication with your roommate.

Chapter 3 Quiz Questions

1. What are the stages of the perception process?
   a. selection, organization, interpretation, and negotiation
   b. stereotyping, punctuation, and perceptual schemata
   c. selection, punctuation, organization, and interpretation
   d. physical, role, and interaction
2. In what phase of the perception process does the recognition of a "*figure*" as standing out from a "*ground*" of other stimuli takes place?
   a. ideation
   b. selection
   c. verification
   d. organization
3. Kristen found that her social worker was compassionate and caring. What type of construct is Kristen using?
   a. interaction
   b. membership
   c. psychological
   d. role
4. When is nonverbal congruency extremely important?
   a. in the perception process
   b. in perception checking
   c. in the pillow method
   d. in the attribution process
5. Which of the following is NOT an attribution error?
   a. We assume that others are dissimilar to us.
   b. We tend to assume others are similar to us.
   c. We cling to first impressions.
   d. We tend to judge ourselves more charitably than others.

6. When someone botches a job, you think that she or he was not listening or trying hard enough to get it right. When you botch a job, you think the directions were not clear or there was not enough time to do it. What does this type of attitude exemplify?
   a. that we are influenced by the obvious
   b. the halo effect
   c. the self-serving bias
   d. that we tend to assume others are similar to us
7. How could you improve this perception checking statement: "When you gave me an F on my essay, I figured you hated me. Right?"
   a. Describe a behaviour.
   b. Give another interpretation.
   c. Request clarification.
   d. Provide a timeline.
8. Some individuals are able to describe situations more thoroughly, have better communication within their marriages, and are more persuasive. What trait do these individuals have?
   a. empathy
   b. sympathy
   c. self-serving bias
   d. cognitive complexity
9. What is communicating to a friend how sorry you are about the breakup of his or her romance an example of?
   a. sympathy
   b. empathy
   c. role taking
   d. perception checking
10. Which behaviour is helpful when you can't find any reason to accept the behaviour of another person?
    a. using perception checking
    b. examining your own self-concept
    c. using a different communication channel
    d. using the pillow method

Chapter 3 Questions for Thought and Discussion

1. Provide examples of how culture and diversity affect the perception process.
2. Describe a subculture to which you belong. Give examples of and explain several misunderstandings you have had with members of another subculture. How do these misunderstandings reflect your view of that subculture?
3. Develop a situation in which one person is confused about another's behaviour, and then explain what the person could do to implement the perception checking process. Write out the things the person should say and indicate the part of the perception checking process that goes with each statement.
4. Select a conflict you have with another person and apply the pillow method.

Answers

1. a; 2. d; 3. c; 4. b; 5. a; 6. c; 7. b; 8. d; 9. a; 10. d

Chapter in Review

MARK RALSTON/AFP/Getty Images

LO1 Describe how the four components of emotions affect the way you feel and, hence, how you communicate.

Emotions and communication have several components. Physiological factors (e.g., increased heart rate, increased adrenaline secretions, pupil dilation) alert us that we're having an emotional moment. Nonverbal factors (e.g., changes in gestures, vocal tone, trembling) can be either a reaction to an emotion or a cause of an emotional state. But it's the cognitive interpretations and how symptoms are labelled that affect our emotions. Trembling hands could be viewed as fear or excitement. In some cases, however, the only way to express deep, complex feelings is through verbal expression.

LO2 Describe how the influences on emotional expression listed have affected your communication in an important relationship.

Several influences affect emotional expression. In terms of personality, extroverts report more positive emotions than do people with neurotic personalities. Expressing negative emotions is discouraged in collectivistic cultures. Even gender has an impact, supporting the unexpressive male and more expressive female stereotypes. Men express emotions with women, married individuals recognize the emotions of their partners, and women are better than men at interpreting emotions. Social conventions discourage emotional expression, and hence, fear of self-disclosure is common. Finally, emotions are transferred from one person to another and this is known as emotional contagion.

LO3 Apply the guidelines for effectively communicating emotions in an important situation.

Constructive emotional expression can be learned. Being able to identify and label your emotions and recognizing the differences between feeling, talking, and acting are helpful. But you don't have to act on every feeling. Expand your emotional vocabulary and recognize that if you have multiple and/or conflicting emotions at the same time, you'll need to express each one. You'll also have to select the proper time to express feelings, take responsibility for your feelings, and be mindful of the communication channel you select.

LO4 Identify and dispute the fallacies that are creating debilitative emotions in an important situation. Explain how more rational thinking can lead to more constructive communication.

Debilitative emotions emerge from irrational thoughts, referred to as fallacies. The fallacy of perfection holds that you communicate perfectly in every situation, a feat that is humanly impossible. The fallacy of approval is based on the idea of seeking the approval of everyone, but this too is not achievable. The fallacy of shoulds focuses on how things

Emotional intelligence The ability to understand and manage one's own emotions and be sensitive to others' feelings. (Page 87)

Reappraisal Rethinking the meaning of emotionally charged events in ways that alter their emotional impact. (Page 89)

Primary emotions Basic emotions such as anger, joy, fear, and sadness. (Page 89)

Mixed emotions Feeling two or more conflicting emotions at the same time. (Page 89)

Emotion labour The notion that managing and even suppressing emotions is both appropriate and necessary. (Page 93)

Emotional contagion The process by which emotions are transferred from one person to another (Page 93)

Facilitative emotions Emotions that contribute to effective functioning. (Page 99)

Debilitative emotions Emotions that prevent a person from functioning effectively. (Page 99)

Rumination Dwelling persistently on negative thoughts that, in turn, intensify negative feelings. (Page 100)

Self-talk The process of thinking. On some level, self-talk occurs as a person interprets another's behaviour. (Page 100)

Fallacies Debilitative feelings that come from accepting irrational thoughts. (Page 101)

Fallacy of perfection The irrational belief that a worthwhile communicator should be able to handle every situation with complete confidence and skill. (Page 101)

Fallacy of approval The irrational belief that it is vital to win the approval of virtually every person a communicator deals with. (Page 102)

Fallacy of shoulds The inability to distinguish between what is and what should be. (Page 102)

Fallacy of overgeneralization Irrational beliefs in which conclusions (usually negative) are based on limited evidence or exaggerated shortcomings. (Page 103)

Fallacy of causation The irrational belief that emotions are caused by others and not by the person who experiences them. (Page 104)

Fallacy of helplessness The irrational belief that satisfaction in life is determined by forces beyond one's control. (Page 104)

Fallacy of catastrophic expectations The irrational belief that the worst possible outcome will probably occur. (Page 105)

"should" be, yet it is unreasonable to expect that the world operate according to your whims. With overgeneralization, conclusions are based on limited information, or shortcomings are exaggerated. Either way, positive attributes are ignored or minimized. Causation occurs when you believe that others cause emotions, but emotions are based on individual interpretations. Helplessness is the irrational belief that satisfaction in life is determined by forces beyond your control. But looking more closely, many "can't" statements are actually "won't" statements. Those believing in the fallacy of catastrophic expectations assume that the worst possible outcome will occur. In many cases, self-fulfilling prophecy drives outcomes. Irrational thinking is minimized when you monitor your emotional reactions, note the activating event, record your self-talk, and reappraise your irrational beliefs.

Chapter 4 Quiz Questions

1. The mood of the party was pleasant but subdued. Then Emma arrived. She was animated, upbeat, and outgoing; before long, most of the people at the party were laughing and joking. What is Emma's impact on the party an example of?
   a. emotional contagion
   b. empathy
   c. presenting self
   d. social values
2. Which of the following behaviours does your text recommend?
   a. expressing all your emotions to your friends
   b. trying to recognize your emotions
   c. being glad you have debilitative emotions
   d. expressing only positive emotions
3. Which two things distinguish facilitative feelings from debilitative ones?
   a. emotions and behaviour
   b. longevity and interpretation
   c. intention and intensity
   d. intensity and duration
4. What can result from subscribing to the fallacy of catastrophic expectations?
   a. self-fulfilling prophecies
   b. erroneous perception checking
   c. reflected appraisals
   d. physical noise
5. What fallacy is the statement "Liam never has a good word to say about anyone" an example of?
   a. should
   b. approval
   c. overgeneralization
   d. causation
6. In individualistic cultures, what are people more likely to do?
   a. keep their emotions to themselves
   b. share emotions only with those they are especially close
   c. feel it is their right to tell others how they feel about things
   d. express emotions such as dislike
7. Which term refers to debilitative feelings that come from irrational thoughts?
   a. perceptual difficulties
   b. cognitive interpretations
   c. fallacies
   d. impression management
8. Which of the following is NOT a step used to minimize debilitative emotions?
   a. Note the activating event.
   b. Engage in identity management.
   c. Monitor your emotional responses.
   d. Dispute your irrational beliefs.
9. You attend a work social function, and after interacting with your boss, you have changed your interpretations of her. At work she is rushed, unfriendly, and demanding, but in a social setting, she is funny, pleasant, and good natured. What is this an example of?
   a. mixed emotions
   b. emotional contagion
   c. social conventions
   d. reappraisal
10. Which of the following does the text offer as a guideline for expressing your emotions?
    a. The sooner a feeling is shared, the better.
    b. Try to avoid sharing negative feelings whenever possible.
    c. Let others know that they have caused you to feel a certain way.
    d. Share mixed feelings when appropriate.

Know Your Fallacies

Insert the fallacy that best fits the following descriptions:
   a. Basing a belief on a limited amount of evidence or exaggerating shortcomings: fallacy of _____
   b. Working under the assumption that if something bad can possibly happen, it will: fallacy of _____
   c. The inability to distinguish between what is and what should be: fallacy of _____
   d. The notion that a worthwhile communicator can handle every situation with complete confidence and skill: fallacy of _____
   e. A belief that emotions are caused by others, not by our own self-talk: fallacy of _____
   f. The idea that satisfaction in life is determined by forces beyond our control: fallacy of _____

Chapter 4 Questions for Thought and Discussion

1. How successful are you at recognizing the emotional messages that are communicated via e-mail, instant messaging, social media, and so forth? How can this chapter help you become more insightful when reading or responding to messages?
2. Identify and provide examples of the three fallacies that are most prevalent in your life. What harm can each one cause if you fail to dispute it?
3. Explain and provide examples of how you use the guidelines for expressing feelings in your life. Which one do you do well and/or often? Where do you need further work? Give examples.

Answers

1. a; 2. b; 3. d; 4. a; 5. c; 6. c; 7. c; 8. b; 9. d; 10. d

Fallacies

a. overgeneralization; b. catastrophic expectations; c. shoulds; d. perfection; e. faulty causation; f. helplessness

Eric Pelaez/Stone/Getty Images

LO1 Analyze a real or potential misunderstanding in terms of semantic or pragmatic rules.

Semantics often cause misunderstandings. For instance, equivocal misunderstandings occur because many words have more than one meaning, and relative language gets its meaning only through comparison. With static evaluation, the verb *is* suggests absolute truth and unchangeability. And then there's abstract language, which is vague at best, while behavioural language is very specific. Pragmatic rules suggest that language is interpreted depending on context. Clearly, with so many semantic variables coupled with the pragmatic rules, it's easy to see how even simple statements can be misunderstood.

LO2 Describe how principles in the section titled "The Impact of Language" operate in your life.

Language affects perception. For instance, people make judgments about others based on whether their name is trendy or old-fashioned. Whether a professor is referred to as Miss, Ms., or Dr. affects how others perceive her credibility. Some individuals establish affiliation with groups by engaging in convergence—that is, using similar vocabulary or slang. Avoiding the use of deferential language markers such as hedges, tag questions, hesitations, or intensifiers can make a person seem more powerful and credible.

LO3 Rephrase disruptive statements in less inflammatory terms.

Fact-inference confusion occurs when opinions and assumptions (inferences) are treated as facts. Instead, you should use perception checking or disclaimers such as "In my opinion . . ." Rather than using emotive language that announces your opinion, use descriptive statements. Because "it" statements distance you from your opinions, take responsibility by using "I" statements. "But" statements cancel preceding messages, so it's better to state the central idea without the "but." While using questions may be a way to be tactful or to hide something, speaking up for yourself is also important.

LO4 Recast "it" statements, "but" statements, and "you" statements into statements that reflect your responsibility for the message.

While "you" statements express judgment of others, "I" statements demonstrate responsibility. "I" statements have four elements that can be stated in any order: (1) the other person's behaviour; (2) your interpretations; (3) your feelings; and (4) the consequences that the other person's behaviour has for you. To avoid overusing "I" statements, make "we" statements that suggest concern and responsibility for both parties. Communicators generally receive I/we combinations (e.g., "I think that we . . .") more favourably.

Semantic rules Rules that govern the meaning of language, as opposed to its structure. (Page 116)

Equivocal language Words, word orders, phrases, or expressions that have more than one commonly accepted definition. (Page 116)

Relative words Words that gain their meaning through comparison. (Page 117)

Static evaluation The tendency to view people or relationships as unchanging. (Page 118)

Abstract language Language that is vague and unclear. (Page 118)

Behavioural language Language that refers to specific things that people do or say. (Page 118)

Abstraction ladder A range of more to less abstract terms describing an event or object. (Page 118)

Syntactic rules Rules that govern the way symbols can be arranged, as opposed to the meanings of those symbols. (Page 120)

Pragmatic rules Rules that help communicators understand how messages may be used and interpreted in a given context. (Page 121)

Convergence The process of adapting one's speech style to match that of others with whom the communicator wants to identify. (Page 124)

Divergence Speech mannerisms that emphasize a communicator's differences from others. (Page 124)

Deferential language A language style in which speakers defer to listeners by using hedges, hesitations, intensifiers, polite forms, tag questions, and disclaimers. (Page 124)

Inference A conclusion that is arrived at from an interpretation of evidence. (Page 125)

Emotive language Language that conveys the speaker's attitude rather than simply offering an objective description. (Page 127)

Euphemisms Pleasant terms or phrases substituted for blunt ones in order to soften the impact of unpleasant information. (Page 128)

"It" statements Statements that replace the personal pronoun *I* with the less immediate word *it*, often with the effect of reducing the speaker's acceptance of responsibility for the statements. (Page 128)

"I" language A statement that describes the speaker's reaction to another person's behaviour without making judgments about the behaviour's worth. (Page 128)

"But" statements Statements in which the word *but* cancels out the expression that preceded it. (Page 129)

"You" language A statement that expresses or implies a judgment of the other person. (Page 129)

"We" statement A statement that implies that the issue is the concern and responsibility of both the sender and receiver of a message. (Page 131)

Low-context cultures Cultures that use language primarily to express thoughts, feelings, and ideas as clearly and logically as possible. (Page 136)

High-context cultures Cultures that avoid direct use of language, relying instead on the context of a message to convey meaning. (Page 136)

Linguistic relativism The notion that the worldview of a culture is shaped and reflected by the language its members speak. (Page 137)

Sapir–Whorf hypothesis This hypothesis suggests that the language we speak affects how we interact with the world around us. (Page 138)

LO5 **Analyze how gender and/or cultural differences may affect the quality of interaction.**
For women, talk can be the essence of their relationships. For men, this is less important. Both men and women use deferential language depending on the situation. Also, the English language is sexist in that the generic pronoun "he" is supposed to refer to women and men but it doesn't at all times, maleness is considered the standard, the use of man-linked language such as mailman or weatherman is common. However, many people are adopting a more inclusive language style. Culture also affects interaction. For example, in high-context cultures, language is indirect, and in low-context cultures like Canada, language is direct. When translated into different languages, words can have different connotations.

Chapter 5 Quiz Questions

1. You learn that your company is hiring someone you knew in grade school. When asked what she was like, you responded by saying that she is pleasant, fair, good humoured, and smart. What have you just engaged in?
   a. behavioural language
   b. convergence
   c. static evaluation
   d. deferential language

2. Which of the following will be noticeable in a low-context language culture?
   a. indirect expression of opinions
   b. that the use of silence is admired
   c. less reliance on explicit verbal messages
   d. that self-expression is valued

3. Which category includes terms like *mailman, fireman, businessman,* and *chairman?*
   a. inclusive language
   b. man-linked terminology
   c. heterosexist language
   d. disruptive language

4. What is the highest-level abstraction?
   a. complaining
   b. complaining about chores
   c. complaining about my housework
   d. reminding me about chores I haven't done

5. What is the notion behind crossword puzzles?
   a. Language can be disruptive.
   b. Language can be powerful.
   c. Language can be equivocal.
   d. Language can be emotive.

6. Which of the following describes the use of a deferential language style?
   a. using hedges, hesitations, intensifiers, and tag questions
   b. avoiding hedges, hesitations, intensifiers, and tag questions
   c. being perceived to be more competent, intelligent, and dynamic
   b. usually showing sympathy and empathy for the listener

7. What does the Sapir–Whorf hypothesis postulate?
   a. All languages share the same pragmatic rules.
   b. Language operates as a perceptual schema.
   c. Language patterns reflect and shape an individual's power.
   d. Men and women use language for different purposes.

8. Which statement does NOT accurately describe language and gender?
   a. Communication can be the essence of a woman's relationship.
   b. Men and women are more similar than different.
   c. Women use deferential language and men use nondeferential language.
   d. Language style depends on the context or situation.
9. Imagine that you have taken an "easy" class your friend recommended but you are finding it to be "hard". Which of the following has created the semantic problem you have encountered?
   a. euphemistic language
   b. relative words
   c. equivocal words
   d. high-level abstraction
10. What term refers to treating something as a fact when it is not?
    a. emotive language
    b. relative language
    c. an inference
    d. low-level abstraction

Know Your Terms

Match the following definitions with the terms below.

1. Way in which languages differ from culture to culture _____
2. Altering your speech to match that of someone with whom you wish to identify _____
3. Language that conveys a speaker's judgment of another _____
4. Rules that help us understand how messages may be interpreted _____
5. Rules that govern the way symbols can be arranged _____
6. Female equivalent of Mr. _____
7. Using pauses, tag questions, polite forms _____
8. Speaking in a way that emphasizes differences _____
9. Where language is used to express thoughts clearly _____
10. Rules that govern the meaning of language, as opposed to its structure _____
11. Language that conveys a person's reaction to another _____

Mrs.	"I" language	Sapir–Whorf hypothesis
inference	low-context culture	pragmatic rules
euphemism	deferential language	divergence
secondary emotions	semantic rules	succinctness and formality
linguistic relativism	Miss	"you" language
convergence	Ms.	"it" statements
syntactic rules	high-context cultures	
emotive language	deferential language	

Chapter 5 Questions for Thought and Discussion

1. Make a list of the words associated with technology (iPod, Skype, Twitter, blog, etc.) that did not exist when you were a child. Find other examples of how your language differs from your parents' and then explain how misunderstandings occur as a result of such differences. Finally, develop a list of some words or language that your grandparents use and indicate what they mean.
2. Should married women retain their last names or change their names to their husband's? How does this concept apply to LGBTQ couples? Share your answers with the class.
3. How do the user names you've selected for various online sites reflect your identity?
4. Describe what abstract language is and how you use unnecessarily abstract language that causes communication problems. Give at least five examples. Tell how you could lower the level of abstraction in each of the examples you have given or explain why the higher-level abstraction is justified and relationally beneficial.
5. Describe why and how a person might make his or her language style more "powerful." What are the pros and cons of using this type of language? What are the gender stereotypes associated with language style?
6. Your friend will soon be going to Korea to teach English as a second language. What information would you provide about the use of language in general in countries such as Japan, China, and Korea? Make sure to use the terminology presented in the chapter.

Answers

1. c; 2. d; 3. b; 4. a; 5. c; 6. a; 7. b; 8. c; 9. b; 10. c

Matching

1. succinctness and formality; 2. convergence; 3. "you" language; 4. pragmatic rules; 5. syntactic rules; 6. Ms.; 7. deferential language; 8. divergence; 9. low-context culture; 10. semantic rules; 11. "I" language

Notes

Chapter in Review

Sam Edwards/Caiaimage/Getty Images

LO1 Explain the defining characteristics of nonverbal communication.

Good nonverbal communicators are thought to possess emotional intelligence and socioemotional well-being. They're considered popular, persuasive, attractive, and successful in careers and romance. All nonverbal behaviour has communicative value and conveys emotions and relational messages as well. Nonverbal communication is used to repeat, complement, substitute, accent, and regulate verbal messages as well as contradict them. Nonverbal indicators of lying are called deception cues, but we're not good at picking up on them. Finally, nonverbal communication is ambiguous and can have several meanings.

LO2 List and offer examples of each type of nonverbal message introduced in this chapter.

Facing someone directly or being at a right angle to another are examples of body orientation, while slumping or sitting up straight are examples of posture. Gestures include illustrators (e.g., making movements to signify a ball or an airplane), emblems (e.g., okay or thumbs-up signs) and adaptors or manipulators (e.g., touching hair, tapping a pen). Many adaptors are similar to courtship gestures—those indicators suggesting an interest in someone. Facial expressions include pouting lips or an open mouth. The eyes are also expressive and send a variety of messages.

LO3 Recognize how individual factors such as voice, touch, and physical attractiveness are related to nonverbal communication.

Emphasis can change a sentence's meaning, tone of voice can create sarcasm, and using vocal fillers (e.g., "um" or "ah") can reduce credibility. People are more comfortable with and more likely to comply with speakers who speak at a similar pace as they do. Women tend to raise their pitch at the end of sentences. Touch can signify a variety of relationships, and its intensity depends on what's being touched, the length and pressure of the touch, movement after contact, and so on. Touch is related positively to power, persuasion, and health. Physical attractiveness is positively related to popularity, higher grades, hiring, promotion, performance evaluation, intelligence, and so forth. Clothing conveys economic level, education level, social background, trustworthiness, moral character, and status.

LO4 Become more aware of how external factors such as distance, environment, and time are related to nonverbal communication.

You can tell how people feel about one another by noting the distance between them. Edward T. Hall describes four spatial zones: intimate, personal, social, and public. Territoriality refers to the area claimed by an individual or a group of

Nonverbal communication Messages expressed by other than linguistic means. (Page 145)

Repeating Nonverbal behaviours that duplicate the content of a verbal message. (Page 148)

Complementing Nonverbal behaviour that reinforces a verbal message. (Page 148)

Substituting Nonverbal behaviour that takes the place of a verbal message. (Page 148)

Accenting Nonverbal behaviours that emphasize part of a verbal message. (Page 148)

Regulating A function of nonverbal communication in which nonverbal cues control the flow of verbal communication between and among individuals. (Page 148)

Contradicting Nonverbal behaviour that is inconsistent with a verbal message. (Page 149)

Mixed message Situations in which a person's words are incongruent with his or her nonverbal behaviour. (Page 149)

Leakage Nonverbal behaviours that reveal information a communicator does not disclose verbally. (Page 149)

Deception cues Nonverbal behaviours that signal the untruthfulness of a verbal message. (Page 149)

Kinesics The study of body position and motion. (Page 156)

Body orientation The degree to which we face toward or away from someone with our body, feet, and head. (Page 156)

Posture How people carry themselves. (Page 156)

Gestures Motions of the body, usually hands or arms, that have communicative value. (Page 156)

Illustrators Nonverbal behaviours that accompany and support verbal messages. (Page 156)

Emblems Deliberate nonverbal behaviours with precise meanings known to virtually all members of a cultural group. (Page 157)

Adaptors Movements in which one part of the body grooms, massages, rubs, holds, fidgets, pinches, picks, or otherwise manipulates another part. Also known as *manipulators*. (Page 157)

Microexpression Brief facial expression. (Page 158)

Paralanguage Nonlinguistic means of vocal expression: rate, pitch, tone, and so on. (Page 160)

Vocal filler A nonlinguistic verbalization; for example, stammering or saying "um," "er," or "ah." (Page 160)

Haptics The study of touching. (Page 161)

Proxemics The study of how people and animals use space. (Page 164)

Intimate distance One of anthropologist Edward Hall's four distance zones, ranging from skin contact to 45 centimetres. (Page 164)

Personal distance One of Hall's four distance zones, ranging from 45 centimetres to 1.2 metres. (Page 164)

Social distance One of Hall's four distance zones, ranging from 1.2 to 3.6 metres. (Page 165)

Public distance One of Hall's four distance zones, extending outward from 3.6 metres. (Page 165)

Territoriality The notion that an area is claimed by an individual or a group of individuals. (Page 165)

Chronemics The study of how humans use and structure time. (Page 166)

people, and those with more status have more territory. Physical environment both sends messages and influences communication (workers are more positive and energetic in beautiful rooms). Even chronemics sends messages. Lower-status people often must wait for higher-status individuals, and the amount of time a person spends with another relates to the importance of the relationship.

LO5 Improve your nonverbal communication in the workplace.

Just landing a job requires certain nonverbal communication (e.g., dressing appropriately, shaking hands, leaning forward, using appropriate facial expressions, mirroring the interviewer's posture). While effective nonverbal communication is important in all professions, students learn more from teachers with good nonverbal skills. These instructors make eye contact, use gestures, move around the room and so forth. Researchers suggest that nonverbal communication is so important in the classroom that all teacher education programs should include instruction on this topic. In health care settings, nurses with good communication skills form better relationships with their clients and patients disclose more information to doctors who make direct eye contact, lean forward, and stand in close proximity.

Chapter 6 Quiz Questions

1. Which of the following is NOT related to nonverbal communication?
   a. your paralanguage
   b. your gender
   c. the language you speak
   d. the rate and speed of your voice
2. When you become aware of nonverbal messages in your everyday life, how should you interpret them?
   a. as reliable facts
   b. as clues that need to be verified
   c. as ways of knowing what a person is thinking
   d. as ways to understand meanings
3. What is the nonverbal function equivalent to telling the person that it's his or her turn to speak?
   a. an adaptor
   b. a regulator
   c. a microexpression
   d. an illustrator
4. Which term includes body orientation, posture, gestures, facial expressions, and eye movements?
   a. kinesics
   b. external factors
   c. the relational dimension of nonverbal communication
   d. a function of nonverbal communication
5. You make an appointment for 3:30 to see your doctor. You arrive on time but find yourself sitting in the waiting room for 45 minutes before you're finally called in. What nonverbal notion is this an example of?
   a. public distance
   b. status
   c. regulating
   d. chronemics
6. What influences how a touch to the shoulder can be interpreted?
   a. the pressure of the touch
   b. whether or not the person is touching both shoulders
   c. whether the touch is intentional or unintentional
   d. what the "toucher" meant by it

7. According to your text, which statement best describes deception cues?
   a. If we watch people very carefully, we can detect their deception cues.
   b. Our ability to pick up deception cues is only a little better than leaving it to chance.
   c. People avoid eye contact when they are lying.
   d. People with nonverbal learning disorders are better detectors of deception.

8. Into which category does the distance we place between ourselves and others fall as a form of nonverbal communication?
   a. social distance
   b. territoriality
   c. kinesics
   d. proxemics

9. From which of the following can you learn about a person's economic level, educational level, social position, or trustworthiness?
   a. their clothing
   b. their nonverbal communication
   c. by watching for leakage
   d. their paralanguage

10. You hear two individuals speaking a language you don't recognize, yet you understand that they're both very sad or distraught about something. Which statement best explains why you could be correct?
    a. Paralanguage is an excellent indicator of a person's emotional state.
    b. Nonverbal cues can give words a particular meaning.
    c. Even if we don't understand a language, we can identify the emotion and its strength.
    d. Emblems have the same meanings in every culture.

Know Your Terms

Match the following descriptions with the terms below.

1. Movements of the arms are called
2. Movements in which one part of the body grooms, rubs, holds, or fidgets are called
3. The way in which individuals carry themselves is called
4. Nonverbal behaviours that regulate the flow of verbal communication are called
5. Nonverbal behaviours that accompany or support verbal messages are called
6. A quick flash that crosses a person's face is called a
7. People's words' being incongruent with their nonverbal behaviour is called a
8. The degree to which we face toward or away from someone is called
9. Nonverbal behaviours that have a precise meaning within a culture are called
10. The ways in which physical setting, architecture, and interior design affect our communication are called
11. Hall's distance zone that ranges from skin contact to about 45 centimetres is called
12. The term used to describe nonverbal vocal messages is
13. The study of the way in which people and animals use space is called

14. Hall's distance zone that is used in conversations and in business is called
15. The study of how humans use and structure time is called
16. A geographical area such as a room, seat, or even a section of the university to which we have made a claim is called
17. The term used to describe the use of stammering or saying "uh," "um," "er," and soon is
18. Nonverbal behaviours that signal an interest in another person are called
19. Signals of deception are called
20. A handshake, a clap on the back, a shove, or a kiss are manifestations of

adaptors	microexpression	public distance
body orientation	mixed message	regulators
chronemics	nonverbal communication	social distance
courtship gestures	paralanguage	territoriality
emblems	personal distance	touch
gestures	physical attractiveness	vocal filler
illustrators	physical environment	
intimate distance	posture	
leakage	proxemics	

Chapter 6 Questions for Thought and Discussion

1. How can you detect deception in computer-mediated communication?
2. In these days of instant messaging, we expect instant responses. Describe how the intentional and unintentional use of time (i.e., the length it takes someone to respond to your messages, etc.) affects your relationships.
3. What misunderstandings have occurred in your electronic communication because of nonverbal communication? Because of a lack of nonverbal communication?
4. Describe some of the intercultural nonverbal differences you have experienced in your life. What nonverbal communication advice would you give someone who will be travelling and working in different cultures?
5. Describe how the knowledge you gained by reading this chapter can influence your life in a positive way in terms of the following:
   • family
   • friends
   • your professional life
   • your student life
   • your ability to find and maintain a romantic relationship

Answers

1. c; 2. b; 3. b; 4. a; 5. d; 6. a; 7. b; 8. d; 9. a; 10. c

Matching

1. gestures; 2. adaptors; 3. posture; 4. regulators; 5. illustrators; 6. microexpression; 7. mixed message; 8. body orientation; 9. emblems; 10. physical environment; 11. intimate distance; 12. paralanguage; 13. proxemics; 14. social distance; 15. chronemics; 16. territoriality; 17. vocal filler; 18. courtship gestures; 19. leakage; 20. touch.

Notes

Rebecca Drobis/Blend Images/Getty Images

LO1 Identify the situations in which you listen actively and those in which you listen passively, and evaluate the appropriateness of each style in a given situation.

Passive listening is superficial and involves giving automatic, routine responses. Because it is impossible to listen to everything we hear, passive listening frees us up to focus on messages that require careful attention. Active listening involves careful, thoughtful attention and responses. Elements in the listening process include hearing, attending, understanding, responding, and remembering.

LO2 Identify the circumstances in which you listen ineffectively and the poor listening habits you use in these circumstances.

Certain circumstances can make listening easier. Nevertheless, many people have bad listening habits. There are several types of ineffective listening: pseudolistening (pretending), stage-hogging (interrupting to make your point), selective listening (listening only to the good parts), insulated listening (ignoring undesirable topics), defensive listening (taking things person-ally), ambushing (gathering information to attack the speaker), and insensitive listening (ignoring nonverbal cues that convey feelings). To improve your listening skills, eliminate these habits, talk less, get rid of distractions, don't judge prematurely, and listen for key information.

LO3 Identify the response styles that you commonly use when listening to others.

There are several different types of response styles: prompting (using silence to prompt the speaker), questioning (seeking additional information about the speaker's thoughts and feelings), paraphrasing (repeating the message in your own words), supporting (showing solidarity), analyzing (offering an interpretation of the message), advising (offering helpful suggestions), and judging (evaluating the message as positive or negative). Being able to offer all the response styles will make you a better listener and a more competent communicator.

LO4 Demonstrate a combination of listening styles you could use to respond effectively in a given situation.

The suitability of a listening style depends on the situation. Begin with prompting, questioning, paraphrasing, and sup-porting to learn more about what's happening. Move on to analyzing, advising, and judging at the individual's request. The best listening style(s) for the circumstance also depends on the other person. Asking how you can help provides insight into which style(s) to use. We generally have one or two default listening styles. Women are good at supporting while men give advice well. You'll be most helpful by excel-ling at each style.

Listening Making sense of others' spoken messages. (Page 176)

Passive listening Reacting to others' messages automatically, without much mental investment. (Page 177)

Active listening Giving careful and thoughtful attention and responses to the messages we receive. (Page 177)

Attending The process of filtering out some messages and focusing on others. (Page 179)

Understanding Occurs when sense is made of a message. (Page 179)

Listening fidelity The degree of congruence between what a listener understands and what the message sender intended to convey. (Page 179)

Responding Giving observable feedback to a speaker. (Page 179)

Remembering The ability to recall information. (Page 179)

Pseudolistening An imitation of true listening in which the receiver's mind is elsewhere. (Page 180)

Stage-hogging A listening style in which the receiver is more concerned with making a point than with understanding the speaker. (Page 180)

Selective listening A listening style in which receivers respond only to the messages that interest them. (Page 180)

Insulated listening A style in which the receiver ignores undesirable information. (Page 181)

Defensive listening A response style in which the receiver perceives a speaker's comments as an attack. (Page 181)

Ambushing A style in which the receiver listens carefully to gather information to use in an attack on the speaker. (Page 181)

Insensitive listening Failure to recognize the thoughts or feelings that are not directly expressed by a speaker. (Page 181)

Prompting Using silences and brief statements of encouragement to draw out a speaker. (Page 185)

Questioning A style of helping in which the receiver seeks additional information from the sender to be sure the speaker's thoughts and feelings are being received accurately. (Page 185)

Closed questions Questions that call for a specific or yes/no response. (Page 186)

Open questions Questions that allow the respondent to answer in a variety of ways and to include a great deal of description and detail. (Page 186)

Sincere questions Questions aimed at soliciting information that enables the asker to understand the other person. (Page 186)

Counterfeit questions Questions aimed at sending rather than receiving a message. (Page 186)

Paraphrasing Repeating a speaker's thoughts and/or feelings in the listener's own words. Also known as *active listening*. (Page 187)

Supporting A helping response that reveals a listener's solidarity with the speaker's situation. (Page 190)

Analyzing A helping style in which the listener offers an interpretation of a speaker's message. (Page 191)

Advising A helping response in which the receiver offers suggestions about how the speaker should deal with a problem. (Page 192)

Judging A response in which the receiver evaluates the sender's message either favourably or unfavourably. (Page 193)

Chapter 7 Quiz Questions

1. Which statement does NOT accurately describe gender and communication?
   a. Men tend to offer more advice.
   b. Women are more likely to give supportive responses.
   c. Men are more skilled at composing supportive messages.
   d. Fraternity men challenge their brothers in order to evaluate their attitudes and values.

2. According to the text, what is NOT a way of listening to help?
   a. analyzing
   b. questioning
   c. prompting
   d. repeating

3. When all your friends tell you something about the person you're seeing that you just don't want to hear, what type of listening will you be most likely to engage in?
   a. pseudolistening
   b. selective listening
   c. insulated listening
   d. empathic listening

4. What are getting rid of distractions, asking questions, and speaking less?
   a. ways to get others to use the correct type of listening response
   b. some of the methods suggested in the text for offering confirming messages
   c. dimensions of supportive listening
   d. ways to help improve your listening

5. According to one study, which behaviour did patients NOT like upon meeting with a doctor?
   a. interrupted the patient
   b. paraphrased what the patient said
   c. looked at the patient when speaking
   d. shook hands with the patient

6. What type of listening are lawyers engaged in when conducting a cross-examination?
   a. defensive
   b. selective
   c. stage-hogging
   d. ambushing

7. What type of question disguises a speaker's true motives?
   a. counterfeit
   b. closed
   c. sincere
   d. open

8. Which two terms describe the process in which you repeat a speaker's thoughts and/or feelings in your own words?
   a. paraphrasing and supporting responses
   b. active listening and paraphrasing
   c. advising and paraphrasing responses
   d. supporting responses and active listening

9. According to your text, what percentage of an original message will you most likely forget after two months?
   a. 25
   b. 35
   c. 50
   d. 75

10. Which term refers to the type of listening that occurs when you give the appearance of being attentive while listening to someone speak?
    a. pseudolistening
    b. selective listening
    c. insulated listening
    d. empathic listening

Chapter 7 Questions for Thought and Discussion

1. Answer the following questions and then compare your results with others in the class.
   a. We live in a world where the media present information in brief segments. What effect will this have on our ability to listen to complex ideas that take time to explain?
   b. Describe ineffective listening styles that you think are more predominant in electronic contexts.
   c. What types of listening may be done more effectively through computer mediated and electronic channels (e.g., informational listening versus listening to help)?
   d. How might you be a more effective listener when you use various channels (e.g., telephone, voice mail, e-mail, chat groups) to receive and respond to others' messages?

2. Read the case below and then answer the following questions. Afterward, share your response with others in the class.

   Jen and Sook-yin have been friends since elementary school and are now in their early 30s. Sook-yin has been happily married for 10 years. Jen has been engaged four times and each time has broken it off as the marriage date has approached. Sook-yin has listened, mainly questioning, supporting, and paraphrasing. Jen has just announced another engagement.

   a. Sook-yin wants to give Jen advice this time. Should she? If she does, what would she say? Evaluate the possible effects on their relationship.
   b. Because Sook-yin has known Jen for such a long time, do you think she should use an analyzing style? If she does, what would she say?
   c. What listening styles do you think would be the most helpful to Jen? What would Sook-yin say in the listening style(s) you have chosen?
   d. Pretend you are Sook-yin. Consider the situation, the other person, and yourself. Given these considerations, how would you listen? Give examples.
   e. Suppose the two friends described here were men. Would your answers to any of the preceding questions change?

3. Review the poor listening behaviours below and identify the ones in which you typically engage. Provide an example of each problem behaviour and then indicate how you can eliminate or minimize your use of these poor listening behaviours.
   a. pseudolistening
   b. stage-hogging
   c. selective listening
   d. insulated listening
   e. defensive listening
   f. ambushing
   g. insensitive listening

4. Which of the listening responses do you most often use when helping someone—paraphrasing, questioning, advising, judging, analyzing, supporting, or prompting? Describe a situation in which you felt that you used the wrong helping style. What happened, and how would you correct the situation if given the opportunity?

5. List your overall strengths and weaknesses as a listener and develop a plan to help yourself become a better listener in the future.

Answers

1. c; 2. d; 3. c; 4. d; 5. a; 6. d; 7. a; 8. b; 9. a; 10. a

Notes

© Arctic Photo/All Canada Photos

LO1 Identify factors that have influenced your choice of relational partners.

Appearance gets a relationship started; other characteristics keep it alive. People like those who share similar values and outlooks. Some relationships are complementary—a dominant person and a passive one make a good team. People also like competent and talented individuals as well as anyone who likes them (reciprocal attraction). Disclosure builds liking, and relationships develop as people learn about each other. With proximity, relationships form because of continued exposure. Finally, relationships offer physical, mental, and social rewards. Therefore, some relationships are based on social exchange theory.

LO2 Use Knapp's model to describe the nature of communication in the various stages of a relationship.

Divided into the broad phases of "coming together" and "breaking apart," Knapp's model consists of initiating (making contact), experimenting (expressing interest), intensifying (having more contact and disclosure), integrating (taking on a single identity), and bonding (denoting the relationship through a symbolic public gesture). In breaking apart, the stages are differentiating (asserting individual values), circumscribing (reducing contact and commitment), stagnating (losing enthusiasm), avoiding (minimizing contact), and terminating (acknowledging the end of the relationship). Of course, not all relationships terminate.

LO3 Describe the dialectical tensions in a given relationship, how they influence communication, and the most effective strategies for managing them.

Some hold that relationships may continue because individuals deal with the dialectical tensions (opposing forces) that exist naturally in relationships. The connection–autonomy dialectic can be managed by spending enough time together to maintain and nurture the relationship but allowing time apart to develop independent interests. The openness–privacy dialectic (needing both communication and privacy) is managed by disclosing information about daily affairs but keeping some things private. The predictability–novelty dialectic is managed by have some routines but also allowing for novelty in terms of social life, vacations, and so forth.

LO4 Describe the possible strategies for repairing a given relational transgression.

Relational transgressions can be minor or significant, social or relational, deliberate or unintentional, or one-time or incremental. Repairing them calls for a discussion of the transgression and an acceptance of responsibility for the transgression. To apologize, acknowledge that the transgression was wrong, offer a sincere apology, and offer some kind of compensation.

Interpersonal relationship An association in which the parties meet each other's social needs to a greater or lesser degree. (Page 203)

Social exchange theory A socioeconomic theory of relational development that suggests people seek relationships in which the rewards they receive from others are equal to or greater than the costs they encounter. (Page 206)

Relational maintenance Communication aimed at keeping relationships operating smoothly and satisfactorily. (Page 207)

Initiating The first stage in relational development, in which the parties express interest in one another. (Page 207)

Uncertainty reduction The process of getting to know others by gaining more information about them. (Page 208)

Experimenting An early stage in relational development, consisting of a search for common ground. If the experimentation is successful, the relationship will progress to *intensifying*. If not, it may go no further. (Page 208)

Intensifying A stage of relational development, preceding *integrating*, in which the parties move toward integration by increasing the amount of contact and the breadth and depth of self-disclosure. (Page 208)

Integrating A stage of relational development in which the parties begin to take on a single identity. (Page 208)

Bonding A stage of relational development in which the parties make symbolic public gestures to show that their relationship exists. (Page 209)

Differentiating A stage of relational development in which the parties reestablish their individual identities after having bonded together. (Page 209)

Circumscribing A stage of relational development in which parties begin to reduce the scope of their contact and commitment to one another. (Page 210)

Stagnating A stage of relational development characterized by declining enthusiasm and standardized forms of behaviour. (Page 211)

Avoiding A stage of relational development, immediately prior to *terminating*, in which the parties minimize contact with one another. (Page 211)

Terminating The concluding stage of relational development, characterized by the acknowledgment of one or both parties that the relationship is over. (Page 211)

Dialectical tensions Inherent conflicts that arise when two opposing or incompatible forces exist simultaneously. (Page 212)

Connection–autonomy dialectic The dialectical tension between a desire for connection and a need for independence in a relationship. (Page 212)

Openness–privacy dialectic The dialectical tension between a desire for open communication and the need for privacy in a relationship. (Page 213)

Predictability–novelty dialectic The dialectical tension between a desire for stability and the need for novelty in a relationship. (Page 214)

Relational commitment An implied or explicit promise to remain and make a relationship successful. (Page 216)

Intimacy A state of personal sharing arising from physical, intellectual, and/or emotional contact. (Page 218)

Self-disclosure The process of deliberately revealing information about oneself that is significant and not normally known by others. (Page 222)

Social penetration A model that describes relationships in terms of their breadth and depth. (Page 222)

Breadth The first dimension of self-disclosure, involving the range of subjects being discussed. (Page 222)

Depth A dimension of self-disclosure involving a shift from relatively nonrevealing messages to more personal ones. (Page 222)

Privacy management The choices people make to reveal or conceal information about themselves. (Page 224)

Benevolent lie A lie defined by the teller as unmalicious or even helpful to the person to whom it is told. (Page 227)

You must be genuine, and your nonverbal and verbal communication must be congruent. To forgive a transgressor, offer an explicit acceptance of the apology and indicate the implications that the transgression has for the relationship.

LO5 Identify the dimensions of intimacy and how they are expressed in a specific relationship.
Intimacy has several dimensions: Physical intimacy involves sexual expression; intellectual intimacy refers to the closeness of sharing thoughts and ideas; emotional intimacy occurs when we share feelings. Sharing activities also provides avenues of intimacy. Women self-disclose for intimacy while men prefer to engage in shared activities, thus causing misunderstandings in heterosexual couples. Intimacy also varies across cultures. In collectivistic cultures, people communicate differently with "in-group" members than they do with "out-groups," whereas in individualistic cultures, the distinctions between personal and casual relationships are blurred. Mediated communication promotes and maintains intimacy in contemporary relationships.

LO6 Use the social penetration and Johari Window models to identify the nature of self-disclosing communication in one of your relationships.
The social penetration model explains self-disclosure in terms of breadth and depth. Greater depth and breadth result in greater intimacy. The Johari Window model examines self-disclosure from four perspectives: information known to you and others (open area); information unknown to you but known to others (blind area); information known to you but unknown to others (hidden area); information unknown to you and others (unknown area). The model allows you to examine the self-disclosure in your relationships.

LO7 Outline the potential benefits and risks of disclosing in a selected situation.
Benefits of self-disclosure include catharsis, self-clarification, self-validation, relationship maintenance and enhancement, and social influence. The risks are rejection, negative impressions, decrease in relational satisfaction, loss of influence, and hurting the other person. To minimize risks, determine if you must disclose, if the risk of disclosing is reasonable, and if the disclosure is relevant. You might also determine if it will be constructive, understood by the listener, and reciprocated.

LO8 Assess the most competent mixture of candour and equivocation in a given situation.
While malicious lying is frowned upon, benevolent lies (ones that may help an individual) are more acceptable. Equivocating is also a viable option as it spares embarrassment and hurt and saves face for both parties ("You're right. That's some outfit!"). Hinting is more direct than equivocating but depends on the listener's ability to pick up on the hint. Lies aren't challenged when we expect someone to lie, when the lie is mutually advantageous, when lying means avoiding embarrassment and confrontation, or when we asked the person to lie.

Chapter 8 Quiz Questions

1. Many couples say their relationship broke up either because they didn't spend enough time together or because they were feeling trapped by the relationship. What are these couples most likely experiencing?
   a. a relational transgression
   b. a predictability–novelty dialectic
   c. an unintentional transgression
   d. a connection–autonomy dialectic

2. What does the openness–privacy dialectic refer to?
   a. the notion that as we form relationships we become more open with that individual and thus experience less privacy
   b. the notion of having a relationship with a very private individual
   c. relationships in which both partners are free to come and go as they please, as long as they respect one another's privacy
   d. a time in a relationship when one partner wants or needs more privacy and the other expects that person to be much more open than he or she currently is

3. According to communication scholars, there are several dimensions of intimacy. Which of the following does NOT fit into this category?
   a. cultural
   b. intellectual
   c. emotional
   d. physical

4. Kyle and Matthew are associates who support one another's businesses. Which of the following best describes their relationship?
   a. managing dialectical tensions
   b. bonding
   c. differentiating
   d. social exchange theory

5. It's odd that Ella and Hanna are friends because Ella is very tidy, conservative, and reserved. What does their continued friendship demonstrate?
   a. reciprocal attraction
   b. complementarity
   c. relational transgressions
   d. metacommunication

6. Which term refers to an association in which the parties meet each other's social needs to a greater or lesser degree?
   a. integrating
   b. relational commitment
   c. connection–autonomy dialectic
   d. interpersonal relationship

7. What are integration, reaffirmation, and balance?
   a. ways to balance dialectical tensions
   b. stages in the development and decline model of relationships
   c. ways to manage dialectical tensions
   d. strategies to repair relational transgressions

8. Which term refers to conflicts that arise when two opposing or incompatible forces exist simultaneously?
   a. predictability–novelty dialectic
   b. recalibration
   c. openness–privacy dialectic
   d. dialectical tension

9. According to Richard Conville, what can you expect about your relationships?
   a. They will change constantly throughout the process.
   b. They will basically remain the same.
   c. They will stay at the same level.
   d. They will not continually move through the stages outlined by Knapp.

10. Jill finds that, every once in a while, her partner will get extremely violent and hit things in the house. What is this an example of?
    a. an unintentional transgression
    b. a significant transgression
    c. violating a social transgression
    d. a one-time transgression

Know Your Knapp

Match the following with Knapp's developmental stages.

1. A stage of relational development characterized by declining enthusiasm and standardized forms of behaviour _____

2. A stage of relational development in which the parties make symbolic public gestures to show that their relationship exists _____

3. A stage of relational development in which parties begin to reduce the scope of their contact and commitment to one another _____

4. The concluding stage of relational development, characterized by the acknowledgment of one or both parties that the relationship is over _____

5. The first stage in relational development, in which the parties express interest in one another _____

6. A stage of relational development in which the parties begin to take on a single identity _____

7. An early stage in relational development, consisting of a search for common ground. If this stage is successful, the relationship will progress to intensifying. If not, it may go no further _____

8. A stage of relational development in which the parties reestablish their individual identities after having bonded together _____

9. A stage of relational development, preceding integrating, in which the parties move toward integration by increasing the amount of contact and the breadth and depth of self-disclosure _____

10. A stage of relational development, immediately prior to terminating, in which the parties minimize contact with one another _____

avoiding	initiating
bonding	integrating
circumscribing	intensifying
differentiating	stagnating
experimenting	terminating

Chapter 8 Questions for Thought and Discussion

1. Using Mark Knapp's model of relationship development and decline, analyze a romantic relationship you once had. Would a knowledge of the dialectical tensions and how to reduce them have "saved" your relationship? Explain your response.

2. We form relationships for a variety of reasons: appearance, similarity, complementarity, reciprocal attraction, competence, disclosure, proximity, and rewards. Match a relationship you've had in your life with each of these rationales for a relationship. Do you recognize any patterns?

3. Think back to some of the relational transgressions that you have experienced. Indicate which category they fell into and examine them in terms of repair. Explain the role that forgiveness played in these transgressions.

4. Draw your Johari Window for each of the following and explain how the differences in the windows compare to the differences in how the relationships affect your life.
   a. a sibling or cousin
   b. a close friend
   c. a boss or supervisor
   d. a romantic partner

Answers

1. d; 2. d; 3. a; 4. d; 5. b; 6. d; 7. c; 8. d; 9. a; 10. b

Matching

1. stagnating; 2. bonding; 3. circumscribing; 4. terminating; 5. initiating; 6. integrating; 7. experimenting; 8. differentiating; 9. intensifying; 10. avoiding

Chapter in Review

oliveromg/Shutterstock.com

LO1 Identify confirming, disagreeing, and disconfirming messages and patterns in your own important relationships and describe their consequences.

Confirming messages convey value and come in the form of recognition, acknowledgment, and endorsement. Disconfirming messages convey a lack of value and come in the form of interruptions or responses that are impervious, irrelevant, tangential, impersonal, ambiguous, or incongruous. Disagreeing messages that say the other is wrong are conveyed through aggressiveness, complaining, and argumentativeness

LO2 Describe how communication climates develop through positive or negative reciprocal communication patterns.

Communication climates develop through reciprocating communication patterns that reinforce the other's messages (spirals). Escalatory conflict spirals build on one another to create negative climates while positive spirals lead to positive communication climates. De-escalatory spirals can also be destructive in that parties slowly lessen their dependence on one another, withdraw, and become less interested in the relationship.

LO3 Use Gibb's categories to create messages that are likely to build supportive rather than defensive communication climates.

To develop supportive climates, use description (focus on speaker's thoughts and feelings) rather than evaluation; take a problem orientation (find solutions together) rather than controlling the situation (imposing solutions); be spontaneous (honest) instead of strategic (hiding ulterior motives); demonstrate empathy instead of neutrality or indifference; recognize equality rather than acting superior; and exercise provisionalism (acknowledging opposing opinions) instead of certainty. In cases where you want to deliver an assertive message, describe the behaviour that bothers you, explain how you interpret it, explain how the behaviour makes you feel, offer a consequence of the behaviour, and explain what you would like the person to do.

LO4 Create appropriate nondefensive responses to real or hypothetical criticisms.

To respond nondefensively, seek more information so you'll understand the critic better. You can do this by asking for specifics and/or making guesses about the specifics, paraphrasing the critic's remarks to help defuse the intensity of the attack, asking what the critic wants, asking about the consequences of your behaviour, or asking if anything else is bothering the other person. You can also agree with the critic even if you disagree with the criticism. For instance, you could agree with some of the facts or with how the critic perceived the situation.

Communication climate The emotional tone of a relationship between two or more individuals. (Page 239)

Confirming communication A message that expresses caring or respect for another person. (Page 240)

Disconfirming communication A message that expresses a lack of caring or respect for another person. (Page 240)

Disagreeing messages Messages that say "you're wrong" in one way or another. (Page 241)

Spiral A reciprocal communication pattern in which each person's message reinforces the other's. (Page 242)

Escalatory conflict spiral A communication spiral in which one attack leads to another until the initial skirmish escalates into a full-fledged battle. (Page 242)

De-escalatory conflict spiral A communication spiral in which the parties slowly lessen their dependence on one another, withdraw, and become less invested in the relationship. (Page 243)

Defensiveness The attempt to protect a presenting image a person believes is being attacked. (Page 244)

Face-threatening act Behaviour by another that is perceived as attacking an individual's presenting image, or face. (Page 244)

Evaluative communication Messages in which the sender judges the receiver in some way, usually resulting in a defensive response. (Page 245)

Descriptive communication Messages that describe the speaker's position without evaluating others. Synonymous with *"I" language.* (Page 245)

Controlling communication Messages in which the sender tries to impose some sort of outcome on the receiver, usually resulting in a defensive reaction. (Page 246)

Problem orientation A supportive style of communication described by Jack Gibb in which the communicators focus on working together to solve their problems instead of trying to impose their own solutions on one another. (Page 246)

Strategy A defence-arousing style of communication described by Jack Gibb in which the sender tries to manipulate or deceive a receiver. (Page 246)

Spontaneity A supportive communication behaviour described by Jack Gibb in which the sender expresses a message without any attempt to manipulate the receiver. (Page 246)

Neutrality A defence-arousing behaviour described by Jack Gibb in which the sender expresses indifference. (Page 246)

Empathy The ability to project oneself onto another person's point of view so as to experience the other's thoughts and feelings. (Page 247)

Superiority A defence-arousing style of communication described by Jack Gibb in which the sender states or implies that the receiver is not worthy of respect. (Page 247)

Equality A type of supportive communication described by Jack Gibb suggesting that the sender regards the receiver as worthy of respect. (Page 247)

Certainty An attitude behind messages that dogmatically implies that the speaker's position is correct and the other person's ideas are not worth considering. Likely to generate a defensive response. (Page 247)

Provisionalism A supportive style of communication described by Jack Gibb in which the sender expresses a willingness to consider the other person's position. (Page 248)

Behavioural description An account that refers only to observable phenomena. (Page 248)

Interpretation statement A statement that describes a speaker's interpretation of the meaning of another person's behaviour. (Page 249)

Feeling statement An expression of a sender's emotions that results from interpretation of sense data. (Page 249)

Consequence statement An explanation of the results that follow either from the behaviour of the person to whom the message is addressed or from the speaker's interpretation of and feelings about the addressee's behaviour. Consequence statements can describe what happens to the speaker, the addressee, or others. (Page 251)

Intention statement A description of where the speaker stands on an issue, what he or she wants, or how he or she plans to act in the future. (Page 251)

Chapter 9 Quiz Questions

1. What is a disagreeing message?
   a. a confirming message
   b. a message consisting of evaluation, strategy, and neutrality
   c. a message consisting of complaining, aggressiveness, and argumentativeness
   d. a nonconfirming message

2. What do you need to do when you decide to agree with your critic?
   a. Agree with the facts.
   b. Agree with the critic's perceptions but not the facts.
   c. Agree with the facts and the critic's perceptions.
   d. Be prepared to offer an apology.

3. According to your text, what should you do when you want to respond nondefensively to criticism?
   a. Seek more information and agree with the critic.
   b. Ask for specifics, guess about specifics, and paraphrase the speaker's ideas.
   c. Make sure to use tangential, impersonal, and incongruous responses.
   d. Be extra aware of escalatory conflict spirals.

4. A new boss arrives at the office and tells the staff that changes are going into effect immediately. The strategy worked at other places and it will work here as well. A couple of employees offer some suggestions, but their ideas are dismissed. Which of Jack Gibb's categories is the boss demonstrating?
   a. evaluation
   b. problem orientation
   c. provisionalism
   d. certainty

5. Which aspect of responding nondefensively does the following example represent?

   Person A: I can't believe you said we'd pick up Sam on the way to the concert.

   Person B: Are you saying that I should call him and tell him he has to get there himself?

   Person A: No, I just wish you'd asked me first.

   a. asking about specifics
   b. paraphrasing the speaker's ideas
   c. asking what the critic wants
   d. asking about the consequences of your behaviour

6. What are you most likely to do when trying to protect your presenting self as a person attacks your behaviour?
   a. Engage in escalatory communication.
   b. Be defensive.
   c. Offer consequence statements.
   d. Paraphrase the speaker's ideas.

7. Jane always feels good after she speaks with Professor MacLean. He listens intently to her ideas and speaks in a very respectful manner. Based on these statements, which of the following best describes Professor MacLean's communication?
   a. He is engaging in what Jack Gibb calls problem orientation.
   b. He is using confirming communication.
   c. He is using intentional statements.
   d. He is sending face-saving messages.

8. Which of the following is a consequence statement?
    a. When you don't pick up the groceries like you said you would, I feel frustrated.
    b. You didn't pick up the groceries like you said you would, you lazy jerk.
    c. You didn't pick up the groceries like you said you would. Were you working late?
    d. You didn't pick up the groceries like you said you would, and now we don't have bread or milk for tomorrow's breakfast.
9. What should you do when using the assertive message format?
    a. Deliver the elements in a specific manner.
    b. Make sure to keep the elements separate and clear for the listener.
    c. Seek more information before you begin.
    d. Word the messages to fit your personal communication style.
10. What is the most visible way that disconfirming messages reinforce one another?
    a. de-escalatory conflict spirals
    b. aggressiveness
    c. escalatory conflict spirals
    d. complaining and argumentativeness

Know Your Terms

Match the descriptions with the terms below.
1. A disagreeing message _____
2. Acknowledgment _____
3. Final element in the assertive message format _____
4. A way to respond nondefensively _____
5. Being completely indifferent to someone _____
6. Finding a solution that satisfies both parties _____
7. A message that challenges the image we want to project _____
8. Providing an objective description of an event without interpreting it _____
9. A factor that is consistently connected to a positive workplace _____
10. Messages that show a lack of regard for the other person _____

argumentativeness
behavioural description
confirming message
disagreeing message
disconfirming messages
encouragement
escalatory spiral
face-threatening act

guess about specifics
intention
interpretation
neutrality
spiral
strategy
problem orientation

Chapter 9 Questions for Thought and Discussion

1. Begin by reflecting on the various types of disconfirming messages: verbal abuse, complaining, impervious responses, interrupting, irrelevant responses, tangential responses, impersonal responses, ambiguous responses, and incongruous responses. Then answer the following questions:
    a. Which types of disconfirming messages do you find the most hurtful or frustrating when they are directed at you?
    b. Are there particular people in your life who give you disconfirming messages? If so, describe how they make you feel and how you tend to react.
    c. Which disconfirming messages are you most likely to use?
    d. To whom are you most likely to direct your disconfirming messages, and how do they respond?
    e. How can you reduce the number of disconfirming messages you send and receive?
2. Think of a time when someone criticized you and it left you feeling bad. Contrast that experience with a time when someone criticized in a way that did not have a negative outcome. What accounted for the differences between the two experiences?
3. How do you respond when someone directs criticism toward you? Is there room for improvement on your part? If so, explain how you will change in future interactions.
4. Print the messages you and a friend or partner exchanged via texting or email over a week-long period. With the printouts in front of you, engage in a face-to-face conversation to explore variations in the intended and received messages. For each message sent, explain how you felt at the time and what your intent was. For each message received, explain your interpretation and how it made you feel. Continue back and forth until every message is reviewed. What did you learn from this exercise?

Answers

1. c; 2. b; 3. a; 4. d; 5. c; 6. b; 7. b; 8. d; 9. b; 10. c

Matching

1. argumentativeness; 2. confirming message; 3. intention; 4. guess about specifics; 5. neutrality; 6. problem orientation; 7. face-threatening act; 8. behavioural description; 9. encouragement; 10. disconfirming messages

Notes

Chapter in Review

BananaStock/Thinkstock

LO1 Identify the conflicts in your important relationships and how satisfied you are with the way they have been handled.

Conflict, an expressed struggle, is an inevitable part of any relationship and comes about as a result of perceived incompatible goals (e.g., wanting different things out of a vacation), perceived scarce resources (e.g., how extra money will be spent), interdependence (we're in this together), or interference from another party. Whatever the cause, conflict is natural and can actually be healthy in a relationship.

LO2 Describe your personal conflict styles, evaluate their effectiveness, and suggest alternatives as appropriate.

When engaging in avoidance (lose–lose), the involved parties ignore the problem. When accommodating (lose–win), one party gives in. These styles are more positively regarded in high-context, collectivistic cultures. When competing (win–lose), parties try to resolve the issue to their own advantage, which can involve direct or passive aggression. When compromising (partial lose–lose), both parties sacrifice to gain a little of what they want. Collaborating (win–win) seeks a solution that meets everyone's needs. Which style to use depends on the relationship, the situation, the other person, and your goals.

LO3 Identify the relational conflict styles, patterns of behaviour, and conflict rituals that define a given relationship.

Relational conflict styles are patterns of disagreement that repeat themselves. In the complementary conflict style, partners use different but mutually reinforcing behaviours. In the symmetrical conflict style, both partners use the same tactics. In the parallel conflict style, the approach varies according to the situation. John Gottman identified four destructive conflict patterns: criticism, defensiveness, contempt, and stonewalling. A conflict ritual is an unacknowledged repeating pattern of interlocking behaviours used by participants in a conflict.

LO4 Demonstrate how you could use the win–win approach in a given conflict.

To use the win–win approach, (1) identify your problem and unmet needs; (2) make a date to discuss the problem; (3) describe your problem and needs by using the assertive message format; (4) consider your partner's point of view; (5) negotiate a solution by identifying and defining the conflict, generating a number of possible solutions, evaluating the alternative solutions, and deciding on the best solution; and (6) follow up the solution. After a "test run," you may decide to alter the solution.

Conflict An expressed struggle between at least two interdependent parties who perceive incompatible goals, scarce resources, and interference from the other party in achieving their goals. (Page 263)

Avoiding A lose–lose conflict style in which the parties ignore the problem at hand. (Page 266)

Accommodating A win–lose conflict style in which the communicator submits to a situation rather than attempting to have his or her needs met. (Page 266)

Competing A win–lose approach to conflicts that seeks to resolve them in one's own way. (Page 267)

Direct aggression A criticism or demand that threatens the face of the person at whom it is directed. (Page 267)

Passive aggression An indirect expression of aggression that occurs when a communicator expresses hostility in an obscure or manipulative way. (Page 267)

Compromising An approach to conflict resolution in which both parties attain at least part of what they wanted through self-sacrifice. (Page 269)

Collaborating A conflict management style that seeks win–win solutions. (Page 269)

Relational conflict style A pattern of managing disagreements that repeats itself over time in a relationship. (Page 271)

Complementary conflict style A relational conflict style in which partners use different but mutually reinforcing behaviours. (Page 271)

Symmetrical conflict style A relational conflict style in which both partners use the same tactics. (Page 271)

Parallel conflict style A relational conflict style in which the approach of the partners varies from one situation to another. (Page 271)

Conflict ritual An unacknowledged repeating pattern of interlocking behaviour used by participants in a conflict. (Page 272)

Dysfunctional conflict Conflict that creates animosity, causes interpersonal stress, and hinders a group's progress. (Page 280)

Functional conflict Positive conflict that focuses on issues rather than personalities. (Page 280)

Chapter 10 Quiz Questions

1. When Hatim and Nicholas have a problem about something, they use the same old behaviours every time to deal with it. What type of conflict style do they have?
   a. compromising
   b. constructive
   c. a complementary
   d. a symmetrical

2. Which statement best describes work teams that have a lot of functional conflict?
   a. They cause people to suffer undue stress.
   b. They make better final decisions.
   c. They tend to use parallel conflict styles.
   d. They are common in high-context cultures.

3. What can be said about the relationship between assertiveness and culture?
   a. People tend to be more assertive in low-context cultures.
   b. People tend to be more nonassertive in low-context cultures.
   c. There is no relationship between assertiveness and the high- or low-context cultures.
   d. Assertiveness is common in collectivistic cultures.

4. What can be said about the act of describing your problems and needs?
   a. It is part and parcel of an assertive communication style.
   b. It is considered a positive conflict skill.
   c. It is a conflict ritual.
   d. It is common in a parallel conflict style.

5. How can you determine which conflict style is best for a situation?
   a. Ask the person what works best for him or her.
   b. Put your goals aside and let the relationship unfold.
   c. Consider the particular situation.
   d. Use the style that has worked best for you in the past.

6. What are you doing when you consider the relationship, your goals, and the other person?
   a. determining which conflict style to use
   b. engaging in a win–win conflict style
   c. becoming more sensitive to the gender dimension of conflict
   d. looking at the elements in the complementary relational conflict style

7. What conflict style commonly includes both direct aggression and passive aggression?
   a. compromise
   b. avoiding
   c. accommodating
   d. competing

8. What is not a characteristic of conflict?
   a. dependence
   b. perceived scarce resources
   c. expressed struggle
   d. perceived incompatible goals

9. What are stonewalling and contempt examples of?
   a. a relational conflict style
   b. destructive conflict patterns
   c. direct aggression
   d. gender differences in dealing with conflict

10. What are character attacks, appearance attacks, and competence attacks examples of?
   a. lose–lose conflict style
   b. passive aggression
   c. direct aggression
   d. a symmetrical conflict style

Know Your Terms

Match the following descriptions with the terms below.
1. Make a date _____
2. Conflict that focuses on the issues rather than personalities _____
3. Continually being defensive and criticizing during conflict _____
4. Repeating patterns of interlocking behaviours by participants in conflict _____
5. The style used by the couple who decided to vacation in PEI _____
6. A crazymaker's approach _____
7. When both parties get at least part of what they wanted _____

accommodating	destructive conflict patterns
collaborating	dysfunctional conflict
compromise	functional conflict
conflict ritual	pseudoaccommodator
constructive conflict skill	relational conflict style

Answers

1. d; 2. b; 3. a; 4. b; 5. c; 6. a; 7. d; 8. a; 9. b; 10. c

Matching

1. constructive conflict skill; 2. functional conflict; 3. destructive conflict patterns; 4. conflict ritual; 5. collaborating; 6. the pseudoaccommodator; 7. compromise